# On Behalf of Their Homeland:
# Fifty Years of SVU

*An Eyewitness Account of the History of the Czechoslovak Society of Arts and Sciences (SVU)*

by

One of the SVU Founders and
SVU President for Many Years

# Dr. Miloslav Rechcígl, Jr.

EAST EUROPEAN MONOGRAPHS, BOULDER
DISTRIBUTED BY COLUMBIA UNIVERSITY PRESS, NEW YORK
2008

# EAST EUROPEAN MONOGRAPHS, NO. DCCXXXII

Copyright 2008 by Miloslav Rechcígl, Jr.

ISBN: 978-0-88033-630-7

Library of Congress Control Number: 2008930295

All rights reserved.

No parts of this document may be reproduced or transmitted in any form or by any means, electronic or mechanical, including photocopy, recording, xerography, or any information storage and removal system, without permission from the compiler.

Printed in the United States of America

*To my wife Eva,*
*to our children Jack and Karen,*
*and our grandchildren Greg, Kevin and Lindsey, and Kristin and Paul*

for their understanding and tolerance when I was spending a great amount of time and effort on SVU matters instead of devoting it to them. Beyond that, my wife, of her own volition, devoted considerable time to the needs of our Society, including the preparation of multiple editions of the SVU Biographical Directory, and was always there when needed.

# Table of Contents

*Preface*     xi

*Foreword*     xv

## Part I:
## The Formative Years

1. Planting the Seed — 3
2. Recruited for SVU — 9
3. The SVU Preparatory Council at Work — 15
4. Vaclav Hlavatý's Presidency — 21
5. The First SVU Congress — 26
6. Editing Congress Proceedings — 30
7. René Wellek's Presidency — 36
8. The Second SVU Congress — 41
9. Wellek's Second Term — 45
10. The Second Congress Collection — 50
11. Hlavatý Returns to SVU Presidency — 55

## Part II:
## After the Prague Spring

12. Jaroslav Němec's Presidency — 63
13. Jan Mládek's Presidency — 71
14. Francis Schwarzenberg's Presidency — 77
15. Beating the Prince — 82
16. As SVU President — 87
17. The Los Angeles Annual Meeting — 96
18. The US Bicentennial SVU Congress — 100
19. My Second Term — 106
20. SVU Conference in Ottawa — 113

| | | |
|---|---|---|
| 21. | The Cleveland Congress | 116 |
| 22. | Jan Tříska's Presidency | 121 |
| 23. | Leopold Pospíšil's Presidency | 126 |
| 24. | Pospíšil's Second Term | 131 |
| 25. | Jiří Nehněvajsa's Presidency | 136 |
| 26. | Nehněvajsa's Second Term | 141 |
| 27. | Igor Nábělek's Presidency | 146 |

## Part III
### The Aftermath of the Velvet Revolution

| | | |
|---|---|---|
| 28. | The Collegium of Presidents Acts | 153 |
| 29. | SVU Commission for Cooperation with Czechoslovakia | 159 |
| 30. | Fact-Finding Mission to Czechoslovakia | 162 |
| 31. | Critical Assessment of Czechoslovak Needs | 177 |
| 32. | Tříska's Return to the SVU Presidency | 192 |
| 33. | Organizing the First SVU Congress in Prague | 198 |
| 34. | Echoes from Prague Congress | 205 |
| 35. | SVU General Assembly in Los Angeles | 210 |
| 36. | Zdeněk Slouka's Presidency | 214 |
| 37. | Organizing the Second Congress in Prague | 225 |
| 38. | Hard Work Bears Fruit – The Second Successful Prague Congress | 229 |

## Part IV
### Twelve Uninterrupted Years as SVU President

| | | |
|---|---|---|
| 39. | Returning to the SVU Presidency | 237 |
| 40. | The Košice Conference | 240 |
| 41. | State of the SVU in 1995 | 245 |
| 42. | SVU World Congress in Brno | 253 |
| 43. | State of the SVU in 1996 | 259 |
| 44. | SVU Goes to Texas | 264 |

Contents vii

| 45. | State of the SVU in 1997 | 268 |
| --- | --- | --- |
| 46. | Organizing the Bratislava Congress | 274 |
| 47. | The Unforgettable Memories | 283 |
| 48. | State of the SVU in 1998 | 288 |
| 49. | Organizing SVU Minnesota Conference | 293 |
| 50. | In the Limelight of President Havel's Visit | 297 |
| 51. | State of the SVU in 1999 | 302 |
| 52. | Organizing the Millennium SVU World Congress | 307 |
| 53. | Beyond Expectations and Our Dreams: Echoes and Reflections from the SVU Millennium Congress | 312 |
| 54. | State of the SVU in 2000 | 318 |
| 55. | The Nebraska Happening | 327 |
| 56. | State of the SVU in 2001 | 332 |
| 57. | Organizing the Plzeň Congress | 338 |
| 58. | Plzeň with Flying Colors | 344 |
| 59. | State of the SVU in 2002 | 350 |
| 60. | Reliving the New World Symphony | 357 |
| 61. | State of the SVU in 2003 | 363 |
| 62. | Organizing the Congress in Olomouc | 370 |
| 63. | The Olomouc Happening | 376 |
| 64. | State of the SVU in 2004 | 382 |
| 65. | Organizing 2005 SVU Conference | 388 |
| 66. | SVU Extravaganza in Florida | 394 |
| 67. | State of the SVU in 2005 | 401 |
| 68. | Organizing the 2006 SVU World Congress | 407 |
| 69. | SVU Scores a Home Run in České Budějovice | 424 |
| 70. | State of the SVU in 2006 | 432 |
| 71. | End of an Era | 439 |

## Part V
## Special Topics

| | | |
|---|---|---|
| 72. | SVU Aims and its Mission | 449 |
| 73. | Organizational Aspects of the Society | 455 |
| 74. | SVU Membership | 464 |
| 75. | SVU Finances | 472 |
| 76. | The Nonpolitical Character of SVU | 477 |
| 77. | SVU Goes International | 486 |
| 78. | Directing SVU Publication Program | 490 |
| 79. | *Zprávy SVU* | 498 |
| 80. | SVU Directory | 506 |
| 81. | *Proměny* | 510 |
| 82. | SVU English Periodical | 516 |
| 83. | The SVU Local Chapters | 523 |
| 84. | In the Background but not in the Shadows | 530 |
| 85. | From an Understudy to a King-Maker | 533 |
| 86. | The Rebellious Local Chapters | 538 |
| 87. | SVU Research Institute Activated | 541 |
| 88. | The SVU Research Institute's First Workshop | 546 |
| 89. | The Second Series of Workshops | 553 |
| 90. | SVU Workshop for the Administrators | 562 |
| 91. | Demands for Autonomy of European Chapters | 569 |
| 92. | Preserving Our Cultural Heritage | 578 |
| 93. | The MZV Grant | 584 |
| 94. | Survey of Czech-American Historic Sites | 589 |
| 95. | Survey of Czechoslovak American Archivalia | 592 |
| 96. | SVU Archives Repository | 596 |
| 97. | Working Archival Conference | 602 |
| 98. | SVU Fellows | 608 |

| | | |
|---|---|---|
| 99. | SVU Website | 613 |
| 100. | Bibliography of SVU Publications | 619 |

**Appendices**

| | |
|---|---|
| Table 1: Chief Executive Officers of the Society | 637 |
| Table 2: SVU General Assembly Meetings | 638 |
| Table 3: SVU World Congresses | 640 |
| Table 4: SVU Local Chapters | 641 |
| Table 5: Major SVU Awards | 642 |
| *List of Illustrations* | 646 |
| *Bibliographic Note* | 649 |
| *Author's Biography* | 650 |
| *Name Index* | 653 |

# *Preface*

This is an eyewitness account to SVU history, not only from the perspective of an outside witness but also as an insider and an active participant, frequently in the leading role. I was on the ground floor when the Society started and participated in most SVU Executive Board meetings, as well as in the meetings of the Council and the SVU General Assemblies. I also partook in all SVU Congresses, many of which I also organized and was responsible for their academic programs. Moreover, as the first chairman of SVU Publication Program, I played a pivotal role in shaping the SVU publications' agenda.

Working in close association with Dr. Jaroslav Němec, who was instrumental in my joining SVU, I was fortunate enough to see the inside workings of SVU from the very beginning, in spite of my relatively young age, being almost twenty years junior to most of my SVU colleagues. Early on, my mentor acquainted me with almost every aspect of the Society work, and we frequently debated the challenges and the opportunities the Society faced. He obviously was grooming me for my future leadership role in the Society.

In the formative days of the Society, the officers were more closely knit together than today, working closely as a team, selflessly, for the common goal to sustain and to enhance the good name of Czechoslovakia on the international forum, especially academically. We were all enthusiastic about our work and whatever we did, we did without any compensation.

I had the opportunity to work closely with such SVU "Greats" as Professor Václav Hlavatý, Prof. René Wellek, Prof. Vratislav Bušek, Prof. Francis Dvorník, the editor Ivan Herben, Dr. Jan V. Mládek, Dr. Ladislav Radimský, Dr. Rudolf Šturm, Dr. Vojtech E. Andic, Dr. John G. Lexa, Dr. Jiří Škvor, Prof. Ladislav Matějka, Prof. Jan F. Tříska, Prof. Leopold Pospíšil, Prof. Jiří Nehněvajsa, Prof. Zdeněk Slouka, Frank Marlow, the writer Josef Škvorecký, as well as with the pianist virtuoso Rudolf Firkušný, the world renown conductor Rudolf Kubelík and the beloved opera singer Jarmila Novotná. Some of them held important

SVU positions, such as Secretary General, SVU President, SVU Treasurer, Editor of the newsletter *Zprávy SVU* or the Czech/Slovak periodical *Proměny* or the English periodical *Kosmas*.

After the Velvet Revolution, my contacts were considerably expanded by the key personalities in Czechoslovakia and the Successor States, such as President Václav Havel, President Václav Klaus, Presidents of the Academy: Otto Wichterle, Rudolf Zahradník and Václav Paces, Rector of Charles University Radim Palouš, Senator /Rector Josef Jařáb of Olomouc, Rectors of ČVUT Stanislav Hanzl and Petr Zuna, Vice Rector Alexander Tkáč of the Slovak Technical University, Senator Václav Roubíček of Ostrava, the new Czech and Slovak Ambassadors to the United States: Michael Žantovský, Sáša Vondra, Martin Palouš, Petr Kolář, Martin Bútora and Rastislav Káčer, pianist Radoslav Kvapil, Deans Ivo Budil and Ivo Barteček of the University of South Bohemia and the Palacký University in Olomouc, respectively, Vice Rector Vladimír Papoušek of the University of West Bohemia and many others. They all were extremely helpful with our various activities in the Czechlands and in Slovakia, to me and SVU.

Thanks to the series of research grants workshops which I organized in various parts of Czechoslovakia and its Successor States, jointly with Dr. Zdeněk Slouka, under the sponsorship of the SVU Research Institute, I came in contact with many other major figures in various universities and research institutions throughout Bohemia, Moravia and Slovakia.

This publication is essentially arranged chronologically, starting with the formative years through the events after the Prague Spring and the aftermath of the Velvet Revolution and ending with the section of my continuous service to the Society as its President for twelve years. The administrative period of each SVU President is covered separately, within the respective chapters. Apart from the chronological arrangement of chapters, I have also included several specific chapters that did not lend themselves to chronological approach because they overlapped several time periods or did not exactly fall into SVU agenda or calendar, such as The Nonpolitical Character of SVU, SVU Goes International, SVU English Periodical, In the Background but Not in the Shadows, From an Understudy to a King Maker, etc.

*Preface* xiii

As for the sources, I used the documents from the "SVU Archives" and the "Miloslav Rechcígl, Jr. Papers," maintained at the University of Minnesota's Immigration History Research Center (IHRC), as well as my own personal archival material. I have, of course, also heavily relied on my own memory and recollections, since I was fortunate enough to partake in most of the Society's events and activities.

As expressed and viewed by most academically-inclined individuals, the creation of SVU has been the greatest achievement of the post-February 1948 exile, which does not have equal in the Czechoslovak history. Although some of the other ethnic groups tried to emulate its World Congresses, none of them came even close to the variety and the breadth of the programs the SVU mustered at its meetings.

This monograph should not be viewed as an official SVU history. That still needs to be written. To make the job for the future historians easier, I have made a deliberate effort to document each important SVU event and activity and identify all the key players by appropriate footnote or reference and provide background to all major decisions that have been made by the Society.

I would like to conclude with an amusing anecdotal episode which actually happened to me not too long ago. Because of my identical name with my father, I usually added "Jr." to my name. Nevertheless, some people still confused us. During my recent conversation with one of my friends – mind you, he was an important SVU officer for several years – I brought up the subject of my writing SVU history, which prompted him to say: "That important fellow in SVU that was your father! Wasn't he?" When I told him that, although he was a member, my father was not active in the Society, and that "the important fellow" must have been me, I presume, his respect towards me must have risen by a couple of notches. This episode shows why it is important to record SVU history, before all the institutional memory is all gone.

Finally, I must convey my gratitude to Mr. Peter Sis for allowing us to use his magnificent illustration of Prague for our book jacket. Thanks are also due to Jiří Eichler for his assistance with the initial formatting of the manuscript and, furthermore, I would like to express my appreciation to Dr. Stephen Fischer-Galati and his highly intelligent and imaginative daughter Nancy Tyson for getting the book ready for the final printing and the preparation of the Name Index. To complete the record, I would also like to acknowledge the indispensible role of my wife, who read individual chapters, as I wrote them, critiqued them, proofread them and, at the end, helped me correct the proofs.

*Miloslav Rechcigl, Jr.*
*Rockville, MD, May 2008*

# *Foreword*

This is a unique book about an unique organization which has now existed for fifty years and which has done a lot for the image and the visibility of Czechoslovakia and its Successor States, the Czech and the Slovak Republics, both during the Cold War and after the Velvet Revolution. The Czechoslovak Society of Arts and Sciences, of which I speak, or SVU in short, an acronym, which stands for" Společnost pro vědy a umění," under which it is generally known, even in the Western World, was officially established in 1958, after several years of preparatory work. It was organized by the Czechoslovak intellectuals abroad who were forced to abandon their native land, after the forceful takeover of Czechoslovakia by Communists in February 1948. The original planning for the Society was done in Washington, DC, the US National Capital, but its establishment was officially announced in New York City.

The main purpose of the Society was to improve Czechoslovakia's image abroad, which was greatly tarnished by the Communist system, and to return dignity to its peoples. The Communist regime obstructed the scientific and artistic development and, in many areas of cultural life, it actually destroyed the wealth of the country's thousand-year-long traditions. As stated in the original Society's Proclamation, "We, in the free world, must maintain viable continuity with the treasures of our European civilization, which took centuries to build. It is our solemn obligation to keep creating moral values, scientific and artistic, so that, one day, they could resuscitate the free culture, when Czechoslovakia again is politically free. It is our obligation to erect one of the bridges which will outlast even the life of its builders, which will link the free generations of the past, the present and the future, across the abyss that opened up among them by today's lack of freedom."

Since its inception, the SVU has grown into a respected international organization with chapters in major cities around the world. To date, the Society has organized twenty-three SVU World Congresses, some twenty European and over twenty American and Canadian conferences, over thirty art exhibits, more than fifty musical and drama productions, and more than twenty book displays. Furthermore, it has published some two hundred monographs and other occasional publications, four periodicals, besides sponsoring or providing support to some fifty other books. There must have been some 4,000 lectures presented at various SVU World Congresses and Conferences, some of which were in the context of symposia or discussion panels. In addition to the above, each Local Chapter has organized meetings, lectures, discussions, exhibits and social functions. This is a remarkable achievement by any standard.

In the opinion of many, SVU does not have an equal in the history of Czechs and Slovaks abroad.

This book, which gives a detailed account of the Society's existence and activities of fifty years, between 1956 and 2006, has been written by one of the Society's founders and for many years its President, Dr. Miloslav Rechcígl, Jr., who more than any one else is qualified to write it. He has been involved with the Society's matters from the very beginning, not only as a passive witness but as an active participant and leader, who guided the Society's path and set its policies for many years, sixteen of which were in the capacity as SVU President. It is beyond the scope of this Foreword to go through his various accolades. Suffice it to say that many of the SVU initiatives came from him, most of which were also single handedly carried out by him to successful completion, including the organization of SVU World Congresses, directing SVU publication program, jointly with his wife preparing SVU Biographical Directories, laying the foundation for the launching of the SVU English periodical, establishing SVU Research Institute, launching concerted effort to preserve Czech and Slovak cultural heritage abroad, surveying Czech American historical sites, making inventory and publishing Czechoslovak American Archivalia, etc. He participated in the 100th Anniversary of the Czech Academy of Arts and Sciences and I am delighted to say that my predecessor Prof. Otto Wichterle awarded him, on that occasion, the Josef Hlávka Medal. I also recall with pleasure my participation in one of the SVU Research Institute's highly effective workshops on research management and granstmanship, which Dr. Rechcígl conducted, jointly with Prof. Zdeněk Slouka, here in the Academy. I have known Míla personally from the time democracy came back to Czechoslovakia and we have maintained a warm friendship ever since.

*Foreword*

As readers will find out for themselves, what the Society has accomplished in its fifty years of existence, boggles the mind and the story is truly inspirational. To be sure, the activities of the Czechoslovak Society of Arts and Sciences clearly reflect the love and the devotion of the Czechs and the Slovaks abroad to the land of their birth and must be viewed as an integral part of our Czechoslovak cultural history.

This is a must reading for everyone, especially for our young generation.

*Václav Pačes*
President, Academy of Sciences of the Czech Republic

# Part I
# The Formative Years

# 1
## *Planting The Seed*

The idea to organize the Czechoslovak scholars, scientists and artists abroad did not obviously originate in the mind of only one individual. It most certainly must have occurred to a number of people who were displaced in various parts of the globe, after being forced to escape from the Communist Czechoslovakia, including Professor Hlavatý,[1] as related in Jaroslav Němec's reminiscences.[2]

Nevertheless, it is the fact that it was primarily due, thanks to the diligent work and perseverance of one particular individual, Dr. Jaroslav Němec,[3] that the idea was actually realized. The rationale for the establishment of an organization of Czechoslovak intellectuals abroad was provided by Němec in his historical article of reminiscences in *Zprávy SVU*.[4]

I heard from Jaroš, as he liked to be called, that he already discussed this matter in 1954, with his friend Dr. Václav Mostecký,[5] who, just as Němec, resided in the US National Capital, Washington, DC.[6] I should point out that there were two other individuals, besides Němec and Mostecký, who were involved in the initial discussion of the planned Society, namely Jaroslav Polach[7] and Branislav Štefánek,[8] but the former subsequently excused himself, because of the pressure of his

---

[1] Václav Hlavatý (1894-1969), a noted Czech mathematician; in the US, he held the position of full professor at Indiana University in Bloomington.

[2] Jaroslav Němec, *Zprávy SVU,* vol. 9, No. 4 (July-August 1987), pp. 6-10 (see specifically p. 8).

[3] Jaroslav Němec (1910-1992), lawyer and librarian, living in Washington, DC.

[4] Jaroslav Němec, *Zprávy SVU, Op. cit.*

[5] Václav Mostecký (1919- 2004), lawyer and librarian, living in Washington, DC, at that time.

[6] There was apparently also Dr. Jaroslav Polach involved in the early discussions.

[7] Jaroslav G. Polach (1914-1993), lawyer and economist by training, who, from 1952 until 1961, worked for the central intelligence service.

[8] Branislav Štefánek (1923-1973), journalist with Radio Free Europe, Munich Germany; he was a native of Slovakia.

job,[9] and with respect to the latter, I could never discern the nature of his involvement.

What Němec and Mostecký had, actually, in mind was organizing the younger generation of refugees who were contemplating entering scientific careers in the US. No thought was given to artists, at that time. They thought of establishing a periodical in English in which the members of the planned organization would publish their works. In that way, the newly established Society would aid the students in getting ahead, while, at the same time, would inform the English public of these rising future scholars. This Society was also to assist its members by providing personal references and by assisting them in seeking employment. Inasmuch as they felt that covering all scientific disciplines in one organization would not be manageable, they decided to focus on social sciences only, i.e., anthropology, economics, philology, history, education, law, psychology and sociology.

Němec and Mostecký had, in fact, drafted invitation letters already in 1955 which they intended to send out to the respective Czechs, Slovaks and Ruthenians abroad.

Their recruitment letter, however, was never sent out because they were concerned that the undersigned were known only to a narrow circle of individuals, fearing that without the support of the leading scholars and scientists of Czechoslovak descent would end with fiasco. Thus the idea was tabled for a time, waiting for a more opportune moment.

The opportunity presented itself when the Czechoslovak National Council of America (CNCA) established a new chapter in Washington, DC and when Němec became its chairman. Mostecký, under Němec's influence, accepted the responsibility for heading the Chapter's newly established Study Section. Němec and Mostecký thought that with these structures they may finally be able to realize their dream to organize Czechoslovak scientists abroad. By holding offices in the largest Czechoslovak organization in the US, they were certain that their proposal would now be taken more seriously.

---

[9] Polach focused his energies for a while on the new Washington DC Local Chapter but soon also left it. Later on, for unknown reasons, he completely dissociated himself from SVU, until I brought him back in 1974, when I became SVU President.

*Planting the Seed*

Without further ado, under Němec's guidance, Mostecký presented their plan at the CNCA Congress, held in Washington on May 3, 1957. The CNCA leadership approved the idea and gave the Study Section the responsibility of preparing a detailed proposal for the establishment of "Československá společnost pro vědy a umění" (SVU) (Czechoslovak Society of Arts and Science). The first task was to gather addresses of Czechoslovak university professors and other scientific and cultural workers. It is noteworthy that the effort was not limited only to America but the organizers encompassed the whole world, where the Czechoslovak refugees were scattered. It should also be pointed out that in this effort, they broadened the scope and began gathering information not only in the area of sciences but covered the other major professions, including the artists.

Although the organizers were convinced of the correctness of their approach, they wanted, nevertheless, to check it first against the opinion of selected Czechoslovak intellectuals abroad. Consequently, some forty persons were contacted in November 1957 regarding this. Most answers already began coming early in December and the rest of the responses came in January 1958, with only a few stragglers in subsequent months. Statistically, thirty-eight replies were positive, of which 26 were accompanied with enthusiastic commentary. Only one person sent in a negative reply, stating that "you don't have any money and consequently you won't accomplish anything."

To be sure, all the individuals contacted were leading Czechoslovak intellectuals abroad who were well known. Most of them had established professional careers already in Czechoslovakia, although several younger persons were also contacted who began establishing successful careers abroad.

They included such people as Dr. Vladislav Brdlík, former professor of the Czech Technical University in Prague, Dr. Vratislav Bušek, former professor, dean and rector of Comenius University in Bratislava, Dr. Milič Čapek, professor at Carleton College in Northfield, MN, Dr. Václav Hlavatý, former professor of Charles University, later at Indiana University in Bloomington, piano virtuoso Rudolf Firkušný, Ivan Herben, former editor of *Svobodné slovo*, later associated with Radio Free Europe, Dr. Karel Boleslav Jirák, noted music composer and conductor, Dr. František Král, former professor and dean of the Veterinary

University in Brno, Rafael Kubelík, world renown composer and former conductor of the Czech Philharmonic, Dr. Jozef Lettrich, Slovak attorney and politician, later VP of the Council of Free Czechoslovakia, Dr. Otakar Machotka, former professor of Charles University, Dr. Victor Mamatey, professor at Florida State University in Tallahassee, František Munk, professor at Reed College in Portland, Dr. Jiří Nehněvajsa, at that time, professor at Columbia University, Jarmila Novotná, famous opera singer with the Metropolitan Opera in New York, Dr. Jan Maria Novotný, former professor of Prague Business College, Dr. Joseph S. Rouček, professor at University of Bridgeport, CT, Dr. René Wellek, professor at Yale University, etc.

Many of them sent lengthy commentary, excerpts of which were reprinted in the *Zprávy SVU*.[10] It is of interest to quote from some of the received comments:

> Prof. Dr. Vladislav Brdlík: Your planned society will fulfill the felt need – uniting the Czechoslovak intelligentsia. Don't get side-tract with unimportant issues. Get going! We'll all help without unimportant debates.
>
> Rudolf Firkušný: I agree with your proposal and welcome every initiative to support and organize scientists, writers and artists of the Czechoslovak origin.
>
> Ivan Herben: I am certainly in favor and agree without reservations with your proposal. I will gladly become a member and if accepted, an active member, indeed.
>
> Prof. Dr. Václav Hlavatý: I wholeheartedly congratulate you on the splendid idea. I personally strode for similar thing but the timing was not right. I will fully support the project with all my strength.
>
> Prof. Dr. František Král: I wholeheartedly welcome your efforts to organize scientific workers and artists of Czechoslovak origin and the friends of the Czechoslovak arts and sciences. I agree to include my name among the persons who support the project.
>
> Rafael Kubelík: I wish to be part of your effort – for the mission of intellectuals and artists abroad I consider: to propagate and maintain the old democratic culture of Czechs and Slovaks and continu-

---

[10] Jaroslav Němec, *Zprávy SVU*, vol. 29, No. 2 (March-April 1987), pp. 5-9.

ously remind the world of it. It seems to me that in the stage of cold war the word should be given to Czechoslovak scientists and artists whose goal is to maintain in the sub-conscience of the free world the free Czechoslovak cultural tradition from the time of the Masaryk Republic.

Jarmila Novotná: I read your proposal indeed with greatest interest and feel that your plans are highly praiseworthy.... Such a project, I feel, should have the support of every Czechoslovakian.

Prof. Dr. Joseph S. Rouček: I shall be glad, of course, to join your effort to organize the scholars of the Czechoslovak background. You may use my name!

Jan Rubeš: I consider your step important, deserving support and also an activity that should bring practical results with the popularization and enhancement of the good name of Czechoslovakia.

Encouraged with such a response, the organizers went ahead with the recruitment of members, by sending out some 500 additional letters addressed to scholars, scientists, artists and students at universities. The response was so overwhelming that by May 1958, the number of members exceeded the 200 mark.

Having relinquished his responsibilities as the head of the Washington chapter of CNCA, Němec was able to take over the leadership of the Study Section, after Mostecký had to leave for personal reasons. In this capacity, he presented a detailed plan for organizing the new SVU at the subsequent CNCA Congress, held in Chicago in February 1958. The new body was to be an integral part of the CNCA. The CNCA approved the preliminary proposal and assigned to the Study Section the responsibility for its implementation.

The Study Section then proceeded to form the 14-member Preparatory Council which would take over its work and work out the necessary organizational details prior to convening the SVU General Assembly meeting. This was done through an election process in which 80% of signed members participated. The outcome of the election was as follows: Dr. Václav Hlavatý, chairman; and Rafael Kubelík, Dr. Vratislav Bušek, Dr. Otakar Machotka, Dr. Eduard Táborský. Dr. František Schwarzenberg, Dr. Jiří Škvor, Dr. Ladislav Radimský, Dr. Václav Beneš, Dr. Vladislav Brdlík, Ivan Herben and Jarmila Novotná, members. They are listed in order of the votes they received. In addition to these members, the Study Section delegated three other individuals, namely Dr. Jaroslav Němec, Dr. Oldřich Černý and Dr. Jaroslav Jíra.

Although the Study Section completed its assigned task, it still was responsible for all the administrative work until the meeting of the Council took place. In August 1958 the New York members of the SVU Preparatory Council met with the representatives of the Study Section to discuss the next steps. The meeting went well except for Dr. Ladislav Radimský's[11] refusal to take on the function of the SVU Secretary General, as was recommended by the Washington people. The Study Section was well aware of the fact that the new Secretary General will carry the major administrative load of the Society and as a consequence wanted to divide the post into two functions, General Secretary who would be responsible for the development of the society and Organizational Secretary who would handle administrative matters, such as membership drive, bylaws, card catalogue, contact with members and local chapters, etc. The Washingtonians had preference to having one Secretary General only, the idea of which prevailed.

On September 17, 1958, the Study Section met for the purpose of preparing the program of the upcoming "Charter" meeting of the SVU Preparatory Council. On the 18th of October the SVU made its first appearance in public at the Jan Masaryk Club in Chicago, where Professor Václav Hlavatý, the newly elected head of the SVU Preparatory Council spoke, followed by Dr. Němec. Both presentations were well received.

The Charter meeting of the new SVU Preparatory Council was scheduled for October 24, 1958 in New York City.

---

[11] Ladislav Radimský (1896-1970), former Czechoslovak diplomat and noted writer.

# 2
## *Recruited For SVU*

My first contact with SVU,[12] as we called the Czechoslovak Society of Arts and Sciences[13] for short, began while I was still at Cornell University working on my doctorate. I was the recipient of one of the early letters Dr. Jaroslav Němec sent informing me about plans to organize a new society of Czechoslovak intellectuals abroad.

This Society seemed a bit different from other Czech organizations, most of which had some political goal. This organization seemed different; completely apolitical with the aim of keeping alive historic traditions which were denied and rejected by the current communist regime. It was music to my ears and I had not to think long before I was "hooked." I could not have imagined that any Czech scientist or scholar would not respond affirmatively to such a noble call.[14] I was delighted by the idea and promptly responded in the affirmative and sent in my filled-out application for membership.

After coming to Washington in the fall 1958,[15] I soon made the acquaintance of Dr. Němec and Dr. Jaroslav Polach who were clearly in the forefront of this effort. As I recall, we invited them to our little rented house in Bethesda, during which time I learned more details about the new initiative.

I do not recall the exact sequence of events but it did not take long after coming to Washington for Eva and me to attend the lectures organized by the Society's Washington-based Study Section, later changed to SVU Washington, DC Chapter.

---

[12] The acronym for "Společnost pro vědy a umění."

[13] The Society was actually originally known as Czechoslovak Society of Arts and Sciences in America. During my SVU Presidency the words "in America" were dropped to denote the SVU international character.

[14] To be sure, there were some doubters, and even opposition, especially coming from the leaders of various Czechoslovak political parties who saw some competition with or even threat to their activities.

[15] I was a postdoctoral fellow at the National Institutes of Health in Bethesda, MD, which was a part of the Washington Metropolitan area.

During the Annual Meeting of the Chapter, convened on June 1, 1960, it was generally expected that Jaroslav Polach, the then chairman, would continue in his function. He, however, decided against it because of the pressure of his job. The members therefore proceeded to elect a five-member working group, including myself, with the responsibility of coming up with the slate of candidates for the new term. Jáša Drábek[16] initially expressed interest in the post of the Chapter's chair, but then changed his mind. The presidency was therefore offered to Dr. Ladislav Feierabend[17] who accepted. I was elected secretary, Miloš Jansa[18] treasurer and Vojtěch Nevlud[19] vice chairman and press officer. Jáša Drábek and Josef Kučera were elected members of the Board without specific functions.

My main job was to write the minutes, send out the invitations and keep track of the membership. These responsibilities, however, were soon augmented to also include the responsibility for correspondence and in addition I became a member of the program committee. For practical purposes, most of the programs were, in fact, prepared by me. We initiated the practice of allowing only SVU members or specifically invited guests to attend. This, of course, increased the interest in our lectures, since nobody wanted to be left out.

Josef Kučera,[20] a kind elderly man who lived with his wife on Park Road, not too far from Jaroslav Němec, usually helped me with the printing of the announcements. He was a journalist by background who published regularly, in monthly intervals, the newsletter, *Zpravodajství z Washingtonu*.[21] As such, he had access and knew how to operate a somewhat primitive mimeo-graphic machine.

Our main activities focused on the lecture series relating to preserving historical documents and memoirs relating to the "Development of the Idea of Czechoslovak State in 1938-1948." The meetings were held

---

[16] Jaroslav Drábek (1932-1992), a graduate student at the time, who later became a lawyer. He was the oldest son of Dr. Jan Drábek who prosecuted Hermann Frank.

[17] Ladislav K, Feierabend (1891-1969), Czech politician, employed by Voice of America in Washington, DC.

[18] Miloš Jansa (1923-), pediatrician, living in Landover Hills, MD.

[19] Vojtěch Nevlud (1920-2005), journalist with the Voice of America, Washington, DC.

[20] Josef Kučera (1896-1982), a journalist.

[21] News from Washington.

in monthly intervals, usually at 7:30 PM, the second Friday of the month, in the Alliance Room of the All Souls Church on 16th & Harvard Sts., N.W., Washington, DC.

We customarily invited prominent politicians of the 1938-1948 period to give us personal and authoritative accounts of their activities and experiences, accompanied with explanations and documentary evidence. In addition to their oral presentation, which was tape-recorded, each participant also had to present his contribution in writing.

Since I saved the minutes from that time period, I know exactly who the speakers were. For the sake of history, they are listed below.

### *Lectures Presented during 1960-1961 Period*

October 7 – Václav Majer: "Trip to Moscow and the Beginnings of the Kosice Program"

November 8 – Dr. Ladislav Feierabend: "Hácha and Experiences in the Government of the Protectorate"

December 9 – Jaroslav Drábek: "Beginnings of Czechoslovak Resistance during the WW II"

January 13 – Dr. Theodore Procházka: "Berlin 1938-1944. My Memories"

February 10 – Dr. Jozef Lettrich: "Recollections from the Czechoslovak Domestic Resistance and Slovakia in 1939-1943"

March 10 – Gen. Josef Schejbal: "Czechoslovak Air Force during the World War II"

April 4 – Dr. Arnošt Heidrich: "International Political Causes of Our National Tragedy – February 1948"

May 2 – Banquet and Reception – Dr. Ladislav Radimský: "Commentary at the Margin of Contemporary Czech Literature"

### *Lectures Presented during 1961-1962 Period*

September 8 – A Discussion Panel: "Goals and Aims of the Czechoslovak Society of Arts and Sciences in America" Panelists: Dr. Jaroslav Němec, Jan Hajda, Čestmír Ješina, Dr. Frank Meissner, Dr. J. Polach, Ivan Herben and Dr. Jozef Lettrich

October 16 – Dr. Karel Steinbach: "Karel Čapek and his Times"

November 10 – Mikuláš Ferjenčik: "Recollections from and Experiences in Moscow and the Slovak National Uprising"

January 12 – Ivan Herben: "Brother Josef – Memories of the Capek Brothers from Lidové Noviny and Josef Čapek from Concentration Camp"

February 15 – Marie Provazníková "The Sokol Contributions to the Origin, Development and Democracy of the Czechoslovak State"

April 20-22 – "First Congress of the Czechoslovak Society of Arts and Sciences in America"

June 22 – Annual Meeting – Discussion Panel: "Comments on the First SVU Congress" Panelists: Dr. Jaroslav Drábek, Dr. Zorka Černá, Josef Hasek, Vojtěch Nevlud, Dr. Zora Procházková, Arch. Emil Royco.

The presentations usually were followed by intensive discussions and commentary from the audience. Because of the frequently controversial nature of the topics some of these discussions were quite lively and even confrontational. The meetings were run with an iron hand so that they never got out of hand. I do recall only one "ugly" incident, when Jozef Čambalík,[22] a Slovak who served in the military, accused Dr. Jozef Lettrich and other Slovaks of stealing the "Slovak Golden Treasure." We sent him a letter subsequently informing him that he won't be permitted to attend future SVU meetings unless he can produce convincing evidence for his accusations.

It should be noted that the referenced series of lectures were actually the first occurrence in the Czechoslovak post World War II exile of having politicians of opposing views talking from the same platform. Until SVU came up with this lecture series, they would hardly ever speak to one another.

During my tenure as secretary, I developed a very close relationship with Ladislav Feierabend who also taught me a lot regarding organization, management and diplomatic skills. He was a kind person and very effective when dealing with people.

To get more people interested and involved, he introduced the practice of having each speaker introduced by a different person who also

---

[22] Jozef Čambalík (1911-1989), Slovak army officer with the rank of Colonel.

moderated the discussion. This required some preparation and the person also gained invaluable experience in public speaking.

To make the meetings more sociable, my wife Eva came up with one innovation, namely to have every meeting followed by refreshments. This practice, which has been kept to date, gave each meeting a friendlier and more sociable atmosphere conducive to opening up and talking to one another.

I remained secretary for two terms (June 1, 1960-June 22, 1962). Subsequently I had to relinquish this function in order to devote attention to publications and other SVU matters at the national level. Upon leaving, as I reported in my report to the General Assembly, the Washington DC Chapter had 83 members, in comparison to 74 in September 1961. The list of officers and members of the Washington DC Chapter from the 1960-61 period is reproduced below.

### Czechoslovak Society of Arts and Sciences, Washington DC Chapter
### Officers 1960-1961

*President:* Dr. Ladislav K. Feierabend, 3821 Newark St., NW, Washington 16, DC
*Vice President*: Vojtěch Nevlud, 3675 Camden St., SE, Washington 20, DC
*Secretary*: Dr. Miloslav Rechcígl, Jr., 1703 Mark Lane, Rockville, MD
*Treasurer*: Dr. Miloš A. Jansa, 7403 Varnum St., Landover Hills, MD
*Board*: L. K. Feierabend, V. Nevlud, M. Rechcígl, Jr., M. A. Jansa, J. Drábek, Jr., J. Kučera

### *Chapter Members*

| | | |
|---|---|---|
| Basch, Antonín, Dr. | Drábek, Jaroslav, Dr. | Hasal, Milan J. |
| Boehmer, Alois, Dr. | Drábek, Jaroslav A., Jr. | Hasalová-White, Dagmar |
| Brodenová, Lída | Eret, Josef P., Gen. | Hašek, Josef, Dr. |
| Černá, Zorka M., Dr. | Feierabend, L. K., Dr. | Heidrich, Arnošt, Dr. |
| Černý, George | Feierabendová, Jana | Hexner, Ervin, Dr. |
| Černý, Oldřich | Fiala, Jiří, Dr. | Ingrová, Cilka |
| Dalecká, Zdenka | Fischmeister, Ladislav, Dr. | Jansa, Miloš A., Dr. |

Jarolím, John S.
Ješina, Čestmír
Jíra, Jaroslav, Dr.
Kaše, František, Dr.
Kaše, Karel, Dr.
Kašpar-Pátý, Jaroslav, Col.
Klímek, Adolf, Dr.
Klimeš, Jan
Klimešová, Naďa
Kočvara, Štefan, Dr.
Koeppl, Evžen C.
Kolafa, Josef, Ing.
Kreysa, Frank J., Dr.
Kučera, Josef
Kybal, Milič, Dr.
Lajda, Brano, Dr.
Lejková, Milada, Dr.
Lettrich, Jozef, Dr.
Liberský, Frank
Lišková, Marta

Majer, Václav
Maňhal, Gertruda
Marynchak, Arnošt
Michal, Jaromír J.
Mládek, Jan V., Dr.
Munz, Otto John, Dr.
Naylor, Herbert, Maj.
Němec, Jaroslav, Dr.
Němcova, Jarmila
Neumann, Matěj
Nevlud, Vojtěch
Nosek, Jindřich, Dr.
Palic, Vladimír, Dr.
Polach, Jaroslav G., Dr
Procházka, Theodor, Dr.
Procházka, Zorka, Dr.
Ptáček, Zdeněk
Rechcígl, Miloslav, Jr., Dr.
Royco, Emil
Sádlík, Josef, Dr.
Schlosberg, Květa G.

Sládek, Jaromil, Dr.
Sládková, Gertrude, Dr.
Slávik, Juraj, Dr.
Slávik, Juraj L. J., Jr.
Šturc, Ernest, Dr.
Šturman, Pavel
Švestka, Miroslav J.
Szalatnay, Louisa
Zenkl, Petr, Dr.

**Outside Washington Area**

Bednar, Charles S. (VA)
Brychta, Ivan (VA)
Cihlář, Antonín (MD)
Hajda, Jan, Dr. (MD)
Hapala, Milan E. (VA)
Hauzenblas, J. W., Dr.(VA)
Hejný, Frank (MD)
Lomský, Igor, Dr. (MD)
Matoušek, Karel (MD)
Švejda, Agnes F. (MD)

# 3
# *The SVU Preparatory Council At Work*

Before Dr. Václav Hlavatý assumed the formal title as SVU President, he headed the Society in the capacity as chairman of the SVU Preparatory Council, which was charged with the responsibility of working out the details of the new Society. The Charter meeting of the Council was held in New York on October 24, 1958. This was a memorable meeting which gave the Society an organizational basis, and which implemented decentralization functions and clarified the goals and by electing regional secretaries and committees it laid the foundation for the actual work.[23]

The functions were divided as follows: Rafael Kubelík[24] and Dr. Vratislav Bušek[25] were elected the first and the second Vice Presidents, respectively; Dr. Jaroslav Němec, Secretary General and Oldřich Černý,[26] Treasurer. Several members were without any specific functions, i.e., Dr. Otakar Machotka, Dr. Edward Táborský, Dr. František Schwarzenberg, Dr. Jiří Škvor, Dr. Ladislav Radimský, Dr. Václav Beneš, Dr. Ing. Vladislav Brdlík, Jarmila Novotná, and Dr. Jaroslav Jíra. There were also two alternates, namely Dr. Viktor S. Mamatey and Marie Provazníková.

To make the job of Secretary General easier, and to enhance the effectiveness of the membership drive, the territory of the US was divided into seven regions, each headed by regional secretaries. The latter were Dr. Vaclav Mostecký for Region I (ME, NH, CT, MA, RI, VT), editor Ivan Herben for Region II (NY, DE, NJ), Dr. Vojtech Andic for Region

---

[23] Jaroslav Němec, "Zpráva o vzniku a činnosti SVU (AVU) v r. 1958," Washington, DC, 1958; *Zprávy SVU* – Special issue, p. 2.

[24] Rafael Kubelík (1914-1996), noted Czech conductor and composer.

[25] Vratislav Bušek (1897-1978), professor of church law and former rector of Comenius University.

[26] Oldřich Černý (1926-), living in Washington, DC at that time; he later moved to Switzerland.

III (PA, VA, MD, WV, DC, MI, OH, IN, KY), Dr. Mojmir Povolný for Region IV (ND, SD, MN, WI, IA, NE), Dr. Joseph Čada for Region V (IL), Region VI, editor Josef Martínek for Region VII (AZ, NM. NE, CA, UT, CO) and Prof. Jan Zach for Region VIII (OR, WA, ID, MT, WY). There was no candidate for Region VI at that time.

Several advisory committees were appointed, including membership (Dr. Vratislav Bušek, chair), finances (Dr. František Schwarzenberg), bylaws and rules and procedures (Dr. Jaroslav Jíra), program (Dr. Ing. Vladislav Brdlík), publications (Dr. Otakar Machotka) and biography and bibliography (Oldřich Černý).[27]

Looking at the elected roster of prestigious names, from the distance of years, one gets the distinct feeling that these early elections were primarily based on the popularity contests, in which people were selected primarily on their public image and celebrity status rather than on their management and organizational abilities, which really mattered most. Otherwise, I cannot imagine why Rafael Kubelík would have been elected the first Vice President, knowing too well that he could not possibly attend any of the Council meetings, not to speak about any other substantive involvement. There might have been, of course, other considerations, such as that the behind-the-scene leaders tried to make the Society more visible by having such people among the SVU officers and thus more acceptable in the public eye. In any case, with experience, they were gradually replaced by more appropriate and more effective officers.

Returning back to the subject of this chapter, the principal outcome of the Charter meeting, apart from giving the newly established society its organizational structure, was the clarification of the SVU mission and its aims, although the details had to await the issuance of the new SVU Bylaws.

The Charter meeting also decided to change the name of the organization to Academy of Arts and Sciences within the CNCA ("Akademie věd a umění při ČSNRA"[28] – AVU) and approved the principles of how the new bylaws were to be written.

---

[27] *Zprávy SVU*, vol. 2, No. 5 (May 1960), p. 34.

[28] ČSNRA is a Czech acronym for the Czechoslovak National Council of America.

Generally, it was contemplated that the new Academy would support and provide incentive for scientific and artistic work, call attention to gaps in knowledge and coordinate the work. The new organization was going to provide assistance to members with publication, lecture and promotional activities, preparation of concerts and exhibits, etc. It planned to function as a free, critical and objective organ to assure the highest quality of work, etc.

A new student fund was in preparation, as was a journalist section, and a pamphlet about the Academy was readied for print. Furthermore, at work was a new publication about the Czechoslovak scientists and artists, a working conference in Bloomington and perhaps a banquet in Washington, DC, and a monograph about Czechoslovak immigrants. The various advisory committees were at work to get things started at the beginning of the year 1959.

Following the executive work session, which was closed to the public, there was a public meeting during which the creation of the new Academy was ceremonially announced by reading the solemn and program proclamation and during which the new officers were introduced. This was the first time the new Academy appeared in public as a live, vigorous new body.

The whole event evoked extraordinary interest, not only in the US but also throughout the free world. The entire Czechoslovak democratic press abroad welcomed the new idea with pleasure and joy, the radio widely spread the word and positively commented on the event and large number inquiries began coming in.

At the start of the new year – 1959 – the regional secretaries began their work and at the same time it was decided to return to the original name "Společnost pro vědu a umění" (Czechoslovak Society for Arts and Sciences) or SVU, in short. In March, the editor Ivan Herben was named the SVU Press Secretary.

SVU was considered as an autonomous unit within the CNCA which was to manage its finances independently, although it had to send its membership dues to CNCA in Chicago. From the total of $2 it would retain only a fourth. It was obvious to SVU leadership that this was not sustainable, considering that the membership dues were the only SVU income.

In the meantime, the Washington-based Study Section appointed Dr. Jaroslav Polach as its new head. The Section became, in effect, the first SVU working group, which subsequently changed its name to Washington DC Chapter, the first of the many local chapters to be established within SVU.

By September 1959, the SVU already had 300 members. In the same month, the SVU began publishing its newsletter *Zprávy SVU*,[29] under the able editorship of Ivan Herben.[30] While lots of activities were generated in Washington, DC, New York and Chicago, it became soon apparent that the other SVU centers did relatively little. This prompted Prof. Hlavatý to send out an urgent memorandum to the members of the Preparatory Council. Here are a few excerpts from his letter:

> ... A lot is expected from our Preparatory Council, not only in terms of establishing a firm organizational foundation for the Society, but also to stimulate the Society's activities, generally. The membership hopes that the Council, through its work, enthusiasm and suitable action, will carry out, what until now, nobody succeeded in doing, especially in terms of actual results. Our intellectuals are generally known for their dilatoriness when it comes to the organizational work. This is understandable since the intellectuals normally focus primarily on their creative work. In the present situation, this tendency can be, however, harmful to our Society. It is necessary, at least, at the beginning to behave differently. The building of SVU is a test of character of Czech and Slovak intelligentsia. It will show how much real effort we are willing to devote to a great idea. This is also our last opportunity. As was rightly stated by one of our members, if we won't be able to establish SVU, nobody else would accomplish anything else that would be worthwhile. The present status is unacceptable.

His letter was quite effective and began bringing fruit in terms of the members' productivity, even though it did not become discernable until the beginning of 1960.

---

[29] As pointed out in Ivan Herben's introductory editorial, the Society did not plan to publish a periodical but rather a newsletter, the link among the members, and the tie which will bind the members with their homeland.

[30] Ivan Herben (1900-1968), noted Czech journalist, associated with Radio Free Europe in New York City; son of the well known writer and journalist Jan Herben.

SVU President played undoubtedly an important role in the Society but, as was anticipated, the greatest load was on the shoulders of the Secretary-General Dr. Jaroslav Němec. It was therefore, with reluctance, that Hlavatý accepted Němec's resignation from his post on October 15, 1959, because of the increased demands of his job at the National Library of Medicine.[31]

He was replaced by Dr. Rudolf Šturm,[32] professor at Skidmore College, Saratoga Springs, NY. Šturm stayed in this role for about half a year until the time of the meeting of the SVU General Assembly in April 1960.

In November 1959, the Washington DC Chapter initiated its lecture series,[33] known as "The Idea of the Czechoslovak State during the Years of 1938-1948," with the lecture by Dr. Ladislav Feierarbend, while in Pittsburgh, PA[34], Dr. Vojtech Andic[35] organized a special lecture program, with the participation of Prof. Bušek, Dr. Němec and Dr. Polach.

Within SVU, the major debate centered on the issue of membership categories, specifically whether there should be two or three, one being regular members, the second, associate members and the third, contributing members. By the end of 1959, the SVU had 325 members and $700 in the bank.

The year 1960 was marked by increased activities. The Washington Chapter continued with its lecture series,[36] while a new chapter was organized in Chicago. New York was also ready to establish their chapter. Czech and Slovak media began regularly publishing news about the SVU activities, on the basis of press releases provided by Ivan Herben and his Press service.

On March 7, 1960 CNCA convened its Congress in Washington, DC to which Prof. Hlavatý delegated four SVU representatives, namely

---

[31] *Zprávy SVU*, vol. 1, No. 2 (October 1959), pp. 1-11.

[32] Rudolf Šturm (1912-2000), professor of Italian and Slavic language, Skidmore College, NY.

[33] *Zprávy SVU*, vol. 2, No. 1 (April 1960), pp. 24-25.

[34] *Zprávy SVU*, vol. 1, No. 4 (December 1959), p. 27.

[35] Vojtech E. Andic (1910-1976), professor of economics at Union University, Albany, NY, a native of Slovakia.

[36] *Zprávy SVU*, vol. 2, No. 2 (February 1960), p. 10.

Dr. Bušek, Dr. Jíra,[37] Dr. Němec and Dr. Polach. Among other, they were instructed to inform the CNCA leadership of the SVU's decision not to pay any dues to CNCA.

The SVU delegation informed the Congress of the situation in SVU but did not have much luck in their stand regarding the nonpayment of dues to the parent organization. The Congress increased the amount of money a CNCA member had to pay for dues, which also included the SVU members. When Němec asked to have the dues lowered for the SVU members, he was largely ignored and the discussion ended by the CNCA President's statement that "SVU members are expected to pay full membership dues like anybody else." This was clearly unacceptable to SVU.

On March 26, a new SVU Chapter was established in New York.[38] By this date, they claimed over 80 members and at their first meeting they already had an announced lecturer.

The SVU Preparatory Council had its last meeting on April 15, 1960. As of that date, based on the report of the new Secretary-General Rudolf Šturm, the Society had a total of 370 members, while the Treasury had $904.70 in assets. The Council discussed the draft Bylaws, prepared by the Bylaws Committee, chaired by Dr. Jíra, and prepared the agenda for the upcoming General Assembly meeting, scheduled for the next day.[39]

---

[37] Jaroslav Jíra (1906-1983), lawyer and librarian, with the Library of Congress, Washington, DC; the drafter of the original SVU Bylaws.

[38] *Zprávy SVU*, vol. 2, No. 3 (March 1960), p. 40.

[39] *Zprávy SVU*, vol. 2, No. 1 (January 1960), p 3.

# 4
## *Václav Hlavatý's Presidency*

As scheduled, on April 16, 1960 in New York City, Prof. Hlavatý called the first SVU General Assembly meeting to order, in which 69 members took part from the US and Canada, with several tens of guests. Among the official greeters was Prof. Zykmund Nagorski, representing the Polish Institute, Emilie Welclová, representing CNCA and Dr. Jiří Škvor, on behalf of the Czechoslovak Association of Canada.[40]

Following the reports of various officers came the report of the Treasurer which was approved. Next point on the agenda was the discussion of the new Bylaws which were approved. There were several proposals for granting honorary membership, i.e., to Zdeněk Němeček (in memoriam), Dr. Jan Lowenbach, Josef Martínek and Albin Polášek, which were all approved.

Based on the new Bylaws, the Society has now become an independent organization and thus severed its ties with the CNCA, which was brought about by the shortsightedness of the CNCA leadership. Frankly, I was a bit concerned about the "marriage" between these two organizations, considering the nonpolitical character of SVU which was difficult to reconcile with the clearly political mission of CNCA.

During the elections, new officers were elected,[41] based on the recommendations of the Nominations Committee. Professor Hlavatý was elected President, Professor Vratislav Bušek, Rafael Kubelík, and Dr. Felix Mikula,[42] Vice Presidents; and Dr. Němec, Secretary-General, Oldřich Černý, Treasurer and Ivan Herben, Press Secretary. In addition to the 7-member Executive Board, 32 members were elected to SVU Council, and 8 regional secretaries (4 for the US, 3 for Canada and 1 for

---

[40] *Zprávy SVU*, vol. 2, No. 5 (May 1960), p. 14
[41] *Zprávy SVU*, vol. 2, No. 6 (June 1960), p. 46.
[42] Felix Mikula (1906-1979 ), the former aide to the Archbishop of Prague Josef Beran.

Italy).[43] General Assembly also increased the membership dues to $5 [44] and in parting the members had the satisfaction that a firm foundation was laid for SVU and that the Society is on the right track.

When the meetings were over, Jaroslav Němec took over the agenda from Rudolf Šturm as the new Secretary General. By this time, the SVU Chapters in Washington and Chicago were winding up their activities, as the summer break was approaching. The Chicago Chapter came up with a new project to publish a collection of papers about the Czechoslovak sciences and culture. This first publication initiative unfortunately was not realized and the first SVU publication did not appear until a year later. The summer months were utilized for translating the SVU Bylaws which was required for the incorporation of the Society. Planning of the SVU future was in the hands of the Program Committee which was unfortunately idle. Consequently, Dr. Němec had no choice but to take over this function.

Frankly, in these early days, all of the administrative and organizational work was really on the shoulders of Jaroslav Němec who spent practically all his free time on Society matters, and, of course, without any compensation. He had full support from his first wife, Jarmila Němcová (1914-1967), an elegant lady, who helped him socially, as they frequently had parties in their house, and more over, many out-of-town visitors stayed with them in their spacious house on Park Road in the downtown Washington. He also received help from Dr. Bohuslav Horák, [45] who lived in their house on Park Road as a tenant. He was rather shy and preferred to stay in the background so as not to endanger his relatives in Czechoslovakia.

Václav Hlavatý's role was largely ceremonial, nevertheless, an important one, as he represented SVU in public and frequently was called on to give speeches or participate in discussions on the aims of the Society. There were many doubters among the Czechoslovak exiles and

---

[43] Dr. V. E. Andic (Pittsburgh), Dr. Joseph Čada (Chicago), Dr. Velen Fanderlík (Western Canada), Dr. Mario Hikl (Toronto), Dr. Zdeněk Petrla (Montreal), Milan Vojtek (New York), Jan Zach (Oregon) and Pavel Želivan (Rome).

[44] Actually, one of the reasons for raising the dues was the large costs of publishing *Zprávy SVU* which amounted to, with 10 issues a year, about $900 annually. Had the dues remained at the $2 per member, the Society would be in the red.

[45] Bohuslav Horák (1899-1976), journalist, living in Washington, DC; he was the widower of Dr. Milada Horáková whom the Communists sentenced to death.

some were rather negative, spreading rumors that Hlavatý was building up a political base for himself. The greatest opposition came from politicians,[46] many of whom were associated with the Council of Free Czechoslovakia. With time, the seeming opposition began to subside and many of the previously opposed critics joined the Society, following the saying "if you cannot beat them, join them."

Hlavatý had a great sense of humor and his talks were very entertaining. Although he professionally worked on rather complex and highly theoretical aspects of mathematics he was able to present it in simple terms so that the listeners could follow him even when he talked about the unified theory of relativity.

Ivan Herben was the third member of the Troika that ran the Society in the formative years. *Zprávy SVU* which he edited were very influential and regularly read by members, as well as nonmembers, and were the major means of communication within and outside the Society.

Both Hlavatý and Herben were very kind persons and I was on the best terms with them. They frequently visited Washington and I had ample opportunity to get to know them on a personal basis. Herben had the custom of periodically sending out postcards to individual SVU members about whom he knew were professionally active, asking them to send him a couple of paragraphs about their work for the inclusion in his *Zprávy SVU*. This way, he always had plenty of material to write. No other editor who came after him used this technique, depending only on what the members themselves sent him. He liked wine and as he got older he frequently brought with him a jug of cheap Californian wine, when he came visiting.

In January 1961, at the invitation of a number of Asian and European universities, Professor Hlavatý undertook a lecture tour around the world[47] which took him to California, Hawaii, Japan, Hong-Kong, Thailand, India, Israel, Italy, France, Belgium, England and Ireland. As was characteristic for him, Hlavatý always addressed the universities in the name of SVU and in his capacity as SVU President. He carried with him a Latin inscribed proclamation bearing the Society greetings to the learned institutions of higher learning. The University Chancellors

---

[46] Hlavatý used to be a member of the Chamber of Deputies of the Czechoslovak Parliament in the post-war Czechoslovakia.

[47] *Zprávy SVU*, vol. 3, No.1 (January 1961), p. 1.

customarily attached their seals and insignia to the document as the sign of friendship and good will.[48] This unique document is maintained in the archives of the Indiana University in Bloomington.

Hlavatý's trip was not only a personal triumph for him but it also provided high visibility to SVU around the globe.[49] When he addressed the assembly of the French Academy of Sciences he greeted them in the name of SVU as SVU President. This was the first time the SVU name appeared on the international forum. His trip gave Professor Hlavatý also a splendid opportunity to meet with numerous Czechoslovak scientists and other intellectuals around the world, including Rome, Paris, Brussels and London and inform them about SVU mission and its activities.

In 1961, the organization was incorporated under the laws of the State of New York as a non-profit cultural organization and it assumed the name: Czechoslovak Society of Arts and Sciences in America, Inc. Although the Society maintained its headquarters in the United States, it was clearly an international organization from the start. The original concept of the Society of Czech and Slovak intelligentsia abroad soon also changed into an organization open to all intellectuals, regardless of national background, who were interested in the advancement of Czechoslovak scholarship.

In the spring of 1961, the Society also began preparing for its first Congress which was to be held in Washington during Easter. The Society's image was further enhanced by establishing new SVU Chapters, i.e., in Toronto and in Munich.

On April 29, 1961, the SVU Executive Board met in New York during which the theme for the upcoming Congress was debated. Discussed were also the publication opportunities, and in conclusion the Board decided to create a separate publication corporation,[50] outside SVU, with the aim of finding financial support for publications. Shares in the amount of $25 were to be offered. Toward this end, Dr. Bušek and Dr. John G. Lexa[51] agreed to take the required legal steps. In August 1961 the Society issued its first publication, as a contribution towards

---

[48] *Zprávy SVU*, vol. 3, No.10 (December 1961), pp. 105-106

[49] *Zprávy SVU*, vol. 3, No. 6 (June 1961), p. 49-50.

[50] *Zprávy SVU*, vol. 3, No. 7 (September 1961), p.56.

[51] John G. Lexa (1914-1977), lawyer, living in New York City; chairman of the SVU New York Chapter and later SVU Secretary-General.

the "Dvořák Year," on the occasion of the composer's 120th anniversary of his birth.[52] It was a slender brochure of 31 pages, written by Professor Jirák.[53]

The proposed Arts & Sciences Publishing Corporation was generally well received among the members and in a relatively short time gathered several thousands of dollars. Unfortunately, because of some legal complications the effort had to be terminated and the money returned.

By the fall,[54] the Society had already some 600 members, and the activities of its local chapters were rapidly expanding. Among these, the most active appeared to be the Washington DC Chapter, which, in addition to its regular lecture program organized a special discussion panel regarding the SVU mission, and, beyond that, it carried the major burden for the logistics of the upcoming SVU Congress.

In November 1961 another SVU chapter was established, this time in Montreal, as a result of Prof. Hlavatý's visit there. He was also an invited speaker in Toronto and Ottawa on October 28th during the commemoration of the Czechoslovak National holiday and in addition appeared twice on the Canadian TV.[55]

On December 18, 1961 SVU General Assembly was convened in New York City.[56] It was more or less a formality to satisfy the laws of the New York State in which SVU was incorporated.

The first few months of the year 1962 was devoted to the preparation of the First SVU Congress, which were to follow the General Assembly meeting, which Professor Hlavatý called for April 20, 1962.[57]

---

[52] *Zprávy SVU*, vol. 3, No. 7 (September 1961, p. 57.
[53] Karel B. Jirák, *Antonín Dvořák, 1841-1961*. New York, NY, 1961.
[54] *Zprávy SVU*, vol. 3, No. 8 (October 1961), p. 73.
[55] *Zprávy SVU*, vol.3, No. 9 (November 1961), p. 90.
[56] *Zprávy SVU*, vol. 4, No. 1 (January 1962), p. 6.
[57] *Zprávy SVU*, vol. 4, No. 2 (February 1962), p. 9.

# 5
## The First SVU Congress

Since my early days in Washington I was in frequent contact with Jaroslav Němec, who then held the position of SVU Secretary-General and was, de facto, the chief executive officer of the Society. We often discussed ways to increase SVU effectiveness and visibility. This brought us to the idea of organizing a special SVU conference at the national level.

Despite some initial doubts, the Executive Board of the Society gave us a green light to proceed with the planning of the conference. The Conference, which I later renamed Congress, was to be held in Washington, DC on 22-24 April 1962. A conference program committee was established, consisting of Prof. Vratislav Bušek, Prof. Václav Hlavatý, Prof. Karel B. Jirák,[58] Dr. Jaroslav Němec, Prof. René Wellek,[59] and myself,[60] serving as the committee's secretary.

After initial consultations with the members of the committee, I proposed that the program of the congress focuses on contributions of Czechoslovakia to world culture. The idea came to me from the Czech book, *Co daly naše země Evropě a lidstvu*[61] (What Did Czechlands Give to Europe and the Mankind), published by Vilém Mathesius during the eventful days in Czechoslovakia at the onset of World War II. Inasmuch as the main aim of the congress was to inform American public about the Czechoslovak contributions, I recommended that all lectures be presented in English. My proposal received spirited approval and, from that point onward, I was essentially on my own. Naturally, I kept the committee informed of what I was doing and from time to time asked

---

[58] Karel B. Jirák (1891-1972), composer and conductor. He held the position of Professor of Musicology at Roosevelt University, Chicago, IL.

[59] René Wellek (1903-1995), noted scholar and professor of comparative literature at Yale University, New Haven, CT.

[60] By this time, I already was a regular member of the staff of the Laboratory of Biochemistry of the National Cancer Institute, which was an integral part of the National Institutes of Health in Bethesda, MD.

[61] 2nd ed. Praha: Sfinx – Bohumil Janda, 1940. 426 p.

them for advice. However, with the increasing correspondence and having satisfied the committee with the quality of my work, they let me do it all.

My plan was to select prominent individuals in different areas and let them speak on some aspect of Czechoslovak arts, letters, science or technology. In those days we did not have our *SVU Biographical Directory,* so I had to start from scratch. Frankly, I did not even have access to the addresses of SVU members.

As a scientist, I was well acquainted with libraries which I considered, together with my laboratory, my second home. I was familiar with various biographical dictionaries and began immediately searching through multiple volumes of the *American Men of Science* and the *Directory of American Scholars* which listed prominent scientists and scholars, respectively. In a matter of weeks I had a respectable list of potential speakers, their addresses, qualifications and accomplishments.

I then began the arduous task of correspondence. We did not have computers in those days so every letter had to be typed individually. Mind you, I had no secretary either. To make matters worse, I was not a typist. I used two fingers and was rather slow, as I had to constantly look for the keys on my keyboard. I managed, nevertheless, and when I got stuck, Eva helped. I should point out that, although some letters were in Czech or Slovak, most of the correspondence was in English.

Practically every evening, for a good half a year, I spent laboriously typing invitation letters and responding to correspondence. The hard work paid off and eventually I assembled some 60 speakers. Each speaker was instructed to submit the title of his/her planned paper together with a short summary of the talk. The summaries were later published under my editorship in the *Abstracts,*[62] commented on in the *Zprávy SVU* editorial.[63]

I neglected to mention that Eva was pregnant at the time and was expecting a child about the time of our congress. I was obviously getting nervous, knowing too well, that my presence at the Congress was essential. Well, my worries came to fruition. Eva had the delivery on April 16,

---

62 *Abstracts.* The First Congress of the Czechoslovak Society of Arts and Sciences in America, Inc. Washington, DC, April 20-24, 1962. Washington, DC–New York: Czechoslovak Society of Arts and Sciences, Inc., 1962. 40 p.

63 *Zprávy SVU,* vol. 4, No. 6 (June 1952).

two days before the Congress started. She gave birth to a beautiful girl, whom we named Karen.

To make the story short, with Eva's consent, I attended to my duties for most of the Congress, sneaking out only here and there to visit Eva and our offspring. Eva stayed in the hospital for the duration of the Congress, one day longer than she was supposed to, for my convenience and for the convenience of SVU. Very few people in the Society knew about this.

The Congress[64] was held in Statler Hilton Hotel, located on 16th and K Streets – a choice location in the heart of Washington, DC. A prestigious hotel, with elegant setting, added festive atmosphere to the whole event. More than 200 people were in attendance, including sixty prominent speakers.

The opening ceremony commenced at 9:30 AM with the National Anthems, performed by the choral society "Antonín Dvořák," Jan Klimeš[65] conducting. Then the business meeting followed, which continued in the afternoon, after a two-hour break for lunch. In the evening there was a reception and a special lecture by SVU President, Václav Hlavatý. He was a fascinating speaker and his topic "Around the World with Abacus" added excitement to the evening.

Individual lectures were scheduled for Saturday and Sunday, starting at 9 AM till noon and again at 2 PM ending after 5 o'clock. The program[66] covered a wide variety of topics, organized, for the sake of convenience, into eight separate sessions dealing specifically with: science, medicine and technology; fine arts; literature and literary criticism; linguistics and Slavistics; law and economics; sociology, theology, and philosophy; history and political science; and, finally, a session devoted to the accomplishments of Czechs and Slovaks abroad. Although there were also a few papers presented which dealt with the problems of today's Czechoslovakia, and several topics were not related to Czechoslovakia at all, except for the speaker's national background,

---

[64] Jaroslav Němec in his editorial, *Zprávy SVU*, vol. 4, No. 2 (February 1962), pp. 9-10, states that the "Congress is apparently the greatest cultural event in the history of Czechs and Slovaks abroad."

[65] Jan Klimeš (1906-1981), teacher, musician and music conductor, living in Washington, DC.

[66] *Zprávy SVU*, vol. 4, No. 3 (March 1962), pp. 27-30.

most lectures were concerned with the past accomplishments of the Czechoslovak peoples.

On Saturday night an official banquet, with František Schwarzenberg,[67] serving as Master of Ceremonies, was held. The renown piano virtuoso Rudolf Firkušný[68] gave a private concert[69] on the occasion, playing music of Bohuslav Martinů, Leoš Janáček, Karel B. Jirák and Bedřich Smetana.

The reputation of the Society was firmly established after its First World Congress. The Congress was a big success and clearly put SVU on the map. In the opinion of many, it was the greatest cultural event in the history of Czechs and Slovaks abroad. According to Jaroslav Němec, our largest organizations or even the former Czechoslovak governments abroad were not capable of accomplishing anything like this, even though they had ample financial resources.

Ivan Herben wrote that the Congress will be the exile's "business card with a golden rim."[70] Hlavatý expressed the view that the success of the Congress was surprising for several reasons.[71] First, SVU succeeded in attracting a younger generation. The Congress was prepared by young people who had the main responsibility for the organization and the success of the Congress. Secondly, it was the high quality of sixty lectures, most of which were to be made available to world forum in published form in English. And thirdly, Hlavatý referred to "unusual cultural hunger" that seemed to prevail throughout the event. The lectures were conducted for two full days, eight hours daily, in two halls simultaneously, overflowing with listeners. After each talk the attentive audience began debates which were all extremely interesting and frequently quite lively. Němec also stated that the organization of the academic program which I prepared could be described only in superlatives.[72]

---

[67] František Schwarzenberg (1913-1992), professor of law at Loyola University, Chicago, IL.

[68] Rudolf Firkušný (1912-1994), the foremost Czech pianist living in exile.

[69] This was listed as private concert for the participants of the Cngress, because otherwise, if it were open to the general public, Firkušný would have been obliged to charge admission according to the Union rates.

[70] *Zprávy SVU*, vol. 4, No. 3 (March 1962), pp. 1-2.

[71] *Zprávy SVU*, vol. 4, No. 4-5 (April-May 1962), pp. 31-32.

[72] *Zprávy SVU*, vol. 4, No. 2 (February 1962), p.10.

# 6
# *Editing Congress Proceedings*

From the day I began preparing the program of the First SVU Congress, I was determined to have the papers presented at the Congress published. I realized that the Society alone could not afford to publish it on its own because it lacked the necessary finances and, furthermore, it did not have sufficient space for storing the books and was not set up, nor had, any experience with distribution of a large quantity of books.

Having this in mind, early on, I began corresponding with various US publishers to see whether I could get them interested in the project. Ideally, I was hoping to find a publisher who would publish the papers at his own expense, without any subsidy from us. I was convinced that a combination of interesting topics, high quality papers and outstanding authors would sell our product without difficulty. At first, I tried several University Presses, but without much success. I therefore began corresponding with several leading commercial publishing houses, specializing in Slavic and East European matters. Among other, I also approached Mr. Peter de Ridder who directed Mouton & Co. in the Netherlands. He expressed great interest in our undertaking when he saw my proposed Table of Contents and the names of the authors. After a few exchanges of correspondence I got him "hooked." I should like to point out that we had no contract and everything was essentially based on my personal agreement with Mr. de Ridder and our mutual trust. I doubt that anything comparable could happen today.

In order to achieve uniformity and harmony in the material covered in the proposed volume, we agreed, in conjunction with the publisher, to include only selected papers which either had a direct bearing on our central theme, as expressed in the title of the book, *The Czechoslovak Contribution to World Culture*, or which were, in some way, related to Czechoslovakia. To make the coverage more complete, it was further decided to include additional contributions on topics which were not covered at the Congress, to the extent that space would permit, to make the coverage more complete.

The first task was to contact the authors and collect their papers and to assure that they meet high standards. Therefore I had them peer reviewed by experts in particular fields. Each paper was usually sent to two reviewers and in case of disagreement it was sent to another. Comments were then summarized and sent to individual authors with the request for revision or to respond to reviewers' comments. When dealing with academics I had no problems, whatsoever, in their acceptance of critical comments and willingness to revise their papers. When dealing with others, who were not accustomed to peer review, it was not always easy. Some of them got emotional and even upset and it took some diplomatic persuasion to convince them that they have to make appropriate changes if they wished to have their papers published. A number of papers were, of course, unacceptable for publication purposes, in which case I had the ominous duty to break the news to them. I am sure I must have lost some friends in the process.

My peer reviewers included such individuals as Josef Anderle, V. E. Andic, Antonín Basch, Vratislav Bušek, Josef Čada, Milič Čapek, Ivo Ducháček, Francis Dvorník, Philipp Frank, Mojmír Frinta, Jan Hajda, Ervin Hexner, Frederick G. Heymann, Václav Hlavatý, Milo P. Hnilička, Karel B. Jirák, Bruno Kisch, Jiří Kolaja, Ferdinand Kolegar, Henry Kučera, John G. Lexa, Otakar Machotka, Ladislav Matějka, Frank Meissner, Jan V. Mládek, Jiří Nehněvajsa, Jaroslav Němec, V. N. Nevlud, Otakar Odložilík, Leopold Pospíšil, Jaroslav J. Pelikán, Theodor Procházka, George J. Staller, Ernest Šturc, Rudolf Šturm, Edward Táborsky, Kurt Wehle, and René Wellek.

The peer review process was quite tedious and time-consuming. It was not just simply sending out instructions and then await responses. Although I would send them general guidelines, the fact of the matter is that many a letter had to be individualized, addressing specific points and issues that required explanation. If you take into account that, on one hand, I had to correspond with the peer reviewers and, on the other hand, with the individual authors, you can well imagine how much effort and time it required, and, above all, patience and keeping one's cool.

When the editing was completed I sent the papers to the Netherlands for typesetting and, in due course, I received the galley proofs. I immediately sent two copies of the proofs to the respective authors together with their original manuscripts with instructions to carefully proof-read them and return them to me within 10 days. I also informed them that their manuscripts were corrected by a linguist to improve the language and the readability. The authors were specifically instructed not to make any alterations or additions except for correcting printer's errors, otherwise they would be charged. There were also additional instructions how to assist with the preparation of the subject index. Since I wanted to also include the authors' biographies, I asked each author to send me his/her *Curriculum vitae* which I used in preparing their biographical sketches.

Of the original 60 papers presented at the Congress, 40 were selected for the inclusion in the book. With the additional 17 papers, which I solicited, this made a total of 57 contributions. The final product was clearly not just Congress Proceedings but a fairly comprehensive volume about "*The Czechoslovak Contribution to World Culture,*" which was also the title of the book.[73]

In his foreword, René Wellek, then President of the Society, wrote: "The Society wants to help keeping alive and making the world aware of the Czechoslovak cultural tradition which dates back to the beginning of Christianity and has consistently upheld the ideals of humanity. The great names of Jan Hus, Jan Amos Komenský (Comenius) and T. G. Masaryk are sufficient evidence that the Czechoslovak peoples were and are a part of the Western civilization. The first Congress, attended by over 200 members, held in Washington in April 1962 elaborated this theme, and we hope that the 2nd Congress which will convene in New York City on September 11-12, 1964 will again testify to the vitality of the Czechoslovak tradition in the free world. This volume is, we hope, a good beginning."

This collection is divided into ten sections, i.e., Literature and Literary Criticism, Linguistics, Music and Fine Arts, History, Political Science and Philosophy, Sociology Economics, Law, Science and Technology and the Czechs and Slovaks Abroad, which approximates, although not exactly, the names of the specific sections of the Congress academic program.

The Literature section comprised contributions from ten authors, namely René Wellek (Yale University), Jiří Škvor (Universite de

---

[73] Miloslav Rechcígl, Jr., *The Czechoslovak Contribution to World Culture*. The Hague-London-Paris: Mouton & Co., 1964. 682 p.

*Editing Congress Proceedings* 33

Montreal), George Pistorius (Lafayette College), Rudolf Šturm (Skidmore College), William E. Harkins (Columbia University), Jaroslav Dresler (Radio Free Europe), Peter Demetz (Yale University) and Jan Tumlíř (Yale University). The Linguistics section had three authors: Henry Kučera (Brown University), Ladislav Matějka (University of Michigan) and Angelika K. Cardew (nee Kruliš-Randa) (University of Michigan). The Music and Fine Arts section consisted of six paper authored by Kael B. Jirák (Roosevelt University), Edith Vogl Garrett (Wheaton College), Mojmír S. Frinta (State University of New York at Albany), Jaroslav Šejnoha (Toronto, Canada) and Jan Zach (University of Oregon). There were seven authors in the History section: Milič Čapek (Boston University), Jerzy Zaborski (Arizona State University at Tempe), Howard Kaminsky (University of Washington at Seattle), Frederick G. Heymann (University of Alberta at Calgary). Joseph Rouček (University of Bridgeport), Theodore Procházka (Voice of America) and Ludvík Němec (Rosemont College at Philadelphia).The Political Science and Philosophy section had three authors: Václav Beneš (Indiana University), Edward Táborský (University of Texas at Austin) and Erazim V. Kohák (Boston University). The Sociology section had four contributions: Otakar Machotka (Harpur College of the State University of New York), Jan Hajda (John Hopkins University), Joseph S. Rouček and Jiří Nehněvajsa (University of Pittsburgh). The section on Economics consisted of five contributions from Jaroslav G. Polach (Resources for the Future), Anthony Cekota (Bata Limited, Toronto), V. E. Andic (Union University at Albany) and Jan Michal (Western Maryland College). The Law section included five papers by Jaroslav Němec (National Library of Medicine), Vratislav Bušek (Radio Free Europe), Adolf Procházka (Christian Democratic Union of Central Europe), John G. Lexa (Waldes Kohinoor, Inc., Long Island) and Jaroslav Jíra (Glenn Dale Hospital Library). The section on Science and Technology had six authors: Karel Hujer (University of Chattanooga), Josef Brožek (Lehigh University), Walter Redisch (New York University School of Medicine), Jaroslav Němec, Joseph Z. Schneider (Chevy Chase, MD) and Miloš Šebor (Tennessee Polytechnic Institute). To the section relating to Czechs and Slovaks Abroad contributed Matthew Spinka, M. Norma Švejda, (Augustine Herman Czech American Historical Society, T. D. Stewart (US National Museum), John M. Skřivánek

(Texas AM College), Milič Kybal (World Bank), V. Andic (University of Pittsburgh), Vojtěch N. Duben (Voice of America) and Vlasta Vráz (Czechoslovak National Council of America).

This was the first book of its kind in the English language, which gave us hope that it would find a sympathetic audience among both students and scholars of Slavic studies in general, and studies of Czechoslovakia in particular. And we were not disappointed, judging by the many book reviews that appeared in a large number of periodicals.

Here are a few typical excerpts:

> *Books Abroad*: ...This volume achieves its goal. It shows that both the Czechs and the Slovaks have given a remarkable impetus to the progress of Euro-American civilization by playing the important. difficult part of mediators between the Slavic and the so-called Western World..[74]

> *The Polish Review*: The editor and the Czechoslovak Society of Arts and Sciences are to be congratulated on producing a volume where there is so much that is both useful and stimulating for all with interest in Czechoslovak learning and culture.[75]

> *The Library Quarterly*: The Czechoslovak Contribution to World Culture is the first book of its kind in the English language and those responsible for its conception and production ought to be commended. The book has an important message to convey, and it presents it well.[76]

> *Slavic Review*: The contents on the whole are objective and solid. The huge volume, which is really an encyclopedia as well as a collection of papers, is very valuable. The editorial work, which must have been staggering, is excellent. Everyone interested in things Czech and Slovak will be grateful for the eighty-page bibliography of the country's history, humanities, and social and natural sciences in Western languages. ...All I can do is to urge the readers of this review to make certain their library has the volume, look through the table of contents, and copy out references to articles in their fields which they might otherwise miss.[77]

---

[74] *Books Abroad*, April 1966.
[75] *The Polish Review*, vol. 11, No. 2 (Spring 1966), pp. 86-88.
[76] *The Library Quarterly*, vol. 36, No. 2 (April 1966), pp. 184-186.
[77] *Slavic Review*, vol. XXIV, No. 3 (September 1965), pp.571-572.

*International P.E.N. Bulletin of Selected Books* : ...magnificently produced book...gives information about the most important cultural achievements of the Czechoslovak nation....[78]

*The Slavonic and East European Review*: In nearly each contribution to this uncommonly rich anthology there is much valuable information, enabling the general reader as well as the scholar to gain a wider and deeper insight into the essential trends of the Czechoslovak national development. Both will also be pleased with the selective but extremely useful bibliography of publications on Czechoslovak culture written in the Western European languages, which contains no less than 1318 titles. This book, soon to be followed by another of the same kind and the same editor, will be found an indispensable vade mecum for every student of Czechoslovak culture.[79]

*Slavic and East European Journal*: In sum, one can say without reservation that the collection is a significant contribution to Slavic studies in the Western world. The book as a whole, then. is an impressive document of the vigor and resourcefulness of the Czech and Slovak exiles, and their ability to establish the ideas of the countries in which they are living without losing the ties with their national traditions.[80]

*Osteuropa*: ...Wie die Themenauswahl und die Aufnahme weitere Studien zeigen, ist es den Herausgeben vielmehr darum gegangen, ein Kompendium des tschechoslowkischen kulturellen Beitrags bis in die juengste Vergangenheit zusammenzustellen, das sowohl der Slawistik im allgemeinen als auch der Tschechoslowakei-Forschung im besonderen als Hilfe in der rundlagenforschung und als Orientierungsstuetze dienlich sein konnte.[81]

---

[78] *International; P.E.N. Bulletin of Selected Books*, vol. 16, No. 2 (1965), pp. 45-48
[79] *The Slavonic and East European Review*, vol. XLIV, No. 103 (1966), pp. 499-500.
[80] *The Slavic and East European Journal*, vol. 10, No. 2 (Summer 1966), pp. 221-224.
[81] *Osteuropa*, No. 10 (1966), p. 728.

# 7
# *René Wellek's Presidency*

The General Assembly, which met in Washington on the occasion of the First World Congress, elected Professor René Wellek of Yale University as the Society's new President and Professor Rudolf Šturm as Secretary-General. Prof. Vratislav Bušek, Rafael Kubelík and Dr. Felix Mikula remained Vice-presidents. In addition to the post of Press Secretary, held by Ivan Herben, the Assembly created a new position of Director of Publications, to which I was elected.

René Wellek's election to SVU Presidency marked a new era in SVU as it enhanced its image in academic circles, both in the US and abroad. He was an internationally renown scholar which added to increasing SVU reputation.

In order to qualify for the exemption of paying taxes, the Society was asked to include certain of its Bylaw provisions in its Articles of Incorporation. This had to be done through a special meeting of the SVU General assembly of members which was convened in New York City for October 12. It was at this meeting that the decision was made to call the next General assembly meeting in Montreal, Canada on Saturday, September 7, 1963. The subsequent General Assembly in 1964 was to be held in New York City, in conjunction with SVU Congress, for which September 11-12 were reserved, also the time of the World's Fair in New York. Several Committees were named, including Education Committee (Marie Dolanská, chair), Publication Fund (Antonín Cekota, chair), and Military History (Gen. Josef Eret, chair). As the chairman of the Publication Committee I was pleased to inform them of my negotiations with the Dutch publishing firm Mouton that agreed to publish the papers from the First SVU Congress.

As was reported in *Zprávy SVU* in November 1962, the US Dept. of Treasury classified SVU as nonprofit, nonpolitical, cultural organization and, as such, exempted it from paying taxes.[82] This was very good news

---

[82] *Zprávy SVU*, vol. 4, No. 9 (Nov. 1962), p. 79.

because this increased our chances of receiving donations from our members.

On August 22, 1963, Professor Wellek celebrated his sixtieth birthday. On this occasion, the Society published a collection of his papers, under the title *Essays on Czech Literature*.[83] I had the pleasure of presenting the first copy to him at the SVU General Assembly meeting in Toronto, Canada in the fall of 1963. The book was published for us by Mouton and Co. in the Netherlands, which I arranged, and was edited by Peter Demetz[84] who also wrote an introduction to the book. The description of the book was given in *Zprávy SVU*.[85] In March 1963, the Executive Board had its regular meeting in New York where the Board reaffirmed to hold SVU General Assemblies on the indicated days. In connection with the planned 1964 Congress it was also proposed to organize an art exhibit. There was also an extensive discussion of the recommendation of the Program Committee regarding the future plans for SVU. Secretary-General Šturm complained of being overloaded with additional work, particularly after the resignation of Dr. Anderle[86] who was handling the logistics of the second SVU Congress. A new makeup of the Program Committee was also announced, which now consisted of Dr. Jiří Škvor, Chair and Dr. L. Radimský and Dr. J. Slávik, members. And finally, approval was given to the Press Secretary to publish Dr. Alice Masaryková's[87] essay "Hudba ve Spillville"(Music in Spillville).

In the midst of the year, we were shocked by the decision of Ivan Herben to step down from his post as Editor of the *Zprávy SVU* and as SVU Press Secretary. He based the decision on account of his poor health. He planned to retire and move to California where his son lived. In his farewell message,[88] he wanted his successor to know that the job of an editor is nothing but drudgery, involving retyping and rewriting

---

[83] René Wellek, *Essays on Czech Literature*. Introduced by Peter Demetz. The Hague: Mouton & Co., 1963. 216 p.

[84] Peter Demetz (1922-), professor of German literature, Yale University.

[85] *Zprávy SVU*, vol. 5, No, 3 (March 1963), pp. 17-18.

[86] Josef Anderle (1924-), assistant professor of history at the University of North Carolina, Chapel Hill.

[87] Alice Masaryková (1879-1966), sociologist and social worker, who lived in the US after 1948; the oldest daughter of President Masaryk.

[88] *Zprávy SVU*, vol. 5, No. 6 (June 1963), p. 51.

news items sent in by members, that it is extremely difficult to gather information from American and ethnic press, to search dictionaries for appropriate translations of highly technical terms and continuous correspondence with members – that it takes all his free time at the expense of personal comfort – however, as a reward, one gets satisfaction for the work well done and satisfaction of fulfilled duty.

On September 7, 1963, the Society had its General Assembly[89] in Toronto, chaired by Professor Wellek. Secretary General Šturm presented a detailed report in which he stressed the ever increasing SVU Agenda, with its 615 members, in five different continents. He reported on the activities of SVU chapters, i.e., Toronto, Montreal, Chicago, Washington, New York, Pittsburgh and Munich, as well as on the work of regional secretaries, Ontario, Quebec, British Columbia, New York, Oregon, Illinois and State of Washington and Italy. Naming additional regional secretaries for California, England, France, etc. was in process. Other reports were presented by Dr. Jiří Škvor for Program Committee, Dr. Miloslav Rechcígl, Jr. for Publication Committee, and Antonín Cekota[90] for the Publication Fund. In addition, there were reports of individual local chapters. There was a discussion of the possibility of combining several existing periodicals into one which would be published under the SVU sponsorship.

There were also the required elections, which was a pro forma process, during which the present officers were reelected. The General Assembly also elected Prof. Francis Dvorník honorary members of SVU, while Ivan Herben was elected a founding member.

The afternoon was reserved for lectures, which were given in Toronto Library. They included a talk by Prof. Bušek about the Munich Agreement, Jaroslav Šejnoha's[91] talk about the Vignettes from the Art world, Václav Hlavatý's talk on Relativity, Universe and Philosophy. The session was concluded by recitation of poetry by their authors, specifically Pavel Javor,[92] Inka Smutná[93] and Miloslav Zlámal.[94]

---

[89] *Zprávy SVU*, vol. 5, No. 7-8 (Sept. -Oct. 1963), pp.59-60.
[90] Antonín Cekota (1899-1982), industrial consultant with Bata Ltd. in Canada.
[91] Jaroslav Šejnoha (1889-1994), painter and graphic artist; former Czechoslovak diplomat, living in Toronto, Canada.
[92] The pen name of Dr. Jiří Škvor (1916-1980), noted Czech poet, living in Toronto, Canada.

In the evening there was a festive banquet in the hotel Westbury, attended by over 200 people, which included Thomas Baťa, Jr., Canadian Minister Grosman on behalf of the Prime Minister of Ontario, representatives of the City of Toronto, officers of various ethnic organizations, etc. Jan Rubeš was the master of ceremonies who during the introduction sang an aria from Dvořák's "Jakobín." The occasion was used to present Professor Wellek the first copy of his *Essays on Czech Literature* which SVU published to commemorate his 60th birthday.[95] After the dinner René Wellek had a lecture on Czech literature which was later published.[96] The enjoyable evening was concluded by a piano composition of Professor Oskar Morawetz[97] who specifically wrote it for SVU and which he also played.

The great success of the Toronto event was largely due to the regional SVU secretary Dr. Josef Čermák[98] who was responsible for the publicity and the press. The event generated lots of publicity in the media[99] and a number of SVU members were interviewed on radio and TV. Professor Wellek and other members of SVU delegation used the occasion to meet with the key representatives of the City and also visited editorial offices of "*Náš domov*" and "*Naše Hlasy*."

As was reported in the November[100] and December[101] 1963 issues of *Zprávy SVU,* starting in 1964, the Society began publishing its literary periodical, *Proměny (Metamorphoses)*[102] under the editorship of Dr.

---

[93] The pen name of Georgina Steinský-Sehnoutka (1923-2006), poet, living in Toronto, Canada.

[94] Miloslav Zlámal (1922-1997), poet, journalist, businessman, living in Toronto, Canada; Slovak native who wrote poetry equally well in Czech, Slovak and English.

[95] *Zprávy SVU*, vol. 6, No. 1 (January 1964), pp. 2-3.

[96] René Wellek, *Czech Literature at the Crossroads of Europe*. Toronto, 1963.

[97] Oskar Morawetz (1917-2007), pianist and music composer; professor of music at University of Toronto.

[98] Josef Čermák (1924-), lawyer, living in Toronto, Canada.

[99] *Zprávy SVU*, vol. 10, No. 7-8 (Sept.-Oct. 1963), p.61.

[100] *Zprávy SVU*, vol.5, No. 9 (November 1963), p 76.

[101] *Zprávy SVU*, vol. 10, No. 10 (December 1963), p. 87.

[102] As reported in *Naše Hlasy*, March 14, 1964, p. 2), the following rationale was provided for its existence: "The Czech and Slovak intellectual must be 'penetrated' with the best tradition of the Nation from which he came and must be on the side of the conquerors,

Ladislav Radimský.[103] It came out quarterly and published articles primarily in the area of literature, philosophy and the arts. The periodical soon gained the reputation as one of the leading Czechoslovak exile periodicals.[104]

SVU Executive Board had its regular meeting on January 18, 1964 in New York, chaired by Professor Wellek. Apart from the Board members also present were the former Secretary General Jaroslav Němec, the organizational secretary of the 2nd SVU Congress Dr. John G. Lexa and myself, as the Congress program chairman. The main agenda was a discussion of organizational and program aspects of the upcoming SVU Congress.[105] Apart from the academic program, the Board decided to include as a part of the congress a special exhibit of the Czechoslovak exile art.[106]

As reported in the April 1964 issue of *Zprávy SVU*,[107] in spite of its relatively short existence so far, our Publication Committee presented a very promising report of its activities, which was well received. Equally well received was my report of the preparation of the program for the 2nd Congress, excerpts of which appeared in the subsequent issue.[108] The organizational aspects, including the local arrangements of the Congress were presented in the June issue.[109]

On September 11-13, 1964, the Society held its Second World Congress. The account of the Congress is in a separate chapter.

---

on the side of experimenters, on the side of change of ages and the thought. And his periodical, even if the fate would give it the most modest role to play, must make an effort to impart this partisan approach on its pages."

[103] Ladislav Radimský (1896-1970), Czech diplomat and writer.

[104] After Radimský died, the editorship was assumed by Jiří Škvor and later by Ladislav Matějka and then by Karel Hrubý.

[105] *Zprávy SVU*, vol. 6, No. 2 (February 1964), pp. 9-10.

[106] *Zprávy SVU*, vol. 6, No. 3 (March 1964, p. 19.

[107] *Zprávy SVU*, vol. 6, No. 4 (April 1964), pp. 25-26.

[108] *Zprávy SVU*, vol. 6, No.. 5 (May 1964), p. 33.

[109] *Zprávy SVU*, vol. 6, No. 6 (June 1964), pp. 41-42.

# 8
# *The Second SVU Congress*

As per the decision of the SVU Executive Board, the 2nd SVU Congress was planned for September 11-13, 1964 on the campus of Columbia University in New York. Specific plans were outlined in the February 1964 issue of *Zprávy SVU*.[110] This was followed by my descriptive article about the academic program,[111] which I organized, and by the local arrangement details, provided by John G. Lexa.[112]

The Congress exceeded all our expectations[113] and with its success it became an important milestone in the history of SVU. Its echoes were heard not only among the Czechoslovaks abroad, but it also received extraordinary recognition in and attention of the American political and scientific world. Governors of Alabama, Delaware, Illinois, Vermont, Washington and Wisconsin proclaimed the days of SVU Congress the "Days of the Czech and Slovak Culture". Governors of California, Maine, Michigan, Montana, New York, Oklahoma, Oregon and Texas sent SVU personal greetings or declarations praising the SVU work, as well as the cultural contributions of Czechs and Slovaks in the US.

Telegrams and greeting notices were received from Senators Clifford P. Case, Everett McKinley Dirkson, Thomas J. Dodd, Paul. H. Douglas, Jacob J. Javits, Kenneth B. Keating, Thomas H. Kuchel, Frank J. Lausche, Wayne Morse, William Proxmire, Margaret Chase Smith, Abraham Ribicoff and Stephen M. Young. Expression of friendship and congratulations were sent by President of US Senate, John W. McCormack and Congressmen Carl Albert, Robert R. Barry, Emanuel Celler, Charles A. Halleck, and Chairman of Senate Education Committee Adam C. Powell. Senator Roman L. Hruska talked about our Congress in the Senate and his remarks were recorded in the *Congressional Record*. Additional greetings came from Ambassador Adlai E. Steven-

---

[110] *Zprávy SVU*, vol. 6, No. 2 (February 1964), pp. 9-10.
[111] *Zprávy SVU*, vol. 6, No. 5 (May 1964), p. 34.
[112] *ZprávySVU*, vol. 6, No. 6 (June 1964), pp. 42-42.
[113] *Zprávy SVU*, vol. 6, No. 8 (October 1964), 63-65.

son, Chairman of New York City Council Paul R. Screvane, Director of USIA Carl T. Rowen and the Ohio State Senator and Nestor of Czech-American journalists Frank J. Svoboda and others.

Numerous greetings also came from American universities, including President of Columbia University Grayson Kirk, Dean of the same University Ralph S. Halford, former President of Harvard University James B. Conant, and others. Other congratulatory messages came from various American cultural and education organizations, such as American Academy of Arts and Letters, American Philosophical Association, National Institute of Arts and Letters, Cultural and Education Section of US State Department and numerous letters from SVU members who could not come. For lack of space I shall only mention some senders: Rudolf Firkušný (from Paris), Jarmila Novotná (Vienna), Egon Hostovský (Denmark), Josef Josten (London), Rev. Arnošt Žižka (Lisle), Prof. Otakar Odložilík (Philadelphia) and Jaromíra Žáčková (Chicago).

The academic part of the Congress was preceded by the meetings of SVU Executive Board, SVU Council and the General Assembly. The General Assembly meeting was held on Friday, September 11th from 8:30 AM to 12:00 o'clock noon and commenced again at 2 o'clock and continued until 6 PM. All meetings were officially presided by Prof. René Wellek. At the beginning of the General Assembly meeting greeting and welcome messages were heard from representatives of Columbia University, Free Europe Committee, spokesmen of New York Mayor Wagner, Russian cultural groups, Polish Science Society, Czechoslovak National Council in America, Czechoslovak National Association of Canada, CSA and the Council of Free Czechoslovakia.

Among various reports heard at the General Assembly, the SVU members were pleased to hear Dr. Rudolf Šturm, in his capacity as Secretary-General, say that the Society's membership reached the number 735. Nevertheless, he made an appeal to membership to recruit additional members, especially outside the US and with particular attention to the younger generation. I reported on behalf of our Publications Committee.

During the noon hours, on Friday, there was an official opening of the Fine Arts Exhibit, introduced by Ladislav Sutnar and Jarmila Dvořáková. Works of 43 artists were displayed, including paintings, sculptures, reproductions of architectural designs and examples of photographic art. This was followed with the opening of the exhibit of books on Czechoslovakia and books and music written by Czech and Slovak authors abroad since World War II. Also shown were periodicals, currently published outside Czechoslovakia. The exhibit was opened by René Wellek and Zdenka Muenzerová.

Friday evening was devoted to a literary and musical evening, organized by Dr. Jiří Škvor. On the program was a lecture by Peter Den on Czech Poetry in Exile, with the readings of works of these poets: Gertruda Goepfertová, Pavel Javor, Inka Smutná, Jiří Kavka, František Listopad, Josef Martínek, Jaromír Měšťan and J. Neresnický, Věra Stárková, Robert Vlach and Mariam Žiar. There were several musical interludes, featuring pianist Igor Horský and soprano Milena Šustrová who sang Czechoslovak songs and arias. It was truly a memorable and enjoyable evening.

The main components of the Congress were, of course, individual lectures presented in various sections, panel discussions and symposia scheduled for September 12 and 13. About 120 papers were presented by scholars – invited guests as well as members of the Society – from all over the United States, Canada, South America, Australia and Western Europe. Although the central theme of the Congress was "Czechoslovakia Past and Present," the papers covered most major fields of intellectual endeavor, including history, literature and linguistics, music and fine arts, social sciences, and the biological and physical sciences. In contrast with the first SVU Congress, when there were two simultaneous sessions, this time, lectures were conducted in three separate lecture halls.

The lecture program was organized according to major subjects, such as Early and Medieval History and Civilization, Modern Czechoslovak History, Linguistics and Literature, Music and Fine Arts, Literature, Social Sciences, and finally Biological and Physical Sciences. Three separate sessions were devoted to the contemporary situation in Czechoslovakia. The first dealt with the social and economic aspects, the second with the political and international aspects and the third with cultural aspects. In addition, two special symposia were organized. One concerned the "First Czechoslovak Republic." in which the accomplishments achieved under Masaryk were discussed in great depth and from every possible angle, by people who knew something about it from their own experiences and knowledge. The second symposium dealt with the subject of "Czechoslovakia and its Neighbors," with the participation of historians and political experts from the respective countries, so that one did not get just one country's point of view. Thus, for example, the relationship between Czechoslovakia and Poland was presented by Piotr S. Wandycz who was a native Pole, while the relationship between Czechoslovakia and Hungary was discussed by Stephen Borsody, who was a Hungarian. A novelty of the program was the inclusion of a session in Czech and Slovak languages, in which the historical development of Czechoslovakia and the relations between Czechs and Slovaks were discussed. Brief summaries of the papers were published in form of the Abstracts.[114]

On the whole, the lectures were well attended and in some cases there was standing room only. The quality of most presentations was high, as we heard from Czech and Slovak listeners, as well as from American professors and students who were present in the audience.

As in the case of the 1st SVU Congress, I was again responsible for the preparation of the program of this Congress. This time, however, I had no committee to help me, or better said to look over my shoulders. I was entirely on my own. It was an enormous job which took twice as much work than the Congress before, which was also reflected in the number of speakers, being twice as many as before. The SVU Press Secretary, in his September editorial of *Zprávy SVU*,[115] expressed his appreciation in these words:

> The circumstance that there were 114 lectures presented at the Congress is sufficient to realize how much correspondence it involved. The correspondence proper was, however, preceded by preliminary planning of the entire lecture program, the selection of suitable speakers, arrangement of the lectures into appropriate sections and series of other related problems. We don't dare to guess how many hundreds of hours Dr. Rechcígl devoted to this work, in addition to his regular employment. SVU will forever be indebted to him for all his work relating to the Congress and the credit for the successful outcome of the Congress must go to him.

---

[114] *Abstracts of Papers. The Second Congress of Czechoslovak Society of Arts and Sciences in America, Inc., Columbia University, New York, September 11-13, 1964.* Washington, DC: SVU, 1964. 66 p.

[115] *Zprávy SVU*, Vol. 6, No. 7 (September 1964), pp. 53-54.

# 9
# Wellek's Second Term

At the General Assembly meeting in New York, on September 11, 1964, before the start of the 2nd SVU Congress, Prof. René Wellek was reelected SVU President. Other elected officers included Rudolf Šturm Secretary General, Josef Korbel,[116] Victor S. Mamatey,[117] Vice Presidents, Rudolf Šturm Secretary General and Michael Šumichrast,[118] Treasurer. Because of illness, Ivan Herben did not wish to continue as an editor of *Zprávy SVU* and the function was taken over by Vladimír Walzel.[119] I was reelected as Chairman of the Publications Committee.

The work of our Publication Committee bore fruits from the very start, when we were able to announce[120] the publication of the Czech version of Egon Hostovský's[121] novel *Tři noci,* which was originally published in London in English. The monograph was published under the SVU sponsorship by the Orbis Printing Co. in New York.[122] *Zprávy SVU* devoted a special editorial to this book in one of its later issues.[123]

On December 29, 1964, the newly elected Executive Board had its first meeting, under the chairmanship of Professor Wellek. Secretary-General Šturm gave an account on the affairs of SVU since its October Congress. It was gratifying to hear that 47 new members have enlarged

---

[116] Josef Korbel (1909-1977), professor of international relations at the University of Denver, CO.
[117] Victor S. Mamatey (1917-2007), professor of history at the University of Georgia.
[118] Michael Šumichrast (1921-2007), chief economist of the National Association of Home Builders, Washington, DC.
[119] Vladimir S. Walzel (1915-1992), bank executive, living in New York City.
[120] *Zprávy SVU*, vol. 6, No. 9 (November 1964), p. 75.
[121] Egon Hostovský (1908-1973), noted Czech novelist, living in the US; former Czechoslovak diplomat.
[122] Egon Hostovský, *Tři noci*. A Novel. New York, NY, 1964. 208 p.
[123] *Zprávy SVU*, vol. 7, No. 3 (March 1965), pp. 17-18.

the SVU rolls. Then came the reports by Miloš Šebor[124] in his capacity as the new SVU Press Secretary, Joža Karas,[125] as music secretary, Jaroslav Šejnoha,[126] as the fine arts secretary. Since I could not attend, Dr. Šturm read my report on the SVU publications.

The Board was gratified by the news that the papers from the First SVU Congress[127] have come out. The proceedings were published by the Mouton and Co. in the Netherlands, under the title *The Czechoslovak Contribution to World Culture*, which I had the pleasure of editing.[128] It was the Society's first publication resulting from the combined efforts of many of its members. The book was also unique in another respect: it was the first major publication in English concerning Czechoslovak culture.

Starting with March 1, 1965, the Society opened its new office in New York City,[129] located at 381 Park Avenue South. The office became a meeting place for the Society's members and for other scholars and intellectuals, including visitors from Czechoslovakia. It was a place where scholars could obtain information and find useful books and periodicals. The office served also as the circulation headquarters for the Society's publications, and as its library and archives. The office was staffed with a full time secretary who also worked for the Secretary General.[130]

In April 1965, in his editorial in *Zprávy SVU*,[131] Professor Bušek elaborated on the existing SVU 800 members and what it meant for the Society, as a whole. The same issue carried also an announcement of publishing Pavel Javor's new volume of poetry, entitled *Nedosněno*,

---

[124] Miloš M. Šebor (1911-1995), associate professor of geography, Tennessee Technological University, Cookeville. TN.

[125] Joža Karas (1926-), violinist, Hartford Symphony Orchestra, CT.

[126] Jaroslav Šejnoha (1889-1982), painter and graphic artist; former Czechoslovak diplomat.

[127] *Zprávy SVU*, vol. 7, No. 2 (February 1965), p. 9-10.

[128] Miloslav Rechcígl, Jr., Ed., *The Czechoslovak Contribution to World Culture*. The Hague: Mouton & Co., 1964. 862 p.

[129] *Zprávy SVU*, vol. 7, No. 3 (March 1965), p. 18.

[130] In the early years, the Society received financial support from the Radio Free Europe to maintain the office.

[131] *Zprávy SVU*, vol. 7, No. 4 (April 1965), pp. 25-26.

*nedomilováno*, published, under the SVU sponsorship, by the Universum Press.

As per the analysis of SVU membership, we learn from the September 1965 issue that the Society had 855 members, as compared to 723 a year ago, indicating that the Society was steadily growing.[132]

On September 17, 1965, the Society held in Chicago, IL the meetings of its Executive Board and its Council, followed by SVU General Assembly on the next day. The Assembly meeting was convened at the University of Chicago in Center for Continuing Education. The meeting was attended by Professor George W. Beadle, a Nobel Prize laureate, who addressed the participants in his capacity as the University Chancellor. A detailed account of the meeting appears in the October 1965 issue of *Zprávy SVU*.[133]

In the afternoon, following the General Assembly meeting, there was a series of lectures, starting with Prof. Hlavatý's talk "From Euclid to Albert Einstein." Other lectures included Edward Stankiewicz talk on "Czech and Slovak Studies at the University of Chicago," Zdeněk Hruban's[134] talk on "Reaction of the Cell to Injury," Miroslav Synek's[135] presentation "Quantum Mechanical Nature of Atoms," Václav Laška's talk[136] "Fortunes of a Poggio's Letter in Czech Translation," and Helena Hrabík's talk about Czech and Slovak folk costumes. The program was concluded with an evening of music and poetry, held in the auditorium of the Morton College in Berwyn, with the participation of the composer Karel B. Jirák.

Professor Wellek, who could not come to Chicago because his wife was seriously ill, was reelected SVU President for the next year, as were all the other officers.

On February 19, 1966 there was a special SVU working conference, with the participation of SVU Council, SVU Executive Board and the representatives of various SVU committees, the outcome of which

---

[132] *Zprávy SVU*, vol.7, No. 7 (September 1965), pp. 51-52.

[133] *Zprávy SVU*, vol.7, No. 8 (October 1965), pp. 57-58.

[134] Zdeněk Hruban (1921-), assistant professor of pathology, University of Chicago.

[135] Miroslav Synek (1930-), associate professor of physics, DePaul University, Chicago.

[136] Václav Laška (1929-1984), Slavic bibliographer, University of Chicago.

was described in detail in the February 1966 issue of *Zprávy SVU*.[137] Among the items discussed was awarding honorary membership to Cardinal Beran[138] who was to visit the US in April. The latter proposal was approved and the official presentation took place upon Cardinal Beran's arrival in New York on April 11 in the Hotel Waldorf-Astoria during a gala banquet the Society organized.[139]

Wellek's Presidency was concluded with the Third SVU Congress,[140] held on September 2-4, 1966 at Columbia University. A total of one hundred and thirty-eight papers were presented. Scientists and scholars from sixty-five universities in the United States, from eight Canadian and eight European universities, as well as from one university each in Australia and Central America participated in the lectures and symposia. Similarly to the earlier congresses, this Congress comprised a balanced program of lectures of general and scholarly interest, designed to document and highlight current research on Czechoslovakia, as well as contributions of Czechs and Slovaks throughout the Western world in such domains as natural and social science, the arts and literature.

In addition to the regular sessions organized according to various disciplines, the program included several symposia, one entitled "The Czechs and the Reformation," the second, "Poland and Czechoslovakia" (organized in cooperation with the Polish Institute of Arts and Sciences in America), the third "ČSSR – The New Economic Model," and the fourth, "Czechoslovakia 1945-1948."

A special feature of the program was a panel discussion on scientific research and the organization of science in present-day Czechoslovakia, which I co-chaired with Professor Hlavatý. Among the panelists were former scientific workers and associates of the Czechoslovak Academy of Sciences, including Drs. F. Chytil, V. Fried, E. Šipoš, etc., and Prof. V. Slámečka of the Georgia Institute of Technology and Dr. R. Urban of the Johann-Gottfried-Herder-Institut.

Those attending the Congress were also able to view two exhibits, one featuring reproductions of documents, publications and engravings

---

[137] *Zprávy SVU*, vol. 8, No. 2 (February 1966), pp.9-10.

[138] Josef Beran (1889-1969), Catholic theologian; Archbishop of Prague, Cardinal; jailed by Communists until his release in 1965, when he was allowed to leave for Rome.

[139] *Zprávy SVU*, vol. 8, No. 3-4 (March-April 1966), pp. 21-24.

[140] *Zprávy SVU*, vol. 8, No. 7 (September 1966), p. 49.

of 17th century Czech and Slovak exile writers and artists in Western Europe who had been forced to leave their native land due to religious persecution, such as Jan Amos Komenský (Comenius), Wenceslav Hollar, and others. The other exhibit displayed Czechoslovak postage stamps from 1918 to 1948.

In honor of the seventieth birthday of Prof. Václav Hlavatý, Indiana University Press published a Society-sponsored Festschrift, entitled *Perspectives in Geometry and Relativity*.[141] I had the pleasure of presenting the first copy of the book to Professor Hlavatý at the banquet of the Society. The visitors at the Third Congress were also able to purchase the Society's first SVU Biographical *Directory of SVU Members*[142] which my wife Eva compiled and edited.

---

[141] *Perspectives in Geometry and Relativity*. Essays in Honor of Václav Hlavatý. Edited by Banesh Hoffman. Bloomington-London: Indiana University Press, 1966. 491 p.

[142] *Czechoslovak Society of Arts and Sciences in America, Inc. Directory*. Compiled and edited by Eva Rechcígl. New York: SVU, 1966. 80 p.

# 10
## *The Second Congress Collection*

This chapter rightfully follows the chapter on the Second SVU Congress, even though the Congress proceedings, which I had the pleasure of editing, did not get published until a few months after 1968.[143]

This collection is primarily based on the papers which were originally presented at the Second Society's Congress, held at Columbia University, September 11-13, 1964. It bears the title *Czechoslovakia Past and Present* which is identical with the theme of the Congress.

Over 110 papers were presented at that Congress by scholars – invited guests, as well as members of the Society – from all parts of the United States, Canada, South America, Australia, and Western Europe. The papers cover most major fields of intellectual endeavor, i.e., history, literature and linguistics, music and fine arts, the social sciences, and the biological and physical sciences.

A special feature of the program was a symposium, "Czechoslovakia and its Neighbors: Nationalism vs. Federalism," in which distinguished scholars of different national backgrounds debated the issues which lead to nationalistic conflicts in East-Central Europe. Another symposium was organized to evaluate the era of the First Czechoslovak Republic. The situation in contemporary Czechoslovakia – cultural, social, economic, political, and international aspects – was covered during three separate sessions.

For this publication, the papers were carefully selected on the basis of their overall quality and subject matter. The material was organized in two separate volumes. The first concerns political, international, social, and economic aspects of Czechoslovakia, past and present, while the second volume includes essays on the arts and sciences, arranged according to various disciplines. The two-volume set has a total of

---

[143] Miloslav Rechcígl, Jr., ed., *Czechoslovakia Past and Present*. The Hague – Paris: Mouton, 1968. 2 vols.1900 p.

almost 1900 pages, the first having 880 and the second, 1020 pages, which, by any standard, is an enormous publication.

The first volume comprises four major sections, i.e., Czechoslovakia through the Second World, Contemporary Czechoslovakia, Czechoslovakia and the World and the Czechs and Slovaks Abroad. The first section was subdivided as follows: 1. Rise and Fall of the First Czechoslovak Republic – Historical Aspects, 2. The First Czechoslovak Republic – Social and Economic Aspects and 3. Czechoslovakia and the Second World War. The section relating to Contemporary Czechoslovakia was, in turn, subdivided into: 1. Political Aspects, 2. Social and Economic /Aspects and 3. Cultural Aspects. The third section on Czechoslovakia and the World has two parts: 1. Czechoslovakia and its Neighbors: Nationalism versus Federalism and 2. Czechoslovakia and the Great Powers.

The second volume, which carried the subtitle *Essays on the Arts and Sciences*, consisted of the following sections: Literature, Linguistics, History, Music, Fine Arts, Social Sciences, Physical, Biological, and Behavioral Sciences and Bibliography.

Of the 118 papers, which appear in the collection, 96 were presented at the Society's Congress. The remaining 22 papers either arrived too late to appear on the program of the Congress, or their authors were not able to attend the meetings. In addition, several new manuscripts were included which were subsequently requested in order to fill a gap in a specific area or historical period. A favorable reception by the reviewers of the selective bibliography of publications on Czechoslovakia which appeared in the Society's First Congress Proceedings' prompted the editor to add to this collection also a comprehensive bibliography of bibliographies concerning Czechoslovakia – probably the first such bibliography to be published in the Western Hemisphere.

Because of the enormous size of the publication, it is beyond the scope of this chapter to discuss the specific papers. However, for the sake of a historical record, I've thought it would be in order, at least, to mention some of the names of the authors, many of whom represent the cream of the crop of the post-February 1948 Czechoslovak exile, as well as the premiere scholars on the thing Czechoslovak. They are in alphabetical order as follows: Karel B. Absolon of the St. Anthony's Hospital in Amarillo, TX, Josef Anderle of the University of North Carolina in

Chapel Hill, Vojtech E. Andic of the Union University in Albany, Antonín Basch of Michigan University at Ann Arbor, Curt F. Beck of the University of Connecticut, Paul Blaho of Radio Free Europe, Stephen Borsody of Chatham College at Pittsburgh, Bohuslava Růžena Bradbrook of St. Mary's College at Bangor, North Wales, John F. N. Bradley of Manchester University, UK, John Wolfgang Bruegel of London, Vratislav Bušek of New York City, a former Rector of Comenius University, Milič Čapek of Boston University, Petr Den (the pen name of Ladislav Radimský) of New York, Zdeněk R. Dittrich of the University of Utrecht, Jaroslav Drábek of Voice of America, the former prosecutor in the trials of war criminals, Vojtěch Nevlud Duben of Voice of America, Leslie C. Dunn of Columbia University, Rev. Francis Dvorník of Harvard University, Andrew Eliáš of the US Bureau of the Census, Keith Eubank of the Queens College of the City University of New York, Philipp Fehl of the University of North Carolina, Ivo K. Feierabend of San Diego State College, CA, Ladislav K. Feierabend of Voice of America, the former Czechoslovak Minister of Finance, Oscar Felsenfeld of Tulane University Medical School, LA, Victor Miroslav Fic, then at the Chinese University Nanyang in Singapore, Radu K. Florescu of Boston College, Marianka S. Fousek of Duke University at Durham, Alfred French of University of Adelaide, South Australia, Mojmír S. Frinta of State University of New York at Albany, George Gibian of Cornell University, Feliks Gross of Brooklyn College of New York, Joseph Hajda of Kansas State University, Harry Hanák of the University of London, Milan E.. Hapala of Sweet Briar College, VA, William E. Harkins of Columbia University, Josef Paul Hodin of London, Karel Holbík of Boston University, Erik Hošek a noted architect in Paris, Roger Howell of Bowdoin College, Brunswick, ME, Wilma A. Iggers of Amherst, NY, Jaroslav Jíra of the University of Paris, Karel B. Jirák of Roosevelt University, Howard Kaminsky of the University of Washington in Seattle, Robert A. Kann of Rutgers University, Guido Kisch of Hebrew Union College of New York, Štefan Kočvara of Library of Congress, Erazim V. Kohák of Boston University, Jiří Kolaja of State University at Brockport, Ferdinand Kolegar of Roosevelt University, Josef Korbel of the University of Denver, Boris Kremenliev of the University of California at Los Angeles, Henry Kučera of Brown University, Rado L. Lencek of Columbia University, Nicholas Lobkowicz of the University of Munich, Victor S. Mamatey of the

University of Georgia, Václav E. Mareš of Pennsylvania State University, Ladislav Matějka of the University of Michigan, Jan M. Michal of the State University of New York at Binghamton, Edwin M. Moseley of Skidmore College at Saratoga Springs, NY, Ludvík Němec of Rosemont College in Philadelphia, Roman Olynyk of the CBS, Montreal, Canada, Ján Papánek of the American Fund for Czechoslovak Refugees, the former Czechoslovak Ambassador to the UN, Stanley J. Pech of the University of British Columbia in Vancouver, Canada, Mojmír Povolný of Lawrence University at Appleton, WI, Adolf Procházka of New York, former Czechoslovak Minister of Health, Bogdan Raditsa of Farleigh Dickinson University, Teaneck, NJ, Jan Roček of Catholic University, Washington, DC, Alois Rozehnal of Radio Free Europe, Hugo Michael Skála of Fairleigh Dickinson University at Rutherford, NJ, Vladimír Slámečka of Georgia Institute of Technology, Josef Peter Stern of the University of Cambridge, Joseph V. Talacko of Marquette University in Milwaukee,. Pavel Tigrid, editor of *Svědectví* in Paris, France, Peter A. Toma of the University of Arizona in Tucson, Jan F. Tříska of Stanford University, Otto Ulč of the State University of New York at Binghamton, Vladimír Vaněk of Rome, a former Czechoslovak diplomat and writer, who died in 1965, Stanislav J. Velinský of Shorter College Rome, GA, Emil Walter of Uppsala Sweden, a former diplomat and writer, who died in 1964, Piotr S. Wandycz of Yale University, Gerhard L. Weinberg of the University of Michigan, Joseph Frederick Záček of the State University of New York at Albany.

The editing of the papers was a mammoth undertaking if you consider that each paper was read at least by two reviewers and in cases where there were disagreements more peer reviewers were consulted. More than seventy peer reviewers were used in the process. They included eminent scholars and scientists, such as Prof. Josef Brožek of Lehigh University, Prof. Francis Dvorník of Harvard University, Prof. Stephen A. Fischer-Galati of the University of Colorado, Prof. Herman Freudenberger of Tulane University, Prof. George Gibian of Cornell University, Prof. William E. Harkins of Columbia University, Prof. Frederick G. Heymann of the University of Alberta at Calgary, Prof. Vaclav Hlavatý of Indiana University, Prof. Howard Kaminsky of the University of Washington, Prof. Stephen Dent Kertesz of the University of Notre Dame Prof. Bruno Z. Kisch of Yeshiva University, Prof. Hans Kohn of the City College of New York, Prof. Ivo John Lederer of Yale

University, Prof. Josef Macek of the University of Pittsburgh, Prof. George Morton of London School of Economics and Political Science, Prof. Philip E. Mosely of Columbia University, Prof. Frank Munk of Portland State College, Prof. Jiří Nehněvajsa of University of Pittsburgh, Prof. Paul Nettl of Indiana University, Prof. Leopold J. Pospíšil of Yale University, Prof. H. K. S. Řezníček of Rijksnniversiteit in Utrecht, Prof. H. Gordon Skilling of the University of Toronto, Prof. Robert L. Škrábánek of Texas A. and M. University, Prof. Roman S. Smal-Stocki of Marquette University, Prof. Matthew Spinka of Claremont Graduate School, Prof. Edward Táborský of the University of Texas, Prof. S. H. Thomson of the University of Colorado, Prof. Piotr S. Wandycz of Yale University, Prof. René Wellek of Yale University, Prof. Z. A. B. Zeman of the University of St. Andrews, Prof. Paul H. Zinner of the University of California, Davis and others. The list reads like Who's Who. Anybody looking at these names will readily agree that the review of the papers was not a *pro forma* process.

The Second Congress collection was received with praise by reviewers, just as were the papers from the First World Congress. Here are a few examples:

> *The Slavonic Review*: The appearance of these two massive volume owes much to the dedication and energy of their editor, Dr. Rechcígl, Jr.. A biochemist by profession, he has enabled historians, philologists, musicologists, literary critics and many others to express their views and publish their findings on a great variety of subjects.[144]

> *Books Abroad*: ...Nearly all contributions exemplify scholarship of high quality. ....The symposium is a significant addition to materials in English pertaining to Czech and Slovak subjects.[145]

> *The Slavic and East European Journal*: Some reviewers have characterized the book as an encyclopedia, others as an anthology. Perhaps it could also be described as Festschrift, *Ad maiorem gloriam Czechoslovakiae.*[146]

---

[144] *The Slavonic Review*, vol. , p. 633.
[145] *Books Abroad*, vol. 45, No. 3 (Summer 1971),
[146] *The Slavic and East European Journal*, vol.15, No. 2 (Summer 1971), pp. 254-255.

# 11
## *Hlavatý Returns to the Presidency*

Since René Wellek did not wish to continue in the position of President, in the 1966 SVU elections the Presidency returned to Professor Hlavatý. Other elected officers included Dr. Ferdinand S. Hoffmeister,[147] Prof. Josef Korbel and Prof. Victor S. Mamatey, Vice Presidents; and Prof. Vojtech E. Andic, Secretary-General and Emil Royco,[148] SVU Treasurer.

The first significant event this period was the SVU Conference in Los Angeles, organized by the SVU LA Chapter. It was held on the occasion of the Czechoslovak national holiday on October 28th which fell on Saturday. The latter was commemorated by the speech of Dr. Francis Schwarzenberg, which was followed by a party at Mr. and Mrs. Bruna's[149] residence. Sunday was devoted to a series of lectures relating mostly to Czechoslovakia, including the talk by J. J. Mráček[150] on Czech and Slovak theatre in the US, Jiří Karger's[151] talk on the contemporary trends in the arts, and Antonín Hradílek's talk about Czech poetry in exile, which all took place in the morning. In the afternoon J. Beleš and A. Materna[152] had a presentation about the role of computers in the contemporary society, followed by talk of George Kubín on the international trade and J. Bruna's discussion of the situation in today's saving institutions against the historic backdrop of the traditional family savings tendencies in Czechoslovakia.

Soon after this conference, one could discern gradual unrest among intellectuals in Czechoslovakia and call for democratization, of which

---

[147] Ferdinand S. Hoffmeister (1914-2004), medical researcher at Roswell Park Memorial Institute, later professor at Albany Medical College.

[148] Emil Royco (1908-1996), architect in Washington, DC.

[149] Joseph Bruna (1924-), Business executive, Beverly Hills, CA.

[150] Jaroslav J. Mráček (1928- 1999), associate professor of musicology, San Diego State College, CA.

[151] George Karger (1924-), painter and creative director, CBS TV, Los Angeles.

[152] Anthony Materna (1925-), business executive, Los Angeles, CA.

the SVU became quite cognizant. Although the Society has traditionally stuck to its non-political character, the changing political situation in Czechoslovakia was not mere politics but it concerned the question of civility and human rights which was clearly something of which the Society wanted to be a part. These matters obviously also affected our planning of the 1968 SVU Congress.

The situation also warranted increased contacts between SVU and the Radio Free Europe and its parent body National Committee for Free Europe. The Society wanted it to be known of its desire and interest to be helpful to intellectuals in communist Czechoslovakia and also request some financial assistance from the Committee regarding this effort.

According to SVU Minutes,[153] in May 1967, Hlavatý met with representatives of Radio Free Europe regarding the support of SVU for the upcoming year. RFE was willing to provide SVU $5,600 towards publication of a memorial volume on the occasion of the 50th anniversary of ČSR. In addition, he discussed with them the RFE's purchase and distribution of the existing SVU publications. They were interested in having the books available to the visitors from Czechoslovakia and also sending them to interested people directly to Czechoslovakia. Hlavatý also mentioned that SVU, together with the Polish Institute were planning a book exhibit at McGill University on the occasion of the international exposition EXPO 67.

In the same meeting I briefed the Board members of my meeting with Mr. Minden of RFE regarding RFE's support for various SVU publication projects that we planned. Mr. Minden expressed a great interest in the proposed projects, particularly the planned Festschrift for Prof. Dvorník, translation of Prof. Fischer's monograph on Socrates (Prof. Fischer lived in ČSR) and a monograph commemorating 50th anniversary of ČSR. We also discussed a literary competition for the best manuscript relating to Czechoslovakia. Mr. Minden also told me that it would not be difficult to obtain funds for organizing an art exhibit of artists living in CSR and he also indicated RFE's willingness to support scholarships and fellowships. Finally, he told me that they would be willing to finance trips of invited scholars to attend the planned SVU Congress in 1968. The SVU Board was generally in agreement with these proposals but cautioned that in case of speakers from Czechoslo-

---

[153] Minutes of the SVU Executive Board, May 13, 1967.

vakia, they would have to be selected by our Society, rather than by the Czechoslovak government.

In June 1967 the Union of Writers in communist Czechoslovakia held its Fourth Congress in Prague, which was attended by L. Vaculík, Pavel Kohout, Ivan Klíma, and Milan Kundera, who were all Communists at that time, as well as non-Party member Václav Havel. Vaculík made an inflammatory speech in which he rejected the leading role of the party as unnecessary and criticized it for its restrictive cultural policies and failure to address social issues. Vaculík's and other writers' speeches at the conference, with their anti-Novotný sentiments, increased the gap between the conservative Novotný supporters and more moderate members of the party leadership, a division that would contribute to Novotný's eventual fall.

It was in this atmosphere that SVU held its Annual meeting and General Assembly at McGill University, Ottawa on June 20–July 1, 1967, at the time of the EXPO 67. At the General Assembly meeting, discussion about the changing situation in Czechoslovakia was obviously the most important subject on the agenda.[154] Questions were raised to what degree should SVU get involved, how to assist the scientists and artists there, how could we make available publications to them, etc. As a result of the deliberations, The General Assembly also issued a special proclamation entitled "Freedom for Everyone."[155]

Among the traditional reports at the General Assembly it was particularly gratifying to hear from the Treasurer that the assets of the Society had risen to $9,354.68.[156] I had the pleasure of presenting the Report of the Publication Committee[157] of which I was the chairman. I was particularly pleased to inform the members that our 2-volume set, *Czechoslovakia Past and Present*, based on the papers presented at the Second SVU Congress will come out in a matter of weeks which was accepted with appreciation and applause.

As mentioned earlier, SVU had a special book exhibit at Mc Gill University in Montreal, during the 1967 International and Universal Exposition (Expo 67), held from April 27 to October 29, 1967. On this

---

[154] *Zprávy SVU*, vol. 10, No. 7-8 (Sept.-Oct. 1968), pp. 1-2.

[155] *Zprávy SVU*, vol 9, No. 7-8 (Sept.-Oct. 1967), p. 49.

[156] *Zprávy SVU*, vol. 9, No. 7-9 (Sept.-Oct. 1967), p. 50..

[157] *Zprávy SVU*, vo. 9, No. 7-8 (Sept.-Oct. 1967), pp. 53-55.

occasion SVU made available its books gratis to the visitors from Czechoslovakia. We made it also known that we would furnish specific books to interested scholars, scientists, educators and artists, writers and others from Czechoslovakia, who were visiting the US, Canada or other western countries. A number of these visitors came to the SVU Office in New York. All SVU Chapters were informed about this new policy and were asked to give us a hand with this new effort.[158]

In the meantime, the political situation in Czechoslovakia was changing rapidly. In September 1967, Alexander Dubček, secretary of the Slovak Communist Party, presented a long list of grievances against the government. The following month there were large demonstrations against Novotný. In January 1968 the Czechoslovak Party Central Committee passed a vote of no confidence in Antonín Novotný and he was replaced by Alexander Dubček as party secretary. Soon afterwards Dubček made a speech where he stated: "We shall have to remove everything that strangles artistic and scientific creativeness."

During what became known as the Prague Spring, Dubček announced a series of reforms. This included the abolition of censorship and the right of citizens to criticize the government. Newspapers began publishing revelations about corruption in high places. This included stories about Novotný and his son. On 2nd March 1968, Novotný resigned as president of Czechoslovakia. He was now replaced by the Dubček's supporter, Ludvík Svoboda.

In April 1968 the Communist Party Central Committee published a detailed attack on Novotný's government. This included its poor record concerning housing, living standards and transport. It also announced a complete change in the role of the party member. It criticized the traditional view of members being forced to provide unconditional obedience to party policy. Instead it declared that each member "has not only the right, but the duty to act according to his conscience."

The new reform program included the creation of work councils in industry, increased rights for trade unions to bargain on behalf of its members and the right of farmers to form independent co-operatives. Aware of what happened during the Hungarian Uprising Dubček announced that Czechoslovakia had no intention of changing its foreign policy. On several occasions he made speeches where he stated that

---

[158] *Zprávy SVU*, vol. 10, No. 5-6 (May-June 1968), p. 32.

## Hlavatý Returns to the Presidency

Czechoslovakia would not leave the Warsaw Pact or end its alliance with the Soviet Union.

In July 1968 the Soviet leadership announced that it had evidence that the Federal Republic of Germany was planning an invasion of the "Sudetenland" and asked permission to send in the Red Army to protect Czechoslovakia. Alexander Dubček, aware that the Soviet forces could be used to bring an end to Prague Spring, declined the offer.

On 21st August, 1968, Czechoslovakia was invaded by members of the Warsaw Pact countries. In order to avoid bloodshed, the Czech government ordered its armed forces not to resist the invasion. Alexander Dubček and Ludvík Svoboda were taken to Moscow and soon afterwards they announced that after "free comradely discussion" that Czechoslovakia would be abandoning its reform program.

The Prague Spring of 1968, which brought unprecedented political changes in communist Czechoslovakia, had also a profound effect on the Society's Fourth World Congress, planned for August 30- September 1, 1968. The Society wanted to use the occasion to commemorate the 50th anniversary of the founding of the Czechoslovak Republic and there were plans to also invite selected scholars from Czechoslovakia. The subsequent takeover of the country by the Soviet troops, unfortunately, changed all that and of the invited individuals only one person came.

I still vividly remember how a few hours before the Congress started, a prominent journalist[159] from *New York Times* was anxiously waiting the arrival of Prof. Ivan Sviták[160] who was expected to address the Congress. Sviták arrived from Austria, where a group of twenty-five Czechoslovak intellectuals drafted a proclamation "Manifest against Aggression,"[161] which he read to an excited audience, in front of TV lights and cameramen and reporters representing major American media, and then gave a series of interviews which made headlines in the US press.

The Society issued on that occasion a special resolution[162] addressed to scientific and art institutions of the free world, reminding them that freedom and peace are inseparable and that any restriction of

---

[159] It was Marvin Kalb. I readily recognized him because he was frequently seen on TV.
[160] Ivan Sviták (1925-1994), Czech Marxist philosopher.
[161] *Zprávy SVU*, vol. 10, No. 7-8 (Sept.-Oct. 1968), p. 48-29.
[162] *Zprávy SVU*, vol. 10, No. 7-8 (Sept.-Oct. 1968), p. 48.

these basic values anywhere in the world, sooner or later, will impact on the entire global society. SVU expressed the hope that the world will finally come to grips with the true substance of international communism and Soviet imperialism, opposed by people who have been subjugated by the Soviet Union.

The Congress otherwise proceeded very smoothly. In addition to the customary variety of scholarly lectures and symposia, this Congress commemorated the 50th anniversary of the establishment of the Czechoslovak Republic in October, 1918 in a section entitled "Fifty Years of Czechoslovakia," with a number of lectures and panel discussions dealing with the relations between Czechs and Slovaks, Czechoslovakia's history, politics, literature, economy, diplomacy, geography, medicine, education, etc.

Several exhibits were organized at the occasion of the Congress: fine arts, architectonic and book exhibits at Georgetown University, and another art exhibit featuring paintings of Koloman Sokol[163] and Oskar Kokoschka[164] at the Smithsonian Institution. A special exhibit of rare documents pertaining to the founding of Czechoslovakia was open to the public in the Library of Congress from August 26 through September 29. Among various memorabilia it contained the original correspondence between Thomas G. Masaryk and Woodrow Wilson, and the Washington Declaration of Czechoslovak Independence of 1918. On Friday, August 30th, an evening concert of organ music at the Washington National Cathedral featured Professor Karel Paukert[165] from Northwestern University.

One of the highlights of the Congress' banquet were the moving addresses of the novelist Marcia Davenport[166] and the physician Dr. Karel Steinbach,[167] both of whom were close friends of the late Jan Masaryk.

---

[163] Koloman Sokol (1902-2003), a noted Slovak painter.

[164] Oskar Kokoschka (1886-1980), b. in Vienna of Czech father. A noted painter, illustrator, poet, and playwright, who is credited with founding Expressionist drama.

[165] Karel Paukert (1935-), curator of musical arts, Cleveland Museum of Arts, OH.

[166] Marcia Davenport (1903-1996), American author and music critic.

[167] Karel Steinbach (1894-1990), a popular Czech gynecologist and general practitioner living in Queens, NY.

# Part II
# After the Prague Spring

# 12
## *Jaroslav Němec's Presidency*

At the General Assembly meeting, which was held during the Congress, Dr. Jaroslav Němec was elected the new President, Dr. V. E. Andic, Dr. George J. Škvor, Dr. Rudolf Šturm, Dr. M. Rechcígl, Vice Presidents; and Dr. John G. Lexa[168] Secretary-General, Emil Royco, Treasurer, Ladislav Radimský, Editor of Proměny and Andrej Eliáš,[169] publications.

The first important project the newly elected Executive Board undertook was the issuance of a special Memorandum addressed to some 2000 major universities around the world.[170] Symbolically, the document was dated October 28. Among other, the Memorandum appealed to sister universities in these words:

> The Czechoslovak Society of Arts and Sciences in America, a non-political organization uniting some 1200 scholars and artists in the Free World, acting on behalf of Prague's famous old Charles University whose voice has once again been stilled, as well as on behalf of the other captive Czechoslovak universities, appeals to all of their sister universities to join them in their protest against the occupation of Czechoslovakia and the decline of public morality throughout the world. Such circumstances have in the past always signaled the impending catastrophe....

The complete text of the Memorandum is appended below, at the end of this chapter.

As for the situation within the SVU, it looked very good. As was reported in *Zprávy SVU*,[171] the Society has reached the number of 1,200 in membership and it was anticipated that the membership would

---

[168] Associated with New York University.
[169] Andrew Eliáš (1920-), economist, statistician, US Bureau of the Census, Washington, DC.
[170] *Zprávy SVU*, vol. 10, No. 9 (Nov. 1968), pp. 57-58.
[171] *Zprávy SVU*, vol. 10, No. 9 (Nov. 1968), p. 60.

steadily grow because of the increased interests in Czechoslovakia due to the dismal events there.

The popular SVU periodical *Proměny,* as it entered its 6th volume, registered a total of 140 authors, which was considered a record among the Czech and Slovak magazines abroad.[172]

I was pleased that I could also add additional favorable news by informing my colleagues on the Executive board, that Eva and I had completed the preparation of the 2nd edition of the *SVU Directory*[173] which should come out soon.

Administratively, the most important issue that surfaced at the time was the need to revise the SVU Bylaws. Prof. Vratislav Bušek devoted the whole editorial in *Zprávy SVU* to the matter.[174] The matter of contention, in his opinion, was the question of the nonpolitical character of SVU and the question of the membership categories.

On January 27, 1969, Prof. Václav Hlavatý would have reached his 75th birthday and plans were to have a banquet in his honor in one of the hotels in New York. But this was not to be, as the news came that Prof. Hlavatý suddenly died on January 11, as a result of a stroke.[175] This was indeed tragic news for SVU and especially those of us who knew him personally.

The question of assistance to students and intellectuals from Czechoslovakia[176] and the problems facing the thousands of Czechoslovak citizens stranded around the world,[177] as the result of the Soviet invasion, was a standard item on the Agenda of the SVU Executive Board. According to the UN Report, some 25,000 Czechoslovak citizens were abroad at the time of the invasion and their number increased rapidly within a few weeks. Thus in Austria alone, the number of Czechoslovak refugees reached the 180,00 level.

Because of the enhanced interest in Czechoslovakia, a number of new cultural events were organized around the country with the focus on

---

[172] *Zprávy SVU*, vol. 10, No. 10 (Dec. 1968), p. 67.
[173] *Zprávy SVU,* vol. 10 , No. 9 (Nov. 1968), p. 58.
[174] *Zprávy SVU*, vol. 11, No. 1 (Jan. 1969), pp. 1-3.
[175] *Zprávy SVU*, vol. 11, No. 2 (Feb. 1969), pp. 9-10.
[176] *Zprávy SVU*, vol. 11, No. 1 (Feb. 1969), p. 10-11.
[177] *Zprávy SVU*, vol. 11, No. 2 (Feb. 1969), p. 11.

Czechoslovakia. One such event was held in New York under the sponsorship of SVU, specifically a concert of Czech and Slovak chamber music by Hartford University which took place at Carnegie Recital Hall on April 28, 1969.[178] In this connection, we should also mention a special performance of the Birmingham Civic Chorus in Alabama, organized in honor of Czechs and Slovaks in America and those who fought against communism in Czechoslovakia. As part of their repertoire were the Czechoslovak National Hymns, sung in Czech and Slovak.[179]

The most important SVU event in 1969 was its Annual meeting and General Assembly scheduled for Saturday, October 4.[180] It was to be preceded by the meeting of the SVU Council and the SVU Executive Board.

The SVU General Assembly was convened in the Prince George Hotel on Madison Ave., in New York City and was followed by the SVU banquet. As a result of the deliberations, the Assembly concurred that the most important mission of the Society is the publication activity[181] and approved the recommendation that 75 per cent of the SVU assets, i.e., approximately $12, 000 be reserved for that purpose. Further, it appointed a new committee to guide the financial policy and management of the Society. Starting with January 1, 1970, the membership fee was raised to $10 for single, $14 couple, $5 for students. In Europe, the corresponding figures were: $7, $11 and $5 and in Central and South America: $4, $7 and $4.

With respect to SVU local chapters, it was gratifying to hear that the Montreal SVU Chapter renewed its activities, under the chairmanship of Dr. Jiří Škvor, while two new chapters were organized, in Cleveland, OH and Albany, NY, respectively. In addition, there was a proposal to establish another chapter in Edmonton, Canada.

On behalf of the SVU Publication Committee, I was pleased to inform the members that the two-volume-set collection, *Czechoslovakia Past and Present*, based on the papers presented at the Second World

---

[178] *Zprávy SVU*, vol. 11, No. 4 (April 1969), p. 25.

[179] *Zprávy SVU*, vol. 11, No. 6 (June 1969), pp. 44-45.

[180] *Zprávy SVU*, vol. 11, No. 7 (Sept. 1969), p. 51 & p. 54.

[181] *Zprávy SVU*, vol. 11, No. 9 (Dec. 1969), p. 65 & p. 67.

Congress, was finally finished and that the first shipment of the books will reach the SVU Office in October.

The General Assembly, on this occasion, also issued the traditional Resolution,[182] in which SVU denounced the suppression of culture in Czechoslovakia.

As was reported by Secretary General John G. Lexa,[183] as an aftermath of the events of the Soviet invasion of Czechoslovakia, his overall responsibilities and the workload have increased enormously.

Programmatically, the most important upcoming event for the Executive Board was the Fifth SVU Congress,[184] which was scheduled for November 13-15, 1970 at New York University. The reason for picking these dates was the desire to have them coincide with the 300th anniversary of the death of John Amos Comenius (Komenský), who died on November 15, 1670. In fact, Komenský was to be the central theme of the planned Congress. Prof. Anthony L. Vaněk[185] was charged with the responsibility for the preparation of the program,[186] while Jaroslav Šabat[187] assumed the responsibility for local arrangements.

Before convening the above Congress, we should mention the Working SVU Conference,[188] June 26-28, 1970, in Horgen, Switzerland, the first such meeting to take place in Europe. Some 150 persons from various European countries, in addition to the American delegation representing the SVU Executive Board, took part in the proceedings. There were altogether twelve panel discussions, including "The Aims and Activities of the SVU," "Czechs and Slovaks Abroad," a panel on the arts, "Contemporary Czechoslovakia," a historical session, "The Prague Spring of 1968," and sessions in the fields of political science, philosophy, education, literature, economics and journalism.

The unique feature of the meeting was that a larger proportion of the participants were individuals who left Czechoslovakia recently,

---

[182] *Zprávy SVU*, vol. 11, No. 9, (December 1969), p. 67.

[183] *Zprávy SVU*, vol. 11, No. 9 (December 1969), pp 74-75.

[184] *Zprávy SVU,* vol. 12, No. 2 (Feb. 1970), p. 13.

[185] Anthony L. Vaněk (1931-), graduate student, University of Illinois, Urbana.

[186] He was later replaced by John G. Lexa.

[187] Jaroslav Šabat (1905-1986), chairman, Manhattan Branch, NY of the CNCA.

[188] *Zprávy SVU*, vol. 12, No. 6, (June 1970), p. 1.

following the "Prague Spring" of 1968. The meeting thus afforded an excellent opportunity for getting to better know the most recent exiles, to get acquainted with their views and to exchange ideas. The Executive Board was represented by Secretary General John G. Lexa and myself. Dr. Němec fell sick and thus he could not come. A detailed account of the SVU Working Conference was published in *Zprávy SVU*.[189] The complete transcript of the Conference also exists.[190]

A month before the SVU Congress, we were saddened by the news that Dr. Ladislav Radimský, the long-time Editor of the SVU periodical *Proměn*y, died on September 9, 1970 in New York.[191] On the positive side, the first shipment of the SVU collection of papers, *Czechoslovakia Past and Present* was received in the SVU office.[192]

As already mentioned the Fifth SVU Congress was convened on the campus of New York University on November 15, 1970, on the occasion of the 300th anniversary of the death of Jan Amos Komenský (Comenius). A commemorative convocation to honor the "Teacher of Nations" was attended by representatives of American universities and colleges and other prominent personalities, including Mrs. Gerta Figulus-Kallik of Los Angeles, a direct descendant of Comenius.[193] Prof. Otakar Odložilík[194] delivered the principal address, followed by a film showing the main works of Comenius and the Comenius Museum at Naarden, The Netherlands.

In addition, two special symposia were organized depicting the highlights of Comenius' life and his works. Apart from this program were the customary lectures on various aspects of Czech and Slovak culture. A special concert was given to commemorate the 100th anniversary of the birth of the Czech composer Vítězslav Novák. The detailed program of the Congress was published in *Zprávy SVU*.[195]

---

[189] *Zprávy SVU*, vol. 12, No. 7 (Sept. 1970), pp. 56-52.

[190] První Evropská konference SVU. Horgen u Curychu (Švýcarsko). 26.-28. června 1970. Transkript pořídila podle zvukového záznamu Libuše Králová. (C) 1970 Czechoslovak Society of Arts and Sciences in America, Inc. 184 p. Mimeographed.

[191] *Zprávy SVU*, vol. 12, No. 7 ( Sept. 1970), p. 53.

[192] *Zprávy SVU*, vol. 12, No, 7 (Sept. 1970), pp. 62-63.

[193] *Zprávy SVU*, vol. 12, No. 8 (October 1970), p. 70.

[194] Otakar Odložilík (1899-1973), a noted Czech historian.

[195] *Zprávy SVU*, vol. 12, No. 8 (Oct. 1970), pp. 65-69.

On the occasion of the Congress, the Society published in a mimeographed form the 72-page play of Jan Amos Komenský, *Diogenes Cynicus Redivivus*, for the first time translated into English by Michael C. Mittelstadt, professor of classics at State Univ. of New York at Binghamton.[196] In addition, SVU published Dr. Miroslav Lokay's[197] monograph *Československé legie v Italii*.[198]

Very few members realize that the Congress almost did not take place due to the sudden heart attack Secretary General John G. Lexa suffered two weeks before its start. Fortunately, the organizers continued the Congress preparation so that it could take place and had, in fact, a very successful outcome.

---

## MEMORANDUM OF NOVEMBER 1, 1968

### Addressed to the Major Universities throughout the World

At a time when armed forces of the Soviet Union and other countries of the Warsaw Pact have invaded Czechoslovakia, when the governments of most of the Western Democracies meet this criminal act by silence, when many members of the United Nations pretend that nothing has happened, the people of Czechoslovakia have but one forum where law and truth cannot be suppressed by bayonets, sold for gold, outsmarted by diplomacy nor forgotten by indifference. Such a forum are the universities throughout the world, the fountains of knowledge and, therefore, also the fountains of truth and, in the words of Jan Amos Comenius, officinae summae humanitatis – the guardians of humanism and morality.

The Czechoslovak Society of Arts and Sciences in America, a non-political organization uniting some 1200 scholars and artists in the Free World, acting on behalf of Prague's famous old Charles University whose voice has once again been stilled, as well as on behalf of the other captive Czechoslovak universities, appeals to all of their sister universities to join them in their protest against the occupation of Czechoslovakia and the

---

[196] J. A. Comenius. *Diogenes the Cynic*. Translated from Latin by M. C. Mittelstadt. New York, NY: SVU, 1970. 73 p.

[197] Miroslav Lokay (1891-1973), former Czechoslovak diplomat.

[198] Miroslav Lokay, *Československé legie v Italii*. New York, NY: SVU, 1981. 31 p.

decline of public morality throughout the world. Such circumstances have in the past always signaled the impending catastrophe.

Neither the institutions of learning, in whose name we are not merely entitled but duty-bound to act, nor we ourselves want to interfere in the internal affairs of Czechoslovakia. What we do have in mind is to assure the freedom of Czechoslovakia whose centuries old culture we are trying to present to the world, to assure the Czechs and Slovaks the right and possibility to determine their own fate and handle their own affairs without Soviet terror. We urge you not to be deceived by statements of the official spokesmen of occupied Czechoslovakia to the effect that allegedly they agree to the occupation and the nullification of their freedoms. They are acting under brutal duress in order to give the appearance of legitimacy to the acts of violence committed against them.

We cannot remain silent when the Soviets and their helpers violate basic human rights in occupied Czechoslovakia – rights, which they themselves had pledged to respect so many times in the past. We reject the so-called "Brezhnev Doctrine" announced on September 25. 1968 in the Moscow Pravda in an article entitled "Sovereignty and International Duties of Socialist Countries," that law and legal norms applicable to the mutual relations of socialist countries are subject to the "laws" of class struggle as defined by the teachings of Marxism-Leninism. This "doctrine" violates not merely all principles of international law and the Charter of the United Nations, but it is, first of all, totally incompatible with the moral bases of European civilization and ominously indicates the probability of further plans to occupy other countries wherever the Moscow brand of communism believes itself in danger.

We urge you to help the people of Czechoslovakia in their new fight for freedom, not by the power of arms, but by the power of the word, by the power of truth, which is always stronger, in the final outcome, than any tanks, which cannot be stopped by the most powerful armies nor arrested by any secret police.

We expect that the August events in Central Europe wilt be a matter of discussion among members of your faculties and among your students; should they be interested in pertinent documentation we will be pleased to make it available to them.

We would guess that they may reach the same conclusion as we do, that the Nazi "Drang nach Osten" has been replaced by an equally ruthless Soviet imperialism. We have no doubts in the outcome of such debates, for it is not difficult to distinguish between the killer and his victim.

May we ask you one special favor: If you can give any assistance to Czechoslovak intellectuals in the impending exodus to enable them to continue the fight for their ideals abroad, you will be assured of the gratitude of the long-suffering people of Czechoslovakia longing for liberty and peace, who have been fighting for these aims again and again for the long centuries of their history, but who lost 200,000 of their intellectuals under Nazism and additional tens of thousands under Soviet Stalinism. Please help to save whatever can be saved today.

Sincerely yours,

CZECHOSLOVAK SOCIETY OF ARTS AND SCIENCES
IN AMERICA, INC.

Jaroslav Němec, J.D., President   John G. Lexa, J.D., Secretary-General

# 13
## *Jan Mládek's Presidency*

On November 13, 1970, following the established practice, during the General Assembly meeting, the Society chose its new officers for the next term. Dr. Jan V. Mládek[199] was elected President; Prof. Vojtech E. Andic, Dr. Thomas M. Messer,[200] Prof. George J. Škvor and Prof. Rudolf Šturm and myself as Vice-presidents, Dr. John G. Lexa as Secretary-General and Prof. Vratislav Bušek, Editor of *Zprávy SVU*. Mr. Emil Royco was re-elected Treasurer.

Dr. Lexa, who could not attend the 5th SVU Congress because of illness was recovering fast so that he could assume his function of Secretary General. In fact, in those days, the major administrative work lay on his shoulders, as one can ascertain by going through the old issues of *Zprávy SVU*.

At its first meting, the newly elected Executive Board named several committees, including Karel Engliš Memorial Committee, headed by J. G. Polach, the Education Committee, headed by Jarmila Uhlířová,[201] the Committee for Cooperation with the Polish Institute, headed by Prof. Jiří Kolaja,[202] and the Employment Committee, headed by Dr. F. S. Hoffmeister.[203] Subsequently another committee was established, namely that of the Bylaws, which was to be headed by Dr. Vratislav Bušek.

The first issue with which the newly elected Executive Board had to deal was the revision of SVU Bylaws.[204] Following the General Assembly's approval to increase the number of the Council members for the purpose of co-opting selected persons from the post-August 1968

---

[199] Jan V. Mládek (1911-1989), economist with International Monetary Fund, Washington, DC.
[200] Thomas S. Messer (1920-), director, Guggenheim Museum, New York, NY.
[201] Jarmila Uhlířová (1902-1988), teacher, New York City. formerly a member of the Czechoslovak Parliament.
[202] Jiří Kolaja (1919-), professor of sociology, West Virginia University.
[203] F. S. Hoffmeister (1914-2004), clinical professor of surgery, Albany Medical College.
[204] *Zprávy SVU*, vol. 13, No. 2 (Feb. 1971), pp. 14-15.

emigration, it was necessary to change the Bylaws. This was done by means of Referendum of the members. Specifically, it was recommended to increase the number from 48 to 60. Another proposed change dealt with the removal of two SVU editors (*Proměny* and *Zprávy SVU*) from the Executive Board which seemed more appropriate. The third change called for giving the Executive Board the right to make decisions which would commit the Society beyond $1,000 , instead of the previously approved amount of $500. There were a few other minor changes of technical nature. It should be pointed out that in those days, the Referendum was simply posted in the *Zprávy SVU*, rather than sending each member a voting ballot by mail.

Because of the nature of his position in the International Monetary Fund, the new SVU President Jan Mládek had the opportunity to travel a lot. This gave SVU a tremendous advantage, particularly since he could visit SVU local chapters in Europe.[205] During his visits to England and Switzerland, the greatest interest among the European members seemed to be in the publication area. Generally speaking, they wanted to speed up the process by which the manuscripts were published. In case of Congress proceedings they preferred to see smaller thematic volumes rather than the voluminous collections of papers. Above all, they preferred cheaper editions in order that more people could afford to buy them.

During another occasion, Dr. Mládek met with the representatives of the Munich Chapter.[206] During the debate about the SVU aims, the local members pointed out while the largest numbers of emigrants who left Czechoslovakia in 1948 settled in America, the 1968 exile seemed to remain in Europe. These people, on the whole, expressed less need for the propagation of Czechoslovak culture, claiming that Europe knows more about Czechoslovakia than America. They are very much interested in the events in Czechoslovakia, which is accentuated by the close proximity to their homeland. For these reasons, they give preference to Czech and Slovak publications rather than English titles. They all seemed to favor the SVU periodical *Proměny*. Because of financial difficulties they were rather skeptical about a larger number of European members being able to take part in the SVU Congresses in America.

---

[205] *Zprávy SVU*, vol. 13, No. 4 (Feb. 1971), pp. 25-26.
[206] *Zprávy SVU*, vol. 13, No. 5 (May 1971), pp. 33-34.

*Jan Mládek's Presidency*

Later on, Jan Mládek paid a special visit to Switzerland, the account of which is given in *Zprávy SVU*.[207] During his stay in Australia, Mládek met with a number of SVU members in Sydney, Melbourne and even at Port Moresby, on the Papuan territory on the island of New Guinea.[208]

As per the decision of the Executive Board at its March and May 1971 meetings, the plans were to organize the next SVU annual meeting and General Assembly in New York on November 6, 1971 in the Prince George Hotel. The subsequent annual meeting was to take place in Washington, DC on November 10, 1972. The Sixth SVU Congress[209] would be convened during November 11-12, 1972. Dr. O. Horna was put in charge of the preparation of the program.

The Executive Board also named an additional committee, i.e., Nominations Committee, chaired by Dr. Karel Steinbach, which had the responsibility for coming up with the candidates for the next year. It was also noted that the Indian Publishing House, which was commissioned to publish the SVU Proceedings from the papers from the Third SVU Congress, sent the SVU Office the first set of proofs. The problem was that the proofs did not contain any diacritical marks which upset the Board considerably. Secretary General was asked to follow up with a strong letter that this was unacceptable. The great delay with which this collection was being published strengthened the resolve of the Executive Board in the future to publish smaller thematic monographs which would speed up the process. Eva and I volunteered to start working on another (3rd) edition of *SVU Directory,* the last having been published in 1968.

During the August 1971 Executive Board meeting, the major point on the agenda was the future SVU publication plans. Following the initial problems with the Indian Publishing House, which was preparing the SVU collection of papers from the 3rd SVU Congress, so far, sent proofs of only a few papers which were without any diacritical marks which the Board found unacceptable. The Indian printer promised that they would obtain the necessary fonts and correct the problem. In the meantime,

---

[207] *Zprávy SVU*, vol. 14, No. 5 (May 1972), p. 35.
[208] *Ibid.*, pp. 35-36.
[209] *Zprávy SVU*, vol. 14, No. 5 (May 1972), pp. 34.

arrangements were made with Prof. Ladislav Matějka, who attended this particular Board meeting, for publishing Roman Jakobson's monograph *Slovesné umění,* by the University of Michigan, in its Slavistic series. The monograph was scheduled to come out in October 1972 on the occasion of Roman Jakobson's 75th birthday. SVU was simultaneously negotiating with the University of Michigan the publication of two additional monographs, i.e., an anthology of translations of Czech poetry by Prof. Alfred French and a thematic collection of papers about Jan Amos Komenský, based on the 5th SVU Congress.

Because of the recurrent questions regarding this issue, the Executive Board issued a statement concerning the nonpolitical character of SVU, emphasizing that regular members of the Society are selected strictly on the basis of their scientific or artistic qualifications. The Society does not screen the applicants for their political past and does not issue judgments about their political activities or political profiles. For these reasons, the Society does not consider it to be its duty to defend its members against recriminations and political attacks. On the other hand, it would be incorrect to interpret the SVU's nonintervention as a concurrence with the attacks on its members.[210]

As scheduled, the 1971 Annual Meeting was held on November 6, following the meeting of the SVU Executive Board and the SVU Council, on the preceding day. At the Board meeting a new publication committee was appointed, with the following members: Dr. Ladislav Matějka,[211] Dr. Jaroslav Němec, Dr. Ernest Šturc, Dr. René Wellek and Miloslav Rechcígl, Jr., who served as its chairman. Based on the committee's recommendation, Matějka was asked to arrange for publication Jan Amos Komenský's opus *Labyrint světa a ráj srdce* in English, translation by Prof. Mathew Spinka.[212] Per recommendation of the Publication Committee, Prof. Vratislav Bušek was given the responsibility for editing papers on Jan Amos Komenský, presented at the 1970 SVU Congress.

---

[210] *Zprávy SVU*, vol. 13, No. 8 (Oct. 1971), p. 58.

[211] Ladislav Matějka (1919-), professor of Slavic languages and literatures at University of Michigan, Ann Arbor.

[212] Matthew Spinka (1890-1972), professor emeritus of church history, Hartford Seminary Foundation, CT.

## Jan Mládek's Presidency

In his report to the General Assembly, Secretary-General[213] gave a detailed account of the SVU membership. In comparison to 1970, when the Society had 1365 members, a year later the total number of members rose to 1482. Interestingly, the increase occurred primarily in Canada (from 144 to 229), Germany (from 38 to 58) and Switzerland (from 35 to 49).In the US, New York State had the largest number of members (165), followed by California (197) Illinois (95), District of Columbia (81), Maryland (41) and New Jersey (37). In Canada, Ottawa claimed 133 members and Quebec 63. General Secretary also informed the members that all the Bylaws revision changes were approved in the last Referendum.

In the evening, following the General Assembly meeting, there was a reception and the banquet, honoring the 75th birthday of Dr. Ján Papánek.[214] The accompanying cultural program included the performance by pianist Jana Spačková who played Antonín Benda's "Rondo D dur," Jozef Kresanek's "Scherzo for piano" and Smetana's "Furiant."

The most significant news among the SVU activities in spring 1972 was the publishing of two new SVU monographs by the University of Michigan. The first was the new English translation of Jan Amos Komenský's *Labyrint světa a ráj srdce*, prepared by Prof. Matthew Spinka, together with the facsimile of the original Czech text. The second monograph, entitled *Studies in Verbal Arts*, was a collection of Roman Jakobson's[215] studies, originally written in Czech, which have now been translated into English.[216]

Mládek's administrative period was concluded with the traditional SVU Congress, sixth in number, held at George Washington University on 10-12 November 1972. The general lectures focused on medieval Bohemia and Moravia, history of the making of modern Czechoslovakia, Czechoslovakia after World War II and Slovakia. Specialized sections featured papers on "Czechoslovak Law and Administration of Justice," "Literature and Linguistics," "Fine Arts," "Musicology," "News Media and Journalism," "Ethnic Studies," "Social and Behavioral Sciences,"

---

213 *Zprávy SVU*, vol. 13, No. 9 (Nov. 1971), pp. 67-68.

214 Ján Papánek (1896-1991), former Czechoslovak diplomat.

215 Roman Jakobson (1896-1982), professor of Slavic languages, literature and general linguistics at Harvard University; the founder of the famed Prague Linguistic Circle.

216 See *Zprávy SVU*, vol. 14, no. 4 (April 1972), pp. 25-26.

"Biological and Physical Sciences," "Engineering and Technology," and "History of Sciences, Technology and Education." In addition, three reading sessions from new works of Czech and Slovak writers were organized. The highlight of the Congress was the reception and banquet at the Atrium of the John F. Kennedy Center for Performing Arts. On this occasion, Honorary memberships to past Presidents Professor René Wellek and Dr. Jaroslav Němec were presented, in recognition for their accomplishments.

In retrospect, the most important of Mládek's contributions were his international trips which brought the distant chapters and members closer to SVU leadership and to American members, in general. During his administration, several new monographs were published or initiated. This included the already mentioned Roman Jacobson's *Studies in Verbal Arts*[217] and Matthew Spinka's translation of Comenius' *The Labyrinth of the World and the Paradise of the Heart*,[218] as well as a collection of essays, *Comenius*,[219] edited by Vratislav Bušek, in commemoration of the 300th anniversary of the death of the Bohemian scholar. The first two books were published jointly with the University of Michigan. In 1972, the newly revised *SVU Directory*, prepared by Eva Rechcígl and myself, was also published. In addition to the customary biographical data, this edition of the Directory also contained the bylaws and a chapter on the milestones in the history of the Society.[220] Alfred French's *Anthology of Czech Poetry*,[221] which was prepared during this period, was published a year later.

---

[217] Roman Jakobson, *Studies in Verbal Art*: Texts in Czech and Slovak, Ann Arbor: University of Michigan, 1971. 412 p.

[218] Comenius, J. A., *The Labyrinth of the World and the Paradise of the Heart*. With a Facsimile of the 1663 Czech Original Translated by Matthew Spinka. Ann Arbor: University of Michigan, 1972. 203 p.

[219] *Comenius*. A Symposium Commemorating the 300th Anniversary of the Death of Jan Amos Comenius (Komenský). Edited by Vratislav Bušek. New York, NY, 1972. 184 p.

[220] *Biographical Directory of the Members of the Czechoslovak Society of Arts and Sciences in America, Inc.* 3rd ed. Compiled and edited by Eva Rechcígl and Miloslav Rechcígl, Jr. New York, 1972. 134 p.

[221] Alfred French, comp., *Anthology of Czech Poetry*. Introduced by René Wellek. Ann Arbor: University of Michigan, 1973. 372 p.

# 14
## *Francis Schwarzenberg's Presidency*

The newly elected officers for 1972-73 period were Prof. Francis Schwarzenberg, President, Prof. V. E. Andic, Prof. Vratislav Bušek, Arch. Emil Royco, Prof. Rudolf Šturm and Miloslav Rechcígl, Jr., Vice Presidents; Dr. John G. Lexa, Secretary-General; Mr. Jaroslav Šabat, Treasurer; and Jiří Škvor, Editor of *Proměny*. The officers were re-elected for another one-year term at the General Assembly Meeting held in Toronto on November 17, 1973.

The election of Francis Schwarzenberg to SVU Presidency came as a surprise and brought some apprehension and concern among some members. This was based on the general perception that Schwarzenberg was viewed primarily as a politician rather than a representative of the intellectual community. To be sure, he was otherwise a popular figure, particularly among the Chicagoans, who saw him frequently at various political rallies and social events which he attended. His selection had lots to do with the makeup of the Nominations Committee which had hardly any university representative or other intellectuals among them.[222] Dr. Jaroslav Němec, who has always been the strongest voice for the nonpolitical character of SVU and who was originally a member of the committee, subsequently resigned from it which might have been due to his opposition to nominate Schwarzenberg to SVU Presidency. This is, of course, a mere conjecture on my part.

Schwarzenberg was obviously aware of the criticisms, and, consequently, made a special point in his acceptance speech of the nonpolitical nature of the SVU mission, the tradition which he intended to follow.[223]

To write about Schwarzenberg's administrative period, in retrospect, is a bit difficult due to the paucity of available information. The newsletter *Zprávy SVU*, which normally abounds with information about the activities of the respective Executive Boards, surprisingly did not

---

[222] The Committee comprised Karel Steinbach, Brano Lajda, Miloš Šebor and Josef Žanda.
[223] *Zprávy SVU*, vol. 14, No. 9, (Nov. 1972), pp. 69.

report much from this time period. The only substantive news items dealt with the notices of John G. Lexa in his capacity as Secretary General.

The first tangible reference to the SVU Executive Board appeared in the January 1973 issue of *Zprávy SVU*,[224] informing the members of the Board meeting on January 6 in which it was decided to hold the SVU Annual meeting on November 17, 1973 in Toronto. Furthermore, the Board recommended that the Seventh SVU Congress be convened on 15-17 November 1974 in New York City at New York University.

The next mention of the SVU Executive Board appeared in the April issue of *Zprávy SVU*[225] regarding the naming of various committees for the year 1972-73. They were : Nominations Committee, chaired by Jan V. Mládek, Membership Committee, chaired by Brano M. Lajda,[226] Publication Committee, chaired by Miloslav Rechcígl, Jr., By-laws Committee, chaired by Dr. Antonín Srba,[227] Music Committee, chaired by Zdenka Fischmann.[228] The Board also reaffirmed their decision to hold the next SVU Congress on November 15-17, 1972 and appointed Rudolf Šturm as the coordinator of the academic program. The latter reported on his progress in the September issue of *Zprávy SVU*.[229]

In the October 1973 issue of *Zprávy SVU*,[230] there is a terse announcement that the Executive Board, with regret, decided to terminate the project "Who's Who" which was on SVU books for the last 10 years. As an explanation, it was stated that no suitable editor could be found. All the volunteers who initially expressed interest in serving in such capacity have eventually given up this task. Inasmuch as $5 was originally requested from the interested people, they have been told they will be given a copy of the *SVU Directory* instead.

---

[224] *Zprávy SVU*, vol. 15, N. 1-2 (Jan-Feb. 1973), p. 4.

[225] *Zprávy SVU*, vol. 14, No. 8 (April 1973), p. 118.

[226] Brano M. Lajda (1917-2000), journalist and economist, associated with Voice of America, Washington, DC.

[227] Antonín Srba (1907-1980), president, Hedwin Corporation, New York.

[228] Zdenka E. Fischmann (1923-1999), music therapist and musicologist, Patton State Hospital, Corona, CA.

[229] *Zprávy SVU*, vol. 15, No. 7 (Sept. 1973), pp. 51-52.

[230] *Zprávy SVU*, vol. 15, No. 8 (Oct. 1973), p. 60.

As per its announcement,[231] the Nominations Committee recommended that the current SVU officers be reelected. This indeed happened during the elections which took place at the General Assembly meeting on November 17, 1979, convened at the University of Toronto. The new slate of officers was reprinted on the first page of the December issue of *Zprávy SVU*,[232] without saying much about the actual proceedings of the General Assembly. Only the report of the Secretary General John G. Lexa is mentioned which was reprinted in full.[233]

A considerable part of Lexa's report dealt with the increased responsibilities and work load put on the SVU office in New York, particularly with reference to the distribution and sales of SVU publications. The initial efforts to involve a commercial firm in the mailing process was unsatisfactory because the firm lacked the appropriate contacts and had incorrect addresses. As a result, Secretary General had no choice but to prepare, on the basis of Slavic library directories, his own listing of addresses to which the office then sent over 1000 letters with SVU leaflets about its publications.

Lexa also informed the members that IRS conducted the review of the SVU finances which, first in its history, were found satisfactory, as was the external audit, carried out by the New York-based firm Spiegler, Niederhoffer & Co. He further commented on the completion and availability of the SVU monograph *Comenius,*[234] edited by Prof. Bušek. He had, however, only harsh words for the Indian printer who has not as yet completed the work on the collection of papers from the Third SVU Congress. In spite of numerous reminders, very little progress has been made and Lexa did not think that filing a law suit in India would be too effective.

As we learned from the December issue of *Zpravy SVU*,[235] Rudolf Šturm, who had the responsibility for the program of the upcoming SVU

---

[231] *Zprávy SVU*, vol. 15, No. 7 (Sept. 1973), p. 52.
[232] *Zprávy SVU*, vol. 15, No. 10 (Dec. 1973), p. 74.
[233] *Zprávy SVU*, vol. 15, No. 10 (Dec. 1973), pp. 74-75.
[234] A detailed announcement about the monograph appeared in *Zprávy SVU*, vol. 16, No. 1 (Jan 1974), p. 5.
[235] *Zprávy SVU*, vol. 15, No. 10 (Dec. 1973), p. 76.

Congress, had to resign, for personal reasons. Prof. Milan Fryščák,[236] who was associated with the New York University, where he taught Czech, took his place.

In browsing through various issues of *Zprávy SVU* during this period, one cannot but be impressed how much Lexa was involved in various SVU activities, which were clearly beyond his responsibilities as Secretary General. Thus in the February issue, he published an editorial concerning the propagation and sale of SVU publications.[237] Although it was up to the SVU Office to handle the technical aspects of this, I am sure, that John Lexa had to wrap many of the parcels himself. Elsewhere, we read his note,[238] on behalf of the editors of SVU periodicals, in which he appeals to the membership to regularly send in information about their work and accomplishments, about their publications, public lectures, complaining that only a limited number of chapters send in news items about their activities. With reference to *Proměny*, he reminded the members to provide manuscripts that are legible and typed, with appropriate diacritical marks, etc. I know from the discussions with him, that many of the submitted manuscripts were so illegible that they had to be retyped and some of them he actually had to retype himself. He also made an appeal to Slovak authors to send in more articles in the Slovak language to assure that the Slovak–Czech orientation is maintained.

The announcement of the Seventh SVU Congress was carried out in the September 1974 issue of *Zprávy SVU*,[239] listing the titles of the various academic sessions. The Congress was held on 15-17 November 1974, at the Washington Square campus of New York University As for its program, it basically followed the same pattern as the previous six Congresses. Apart from sections along the disciplinary lines, there were several thematic symposia, including lectures and discussions on the Hussites; an overview of the controversial manuscripts of Dvůr Králové and Zelená Hora; Czech politics between the Revolutions of 1848 and 1918; politics and politicians of the 1920s; nationality problems in

---

[236] Milan Fryščák (1932-), associate professor of Slavic languages and literature at New York university.

[237] *Zprávy SVU*, vol. 16, No. 2 (Feb. 1974), pp. 9-11.

[238] *Zprávy SVU*, vol. 16, no. 4 (April 1974), p. 28.

[239] *Zprávy SVU*, vol. 16, No. 7 (Sept. 1974), p. 50.

Slovakia and Ruthenia; the Jews in Czechoslovak history and culture; Czechoslovak-Ukrainian relations, etc.

There was a special showing of a full-length film of the opera "Krutnava" by the contemporary Slovak composer Evžen Suchoň.[240] At the banquet, held in the Prince George Hotel, a concert featured music by Czechoslovak composers Karel Boleslav Jirák, Leoš Janáček and Karel Husa, performed by Rudolf Firkušný, František Smetana[241] and Karel Husa.[242]

The Congress itself was preceded by SVU General Assembly meeting[243] which was held on Friday, November 15, 1974. The Assembly approved the recommendation to hold the next SVU Congress in summer 1976, with the general theme "Contributions of Czechs and Slovaks to the USA," which would be convened as a part of the 200th anniversary of the founding of the United States. Among various reports, the most dramatic presentation came from the SVU Treasurer Jaroslav Šabat who shocked the members with his statement that, as of September 30, 1974, the Society was $5000 in red. The deficit apparently occurred, partly because of the increased expenses and partly due to reduced income.[244]

---

[240] Evžen Suchoň (1908-1993), one of the greatest Slovak composers.

[241] František Smetana (1914-2004), a notable Czech cellist.

[242] Karel Husa (1921-), noted composer, conductor and professor of music at Cornell University, Ithaca, NY.

[243] Report of the meeting appears in *Zprávy SVU*, vol. 16, No. 10 (Dec. 1974), pp. 76-79.

[244] *Zprávy SVU*, vol. 16, No. 10 (December 1974), pp. 76-79.

# 15
## *Beating the Prince*

It must have been in the second year of Schwarzenberg's SVU Presidency, when I was first approached by Jaroš Němec and Jan Mládek whether I would be interested in being nominated for the next SVU President. The suggestion did not really take me by surprise because, by then, I was immersed in SVU activities so earnestly and extensively that I felt in my bones that I could do a good job. It was no secret that Jaroš was grooming me for the high SVU office which I knew would sooner or later be offered to me. Ivan Herben, one of my early mentors, long predicted that one day I would "take over the reigns of SVU."

The situation in SVU, at the time, was not really the best; it was actually precarious. In terms of activities, nothing exciting was happening and in terms of finances the Society was in a bind. Most of the savings had been used up for the maintenance of the SVU office in New York and for the salaries of two secretaries. The SVU membership dwindled and the dues were hardly enough for paying the postage and other basic expenses. František Schwarzenberg, who was otherwise a very nice person,[245] did not take any steps to circumvent the status quo, partly because he probably was not even aware of what was happening. The Society was then largely in the hands of Executive-Secretary Hanuš Lexa,[246] while the SVU President was largely a figurehead.

Neither Mládek nor Němec tried to hide the seriousness of the situation the Society was facing. They told me point blank that Schwarzenberg has to be replaced by a younger and more agile person who would bring the Society back on the right track. They thought that I was the man. After discussing the matter with Eva, who thought that I would do a credible job and promised her support, I told Jaroš and Jan that I was ready and willing.

---

[245] He had a very good public image, being a member of the old aristocratic family from the times of the Kingdom of Bohemia.

[246] John G. Lexa was usually known among his Czechoslovak friends as Hanuš.

The SVU Nominations Committee, consisting of three past SVU Presidents, namely Jan Mládek, chairman and Jaroš Němec and René Wellek, did indeed nominate me for the next SVU President. In their statement,[247] they stated the following:

> Some societies and institutions adhere to the principle of changing the entire leadership at the start of a new term. Other associations make a selection bearing in mind effective continuity and effective exchange or rotation. The Nomination Committee is convinced, in part, because of age of the Society (16 years), and, in part, because the growing membership from the ranks of the 68th emigration requires that more emphasis than in the previous years be put on the change and filling the position with new people. This attitude is not a critique of the present leadership but rather an expression of our conviction that it is only right to give a chance to new people and enable the transition between generations. If the General Assembly will accept the proposal of the Nominations Committee, it would result in the departure from the Executive Board and the Council of several individuals who unquestionably played a role in the formative years of SVU. This should not be interpreted as a sign of ingratitude but the application of the principle that office functions are temporary and that every member is entitled to be considered for a temporary role in the working circle of SVU Executive Board, SVU Council, committees, etc. In recommending a number of changes, the Committee is fully aware that experience and a creditable record of the candidates cannot be overlooked and its conception of the principle of rotation is fully justifiable in the future administrative periods and the return to SVU offices of people who are dedicated, experienced and capable.[248]

As the news became known, some rumbling began to be heard from certain corners. It was partly my age which had them worried. After all, in my early forties I was still considered a greenhorn by SVU standards, the majority of the membership being at least 20 years my senior. Stories began to be circulated, particularly among the extreme "right-wingers" that I would take radical steps and bring SVU astray. An opportunity that

---

[247] Published in *Zprávy SVU*, Volume 17, No. 7 ( September 1974), pp. 2-3.
[248] *Zprávy SVU*, vol. 16, No. 7 (September 1974), pp. 50-51.

added ammunition to their case lent itself as a result of a private party given by Dr. Karel Absolon[249] in his house. Among his guests was the newly then named Czechoslovak Ambassador to the US Dušan Spáčil. None of the guests, including myself, had been informed of this beforehand. This was obviously embarrassing to most of us but, frankly, the whole thing was of no consequence because hardly any of us actually talked to him. Absolon, of course, thought nothing of it and considered Spacil's invitation, who was his classmate from Brno, a personal matter.

The news of this got around fast and my opponents had an additional argument against me. They began to spread rumors that if I were to become SVU President that I would establish relations with the communist Czechoslovakia and, above all, that I couldn't be trusted.

In this climate, my opponents began putting pressure on Schwarzenberg to enter the race as my opponent, telling him that it is a matter of utmost urgency, a matter of honor and patriotism,. etc. Under such pressure, Schwarzenberg finally agreed to run against me "to save the Society from possible disaster." At this point, some members thought that it would be in the interest of the Society if I would simply withdraw my candidacy. To my amazement, even Dr. Karel Steinbach[250] came to me with such a proposition. I must say, it was primarily Jan Mládek who stuck with me all the way and who gave me his unequivocal support from the beginning to the end.

In those days, elections always took place at the General Assembly meetings which were frequently the witness of immense politicking, outrageous speeches, excitement, confrontations and the final tense and thrilling voting. It was truly "the most exciting show in town" to which many a member was looking forward the entire year. Those members who could not participate could give their proxies to other members. There was no limit to the number of proxies a member could have. This gave opportunity to both sides to get ready for the battle.

---

[249] Karel Absolon (1926-) was a reputable heart surgeon who held the position of Chief of Department of Surgery at the Washington Hospital Center. He was a native of Brno, son of the famous Czech archeologist of the same name.

[250] Dr. Karel Steinbach (1893-1990) was a well-known gynecologist in Prague; a close friend of Ferdinand Peroutka, Karel Čapek and Jan Masaryk and a member of the famous Friday group ("pátečníci"). In the US he lived in New York where he worked for the US Army.

*Beating the Prince* 85

The stage was set. On November 14, 1974, SVU General Assembly meeting was convened in one of the halls of New York University School of Law, Washington Square South, New York City, the place of the Seventh SVU Congress. The hall was filled to capacity by SVU members. Everybody was in anticipation of an exciting battle that had no precedence in the entire history of SVU. In the cases of past SVU Presidents, there was always an agreement on the candidate and consequently there was no controversy. All the battles in the past related to other offices. To add to the drama was the realization that František Schwarzenberg, with his aristocratic background and princely title, provided mystique to the whole proceedings and there seemed to prevail a general opinion that a man of such qualities and distinction cannot be beaten by any challenger, particularly by such a "young Turk" like myself.

The actual voting was preceded by speeches by opposing sides, including those of the nominees. Karel Absolon and Miša Šumichrast[251] came especially to New York to voice their opinion and give me support. To give the proceedings some order and impartiality, the Assembly voted to have it presided by Jan Stránský,[252] an able attorney, who was in the employ of Radio Free Europe in New York. I do not recall all details and who spoke for or against. One incident stuck in my mind, however. Just before the voting was to begin, a group of Slovaks, associated with the "Stálá slovenská konferencia,"[253] came to me to tell me that they all decided to oppose Schwarzenberg and vote for me.

When all the speeches were exhausted, the Presiding Officer called for a vote. Instead of quieting down, "all hell seemed to break loose." All of a sudden, member after member hurried forward toward the presiding officer's desk bringing his proxies. There was a lot of confusion, like a circus. After the chairman restored order, the tellers were called in to start counting the votes. It must have taken at least half an hour for things to get sorted out, since some of the proxies were contested, before

---

[251] Chief economist with the Home Builders of America. He and his wife Marika were our very close friends.

[252] Jan Stránský (1913-1998), in the US journalist with Radio Free Europe; the son of Dr. Jaroslav Stránský, Minister of Justice of Czechoslovakia.

[253] In English: Permanent Slovak Conference; an association of the democratic Slovaks abroad, founded by Martin Kvetko and Jozef Lettrich.

the results were finally announced. In spite of general expectations, I was declared the winner, beating my opponent by a landslide, i.e., 2:1 margin[254] or in terms of actual numbers, I received 162 votes against Schwarzenberg's 82. The outcome was so embarrassing that the actual numbers were never reported in *Zprávy SVU*, and, in fact, no mention was even made in the SVU newsletter that Schwarzenberg ran against me.[255]

As reported in the November 1974 issue of *Zprávy SVU*, [256] the newly elected SVU Executive Board comprised the following members: Miloslav Rechcígl, Jr.,[257] President; Dr. Alexej Bořkovec,[258] Ing. Ján Gavora,[259] Prof. Josef Škvorecký,[260] Dr. Ernest Šturc[261] and Prof. Zdeněk Suda,[262] Vice Presidents; Dr. John G. Lexa,[263] Secretary-General, Dr. Frank Meissner,[264] Treasurer and Dr. Jiří Škvor,[265] Editor of *Proměny*.[266] In retrospect, this was truly an outstanding team.

---

[254] "Valné shromáždění SVU dne 25. listopadu 1974 v Novém Yorku, NY. Výtah z transkriptu pořízeného Dr. John G. Lexou, gen. sekretářem SVU."

[255] *Zprávy SVU*, vol. 16, No. 10 ( December 1974), pp. 76-79.

[256] *Zprávy SVU*, vol. 16, No. 9 (November 1974), pp. 65-67.

[257] I was then associated with the US Agency for International Development, which was then an integral part of US Department of State, Washington, DC.

[258] Alexej B. Bořkovec (1925-), organic chemist with the U.S. Department of Agriculture, Agricultural Research Center, Beltstville, MD.

[259] Ján Gavora (1933-), animal scientist associated with the Canada Department of Agriculture, Ottawa, Canada. He was a native of Brezová, Slovakia.

[260] Josef Škvorecký (1924-), a well-known Czech writer living in exile in Canada. He was Professor of English at the University of Toronto, Erindale College, Mississauga, Ont., Canada.

[261] Ernest Šturc (1915-1980), economist of Slovak origin, with the International Monetary Fund, Washington, DC.

[262] Zdeněk Suda (1920-), a sociologist with University of Pittsburgh, Pittsburgh, PA.

[263] At this time, Lexa was employed as a lawyer with Waldes Co. in New York and, in addition, he was associated, as a lecturer, with the New York University Law School.

[264] Frank Meissner (1923-1990), an agricultural economist associated with the Inter-American Development Bank, Washington, DC.

[265] Jiří Škvor (1926-1980), a well-known Czech poet who wrote under the pseudonym Pavel Javor. He was associated with the Radio Canada International as a broadcaster.

[266] Complete list of newly elected SVU officers, together with my biography, is in *Zprávy SVU*, vol. 16 (Nov. 1974), No. 9, pp. 65-67.

# 16
# *As SVU President*

At the onset of my term as President,[267] each of our Vice Presidents was given responsibility for a specific task, i.e., Alexej Bořkovec for preparation of the program of SVU Congress, Jan Gavora maintaining contact with local chapters, Zdeněk Suda liaison with professional organizations and institutions, Josef Škvorecký to maintain contact with post-August 1968 emigration and the distribution of SVU publications and Ernest Šturc for seeking external sources of funding.

Early on, we constituted a number of advisory bodies, including membership committee, ethnic studies committee, membership drive committee, committee for evaluating Czechoslovak academic degrees, employment service committee and the SVU Speakers Bureau.[268]

To be sure, the Executive Board members, as well as the members of various SVU committees, performed all their duties without any compensation. Paid assistance was used only in exceptional cases for work which required special expertise or experience which we lacked.

Faithful to the promise I made in my acceptance speech,[269] we established a number of professional and interest groups within the SVU organizational structure, starting with historical and journalist sections. Moreover, we asked Rudolf Šturm to constitute a bibliographical section, Prof. Peter Toma[270] a political science section, Dr. Zdenka Fischmann[271] a musicological section, Dr. Zdenka Muenzer[272] an art

---

[267] This chapter is based in part on my annual reports to General Assembly, published in *Zprávy SVU*, vol. 18 (Jan-Feb. 1976), no. 1, pp. 1-6; *Ibid.*, vol. 18 (Sept.-Oct. 1976), No. 5, pp. 1-6.

[268] *Zprávy SVU*, vol. 17, N o. 2 (February 1975), pp. 9-11.

[269] *Zprávy SVU*, vol. 16 (Dec. 1974), No. 10, pp. 1-3.

[270] Peter A. Toma (1925-), professor of government at the University of Arizona at Tucson.

[271] Zdenka E. Fischmann (1923-1999), musicologist and music therapist, Patton State Hospital, Corona, CA.

[272] Zdenka Muenzer (1902-1986), art historian, associated with the Metropolitan Museum of Art in New York City.

history section, Dr. Antonín Kratochvíl[273] a literary history section and Dr. O. Turchan[274] a science and technology section. At the same time we asked the membership for suggestions for additional interest sections and called for volunteers, especially among the younger generation.

Administratively, my first task was to undertake, jointly with the Executive Board, a thorough analysis of management and fiscal affairs of the Society.[275] Partly because of financial losses on earlier publication projects and partly due to a slack of income from membership dues, the Society faced a critical situation inasmuch as its yearly expenses began to exceed its annual income. The financial situation was precarious and it was clear to me from the beginning that some drastic steps must be taken to keep the Society afloat. I knew that the biggest drain on our finances was our SVU New York office which eventually would have to close. As a consequence, it was apparent to me that SVU would have to undergo a large decentralization. This was a tall order which I could not very well accomplish on my own without some external help. I decided therefore to turn to past officers who held the office of Secretary-General and SVU President for assistance.

In an effort to maintain continuity and not to lose experience gained in the past, as I rationalized, I established a special advisory committee, composed of Past Secretary-Generals, i.e. Rudolf Šturm, Jaroslav Němec and Vojtech Andic. I asked them to carefully evaluate the decentralization question, having in mind the financial difficulties of the Society, and come up with specific plans. In the same vein, I felt that the Society never took advantage of all the wisdom and experiences of its past presidents. Consequently, I constituted another advisory body, comprised of Past Presidents, i.e., Prof. René Wellek, Dr. Jaroslav Němec, Dr. Jan V. Mládek and Prof. František Schwarzenberg, who were henceforth regularly invited to our Executive Board meetings. Furthermore, I convened

---

[273] Antonín Kratochvíl (1924-2004), research analyst, associated with the Radio Free Europe, Munich, Germany.

[274] Otto Charles Turchan (1925-), physicist, Beverly Hills, CA.

[275] *Zprávy SVU*, vol. 17 (Jan. 1975), No. 1, pp. 1-6.

*As SVU President*

a special meeting with them to discuss serious problems that confronted SVU and sought their counsel.[276]

The greatest attention was given to SVU financial problems with the aim of reducing SVU expenses and increasing SVU income. From the meticulous analysis of our Treasurer[277] it was clear that the SVU reserves would be exhausted in a two-year period unless some drastic action be taken. The largest expenses were related to the cost of renting the SVU New York office – which amounted to about $10,000 per year. After careful analysis, our decentralization committee recommended that the office be abolished and the agenda of the office be transferred to and distributed among volunteers. The Past Presidents had the same recommendation.

With these recommendations from such distinguished bodies I did not have much problem in selling the idea to the Executive Board. Most affected by the decision was SVU Secretary-General John G. Lexa, who did not bear it lightly because he heavily depended on the office and the paid secretary for his work.[278]

As a result of the Executive Board's ruling, the office was terminated as of January 1975 and the position of SVU secretary was not renewed. We were hoping that this action would remove our deficit which threatened the very existence of the Society. Abolishing our office was not a popular step and we had to carefully explain to our membership that this was a step to put the Society on firm foundation because otherwise the Society's future was doomed.

Apart from the expenses relating to our office, substantial sums were also expended on our periodicals, *Zprávy SVU* and *Proměny* which had to be checked. In the case of *Proměny*, which had to be heavily subsidized by the Society, we cut down a number of unnecessary expenses, such as retyping illegible manuscripts, and moved the whole operation to

---

[276] To legitimize this body's existence, we later included a special paragraph in the newly revised SVU Bylaws, on the establishment of the "Collegium of Presidents." It comprised Past Presidents as an independent advisory body to SVU on matters of policy.

[277] *Zprávy SVU,* vol. 18 (March-Apr. 1976), No. 2, pp. 1-8.

[278] Actually he was going to challenge our decision at the SVU General Assembly meeting in Los Angeles, scheduled for October, 1975. Fortunately I got wind of it and called him and asked him to be a team player and accept the democratic decision of the Executive Board or otherwise I'd be forced to ask for his resignation. He consented to my request and the trouble was over.

Canada. Simultaneously we appealed to the membership to subscribe to the periodical to help us pay for production costs with the hope that one day *Proměny* could stand on its own feet.

The costs of publishing SVU newsletter *Zprávy SVU* also steadily increased to $2,500 for 10 issues of 8 pages each annually. Apart from the increased cost, the printing firm did not keep up with the newsletter's schedule. As a consequence some issues came out several months late which caused rumbling among SVU members. After an unsuccessful search for a cheaper and more reliable firm, we decided to purchase our own typesetting equipment ("Veritype") and do the typesetting by ourselves. Although it was a second-hand machine, it did its job and reduced our production costs by half and very soon we were caught up with our schedule.

The decentralization of our agenda that followed the abolishment of SVU New York office saved a substantial sum but also brought some confusion, especially at the beginning, before our volunteers became fully accustomed to their new responsibilities and before new procedures became routinized.

To appreciate the magnitude of decentralization let me mention a few examples. First, it was necessary to transfer the entire operation to Washington, DC, including finances, membership record keeping, storage of SVU published books, as well as SVU library which had to be liquidated. This meant finding space and people. Moreover, we maintained our SVU editorial office in Washington, typesetting as well as distribution – which by itself was quite an undertaking. Moving the editorial function and printing of *Proměny* to Canada also gave us more breathing space.

Apart from our concerted effort to reduce our expenses, I should point out that we also launched a systematic campaign to increase SVU income by urging members to pay their back dues, by enlarging the membership rolls and from donations. In this connection, it should be noted that the Washington DC Chapter donated its entire proceeds from their US Bicentennial Bazaar to SVU in support of its growing publication program.

On 24-26 October 1975, we held, in Los Angeles, CA, our traditional annual meeting with General Assembly and a Conference in Los

*As SVU President*

Angeles, CA.[279] In my capacity as President I presented to the Assembly a detailed annual report which was reprinted in full in the first 1976 issue of *Zprávy SVU*.[280]

The SVU Los Angeles Chapter, jointly with the Center for Russian and East European Studies of the University of California at Los Angeles (UCLA), organized a day-long Symposium in celebration of the 125th anniversary of the birth of Thomas Garrigue Masaryk. It was opened by Frank Marlow for SVU and Prof. Birnbaum for the Center. Prof. Worth acquainted the participants with the program of Czech Studies at the University of California in Los Angeles.

The Symposium speakers included Prof. Michael Heim,[281] who talked about K. H. Borovský in relation to the development of Masaryk's *Česká otázka*, Dr. Pavel Machotka,[282] who discussed Masaryk's philosophy and sociology, Dr. Jaroslav G. Polach who analyzed Masaryk's contributions to economics, Ms. Draga Shillinglaw,[283] discussed Masaryk's stay at the University of Chicago in 1902, Dr. Stanislav Segert,[284] who evaluated the influence of Masaryk's ideas in Czechoslovakia in the fifties and sixties and Dr. Jiří Liška[285] talked about Masaryk's relation to Sokol.

On October 25th there was a festive dinner held in Del Rey Marina, during which five students were awarded stipends for the best essays. The competition was initiated by Dr. Zahradka,[286] who was the first chairman of the Los Angeles Chapter. I had the honor to address the

---

[279] A detailed report about the conference can be found in *Zprávy SVU*, vol. 17 (Nov.-Dec. 1975), No. 9-10, pp. 64-72.

[280] *Zprávy SVU*, vol. 2 (January-February 1976), pp. 16.

[281] Michael H. Heim (1943-), associate professor of Slavic Languages, University of California at Los Angeles.

[282] Pavel Machotka (1936-), professor of psychology at the University of California at Santa Cruz.

[283] Draga B. Shillinglaw (1927-), translator, associated with the University of Chicago.

[284] Stanislav Segert (1921-2005), professor of Biblical studies and Near-Eastern languages at the University of California at Los Angeles.

[285] Jiří Liška (1916-), management consultant, Thousand Oaks,, CA.

[286] Joseph A. Zahradka (1909-1977), attorney, senior partner of law firm Zahradka & Glines, Los Angeles, CA.

audience with a talk on the Czechoslovak contributions to the United States of America.

The Conference was concluded with a festive assembly during which the Honorable Tom Bradley, Mayor of Los Angeles, issued a proclamation, declaring October 28, 1975 the Czechoslovakia's Independence Day. In the evening the SVU members participated in the celebrations of the October 28th anniversary in the Sokol Hall.

In reference to the future of SVU, the most important event in Los Angeles was a joint meeting between our Executive Board and the leadership of the SVU LA Chapter. On one hand, the Board had the opportunity to get acquainted with SVU members in our largest Chapter in the West and the type of problems distant SVU chapters have to deal with. The Los Angeles members, in turn, were informed about the responsibilities of SVU Executive Board and its aims and the challenges they have to confront. A friendly meeting between the SVU Executive Board and the leadership of the LA Chapter led to a joint "Program Declaration"[287] and the commitment of the LA Chapter in several SVU publication projects, both editorially and financially, specifically the T. G. Masaryk Symposium and the Symposium about the Czech Music. LA Chapter thus became, after Washington DC Chapter, the second SVU chapter to cooperate with the SVU headquarters on joint projects.

With the gradual improvement of our financial situation, the Society was again able to broaden its activities, particularly in the area of publishing. This was reflected in our new extensive publication plan.[288] In a relatively short time, SVU published selected papers from the Law Symposium held at the Sixth SVU Congress, under the title *Czechoslovak Military Justice Abroad during the Second World War* [289] and launched a new series of *Occasional Papers*,[290] under the general editorship of Dr. Jaroslav G. Polach. In press was also an extensive bibliogra-

---

[287] *Zprávy SVU*, vol. 17 (Nov.-Dec. 1975), No. 9-10, pp. 68-70.

[288] "O publikační činnosti. Zpráva Ediční a publikační komise SVU," *Zprávy SVU*, vol. 17 (Sept.-Oct. 1975), No. 7-8, pp. 48-51.

[289] Keith Ewing and John H. Fisher, eds. *Czechoslovak Justice Abroad during the Second World* War. New York, NY, 1975. 47 p.

[290] The first study was that of Victor S. Mamatey, *Building Czechoslovakia in America*: 1914-1918. Washington, DC, 1976. 17 p.

*As SVU President* 93

phy of *Czechs and Slovaks in North America,*[291] a life-long work of Esther Jeřábek[292] of Minnesota. As was related elsewhere, the Washington DC Chapter offered to finance its lecture series[293] while the Los Angeles Chapter made the commitment to pay publication costs for the planned symposia collections on Czech Music and T. G. Masaryk. Plans were also made to publish an English version of Karel Engliš' monumental monograph on *Economic Systems,* and to cosponsor the University of Michigan's planned publication about the Prague Linguistic Circle. The new Publication Committee had every intension to also publish selected papers from various SVU congresses and other worthy materials SVU accumulated throughout its history. As the first step, it decided to catalogue the known and available manuscripts[294] under the editorship of Mrs. Eva Polach.[295]

With reference to book sales, we established a new service and put Bohumil Jaroš[296] and his wife in charge. Our newsletter periodically printed lists of books that were available for sale, including our own, as well as volumes from our former NY library and urged the members to buy them.

We also paid special attention to SVU publicity and launched a membership drive. A special publicity leaflet was prepared for that purpose which was sent with an invitation letter to potential SVU members. Josef Škvorecký also kindly offered to include our publicity pamphlet in his correspondence with his readers and subscribers of 68 Publishers[297]

---

[291] *Czechs and Slovaks in North America: A Bibliography.* By Esther Jeřábek. New York, NY: SVU, 1976. 448 p.

[292] Esther Jeřábek (1897-1979), retired librarian living in Minneapolis, MN.

[293] The series has been enlarged to include the time period until 1968, under the title "Idea of the Czechoslovak State 1938-1948-1968." The Washington DC Chapter which committed its funds for this project set up its own committee, consisting of Dr. B. Lajda, Dr. C. Ješina and J. Novotney, to get the manuscripts ready for publication.

[294] The bibliography was later published under the title *The SVU List of Lectures, Studies and Other Materials.* Eva B. Polach. Washington, DC: Czechoslovak Society of Arts and Sciences in America, Inc, 1976. *Occasional Paper* No. 2. 34 p.

[295] She was associated with the Library of Congress, Washington, DC.

[296] Bohumil Jaroš (1907-died), active in the Sokol Washington.

[297] The publishing firm Sixty-Eight-Publisher was established by Josef Škvorecký and his wife Zdena Salivarová in Toronto. Ont., Canada in 1969 and remained in operation until 1994.

which he directed with his wife. In this connection I also urged SVU members representing different disciplines and professions to volunteer and form a sort of information corps with the aim of helping us assemble names and addresses of their peers who had roots or interest in Czechoslovakia, such as physicians, microbiologists, physicists, botanists, sociologists, philosophers, historians, painters, musicians, etc. Such lists would not only serve as a useful source for potential members but it would also help us map Czechoslovak intelligentsia abroad. In addition, it could be the basis for forming specialized "academic" sections within SVU, along the lines of the prestigious Academies of Sciences.

Having been sensitized by the confusion with the proxies at the General Assembly meeting during my own election as President, I was determined to reform the SVU election process. I requested our Bylaws Committee to prepare a revision of SVU Bylaws to replace the haphazard election procedure and frequent personal confrontations at SVU General Assembly meetings by having elections by mail, thus eliminating the need for proxies altogether. The newly proposed election process was accepted in a special referendum of members[298] and became part of our Bylaws. Our procedures are now comparable to those of major organizations whose membership is geographically widely spread out like ours. It is a democratic measure that saves General Assemblies considerable time and removes potential personal disputes and confrontations among individual members which are undignified for our organization.

In the latter part of my term we also spent considerable time on the preparation of the 8th SVU Congress in Washington, DC.[299] One of the features of the Congress were the Bicentennial Distinguished Awards presented to selected personalities who made contributions toward scientific, artistic, economic or cultural development of the US. The Congress culminated with a festive banquet and a Grand Ball. A detailed account of the Congress is given in a separate chapter.

I personally felt a sense of satisfaction with our accomplishments during the two-year period.

---

[298] The referendum was dated February 11, 1976.

[299] Preliminary announcements appeared in *Zprávy SVU*, vol. 17 (Apr. 1975), No. 4, pp. 24-25; *Ibid.*, vol. 18 (June 1975), No. 6, p. 40; and *Ibid.*, vol. 18 (March-Apr. 1986), No. 2.

When I presented my State of the SVU Report[300] to SVU General Assembly at the end of my first term Presidency on August 12, 1976, I was pleased to report that SVU stood on its own feet and that our income was based entirely on our membership dues and donations and work of our members. We didn't owe anything to anybody and had to obey only our own members. Financially, SVU stood on firm foundation, we operated again in the black and our income was rising.

During the General Assembly meeting, two resolutions were approved. One was in the form of a proclamation, congratulating the US on the occasion of its 200th anniversary,[301] while the other dealt with the desirability of preserving the Czech and Slovak languages abroad.[302]

---

[300] "Zpráva předsedy SVU," *Zprávy SVU*, vol. 18, No. 5 (Sept.-Oct. 1976), pp. 6-10.

[301] "Prohlášení SVU," *Zprávy SVU*, vol. 18, No. 6 (November-December 1976), p. 8

[302] "Rezolúcia SVU za dalšie rozvijanie češtiny a slovenčiny v zahraničí," *Zprávy SVU*, vol. 18, No. 6 (November-December 1976), p. 9.

# 17
# The Historic SVU Annual Meeting in Los Angeles

As per the decision of our Executive Board, it was decided to hold our first annual meeting and the General Assembly on the West Coast. The meetings were scheduled for 24-26 October 1975 in Los Angeles.

As was narrated in the preceding chapter, in 1974, the Society was practically broke and at the brink of possible dissolution. The imminent financial crisis, the Society was facing, was brought about, partly because of financial losses on earlier publication projects, partly due to the slack of income, and above all, because of enormous administrative expenses.

The delicate situation required cool heads and quick action. Very few SVU members were aware of the role the Los Angeles Meeting played in those tumultuous days and in the eventual resolution of the predicament of the Society.

After consultation with the Past Presidents and the Past Secretaries-General, the newly elected Executive Board decided to undertake a series of drastic administrative steps in an effort to overhaul the dismal financial balance, and thus save the Society from extinction. The most radical step was abolishing the New York SVU office and the termination of employment of two secretaries. Other steps included cutting down on all expenses and initiating broad decentralization plans of the Society's agenda. It was the spirit of the decentralization policy which also led the Executive Board to hold the Society's 1975 annual meeting in Los Angeles.

The meeting in Los Angeles was an important task case and historical milestone for the Society. Until then, all of the Society annual meetings took place on the East Coast, the majority having been held either in Washington, DC or in New York City. The prevalent view, in those days, was holding meetings outside the East Coast "center" a fantasy, which must inevitably end in failure.

The successful outcome of the meeting clearly dispelled the falsehood of this view once and for all. Secondly, it was a crucial testing ground for examining and judging the soundness of the new directions, initiated by the Executive Board, by the membership-at-large. We were well aware that many of the steps taken were quite unpopular and that there was a distinct possibility that the General Assembly could override our actions. Although I personally did my "homework," and was prepared to defend our judgments with fully documented figures and critical analyses, and supported by written recommendations of the respected Past Presidents of the Society, as well as Secretaries-General, I had some trepidations when I first faced the General Assembly during the presentation of the President's Annual Report.[303]

I informed the Assembly of the specific steps the Executive Board had undertaken, including abolishing the SVU Office in New York, not filling the secretary's position after the current secretary left the office, drastically cutting the publishing costs by purchasing appropriate equipment so that we could do the printing ourselves which was considerably cheaper than what the commercial printers charged, etc. The Assembly was also presented a detailed Treasurer's report which convincingly showed the fiscal predicament the Society faced, as well as the "light at the end of the tunnel," if the Society would follow the newly charted course, based on the balanced budget.[304]

As it turned out, the annual meeting was an unqualified success[305] and my anxiety was soon dissipated when I realized that I was addressing a sympathetic audience. The traditionally business-oriented members of the Los Angeles Chapter immediately grasped the gravity of the situation in which the Society found itself and completely endorsed the efforts undertaken by the new Executive Board. In the follow-up meeting between the representatives of the Executive Board and the Council of the Los Angeles Chapter a joint communiqué[306] was issued which further elaborated on the Executive Board's policy of decentralization and detailed the role of local chapters. The document emphasized the

---

[303] *Zprávy SVU*, vol. 18, No. 1 (January-February 1976), pp. 1-6.

[304] *Zprávy SVU* 18, No. 2 (March-April 1976), pp. 1-8.

[305] *Zprávy SVU*, vol. 17, No. 9-10 (November-December 1975), pp. 64-70.

[306] *Zprávy SVU*, vol. 17, No. 9-10 (November-December 1975), pp. 70-72.

necessity for financial self-sufficiency at the local level and underlined the importance for developing individual identity of each chapter in an area of its choice. Furthermore, it stressed close contact and cooperation with the Executive Board and encouraged joint funding of projects which are of mutual interest, particularly in the publication sphere.

Apart from strictly management and administrative matters, the Los Angeles meeting produced another "first". At the request of the Executive Board, at the occasion of the SVU annual meeting, the Los Angeles Chapter organized a full day symposium commemorating the 125th anniversary of Thomas Garrigue Masaryk's birth. The symposium, which was co-sponsored by the East European Center of the University of California, was entirely organized locally and drew a large audience not only from the SVU membership, but also from the University faculty and students. It was, by any standard, a first-rate conference.

There were also social events on this occasion. Prior to the General Assembly Meeting, there was a social hour, hosted by the Dept. of Slavic Languages of UCLA.[307] After the TGM Symposium on the next night, the Los Angeles Chapter organized a splendid banquet featuring the address of the President of SVU at the elegant California Yacht Club, followed by dancing and scholarship award presentations. The following afternoon, the SVU participated with the other Czechoslovak organizations at the ceremonies commemorating the founding of Czechoslovakia in 1918. These ceremonies included the solemn raising of the Czechoslovak flag in front of the Los Angeles City Hall.

The combination of the SVU Annual Meeting with the varied cultural and social programs, as organized by the L.A. Chapter, has become a sought-out prototype for future annual meetings to mimic.

The 1975 meeting in Los Angeles clearly plowed new ground and significantly contributed to subsequent growth and development of the Society. The face-to-face meetings between the Los Angeles Chapter and the representatives of the Executive Board provided better understanding and mutual respect between the two bodies and fostered everlasting friendships and cooperation between individual members and officers. This aspect too, as many a past or present officer can testify, has been a crucial element in minimizing costly misunderstandings and

---

[307] The acronym for the University of California in Los Angeles.

strengthening the spirit of collaboration in the Society. The Los Angeles Chapter deserves our thanks and gratitude for showing us the way.

Some of the individuals I recall who made the Los Angeles Meeting successful included Dr. Otto Turchan, Prof. Stanislav Segert, Frank Marlow,[308] Dr. Marie Husák,[309] Jindra H. Lasch,[310] Jarmila Kracíkova,[311] Ing. Ladislav Krátký,[312] Zdenka E. Fischmann and Josef A. Zahradka. One unforgettable and unexpected moment also comes to mind when during the banquet Jan Filípek[313] came to me and remarked "Hello friend, you and your group are doing a fine job. Here is something to make your job a little easier" and discretely handed me a sizable check payable to the Society.

---

[308] Frank J. Marlow (1911-1996), President, Royal Leasing Corp., Los Angeles, CA.

[309] Marie Husák (1915-), lawyer with American Express, Los Angeles, CA.

[310] Jindra H. Lasch (1909-2006), CEO, Henry Lasch Associates, Oceanside, CA.

[311] Jarmila Kracík (1910-1996), Dept. of Justice, Los Angeles.

[312] Ladislav A. Krátký (1901-1991), auditor and business counselor, Laguna Hills, CA.

[313] Jan Filípek (1913-2004), realtor, Palm Spring, CA; a close friend of my father's.

# 18
# *The US Bicentennial SVU World Congress*

### THE WHITE HOUSE
### WASHINGTON

*August 10, 1976*

*My warmest greetings to the members of the Czechoslovak Society of Arts and Sciences in America as you hold your Eighth Congress in our Nation's Capital.*

*The contributions of Czechs and Slovaks to North America span the entire history of our national life. This year our celebration of two hundred years of independence provides an especially appropriate setting for a tribute to Czechoslovak Americans in whose ancestral homeland the spirit of freedom and independence has never been broken.*

*Czechoslovaks have brought this same spirit to America – and along with it a deep-rooted devotion to scientific, artistic and cultural accomplishment. With this in mind, I want to commend your Society on its full and open support and strong encouragement for the development of the arts and sciences in the Czechoslovak American community. You have preserved and perpetuated a noble faith in the freedom of inquiry and expression and an undiminished quest for excellence.*

*Mrs. Ford joins me in the hope that these sessions will be rewarding and memorable for each of you.*

**Gerald R. Ford**

In 1976, by far the most important event of the year was the Eighth World Congress[314] of the Society, which formed a part of the Bicentennial celebrations of the United States, and was held August 12-15, 1976

---

[314] *Zprávy SVU*, Vol. 18, No. 5 (September-October 1976), pp. 1-6.

in Washington, DC, at Georgetown University. The central theme of the Congress was "Contributions of Czechs and Slovaks to North America." The program was printed as the fourth issue of *Zprávy SVU*,[315] as well as a separate publication. The *Abstracts* of the presented papers were also published.[316]

Featured were symposia "Czechoslovak Immigrants in the U.S. and Canada from a Regional Point of View," "Religious and Spiritual Life of Czechs and Slovaks in North America," "Prominent Americans of Czechoslovak Origin," "Czechoslovak Economists in North America, " "Czechoslovak Ethnic Studies in North America," and others. In addition, there was an International Symposium on František Palacký (1798-1876) in commemoration of the centenary of the death of the "Father of the Nations," six separate history sections and a symposium "Fifty Years of the Prague Linguistic Circle." The academic sessions ran from Friday morning till Sunday noon.

On Thursday night, August 12, a reception for the SVU Congress participants and their guests was held in the magnificent Caucus Room of the U.S. Senate on Capitol Hill. Following the reception, the Congress participants visited the U.S. Library of Congress where a special exhibit of documents, books and periodicals relating to Czechs and Slovaks in the United States was featured. The displayed materials traced the history of Czech and Slovak immigrants from colonial times to the present: (a) first maps of Maryland and Virginia, drawn in 1673 by Augustine Herman, Lord of Bohemia Manor and one of the founders of the State of Maryland; (b) documents relating to the arrival of the Moravian Brethren in the 1740s, the period between mass migration beginning after 1848 and up to the political immigrations after 1938; (c) also on display was an 1862 issue of *Slavie,* one of the earliest Czech newspaper in America, a 1905 edition of a grammar and phrase book for new Slovak immigrants, a phonograph record of one of the Texas Bata family bands, a holograph score of the composer Bohuslav Martinů, a printed volume of

---

[315] *Czechoslovak Society of Arts and Sciences in America, Inc. 8th Congress Program.* Georgetown University, Washington, DC, August 12-15, 1976. *Zprávy SVU*, vol. 18, No. 4 (July-August 1976). 28 p.

[316] *Contributions of Czechs and Slovaks to North America. The Central theme of the Eighth Congress of the Czechoslovak Society of Arts and Sciences in America. Abstracts of Papers.* Washington, DC: SVU, 1976. 70 p.

the anthropologist Aleš Hrdlička's *Alaska Diary*, and many other memorabilia. On Friday night, August 13, the U.S. Army Band played a special concert of Czech and Slovak music on the steps of the U.S. Capitol.

On Saturday morning, August 14th, the Society saluted the USA Bicentennial at the ceremonial Plenary Session, held in the Hall of Nations of Georgetown University. Some fifty welcoming messages and greetings, including those of the President of the United States, as well as Governors, Senators, Congressmen, Mayors, etc., were read. A number of State Governors, including those of Maryland, Connecticut, Pennsylvania and Virginia declared Czechoslovak Days in their States for the duration of the SVU Congress. The event was also announced, with a lengthy statement about SVU, in *Congressional Record*[317] by Senator Roman Hruska.

Following the official greetings, the leaders of the major Czechoslovak organizations and community groups in the United States and Canada, who were especially invited for the event, were introduced. This was followed by presentations of the Bicentennial Distinguished Awards to selected personalities of Czechoslovak descent. The ceremonies were concluded with a keynote address by Dr. Michael Novak, a prominent publicist of Slovak descent.

Other special events included an art exhibit, "SVU Contributions of Arts," an exhibit of books by the members of the Society, a boat cruise on the Potomac River, etc. The social activities culminated on Saturday night at the SVU reception and banquet, followed by the Bicentennial Grand Ball in the elegant L'Enfant Plaza Hotel.

*Washington, D.C.*     *Georgetown University*
*August 12-15, 1976*     *1221 36th St., N.W.*

## "CONTRIBUTIONS OF CZECHS AND SLOVAKS TO NORTH AMERICA"

---

[317] *Congressional Record*, Vol. 122, Washington, Friday, July 23, 1976, No. 111, pp. 1-2.

*Announcing*
*A Major Event in "Bicentennial Setting"*

**The Central Theme of the Eighth Congress
of the Czechoslovak Society of
Arts and Sciences in America**

## PROGRAM

**Thursday, August 12, 1976**

All Day: Registration

    Morning: General Membership Meeting

    Afternoon: Panel Discussion of the Role and Responsibilities of the Local Chapters of the Society

    Evening: Reception- Society Smoker- Buffet & Wine

    Russell Senate Office Bldg. Caucus Room

    Opening Exhibit of Documents Czechs and Slovaks in the U.S.

    U.S. Library of Congress, T. Jefferson Bldg., 5th Floor

**Friday, August 13, 1976**

Morning: Sessions

    1    Symposium on Czechoslovak Immigrants in U.S. and Canada – Regional Approach

    2    Symposium on Czechoslovak Economists in North America

    3A   Religious and Spiritual Life of Czechs and Slovaks in North America

    3B   History I

    4    Contemporary Contributions: Biology & Medicine

Afternoon:

    1    Symposium on Prominent Americans of Czechoslovak Origin

    2A   History II

    2B   History III

    3A   Czech and Slovak Music in North America

    3B   History IV

    4    Contemporary Contributions: Literature & Language

Evening:    Concert by the U.S. Army Band (Pershing's Own) Featuring "Evening of Czech and Slovak Music" – U.S. Capitol, West Terrace

**Saturday, August 14, 1976**

Morning: Plenary Session "The Society Salutes the Bicentennial"

Afternoon: Sessions
- 1 Presidential Symposium on Czechoslovak Organizations in North America
- 2 International Symposium on Frantisek Palacky
- 3 Prague Linguistic Circle: 50 Years

Evening: Reception and Banquet at L'Enfant Plaza Hotel
Bicentennial Grand Ball at L'Enfant Plaza Hotel

**Sunday, August 15, 1976**

Morning: Sessions
- 1A History V
- 1B History VI
- 2 Czechoslovak Ethnic Studies in North America
- 3 Contemporary Contributions: Scientific and Social Thought

All meetings, except social functions, will he held at Edmund A. Walsh Building, Georgetown University, 1221 36th St. N., Washington, D.C.

Exhibits featuring works of the Society scholars, scientists and artists and a sales booth for SVU books will be open during the duration of the Congress.

Congress pre-registration, accommodations, tickets for special events, inquiries to: Mrs. Anna Faltus, Melbourne House #414. 1315 16th St., NW., Washington. DC. 200.36; Phone: 872-1910; evenings: 387.8066.

For further information write to: Mrs. Emilia Royco. 6612 Tulip Terrace, Washington, DC. 20116. Phone: 229-6315.

## CZECHOSLOVAK SOCIETY OF ARTS AND SCIENCES IN AMERICA (SVU)
## SALUTES THE BICENTENNIAL

### The Ceremonial Opening

Saturday, August 14, 1976, 9 am -12 noon,
Hall of Nations, Walsh Building, Georgetown University
Chairman: Dr. Miloslav Rechcigl, Jr., President SVU

*Opening Remarks* ................................... *Dr. Miloslav Rechcígl, Jr., President SVU*

*Greetings from Georgetown University* ................................ *Miss Virginia Keeler,*
*Secretary of the Corporation,*
*Georgetown University*

*The National Anthems* ......................................... *Dagmar Hasalová-White, soprano*
*Lída Brodenová, piano*

*Invocation* ................................................................ *Rev. Andrew. J. Novotney, S.J.*

*Readings. of Messages and Greetings* ...........................................*Dr. John G. Lexa,*
*Secretary General SVU*

*Introduction of, and Addresses by the*
*Leaders of Czechoslovak Organizations*                 *Dr. Alexej B. Bořkovec,*
*and Community Groups in North America* ............................... *SVU Vice President*

*Representing:*

*National Czechoslovak Association of Canada, its President,*
*Dr. Louis Urban*

*Czechoslovak National Council of America, its Vice President,*
*Dr. Štefan Papánek*

*Czechoslovak Society of America , its. President,*
*Mr. Frank J. Vodrážka*

*Slovak Gymnastic Union, its Vice President,*
*Mrs. Mary Kadrik*

*Czech Catholic Union, its President,*
*Mrs. Anna M. Veverka*

*Presentation of Bicentennial*
*Distinguished Awards* ...................................................... *Dr. Miloslav Rechcígl, Jr.*

*Introduction of Award Recipients:*

*Mr. Thomas J. Baťa – Introduced by Dr. Jan V. Mládek, Past SVU President*

*Prof. Francis Dvorník in Memoriam – Introduced by Dr. F. Schwarzenberg,*
*Past SVU President*

*Ms. Frances Gladys Knight – Introduced by Mrs. M. Meissner*

*Dean Jaroslav J. Pelikán – Introduced by Dr. Ernest Šturc,*
*SVU Vice President*

*Hon. John Slezák – Introduced by Maj. Gen. W. Stanford Smith*

*Keynote Address "The New Ethnicity"* ....................................... *Dr. Michael Novak*

*Adjournment*

# 19
# My Second Term

My nomination for the second term was no surprise to me as the Nominations Committee[318] told me at the outset of their intention to renominate me.[319] I was willing to serve the second term because I wanted to further advance the SVU agenda started during my first term Presidency. I was easily reelected without opposition.[320] The other elected members of the Executive Board were Dr. Alexej Bořkovec, Ing. Ján Gavora, Prof. Miloš M. Šebor,[321] Prof. Josef Škvorecký and Dr. Ernest Šturc, Vice Presidents; Dr. John G. Lexa, Secretary-General, Frank Meissner, Treasurer and Dr. Jiří Škvor, Editor of *Proměny*. Most of them served with me in the previous term. Our second term commenced at the SVU Annual Meeting on August 12, 1976, on the occasion of the 8th SVU World Congress in Washington, DC.

Apart from continued emphasis on stabilizing our finances we again paid special attention to further decentralize our agenda and to long-term planning. Early on, we created a special search committee for the purpose of selecting potential officers. To avoid bias we purposely chose for this purpose individuals who had no previous ties with the SVU leadership.[322]

Furthermore we proceeded with the revision of SVU Bylaws, the question of providing for the future of the Society, preparation of the management guidelines, the renewal of the Press function and reorganization of the SVU periodicals. In addition, we laid a foundation for a new international English scholarly periodical.

---

[318] The Committee comprised Dr. Bohuslava Bradbrook, Dr. Brano Lajda, Dr. František Schwarzenberg, Dr. René Wellek and Dr. Jaroslav Němec, Chairman.

[319] The complete slate of candidates is printed in *Zprávy SVU*, vol. 18. No. 2 (March-Apr. 1976), p. 10 ff.

[320] *Zprávy SVU*, vol. 18, No. 5 (December-October 1976), pp. 10-12.

[321] Miloš M. Šebor (1911-1995), professor of geography, Eastern Kentucky University, Richmond, KY.

[322] *Zprávy SVU*, vol. 19, No. 1 (Jan.-Feb. 1977), pp. 4-5.

In the spirit of decentralization, the SVU agenda was again shared with vice presidents. Dr. Alexej Bořkovec was assigned responsibility for a membership drive and membership matters, in general, Ing. Ján Gavora maintained contacts with local chapters and Dr. Miloš Šebor was a liaison with professional organizations. Dr. Josef Škvorecký was responsible for the relations with the post-August 1968 emigration and for advising on publicity and distribution of SVU publications and Dr. Ernest Šturc was responsible for coordination of SVU efforts to seek external funding assistance.

The whole series of functions that were previously performed by SVU New York Office and controlled by Secretary-General were decentralized and taken over by individual members of the Executive Board, editors, committees and other specifically designated individuals. To assure continuity and avoid duplication and possibly misunderstandings between so many different players it was necessary to set up specific procedures and provide guidelines.

As a result of our February 1977 meeting,[323] our Executive Board issued a special SVU proclamation regarding the Charter 77,[324] which started with the words: "The Czechoslovak Society of Arts and Sciences (SVU) is not a political organization, but just as any other organization, it is concerned whenever human rights are being violated. SVU has issued the following proclamation on the occasion of the manifesto of the Czechoslovak intellectuals, the Charter 77...."[325]

In the spirit of decentralization the Executive Board chose Ottawa, Canada for its 1977 Annual meeting with a Conference, held on 7-9 October 1977.[326] In contrast to previous conferences that dealt primarily with history or social sciences, the present Conference featured a symposium on "The Contributions of Czechs and Slovaks to Natural and Medical Sciences." Another symposium commemorated "Fifty Years of Czechoslovakia: Selected Historical and Political Topics." Special

---

[323] *Zprávy SVU,* vol. 19, No. 2 (March-April), pp. 1- 6.

[324] The Charter 77 was an informal civic initiative in Czechoslovakia from 1977 to 1992, named after the document Charter 77 from January 1977. Founding members and architects were Václav Havel, Jan Patočka, Zdeněk Mlynář, Jiří Hájek, and Pavel Kohout.

[325] *Zprávy SVU,* vol. 19, No. 2 (March-April 1977), pp. 1-2.

[326] *Zprávy SVU,* vol. 19, No. 4 (July-August 1977), pp. 1-2.

events included an art exhibit of paintings by SVU members and a concert, with Mme. Martine Kouba, Prof. Zdeněk Koníček and Dr. Francis Stein participating.

As a consequence of the premature death of the Secretary-General, Dr. John G. Lexa,[327] two months prior to holding the Society Annual Meeting in Ottawa, there was a need to appoint a new Secretary-General. At a special meeting of the SVU Council, which convened in Ottawa on October 7, Dr. Věra Žandová Bořkovec[328] was elected to complete the current term of the office.

Increased attention was also given to the role of Local Chapters and the ways to enhance closer relationship between the Chapters and the Executive Board. With this in mind, Ján Gavora was given the responsibility for coordinating the work of local chapters.[329] As a result, substantial revitalization occurred in most chapters. The following chapters: Chicago. Montreal and Melbourne were particularly noted for their efforts and initiatives. Moreover, two new chapters sprang into existence, one in Vancouver, B.C., Canada[330] and another in Wellington, New Zealand. Of the old-time regulars, the Washington DC Chapter was again in the forefront with its new initiative to organize Czechoslovak Christmas Bazaars on an annual basis and contributing its proceeds to SVU Treasury towards funding various SVU publications.

Among the European Chapters, the Swiss Chapter's activities were noteworthy. On October 17-19,1976, the Chapter organized in Interlaken, Switzerland an European Conference[331] on the "Meaning of Czech and Slovak History," attended by eminent scholars from various West European countries. Presentations included contributions from Prof. Milan S. Ďurica,[332] Dr. Milan Hauner,[333] Dr. Karel Hrubý,[334] Prof.

---

[327] Zprávy SVU, vol. 19, No. 5 (Sept.-Oct. 1977), pp. 1-2.

[328] Věra Žanda Bořkovec (1926-), associate professor of Russian, American University, Washington, DC.

[329] Zprávy SVU, vol. 19, No. 2 (March 1975), pp. 6-12.

[330] Zprávy SVU, vol. 19, No. 3 (M ay-June 1977), pp. 1-2.

[331] Zprávy SVU, vol. 18, No. 6 (November-December 1976), pp. 1-4.

[332] Milan S. Ďurica (1925-), Slovak historian who lived in Italy until 1998, after which he returned to Slovakia.

[333] Milan Hauner (1940-), historian who was doing research in London at that time.

[334] Karel Hrubý (1923-), sociologist with CIBA-GEIGY International, Basel, Switzerland.

Jaroslav Krejčí,[335] Prof. J. M. Lochman,[336] Mikuláš Mičátek,[337] Prof. K. Skalický,[338] publicist Pavel Tigrid[339] and Prof. Mojmír Vaněk.[340] The report of the conference can be found in *Zprávy SVU*.[341] The Conference proceedings were subsequently published in *Proměny*.[342]

On October 28, 1978, on the occasion of the 60th anniversary of the founding of Czechoslovakia, the same Chapter organized an international "table ronde" on "Culture and Freedom."[343] The enormously successful event took place at the University of Geneva with participation of a number of prominent personalities of Swiss and French cultural life. Among speakers were Jeanne Hersch,[344] Roland Ruffieux,[345] Andre Reszler,[346] Georges Cotier,[347] Francois Bondy[348] and Bernard Dorival.[349] It is noteworthy that the entire proceedings were conducted in the French language.

The Executive Board gave special attention to *Proměny*. To make the periodical pay for itself we felt it necessary to increase its subscrip-

---

[335] Jaroslav Krejčí (1916-), professor at School of European Studies, University of Lancaster, Lancaster, UK.

[336] Jan Milič Lochman (1922-2004), Rector, University of Basel, Switzerland.

[337] Basel, Switzerland.

[338] Karel Skalický (1934-), professor of theology, Universita Lateransis, Rome, Italy.

[339] Pavel Tigrid (1917-2003), writer, publicist, Editor of *Svedectv*i, Paris, France.

[340] Mojmír Vaněk (1911-1992), professor of art history, Universite de Geneva, Switzerland.

[341] *Zprávy SVU*, vol. 18 (Nov.- Dec. 1976), No. 6, pp. 1-4.

[342] *Proměny*, Vol. 14, No. 2 (1977).

[343] *Zprávy SVU*, vol. 20, No. 6 (November -December 1978), pp. 12-13.

[344] Professor of Philosophy at the University of Geneva; later a Swiss delegate to UNESCO.

[345] Professor of Contemporary History and Political Science at Fribourg and Lausanne and President of the Swiss Federal institution "Pro Helvetia."

[346] Professor of Modern European Cultural History and Director of Centre Europeen de la culture in Geneva.

[347] Professor of Philosophy at the University of Geneva and Fribourg and publisher of the renown revue *Nova et Vetera*.

[348] Leading literary and drama critic, from Zurich.

[349] Professor of Art History at the University of Paris IV (Sorbonne); former director of Musee national d'art moderne in Paris, and a recognized expert on Czech modern art.

tion base. In our opinion, this could best be achieved by publicizing it and making its content more interesting. Having this in mind, the Executive Board decided to augment the editorial office by appointing three assistant editors and 7-member editorial board. The stylistic editing was entrusted to a language editor and the design to a graphic artist.[350]

With reference to the SVU newsletter, *Zprávy SVU*, most of the technical difficulties were resolved and the newsletter was again coming out every second month, on schedule. Each issue contained an editorial, followed by news from the Executive Board, reports from individual chapters, news from SVU interest sections and the accounts of activities of individual members.

We also gave considerable thought to the idea of launching a new scholarly periodical in English for publishing comparative studies and analyses relating to Czechoslovakia and its culture. SVU would thus offer scholars, members and non-members, a new publication forum. With this aim, we also named a special three-member committee to prepare the groundwork and the plan for such journal which would be within financial means of the Society.

In 1976, as our special contribution to the USA Bicentennial, the Society published the monumental bibliography, *Czechs and Slovaks in North America*,[351] the result of meticulous research by the librarian Esther Jeřábek, a second generation American of Czech descent. As the Chief of the Slavic Division of the U.S. Library of Congress put it: "With unparalleled thoroughness this bibliography provides a remarkably full inventory of published, and to some extent, also unprinted documents, on Czechs and Slovaks in North America, opening a panoramic view of their immigration to this [U.S.] country, the often arduous first steps in a new and unaccustomed environment, the taking root and settling down, and the richness of their contribution to the development and growth of their adopted country."

---

[350] *Zprávy SVU*, vol. 19, No. 3 (May-June 1977), pp. 4-5.
[351] Esther Jerabek, *Czechs and Slovaks in America: A Bibliography*. New York: SVU, 1976. 448 p.

Another publication which was published during my second administrative period as President, was *SVU Directory*.[352] As in the case of earlier editions, the information was gathered, compiled and edited by my wife, Eva, and myself.

In addition to Victor S. Mamatey's study on *Building Czechoslovakia in America: 1914-1918*, we have issued four additional occasional papers, i.e., that of Eva B. Polach's *The SVU List of Lectures, Studies and Other Materials*,[353] Brackett Lewis'[354] study, *Eyewitness Story of the Occupation of Samara, Russia, by the Czechoslovak Legion in June 1918*,[355] Vojtěch N. Duben's[356] *Czech and Slovak Press: Its Status in 1978*[357] and František Schwarzenberg's study on *František Palacký*.[358]

Among my various goals as President, I felt it necessary to also resolve the jurisdictional question between SVU President and Secretary-General. Until then, it was generally assumed that the type of people who would be selected for Presidency would not usually have time nor desire to serve as chief executive officers and consequently the SVU Bylaws prescribed to them essentially a ceremonial function. The main responsibility for managing the Society was allotted to Secretary-General who for a number of years also had an office and a secretary to his disposal.

During my Presidency all of this radically changed. In my capacity as President I certainly contributed my share to practically all administrative, management and fiscal aspects of the Society, while Secretary-General essentially only handled correspondence. This led us to propose

---

[352] *Biographical Directory of the Members of the Czechoslovak Society of Arts and Sciences*. 4th ed. Compiled and edited by Eva Rechcígl and Miloslav Rechcígl, Jr. Washington, DC: SVU, 1978. 137 p.

[353] Eva B. Polach, *SVU List of Lectures, Studies and Other Materials*. Washington, DC: SVU, 1976. 34 p.

[354] Brackett Lewis (1894-1979), research analyst with Library of Congress, Washington, DC.

[355] Brackett Lewis, *Eyewitness Story of the Occupation of Samara, Russia, by the Czechoslovak Legion in June 1918*. Washington, DC: SVU, 1977. 20 p.

[356] Vojtěch N. Duben was a pen name of Vojtěch Nevlud, journalist with Voice of America, Washington, DC.

[357] Vojtěch N. Duben, *Czech and Slovak Press: Its Status in 1978*, Washington, DC, 1978. 62 p.

[358] František Schwarzenberg, *František Palacký*. Washington, DC, 1978. 26 p.

a revision of SVU Bylaws which were subsequently approved. SVU President henceforth has become a real head and the principal spokesman for the Society, with prescribed responsibility over all SVU organs, while Secretary-General's role was reduced to writing minutes, sending out notices of General Assembly meetings and handling those organizational and administrative matters assigned to him/her by SVU President. Our revision of SVU Bylaws also included dropping the word "in America" from the official name of the Society to better reflect the international character of SVU whose membership was represented on every continent. My final act was to move the official seat of the Society from New York City to the Nation's Capital, Washington, DC. which *de facto* already functioned, as such, after the New York SVU Office was abolished.[359]

---

[359] *Zprávy SVU*, vol. 20, No. 3 (May-June 1978), pp. 8-9.

# 20
# SVU Conference in Ottawa

The 1977 SVU annual meeting was held on 7-9 October in connection with a special conference and exhibit in Canada's Capital Ottawa. The Conference was organized by the Society's Local Chapter in Ottawa, whose membership was comprised predominantly of the immigrants from the post-1968 period. The description of the program appeared in the 4th issue of the 1977 *Zprávy SVU* [360] and the Conference evaluation in the January 1978 issue.[361]

The program started on Friday evening with the official opening of the exhibit, held in the spacious exhibition hall of the Ottawa State Library. Some forty Czech and Slovak artists living abroad exhibited their works which enjoyed great attention by the Canadian public.[362]

After the opening, there was a meeting of the SVU Council to elect a successor for the recently deceased Secretary-General Hanuš Lexa. After a short debate, the vacancy was filled by Prof. Věra Bořkovec of the American University in Washington. This was an unprecedented act in the history of SVU since she was the first woman to hold such a key position in the Society.

The Council also recommended to award honorary memberships[363] to three distinguished persons, namely Dr. Carleton Gajdusek,[364] Dr. František Král[365] and Ferdinand Peroutka,[366] the foremost living Czech journalist of Radio Free Europe. In addition, the Council voted Founding

---

[360] *Zprávy SVU,* vol. 19, No. 4 (July-August 1977), pp. 1-8.
[361] *Zprávy SVU*, vol. 20, No. 1 (January-February 1978), pp. 1-3.
[362] *Zprávy SVU*, vol. 20, No. 2 (March-April 1978), p. 6.
[363] *Zprávy SVU*, vol. 20, No. 1 (Jan.-Feb. 1978), pp. 1-5.
[364] Daniel Carleton Gajdusek (1923-), noted medical researcher and Nobel Prize laureate at the National Institutes of Health, Bethesda,. MD.
[365] Frank Král (1892-1980), professor of veterinary medicine at the University of Pennsylvania.
[366] Ferdinand Peroutka (1895-1978), the foremost living Czech journalist, now associated with the Radio Free Europe.

Membership to Rev. Přemysl Pitter,[367] and a Founding Membership in memoriam to the deceased Secretary General Hanuš Lexa. The General Assembly, which met the following day, concurred with the Council's recommendations.

At the Assembly were reports of various officers. In my detailed State of the SVU Report,[368] I was glad to inform the membership of the greatly improved status of the Society, as judged by the growing new membership, the newly established SVU chapters and, above all, by the improved financial situation. The members were impressed by the newly published Bibliography of Esther Jeřábek. The publication, bearing the title *Czechs and Slovaks in the US and Canada: A Bibliography* is the largest bibliography of its kind, listing publications of Czechs and Slovaks in the US and Canada.[369]

The Conference lecture program was held on Saturday at the University of Ottawa. It comprised of two symposia, one on the "Contribution of Czechs and Slovaks to Natural and Medical Sciences" and the other on "50 Years of Czechoslovakia: Selected Historical and Political Topics." I had the pleasure of opening the former symposium, with a historical overview of natural sciences in Czechoslovakia and the contributions of Czech and Slovak scientists abroad." Then came presentations by Dr. John D. Čipera[370] on the origin of the carbonate moiety in the avian shells, Dr. Vladimír Krajina's paper[371] on bio-geoclimatic zones of British Columbia, Dr. Alexej Bořkovec's presentation on modern approaches to pest control and Ing. Ján Gavora's paper on the genetic resistance to the avian leukosis complex.

The afternoon session was devoted to medical and clinical sciences. Vladimír Šístek[372] talked about the new horizons in medical education,

---

[367] Přemysl Pitter (1895-1976), former chairman of the Swiss SVU Chapter.

[368] *Zprávy SVU*, vol. 19, No. 6 (November -December 1977), pp. 1-7.

[369] Esther Jeřábek, *Czechs and Slovaks in America: a Bibliography*, New York: SVU, 1976. 448 p.

[370] John D. Čipera (1923-1963), chemist with the Canada Dept. of Agriculture.

[371] Vladimír Krajina (1905-1993), professor of botany, University of British Columbia, Vancouver, Canada.

[372] Vladimír Šístek (1931-), professor of anatomy, University of Ottawa Faculty of Medicine.

Silvio Fiala[373] on carcinogenesis and anti-carcinogenesis, Otakar and Anna Šístek[374] discussed their work in experimental diabetes, Karel Rakušan[375] talked about postnatal development of the heart and Bořivoj Korecký[376] discussed his experimental studies on depression and anti-depression.

All papers, which were presented in English, were of high quality. Each paper was followed by a discussion and the lecture hall was invariably full.

The Canadian TV broadcasted parts of the symposium and they also interviewed me about the contributions of Czechs and Slovaks to world culture. I was also queried about the current situation in Czechoslovakia. In connection with the question regarding the SVU's stand toward the current situation in Czechoslovakia in the light of the Helsinki Accords, I referred them to the 1976 SVU Proclamation "An Assertion of the Need to Intensify the Pursuit of Free Inquiry and Exchange of Ideas," approved by the SVU General Assembly at the Bicentennial SVU Congress in Washington[377]. My interview, as well as the reports from our Conference, was part of the evening news that very day.

On Saturday evening there was a gala banquet with a reception at the National Art Centre. The participants could hear a concert, performed by soprano Martina Kouba,[378] cellist Zdeněk Koníček[379] and pianist Dr. František Stein.[380] There were several prominent guests in the audience, including a member of the Canadian Parliament Cyril Lloyd Francis and his wife, Director of the Institute for East European Studies

---

[373] Silvio E. Fiala (1912-1982), research physician with the Veterans Administration, Martinsburg, WV.

[374] Otakar V. Sirek (1921-2006) and Anna Sirek (1921-), a husband-and-wife team, both physiologists, associated with the University of Toronto; both were natives of Slovakia.

[375] Karel Rakušan (1935-), Professor of physiology, University of Ottawa Faculty of Medicine.

[376] Bořivoj Korecký (1929-), professor of physiology, University of Ottawa Faculty of Medicine.

[377] *Zprávy SVU*, vol. 19, No. 2 (March–April 1977), pp. 2-3.

[378] Martina Kouba (1938-), singer, residing near Ottawa; a Belgian native, wife of Jaromír A. Kouba.

[379] Zdeněk Koníček (1918-), professor of music, McMaster University, Hamilton, Canada.

[380] Frantšek Stein (1896-1989), concert pianist residing in Ottawa, Canada.

at Carleton University and other representatives of the public cultural and political establishment. As a keynote speaker, I acquainted the audience with the origin and the aims of SVU and enumerated the contributions of Czechs and Slovaks to their new homeland in the US and Canada. The listeners seemed to be quite impressed with the large list of our people who impacted the progress in North America.

The conference followed on Sunday with the symposium "Fifty Years of Czechoslovakia: Selected Historical and Political Topics," which again convened at the University of Ottawa's University center. The presentations comprised papers by Miloš Šebor on Czechoslovakia: Positive aspects of Austro-Hungary, by Victor M. Fic[381] on Russia and creation of Czechoslovakia, by Jaroslav A. Bouček[382] on Impact of Munich on 1948 Coup d'état in Czechoslovakia and by Jiří J. Fabšic[383] on 1968 – Czechoslovakia's Return to Europe.

All in all, it was an outstanding meeting, thanks to our Ottawa member co-organizers. The organization of a technical symposium on natural and medical sciences on the SVU platform with the participation of the first-rate scientists was a real "first." The organizers succeeded to arouse attention not only of the local SVU members but of the wider Czech and Slovak community in Canada, and more importantly interest of the Canadian academic circles.[384]

---

[381] Victor M. Fic (1922-2005), professor of political science, Brook University, St. Catharines, Canada.

[382] Jaroslav A. Bouček (1916-1996), economist and historian associated with the University of Carleton, Ottawa.

[383] Jiří J. Fabšic (1940-), professor of history, McMaster University, Hamilton, Canada.

[384] The report on the Conference was published in *České Slovo*, November 11, 1977, p. 4.

# 21
## *The Cleveland Conference*

**THE WHITE HOUSE**
**WASHINGTON**

*October 24, 1978*

*On the occasion of your Ninth World Congress, I send greetings to the members of the Czechoslovak Society of Arts and Sciences in America, and I extend a warm welcome to your distinguished delegates from abroad.*

*Twenty years ago your prestigious organization was founded to provide a forum from which intellectuals, scholars and artists of Czech and Slovak descent could perpetuate and advance their ancestral heritage and democratic traditions. Incorporated in the United States, this highly regarded organization has in the past two decades expended to many other nations and exerted a positive influence on peoples and institutions throughout the Western World.*

*Its members and friends can be proud of the useful books and periodicals it has published and of the incentive it has given to the advancement of Czechoslovak scholarship abroad.*

*I am pleased for this opportunity to applaud the international impact of Czechoslovak arts and sciences and the dynamic leadership role of this organization on marshaling some of the finest talents of Eastern European origin in service to all nations.*

*May this be a highly stimulating and productive session.*

                              ***Jimmy Carter***
                                 ***President***

It was the spirit of decentralization that prompted the Executive Board and me to hold the Ninth SVU World Congress in Cleveland, Ohio, instead of its traditional locations such as Washington, DC or New York City. The main rationale for selecting Cleveland was the recognition of the role Cleveland has played in the history and lives of the Czech and Slovak immigrants from the middle of the last century to date. The program of the Congress appeared as the 4th issue of *Zprávy SVU* [385] and was also published separately. The *Abstracts* were also published as a separate monograph.[386]

The Congress was convened on the modern, newly opened campus of the Cleveland State University during October 26-29, 1978, under my Presidency and program chairmanship of Ing. Stanley J. Maršík and local arrangements of Mrs. Dagmar Poseděl.[387] The Congress marked the twentieth anniversary of SVU,[388] which was commemorated by several special events. First there was a historical Society symposium, chaired by Past President Jan V. Mládek and vice-president Ján Gavora. As a part of the symposium Dr. Jaroslav Němec gave a detailed account of the beginnings of the Society. This was followed by individual presentations by the Presidents of the local chapters of the Society throughout the world on the development, current status and activities of their respective chapters. Another commemorative event, "Salute to the Twentieth Anniversary of the SVU," took place on Saturday in the Cleveland City Hall, where it had maximum exposure and publicity. It was an extraordinary event, with the participation of the Mayor and the members of the Council of the City of Cleveland and other public officials. Countless number of congratulatory messages were received from various parts of the United States and Canada, including those from U.S. senators and congressmen, governors, mayors and others. President Jimmy Carter, in his letter to Dr. Rechcígl, praised the international impact of SVU and its dynamic leadership role in attracting the best talents of central Europe.

---

[385] *20th Anniversary of the Czechoslovak Society of Arts and Sciences 9th World Congress Program. Zprávy SVU*, vol. 20, No. 4 (July-August 1979), 36 p.

[386] *Abstracts of Papers. The Ninth World Congress,* Cleveland State University, Cleveland, OH, October 26-29, 1978. Cleveland: Cleveland State University Press, 1978. 80 p.

[387] The wife of Dr. Miroslav Poseděl (1933-2002), physician in Cleveland, OH.

[388] *Zprávy SVU*, vol. 20, No. 2 (March-April 1978), pp. 1-3.

*The Cleveland Conference* 119

It should be noted that all the living SVU Presidents, past and present, were present during the ceremony, i.e., René Wellek, Jaroslav Němec, Jan Mládek, František Schwarzenberg and Miloslav Rechcígl. Festivities culminated with the moving address by Hon. Charles A. Vanik.[389] The Society gave Congressman Vanik, who is of Czech extraction, a distinguished award at that occasion, in recognition of his contributions to social and immigrant legislation.

The major part of the Congress was devoted to scholarly and scientific lectures and discussions, organized in six concurrent sections for most of the last three days of the Congress. The subject matter was unusually broad, covering modern and medieval history, philosophy, literature and linguistics, social and behavioral sciences, economics, biomedical sciences, physical sciences, creative and performing arts, etc. There were also special symposia organized, such as that on contemporary Czechoslovakia, another on "Future Alternatives for Czechoslovakia," on the composer Leos Janacek and his work, on Bishop St. John Nepomucene Neumann,[390] on world energy crisis, on women in retrospect and perspective, and so on. There was also a symposium on the contributions of Jews from Czechoslovakia, and another on Czech and Slovak archival and library resources in America, and one on general systems research. In addition, the program included a panel discussion on Czech and Slovak literature at home and abroad, one on political history of Czechoslovakia, one on science and society, and another on cancer research and treatment. A separate session was devoted to the traditional readings by Czech and Slovak writers from their new works.

A variety of cultural and social events were scheduled for the evenings. On the first night there was a special documentary in Czech and Slovak, "A to, co neumírá,"[391] arranged by Jaromír Zástěra[392] of Voice of America. It was a variety show, comprised of poetry reading, music, songs, movie shorts and stills, depicting the last 60 years in the eventful history of Czechs and Slovaks-at the height of their glory and triumph, and at the time of their distress and suppression.

---

[389] Charles A. Vanik (1913-), U.S. Representative from Cleveland.
[390] American Saint of Czech descent.
[391] In translation: "And that what does not die."
[392] Jaromír Zástěra (1930-1984), Czech-American journalist with Voice of America.

In observance of the fiftieth anniversary of Leoš Janáček's death, the Cleveland Museum of Arts paid the composer a fitting tribute by performance of his works. Performers included the Kent State University chorale, organist Karel Paukert,[393] pianist Antonín Kubálek,[394] and others.

Among other special events there was an art exhibit of SVU members, organized and arranged by Antonín Švehla[395] and Líba Puchmajer;[396] exhibits of books as well as a display of documents relating to Czechoslovak legions in Siberia and another one to canonization of St. John Nepomucene Neumann. Among the exhibited SVU publications was also a newly revised edition of the Biographical Directory of the Members of the Society.[397]

The Congress activities reached their peak with the traditional banquet and Grand Ball held at the Cleveland Plaza Hotel on Saturday night. This was the occasion for the outgoing President to give his farewell address and for the new President to outline some of his plans.

As an outgoing President, I received special recognition for my efforts on behalf of the Society by being elected an honorary member. It was a nice parting present.

---

[393] Karel Paukert (1935-), organist with the Cleveland Museum of Art.

[394] Antonín Kubálek (1935-), a famous Czech-Canadian pianist.

[395] Antonín Švehla (1935-), artist, living at that time in Silver Spring, MD; grandson of the late Czechoslovak Prime minister Antonín Švehla.

[396] Líba Puchmajer (1936-), graphic artist, Briarcliff Manor, NY.

[397] *Biographical Directory of the Members of the Czechoslovak Society of Arts and Sciences*. 4th ed. Compiled and edited by Eva Rechcígl and Miloslav Rechcígl, Jr. Washington, DC: SVU, 1978. 137 p.

# 22
## Jan Tříska's Presidency

Since I wished to step down from the SVU Presidency at the conclusion of my second term, the Society elected, as my successor, Prof. Jan F. Tříska whom I knew quite well. The other elected officers[398] included Professor William E. Harkins,[399] Stanley Maršík,[400] Professor Ladislav Matějka, Michael Šumichrast,[401] and Professor Milan Trpiš,[402] Vice Presidents; Professor Věra Ž. Bořkovec, Secretary-General and Herbert Naylor,[403] Treasurer. Jaroslav Pecháček[404] was elected the new editor of *Zprávy SVU*,[405] while Jiří Škvor was elected editor of *Proměny*.[406]

With the greatly improved financial status of the Society, Professor Tříska's Presidency was conducted, from the start, in an atmosphere of relaxed optimism and promise.[407] Thanks to the initiative and efforts of Professor Matějka, who had the responsibility for SVU publication program, several new titles appeared in print under the Society's sponsorship. There was a new edition of Alfred French's *Anthology of Czech Poetry*, followed by Jaroslav Seifert's *Morový sloup – The Plague*

---

[398] *Zprávy SVU*, vol. 20, No. 6 (November-December 1978), pp. 9-11.
[399] William E. Harkins (1921-), professor of Slavistics at Columbia University.
[400] Stanley J. Maršík (1927-), physicist with NASA, Cleveland, OH.
[401] Michael Šumichrast (1921-2007), economist and VP, National Association of Home Builders, Washington, DC.
[402] Milan Trpiš (1930-), associate professor of medical entomology, Johns Hopkins University School of Public Health, Baltimore, MD.
[403] Herbert Naylor (actually Němec) (1915-2001), with National Library of Medicine, Bethesda, MD.
[404] Jaroslav Pecháček (1911-1997), the former director of the Czechoslovak Broadcasting Dept. of Radio Free Europe, Munich.
[405] He was later replaced by his son Pavel Pecháček (1940-), who was, at that time, working for Voice of America in Washington, DC.
[406] Since he subsequently resigned, he was replaced by Ladislav Matějka.
[407] *Zprávy SVU*, vol. 21, No. 1 (January-February 1979), pp. 1-2.

*Monument,*[408] translated by Lyn Coffin and with collages by Jiří Kolář, and Jiří Orten's Elegie-Elegies.[409] In addition, funds were authorized for publication of Joseph Čada's *The Czechs in U.S.*[410] and T. G. Masaryk compendium[411] under the editorship of Milič Čapek[412] and Karel Hrubý. Furthermore, at the request of the Executive Board, I prepared an extensive directory of American and Canadian university professors of Czech/Slovak origin and other educators who had professional ties with Czechoslovak culture. The book, which came out under the title *Educators with Czechoslovak Roots*[413] was subsequently used as a premium in the Society new membership drive, organized by Stanley Maršík.

In an effort to make the Society more accessible to the public as well as to provide better integration of its English speaking members, SVU launched, in 1980, a new English news bulletin, *SVU Bulletin,*[414] published three times a year. Plans to publish a new scholarly periodical in English, unfortunately, could not be materialized at that time, for a variety of unforeseen organizational and administrative problems.

Three new SVU chapters were founded during this time, one in Pretoria, South Africa (1979), one in San Francisco-Bay Area (1980), and another in Vienna, Austria (1980).

In the continuance of the SVU policy of decentralization, the 1979 annual meeting was convened in Los Angeles October 26-28. The preliminary program appeared in the September issue of *Zpravy SVU*.[415] The proceedings of the General Assembly were reported in the subsequent issue of the *Zprávy SVU*.[416]

---

[408] Jaroslav Seifert, *Morový sloup – The Plague Monument*. New York, NY: SVU, 1980. 57 p.

[409] Jiří Orten. *Elegie – Elegies*. New York, NY: SVU, 1980. 111 p.

[410] Joseph Chada, *The Czechs in the United States*. New York, NY: SVU, 1981. 292 p.

[411] Milič Čapek and Karel Hrubý, eds., *T. G. Masaryk in Perspective: Comments and Criticism*. New York, NY: SVU, 1981. 282 p.

[412] Milič Čapek (1909-1997), professor of philosophy at Boston University.

[413] Miloslav Rechcígl, Jr., *Educators with Czechoslovak Roots: A US and Canadian Roster*. Washington, DC: SVU, 1980. 122 p.

[414] The first issue, as *SVU Bulletin,* Vol. 1, No. 1, appeared in January 1980, with an editorial "Greetings and Welcome from the US President."

[415] *Zprávy SVU*, vol. 21, No. 5 (September -October 1979), pp. 1-2.

[416] *Zprávy SVU*, vol. 1, No. 6 (November- December 1979), pp. 1-7.

Following the established practice, the local chapter had the sole responsibility for arranging the cultural and social program. The Los Angeles Chapter, jointly with the Center for Russian and East European Studies and the Department of Slavic Languages at the University of California-Los Angeles, organized an eminently successful symposium entitled "Czechoslovakia 1979." Professor Stanislav Segert was responsible for the program content, while Frank Marlow was in charge of local arrangements. Participants included Dr. Boris Krekic, Director of the Center for Russian and East European Studies at UCLA, Professor Andrzej Korbonski,[417] chairman of the Department of Political Science, UCLA, Professor Jiří Valenta of Naval Post Graduate Academy at Monterey, Professor Jan F. Tříska of Stanford University, Professor Michael S. Flier, Chairman of the Slavic Department at UCLA, Professor Michael Heim of the same department, Professor Stanislav Segert, UCLA, Professor Jaroslav Mráček of California State University at San Diego and Dr. Zdenka Fischmann of Corona, California. The details of the Symposium and the cultural activities were published in *Zprávy SVU*.[418]

On Saturday night the traditional SVU banquet was held at the Los Angeles Athletic Club. On Sunday, October 28, which was declared by the Mayor of the City of Los Angeles Czechoslovak Day, the Society took part in the commemorative ceremonies of the anniversary of the Czechoslovak independence.

During May 15-18, 1980, the Swiss Chapter organized the Second European Conference in Interlaken, entitled "The Humanitarian Legacy of T. G. Masaryk."[419] One hundred and twenty participants from ten countries attended the meetings. Masaryk's philosophical and political writings, which have played a major role in the development and identity of the modern Czech and Slovak nations, were appraised in the light of the world's events following Masaryk's death. Speakers included Prof. Mojmír Vaněk,[420] Prof. Erazim Kohák,[421] Prof. J. M. Lochman, B.

---

[417] Andrzej Korbonski (1927-), professor of political science at the University of California at Los Angeles; he was an SVU member.

[418] *Zprávy SVU*, No. 6 (November-December 1979), pp. 4-7.

[419] *Zprávy SVU*, vol. 22, No. 4 (January-August 1980), pp. 15-16.

[420] Mojmír Vaněk (1911-1992), professor of art history, Universite de Geneva, Switzerland.

Štefánek (Munich), Ant. van den Beld, Dr. Karel Hrubý, Dr. Miroslav Novák,[422] Dr. F. Schwarzenberg, and Prof. J. Krejčí. The papers were later published in a special issue of the SVU periodical *Proměny*.[423]

The months that followed were spent primarily on the preparation for the Tenth World Congress[424] scheduled for October 17-19, 1980 at Georgetown University, Washington, DC. Professor William E. Harkins was responsible for the substantive content of the program while Mr. and Mrs. Royco were in charge of the local arrangements.

At the General Assembly meeting, on October 16, Tříska presented the customary SVU President's report, which was printed in the November issue of *Zprávy SVU*.[425] The detailed account of the Congress proceedings appeared in the September 1980 issue of *Zprávy SVU*.[426] It is noteworthy that President of the US Jimmy Carter sent his greetings and message to the Congress which included the following statement: "I am proud to welcome you to our Nation's Capital and equally proud to acknowledge and applaud your important contributions to the enrichment of our American way of life."[427] A telegram also came from the Republican candidate for President Ronald Reagan who, three weeks later, was elected President of the United States.

The lecture program of the Congress began on Friday afternoon (October 17) and continued through Saturday and Sunday. The Friday program comprised of a panel discussion of the future of the SVU and two symposia, one on the "Perspectives of Nationalism," and the other on "The Role of Women in the Arts and Sciences." The Saturday program was quite varied, encompassing such topics as the role of Czechoslovakia in world trade, Czech literature and culture, Czechoslovak industrial and agricultural development, philosophy of Czech history, technology and the contemporary world, Kafka in East European literature, religion and the world today, a panel discussion on Charter 77

---

[421] Erazim V. Kohák (1933-), professor of philosophy, Boston University.

[422] Miroslav Novák (1953-), sociologist, associated with the Universite de Geneva, Switzerland.

[423] *Proměny*, Vol. 17, No. 4 (1980).

[424] *Zprávy SVU*, vol. 22, No. 2-03 (March-May), pp. 2-3.

[425] *Zprávy SVU*, vol. 22, No. 6 (Nov.-Dec. 1980), pp. 1-4.

[426] *Zprávy SVU*, vol. 22, No. 5 (September-October 1980), pp. 2-19.

[427] Reprinted in *Zprávy SVU*, vol. 22, No. 6 (November-December 1980), p. 9.

*Jan Tříska's Presidency* 125

and its aftermath, music and the modern world, two sections on musicology and music history, a section on earth sciences and another on natural sciences. In addition, there was a panel discussion on Czech and Slovak films and readings from new works by Czech and Slovak authors.

The Sunday program was just as diversified. A number of sections were arranged by discipline, such as psychology and psychiatry, biology and medicine, economics, arts, history, literature etc. Others were organized into topical groups, i.e. Czechoslovakia and Eastern Europe, Rusyns and the First Czechoslovak Republic, Slovak literature and culture, Czechoslovak-Ukrainian relations, the ethnic approach to the teaching of Czech and Slovak languages and culture, the Bohemian-Jewish milieu and its cultural creativity, global foreign policy issues, such as "After Afghanistan and Iran What?"; a symposium on cancer research and treatment, another session on Czechoslovak and East European history and more readings from new works by Czech and Slovak authors.

Other cultural events included an SVU book exhibit and two art exhibits by SVU members. On Saturday evening a concert of Czech and Slovak music in honor of the 100th anniversary of birth of Jan Kubelík, took place. The SVU Banquet and the Ball was held on Saturday night in the L'Enfant Plaza Hotel under the Honorary Chairmanship of Col. John Slezák.[428] The banquet program included an address by the newly elected SVU President Leopold Pospíšil and brief remarks by the outgoing President Jan F. Tříska.[429] On this occasion, Dr. Miloslav Rechcígl, Jr., the President of the Society during 1974-1978, was formally presented the diploma of honorary SVU membership, while Rudolf Šturm, Jiří Škvor, Lída Brodenová, and the husband-and-wife team Emil and Emilia Royco were given certificates of founding members. The founding membership was also awarded to the late Msgr. Alexander Heidler in memoriam.[430]

---

[428] Col. John Slezák (1896-1986), chairman of the board, Kable Printing Co.; former Undersecretary of the Army.

[429] The outgoing President Tříska also addressed SVU membership in his editorial in *Zprávy SVU*, vol. 22, No. 5 (September-October 1980), p. 1.

[430] *Zprávy SVU*, vol. 22, No. 6 (November-December 1980), pp. 4-6.

# 23
## Leopold Pospíšil's Presidency

Třiska's successor was Prof. Leopold Pospíšil[431] of Yale University. Other members of his Executive Board included Dr. Karel B. Absolon, Milan Getting, Jr.,[432] Prof. Henry Kučera,[433] Prof. Jiří Nehněvajsa, and Prof. Peter A. Toma, Vice-presidents; Mrs. Blanka Glos,[434] Secretary-General; and Mr. Frank Marlow, Treasurer. The new officers were elected on the basis of the recommendations of the Nominations Committee which I had the pleasure of chairing.[435] The rationale for our selection, together with biographies of the candidates, was published in the June issue of *Zprávy SVU*.[436]

Pospíšil introduced himself in his editorial in the January issue of *Zprávy SVU*.[437] A major effort of the new Executive Board was expended on the realization of a new scholarly journal in English, along the lines initially proposed two years earlier by the SVU leadership. It was necessary to establish editorial policy regarding the aims and the content of the journal as well as to assure financial support and make the necessary arrangements for printing and distribution. Most of the organizational responsibility for these matters rested on the shoulders of Vice-President Karel B. Absolon. The idea was formalized in the fall of 1981 when the SVU Council voted the necessary funds for the new endeavor. The new periodical was to bear the title *Kosmas: The Journal of Czechoslovak and Central European Studies*. The name *Kosmas* was

---

[431] Leopold Pospíšil (1923-), Professor of Anthropology at Yale University.
[432] Milan Getting, Jr. (1908-1990), Engineer with Allis-Chalmers Corporation, Pittsburgh, PA.
[433] Henry Kučera (1925-), Professor of Slavic Linguistics, Brown University, Providence, RI.
[434] Blanka Glos (1921-2006), librarian, formerly of St. Mary's University.
[435] The other members included Dr. Pavel Albrecht, Dr. Josef Škvorecký, Dr. Ernest Šturc, and Prof. René Wellek.
[436] *Zprávy SVU*, vol. 22, No. 4 (June-August 1980), pp. 5-14.
[437] *Zprávy SVU*, vol. 23, No. 1 (January-February 1981), pp. 1-2.

*Leopold Pospíšil's Presidency* 127

patterned after the first Bohemian chronicler who lived in the Czech lands in the years 1045-1125. Dr. John F. N. Bradley of the University of Manchester was appointed editor, to be assisted by an international editorial board. Arrangements were simultaneously made with Dr. Stephen Fischer-Galati of the University of Colorado for printing and distribution of the new periodical, which was initially to be published twice a year.

In order to provide firmer stability to its finances, the Society voted to set aside $40,000 from its reserves to be used as seed money for attracting additional monies for the newly established Society Endowment Fund.

With reference to new monographs, the Society contributed financially toward publication of Prokop Drtina's *Memoirs* and of the *Directory of Czech Writers*, to be published by 68-Publishers in Toronto. It was also decided to co-sponsor William E. Harkins' *Anthology of Czech Prose*.

The Executive Board had further resolved to initiate immediate steps toward systematic collection of information about Czechs and Slovaks abroad and their contributions, including living as well as deceased individuals plus other persons professionally engaged in studying things Czechoslovak. Past President Dr. Rechcígl was put in charge of this new endeavor.[438] Apart from its historico-cultural value, the inventory will be of great assistance in the preparation of "Who's Who among Czechs and Slovaks Abroad," which has been on the Society's drawing board from its inception.

The decision was made to hold the 1981 SVU Annual Meeting in Montreal during 23-25 October 1981.[439] The local chapter, under the chairmanship of Dr. Richard Drtina,[440] was charged with the responsibility for making the necessary arrangements and for organizing a suitable cultural and social program.

By all accounts, the meeting was an unqualified success. It began with the official opening of an art exhibit of paintings, graphic art and ceramics by Czech and Slovak artists from the Montreal and Quebec area. In addition to some 40 exhibited objects of art, a special place of

---

[438] *Zprávy SVU*, vol. 23, No. 2 (March-April 1981).
[439] *Zprávy SVU*, vol. 23, No. 4 (September-October 1981), pp. 1-4.
[440] Richard Drtina (1935-), professor of philosophy, John Abbott College, Kirkland Campus, Montreal, Canada.

honor was given to a literary exposition of Pavel Javor's work, kindly prepared by Mrs. A. Škvor, the widow of the recently deceased poet.

The General Assembly, which was convened on Friday, October 23, included the annual report of the SVU President which was reproduced in full in the November issue of *Zprávy SVU*.[441]

The Saturday program[442] consisted primarily of the symposium "Energy – The Challenge for the World," organized by Professor V. Zajíc.[443] The program speakers, who were exclusively from Montreal, included Professor T. J. F. Pavlásek[444] of McGill University, Dr. V. Fuchs and V. Zajíc of Hydro-Quebec Institute of Research, and Professor V. Zeman[445] of Concordia University. Following the lectures and stimulating discussion, the audience had the opportunity to browse through an attractive and varied book exhibit (Distribution Bohemicum), arranged by L. Křivánek.[446]

The Montreal Conference culminated with an evening banquet and a cultural program. As part of the program there was a presentation of a SVU honorary membership diploma to Prof. H. Gordon Skilling[447] of the University of Toronto, an authority on Czechoslovakia and an author of the recently published Charter 77 and Human Rights in Czechoslovakia.

Another memorable event was in the making on the European continent. In conjunction with the 1982 Sokol Slet in Vienna, the determined Dr. Jan Krupka[448] together with the members of the recently founded Viennese SVU Chapter, organized an immensely successful "Week of Czechoslovak Culture in Exile" held July 1-7. The program was varied, including an art exhibit, a series of musical performances (classical as well as modern), exhibits of books, newspapers, photo-

---

[441] *Zprávy SVU*, vol. 23, No. 5 (November-December 1981), pp. 1-4.
[442] See *Zprávy SVU*, vol. 23, No. 5 (November-December 1981), pp. 4-6.
[443] Vladimír D. Zajíc (1942-), political scientist
[444] Tomáš J. F. Pavlásek (1923- ), professor of electrical engineering at McGill University, Montreal, Canada.
[445] Professor of philosophy, Concordia University.
[446] Ladislav Křivánek (1914-), chief chemist, Citosan Canada Ltd.
[447] H. Gordon Skilling (1912-2001), professor of political science at the University of Toronto, Canada.
[448] Jan Krupka (1946-), psychologist, associated with the University of Vienna, Austria.

graphs, and recordings, readings from contemporary writings, showing of movies, plays, humor, discussions, singing and more music.[449]

The Eleventh World Congress of the Society took place soon after, on October 28-31, 1982 at the University of Pittsburgh. The preparatory steps were outlined in the March issue of *Zprávy SVU*.[450] The selection of Pittsburgh was not an accident by any means. Pittsburgh has been a center of American Slovaks for many years and at one time it was the largest Slovak city in the world. It was also the site of the historical signing of the Pittsburgh Agreement by President Masaryk and the American Slovak representatives.

Honorary sponsorship of the Congress was provided by Hon. Richard S. Caliguiri, Mayor of the City of Pittsburgh, Hon. Joseph M. Gaydos, U.S. Representative of Pittsburgh, Hon. John Heinz, U.S. Senator from Pennsylvania, and Hon. Richard L. Thornburgh, Governor of the State of Pennsylvania.

The academic program of the Congress was organized by Professor Zdenka Pospíšil,[451] the wife of SVU President Pospíšil. The local arrangements were under the care of Professor Zdeněk Suda of the University of Pittsburgh. As noted in the *Zprávy* editorial, the Congress was a great success.[452] The audience was delighted when the telegram greetings were read from the President of the US, Ronald Reagan.[453]

More than 150 lectures were delivered at the Congress by scholars and educators from the U.S., Canada, and other parts of the world. The talks covered a wide array of subjects, ranging from political science, sociology, economics, history, philosophy, theology, to arts, musicology, medicine, physical and biological sciences, physical education and sports. A number of sections dealt with special topics, such as the women question, a symposium on "Initial Unionistic Endeavors toward Church Unity," "The Philosophical and Political Foundations of the Czechoslovak Foreign Policy," a round table discussion on "Czechoslo-

---

[449] *Zprávy SVU*, vol. 24, No. 2 (March-April 1982), pp. 7-8.

[450] *Zprávy SVU*, vol. 24, No. 2 (March-April 1982), pp. 3-5.

[451] Zdenka Pospíšil (1923-), professor of history of art at the Southern Connecticut State College, New Haven, CT.

[452] *Zprávy SVU*, vol. 14, No. 6 (November- December 1982), pp. 1-2.

[453] *Zprávy SVU,* vol. 24, No. 6 (November -December 1982), p. 8.

vakia, Eastern Europe, the U.S.S.R. and the West," "Czechoslovak Economy at Crossroads: Stagnation or Reform?," "Contemporary Poland and Czechoslovakia" and finally a symposium on "Reanimatology and New Definition of Death."

Besides lectures, there were the customary readings of excerpts from new works by writers of Czech/Slovak origin and a Czechoslovak Writers Forum with the participation of Arnošt Lustig,[454] Josef Škvorecký, and Jiří Kovtun.[455]

Following the Writers Forum and a joint buffet, there was an organ recital by Karel Paukert, assisted by his wife Noriko Fugii, soprano. The program presented compositions by Mikuláš Moyzes, Petr Eben, Karel Paukert, Bohuslav Matěj Černohorský, Jan Michalička, Jan Křtitel Kuchař, Karel Boleslav Jirák, Bedřich Antonín Wiedermann, Antonín Dvořák, and Leoš Janáček.

Under the joint sponsorship of the Society and the University of Pittsburgh Arts Department, there was also an art exhibit, organized in the beautiful halls of the Frick Fine Arts Building. Some twenty-five members from North America and Europe participated, including a number of young artists. The exhibit was a success, thanks to the organizational ability of Ladislav Haňka,[456] Jr. Integrated in the Congress program was also the commemoration of the Czechoslovak Independence Day, celebrated by an evening of Slovak folk dancing. The peak of the social events was the Society Banquet and Grand Ball held at the Pittsburgh Athletic Association Club. At the banquet, honorary membership was presented to two outstanding personalities from the Pittsburgh area, namely Professor Wesley W. Posvar[457] and Dr. Ivan A. Getting,[458] of Czech and Slovak descent, respectively.

As the SVU Bylaws require, Pospíšil presented his State of the SVU report at the SVU General Assembly meeting, held on October 29, 1982, which was published in the September issue of *Zprávy SVU*.[459]

---

[454] Arnošt Lustig (1926-), a noted Czech writer, living in Washington, DC.
[455] Jiří Kovtun (1927-), Czech poet and area specialist at the Library of Congress.
[456] Ladislav R. Haňka (1952-), graphic artist, Kalamazoo, MI.
[457] Wesley W. Posvar (1925-2001), chancellor of the University of Pittsburgh.
[458] Ivan A. Getting (1912-2003), President of Aerospace Corporation, California.
[459] *Zprávy SVU*, vol. 24, No. 5 (September-October 2982), pp. 1-5.

# 24
## *Pospíšil's Second Term*

At the recommendation of the Nominations Committee,[460] which I chaired, Pospíšil was reelected to SVU Presidency at the General Assembly meeting in Pittsburgh on October 29, 1982, together with the following: Dr. Karel B. Absolon, Professor Charles S. Bednar,[461] Professor Igor Vojtech Nábělek,[462] Professor Jiří Nehněvajsa and Professor Thomas G. Winner,[463] Vice Presidents; and Mr. Josef Staša,[464] Treasurer. The remainder of the new team included Ing. Miloš Kučera,[465] Secretary-General, Dr. Karel Hrubý, Editor of *Proměny*, Dr. Jaroslav Němec, Editor of *Zprávy SVU*, Dr. Zdenka Fischmann, Editor of *SVU Bulletin*, and Professor Zdeněk Suda, Editor of *Kosmas*.

The Pittsburgh Congress gave impetus for establishing a new SVU chapter in that city. Another chapter came into existence at Hartford, Conn. Discussions also started regarding the possibility of organizing additional chapters in Utrecht, the Netherlands, and Perth, Australia.

By soliciting additional funds to increase the endowment, the newly elected Executive Board continued the efforts of its predecessors of further stabilizing the publication of SVU periodicals. The move of the Editorial offices of *Proměny* from the U.S. to Europe was a significant and wise move, considering that a large number of the Czech and Slovak contributors to this periodical reside in Europe. Similarly, it was anticipated that the currently U.S.-based *Kosmas* will draw primarily on the English-language contributors in North America.

---

[460] Other members included Dr. Milan Fryščák, Dr. Michael Šumichrast, Dr. Jan F. Tříska and Dr. René Wellek. The rationalization of the selection with the biographical sketches of the candidates was published in *Zprávy SVU*, vol. 14. No. 3 (May-June 1982), pp. 1-8.

[461] Charles S. Bednar (1930-), professor of political science and Associate Dean at Muhlenberg College.

[462] Igor V. Nábělek (1924-), professor of audiology at the University of Tennessee.

[463] Thomas G. Winner (1917-2004), professor of Slavic Languages, Brown University.

[464] Josef Staša (1923-), architect with Harvard University Planning Office.

[465] Miloš K. Kučera (1944-), engineer with Brooklyn Union Gas. Co.

During the period 1983-84, the Society issued a new edition of the *Biographical Directory of Members*,[466] which was again prepared for publication by the Rechcígls. The Executive Board also voted to provide financial assistance and sponsorship to Jiří Kovtun's[467] *Slovo má poslanec Masaryk*[468] and to Sylvie Richterová's[469] *Slovo a ticho*.[470] Approval was also given for the preparation of an updated index to the first ten volumes of the *Zprávy SVU*, to be compiled by Dr. Jaroslav Němec and Irena Lettrich.

At the recommendation of the By-Laws Committee, chaired by Dr. George Glos,[471] the Executive Committee submitted a Referendum to members to vote on a number of important changes in the SVU Bylaws. The subsequently approved revisions included a provision to broaden the Executive Board and enlarge the responsibility of its members. Specifically, the future Executive Boards would consist of: President, Executive Vice-President, six Vice-Presidents with specific responsibilities, Secretary-General, and a Treasurer. The editors of various periodicals would, henceforth, be appointed by the Executive Board. Other changes related primarily to a better definition of various types of membership in the Society and the delineation of the criteria for the selection of the honorary and founding members.

The two single most important external events of 1983 were the Third SVU European Conference in Bern and the SVU Annual Meeting in Cambridge, MA.

The European Conference,[472] organized by the Swiss Chapter, took place on Aug. 26-28 at Bern's Waldhotel Gurten with the central theme "Our European Destiny." It was an immensely successful event, with the

---

[466] *Biographical Directory of the Czechoslovak Society of Arts and Sciences*. 5th ed. Compiled and edited by Eva Rechcígl and Miloslav Rechcígl, Jr. Washington, DC: SVU, 1983. 193 p.

[467] George J. Kovtun (1927-), area specialist, Library of Congress, Washington, DC.

[468] Jiří Kovtun, *Slovo má poslanec Masaryk*, Munich: Edice Arkýř, 1985. 211 p.

[469] Sylvie Richterová (1945-), professor of Czech and Slovak literature, Universita Padova, Italy.

[470] Sylvie Richterová, *Slovo a ticho*. Munich: Edice Arkýř, 1986. 155 p.

[471] George Glos (1924-), lawyer, associated with European Law Division, Library of Congress, Washington, DC.

[472] *Zprávy SVU*, vol. 25, No. 5 (September-October 1983), pp. 4-6.

participation of some 150 members and friends of the Society from England, Belgium, Denmark, France, Netherlands, Italy, Germany, Norway, Austria, Sweden, Switzerland and the U.S. The lectures included presentations by K. Hrubý (Basel), J. Mlynárik (Munich), A. Měšťan[473] (Freiburg), F. Munk[474] (Portland), V. Bělohradský (Genoa), K. Skalický (Rome), L. Ďurovič[475] (Lund), L. Pospíšil (New Haven), Z. Suda (Pittsburgh), B. Štefánek (Munich), F. Marlow (Sherman Oaks), V. Škutina[476] (Zurich), J. M. Lochman (Basel), E. Kohák (Boston), P. Tigrid (Paris) and J. Krejčí (Lancaster). The organizers also prepared a special booth featuring the SVU publications and the art exhibit of Čeněk Pražák's[477] paintings. The Conference provided an excellent opportunity for SVU officers from Europe and the U.S. to exchange views and to strengthen co-operation between the two continents. The texts of the conference were published in *Proměny*.[478]

On the weekend of November 4-6, 1983 the Society held its Annual Meeting in Cambridge, MA, with the General Assembly meeting on the first day, followed by a special Conference on Robotics on the following two days.[479] At the General Assembly, SVU President presented his traditional annual report,[480] followed by the reports of the other officers.

The aim of the Conference was to examine the meaning and the consequences of Robotics from the broadest point of view, encompassing not only scientific and technological aspects, but also the social and economic dimensions as well as philosophy, creative arts and literature. The last paper on the program dealt appropriately with Karel Čapek's play *R.U.R.*, in which the word robot was coined. The conference ended with organ music by Czech composers, performed by the Czech organist

---

[473] Antonín Měšťan (1930-2004), professor of Slavistics, University of Freiburg, Germany.
[474] Frank Munk (1901-1999), professor of political science at Portland State University, and Reed College, OR.
[475] Lubomír Ďurovič (1925-), professor of Slavistics, Universitet Lund, Sweden.
[476] Vladimír Škutina (1931-1995), writer, living in Zurich, Switzerland.
[477] Čeněk Pražák (1914-), painter, living in Dittingen, Switzerland.
[478] *Proměny*, vol. 21, No. 1 (1984).
[479] *Zprávy SVU*, vol. 25, No. 4 (June-August 1983), pp. 1-2,
[480] *Zprávy SVU*, vol. 25, No. 6 (November-December 1983), pp. 1-5.

J. Tománek[481] and his Cecilia Chorus. As noted in the *Zprávy SVU*,[482] the outcome of the Conference was described in superlatives.

No sooner was the annual meeting over, when the major focus of the Executive Board's attention was put on the preparation of the Twelfth World Congress, scheduled for October 25-28, 1984 in Toronto. Prof. Thomas G. Winner was appointed Program Chairman[483] of the Congress and Anthony Krondl[484] was given the responsibility for local arrangements. This Congress was the first Society Congress organized outside the borders of the US. SVU availed itself of the hospitality of Canada, following the summer festivities celebrating Ontario's Bicentennial and Toronto's 150th birthday.

All organizational meetings and academic sessions took place in the comfortable convention rooms of the Royal York Hotel. This made "circulation" among various lecture rooms easier and facilitated contacts of all participants. The central meeting point was, of course, the Registration Desk, unselfishly attended by members of the local arrangements committee. The nearby display of books "for sale" also became very popular, and one afternoon the magnificent handmade textiles and Czechoslovak national costumes could also be viewed.

The academic program consisted[485] of some thirty sessions, mostly averaging six papers each. Anthropology, philosophy, economics, history of art, women's studies, political science, film, psychology, history of science, church history, and poetry readings had one session each. Natural sciences, musicology, sociology and Czechs and Slovaks abroad had two sessions, history and linguistics had three and medicine had five sessions. The film session included the viewing and discussion of "The Wind in the Pocket" (Vítr v kapse). One of the high points of the Congress was a joint session, chaired by Prof. René Wellek, in honor of the recently announced Nobel Laureate, the Czech poet Jaroslav Seifert.

---

[481] Godfrey Tománek (1925-), organist, associated with the University of Connecticut.
[482] *Zprávy SVU*, vol., 25, No. 6 (November-December 1983), p. 5.
[483] *Zprávy SVU*, vol. 26, No. 1 (January-February 1984), pp. 1-2.
[484] Anthony Krondl (1914-1995), assistant professor of medicine, University of Toronto, Canada.
[485] The program was published under the title 12th World Congress Program, as the fourth issue (June-August) of the 1984 *Zprávy SVU*. It is an impressive document of 42 pages.

Another important event was the Mendel Memorial Symposium on the occasion of the centennial of J. G. Mendel's death. The session was organized in conjunction with the Mendel-Frimmel Society for Applied Genetics, Freising, Federal Republic of Germany. A Mendel exhibit accompanied the symposium, in which four speakers from West Germany and one each from Sweden and the U.S. participated.

Special events included an exhibition of fine arts, a piano and flute recital at the Royal Conservatory of Music, and a Czech theatrical group's presentation of a Czech version of Thornton Wilder's "The Skin of our Teeth," and the traditional SVU Banquet.

As has been the tradition, the General Assembly meeting preceded the actual Congress and was held on October 25, 1984. Pospíšil, in his capacity as President, presented his report covering the two-year administrative period.[486] The overall assessment of the Congress was written by Vladimír Kabeš.[487]

---

[486] *Zprávy SVU*, vol. 26, No. 6 (November-December 1984), pp. 1-4.

[487] *Zprávy SVU*, vol. 26, No. 6 (November- December 1984), pp. 5-8.

# 25
## Jiří Nehněvajsa's Presidency

As per recommendation of the SVU Nominations Committee,[488] at the conclusion of Pospíšil's two terms, Prof. Jiří Nehněvajsa was elected as the new President. With him were elected Prof. Igor Nábělek, Executive Vice President; Prof. Anton Novacký,[489] Vice President for the Sciences; Emil S. Purgina,[490] Vice President for the Arts; Prof. Věra Ž. Bořkovec, Vice President for Student Affairs; Dr. Čestmír Ješina,[491] Vice President for Local Chapters; Prof. J. Škvorecký, Vice President for Publications; Dr. Vladimír M. Kabeš,[492] Vice President for Press Relations; Ing. Miloš K. Kučera, Secretary-General; and Josef Staša, Treasurer. The entire slate of elected officers, including the members of the Council, etc., appears in the November 1984 issue of Zprávy SVU.[493] Their term commenced at the General Assembly meeting in Toronto on October 25, 1984.

Nehněvajsa started his term with an inspiring speech, which was reprinted in full in Zprávy SVU.[494] One of the first actions of the Executive Board was to authorize the expansion of the quarterly Proměny. The Society's SVU Bulletin began appearing four times rather than three times a year. The decision was also made to financially assist the new edition of Arne Novak's Czech Literature,[495] to be published by the University of Michigan Press. Furthermore, arrangements were made for Columbia University Press to publish, under SVU sponsorship, Karel

---

[488] Zprávy SVU, vol. 26, No. 3 (May-June 1984), pp. 16-28.
[489] Anton J. Novacký (1930-), professor of plant pathology, University of Missouri, Columbia, MO.
[490] Emil S. Purgina (1937-), artist, Lecturer, University of Ottawa.
[491] Cestmir Ješina (1924-2001), senior analyst, US Dept. of Energy, Washington, DC.
[492] Vladimír Kabeš (1918-), lawyer and businessman, Washington, DC.
[493] Zprávy SVU, vol. 26, No. 6 (November–December 1984), pp. 9-10.
[494] Zprávy SVU, vol. 26, No. 6 (November-December 1984), pp. 10-13.
[495] Arne Novák, Czech Literature. Revised ed. Edited with Supplement by William E. Harkins. Ann Arbor: University of Michigan, 1986. 382 p.

*Jiří Nehněvajsa's Presidency* 137

Engliš' *Economic Systems*,[496] translated by Prof. Ivo Moravčík.[497] Approval was also given for the publication of my book, *Legislators with Czechoslovak Roots from Colonial Times to the Present* [498] and for assisting Sixty-Eight Publishers with Antonín Měšťan's *Česká literatura*[499] and Helena Kosková's[500] *Hledání ztracené generace.*[501] In addition, with the SVU financial support, Vladimír Veit[502] put out a record entitled "Ve lví stopě" which contains his own musical renditions of a number of classical and more modern Czech poems.[503] Eva and I also began working on the 6th edition of SVU Directory.[504]

The January 1985 issue of *Zprávy SVU*[505] brought in some interesting figures about the SVU finances. According to the proposed budget it was estimated that the Society was anticipating $43,000 of income and $42,000 of expenses. The income came largely from membership dues (42%), from the sale of its publications (25%), and from the interest (24%), the gifts being less than 10%. The expenses were due primarily to publications which amounted to about 60%.

Interestingly, the actual financial balance for the year 1985 turned out a bit differently, with the total income equaling $61,220 and the total expenses to $49,440. The higher income was due primarily to increased gifts which amounted to 22% of the income.[506]

After consultation with the Swiss Chapter, the Executive Board decided to convene the upcoming 1985 Annual Meeting in Thun,

---

[496] Karel Engliš, *An Essay on Economic Systems: A Teleological Approach*. Translated by Ivo Moravčík. Boulder, CO: East European Monographs, 1986. 68 p.

[497] Ivo Moravčík (1926-), professor of economics, University of Alberta, Edmonton, Canada.

[498] Miloslav Rechcígl, Jr., *U.S. Legislators with Czechoslovak Roots from Colonial Times to Present*. With Genealogical Lineages. Washington, DC: SVU, 1987. 65 p.

[499] Antonín Měšťan, *Česká literatura. 1785-1985*. Toronto: 68 Publishers, 1987. 456 p.

[500] Helena Kosek (1935-), language teacher and translator, living in Sweden.

[501] Helena Kosková, *Hledani ztracene generace*. Toronto: 68 Publishers, 1986. 368 p.

[502] Vladimír Veit (1948-), song composer, living in Vienna, Austria.

[503] Vladimír Veit, "Ve lví stopě". Recorded in Vienna, Austria, April 1985.

[504] *Zprávy SVU*, vol. 27, No. 4 (July-August 1985), pp. 1-2.

[505] *Zprávy SVU*, vol. 27, No. 1 (January-February 1985), pp 4-5.

[506] *Zprávy SVU*, vol. 28, No. 1 (January-February 1986), pp. 3-5.

Switzerland.[507] This was the first time in the SVU history that such a meeting was held outside of the North American continent. Delegates from fourteen different countries took part, in addition to a sizeable delegation from America, led by President Jiří Nehněvajsa, Executive Vice-President Igor Nábělek and Secretary-General Miloš Kučera. The face-to-face meetings between the European and American delegates unquestionably improved the understanding of the specific problems facing the members on each continent and strengthened the ties between the two sides.

In conjunction with the Annual Meeting, there was a topical conference,[508] organized by the Swiss Chapter, "The Threatened Heritage of Central Europe." It was also an occasion for commemorating the fortieth anniversary of the end of World War II. Lectures and discussions focused on the dangers to the identity of the Central European countries that are under the pressure of Sovietization, which is gradually undermining their historical social structure and values, such as democratic human rights. Perspectives for future development of this region were explored as well. It was gratifying to see a number of noted exile scholars from other countries among the speakers, including the Hungarian historian P. Gosztony, living in Bern, the Hungarian sociologist A. Reszler, living in Geneva, and the Polish sociologist B. Cywinski from Freiburg.

The lectures, which were uniformly of high quality, were subsequently printed in a special issue of *Proměny*.[509] In addition, the Executive Board supported, on a post hoc basis, the production of a video-cassette, "Ohrožené dědictví Střední Evropy," largely based on the Thun Conference, prepared by Vladimír Škutina and Jindřich Bernard.[510] In 1985, the SVU Executive Board issued two declarations, one on the fortieth anniversary of the end of World War II, and another regarding its position on culture and science, as input into the Budapest Conference on the Helsinki Accords.

---

[507] *Zprávy SVU*, vol. 27, No. 4 (January-August, 1985), p. 8.

[508] *Zprávy SVU*, vol. 27, No. 5 (September-October 1985), pp. 1-4.

[509] *Proměny*, vol. 21, No. 1 (1984).

[510] "Ohrožene dědictví Středni Evropy." Video cassette Prepared by Vladimír Škutina and Jindřich Bernard, largely based on the Thun Conference

Through the efforts of Dr. Zdeněk Hruban and his friends, a renewed chapter of SVU in Chicago sprang into existence. Led by Dr. Eduard Dvořák,[511] it again began a series of high quality and successful activities. There was also a thought of establishing new chapters in France and Israel, but nothing came of it.

On the basis of excellent proposals, SVU was able to acquire significant financial support from the National Endowment for Democracy for the work of the new Documentation Center,[512] for the Jan Palach Trust and the Jan Hus Foundation, the former in Germany, the latter two in London.[513]

The National Endowment for Democracy's funds were also instrumental in the support of Sixty-Eight Publishers' publication of a number of important books, written by authors living in Czechoslovakia; the Society's own "Living History Project," which helps finance the production of video cassettes also benefited. Cassettes on some artists and painters-abroad, on some key Slovak personalities throughout the world, and on Jaroslav Seifert's impact in the West were produced in 1987.

The major event in 1986 was the Thirteenth World Congress, convened on September 18-20th, on the campus of Northeastern University, Boston, Mass. Prof. Ladislav Dolanský,[514] who held professorship at that institution, had the responsibility for local arrangements and Prof. Anton Novacký from the University of Missouri was in charge of preparation of the academic program. The preliminary announcement appeared in the January 1986 issue of *Zprávy SVU*.[515]

The program, which was published as a separate issue of *Zprávy SVU*,[516] consisted of over thirty scientific, scholarly and artistic sessions, covering practically every area of human endeavor. Apart from the individual disciplines, there were also topical symposia, such as "Czechs and

---

[511] Eduard Dvořák (1943-), radiologist, University of Illinois College of Medicine.
[512] Dr. Vilém Prečan, Director.
[513] *Zprávy SVU*, vol. 28, No. 4 (July-August 1986), p. 1.
[514] Ladislav Dolanský (1919-1993), professor of electrical engineering, Northeastern University, Boston, MA.
[515] "XIII. Mezinárodni sjezd SVU," *Zprávy SVU*, vol. 28, No. 1 (January-February 1986), pp. 7-9.
[516] *Zprávy SVU*, vol. 28, No. 2 (March-April 1986) 32 p.

Slovaks Abroad," "The Czechoslovak-Polish Relationship," "The Cyrillo-Methodian Symposium," "The Seifert Symposium," and others.

In addition to the varied lecture program, visitors had an opportunity to view an admirable art exhibit,[517] organized by Emil Purgina, and a unique exhibit of Czechoslovak stamps prepared by Henry Hahn.[518]

The Boston Congress was also the site of the American premiere of the film "Honička," with personal commentary by Jaroslav Vejvoda, the author of the script. Among special events was a Gala Social Evening held at the Isabella Stewart Gardner Museum. The Museum's magnificent and unique collections could be seen as the delightful chamber music was heard. The festivities culminated with a banquet and ball featuring the address of Earl W. Foel, editor-in-chief of the *Christian Science Monitor*, who, as it turned out, had some Czech ancestors.[519]

The final evaluation of the Congress was published in *Zprávy SVU*.[520]

---

[517] *Zprávy SVU*, vol. 28, No. 5 (September-October 1986), pp 5-6.
[518] Henry Hahn (1928-2007), materials science engineer and avid stamp collector, living in Falls Church, VA.
[519] *Zprávy SVU*, vol. 28, No. 5 ((September-October) 1986), pp. 1-2.
[520] *Zprávy SVU*, vol. 28, no. 5 (September-October 1986), 13-14.

# 26
## *Nehněvajsa's Second Term*

The new Executive Board, as per recommendations of the Nominations Committee,[521] remained essentially the same as the previous one, with Nehněvajsa as SVU President. Among the new members were Ing. Stanley Maršík, Vice President for the coordination of local chapters and Prof. Ladislav Dolanský, who was elected the new Treasurer. The two year administrative period of the newly elected Executive Board commenced from the point the outcome of the elections was announced at the General Assembly meeting in Boston on September 18, 1986.

On the occasion of the tenth anniversary of the Charter 77 movement, the Swiss Chapter convened in Zurich on May 17, 1987 a one-day conference with international participation. Various aspects of the aims and the mission of the Movement were presented and discussed by well-known figures, including Jiří Gruša[522] (Germany), Vilém Prečan[523] (Germany), Jiří Němec[524] (Austria), Ján Mlynárik (Germany), Miroslav Novák (Switzerland) and Karel Hrubý (Switzerland). Some 90 attendees from Germany, France, Switzerland, Austria and the U.S. took an active part in the lively discussions concerning the importance and the strategic role of Charter 77 which had generally been viewed as. the most articulate manifestation of the democratic movement in Czechoslovak society.

As a result of the decision by the Executive Board, the 1987 SVU annual meeting was held in Los Angeles, California, during 18-20 September, together with a conference on the "Contributions of Czech and Slovak Immigrants to the US." [525] All activities took place at the International Student Center of the University of California-Los Angeles,

---

[521] *Zprávy SVU*, vol. 28, No. 3 (May-June 1986), pp. 1-13.
[522] Jiří Gruša (1938-), journalist and dissident, living in Germany at the time.
[523] Vilém Prečan (1933-), executive director, Documentation Center for the Promotion of Independent Czechoslovak Literature, Schwarzenberg, Germany.
[524] Jiří Němec (1932-), psychologist, living in Vienna, Austria.
[525] *Zprávy SVU*, vol. 29, No. 3 (May-June 1987), pp. 1-2.

which offered conference rooms, a gallery, and expert advice for arranging the art exhibits as well as catering and refreshments.

Prior to the General Assembly meeting which was scheduled for the evening of September 18, the organizers inaugurated the fine arts exhibition of Czech and Slovak artists,[526] to the accompaniment of violin music. The conference per se took place September 19-20, the first part dealing with the problems of the immigrants' adjustment and acculturation, followed by discussions of the immigrants' achievements in literature, music, science and industry.[527] The evaluation of the Los Angeles meeting appeared as an editorial in the November issue of *Zpravy SVU*.[528]

For years, I have been toying with the idea of creating within the Society an autonomous SVU Research Institute. I was therefore elated when the Nehněvajsa's Executive Board finally accepted my idea and went ahead with the Referendum of members to incorporate it into the SVU Bylaws. It was sent as a part of the March 1988 issue of *Zprávy SVU*.[529]

The year 1988 was eventful. It marked not only the 70th anniversary of the founding of the Czechoslovak Republic, but also a sequence of fateful events that dealt heavy blows to her freedom and democratic spirit, fifty years since Munich, followed by the Nazi occupation, forty years since the February Communist takeover and twenty years of Soviet occupation.

On August 20-21, the Swiss Chapter organized the Fifth European Conference in Bern, Switzerland. Entitled "Culture and Force" (*Kultur and Gewalt*), the conference was conducted in German, English and French. The speakers included Z. Dittrich[530] (Utrecht), J. Krejčí (Lancaster), H. Lemberg[531] (Marburg), K. Chvatík[532] (Konstanz) and J.

---

[526] The list of artists who took part in the Los Angeles exhibit was published in *Zpravy SVU*, vol. 29, No. 6 (November-December 1987), pp. 4-5.

[527] *Zprávy SVU*, vol. 29, No. 4 (July-August 1987), pp. 1-4.

[528] *Zprávy SVU*, vol. 29, No. 6 (November-December 1987), 1-4.

[529] *Zprávy SVU*, vol. 30, No. 2 (March-April 1988), pp. 12-14.

[530] Zdeněk R. Dittrich (1923-), historian, University of Utrecht, The Netherlands.

[531] Hans Lemberg (1933-), historian, Philipps-Universität Marburg, Marburg, Germany.

[532] Květoslav Chvatík (1930-), philosopher, Universität Komstanz, Germany

Rupník[533] (Paris). Part of the conference was a public meeting in Hotel Bellevue to protest against the invasion of Czechoslovakia by the Warsaw Pact armies twenty years ago and the ensuing occupation of the country by the Soviet troops. The meeting which was attended by many important personalities was under the aegis of the Swiss Minister of Culture, F. Cotti. The Charter 77 spokesman, Václav Havel, SVU honorary member and honorary patron of the Conference, could not attend the meeting for fear of not being allowed to return back to Czechoslovakia by the Communist authorities. Some three hundred participants and representatives of Swiss public life were present. Among the guest speakers was the former Minister of Justice of the Swiss Confederation, Rudolf Friedrich. The premiere of Jan Novak's composition "Quadricinium Fidium" and Antonín Dvořák's "American Quartet (Op. 96)" performed by the Lausanne String Quartet, followed. On the morning of August 21 there was a panel discussion on the topic "Culture as a Duty and Responsibility." The proceedings of the Conference were published in German in a brochure entitled *Kultur und Gewalt*, with the financial assistance of Foundation Europeenne de la culture. A detailed account of the Conference was published in the September 1988 issue of *Zpravy SVU*[534] and in *SVU Bulletin.*[535]

The number "eight" was also the major theme of the Fourteenth World Congress,[536] scheduled in Washington, DC Metropolitan area, i.e. at the National 4-H Center, Chevy Chase, MD, during September 15-18, 1988.[537] Dagmar Hasalová White[538] was put in charge of the local arrangements, while Dr. Frank Meissner[539] handled the program.

On the occasion of the Congress, President of the US, Ronald Reagan sent a special message which is reproduced here:

---

[533] Jaques Rupník (1950-), director of research, Centre d'Etudes et de Recherches Internationales (CERI), Paris, France.

[534] *Zprávy SVU*, vol. 29, No. 5 (September-October 1988), pp. 9-11.

[535] *SVU Bulletin*, vol. 10, No. 1 (February 1989), pp. 9-11.

[536] *Zprávy SVU*, vol. 29, No. 5 (September-October 1987), pp. 5-8.

[537] *Zprávy SVU*, vol. 29, No. 6 (November-December 1987), pp. 6-9; *Ibid.*, vol. 30, No. 1 (January- February 1988), pp. 6-8.

[538] Dagmar Hasalová White (1926-), concert singer and musicologist, living in Virginia.

[539] Frank Meissner (1923-1990), economist, associated with Inter-American Development Bank, Washington, DC.

**THE WHITE HOUSE**
*Washington*
September 12, 1988

*I am pleased to greet everyone gathered for the 14th World Congress of the Czechoslovak Society of Arts and Sciences.*

*Your Society perpetuates the traditions of the many millions of Czechs and Slovaks who have contributed much to artistic and scientific life in the United States over the past two centuries. You can be proud of all you have done and all you continue to do in this regard. You can be proud as well of your particularly important role in speaking for the Czechs and Slovaks who today are denied the right to engage in free expression and scholarship in their own country. We all remember that this year makes the 40th anniversary of the communist takeover of Czechoslovakia and the 20th anniversary of the brutal Soviet-led invasion that stifled efforts at reform. You exemplify what Czechs and Slovaks can accomplish when able to live in freedom and make full use of their creativity, inspiration, and talent.*

*Such freedom will one day come again to Czechoslovakia and until then you will keep alive the flame of free artistic and scientific achievement by Czechs and Slovaks around the world. You have my heartfelt appreciation and very best wishes. God bless you.*

*__Ronald Reagan__*

Almost one-third of some 200 individual presentations dealt with the above scheme, covering historical, political, economic and social aspects. The remainder of the program was devoted to agriculture, food and nutrition, medicine, natural sciences, literature, linguistics, art, theater, musicology, education, religion and theology, librarianship, and women studies. In addition, there were special symposia on "Karel

Čapek and His Works," "Czechs and Slovaks in America," and "The Czechoslovak Jewry." There was also a panel discussion on "Contemporary Slovak Culture" and another on "Youth: Roads Ahead." Last, but not least, there were the customary poetry and prose readings from works of contemporary Czech and Slovak writers. Special events included art exhibits, book-mart, film screening, a concert, excursion to Mount Vernon, and a guided tour at the National Gallery of Art.

The critically acclaimed Choral Group, "Columbia pro Cantare," consisting of one hundred and ten singers, together with a fifty-piece orchestra presented an American premiere of Dvořák's "Hymnus, (Op. 301," "Heirs of the White Mountain," and Smetana's "Bohemia Song." Contemporary music was represented by Karel Husa's "Serenade," based on Slovak melodies for wood-wind quintet, strings, harp and xylophone. Further, there were arias and duets from Jenufa, Dalibor, and Rusalka. The entire program, sung in Czech, was conducted by Francis Motyca-Dawson, Director of the "Columbia pro Cantare." The traditional banquet featured two guest speakers: the Hon. Robert W. Farrand[540] and Dr. Martin Harwit.[541]

In the morning of September 15, 1988, the SVU Executive Board held its meeting, followed by the meetings of the SVU Council and that of the General Assembly, during which the officers presented their final reports. At the General Assembly meeting, the members approved a special Resolution in which they memorialized, with pride, the moral, philosophical and cultural legacy of Tomas Garrigue Masaryk.[542] The outcome of the elections, based on the recommendations of the Nominations Committee[543] and which was announced at the meeting, is reported in the following chapter.

---

[540] Deputy Assistant Secretary for Human Rights and Humanitarian Affairs, U.S. Department of State.
[541] Director of the National Air and Space Museum, Smithsonian Institution.
[542] *Zprávy SVU*, vol. 30, No. 5 (September-October 1988), pp. 1-2.
[543] *Zprávy SVU*, vol. 30, No. 2 (March-April 1988), pp. 1-12.

# 27
## Igor Nábělek's Presidency

Nehněvajsa's successor was Prof. Igor V. Nábělek who was elected together with Dr. Thomas G. Gibian,[544] Executive Vice President; Dr. George Keleti,[545] Prof. Zdenka Pospíšil, Prof. Věra Bořkovec, Mr. Stanislav Maršík, Prof. Lubomír Ďurovič and Dr. Michael Šumichrast, Vice Presidents; Ing. Miloš Kučera, Secretary-General and Prof. Ladislav Dolanský, Treasurer. Their term started on the day of the SVU General Assembly meeting, September 15, 1988, where the outcome of elections was announced.[546]

A month later, October 24, 1988 marked the 30th anniversary of the Society, which the Executive Board, for unexplained reason, forgot to acknowledge with any kind of ceremony or announcement. It was not until Jaroslav Němec brought it to the attention of members in his unsigned editorial in the January issue of *Zprávy SVU*.[547]

To mark the 70th anniversary of the Czechoslovak Republic, the SVU British Chapter, in cooperation with Professor Roger Scruton of Birkbeck College, University of London, organized on the 15th October 1988, on the premises of the London School of Economics and Political Sciences, one day conference, "Czechoslovakia – Past, Present and Future." Altogether six papers were presented: Prof. Z. Dittrich of the University of Utrecht, Prof. Jaroslav Krejčí of the University of Lancaster, Dr. B. Hnízdo of the Royal Institute of International Affairs, London, K. Kyncl, associated with the Index on Censorship, A. Tomský, associated with the Church in Need and Prof. Roger Scruton.[548]

On March, 1989, the Executive Board issued the statement protesting the "shocking arrest and sentencing in Prague of one of its honorary

---

[544] Thomas G. Gibian (1922-), Chemical Executive with the Henkel Corp.
[545] George Keleti (1925-2000), Assoc Professor of Microbiology, University of Pittsburgh School of Public Health.
[546] *Zprávy SVU*, vol. 30, No. 5 (September-October 1988), pp. 3-4.
[547] *Zprávy SVU*, vol. 31, No. 1 (January-February 1989), pp. 1-2.
[548] *SVU Bulletin*, vol. X, No. 1 (February 1989), pp. 11-12.

*Igor Nábělek's Presidency* 147

members, the playwright Václav Havel," stating that "this persecution is even more deplorable at this time when writers can speak with considerably more freedom in other parts of the Soviet Union and Václav Havel's plays, forbidden to be performed in his homeland, are played in the neighboring socialist countries and applauded by their government officials."[549]

On August 7, 1989, former SVU President Dr. Jan V. Mládek died which was shocking news for all of us who knew him well and who worked closely with him on various SVU matters.[550]

At my recommendation, the 1989 annual meeting of the Society was held in Bethlehem, PA, in conjunction with a conference on "Moravian Brethren: History and Traditions."[551] The Conference was convened during 13-15 October on the Moravian College campus which co-sponsored the meeting with the Moravian Seminary. Zdenka Pospíšil, with my help, was put in charge of the program. The theme of the Conference was close to my heart, the subject about which I knew quite a bit.

The program[552] dealt with the relationship of the Moravian Brethren and the Unitas Fratrum, the formative years of the Moravian Church and the early days of the Brethren in America. In addition to historical and theological topics, several papers dealt with art, music and literature. It was an immensely successful event with the participation of such scholars as Jan Milič Lochman,[553] Prof. David R. Holeton,[554] Prof. Murray L. Wagner,[555] Prof. David A. Schattschneider, [556] Prof. Stanislav Segert, Ján Liguš,[557] Prof. Josef Anderle,[558] Prof. Louise Scott,[559] and

---

[549] *SVU Bulletin,* vol. 10, No. 2 (May 1989), p. 6.
[550] *Zprávy SVU,* vol. 31, No. 3 (July-August 1989), p. 1; *SVU Bulletin,* vol. 10, No. 4 (October 1989), pp 13-14.
[551] *Zprávy SVU,* vol. 31, No. 1 (January-February 1989), pp. 2-3.
[552] *Zprávy SVU,,* vol. 31, No. 2 (March-April 1989), pp. 1-2; *SVU Bulletin ,* vol. 10, No. 4 (October 1989), pp. 5–8.
[553] Jan Milič Lochman (1922-2004), Rector, Basel University, Switzerland.
[554] David R. Holeton (1948-), lecturer, Trinity College, Toronto, Canada.
[555] Professor, Bethany Theological Seminary, Oakbrook, IL
[556] Professor, Moravian Theological Seminary, Bethlehem, PA.
[557] Professor, Comenius Theological Faculty, Prague.
[558] Josef Anderle (1924-), professor of history, University of North Carolina.

Prof. Thomas Sovík.[560] I also took part in the program, talking about the Formative Years of the Moravian Church in America. The program concluded with a concert of Czech organ music, with Godfrey Tománek at the organ.

Sunday morning participants were invited to attend the services at the Moravian Brethren Central Church in Bethlehem, featuring traditional Moravian music and the Rev. Dr. Jan Milič Lochman, who specifically flew in for the occasion from Switzerland, at the pulpit. In the afternoon, during a visit to the famous Moravian Archives, the participants had an opportunity to see old hymnals in the Czech language and one of the original copies of the Kralice Bible ("Kralická bible").

The Bethlehem Conference was an uplifting experience for everyone. Moreover, the discussions have conclusively shown that the Moravian Church is a spiritual heir of the ancient *Unitas Fratrum*, and that the renewed Church was a direct result of the perseverance and diligent efforts of the descendants of the Bohemian Brethren from Czech Lands, which has not been heretofore known. The Conference also set the foundation for President Havel's 1991 visit to Bethlehem, when he was awarded the Comenius Medal there. An interesting commentary on the Conference was published in the November-December 1989 issue of *Zprávy SVU*.[561]

On November 4, 1989, at St. Antony's College at Oxford, the SVU British Chapter organized a one-day conference, bearing the title "Czechoslovakia in Europe." The morning session focused on the role of literature, with active participation by Dr. B. Bradbrook[562] (Cambridge), Robert Porter (University of Bristol), Dr. James Naughton (University of Oxford) and Dr. Igor Hájek.[563] (Glasgow). The afternoon session dealt with Czechoslovakia's international position. The speakers included

---

[559] Professor, Southern Connecticut State University.
[560] Thomas P. Sovík (1953-), chairman, Division of Music History, University of North Texas.
[561] *Zprávy SVU*, vol. 31, No. 6 (November-December 1989), pp. 9-10; *Ibid.*, pp. 10-12.
[562] Bohuslava R. Bradbrook (1922-), lecturer, University College of North Wales, Bangor, UK.
[563] Igor Hájek (1931-1995), Professor, Slavonic Dept., University of Glasgow, Scotland.

Harry Hanák[564] (University of London), Dr. Borek Hnízdo[565] (London), Dr. Alex Pravda[566] (Oxford) and Dr. Jaroslav Krejčí (Lancaster).

November 1989 was a remarkable and eventful month in the history of Czechoslovakia. After forty years of monopolistic misrule by the Communist Party, democracy was restored to this traditionally democratic land, thanks to the bloodless Prague "Velvet Revolution." This was also a turning point in the major aims and the activities of the Czechoslovak Society of Arts and Sciences.

The Executive Board did little, at first, in response to what was happening in our homeland, except sending out congratulatory telegrams. Finally, at Jaroš Němec's and my urging, they agreed to create a special fund[567] to assist Czechoslovakia. When our Collegium of Presidents got into the act in early February 1990,[568] responding favorably to Past Presidents' recommendation, they also concurred with the establishment of the new Commission for Cooperation with Czechoslovakia and the governing Policy, Planning and Coordination Council, with Zdeněk Slouka[569] in charge. Since then, it was this Council where the action was. To be sure, Nábělek, together with several Board members, had the opportunity to visit President Havel at the Prague Castle, as arranged by Pavel Pecháček, but this was essentially a social call.

The last major event of Nábělek's Presidency was the SVU World Congress, held at the Royal York Hotel in Toronto, Ontario, Canada on 11-14 October 1990. The preliminary announcement of the Congress and the planned program appeared in the August issue of *SVU Bulletin*[570] and the September 1989 issue of *Zprávy SVU*.[571]

---

[564] Harry Hanák (1930-), Reader, School of Slavonic and East European Studies, University of London, UK.

[565] Borek Hnízdo (1952-), historian with the University of London.

[566] Alex Pravda was a Fellow of the Russian and East European Centre, St. Antony's College, University of Oxford, UK.

[567] *Zprávy SVU*, vol. 31, No. 6 (November-December 1989), pp. 2-3.

[568] *Zprávy SVU*, vol. 32, No. 1 (January-February 1990), pp. 7-8.

[569] Zdeněk J. Slouka (1923-), professor of international law and relations, Lehigh University, Bethlehem, PA.

[570] *SVU Bulletin*, vol. 10, No. 3 (August 1989), pp. 5-8.

[571] *Zprávy SVU*, vol. 31, No. 4-5 (September-October 1989), pp. 1-5.

The Congress was convened in an atmosphere, refreshed by the pleasant breezes, emanating from the unprecedented changes in Czechoslovakia, where many SVU members had their roots. Its academic program offered[572] sessions on history, economics, sociology, biology/medicine, science/technology, literature, linguistics, musicology, fine arts, performing arts, etc. There were also several symposia on a variety of topics, such as "Karel Čapek's World," "Bohuslav Martinů," "Czechoslovak Jewry," "Czechs and Slovaks Abroad," "Cancer Research," "Czechoslovak Sokol," "Free Market and Constrained Conditions," "Native Lands in Last Two Centuries" and "Contemporary Czechoslovakia." In addition, there were the traditional readings from contemporary Czech and Slovak writers, art exhibit, concert of Czech and Slovak music, guided tours and a gala evening with a banquet and dance.

During the banquet several distinguished guests gave addresses, including the Hon. Rudolf Schuster,[573] Dr. Jiří Šetlík,[574] the Hon. Pauline Browes, MP,[575] the Hon. Art Aggleton,[576] Prof. Josef Jařáb[577] and Prof. Milan Štefanovič.[578]

---

[572] Counselor for Cultural Affairs, Embassy of ČSFR in the US.

[573] Rudolf Schuster (1934-), Ambassador of ČSFR in Canada; he later became the 2nd President of the newly established Slovak Republic (1999-2004).

[574] Jiří Šetlík (1929-), Counselor for Cultural Affairs, ČSFR Embassy, Washington, DC.

[575] Prime Minister of Canada.

[576] Mayor of Toronto.

[577] Josef Jařáb (1937-), Chancellor of Palacký University, Olomouc.

[578] Chancellor of Comenius University, Bratislava.

# Part III
# The Aftermath of the Velvet Revolution

# 28
## The Collegium of Presidents Acts

The unprecedented evens in Czechoslovakia during the memorable six-week period between November 17 and December 29, 1989, for which the term "Velvet Revolution" was coined, led to the bloodless overthrow of the hated Soviet regime and return to democracy to this traditionally democratic land. The new situation afforded the Society formidable challenges, as well as unparalleled opportunities. It also made a great impact on me personally and influenced my decision to become again active in SVU, after eleven years of "retirement."

Frankly, neither I, nor any other Past SVU President, were particularly happy with the relative inactivity and slow responsiveness of the then Executive Board to the fast moving events in the old country. It was only at Jaroš Němec's and my initiative that the Executive Board finally established a special fund to aid Czechoslovakia, which gave the impetus to individual SVU Chapters worldwide to follow suit and proceed with their own fund-raising activities.[579]

Under the circumstances, we saw it appropriate to convene a special meeting of the Past Presidents, in their capacity as members of the Collegium of Presidents,[580] to discuss the situation and make recommendations, as they saw fit.

The Collegium, consisting of Dr. Jaroslav Němec, Dr. Leopold Pospíšil, Dr. Jan F. Tříska and myself,[581] met on 2 February 1990 in my residence in Rockville, and again the next day with an enlarged group, including Dr. A. B. Bořkovec, Dr. A. Eliáš, Dr. T. Gibian, Dr. Zdeněk

---

[579] *Zprávy SVU,* vol. 31 (Nov.-Dec. 1989), No. 6, pp. 2-3.

[580] Special SVU organ composed of the Past SVU Presidents, to provide counsel to the SVU leadership in matters of basic importance to the Society. The SVU Bylaws empower the Collegium to convene its own meetings and through its initiative develop and send specific recommendations to any organ of the Society, if it deems it appropriate.

[581] The remaining members: Dr. René Wellek, Dr. Schwarzenberg and Dr. Nehněvajsa, could not attend because of illness.

Slouka and Ms. G. B. Lovecky[582] and later Dr. Madeleine Korbel Albright.[583] The result of the meetings led to a Memorandum which was circulated to SVU leadership and made public.

The Memorandum[584] advocated the reorientation of the Society's aims toward assisting the new democratic Czechoslovakia with its needs. Apart from strengthening the newly established Fund for Free Czechoslovakia, it recommended that an official delegation of experts be sent to Czechoslovakia to make initial contacts with the major scientific and cultural institutions and make preliminary assessment of the magnitude of problems the country was facing, particularly in those areas where the Society had a comparative advantage.

It further advocated establishing a Coordinating Council for the purpose of determining priorities and specific actions in concert with related activities of other organizations, working on behalf of Czechoslovakia.

Because of its historical significance, the English translation of the Memorandum is reproduced below:

### Memorandum of the Collegium of SVU Presidents

The memorandum is the result of the meeting of the Collegium of SVU Presidents convened on 2-3 February 1990 in Rockville. MD, in the presence of former SVU presidents: Dr. J. Němec, Dr. L. J. Pospíšil, Dr. M. Rechcígl and Dr. J. F. Tříska. Because of illness or other pressing matters, Dr. R. Wellek. Dr. F. Schwarzenberg and Dr. Nehněvajsa could not attend.

For discussion several guests were invited, namely Dr. A. B. Bořkovec, Dr. A. Eliáš. Dr. T. Gibian, Dr. Z. Slouka. Ms. G. B. Lovecky and later also Dr. Madeleine Korbel Albright.

As the outcome of the discussions came the realization that the revolutionary events in the Central and Eastern Europe place our

---

[582] Georgine B. Lovecky held the position of area chief for Eastern Europe, Council for International Exchange of Scholars, Washington, DC. She had responsibility for the Fulbright Program.

[583] Madeleine Korbel Albright (1937-), at that time, professor of international relations and director for Women in Foreign Service Program, School of Foreign Service, Georgetown University, Washington, DC; later US Secretary of State.

[584] *Zprávy SVU,* vol. 32, No. 1 (Jan-Feb. 1990), pp. 7-8.

native Czechoslovakia, as well as SVU and, in fact, every one of our members into a new situation with new responsibilities.

At the time SVU was established, we stood in the promontory of the free Czechoslovak culture. We tried, and still continue to do so, to defend the good name of Czechoslovakia in the free world and the right of its peoples for independence. We opened, and still do, to the free world the doors to Czechoslovakia, which were closed to the democracies by the Communists.

We will continue in our heretofore activities even hereafter, however, our new and the main goal must be, above all, the help to our homeland. We realize that the material assistance of the country, impoverished through forty years in bondage, is the main focus, but we must also think about the future and contribute to the liberated land with the know-how of our members, especially in areas of arts and sciences of which it was deprived during the Communist era, when they were ignored or suppressed.

The question of material help has been, at least partially, addressed by the SVU Executive Board. by the establishment of a special Fund for Free Czechoslovakia. We hope that our members will fully endorse this action and generously support it. With reference to the assistance to Czechoslovak sciences and arts, or more specifically to scientists and artists, the dimension of the needs. the priorities, location and competent persons for contact have, at this point not as yet been determined

The Collegium of SVU Presidents therefore recommends that an official SVU delegation be sent to Czechoslovakia, consisting of the representatives of the Executive Board, the Collegium of Presidents and several additional known members of the Society. The assignment of the delegation will be to meet with the representatives of the leading Czech and Slovak institutions, especially universities, the Academies, spokesmen of the Ministry of Education and other important organizations relating to arts and sciences. For such meetings and exchange of views, the work conferences would probably be best suited, especially in Prague, but also in Brno and Bratislava.

The Collegium of SVU Presidents feels that the most suitable time for such conference is September, since it will be after the elections and the summer rush of tourists in the cities will be over.

It is assumed that each member of the delegation will pay his own expenses, including transportation. The appropriate number of the delegation seems a group of fifteen persons.

It is probable that the working conference in Czechoslovakia will bring detailed information on the type of assistance the Czechoslovak arts and sciences need and also explain in Czechoslovakia what they can reasonably expect from the SVU.

The SVU Executive Board is immediately urged to establish a coordinating council which will be given the responsibility for establishing priorities in the framework and possibilities of our Society and at the same time, it should follow the action of other organizations on behalf of Czechoslovakia to avoid unnecessary duplication. Furthermore, if our recommendation of sending an official delegation to Czechoslovakia is approved, this Council should assume responsibility for the preparation of the agenda for the working conference in Czechoslovakia.

We appeal to all our members, without delay, to fill out the biographical questionnaire so that the new *SVU Biographical Directory* can be completed which will become an indispensable tool in the work ahead. Individual members should particularly pay special attention to the category of their expertise in connection with the needs of new Czechoslovakia and concrete suggestions for possible assistance that should be organized.

As for the current agenda of the Executive Board, the Collegium of Presidents is of the opinion that issuance of the English periodical is absolutely essential and is convinced that in the future such periodical will gain considerable importance in the work of SVU. It is necessary to find a suitable editor and give him assistance by appointing at least a six-member Editorial board, consisting of qualified persons. Enhancing the quality and diversifying the contents would undoubtedly widen the readers' community, and, above all, an important role be vested in the "managing editor." That is where in the past was our weakness.

Another recommendation the Collegium makes is to open the membership to scientists and artists in Czechoslovakia with a lower membership fee (for example $5). It could be paid in Czech crowns, money deposited in a new SVU account in Czechoslovakia, which could be used for paying SVU expenses in that country.

The Collegium of Presidents presents this Memorandum with the request that the SVU Executive Board give it the attention it deserves.

In the name of the Collegium, of Presidents

> Dr. Jaroslav Němec
> Dr. Jan F. Třiska
> Dr. Leopold Pospíšil
> Dr. Miloslav Rechcígl, Jr.

*In Washington, DC, 7 February 1990*

The reason for the inclusion of the strong language in the Memorandum about the English periodical was the concern that the Executive Board may decide to stop publishing the periodical, as some of the Board members proposed.

Two issues that were also discussed at some length, although there is no mention of it in the Memorandum, namely that the official delegation bring up the subject with the appropriate people in Prague of the suitability of holding the next SVU World Congress in Czechoslovakia and also set the stage for establishing a new SVU Chapter in Prague.[585]

As a result of this initiative, the Executive Board approved the creation of SVU Commission for Cooperation with Czechoslovakia and a narrower Planning, Policy and Coordination Council.[586] The latter body comprised Prof. Zdeněk Slouka, Chairman, and Dr. Alexej B. Bořkovec, Dr. Andrew Eliáš, Dr. Thomas Gibian, Prof. Jiří Nehněvajsa, Dr. Miloslav Rechcígl, Jr., Dr. Zdeněk Suda, Dr. Michael Šumichrast, and Prof. Jan F. Třiska.

Immediately after the Velvet Revolution, the Czechoslovak borders opened and various Czechoslovak groups began arriving in the US Capital and frequently also met with the key members of our SVU Commission. One of the earliest such meeting was held with the young representatives of the Civic Forum. At the request of the Czechoslovak Embassy, I arranged a meeting between them and the SVU leadership in

---

[585] Actually both of theses issues were brought up, by Slouka and myself, during our official visit in Prague which led to the realization of both ideas.

[586] *Zprávy SVU*, vol. 32 (March-April 1990), No. 2, p. 15.

the Cosmos Club,[587] of which I was a member. The group included President Havel's brother Ivan[588] and his wife Dáša, Martin Palous,[589] publicist Zdeněk Urbánek[590] and several members of the Czechoslovak Society of Arts and Sciences, including Thomas Gibian, Alexej Bořkovec, Vladimír Kabeš and myself.

Through my own contacts, SVU established ties with the Czechoslovak Council of Scientific Societies,[591] a supreme coordinating body of some sixty most important scientific and scholarly societies in Czechoslovakia, associated with the Czechoslovak and Slovak Academies of Sciences. The Society officially became a foreign member of the Council of Scientific Societies and I was appointed a member of its governing board.

The first official contact with the Czechoslovak Embassy occurred upon the arrival in the US of Rita Klímová[592] and her appointment as the first Ambassador of the democratic Czechoslovakia to the US. She arrived in Washington, DC with President Václav Havel in his Presidential plane. The Czechoslovak Washington community went out in full force to welcome them at the airport. We were subsequently invited to the Czechoslovak Embassy where a party was held on which occasion Eva and I had the opportunity to exchange a few words with President Havel and Ambassador Klímová.

---

[587] The meeting took place on Friday, January 26, 1990.

[588] Ivan Havel (1938-), computer scientist; he became director, Center for Theoretical Study, Charles University, Prague.

[589] Martin Palouš (1950-), dissident, former spokesman for Charter 77; he later became Ambassador of the Czech Republic to the US.

[590] Zdeněk Urbánek (1917-), Czech writer, publicist and former dissident.

[591] In Czech: Rada vědeckých společností.

[592] Rita Klímová (1931-1993), a former dissident and later Ambassador of Czechoslovakia to the US, Washington, DC.

# 29
# SVU Commission for Cooperation with Czechoslovakia

Responding to the dramatic changes in Czechoslovakia and to the new opportunities for close cooperation between our Society and Czech and Slovak institutions, groups and individuals, at the urging of the Past SVU Presidents, the Executive Board created, in March 1990, a Policy, Planning and Coordination Council and its parent SVU Commission for Cooperation with Czechoslovakia.[593]

The responsibility of the Council, with its members appointed by the Board, was to establish priorities among the many tasks newly facing the society in Czechoslovakia; to initiate, direct and coordinate supportive and cooperative projects; and, in order to expand the society's capabilities, to develop a working liaison with other organizations with compatible goals.

The function of the broader Commission, with members co-opted according to their specific interests, talents and willingness to serve, was to assume responsibility for the implementation of discrete tasks.

Within the normal range of difficulties characteristic for all organizations functioning on an entirely voluntary basis and without an operating budget, the Council and the Commission, in its opening six-month phase, achieved several of its initial goals.[594]

As a matter of policy, the Council decided to concentrate its primary efforts not on individual requests for assistance, whether from Czechoslovakia or elsewhere, but on broader, largely institutional projects and actions contributing to the long-term process of restoring and reforming Czechoslovak education, sciences and arts. Regarding aid to individuals, the Council referred individual requests to our Society

---

[593] *Zprávy SVU,* vol. 32, No. 2 (March-April 1990), p. 15; *SVU Bulletin,* vol. 11, No. 2 (May 1990), p. 9.

[594] *Zprávy SVU,* vol. 30, No. 4 (July-August 1990), pp. 8-9; *SVU Bulletin,* vol. 11, No. 3 (August 1990), pp. 6-7.

members, who were in a position to help or advise, or to appropriate organizations.

The Council broadened its operational range by establishing close cooperation with several institutions and agencies: the Institute of International Education, the Charter 77 Foundation, The Soros Fund, the National Endowment for Democracy, several university centers and programs, US Federal Agencies, the Czechoslovak Embassy in Washington, and some business organizations active in the educational sphere.

These links and contacts assisted the Council in the accomplishment of several tasks high on the list of priorities:

1. In July, a month-long seminar in economics, with some thirty Czech and Slovak professors of economics as participants, was held at Charles University in Prague. Its coordinator, a Society member and an outstanding American economist, was selected on the Council's advice by the sponsoring agency, the Institute of International Education.

2. In July-August, another month-long seminar for Czech and Slovak professors of social sciences, sponsored by the Charter 77 Foundation and the Soros Fund, was held at Palacký University in Olomouc. Again with some thirty participants, the seminar was entirely organized by the Council, led and coordinated by a prominent American sociologist from the Society's ranks, and taught by four economists with recognized competence in their fields, all of them again the Society's members.

3. Through direct contacts with the director of the European office of the Apple Computer Co. in Paris, the Council was instrumental in arranging an outright donation by the company to Czechoslovak universities of three top-line Macintosh computers with two laser printers; through private solicitation of funds, the Council also obtained three more Macintosh computers of a lower order and a FAX machine for universities' use. All equipment is now in place.

During the summer, Council members established extensive contacts with most Czech and Slovak universities, academies of science, federal and state ministries, President Havel's office, and a number of other Czech and Slovak institutions, including the Czechoslovak Foreign

Institute and Matica slovenská. As a result of this preparatory work, the following activities were undertaken:

a) The Council secured full cooperation of the congressional office of Charles University and of other organizations for preparing the Society's 16th World Congress in 1992 in Prague;. At the Council's request, the Executive Board approved in July the location of the Congress in the Czechoslovak capital.

b). At the request of the Institute of International Education, Chairman of the Council wrote an extensive analytical report on models of international educational cooperation in central Europe; much of this work was based on the Council's familiarity with the Czechoslovak educational setting. The report was published by the Institute for distribution to several thousand professionals at some 600 universities associated with the Institute.

c). President Havel accepted the invitation, extended to him by Slouka, on the Council's behalf, to come to the United States for an 11-day unofficial visit under the aegis of the Society. The President was to arrive on 10 April 1991. The President's itinerary was prepared by Z. Slouka, in cooperation with several of us, the President's office, and the Czechoslovak Embassy in Washington. Unfortunately, Slouka's sudden heart attack changed the entire planning process and the SVU, as such, was completely left out.

# 30
# Fact-Finding Mission to Czechoslovakia

The most important undertaking of the SVU Commission for Cooperation with Czechoslovakia was the fact-finding mission in Czechoslovakia, carried out by its Working Group in 1990.

From my perspective, the ball began rolling with the official invitation letter from the head of the Working Group Zdeněk Slouka sent to me at my AID address. For its historical importance, its contents are reproduced below in full:

.......

*Lehigh University – Department of International Relations*
*Maginnes Hall 9*
*Bethlehem, Pennsylvania 18015*
*telephone (215) 758-3390*
*August 8, 1990*

Dr. Miloslav Rechcígl
Office of Science Advisor
Agency for International Development
Washington, DC 20523

During the two weeks between 15-28 September 1990, a small group of professionals from the United States will be visiting Czechoslovak academic, research and other related institutions to assess their capabilities and needs with a view towards a variety of cooperative and supportive projects. I am writing now to invite your participation in the group. As a matter of fact your expertise in research management and your intimate knowledge of the Czechoslovak scientific landscape make your participation quite vital; I sincerely hope you will be able to join us.

I am writing this letter under my various hats as the chairman of the Commission for Cooperation with Czechoslovakia of the Czechoslovak Society of Arts and Sciences (SVU); as a board member of the Charter 77 Foundation; as a consultant for the Institute for International Education (I.I.E., New York); and, finally, as a member of President Havel's Board of International Advisors with a specific mandate in the area of academic and research undertakings. Nominally, the working visit will be sponsored by SVU; however, the other institutions are keenly interested in the process and product of the assessment and are supportive of the effort.

Apart from fairly intensive learning about a variety of aspects of Czechoslovak scientific and academic life, we hope to accomplish two things: (1) to evaluate the capacity of individuals and institutions in Czechoslovakia to effectively absorb various forms of future assistance from abroad; (2) to set the stage for a small number of cooperative projects with our Czech and Slovak colleagues and institutions (e.g., seminars, workshops, training courses). I would hope that throughout the trip you would be able to concentrate on the area of scientific research and its management.

If you accept this invitation – and I most fervently hope you will be able to do so – I will furnish you with all other particulars.

Cordially yours,

Z. J. Slouka
Cohen Professor of International Relations

My superiors were sympathetic to the idea of my participation and within a few days we sent a cable to US Embassy to Prague about my impending visit. After getting the necessary clearances from the various parts of the State Department, I did not anticipate any problems from the higher ups. So without further ado I began making the necessary plans.

From the very beginning, we felt that Charles University should be the center of our operations in Prague where most of the meetings took place. In order to make our mission effective I suggested to Zdeněk Slouka that we organize two separate meetings, one with the rectors and other high level university officials and the other with scientists and researchers. Ing. Ladislav Ševela who was our principal contact at the University, sent Zdeněk Slouka the following letter[595] in response to our suggestions:

---

[595] Translated from the Czech original by M.R.

*In Prague, August 23, 1990*

Dear Zdeněk:

Thank you for your FAX of August 15, 1990. Your suggestion to arrange two conferences with the representatives of the Commission for Cooperation with Czechoslovakia was discussed with the Rector of Charles University Prof. Palouš. Vice Rector Prof. Lojda and JUDr. Winkler, the University Questor, all of whom expressed great interest and offered full support for the idea. We have in the meantime sent out in the name of the Rector a letter addressed to deans of all faculties of Charles University, as well as to Rectors of VŠZ[596], ČVUT,[597] VŠCHT[598] in Prague, Masaryk University in Brno, Palacký University in Olomouc and the presidium of the Czechoslovak Academy of Sciences in Prague with the request to send their responsible representatives to our two conferences arranged as follows:

1. Conference with the university representatives will be held on September 28 from 9-11 AM in the small auditorium at Karolinum.

2. Conference with researchers will take place on September 29 from 9-12 AM in the Karolinum on the second floor.

The address is: Charles University, Ovocný trh 3-5, Praha 1

The information is also being sent to MSMT CSF and Rada vysokých škol CR.[599]

Simultaneously I would like to inform you that we have reserved for you room No. 408 in the hotel of Charles University from September 15-22. and for Dr. Rechcígl and his wife a twin bedroom for the same period.

Cordially,

*Ing. Ladislav Ševela*

.......

---

[596] Vysoká škola zemědělská – Czech University of Agriculture, Prague.
[597] Vysoké učení technické – Czech Technical University, Prague.
[598] Vysoká škola chemicko-technologická – University of Chemical Technology, Prague.
[599] Council of Czechoslovak Institutions of Higher Learning.

To keep the SVU leadership informed about our planned visit, Zdeněk Slouka sent the following memorandum to SVU President and Secretary-General with copies to members of the SVU Council.

*Czechoslovak Society of Arts and Sciences*
*Commission for Cooperation with Czechoslovakia*
*Policy, Planning and Coordination Council*

To: Igor Nábělek, Miloš Kučera; cc: Council members

From: Zdeněk Slouka

Date: 28 August 1990

This interim memorandum, for the record, refers to the forthcoming visit to Czechoslovakia by a working delegation organized by the SVU Policy, Planning and Coordination Council within the Commission on Cooperation with Czechoslovakia (CCC). The initial plans for the visit was unanimously approved on 3 May 1990 by CCC, as recorded in the minutes of that meeting. The general itinerary and the objectives of the visit were discussed in June and in August with the representatives of interested academic institutions in Czechoslovakia, as well as with the staff of the office of President Havel on whose International Board of Advisors the chairman of the Council serves.

The working visit will take place between 17 and 28 September 1990; some members of the group will stay in Czechoslovakia the entire two weeks, others for shorter periods. No SVU funds will be expended for the visit. Some members of the group already are in Czechoslovakia on their own business. The composition of the group is now being finalized in conformity with the disciplinary preferences of our Czech and Slovak colleagues and according to the ability of the members to be in Prague at the scheduled time.

The primary goal of the visit is to establish professional contacts between the respective peers at home and abroad in order to determine the appropriate forms of future cooperation, i.e., the holding of professional seminars or workshops, joint research projects, special lectures, professional exchanges, distribution of print and non-print media, etc. For projects mutually agreed upon, the CCC and the council will seek funding from all appropriate sources. The disciplinary fields initially designated by our Czech and Slovak contacts as deserving specific attention include research management, environmental studies, international studies, political economy, American studies, sociology, and comparative politology. Members of the SVU-CCC group will visit academic and other related institutions throughout Czechoslovakia.

(The use of English in this memorandum reflects the linguistic diversity of CCC membership.)

*Dr. Zdeněk J. Slouka*
*207 Maginnes Hall 9,*
*Lehigh University, Bethlehem, PA 18015*

.......

Initially, we considered the following individuals for our working group: George Kvídera, George Klír, Andrew Eliáš, Vladimír Slámečka. Milan Trpiš, Anton Novacký, Vladimir Novotný, Jaroslav Němec, Jan Tříska, Zdeněk Suda, Zdeněk Slouka and myself. Because of various conflicts the number of participants was reduced to six official representatives. The final makeup of the working group[600] comprised the following individuals: Prof. Zdeněk Slouka,[601] Prof. Jan F. Tříska,[602] Prof. Paul Trenský,[603] Dr. Miloslav Rechcígl, Jr.[604] and Prof. Anton Novacký.[605] Prof. Novacký and I were accompanied by our wives. This working group further extended the Society's cooperative links with the Czech and Slovak universities, academies of science, governmental agencies, and a variety of institutions.

The working group's visit was scheduled between 17th and 28th September 1990. Some members of the group were to stay in Czechoslovakia the entire two week period while others for shorter time.

---

[600] As reported in *Zprávy SVU*. vol. 33 (May-June 1991), No. 3, pp. 14-15.

[601] Lehigh University; international law and relations, international transfer of knowledge, academic management; group coordinator.

[602] Stanford University; political science, international law, comparative politics.

[603] Fordham University; comparative literature, philology, dramatic arts, Slavic studies.

[604] U.S. Agency for International Development; natural sciences, biotechnology, international development, research management.

[605] University of Missouri, natural sciences, environmental sciences.

*Fact-Finding Mission to Czechoslovakia* 167

My own travel plan was to leave on Friday September 14 at 5:05 PM from Dulles Airport via Lufthansa 1404, arriving at Frankfurt at 9:20 AM the following day and then taking another flight which would get us to Prague at 10:25 AM. Our return to the US was slated for October 1, leaving Prague at 7:55 AM via Pan Am, with a stop in Frankfurt and arriving in Washington at Dulles Airport at 4:05 PM.

We[606] arrived in Prague on Saturday, September 15, while others came a day later. We stayed at a small hotel at Karolinum, belonging to Charles University, on the Celetná Street. As noted from the agenda below, we had a very busy schedule from the day we arrived until we left, with little time to spare.

Except for a rather sketchy report in the July 1991 issue of *Zprávy SVU*,[607] there was hardly anything written about this important mission the Working Groups of the SVU Commission for Cooperation with Czechoslovakia had undertaken. I am therefore describing it in some detail, based on my personal notes.

**AGENDA**

<u>Monday – September 17</u>

8:00 AM   Breakfast at Karolinum

9:00 AM   Meeting with Ing. Ladislav Ševela, head of the International department of Charles University to discuss details of our stay.

12:00 PM  Lunch with Vice Rector Zdeněk Lojda in the restaurant "U pavouka" on the Celetná Street.

*Afternoon*
US Embassy
   Meeting with Russell Baker and Timothy Savage

Ministry of Foreign Affairs –
   Meeting with Minister Jiří Diensbier and Deputy Minister Zdeněk Pírek

Editorial Offices of the important Czech daily newspaper "*Lidové noviny*" –
   Meeting with Ing. Michal Klíma, Director, Ing. Miloš Lexa, of International department and J. Ruml.

---

[606] My wife Eva accompanied me on this trip.
[607] *Zprávy SVU*, vol. 38, No. 3 (May-June 1991), pp. 14-15.

7:30 PM   Supper in Chinese restaurant, Janáčkovo nábřeží, Praha 5.

*Tuesday, September 18*

8: 00 AM   Breakfast at Karolinum

9:00 AM   Conference – Small Auditorium of Karolinum
Meeting with top officials of universities and other institutions in charge of the programs in the field of natural sciences, environmental sciences, health, biotechnology and agriculture.

11:30 AM Reception Hall of Karolinum –
Private meeting with Prof. Radim Palouš, Rector of Charles University

12:00 PM Official dinner – Restaurant "U Pavouka"

12: 30 PM Sightseeing of Prague

7:00 PM   Supper in the Restaurant "Barjožka"

*Wednesday – September 19*

8:00 AM   Breakfast

9:00 AM   Small Auditorium of Karolinum

Meeting with Researchers and Scientists

1:00 PM   Meeting with Rector of CVUT, S. Hanzl

3:00 PM   Meeting at the Czechoslovak Academy of Sciences with Ing. Vladislav Hančil, Ing. Jiří Niederle and Pavel Vlasák

7:00 PM   Supper at Restaurant "Berjožka"

*Thursday – September 20*

8:00 AM   Breakfast

9:30 AM   Meeting with Dr. Landa of Czechoslovak Academy of Sciences

10:00 AM Meeting with Prof. Kabert of University of Nitra

11:30 AM Large Auditorium Karolinum –
Awarding honorary doctorate to J. J. Delors, Chairman of the Committee of European Societies

*Afternoon*
    Departure by the University car for Bratislava. There were six of us: Prof. Tříska and his wife, Prof. Novacký and his wife, myself and Eva.

*Evening*
    Upon arrival late at night we were awaited by Ing. F. Hanic, Vice President of the Slovak Academy of Sciences with some refreshments who then escorted us to the University dorms where we stayed over night.

<u>Friday – September 21</u>

The meeting took place at the Slovak Academy of Sciences, Bratislava.
Present were:

Ministry of Education –
    Dr. Vladimír Cholrad, Deputy Minister
    Dr. Fryštacký, Rector, Slovak Technical University

Slovak Academy of Sciences –
    Dr. Ladislav Macho, President
    Dr. Hajduk, Science Secretary
    Ing. F. Hanic, Vice President

Meeting with scientists and researchers, representing Comenius University and other institutions of higher learning

At the conclusion of the meetings, we drove to Martin – because I wanted to have a look at the famous cultural institution – Matica slovenská, where we met with Ing. Jozef Markuš, Chairman of the Board

Subsequently we were invited to Smolenica Mansion where we were all treated to their famous "palačinky"(blintzes).

<u>Monday – September 24</u>

*Morning*
Visiting Czechoslovak Foreign Institute –
    Meeting with Ing. Opatrný, President; Ing. Šimerka, International Relations; Ing. Kolinský, Vice President

<u>Tuesday – September 25</u>
*Morning*
Office of the President –
    Meeting with Karel Schwarzenberg

<u>Wednesday – September 26</u>
Biological Center, České Budějovice, Czechoslovak Academy of Sciences –
    Meeting with Prof. Vladimír Landa and other research scientists

<u>Thursday – September 27</u>
*Morning*
Czech University of Agriculture, Praha – Suchdol

*Afternoon*
Náprstek Museum
Ethnographic Institute, Czechoslovak Academy of Sciences – Dr. Brouček
Institute for Contemporary History – Dr. Vilém Prečan
Czechoslovak Society for History of Science and Technology
National Technical Museum

<u>Friday – September 28</u>
Ministry of Education (Tříska and I met with Prof. Dr. Libor Pátý, Deputy
    Minister)
Law School
Club "Všehrd"
Meeting with representatives of the Brno Institute of Technology

..............

    At the outset of the visit, the working group held two conferences at Charles University. The first one, on September 18, which was limited to top echelons of the major institutions of higher learning in Czechoslovakia, was attended by about 30 Rectors, Vice Rectors and Deans of most Czech and Slovak universities and by officers of both Academies of Science. The second conference included forty-two leading scholars, scientists and working researchers. As I recall, the idea of dividing the participants in this matter was my idea.
    According to the attendance sheet, which I have, the first day was attended by the following individuals:

Charles University:
> Prof Dr. Radim Palouš, CSc. – Rector
> Prof. MUDr. Zdeněk Lojda, DrSc. – Vice Rector
> Ing. L. Ševela
> Ing. J. Kofroň – OZS

Pedagogic Faculty:
> Prof. Černá

Pharmacy Faculty:
> Doc. Semecký, CSc.
> Prof. Voráček

Medicine Faculty:
> Prof. Herget
> Prof. Jodl
> Dr. Dvořák
> Doc. Provazník
> Doc. Rokyta

Medicine Faculty, Hradec Kralove:
> Doc. Červinka

Medicine Faculty, Plzen:
> Doc. Aujedská

Physical Education Faculty:
> Dr. J. Soukup
> Dr. M. Ulbrichová

Palacky University in Olomouc:
> Prof. Hejtmánek

Masaryk University in Brno:
> Doc. Němec
> Dr. J. Beneš

University of Chemical Technology in Prague:
> Ing. Josef Korbel
> Doc. RNDr. J. Staněk

On September 19, the following individuals attended:

Charles University:
    Prof Dr. Radim Palouš, CSc. – Rector
    Prof. MUDr. Zdeněk Lojda, DrSc. – Vice Rector
    Ing. L. Ševela
    Ing. J. Kofroň – OZS

Natural Sciences Faculty:
    V. Štulík
    Doc. Kűhnl
    Doc. Ladislav Jánský
    Prof. Jeník

Mathematics & Physics Faculty:
    Josef Brechler

Medicine:
    Doc. K. Provazník
    Prof. Masopust
    Dr. Eva Seemanová
    Dr. Rokyta
    Dr. Dvořák
    Petr Goetz
    Milan Macek

Medicine, Hradec Králové:
    Doc. Červinka
    Prof. Fixa
    Doc. Hubková
    Dr. J. Cerman
    Dr. Žďárský
    Dr. Lomský
    Doc. Smejkalová
    Ivo Přiznal

Medicine, Plzen:
    Doc. Topolčan
    Doc. Koutenský
    Doc. Aujedská

Pharmacy Faculty:
    Doc. Dr. Semecký

Philosophy Faculty:
   J. Ottová

Social Sciences:
   Dr. Zora Stejskalová
   Dr. Hermenegilda Šimunková

Physical Education Faculty:
   MUDr. J. Pařízková
   Dr. Jan Heller
   Dr. Marie Ulbrichová

Czech Technical University, Prague:
   Vice Dean Miroslava Vrbová

Czech University of Agriculture:
   Prof. Svarlata
   Prof. V. Táborský
   Doc. A. Slabý
   P. Mader
   Doc. J. Cibulka
   Prof. V. Švachula

Czech University of Chemical Technology:
   Prof. Koutel
   Vice Rector Staněk

Czechoslovak Academy of Sciences:
   RNDr. Miloslav Lapka
   Vice President Milan Straškraba
   Jiří Olejníček

Palacký University, Olomouc:
   Doc. Evzen Weigl
   Ing. Jiri Kovařík
   RNDr. Jan Steigl
   Doc. Zdenek Stránský
   Doc. Jan Naus
   Doc. Vratislav Bednář

Masaryk University, Brno:
   Dr. Ivan Holoubek
   Doc. Jaroslav Benedík
   Jiřina Relochová
   Milan Dressler

University of Agriculture, Brno:
: Vice Rector Dalibor Povolný

Research Institute of Preventive Medicine, Bratislava:
: Anton Kočan

University of Maryland, European Division:
: Prof. Jiří Březina

..............

Before leaving for Prague, I prepared some "talking points," for our first organizational meeting in Prague. I should point out that they referred primarily to my own role and presentation:

### General Talking Points
### for SVU Organizational Meeting
### Scheduled for Monday, September 17

1. Composition of CCC Group: Slouka, Rechcígl, Tříska, Suda, Trenský, Novacký
(Eliáš and Hrubý may be added)
2. Purpose of Visit
3. Prepare Agenda for Tuesday Meeting
4. General Itinerary for the Visit
    a) Joint vs. Individual
    b) Principal Contacts (universities, Academies, Ministries, cultural institutions, professional organizations, research institutions, individuals)
    c) Geographical Areas (Prague, Brno, Olomouc, Bratislava, Nitra)
    d) Specific Assignments and Responsibilities
    Rechcígl – Science and research
    e) Discussion Topics
        (1) Major problems ČSFR is facing where SVU could be helpful
        (2) Options for the solution of the problems
        (3) Priorities
        (4) Establish contacts with institutions and individuals
        (5) ČSFR – SVU Information Center
        (6) Determine appropriate forms of cooperation
            Seminars or workshops
            Joint research projects
            Special lectures

Professional exchanges
Participation and organization of SVU World Congress
Distribution of publications
Computers
Fellowships, scholarships, grants
- (7) Printing and Publishing
- (8) SVU Chapter in ČSFR – liaison – open a bank account
- f) Possible Contacts: Charles University, Masaryk University, Komenský University, Palacký University, Czech University of Agriculture, Czech Institute of Technology, Czechoslovak Academy of Sciences, Slovak Academy of Sciences, Náprstek Museum, Památník národního písemnictví (National Museum of Czech Literature), Matica slovenská, Československý ústav zahraniční (ČSÚZ).

**Tentative Agenda and Talking Points for Tuesday Meeting with the University Leaders, Science Policy Makers, etc.**

1. Introduction of Participants
2. Purpose of the Visit
3. What is SVU
4. Miloslav Rechcígl – Science and Research
   a) came to learn and get acquainted, to listen and not to preach or tell what to do.
   b) get full understanding of the nature and magnitude of problems before considering possible solutions
   c) before leaving would like to obtain the following:
      (1) list of problems where science and research can help – arrive at some priorities
      (2) basis for justification of scientific research
      (3) understanding ČSFR science and technology infrastructure
      (4) list of ČSFR research institutions with addresses, telephone and FAX numbers
      (5) list of leading ČSFR researchers
      (6) set up a framework for future cooperation
5. Miloslav Rechcígl – Importance of Science and Research in Solving Pressing Problems of ČSFR
   a) Research Priority areas
      (1) Environmental restoration (global warming, pollution, etc.)

(2) Agricultural sustainability and production of save and wholesome nutritious food crops; utilizing ecological principles, biotechnological approaches, biological control measures.
(3) Biological diversity (chronic shortages of vegetables and fruits)
(4) Environmental health
(5) Automation, modeling, computer science
b) Specific researchable problems where ČSFR has expertise

..............

Our trip generated quite a bit of interest in Czechoslovakia, even in the press and radio and some of us gave interviews.[608]

---

[608] For example, Tříska and I were interviewed by Andrea Vernerová in *Demokrat*, November 19, 1990, p. 5, under the heading "Top Representatives of SVU in Czechoslovakia – Information as an Art."

# 31
# *Critical Assessment of Czechoslovak Needs*

This report[609] evaluates some of the needs and opportunities of the Czechoslovak academia in its efforts to re-establish its links with the institutions of higher education and research in other advanced democratic countries. The report is based on knowledge accumulated between January and August 1990 by individual members of the working group of the SVU Commission for Cooperation with Czechoslovakia during their extensive trips throughout Czechoslovakia, and by the group's two-week study trip in the Czech lands and Slovakia in September 1990.

The report is intended for the use by U.S. institutions and individuals involved in cooperative and assistance projects with Czech and Slovak academics, their Institutions and related private and public agencies.

### INTRODUCTION

Powerful social forces unleashed by its winter revolution are propelling Czechoslovakia along a trajectory that may carry it toward an advanced social system: a system in which those who combine knowledge, skills and an entrepreneurial spirit with tolerance and capability of sharing will be the cutting edge of positive social change.

The rites of passage are rigorous, complex and compelling. Strengths and weaknesses must be assessed. Needs and opportunities ranked. Priorities established, and skills honed to attend to them. Talents counted, cultivated and mobilized. The Czechs and the Slovaks must do it all and no one else can do it for them.

Those two nations in one state can do it in the same way – the only way – in which others, now in advanced stages of development, have done it before them and are doing it now. by incessant learning across national boundaries. They need to join the free transnational flows of knowledge about all things, and to take all they will have learned and

---

[609] Based on "Czechoslovakia, Knowledge, Skills, and Learning. Critical Assessment of Needs and Absorptive Capacity." First Report of the Working Group of the SVU Commission for Cooperation with Czechoslovakia.

then shape and sharpen it and make it fit their own image of a satisfying human and social life.

This report is about the process through which the Czechs and the Slovaks are joining the transnational community of learning, about their re-entry into, and blending with, the advanced civilization to which they can contribute and from which they can take. We do not stipulate what they should seek first and what second. We only record what we have learned from them about their needs as they see them. Only then, on the basis of our understanding of their perceived needs, we seek to critically assess the viability of their efforts to satisfy those needs through transnational communication, cooperation and sharing. Nor is this report addressed to Czechoslovakia. Its target is us. How can we best help in opening to the Czechs and the Slovaks the doors to post-industrial knowledge? Which of the doors? In what areas of knowledge can they find things most essential for their immediate and future needs, and at the least cost? What is their absorptive capacity in various fields? Where can we learn from them?

Purposes of Study Trip

The Working Group of the SVU Commission for Cooperation with Czechoslovakia visited Czech and Slovak academic and research institutions in September 1990 with a set of broad purposes:

- To learn directly from Czech and Slovak academics, scientists and administrators in various institutions of higher learning and research how they perceive their needs while striving to restructure and revitalize their common enterprise in its new setting of social – pluralism and free market economy.
- To judge the extent to which such needs can be served at least partly by re-aligning Czech and Slovak institutions of higher learning and research with their Western counterparts and sources of support, particularly but not exclusively in the United States.
- To assess the overall capacity of Czech and Slovak institutions of higher learning and research and of their professional personnel to benefit from transnational cooperative undertakings and projects of assistance, given the fact that the social, economic, institutional, technological and attitudinal infrastructures are still inadequate and in the process of major reconstruction.

- To offer to appropriate Western and particularly U.S. institutions and agencies an initial set of recommendations for cooperative and assistance projects that would be most cost-effective and mutually beneficial in areas of greatest need.

Participants, Time, Field

The SVU Working Group consisted of six American experts of Czech and Slovak origin. As a whole, the group represented some 150 man-years of professional experience chiefly in U.S. academic and research or research-related institutions. The participants' professional fields, subfields and specialties included social sciences (sociology; sociology of education; comparative government; international relations, law, and organization; transnational flows of science and technology; research management; academic management), humanities (linguistics: philology: comparative literature; dramatic arts), and natural sciences (biology; biochemistry; nutrition; plant pathology; subfields of agronomy; aspects of environmental management). All participants hold terminal degrees in their fields, and all are fluent in English and in Czech or Slovak. Additionally, this report also incorporates extensive observations made by economists who, as members of the Society, spent considerable periods during 1990 in Czechoslovakia but were unable to participate in the group study trip.

The working visit commenced on 17 September and was concluded on 29 September 1990. Some members of the group left earlier, with the minimum stay of one week for any member. However, five of the six members visited Czechoslovakia individually earlier in 1990, often for extended stays and in one case on five separate trips; thus the group visit itself benefited from previously established contacts, experiences and a broader understanding of Czechoslovak conditions.

The working contacts comprised all major academic and research institutions in the Czech lands and in Slovakia as primary targets, and governmental agencies relevant to education and research as secondary targets. The group met with high officials, faculty and research scientists at Charles University, the Czech Technical University and the Agricultural University, all in Prague; at Masaryk University, Technical University and Agricultural University in Brno and at Palacký University in Olomouc (both cities covered separately on a previous visit); at Komenský University, the Slovak Technical University and the university-level school of Transportation in Bratislava and at the Agricultural University in Nitra. The group and its individual members also met with the President and top officials and scientists of the Czechoslovak Academy of Sciences at its headquarters in Prague, at the South Bohemian Biological Center, and at the Nuclear Research Institute in Rez, as well as with Academicians from the Institutes of Sociology and of Economics. Similar substantive contacts were made with high level officials of the Slovak Academy of Sciences and its various institutes. Finally, the group had several discussions with top officials of both the Czech and Slovak ministries of education, with the Minister of Foreign Affairs and his deputies, and with top members of President Havel's office. Supplementary discussions were held at various independent agencies – the Czechoslovak Foreign Institute, Matica slovenská (cultural organization in Slovakia), the Society for the History of Science and Technology, the Charter 77 Foundation, and the daily *Lidové noviny*.

## SUBSTANTIVE FINDINGS AND ASSESSMENTS
BASIC NEEDS IN INFRASTRUCTURE

Before identifying an initial set of substantive needs in the Czechoslovak educational and research system and recommending appropriate responses to them, we need to raise the issue of infrastructure: the underlying sources, means, channels and technologies of communication without which the system as a whole cannot be effectively integrated into the educational and research systems of the advanced countries

The Czechoslovak communication infrastructure is weak, in some areas weaker than in others. Our Czech and Slovak respondents uniformly agreed that in order to cross the bridges to post-industrial knowledge and skills, they need better access to information about academic and research developments abroad and about the related learning opportunities. To mobilize talents from all institutions of higher learning and all research enterprises, more effective means of dissemination of relevant data are needed. Next, linguistic abilities, availability of foreign academic literature and other repositories of information and knowledge, and means of transnational personal communication, all need considerable strengthening.

Information, Dissemination. The flow of essential and accessible information into the Czechoslovak academic and research establishment from abroad is inadequate and uneven across the disciplines. One exception to this generalization are some scientific and technical programs of excellence which, having been politically unobtrusive, have developed over the years reasonably full communication links with their foreign counterparts. The second exception are a few individual scholars and researchers who, in various ways and often by chance, profit from personal contacts with professional colleagues abroad; these contacts and their information yields are, however, a jealously guarded commodity. The vast majority of research scientists, scholars, teachers and, in particular, students, are still largely cut off from information about foreign institutions and programs relevant to their fields, about access routes to such programs, and about new developments in various disciplines of learning. In general, students learn much less than faculties and researchers, and academic professionals in Prague and Bratislava learn much more than those in Brno or Košice. The windows have been so far opened but a crack, and some still remain tightly shut. Even the trickle of incoming information does not get far beyond its initial recipient.

Linguistic Abilities. This segment of the infrastructure is, in highly relative terms, considerably more cheerful. There is an almost obsessive ambition among the inhabitants of the Czechoslovak educational and research establishment to cross the language barrier, in particular and almost exclusively by learning English. Due to the sizeable "do-it-yourself" dimension in foreign language learning, at least passive knowledge of English is not uncommon; in the summer of 1990, for instance, it was possible to run in Czechoslovakia two English-language, month-long seminars for teachers of economics and of social sciences, and several more seminars requested by various disciplines are being organized and are likely to be over-subscribed. As seen by most of our respondents, however, and as we observed, the need for more extensive and intensive learning of English is still vast and, in particular, "specialized" English instruction – e.g., English-for-biologists – is in high demand.

Academic Literature. Little comment is needed here. Academic literature, books, serials and other repositories of information and knowledge from abroad, are in very short supply across the fields. The lacunae in social sciences and humanities, due to four decades of strict political and ideological controls, are larger than those in scientific and technical fields; the price of filling them all is prohibitive.

Personal Communication. In addition to technological inadequacies, cost is again the main barrier to intellectual communication across national boundaries be it by personal travel (the most effective and most desired mode), by telephone or Relefax, or by computer networks.

## LIVING LINKS: TEACHING, RESEARCH, APPLICATION

Among all the issues raised in our discussions and conferences in Czechoslovakia, two stand out as particularly poignant in the context of this report.

One is the question of institutional, intellectual and operational links between academic instruction, scientific research, and the non-academic application of their product. The second is the problem of research design and process and their management for maximum effect.

Each of them directly affects the capacity of the Czechoslovak academic establishment to absorb knowledge and skills from transnational sources. Analytically, both issues should be considered as elements of the infrastructure. They are singled out in a separate section because they loom so large on the academic horizon of Czechoslovakia.

### Academic Discontinuities

The Czechoslovak academia is riddled by sharp discontinuities. In many areas, advanced research is separated from higher learning. In turn, this rift reinforces the academia's ivory-tower tendencies and diminishes its responsiveness to social needs. By saying this we do not mean to downgrade the crucial importance of basic research. We are simply commenting on the absence of channels that would allow an imaginative application of those products of learning and research that are convertible into social goods.

The discontinuities between teaching, research and application have cultural, political and institutional underpinnings. Here we can only note some of the sources of the problem. Historically and culturally, the walls separating the academia from social life have always been lower in the United States than in Europe as a whole, and there has also been a similar, if less conspicuous, separation between instruction and research. In Czechoslovakia, these discontinuities were further aggravated by the politics of the communist decades. Under close ideological and political controls of the regime, many in the professoriate were pushed out of the classroom lest they contaminate younger minds with their heresies, and some of them found a refuge in research. An institutional structure to accommodate and sharpen the rift was at hand: the Academies of Science with a vast in-house research capability stand starkly apart from the classrooms of higher learning.

These sweeping generalizations are, of course, dotted with exceptions. In some areas, instruction and research are indeed integrated. In others, research flows into application. However, the generalization stands and the problem is recognized by Czechoslovak academic leaders as well as by the state apparatus, including the office of the President. We have become fully aware of the problem during the preparatory work for the visit, and in our September meetings it manifested itself again in a great number of contexts. The manifestations were mixed. Since so many vested interests now surround the institutional divisions between instruction, research and application, there was a noticeable tension between the professoriate and the research scholars. Simultaneously, the sense that there really is a problem and that it must be faced was equally pervasive.

How the Czechoslovak academia deals with this issue in institutional terms is, of course, their business, and theirs alone. Our concern is with the effect of the discontinuities on the transnational flows of advanced knowledge and transfer of skills. Together with our colleagues in Czechoslovakia, we are aware that the research-instruction fissure may not only inhibit intellectual discourse within the disciplinary fields that could be otherwise more fully enriched by transnational inputs; it also limits the dissemination of newly obtained knowledge into the classroom. And we also recognize that without imaginative ways of linking research with application, still more may be lost. The society will miss opportunities for improving its over-all performance if it cannot use the products of research for the incubation of new, private, high-technology enterprises and services. And the academia will be a loser as well since the research-generated private sector could well become its source of new support.

Research Management

The forty years of relative isolation of the Czechoslovak academia from its counterparts in advanced societies have left gaping holes in the ability of Czech and Slovak academics and researchers to manage their research. This is not merely a question of the technique of designing a research project, working out its time-table, estimating and controlling its costs, determining an appropriate methodology, providing for an on-going quality control, reporting results and testing them. A larger, non-technical issue lies in the setting of research strategy.

The problem of research strategy has roots somewhat similar to those of academic discontinuities discussed in the previous section. Here, institutionalized discontinuities between instruction, research, and application, are replaced by personal and intellectual discontinuities. Having lived for so many years in a politically tense atmosphere, many scholars and scientific workers learned the safe habits of isolated professional existence. Intellectual discourse was subdued; professional sharing and partnerships were fraught with dangers; interdisciplinary communication became intellectually uncomfortable and politically risky. A system extolling teamwork destroyed its essential pre-conditions. A few discussions – too few to allow generalization – with Czech and Slovak colleagues about their research projects and plans seem to suggest that unidisciplinary, lone-wolf research, un-sharing in process and with results unshared, is still the preferred or at least habitual mode in academic inquiry.

There is, among Czech and Slovak academics and researchers, a high level of awareness that they need training and experience in research management if they are to do progressively better research and if they are to compete successfully, in transnational settings, for research funds and partners. In a conference with 42 Czech and Slovak colleagues, most of them working scientists, we asked how many felt they lacked solid understanding of and experience in the management of research. The circulated response sheet coincided exactly with the list of conference participants present.

## REBUILDING DISCIPLINES OF KNOWLEDGE
### Economics and Business, Social Sciences, and Humanities – Notes

Saying little about the need in the Czechoslovak academia to rebuild, often from ground zero, an entire spectrum of disciplines that have suffered most since 1948, does not detract from the urgency of the tasks ahead. It merely means that the need is as great as it is notorious. In social sciences, including economics, as well as in humanities, everything is needed, in instruction and training even more than in research: development of new faculty, mobilization of student interest, institutional framework, textbooks and libraries, instructional technology, research methodologies.

We have made no attempt at a systematic survey of those needs nor have our discussions touched every field and subfield. We have noted, however, that when it comes to questions of possible transnational cooperation and assistance, Czech and Slovak faculty, researchers and advanced students tend to single out specific and often narrow areas of social sciences, and humanities for special attention and effort. All of such areas most often mentioned in random discussions have a common denominator: they are linked to current problems, pre-occupations and interests of Czechoslovak society. Quite understandably, a particular stress was placed on such subfields of economics as market economics, energy economics, environmental economics and economics of public goods, managerial economics, and on comparative economic systems, plus on practically everything along the interface of economics and business studies. In social sciences, the emphases were no less clear as to their social motivation. Within political science, higher interest manifested itself in comparative government, legislative politics, constitutional and administrative law, and role of interest groups in pluralistic systems. In sociology and social psychology, singled out were political sociology, social change, sociology of organizations, and social psychology of groups and of politics. In international relations, more attention was focused on international organization, international law, international political economy, the politics of European integration, and on American foreign policy, than on other aspects such as theories of international relations or strategic studies. In humanities, attention seemed fairly evenly spread across the disciplines but there was displayed a high interest in a difficult specialty known here as American studies and in Germany as Amerikanistik – a specialty grounded in literature studies but encompassing a whole gamut of other disciplines ranging from anthropology and history through religion studies to politics and economics; thus it probably is, at the present stage; well beyond the reach of most scholars and programs in Czechoslovak academia. There is no doubt that this particularization of academic interests is legitimate and, in any case, motivation is indeed the engine of learning. Yet one must also ask whether those seeking the more specialized knowledge have the capacity to absorb it in cases where they still lack adequate grounding in the fundamentals of the disciplines involved.

Academic Responsiveness to Social Needs

In its transitional and reconstructive stage, the Czechoslovak academia is driven by social forces with considerable momentum and seeks to be responsive, in its instructional emphases as well as in research directions, to dominant social needs. The demand for relevance is not as shrill as that in American universities of the late nineteen sixties, but it is more pervasive and has a broader base among the faculty and students.

In this section, we briefly touch on some of the areas of social urgency which elicit academic interest among the Czechoslovak professoriate and researchers and which are also amenable to transnational inputs. They will be additionally treated in the final section summarizing our recommendations. The highest sense of social urgency pervading the academia is generated by the arduous tasks of transforming Czechoslovak economy. The need is most keenly felt by Czech and Slovak economists themselves: they are very much aware that they often lack the most fundamental intellectual and pedagogical tools that would enable them to take to their classrooms the knowledge and the understanding of economic institutions and processes that need to be known and understood by those who will have to operate the new market economy of the future. The economic professional as well as entrepreneurs responsible for the training of their staff recognize that the need to learn spans the field: from basic knowledge about economic systems and their underlying theories to the specifics of business management, the processes of privatization, and the incubation of new enterprises. Above all, they realize that they have to learn it all now and in numbers because the need is everywhere and there is no time to lose: the economic transformation is already underway and needs to be accelerated, guided and sustained.

The transformation of a centrally directed or "command" society into a pluralistic system with the interplay of numerous forces and interests demands new and more adequate understanding of the processes of social decision making at all levels where social choices must be made. In addition to such obvious needs as improvements in economic and environmental policy and decision making, the Czechoslovak academia has a pressing task in developing broader ranges of expertise, academic and applied, in the operative fields of international relations, such as diplomatic processes, foreign policy making, conflict management, and other cognate areas.

The Czechoslovak academic establishment is clearly expected and expects to play several roles in dealing with the problem of environmental management. On the scientific side, research into environmental degradation, conducted at Czech and Slovak institutions, is quite advanced, particularly in methodology, measurement, monitoring and modeling. Significantly less developed is the understanding of the processes of social, political, economic, and legal decision making in environmental issues.

In academic as well as applied terms, the entire field of agricultural sciences with its close links to, and implications for, food production and nutrition, is another center of intense interest and potential for development. Again, scientific standards of agricultural research are high, but considerable work needs to be done on the problem of agricultural sustainability, exploration of unused genetic sources, and on the entire area of nutrition (with the indirect concern for substance abuse).

Finally, there is both room and urgency for intensified academic and research work in disciplines related to energy production and management, particularly in energy economics, in alternate energy sources and all along the interface of energy and environmental management.

All of the above areas are characterized by high interest on the part of Czech and Slovak professoriate and research workers; by their "interdisciplinarity," by relative inadequacy of understanding their social and political aspects as opposed to the scientific and technical dimensions; and by the wealth of opportunities for their reinforcement through transnational cooperation and assistance.

## RECOMMENDATIONS

These recommendations are addressed to public and private institutions, agencies, endowments, foundations, universities, research centers and programs, professional associations as well as to groups and persons involved in cooperative and/or support the projects with Czechoslovak institutions and individuals.

Prerequisites and Infrastructure

\*1     We recommend support for an expansion of and greater accessibility to sources of information needed by Czech and Slovak academics and researchers seeking to establish transnational links in their professions.

Note: The needs include information about foreign sources of professional support; about events abroad with professional substantive content, such as disciplinary or issue-oriented conferences, workshops, etc.; about developments in the whole range of academic disciplines and research undertakings; about opportunities for joint research projects, research assistance, or specialized study. The U.S. Information Service, the International Research and Exchanges Board, the Charter 77 Foundation, the Institute of International Education, and a host of other institutions already do or are about to offer various types of information services. However beneficial, these sources are still vastly insufficient in terms of information volume, specificity and accessibility.

\*2     We recommend that specialized training in the English language be supported in all of its appropriate forms.

Note: Foreign language training in general and training in English in particular are needed and demanded across Czechoslovakia. Many programs of varying quality are under way, alongside a massive effort in self-instruction with the aid of texts and audio tapes. In addition to all of this there is an urgent need for specialized training in English geared specifically for academics, researchers and university students.

*3  We recommend that sustained effort be made to provide collections of academic literature in English and other foreign languages for the use by Czech and Slovak professors and researchers and their libraries.

Note: Some flow of such literature is already on, particularly from the United States. It would appear most desirable and cost-effective that provisions for shipments of specialized literature be made in conjunction with various cooperative and supportive projects involving Czech and Slovak academics, ensuring that the materials received are put to an early use. Czechoslovak libraries, public, as well as at universities, are short on space and manpower and thus find it difficult to effectively process shipments of general literature.

*4  We strongly recommend the utilization of most advanced technologies that lend themselves to pedagogical ends and are capable of reaching large audiences for the purposes of instruction, dissemination of information and generation of knowledge, such as various audio-visual electronic transmission technologies.

*5  We recommend support for projects, mostly conferences, seminars and workshops, designed to acquaint Czech and Slovak educational leaders with a variety of tested models of the linkage between research and instruction; we also strongly recommend support for undertakings exposing Czech and Slovak academics and researchers to models of cooperative linkages between the academia and industry with a potential both to diversify the domestic sources of support for academic programs and to intensify the process of privatization.

Note: There are under way in the United States several cooperative programs between universities, industry and business. Among these, the

Ben Franklin Partnership program in Pennsylvania provides one of the more pertinent models for Czechoslovakia's needs.

*6    We strongly recommend support for programs, especially in the form of workshops, designed to train Czechoslovak academics and researchers in research management techniques in general and in the management of interdisciplinary team research projects in particular.

Note: Apart from workshops and other group-training forms, it is desirable that sponsors of joint research projects linking American with Czech or Slovak researchers encourage or require full and continuous sharing by both sides in the research management processes.

Disciplines of Learning and Selected Research Fields

*7    We strongly and urgently recommend the launching of diverse programs designed to equip economic and business faculties for their new tasks in preparing their students for a market-oriented economic system.

Note: Programs should also be aimed at supervising business managers who are responsible for instructing their staffs. Their training is no less urgent than the training of teachers of economics. By 1 September 90, according to Prague newspapers, Czechoslovakia had 199,060 private businessmen, of whom more than one half were organized in the Union of Czechoslovak Entrepreneurs. Also see note to Recommendation *8 below for comments on summer 1990 Prague seminar for professors of economics.

*8    We strongly recommend sustained support for a continuing series of survey seminars conducted in Czechoslovakia by U.S. and other Western scholars in social sciences and humanities and designed specifically for Czech and Slovak faculty and for advanced students heading for academic careers.

Note: Several seminars of this type were offered in various Czech and Slovak localities since the spring of 1990. Two of them, particularly well received, were month-long undertakings, each with a coordinator and with four experts in selected sub-fields who were teaching weekly segments; each seminar had about thirty participants from across Czechoslovakia. All instruction was in English with review sessions aided by Czech or Slovak. The first, a seminar in economics, was offered at Charles University in Prague and was sponsored and monitored by the Institute of International Education. (The coordinator of the presently reporting SVU Working Group was commissioned by I.I.E. to evaluate the seminar through extensive interviews with its participants.) The second, a seminar in social sciences held at Palacký University in Olomouc, was organized by the SVU Commission for Cooperation with Czechoslovakia and sponsored by the Charter 77 Foundation and the Soros Fund.

*9   We recommend support for Czechoslovakia-based survey seminars in operative subfields of international relations, opened to mixed groups of participants: faculty, advanced students and officials from the Ministry of Foreign Affairs.

Note: These seminars are particularly needed in support of programs in international studies newly established at Charles and other Czech and Slovak universities, and for staff officers of the Ministry of Foreign Affairs. They can be modeled after seminars described in the note to Rec. *8 above, except that they may have to be offered in staggered segments instead of continuous one-month periods.

*10  We strongly recommend support for seminars, workshops and conferences, preferably held in Czechoslovakia, and addressing the social, political, economic, and legal dimensions of environmental management.

Note: There are no coherent programs in Czechoslovakia, in research or in instruction, examining the complex social dimensions of environmental management. Scientific and technical understanding of environmental degradation is a necessary but insufficient condition of its reversal; there still remains a crucial need for better understanding of the social domain of the problem. Seminars and workshops exploring that domain, e.g., using the methodology of technology assessment, would stimulate new research and curricular development.

*11  We strongly recommend support for joint research projects, linking Czech or Slovak and American experts, in a variety of scientific inquiries into the properties of environmental degradation and its reversal.

Note: Due to the highly developed state of Czech and Slovak knowledge and skills in some areas of environmental sciences, particularly with reference to heavy metals, their measurement, monitoring, and modeling, projects of this type may result in mutual learning. Notes I and II below also apply to this recommendation.

*12   We recommend support for joint Czech or Slovak and U.S. research projects aimed at agricultural sustainability, application of biological controls in agriculture, diversification of agricultural production (also in relation to nutrition), development of unused genetic sources, and at reducing negative impact of agricultural methods on environment.

Note: see notes I and II below.

*13   We recommend support for joint research projects in energy related sciences, particularly for projects aiming at alternate energy sources and energy-saving technologies.

Note I: Excellent models for such joint research projects and for scientific collaboration in general can be found in the existing Program on Scientific and Technical Cooperation (PSTC), administered by the AID–Office of the Science Adviser. This program, seeking to stimulate new and innovative research on problems of developing countries, has been so far focused on the Third World. It would be only natural and highly beneficial from a developmental perspective to include in the program the countries of Central and Eastern Europe or, even better, to set up for them a separate program to avoid unnecessary and uneven competition.

Note II: We do not claim adequate knowledge about the needs of scientists in other European countries; however, the propensity of Czech and Slovak scientists for embarking on new, innovative research would be greatly stimulated by the availability of a special fund facilitating their short-term visits with their U.S. counterparts to begin the preparation of joint research projects. The fund should also provide for a mechanism enabling scientists from both sides to identify their counterparts with shared research interests.

# 32
## Tříska's Return to the SVU Presidency

At the beginning of the second year of Nábělek's Presidency, the Velvet Revolution broke out in Czechoslovakia which led to the return of democracy there. With the rapidly changing political scene in Central and Eastern Europe, there was a consensus among the SVU "elders" that the Society will need an entirely new leadership, capable of coping with the new situation in the democratic Czechoslovakia. They felt that they cannot risk putting someone in the president's place without experience or who had not a proven record. Consequently, they recommended to the Nominations Committee to offer the nomination to Past President, Prof. Jan F. Tříska, who was willing to accept it, this time more readily, realizing too well the challenges and opportunities offered by the new era.

The problem was that Nábělek's Executive Board wanted to stay in their places. Andrew Eliáš, as chairman of the Nominations Committee, was reluctant to replace them with a new slate of officers not to offend them. His reluctance was magnified by the fact that, like Nábělek, he was also a Slovak. To get out of his dilemma, we recommended that we have a two-man race, Nábělek vs. Tříska. Eliáš liked the idea and the Nominations Committee eventually came with two candidates for every position, i.e., new candidates vs. the old Executive Board. As it turned out, Tříska decisively won the elections, receiving 62 votes against Nábělek's 42.[610] Nábělek subsequently contested the election results on the basis of some technicalities. SVU Bylaws committee, after examining the matter, determined that it did not find any fault in the election process and concluded that his claim was without foundation.[611]

---

[610] What could have also helped the new slate of officers to be elected was the fact that a couple of the previous Board members were listed in the infamous Cibulka's list of former collaborators of STB.

[611] Komentář Komise SVU pro stanovy a jednací řády k dopisu předsedy SVU prof. Nábělka o možných iregularitách při volbach SVU.

## Tříska's Return to the SVU Presidency

With Tříska[612] at the helm of SVU, I again began working closely with the newly elected Executive Board. I knew them all well. Besides Jan Tříska, the Executive Board comprised Lubomír Ďurovič, Thomas G. Gibian, Dr. Karel Hrubý, Prof. Zdenka Pospíšil, Prof. Vlado Šimko,[613] Prof Zdeněk Slouka and Dagmar Hasalová-White, Vice Presidents; George J. Kvídera,[614] Secretary-General and Stanley J. Maršík, Treasurer. Because of personal reasons, Prof. Pospíšil and George Kvídera had to resign and were replaced by Dr. George Karger[615] and Frank Marlow, respectively.[616] After his appointment to Directorship of the SVU Research Institute, VP Slouka was later replaced by Prof. Anton J. Novacký[617] to avoid possible conflict of interest. The composition of the new Executive Board was announced, in the November issue of *Zprávy SVU*, together with the acceptance speech of the new President at the 15th SVU World Congress.[618]

My closeness with the Board is indicated by the fact that a number of the Board meetings were held in our house in Rockville, MD for convenience and because my wife Eva put up with it. Actually a better characterization would be that it was her generous hospitality which made the meetings in our house desirable. Moreover, several of the out-of-town members usually also stayed in our house during the days of the meetings, which in those days usually lasted two days. It should be noted that in all these meetings Eva would completely stay out and focused entirely on her role as the "hostess with the mostest."

From the beginning, the new Executive Board was very much aware of the fact that the revolution for democracy in Czechoslovakia brought a sea-change to SVU as well a sea-change which would demand deep structural and functional changes in our Society.

---

[612] He assumed SVU Presidency at the General Assembly Meeting in Toronto, Canada, October 11, 1990, on the occasion of the 15th SVU World Congress, after beating Igor Nábělek in a two-man race, with a large margin.

[613] Vlado Šimko (1931-), Associate Professor of Medicine, State University of New York.

[614] George J. Kvídera (1932-), Business executive.

[615] George Karger (1924-), creative director, CBS TV, Los Angeles.

[616] Both were from California and close friends of Tříska.

[617] Anton J. Novacký (1933-), Professor of Plant Pathology, University of Missouri, Columbia.

[618] *Zprávy SVU*, vol. 32, No. 6 (November-December 1990), pp. 1-3.

The Board realized the new opportunities and challenges as well as the new responsibilities which would be enormous. In order to do what the new imperatives demanded, the Board made an effort to increase the Society's income and to decrease its expenditures as much as possible. Fund-raising, recruitment of new members, and effective control of all routine expenses were considered to be of utmost priority. At the same time, a high value was placed on modernization of the Society, i.e., utilization of FAX machines, which would speed up communications; computers, which would provide a comprehensive, up-to-date database of all members and thus facilitate vertical as well as horizontal communication networking.

Because of new demands on the Society, in the light of political changes in Czechoslovakia, there was an urgent need to revise the SVU Bylaws to make the Society more responsive, more flexible and more effective. In a referendum in late spring of 1991,[619] the Bylaws were amended by an overwhelming vote of the SVU membership.

At my initiative, SVU established formal ties with the Czechoslovak Council of Scientific Societies,[620] a supreme coordinating body of some sixty of the most important scientific and scholarly societies in Czechoslovakia, associated with the then Czechoslovak and Slovak Academies of Sciences. SVU became officially a foreign member of the Council of Scientific Societies and I was appointed a member of their governing board.

In cooperation with the Council of Scientific Societies, the SVU Executive Board established an SVU office, staffed and open daily in Prague, on the premises of the Czechoslovak Academy of Sciences. Steps were also taken, based on my Prague contacts, to establish, for the first time, a local chapter of SVU in Czechoslovakia.

Under the aegis of the SVU Research Institute, a series of workshops[621] was also carried out in Czechoslovakia, the details of which are discussed in a separate chapter.

In the early days of Tříska's presidency, on the first anniversary of the "Velvet Revolution," the SVU British Chapter, under the chair-

---

[619] *Zprávy SVU*, vol. 32, No. 2 (March-April 1991), pp. 1-4.

[620] In Czech: Rada vědeckých společností.

[621] *Zprávy SVU*, vol. 33, No. 6 (November-December 1991), pp. 8-9.

manship of Prof. Jaroslav Krejčí[622] organized a one day conference entitled "Czechoslovakia One Year On." The conference was held at St. Anthony's College, Oxford University, on Saturday, November 17, 1990. After the welcoming address by the Warden of the College, Sir Ralf Dahrendorf, individual presentations by distinguished visitors from Czechoslovakia followed, starting with Prof. Josef Jařáb, Rector of Palacký University, Olomouc on "Changes in Higher Education." Pavel Šimek, representing the Czechoslovak Prime Minister's office, spoke on "Changes in Legal Structures," and Ing. Věra Kameníčková of the Czechoslovak Federal Ministry of Finance, discussed "Changes in Economy." The afternoon session was devoted to "Changes in Politics." The principal speakers were Judy Batt of the University of Birmingham and Dr. Alex Pravda of St. Antony's College, Oxford.

The 1991 SVU Annual Meeting was held on September 21 in Chicago[623] at the International House of the University of Chicago. Following the reports of SVU officers, the participants visited the Czech and Slovak areas of Regenstein Library (over 20,000 books), and the Archives of Czechs and Slovaks Abroad, housed and maintained at the University Chicago Library. The latter comprise some 250 shelves of publications and documents – the result of painstaking labors of Prof. Zdeněk Hruban.

The afternoon was devoted to the presentations and discussions of various topics concerning the lives and activities of selected Czech and Slovak personalities in the U.S. The program included papers on the sculptor Albin Polášek and Dr. Milan Hodža and readings from the works of Jan Novák and Prof. K. B. Jirák. In the evening, the dinner guests heard an address by Prof. Joseph Ceithaml, Dean of the University of Chicago, who proudly recalled his Czech roots. The evening program was concluded with a debate on technical and financial help to Czechoslovak science.

On 25-27 October 1991, following his state visit in Washington, DC, President Václav Havel made two more stops, in Los Angeles and in Bethlehem, PA. The programs in both cities had been pre-arranged in a late summer meeting at the President's office in Prague by SVU mem-

---

622 Jaroslav Krejčí (1916-), Professor, University of Lancaster, England, UK.
623 *Zprávy SVU*, vol. 33, No. 4 (July-August 1991), p. 5.

bers, Mrs. Mia Valert,[624] the founder and Director of LA Czechoslovak Institute, and Prof. Zdeněk Slouka, Director of SVU Research Institute. The Los Angeles and Bethlehem "town meetings" with the President, open to members of Czech and Slovak communities in America, were attended by more than two hundred SVU members from the West and East coasts. In Bethlehem, the President received Moravian College's highest honor, the Comenius Medal, and a Doctor of Humane Letters honorary degree from Lehigh University. The President also delivered an address, "On Civic Society," as the Sixth Cohen International Lecturer in a distinguished series organized annually at Lehigh University by Prof. Slouka. The President was accompanied by Prof. Radim Palouš, Rector of Charles University and a prominent Comenius scholar, who received an honorary doctorate from Moravian College.

Sponsored by SVU, another significant event – a round table entitled "Czechoslovakia Today and Tomorrow" took place on Saturday, November 23, 1991, at the Hyatt Regency Hotel in Miami, Florida, on the occasion of the 1991 International Convention of the American Association for the Advancement of Slavic Studies. The six distinguished participants in the roundtable discussion included Prof. Radomír Luža[625] on politics and society; Prof. Catherine Albrecht[626] on economics; Prof. Bronislava Volek[627] on culture; Prof. Milan L. Hauner[628] on foreign policy; Prof. Victor Mamatey[629] on Slovaks in the Federal Republic; and Prof. Josef Anderle[630] on law and order. Prof. Jan F. Tříska chaired the very successful meeting, which attracted a standing-room audience.

On January 15, 1992, the Society was granted a permit by the Federal Ministry of the Interior of the CSFR to extend its activities to the

---

[624] Mia Valert (1941-), associated with the University of California at Los Angeles.

[625] Radomír Luža (1927-), professor of history, Tulane University, New Orleans, LA.

[626] Catherine Albrecht, historian, associated with the University of Baltimore.

[627] Bronislava Volková (1946-), Associate Professor, Slavic Dept., Indiana University, Bloomington, IN.

[628] Milan Hauner (1940-), research historian, then associated with Georgetown University, Washington, DC.

[629] Victor S. Mamatey (1917-2007), research professor of history, University of Georgia, Athens, GA.

[630] Josef Anderle (1924-), professor of history, University of North Carolina, Chapel Hill, NC.

*Třiska's Return to the SVU Presidency*

Czech and Slovak Federal Republic.[631] On February 19, 1992, a meeting was held in Prague regarding the plans for establishing the Czechoslovak SVU Chapter. Dr. J. Ullschmied[632] who chaired the meeting was appointed the chairman of the organizing council.[633] I knew him well from my professional contact with him when he worked for President Havel in the Prague Castle. About the same time, by courtesy of the Council of the Czechoslovak Scientific Societies, SVU opened its office in the building of the Czechoslovak Academy of Sciences on Národní třída in Prague. The new Chapter was formally established on April 26.[634]

The most important event of the Třiska's Presidency was the 16th SVU World Congress in Prague which is discussed in detail in a separate chapter.

---

[631] *SVU Bulletin*, vol. 13, No. 2 (May 1992), p. 9-10.

[632] J. Ullschmied (1942-), physicist, associated with the Czechoslovak Academy of Sciences.

[633] *Zprávy SVU*, vol. 34, No. 2 (March-April 1992), p. 18.

[634] *SVU Bulletin*, vol. 13, No. 2 (May 1992), pp. 10-11.

# 33
## Organizing the First SVU Congress in Prague

The most important event of Tříska's presidency was the SVU Congress in Prague, scheduled for June 1992. This was the first time in the history of the Society that its Congress was held on Czechoslovak territory.

Although other people could have thought of it, the official impetus for holding the first SVU World Congress in Prague, following the Velvet Revolution, came from the Past Presidents of the Society during their special meeting in my house in February 1990. The idea was further explored by the members of SVU Commission for Cooperation with Czechoslovakia, especially by Tříska, Slouka and myself, with the interested parties in Prague, during the Commission's fact-finding mission in Czechoslovakia during 17-28 September 1990.

As a person who had long experience with previous Congresses, it was only natural that the Executive Board would turn to me for assistance with the initial planning and organization. I drafted the original announcement, which was sent out with the registration forms, and I also had something to do with picking the chief Congress organizers. On the American end, we divided the Congress organizational functions between Andrew Eliáš and Pavel Trenský,[635] the former to coordinate the program, the latter registrations and finances.

The first step was to compile names and addresses of potential speakers which was my job. Using information which I had accumulated in my personal archives and as a result of new search through various university catalogues and directories of scientists and scholars, I was able to amass a list of some one thousand names, mostly from the US and Canada, and other Western countries. The list of invitees from Czechoslovakia was to be prepared by our colleagues in Prague. Based

---

[635] Pavel I. Trenský (1929-), professor of comparative literature and drama at Fordham University, New York,

*Organizing the First SVU Congress in Prague* 199

on my list, Trenský, who had access to computer, prepared the address labels.

The invitation letters to potential speakers were sent out with Tříska's signature with the instructions to mail their acceptances, with the titles of their proposed talks to Eliáš, while the registration material, together with the payment were to go to Trenský. Andrew Eliáš, with whom I maintained almost daily contact, had received an avalanche of responses. It seemed as if practically every invitee wanted to participate in the historic congress in Prague. I helped him with classifying the responses by subject areas and organizing them into possible panels, as well as with the selection of panel chairs. Unfortunately, because of some personal reasons, Eliáš could not complete the entire task, so that the job had to be completed by Jan F. Tříska.

While this was going on, our co-organizers in Prague were not exactly idle. Actually, they began working on the program almost immediately, following my visit to Prague in May 1991, on the occasion of the 100th anniversary of the Czech Academy.[636] On May 14, I was invited to address the plenary meeting of the Council of Scientific Societies,[637] during which I informed them about the planned Congress, with the request that they assist us with the endeavor. They were intrigued with the idea which they fully endorsed, offering their co-sponsorship of the Congress. While I was still in Prague, individual societies began sending me their suggestions for their participation in the Congress, some even listing potential speakers.

Thus, already on May 15, Dr. I. Hrdý, President of the Czechoslovak Entomological Society, was offering to organize a symposium on the ways of solving global problems and two days later, a letter came from the Czechoslovak Sociological Society, expressing interest in par-

---

[636] President of the Academy, Dr. Otto Wichterle, awarded me, on that occasion, at the special ceremony in the National Theatre in Prague, Josef Hlávka Commemorative Medal.

[637] The Council of Scientific Societies, which was affiliated with the Czechoslovak Academy of Sciences, was an umbrella organization of major scientific societies in Czechoslovakia. It comprised 11 societies in physical sciences, 17 in biological and chemical sciences and 18 in social sciences, representing over 33,000 scientists at that time.

ticipation in our Congress. Then came a letter from Dr. Jaroslav Folta[638] with the proposal, in the name of the Czechoslovak Society for History of Science and Technology, to organize two separate symposia, one relating to the Czech and Slovak Science and Technology in Global Context, and another, on the Milestones in the Development of Czech and Slovak Sciences and Technology, involving 30 participants.

On May 23, Dr. Lenka Měchurová,[639] who held the position of Executive Secretary of the Council of Scientific Societies, sent me an exhaustive list of other societies, affiliated with the Council, who expressed interest in active participation. These included the Association of Czechoslovak Mathematicians and Physicists, Czech Geographical Society, Czechoslovak Meteorological Society, Czech Immunological Society and the Society of Ethnography. Detailed proposals were included from Ing. Jitka Pantůčková, CSc., President of the Czech Oriental Society, Ing. Čestmír Falk, CSc., President of the Czechoslovak Zoological Society and Prof. MUDr. Jiří Kraml, DrSc., Science Secretary of the Czechoslovak Biochemical Society.

A separate offer came from the Czechoslovak Biological Society, signed by its President Prof. MUDR. Oldřich Nečas, DrSc. and Science Secretary doc. MUDr. R. Janisch, DrSc. They wrote that their Society comprised some 1,700 members, many of whom were intimately involved in working on the burning issues of environmental pollution, environmental health and ecological questions. Specifically, they proposed several panels, i.e., Experimental and Clinical Cytogenesis, Genetics of Viruses with Emphasis on Retroviruses, Cell Motility Ecology, Agriculture in Czechoslovakia, Cryobiology and Human Health Protection and Environmental Influences on Health. Another proposal came from PhDr. František Šmahel, DrSc., Director of Historical Institute to organize panels on J. A. Komenský and Moravian Brethren and The Emigration Trauma.

The response was truly overwhelming, beginning to reach geographic proportions. It was clear to me that we could not possibly handle the entire congress program from abroad. It was therefore decided to let

---

[638] Jaroslav Folta (1933-), historian of science, associated with the Czechoslovak Academy of Sciences (CSAV), Prague.

[639] Lenka Měchurová (1948-), executive secretary, Council of Scientific Societies, ČSAV, Prague.

*Organizing the First SVU Congress in Prague* 201

our Czech colleagues organize panels with participants from Czechoslovakia, while we would concentrate on the speakers from abroad. Dr. Jaroslav Folta and Dr. Lenka Měchurová assumed the responsibility for the former.

I had another opportunity to do some work on the logistics of our Congress during the workshop SVU Research Institute organized in Prague in September 1991 in which I played a significant role. I talked to a number of key people, including Rector Radim Palouš[640] and Vice Rector Zdeněk Lojda[641] of Charles University, Vice President of the Czechoslovak Academy of Sciences Ing. Vladislav Hančil,[642] Chairman of the Council of Scientific Societies Jaroslav Valenta,[643] President Havel's Advisor Pavel Tigrid, Director of History Institute Frantisek Šmahel,[644] Director of Ethnographic Institute Stanislav Brouček,[645] President of the Czechoslovak Society for History of Science and Technology Jiří Majer[646] and others. Above all, I had several important meetings with Jaroslav Folta, Lenka Měchurová and Jiří Ullschmied.[647]

I also had a special meeting with Dr. Jaroslav Skolek[648] and other representatives of the National Library regarding the planned exhibit about SVU during the upcoming Congress and a special session on librarianship. At their request I subsequently sent them various material for the exhibit, including photographs, documents regarding the founding and the beginnings of SVU, list of SVU Presidents and other important members, list of Local Chapters, list of SVU publications and conferences, etc. I also provided a few examples of our publications,

---

[640] Radim Palouš (1924-), Rector, Charles University, Prague.

[641] Zdeněk Lojda (1927-2004), Vice Rector, Charles University, Prague; he was a histologist of note.

[642] Vladimir Hančil (1941-), Vice President of the Czechoslovak Academy of Sciences, Prague.

[643] Jaroslav Valenta (1927-), professor at the Czech Technical University, Prague.

[644] Frantisek Šmahel (1934-), historian with the Czechoslovak Academy of Sciences.

[645] Stanislav Brouček (1947-), historian and ethnographer with the Czechoslovak Academy of Sciences, Prague.

[646] Jiří Majer (1922-), historian of science and technology, Prague.

[647] Jiří Ullschmied (1942-), physicist, Institute of Plasma Physics of the Academy, who, at that time, was assigned to the President Havel's Office at the Prague Castle.

[648] Jaroslav Skolek (1933-), director of research, National Library, Klementinum, Prague.

such as SVU directory and SVU periodicals and newsletters. The exhibit was actually organized by Paul Trenský's wife Michaela Harnick,[649] who with her husband were in Prague at that time.

During this trip I also met with representatives of the Czech media, including Karel Pacner[650] of *Mladá Fronta Dnes* and Ivo Budil[651] of the Prague Radio to assure adequate coverage of the Congress events. The logistical arrangements, as announced in the November 1991 issue of *Zprávy SVU*,[652] were made entirely by our colleagues in Prague and Bratislava. They also picked the theme, "Czechoslovakia, Europe and the World: Arts and Sciences in the International Setting."

I did not get to see the final program until our arrival in Prague when Eva and I came two weeks before the Congress started. I came earlier because Zdeněk Slouka and I scheduled two one-week workshops, sponsored by our SVU Research Institute. Although we were quite busy during the day, we had ample time in the evening "to check on things" regarding the organizational and programmatic aspects of the Congress. To our dismay, we soon discovered that the general description of the Congress program, including social and cultural events and logistical arrangements and instructions to the participants were printed only in Czech. This would have created a major problem, considering that the larger proportion of the overseas speakers and attendees knew no Czech. We had no recourse but to sit down and prepare with Eva an English version which Jaroslav Folta then laboriously transcribed on the computer. In retrospect, I am still amazed that we were able to finish it before the Congress started.

Nevertheless, I must say, with all honesty, that the Prague organizers otherwise did a fantastic job. The key player in Czechoslovakia was Dr. Jaroslav Folta[653] who assumed overall responsibility over the academic program. He worked closely with the Council of Czech Scientific Societies, headed by Prof. J. Valenta, and the Council of Slovak Scien-

---

[649] Michaela Harnick (1949-), librarian, cataloging supervisor, Columbia University Libraries, New York.

[650] Karel Pacner (1936-), science editor, *Mladá Fronta Dnes*, Prague.

[651] Ivo Budil (1933-), journalist with the Radio Prague.

[652] *Zprávy SVU*, vol. 33, No. 6 (November-December 1991), pp. 1-7.

[653] It was he who first put me in touch with the Council of Scientific Societies and its President Dr. Jaroslav Valenta.

tific Societies, headed by Ing. Jozef Brilla,[654] as well as Presidents of individual societies. The Council and its affiliated societies played the pivotal role in the organization of the program.

On the administrative and organizational end, the responsible person was Dr. Lenka Měchurová who headed the secretariat of the Council of Czech Scientific Societies at the Czechoslovak Academy of Sciences. She was a very capable organizer who seemed to know everybody and had the needed skills to resolve almost any organizational problem. She was assisted by a large assemblage of ladies, i.e., Yveta Moulisová, Dana Pánková, Ing. Alena Kovaříková, Zora Brodská, Libuše Hlaváčková, Dr. Miroslava Holanová, Jana Šlechtová, Bohuslava Jedličková, Dr. Dagmar Křikavová and Ivana Svobodová. She also arranged for the Congress participants to be met at the Prague Airport and to be welcomed and given assistance by student helpers. There were almost fifty of them, under the supervision of Hana Štěpánková and Marie Skalická.

An important role was also played by Ing. Jiří Ullschmied whom I knew from my professional contacts in AID, when dealing with President Havel's Office on research grants. He, together with Ing. Vaclav Babický, and the firm Technologie 2000 from Jablonec nad Nisou, put all the Congress participants' names on computer which simplified the registration process.

From Charles University we had effective help from Václava Kupová and Veronika Bínová,[655] and above all, Vice Rector Prof. Zdeněk Lojda, whom I knew quite well and who always invited me for lunch whenever I was in Prague.

The large number of lecture rooms for various Congress sessions were arranged, thanks to Deans of the Pedagogic and Law Faculties, Profs. Votásek and Urfus, respectively. Directors of J. A. Komenský Museum, the National Museum and the National Library, Dr. Tomáš Pasák, Dr. Milan Stloukal and Dr. Jaroslav Skolek, respectively, together with Dr. A. Mišková from the Academy Archives and Dr. L. Karfík of Náprstek Museum, in turn, provided the space and their staff for installation of three exhibits opened during the Congress.

---

[654] Jozef Brilla (1927-), Slovak mathematician, represented Slovakia on the Council of Scientific Societies

[655] Veronika Bínová (1953-), assistant, Rectorate, Charles University, Prague.

In Bratislava, where the second part of the Congress was to take place, the organizational and logistical arrangements were in the hands of Prof. Jozef Brilla, Mgr. Milec and Mrs. Maková.

# 34
# *Echoes from the Prague Congress*

The SVU Congress was convened on June 25 until July 2, 1992, first in Prague and then in Bratislava, with the central theme "Czechoslovakia – Europe – World: Arts and Sciences in International Context." It was held under the aegis of President Havel and sponsored by Charles University in Prague and Comenius University in Bratislava, in cooperation with the Council of Czech and Slovak Scientific Societies. Altogether, some 1,380 participants took part, of which almost 600 came from abroad. The program of the Congress appeared as a separate issue of *Zprávy SVU*[656] and the Congress evaluation was published in one of the subsequent issues.[657]

The impressive welcoming ceremony was open primarily to visitors from abroad. In the overcrowded auditorium of the ancient Karolinum, it gave the Congress a festive tone. The arrival of President Havel, accompanied by long-lasting applause, the spontaneously sung Czechoslovak national anthems, the official greetings by the Chancellors of Charles and Comenius Universities, the words of the two Presidents of the Council of Scientific Societies were enthusiastically received. This was followed by a heart-felt address by US Ambassador Shirley Temple Black in which she expressed her love for Czechoslovakia, wishing the best to the Czech and Slovak nations on their journey to democracy and prosperity. The audience responded with a standing ovation. The ceremony ended with tunes from Antonín Dvořák's Quartet.

During the ceremony, SVU Executive Board members were seated on the elevated benches above the platform, alongside Rectors and other university dignitaries in their academic gowns. Although I now had no official function in the Society I was included among them and sat on the immediate left of President Havel's box.

---

[656] *16th World Congress. Program Prague-Bratislava, ČSFR, June 26-July 2, 1992. Zpravy SVU*, vol. 34, No. 3 (May-June 1992, 44 p.

[657] *Zprávy SVU*, vol. 34, No. 4 (September-October 1992), pp. 25.

President Havel did not actually stay for the entire ceremony and left immediately after the US Ambassador's address. When he arrived he bowed and smiled to the audience but did not say anything during the entire ceremony.[658] As I looked at him from my seat, he appeared somewhat ill at ease, suggesting that he was under great stress and he might have been somewhat ill as well.

It was symbolic that the official opening of the Congress took place on the premises of Charles University, the bearer of the best traditions of science and learning in Czechoslovakia in the presence of President Václav Havel of Czechoslovakia and Ambassador Shirley Temple-Black of the US.

After the official opening and welcome of visitors from abroad in the ancient hall at Karolinum, the visitors from abroad were hosted in "Obecní dům" on Příkopy. Immediately after, followed a plenary session at the Prague famed Rudolfinum.

The speakers were President of the Czechoslovak Academy of Sciences Otto Wichterle[659] who talked about the problems of basic research in Czechoslovakia without which a prosperous nation cannot exist. He was followed by the newly elected President of the Slovak Academy of Sciences Branislav Lichardus[660] who discussed the future of research at the Slovak Academy of Sciences. Then there was my turn. I chose to speak about the Czech and Slovak immigrants in the US and their impact on the development of the United States. Pavel Tigrid, in his presentation, appealed to SVU members and others to remain faithful to the principles on which SVU was founded and which has relevance to Czechoslovakia even today. Daniela Fischerová discussed the contemporary Czech literature and Peter Eben. in turn, talked about the current developments in music and art. Vice Premier of Czechoslovakia Josef

---

[658] Later on, when Czech press commented on this, they stated that SVU did not let him speak. This was, of course, utter nonsense. Being close to the organization of the Congress, I know for a fact that President Havel, because of his heavy schedule, did not actually plan to come at all and it was only at Pavel Tigrid's prompting that he finally agreed to come, provided he would not have to speak.

[659] Otto Wichterle (1913-1998), President of the Czechoslovak Academy of Sciences; chemist who invented hydrogel contact lenses.

[660] Branislav Lichardus (1930-), deputy director of the Institute of Experimental Endocrinology, Slovak Academy of Sciences, Bratislava.

Mikloško addressed the question of how education and learning can help in solving societal problems.

When this ended, the participants spent a charming evening at Valdštejnská zahrada (Waldstein Gardens) where Children's Choir "Joy of Prague" was featured, followed by a gala buffet at "Rytířský sál" (The Knights' Hall) at the Prague Castle.

The subsequent three days were devoted to individual panels in 24 parallel sessions. Because of their large number, the panels had to be placed in several buildings, generously provided for the occasion by the Law Faculty, the Pedagogic Faculty and Philosophical Faculty, as well as lecture halls at Karolinum, National Museum and the National Library at Klementinum. The list of lectures alone filled 100 pages of the Congress Program.

Among others, the panel on "Learning and Education" attracted great interest, as did the panel devoted to scientific cooperation between Czechoslovakia and the US. The latter included representatives from the National Science Foundation (NSF), U.S. Environmental Protection Agency (EPA), National Institutes of Health (NIH), US Agency for International Development (AID) and the US Embassy. Special attention was also paid to the panel on the role of science policy in society.

During the Congress three special exhibits were on display. One exhibit, devoted to the history and activities of SVU and the book output of its members, was displayed at the National Library at Klemetinum. The second exhibit was at the Náprstek Museum with the theme, "There Beyond the Ocean in America". The third, held in the main building of the Czechoslovak Academy of Sciences, featured the most important documents relating to the development of Czech science, including those bearing on the establishment of Charles University and the Bohemian Learned Society, the predecessor of the Czech Academy.

As to cultural programs, the performance of Smetana's "Bartered Bride," the unforgettable concert of the Czech. Philharmonic, under the baton of Jiří Bělohlávek and Liga Pragensis evening devoted to the life and the works of Jaroslav Seifert also deserves mentioning. The Prague social program, culminated with the gala reception in the Spanish Hall at the Prague Castle.

The second part of the Congress took place in Bratislava, immediately after the proceedings in Prague ended. Most participants arrived by previously arranged buses.

The Bratislava program began with small group excursions to the Slovak Technical University, Comenius University and various institutes of the Slovak Academy of Sciences. The aim of these visits was to establish contacts and possible collaborative arrangements between the scientists on both side of the Atlantic.

The following day, the participants assembled in the beautiful Hall of Comenius University where they were welcomed by representatives of Slovak institutions of higher learning. Minister of Culture and Education Dušan Slobodnik, in his address, asked the participants for understanding in interpreting events in Slovakia in its struggle for freedom which should not be misconstrued with chauvinism. Alexander Tkáč[661] from the Slovak Technical University discussed seventy years of centralist oppression while Jozef Brilla, representing the Faculty of Mathematics and Physics, reviewed serious problems that confronted the Slovak scientific community. He noted how in the past Ministry of Education misinformed the government and the way the nearsighted politics interfered in science and how unlawful means were used in filling science positions, based on political background rather than on scientific competence.

Then came a press conference during which the debate focused on the future role and the responsibilities of government in dealing with scientific institutions and the scientists, in general. There was a consensus that Slovak scientific institutions have had very little effect on government, while the latter has generally been misinformed about the importance of science in the development of society. Minister Kusý, in evaluating the Slovak meeting, stressed two aspects: mutual relations between Czechoslovakia and its emigrants, and the relations between Czechs and Slovaks, generally, both of which have long been ignored. He further commented that during the Communist era in Slovakia the contacts with Prague were persecuted more than the contacts with the émigrés and that this situation has not as yet been corrected, at least in the area of humanities and social sciences. At the end there seemed to prevail the notion that the mutual relations between scientists and the

---

[661] Alexander Tkáč (1922-), Vice Rector, Slovak Technical University, Bratislava.

public in the Czechlands and Slovakia are not dependant on any official organ and that they should be viewed as a natural phenomenon.

On a social level, there were boat excursions along the Danube River to view the remnants of the ancient Devin Castle at the point where the Morava River joins Danube. The participants also had the opportunity to view the manufacture of the unique Slovak ceramics in Modrá.

At the evening gala banquet the participants could rub shoulders with important Slovak personalities, including Minister of Culture Slobodnik and the representatives of Slovak Academy, Universities and the Council of Slovak Scientific Societies.

The Congress was an excellent opportunity to rethink the milestones in the development of Czech and Slovak science and culture and give evidence of the high level of Czechoslovak learning and scholarship and the great scientific accomplishments in the international context.

The Congress also led to fostering international cooperation in arts and sciences on a high social level. It was also self evident that SVU can serve as a global platform for publicizing Czech and Slovak culture throughout the world and provide assistance to Czech and Slovak scientists and artists more than any other institution.

## 35
# SVU General Assembly in Los Angeles[662]

The 1992 annual meeting of SVU took place on October 24,[663] at the Ramada Renaissance Hotel, Los Angeles, California. The agenda followed the program outlined in the August 1992 *SVU Bulletin*[664] and the July 1992 issue of *Zprávy SVU*,[665] with all necessary details. Ballots for voting, either in Czech or in English, were inserted for all SVU members to fill out and mail the form to the Election Inspection Committee for the count.

Minutes of the Los Angeles meeting were taken by two candidates for the new Executive Board 1992-94, Pavel Machotka and Frank Ladislav Mucha,[666] to preserve word-accurate formulations of any propositions and decisions discussed or approved. It will be the duty of the new officers to communicate with the membership about specifics, through the SVU periodicals, as need be.

One discussion which will require further elucidation concerns the SVU Council and the proposition to restructure that body differently from the past, by making it more active. As only two nominated members of the Council were present, i.e., Zdenka E. Fischmann from California and Thomas G. Gibian from Washington, DC, no decision was made about the feasibility of the proposed new role. Miloslav Rechcígl, Jr., as past SVU President, and Jiří Karger, as Chairman of the Los Angeles Chapter, are automatically members of the Council.

Since geographic distances were serious obstacles for SVU, the only members of the Executive Board for the period 1990-92 present were Jan Tříska, President; Thomas G. Gibian, Executive Vice-

---

[662] *SVU Bulletin*, vol. 13, No. 4 (October 1992), pp. 4-5.

[663] A couple of weeks before the meeting, on October 7, 1992, we were saddened by the news of the sudden death of Dr. Jaroslav Němec.

[664] *SVU Bulletin*, vol. 13, No. 3 (August 1992), pp. 1-2.

[665] *Zprávy SVU*, vol. 34, No. 4 (July-August 1992), p. 20.

[666] Frank L. Mucha (1939-), deputy administrative director, Research Foundation for Mental Hygiene, Columbia University, New York.

President; Frank Marlow, Secretary General, and George Karger, Vice-President. They took care of all the issues of the agenda and communicated information received from the absent officers. The minutes from the past annual meeting, awards of Honorary and Founding memberships, as well as the orally presented reports were approved by the Assembly and an "absolutorium"[667] was granted to the outgoing Board.

Next, the results of the election of the SVU Executive Board, SVU Council, Auditors of the Accounts and the Conciliation and Arbitration Committee, were read. All candidates on the ballot were elected by majority of votes. Only few written in substitutions were reported. The newly elected officers who traveled to Los Angeles were introduced in person.

In the afternoon three lectures were given. They were: Michael H. Heim's paper on "Central Europe and the American Intellectual," Andrzej Korbonski's paper on "Czechoslovakia, Eastern Europe and the New International Order," and Stanislav Segert's paper on "400th Anniversary of John Amos Komenský." They all were associated with the University of California at Los Angeles. Josef Anderle from the University of North Carolina, who was supposed to talk on Czechoslovak historiography in America could not attend.

The new elected officers present in Los Angeles were: Zdeněk Slouka, President; Ivan M. Viest,[668] Executive Vice President; Pavel Machotka; Josef A. Mestenhauser,[669] Vice Presidents; Frank L. Mucha, Treasurer.

To the outgoing SVU officers thanks were expressed for their past work. They were active in an unprecedented position of organizing the transatlantic 16th SVU World Congress in Prague and made it their priority to showcase the Society. The task was complicated and at times seemingly hopeless because of the ongoing changes in the ČSFR and the necessity of a flexible search of cooperation while various plans had to

---

[667] The term used by the Europeans, signifying that the retiring officers are discharged of liability, upon the approval of Treasurer's report and the recommendations by the auditors of the accounts.

[668] Ivan M. Viest (1922-), structural engineer, living in Bethlehem, PA.

[669] Josef A. Mestenhauser (1925-), professor of educational policy, University of Minnesota, Minneapolis.

be realistically coordinated by SVU. It was almost a miracle that the Congress could be realized so well.

It meant some major personal sacrifices (especially time and self-financing) by the Board members, but also benefits in terms of successful contacts with the academic community of Czechoslovakia. That some errors, conflicts, miscalculations, stormy moments and hasty decisions were part of the lengthy negotiations, is only natural. It seems the whole event, requiring care of so many details and unfamiliar situations, was stressful for all organizers, but the final results were worth the energy spent. One specifically lucky strike was the cooperation of Dr. Lenka Měchurová, Executive Secretary, Council of Czech Scientific Societies, who provided the knowledge of the Prague scene, as well as an office and clerical help. Another person who provided great help, particularly with reference of the Congress program, was my good friend Jaroslav Folta, science historian with the History Institute of the Czechoslovak Academy of Sciences.

Following the General Assembly meeting, the outgoing President Tříska sent the following letter to Eva and me:

Dear Mila and Eva:

It is with real pleasure that I am writing to you to inform you of the Resolution presented to the General Assembly of SVU by myself, jointly with the Secretary-General of SVU, Frank Marlow, on October 24, 1992, in Los Angeles. The assembled SVU membership greeted the Resolution with applause and approved it by acclamation.

The Declaration reads as follows:
"We wish to thank Dr. Miloslav Rechcígl, Jr., the dedicated and faithful pillar of the Society, for his extraordinary help and assistance to SVU since its foundation almost forty years ago, and in particular to his Executive Board in the last two years; for his remarkable initiative in recruiting several hundred new members for SVU in connection with the 16th World Congress in Czechoslovakia; for his happy discovery of the Council of Learned Societies in Prague, our loyal and energetic partner in the organization of the Congress; for his dedicated labor of love, together with his exceptional and gifted collaborator, Mrs. Eva Rechcígl, on the *1992 SVU Directory*, the best business card our Society ever had;

and to the full, sustained, and selfless support of both of them to the Society and its goals and aspirations over all these years."

With congratulations and best wishes from us all at the SVU General Assembly, I remain

As ever, yours

Jan F. Tříska

# 36
## Zdeněk Slouka's Presidency

Since the Society never had its annual meeting in Czechoslovakia, and only once it was held outside the territory of North America, Tříska was a little concerned about the outcome of a General Assembly meeting held in Prague, in conjunction with SVU World Congress. Consequently, he decided to hold the meeting separately after the Congress. It was scheduled four months later in Los Angeles, on his home territory, on October 22, 1992. In a number of ways it was a fortuitous decision. Among other, it gave me more time to put together a new slate of candidates for the next SVU administrative period, as I was designated chairman of the Nominations Committee.[670]

From my close association with him, in connection with the SVU Commission for Cooperation with Czechoslovakia and the SVU Research Institute, I knew that the most agile person in SVU was Prof. Zdeněk Slouka and, as such, I considered him the best candidate for the next SVU President. During our workshop, sponsored by the SVU Research Institute, and the SVU World Congress in Prague, I had ample opportunity to discuss with him the aims of SVU and his ideas for the future course of the Society. Slouka was clearly committed to do his part and readily consented to accept the nomination, when I posed the question.

Once we had the candidate for Presidency, the rest was relatively easy, except that there was very little time. Nevertheless, within days after my return to the US, our Nominations Committee hurriedly put together the slate of candidates which I then forwarded to Secretary-General Frank Marlow to start the election process. In those days, the process was relatively simple, consisting of publishing the names of the

---

[670] The original Nominations Committee consisted of Prof. Josef Anderle, Prof. Zdeněk Hruban, Dr. Miloslav Rechcígl, Jr. (Chairman) and Prof. Zdeněk Slouka. After accepting the nomination, Dr. Slouka subsequently resigned from the Committee.

candidates in *Zprávy SVU*[671] and having the members return their choices in marked ballots to the previously appointed Committee of the Election Officers. Everything went smoothly.

About the same time, clouds appeared on the horizon. Without any warning, we learned from Tříska that a lawsuit was filed against the Society and against him personally, in his capacity as SVU President, by two SVU members. As part of the legal proceedings, Secretary-General Marlow was requested to submit all sorts of documentation, including the minutes of the Executive Board meetings, and respond to a large number of specific questions by the other side regarding management and administrative matters of the Society, all from the time of Tříska's Presidency. In time, the complaint was narrowed to one specific charge, namely that some of the Board decisions were made by telephone rather than in the official meetings, in the presence of adequate quorum, which was in contradiction with the Articles of Incorporation of the District of Columbia, where the Society was officially registered. I shall not dwell into the merits of the lawsuit nor do I wish to discuss the motivation of the members who brought the lawsuit against the Society. The fact is that the matter could have been resolved in an orderly manner had the principal parties been willing. Instead it went before a judge to arbitrate the dispute.

In the meantime, Slouka and the rest of the candidates, proposed by the Nominations Committee,[672] were elected by SVU membership, without opposition, and the results of the election were announced in Los Angeles at the SVU General Assembly meeting.[673] In our justification for the candidates by the Nominations Committee, we wrote the following:[674]

> The list of candidates for the Executive Board and the SVU Council reflects the process the Society currently experiences: as an overseas branch of the Czech and Slovak culture, the Society

---

[671] The slate of the proposed candidates with their biographical sketches and introductory comments from the committee was published in *Zprávy SVU*, vol. 34 (July-Aug. 1992), No. 4, pp. 1-11.

[672] *Zprávy SVU*, vol. 24, No. 4 (July-August 1992), pp. 1-11.

[673] *SVU Bulletin*, vol. 3, No. 4 (October 1992), pp. 4-5.

[674] *SVU Bulletin*, vol. 13, No. 3 (August 1992), pp. 4-5.

cannot but be affected by the cultural and political revival in the CSFR and must react to her many needs.

The basic mission of the Society has not been changed by the November of 1989. It still wants to represent Czech and Slovak culture abroad, and from there support the cultural development in the home country. However, the conditions of our work have been essentially modified, new prospects for our activities have been opened and our tasks have multiplied. It is necessary to do more, abroad and at home, work more effectively, raise our organizational professionalism, broaden and improve our membership base, mobilize new and younger workers.

During the past period of the chairmanship of Jan Triska, our efforts have already moved in that direction. The goal of the submitted ballot is to go forward and accelerate the tempo of the modernization of the SVU.

Behind the proposed ballot, there is the idea of a unified team whose members will fulfill their tasks according to their specific capabilities, talents and experiences, be it publications or information activities, the strengthening of the membership base, contact with various foundations and governmental agencies, or the cooperation with individuals and organization in Czechoslovakia or abroad.

Even though the selection of the candidates was done with the above functional necessities in mind, it also had to consider their willingness and possibility to serve on a voluntary basis. The Society does not pay its officers and does not provide funds for their travel and other expenses incurred in the performance of their functions.

The newly elected Executive Board consisted of Zdeněk Slouka, President, Ivan Viest, Executive Vice President, Catherine Albrecht,[675] Joseph J. Kohn,[676] Jan Krč,[677] Hana F. Romováček,[678] Pavel

---

[675] Catherine Albrecht, associate professor of history, University of Baltimore, MD

[676] Joseph J. Kohn (1932-), professor of mathematics, Princeton University, NJ.

[677] Jan Krč (1967-), international exchange specialist, U.S. Information Agency, Washington, DC.

[678] Hana F. Romováček (1925-), research associate, University of Pittsburgh, PA.

Machotka,[679] Josef Mestenhauser and Vlado Šimko, Vice Presidents, Halina Břeň,[680] Secretary-General and Frank Mucha, Treasurer. I had previously discussed all these candidates with Zdeněk Slouka and had the greatest expectations from this team. Zdeněk Slouka's public statement, "Quo Vadis SVU," in which he outlined his thoughts and aims was full of promise and gave every indication that the next two years would be successful.[681]

December 30, 1992 marked a sad day in the history of Czechoslovakia, which took Masaryk and his associates so much effort to build. The announced breakup of the State into two separate entities, the Czech Republic and the Slovak Republic, although dubbed the "Gentle Divorce" in Slovak and the "Velvet Divorce" in Czech and other languages, it was a serious blow to all of us who grew up in the Masaryk Czechoslovak Republic. The SVU made its position known in its statement in the January 1993 issue of *Zprávy SVU*[682] and its editorial in *SVU Bulletin*.[683]

The newly elected SVU Executive Board also started on the wrong foot. The problems already began brewing in its first meeting, held at Columbia University, which I attended. At the beginning of the meeting, Halina Břeň announced that she did not want to be Secretary-General and preferred to be a Vice President instead. Pavel Machotka was asked to trade with her and he willingly accepted and immediately took over the task as the minutes taker.

From the way Zdeněk Slouka handled the meeting, it was apparent that he was not entirely himself and at times he seemed unable to respond to questions or to take decisive action. Some of us soon realized that he was not well but none of us could anticipate that his poor health would have such disastrous effect on his Presidency.[684] He began to be

---

[679] Pavel Machotka (1936-), research professor of psychology and art, University of California, Santa Clara.

[680] Halina Břeň (1942-), computer programmer, New Hyde Park, NY.

[681] Published in *Zprávy SVU*, vol. 35, No. 1 (January-February 1993), pp. 1-4.

[682] *Zprávy SVU,* vol. 35, No. 1 (January-February 1994), p. 5.

[683] "Goodbye, Czechoslovakia," *SVU Bulletin*, vol. 13, No. 4 (October 1992), p. 2.

[684] His symptoms may have been due to the side effects of some of the medicine he was taking because some time later, when he changed doctors and his prescriptions, his health returned to normal.

more and more dependent on individual Vice Presidents, some of whom were mere novices, with little knowledge of or experience with SVU matters.

As a result of the Executive Board's decision in their meeting of December 12, 1992, a Referendum of the membership was conducted to change SVU Bylaws. It included the provision to increase the number of Vice Presidents by two due to the expanding functions of the Society. Because many functions of the Vice Presidents overlap and the needs of the Society change, the division of labor within the Executive Board, were to be determined by consensus within the Board itself. Because of the laws of Washington, DC, where SVU was incorporated, the Executive Board's decisions henceforth would be made only in a meeting or in a telephone conference. Due to the fact that the members of the Board were geographically widely dispersed, the previous requirement that the quorum consists of more than one half of its members was to be changed to one third of members.

I could not attend their Board meeting on April 3, 1993, held at the Columbia University Medical Center in New York. According to the minutes,[685] the first part of the meeting was spent on discussing the status of the lawsuit against SVU, on establishing a committee to evaluate the content and the format of the *SVU Bulletin* and *Zprávy SVU*, appointing Mojmír Grygar[686] as the new editor of the periodical *Proměny*, and Trenský as editor of the *Czechoslovak and Central European Journal* would continue.

After considerable discussion, the Board also approved a tentative calendar for the next SVU Conferences and Congresses:

Fall 1993 – A conference at Princeton, NJ, if possible, in connection with a visit by President Havel to the Institute of Advanced Study, to be organized by Washington, DC Chapter.

June 1994 – The 17th SVU World Congress in the Czech Republic or Slovakia to be organized by J. Mestenhauser with the help of Vlado Šimko. The suggested theme was "Relations between the Czech-

---

[685] *Zprávy SVU*, vol. 35, No. 3 (May-June) 1993; *SVU Bulletin*, vol. 14, No. 1 (February 1993), pp. 1-3.

[686] Mojmír Grygar (1928-), scholar with Slavisch Seminarium, University of Amsterdam, The Netherlands.

lands and Slovakia, on one hand, and the US, on the other". This theme, perhaps defined by a broad title, such as "You and We," or "Vy a My," would both narrow the focus and offer papers and symposia of general interest. It would offer scope to analyses from the various social sciences and history. "The Board agreed that a Congress with no focus, such as the past one in Prague, attracted too many speakers without interest in any presentations but their own. The organizers will pick the site and define the theme more narrowly with colleagues in Prague and Bratislava."

Fall 1994 – A conference in New York City to be organized by the New York Chapter.

June 1995 – A congress in Prague devoted to the arts and humanities, to be organized by Pavel Machotka.

The Board then voted to allot up to $2,500 for expenses in connection with planning the Congress, which may include a trip to the site, and $1000 for each of the other three meetings or congresses.

Secretary Machotka then reported on the results of the votes on cooption and the Bylaws changes, both of which passed. The Board also acted on a suggestion to re-examine some of SVU internal structures and appointed J. Kohn and J. Mestenhauser to look specifically into the relation between the Executive Board and the Council. The Board then turned to the matter of membership criteria and the relations between the local chapters and SVU itself.

President Slouka then outlined a possible role of SVU, as an umbrella organization for a number of foundations in the Czech Republic and Slovakia. Under the plan any grants obtained by them through SVU would realize 10% to SVU, which would then go for the salary of a grants person. Interestingly, this passage was omitted from the referenced *Zprávy SVU* report,[687] although it was included in the official minutes prepared by Pavel Machotka.

I always regretted that I could not attend the above meeting, due to severe flu. Frankly, I thought that the proposed calendar of meetings was not realistic and the idea of having two congresses in successive years was outright foolish. I also felt it was a waste of money to send someone

---

[687] *Op cit.*

to the Czech Republic for the purpose of visiting various sites. Be that as it may, based on the Board's action, J. Mestenhauser then went to the Czech Republic, first to Prague and from there to Luhačovice,[688] which was his favored location for holding the Congress. It stands to reason that most people he talked to did not think Luhačovice was an ideal place for holding the Congress, partly because of its remote location, not to speak of the high costs.

At the subsequent Executive Board meeting, Mestenhauser came up with some theoretical ideas on how a successful congress should be run, which would have required enormous sums of money which the Society did not have. There was not enough time to solicit financial support from external sources and, furthermore, neither Mestenhauser nor any other member of the Board was anxious to start writing grant proposals. We did not hear much about the outcome of Mestenhauser's trip to Luhačovice and thus were left with the thought that his trip must have been a failure.

When the Executive Board probed further, it became obvious that Mestenhauser had no concrete plans for the Congress. He expressed his frustrations and helplessness as what to do next and finally recommended that the Congress be postponed at least for a year, if not longer. Břeň supported his view, commenting that there was really no need for any Congress, since the New York SVU Chapter was planning a special conference in New York in 1994 anyhow, for which preparations were well in hand.[689]

At this point I stepped in. It was apparent to me that the Board would have given up on the Congress altogether because nobody was eager to pitch in. I used all my skills to turn the opinion around, pointing out the potential negative impact of such decision for SVU and its public image. It was only after I indicated that Slouka and I would actually take on the responsibility for the Congress that they finally consented.

Zdeněk Slouka's physical condition seemed to be steadily getting worse. Most Executive Board members who were either unaware of his poor physical state or acted as if they did not know, blamed him for every problem that arose, while making little effort to lessen his burden

---

[688] A renowned spa in Moravia.

[689] As it later turned out, hardly any preparations were made since Chapter's Chairman Fryščák was on an overseas assignment.

or responsibilities. They were also critical of the way he managed the SVU Research Institute, demanding detailed accounting, even after he satisfied all the reporting requirements of the granting agency. It seemed that only Mucha and I remained Slouka's loyal friends, while the majority of Board members had turned against him.

Executive Vice President Ivan Viest, who would have been the logical person to assist Slouka in the most critical point of his Presidency, decided to step down, claiming that he actually never gave his consent for his election as Executive VP. Interestingly, he came up with this surprising statement after being in the position for over half a year. He soon was followed by the resignation of Secretary-General Pavel Machotka who gave as a reason for his resignation his appointment to his University's Senate.

These turbulent events inevitably led to convening a General Assembly meeting in Washington, DC. on December 11, 1993,[690] during which Tom Gibian was elected the new Executive Vice President and Věra Bořkovec the new Secretary-General for the remainder of the two-year administrative period.[691] The latter two, de facto, then ran the Society until the two-year administrative period of the Executive Board was over. For reasons unknown to me, there is no mention of Gibian's and Bořkovec's elections in the report of the Washington General Assembly meeting in the *Zprávy SVU*.[692]

Good news came from the Swiss SVU Chapter which reported conducting the 3rd Summer Seminar for Czech and Slovak university students in Switzerland on August 21-28, 1993. A detailed account of this event was given in the September 1993 issue of *Zprávy SVU*.[693]

Good news also came from Bratislava and Kosice in Slovakia where formal SVU chapters were established on March 3, 1994.[694] The Bratislava Chapter immediately went to work and already during 20-21

---

[690] *Zprávy SVU*, vol. 35, No. 5 (September-October 1993), p. 1.

[691] They replaced Ivan Viest and Pavel Machotka, respectively.

[692] *Zprávy SVU*, vol. 36, No. 1 (January-February 1994), pp. 1-2; "Report on the Yearly General Assembly of the Society, Saturday, December 11, 1993," *SVU Bulletin*, vol. 14, No. 4 (November 1993), p. 3.

[693] *Zprávy SVU*, vol. 35, No. 5 (September -October 1993), 3-5.

[694] "Welcome to SVU Local Chapters in Bratislava and Kosice," *SVU Bulletin*, vol. 15, No. 2 (May 1994), p. 5.

October 1994, organized a two-day Conference in Smolenice, Slovakia on the theme, "Science and Arts Do Not Know Borders,"[695] in which Zdeněk Slouka took part.

It was an extraordinary meeting. It was opened by Prof. Alexander Tkáč, who after welcoming the participants, outlined the goals and aims of the Conference, followed by a major address by SVU President Slouka. The representatives from the Prague (P. Mader[696] and Lenka Mechurova) and the Kosice SVU Chapters (M. Gálová[697]) reported on their activities. The academic part of the Conference comprised five panels. The first on Culture and History had three speakers: L. Ďurovič, who gave an analysis of the historical facts influencing the coexistence of Czechs and Slovaks; J. Morovič,[698] who talked on the relations of sciences and arts from the standpoint of science and technology; and R. Fiala on the relations of sciences and arts from the standpoint of arts. The panel on Sciences included papers by M. Gálová on motivating factors in scientific work, J. Morovič on transformation of society, management and economics, M. Greksák[699] on "Ecce scientia Slovacca," L. Borecký[700] on basic research in Slovakia, L. Ebringer[701] on cooperation of Slovak and Czech scientific societies, I. Hudoba[702] on convergence of science and education and L. Macho[703] on dialogue between the university and academy. The panel on Arts had papers by D. Kováč on Czechs and Slovaks in modern history, Z. Macků[704] on Slovak influences on

---

[695] *Zprávy SVU*, vol. 36, No. 6 (November-December 1994), p. 7-8.

[696] Pavel Mader (1941-), associate professor of chemistry; Czech University of Agriculture, Prague; chairman of the SVU Prague Chapter.

[697] Miriam Gálová (1935-), professor of chemistry, University of Pavel Jozef Šafárik in Košice.

[698] Jan Morovič (1945-), advisor for international cooperation, with the Agricultural Minister, Bratislava.

[699] Miloslav Greksák (1936-), animal biochemist and geneticist, with the Slovak Academy of Sciences, Bratislava.

[700] Ladislav Borecký (1924-), director, Institute of Virology, Slovak Academy of Sciences, Bratislava.

[701] Libor Ebringer (1931-), professor of microbiology, Comenius University, Bratislava.

[702] Vice Rector, Slovak Technical University, Bratislava.

[703] Laco Macho (1930-), endocrinologist, with the Slovak Academy of Science, Bratislava.

[704] Zdeněk A. Macků (1943-), painter and writer, living in Prague.

Czech art, V. Bílek on Talich and Slovakia and D. Valocký[705] on cultural servility and cultural prizes. The panel on Spiritual Issues contained contributions by F. Hanic[706] on the role of the intelligence in suppressing aggression, J. Škodáček on ethics in psychiatry, A. Srholec[707] on Europe in the crossroads – between hope and fear and O. R. Halaga on memory of the continuity or setbacks in the progression of the Nation. The fifth panel was a Round Table, in which Z. Slouka, V. Šimko participated. In the evening of the first day there was a piano recital by Doc. E. Fischerová,[708] featuring works of Slovak composers.

The third good news was a special SVU Conference, entitled "Contemporary Czech and Slovak Culture," which the SVU New York Chapter organized at the International House of New York on October 29-30, 1994,[709] in conjunction with the SVU 1994 Annual Meeting.[710]

This was also an excellent Conference which comprised eight panels along the disciplinary lines, including music, social sciences, visual arts, architecture, two panels on literature and finally a session of readings from contemporary works of Czech and Slovak authors and another on teaching Czech and Slovak languages, literature and culture. It was gratifying to see a number of speakers from the Czech Republic, i.e., Petr Bílek, Jiří Hasil, Jan Kuklík, and Oldřich Uličný, all from Charles University in Prague and Vladimír Papoušek of the University of South Bohemia in České Budějovice. In the evening there was a commemoration of the Czech National Holiday with the address of H.E. Karel Kovanda, Ambassador of the Czech Republic to the UN. Afterwards I had the pleasure of addressing the audience in my capacity as the newly elected SVU President.

---

[705] Dušan Q. Valocký (1928-), artist living in Bratislava.

[706] František Hanic (1927-), chemist, associated with the Slovak Academy of Science, Bratislava.

[707] Anton Srholec (1929-), Catholic priest and humanitarian, living in Bratislava.

[708] Eva M. Fischerová (1922-), pianist, associated with the Janacek Academy of Music Arts, Brno.

[709] *Zprávy SVU*, vol. 36, No. 6 (November-December 1994), pp. 8 - 10; *SVU Bulletin*, vol. 15, No. 4 (November 1994), pp. 8-10; *SVU Bulletin*, vol. 15, No. 4 (November-December 1994), pp. 8-10.

[710] *Zprávy SVU*, vol. 36, No. 6 (November-December 1994), pp. 2-3.

The most significant thing that was accomplished during the 1992-94 period for which the Executive Board could specifically claim credit was settling the ongoing legal dispute against the Society.[711] The suit was very costly for SVU, not only in terms of money spent on lawyers but also in terms of time and effort. The matter preoccupied the agenda of most of Executive Board meetings in that period. In fact, until the matter was settled, it almost paralyzed the Society from doing anything significant.[712] At the onset of Slouka's presidency it was planned, among other, to convene a special conference in Princeton relating to education. However, because of the turmoil, the idea had to be scrapped altogether, as were other initiatives. I had, of course, been working on the program of the 1994 Congress, while Zdeněk Slouka worked diligently on the organizational and logistical aspects of the upcoming Congress. We made a good team, which was strengthened by the fact that we liked and also implicitly trusted each other. The account of the 17th SVU World Congress is written in a separate chapter.

The Executive Board itself could hardly claim any credit for the successful outcome of the Congress. The relatively low productivity of the Board is also evident if one examines the contents of *Zprávy SVU* from this period. The SVU newsletter, which abounds with historical material, has hardly any information on the activities of the Board, except for our periodic announcements relating to the upcoming Congress.[713]

---

[711] As a result of this settlement, the Society was directed to change its Bylaws, following the approval of the Referendum by the SVU members.

[712] To be sure, the problem, for which they were not responsible, had its start during the administrative period of the Executive Board that preceded them.

[713] *Zprávy SVU*, vol. 35, no. 6 (November-December 1993), pp. 1-2; *Ibid*, vol. 36, No. 2 (March-April 1994), pp. 1-7; "The Seventeenth SVU World Congress, Prague, June 26-29, 1994), *SVU Bulletin*, vol. 15, No. 1 (February 1994), pp. 1-4.

## 37
## *Organizing the Second SVU Congress in Prague*

As noted earlier, I was given the responsibility for organizing the 1994 SVU Congress quite late, i.e., almost at the end of the year 1993. The Executive Board actually, expressed preference for scrapping the idea altogether and postponing the Congress by two years. It was only after Slouka and I raised objections, they were willing to reconsider, providing that Slouka and I would assume complete responsibility for its organization and the program. Considering the repercussions and damage the Board's decision would have on SVU reputation, Slouka and I accepted the challenge.

I focused on the preparation of the program with the overseas participants, while Slouka dealt primarily with the logistics and maintained liaison with the local organizers. In this connection, I had already negotiated an agreement with Prof. Petr Zuna, Dean of the Faculty of Mechanical Engineering at the Czech Technical University, to hold our Congress on their Dejvice Campus in Prague. The conditions of the agreement were very advantageous to us, as they offered their facilities to us, practically free.

The Prague Organization Committee was headed by Dr. Lenka Měchurová, the Executive Secretary of the Council of Czech Scientific Societies. The program aspects were locally handled by Dr. Jiří Ullschmied and Dr. Jaroslav Folta. After the former's overseas assignment, the entire responsibility for the program with the Czech and Slovak participants fell on the shoulders of Dr. Folta.

The preliminary announcement of our plans for the Congress appeared in *Zprávy SVU* in November-December 1993[714] and again in the March 1994 issue.[715] In the latter issue was a brief outline of major events of the Congress, together with a pre-registration form and the

---

[714] *Zprávy SVU*, vol. 35, No. 6 (November-December 1993), pp. 1-2.
[715] *Zprávy SVU*, vol. 36, No. 2 (March-April 1994), pp. 18.

registration form for speakers. Comparable information in English appeared in SVU Bulletins.[716]

My work in the US was conducted in two phases. The first phase involved the preparation of the list of potential speakers in various fields, some 700 persons in total. With the help of Dr. Blanka Kuděj, we then sent out invitation letters to the persons on our list with the request that they give a talk on some topic in their area of expertise. In contrast to the previous SVU Congress in Prague, the response to our mass mailing was negligible. While two years earlier, more than 400 persons responded in the affirmative, this time less that one tenth of that number replied. This was clearly a reflection of the apathy that beset our membership and Czechs and Slovaks abroad, generally, after the euphoria that followed the Velvet Revolution, subsided. This time it was not a novelty to see one's old homeland or to visit the memorable sites of Prague, because most of the individuals who wanted to see it already went there. Furthermore, judging by some of the negative comments we received, a number of our members resented the paucity of the audience they faced when they presented their talks during the first Congress in Prague which they assigned to the lack of interest by the local Czechs and Slovaks. They did not want to go through another humiliation of this kind.

Under the circumstances it was necessary to change our overall strategy. Two years earlier, the process was relatively simple. The main task was simply to divide the offered talks into appropriate sections and panels and then find suitable chairpersons. This time it was more complex. The relatively few positive responses and suggestions for talks were too sparse and variable, making it impossible to form any meaningful panels on the basis of such information. We had thus no choice but to start from scratch. Based on my knowledge and personal contacts, I made a deliberate effort to find suitable individuals who could organize specific sections in the area of their specialization or expertise.

The second alternative was to organize such panels by myself. I was lucky enough to find a number of professionals who were indeed willing to organize panels, either by themselves or with my help. Nevertheless, this did not cover all the subject areas so that I had to organize the missing panels on my own. With some experience, I soon

---

[716] *SVU Bulletin*, vol. 14, No. 4 (November 1993), pp. 1-2; *Ibid.*, vol. 15, No. 1 (February 1994), pp. 1-4.

discovered that I had more luck in locating speakers for general and multi-disciplinary symposia on some unified topics. Consequently I focused my energies on organizing symposia with timely or retrospective topics.

Based on my calculations, I figured we would need at least 200 participants from abroad to be able to pay for the Congress expenses. At the end, I indeed succeeded in reaching this quota, and, in fact, exceeded it, so that, against all expectations, we actually made a profit.

It was, however, not easy, by any means. Together with my wife, we worked hard on this, almost without stopping, from January until the end of May.

Inasmuch as Blanka Kuděj had to leave for Europe for almost a month, besides the program organization, we were also stuck with the responsibility for the receipt of the registration forms and the fees, as well as for answering individual queries from the potential participants. It was obvious from the correspondence that each letter had to be answered individually because otherwise we might have lost a potential participant. Without my wife's help I would not have been able to manage it all by myself. After Blanka Kuděj's return, she continued in the work we started and carefully handled the financial aspects of the Congress until the end.

Apart from organizing individual panels, it was also necessary to coordinate the overseas program with that of our counterparts in Prague. This coordination was done either by individual panel organizers themselves or between Dr. Folta and me. There was very little time for this and had it not been for the use of FAXes we couldn't have finished on time.

I should mention that I also handled the publicity campaign and drafted the press releases. abroad. Altogether, I prepared ten different press releases in Czech, as well as in English, which were published in various papers. In this connection, our good friend, Petr Bísek, the publisher of *Americké Listy*, regularly printed in his newspaper news about the progress we were making in organizing the Congress.

The result of our efforts was a voluminous and impressive program, comprising 68 pages of the 3rd issue of the 1994 *Zprávy SVU*,[717] which was printed separately.

---

[717] *SVU 17th World Congress Program. Prague, Czech Republic, June 26-June 28, 1994.* Zprávy SVU, vol. 36, No. 2 (May-June 1994),. 68 p.

## 38
# *Hard Work Bears Fruit –*
# *The Second Successful Prague Congress*

As the last words of Rev. Jan Milič Lochman echoed from the walls of the ancient Bethlehem Chapel in Prague, clouds rapidly gathered above the city and a strong rain began pouring down, marking the end of several days of persistent heat that accompanied the entire 17th SVU World Congress.[718] Even though heat might have increased the exhaustion of the participants, it did not disrupt the Congress proceedings and the atmosphere of the meeting, attended by some 600 participants.

The Congress, with its central theme "Contributions of Czechs and Slovaks to World Culture," was convened at the Faculty of Mechanical Engineering of the Czech Institute of Technology in Dejvice, a borough of Prague, which celebrated its 130th anniversary. Under the leadership of its Dean Prof. Petr Zuna, the Faculty provided the Congress all sorts of services and assistance, practically free of charge, including the use of their lecture halls. They also provided more than forty students who for the duration of Congress rendered indispensable service for the Congress. All twenty lecture halls, which were at our disposal, were filled to capacity with participants listening to papers presented at various panels, micro-conferences, round tables, symposia or workshops.

The Congress was ceremoniously opened in the Prague Rudolfinum, in the presence of prominent personalities of Czech public life, with a message from President Havel, followed by the remarks of Prof. Zdeněk Slouka, SVU President, Prof. Jaroslav Valenta, President of the Council of Scientific Societies, and Ministers of the Czech Government, Igor Němec, Pavel Tigrid and Ivan Pilip. Then came the greetings from Zdeněk Kessler, Presiding Judge of the Czech Constitutional Court and His Excellency Adrian Basora, Ambassador of the US. Among the representatives of scientific and cultural organizations who addressed the meeting were Rudolf Zahradník, President of the Czech Academy of

---

[718] This chapter is based, in part, on my article, "Dobrá věc se vydařila," *Zprávy SVU*, vol. 36, No. 4 (July-August 1994), pp. 1-4.

Sciences, Pavel Klener, Vice Rector of Charles University, František Hron, Rector of the Czech University of Agriculture, Jiří Stránský, President of the Czech Center of the International PEN Club and Petr Zuna, Dean of the Faculty of Mechanical Engineering. The words of Prof. Alexander Tkáč, President of SVU Bratislava Chapter and the chief spokesman for Slovakia, were accompanied by an enthusiastic applause. The verbal part of the ceremony was concluded by Miloslav Rechcígl, President of the SVU Congress.

Then came "Missa brevis," composed by Zdeněk Lukáš, who was present, by a brilliant performance of the ČKD Prague Chorus, Miroslav Košler conducting. The national anthems of the Czech and Slovak Republics concluded the official opening of the Congress, accompanied by the academic procession led by President of the Czech Conference of the University Rectors, Stanislav Hanzl, Rector of the ČVUT.

The Congress proceedings began with a plenary session devoted to "The Aims and the Mission of the Czech Exile and Émigré Organizations on Behalf of their Homeland" in the spacious Assembly Hall of the University. Under the direction of the former SVU President Mila Rechcígl and the past President of the Council of Free Czechoslovakia Mojmír Povolný, the participants heard presentations by the representatives of the main organizations abroad that played a role in assisting Czechoslovakia in the past years.

In the evening of the same day there was a social gathering in the Prague Castle ballroom and in the adjacent Royal Gardens. Here the Congress attendees had the opportunity to meet various dignitaries, including Minister of Foreign Affairs Josef Zielenec, Minister of Culture Pavel Tigrid, Minister of Education Ivan Pilip and Vice Premier of the Czech Republic Jan Kalvoda. One would frequently meet an old acquaintance or a friend here whom he or she did not see for many years or make new professional contacts and establish new friendships.

The following Monday most of the Congress participants congregated in one of the numerous scheduled academic sessions. In the course of five half day sessions, individual panels, running concurrently for three hours each, encompassed some 300 working hours, with the participation of more than 600 lecturers and discussants.

In terms of the content and the overall quality, most presentations dealt with the subject in greater depth and more thoroughly than was the

*Hard Work Bears Fruit –*
*The Second Successful Prague Congress* 231

case in the previous Congresses. Even though the organizers did not have enough time to completely merge the US-organized panels with the domestic presentations, this did not pose serious problems. The good will of the participants largely overcame occasional language problems as the domestic speeches, for the most part, were in Czech or Slovak, while the overseas participants gave their talks in English. It was touching to listen to some foreigners who, in an effort to oblige the local audience, made their presentations in Czech or Slovak languages which was obviously not easy for them.

Every Congress participant received Congress Proceedings consisting of the program and the Abstracts of Papers.[719] A preliminary program, with the list of participants and the location of individual panels, appeared previously in the *Zprávy SVU* [720] and *SVU Bulletin*.[721]

It is not possible to provide a detailed account of every panel. There was hardly a single major area that was not represented, from the arts and letters to social sciences, biological and physical sciences, applied sciences and technology.

A number of talks dealt with the life and contributions of Czechs and Slovaks abroad. Besides the already mentioned plenary session devoted to the Czechoslovak exile, there was a separate one-day symposium on the role of Czechs and Slovaks in World War I and World War II. Another symposium commemorated the 350th anniversary of the legendary Augustine Herman who landed in New Amsterdam in 1644.

A novelty of the Congress was a mini-conference devoted to Czech and Slovak contributions in prenatal research, arranged by physiologists.[722] The field of medicine was represented by a series of sessions and discussion panels, covering nutrition, metabolism, application of the latest biological advances in medicine, public health, heart disease, gynecology, rehabilitation medicine and schooling of physicians. Spe-

---

[719] *17th World Congress if the Czechoslovak Society of Arts and Sciences , in cooperation with the Council of Learned societies of CR, under the auspices of Vaclav Havel, President of the CR. Czech and Slovak Contribution to World Culture. Abstracts.* Prague, 1994. 137 p & 64 p.

[720] *Zprávy SVU*, vol. 36, No. 2 (March-April 1994), pp. 18;

[721] *SVU Bulletin*, vol. 14, No. 4 (November 1993), pp. 1-2; *Ibid.*, vol. 15, No. 1 (February 1994), pp. 1-4.

[722] The papers were later published in *Physiological Research*, vol. 44, No. 6 (1995), pp. 339-360.

cialists in forestry organized a day-long symposium[723] about sustainable forestry in the Czechlands and Slovakia and in the world as a whole, combined with a two-day excursion to view selected forestry projects in Bohemia and Moravia. The most ambitious program was organized by the Czech agronomists, thanks to the efforts of Prof. Rudolf Jánal.[724] The problems of ecology were discussed in several panels with participation of American specialists. In this connection mention should be made of a special symposium and a roundtable about atmospheric pollution.

Among physical sciences there was a symposium about Czech astronomy in the world- past, present and future, organized by Mirek J. Plavec and Jiří Grygar and another about Czech and Slovak contributions in mechanics and thermomechanics, organized by Jan Ježek. Another symposium dealt with global tectonics and the ore research with a roundtable about mining of gold in the Czechlands. Another interesting program was prepared by domestic and overseas engineers. Separate panels were devoted to computer technology and technology transfer.

In the area of humanities and social sciences, there was an interesting symposium about Bohemian Reformation and religious practice,[725] symposium about the First Czechoslovak Republic, Slovak National Uprising, four panels devoted to history of science and technology, a symposium about women of yesterday and today, symposium about the Sokol movement, a mini-conference about the advantages and limits of nationality in the post-communist thought in literature, linguistics and information sciences.

The questions of international relations were discussed in four discussion panels, one roundtable and a separate symposium was devoted to Dr. Ján Papánek and his role in international politics. Well attended were

---

[723] The symposium was published under the title *Sustainable Forestry in the Czech Republic, Slovakia and the World.* Proc. of the Conference of the Forestry Section, held in Prague, June 26, 1994 in association with the 17th World Congress of the Czechoslovak Society of Arts and Sciences. Prague, Zbraslav: Národní lesnický komitét, 1996. 78 p.

[724] Published as *Sborník Československé společnosti pro vědy zemědělské, lesnické a potravinářské: Sborníik příspěvků ze 17. světovéhp kongresu.* Edited by Rudolf Janál. Prague, 1994. 238 p.

[725] These papers were published as a monograph, *The Bohemian Reformation and Religious Practice.* Papers from the XVIIth World Congress of the Czechoslovak Society of Arts and Sciences, Prague, 1994. Prague: Academy of Sciences of the ČR, 1996. 95 p.

also panels dealing with economics and trade, and management in the transformation process. Of special interest was a discussion panel about science policy and a session on education, learning and teaching.

The arts were represented by sessions on history of music and musicology, art history and art education, and the readings from the works of Czech and Slovak writers.

Taken as a whole, we can be more than satisfied with the outcome of the Congress. In its multi disciplinary approach, which was a novelty in the Czechlands and Slovakia, the Congress demonstrated the importance of such approaches in meetings of Czech and Slovak intellectuals and their peers worldwide.

# Part IV
# Twelve Uninterrupted Years as SVU President

# 39
## *Returning to the SVU Presidency*

With Zdeněk Slouka's illness, it was evident that he could not run again and that the Society would need to search for a suitable successor at the conclusion of his term. The responsibility rested on the newly named Nominations Committee, consisting of Sáša Bořkovec, Andrew Eliáš, Zdenka Pospíšil, Zdeněk Suda and Jan F. Tříska. Bořkovec assumed the role of Committee chairman and after some preliminary checking he had a meeting of the Committee to decide on the new slate.[726]

To be sure, I was initially urged by Tříska to throw my hat into the ring but I had no desire of returning to SVU presidency and proposed Leopold Pospíšil instead. I was hoping that the Committee would select him because, in my judgment, he was probably the strongest candidate the Committee could find. To my dismay, I soon learned through the grapevine, that Bořkovec had no intention of nominating Pospíšil and was planning to push for Tom Gibian instead.

This was a real shock to me. I have known Tom Gibian quite well and considered him a friend. He was a nice guy, with a pleasant personality, but, in the judgment of many, he was not suitable for President. He had a rather limited exposure to SVU and his knowledge of the Society was very superficial.

I had a valid reason to worry about the future of SVU if his election to Presidency were to materialize. I expressed my reservations to the Nominations Committee and suggested my willingness to run again under these circumstances. Actually, I went beyond that and proposed my willingness to run against Gibian in a two-man race, if the Committee would prefer that.

I do not know what happened during the Committee's deliberations, except that Sáša Bořkovec apparently stuck to his guns and persuaded the other members to accept his recommendation to nominate

---

[726] *Zprávy SVU*, vol. 36, No. 4 (July-August 1994), p. 5.

Gibian for the next President. The option of having a two-man race was apparently not even considered.

When the news broke out about the Committee's intentions of proposing to SVU membership a slate headed by Gibian rather than by me, it created quite a bit of rumblings among the members and it did not take long and an organized effort was afoot for my draft. A large number of signatures were collected on my behalf, which would permit me to run independently of the Nominations Committee against their candidate. When Tom Gibian got wind of what was happening, he asked the Committee to withdraw his name.

This put the Nomination Committee into a precarious position and Bořkovec chose to resign. The rest of the Committee, which then reassembled under Jan F. Tříska's chairmanship, decided to back my candidacy for the next SVU President. They also scrapped the initial choices recommended by Bořkovec, and replaced them with new candidates to assure better teamwork and greater effectiveness of the new Executive Board.[727]

In their reasoned statement,[728] Tříska wrote, on behalf of the Nominations Committee, the following:

> SVU is entering a critical period in its development. The new leadership must not only be exceptionally able but must be also willing to work hard. SVU should avail itself of all the promising opportunities that were never available before. To take advantage of these possibilities is a difficult task and a great responsibility. To find a new – and correct – direction for the Society in this historic phase won't be easy. Under the circumstances a strong experienced, imaginary, inventive a self-sacrificing leadership is a must.
>
> It is for these reasons that the Nominations Committee has returned to the tested SVU worker and professional – Dr. Miloslav Rechcígl – whom it considers, under the current circumstances, the most capable candidate for SVU President. Dr. Rechcígl stood at the cradle of the Society and for more than thirty-five years worked on its behalf. The candidates for the other offices have also been selected with care to assure that the new Executive Board has all

---

[727] *Zprávy SVU*, vol. 36, No. 5 (September-October 1994), pp. 2-11; "SVU General Assembly and Elections," *SVU Bulletin*, vol. 15, No. 3 (August 1994), pp. 1-2.

[728] *Zprávy SVU*, vol. 36, No. 5 (September-October 1994), p. 1.

the expertise, experience and skill it needs to guarantee that the officers will work together as a team. To make it easier to carry out the demanding agenda the candidates for Vice Presidents have been assigned specific set of duties and responsibilities about which they have previously been informed.

The Nominations Committee hopes that the proposed candidates, if elected, will fulfill the new and uneasy SVU role with success.

My election as the new SVU President was a far gone conclusion. I was elected without opposition[729] and my election was formally announced at the SVU General Assembly meeting in New York on October 29, 1994.[730]

Below is the text of my acceptance speech:

Allow me to first thank you for the trust you have shown me by voting me in as the new SVU President. In the past there was a tradition that the newly elected President would give a speech during the banquet, but the format of the New York Conference does not allow it. Nevertheless I would like to use this opportunity to say at least a few words about the current state of SVU, as I see it, and at the same time about my plans for future SVU activities.

It is clear that SVU has entered a critical phase of its development. In view of the political changes in the old country certain apathy manifests itself in our membership, and there are even voices heard that the Society *de facto* has accomplished its mission and that the moment of cease and desist has come. Personally, I disagree with such an opinion. The euphoria of the first post-revolution years in our native country has evaporated quite a long time ago, and it appears that the development in the Czechlands and also in Slovakia will be a long-term process. Despite the undoubted abilities and efforts of our people at home, both Republics will need assistance from abroad to reach a standard on the level of the first Czechoslovak Republic.

---

[729] *SVU Bulletin*, vol. 15, No. 4 (November 1994), pp. 1 & 3.
[730] SVU Bulletin, vol. 15, no. 4 (November 1994), pp. 3-4; *Zprávy SVU*, vol. 36, No. 6 (November-December 1994), pp. 2-3.

I believe that SVU, with its enormous capital of intellect, knowledge and experience, is more than competent to offer such assistance. However, it surely would be inappropriate to force our ideas and plans upon our people at home; on the other hand, we are in a very favorable position to offer information and facilitate contacts on the world-forum, especially in the academic circles, if it will be desired. In this area is our strength and there exists a great potential not yet fully exploited. I am firmly convinced that SVU, by far, has not yet finished its mission and that its golden era still lies ahead....

I am fully cognizant of the worsening financial situation of the Society, as well as of other administrative problems that are making its activity more difficult. To remedy this situation will be our first priority, to make SVU capable to dedicate itself to new tasks that await us.

As the first step of the new administration, I consider a critical assessment of today's state of the Society and the preparation of an agenda for future activities. As soon as possible, we will have to carry out a fiscal reform in our management, based on economic principles and a balanced budget. We will make an effort to keep our membership informed on regular basis about the steps we have taken and results obtained, as well as any new challenges that may confront us.

It is understandable that the Executive Board will not be able to do all such work alone. Therefore, I appeal to all our members to join together for the work on common goals in spreading the Czech and Slovak cultural traditions in the world, and also to make our native country a prominent place in Europe, as it was before the World War II, which is where it historically belongs.

# 40
## *The Košice Conference*

The greatest SVU event of 1995 was, without doubt, the SVU Conference in Košice, held on the occasion of the 200th anniversary of the birth of the great scholar Pavel Josef Šafařík.[732] The Conference was convened at the Jozef Pavol Šafárik University's Institute of Veterinary Medicine, during 21-24 August 1995, under the general theme "Technology – Humanity – Art – Tolerance." The responsibility for the logistics and the program was in the hands of the Košice SVU Chapter, under the chairmanship of Prof. Dr. Karol Marton.[733] Some eighty SVU members and guests from Slovakia (Košice, Bratislava, and elsewhere), the Czechlands (Prague, Brno, Ostrava), United States, Canada, Austria, and Sweden took part in the meetings.

The selection of Košice was not accidental. After holding two Congresses in Prague, I felt it was time to hold our next event on the Slovak territory. Košice appeared as the logical site. It abounds with history and for centuries is widely known for its cosmopolitan cultural and social life. The close attachment and love of the city with its architecture and artistic monuments, which transcends centuries, bears witness to the fact that people of different ethnic background and religious beliefs can coexist with each other and jointly create remarkable and long-lasting values. Košice is also a city pulsating with scientific life of four institutions of higher learning that continue the tradition of the first Košice University confirmed by the Golden Bulla of Leopold I in 1660. The high standards of the ten Institutes of the Slovak Academy of Sciences based in the city have found their place among the leading European research institutions.

---

[732] "The Košice Experience," *Zprávy SVU*, vol. 37, No. 5 (September-October 1995), pp. 5-6; *Ibid.*, vol. 37, No. 6 (November -December 1995), pp. 4-8.

[733] Karol Marton (1933-), professor of electrical engineering, Technical University of Košice.

With the conference theme, "Technology – Humanity – Art – Tolerance," the organizers had the idea of integrating intellectuals from different worlds of learning, educators, scholars, scientists and artists, as well as benefactor of everything that is beautiful and that brings us all together. The central theme of the Conference was also reflective of the then current developmental trends in technology, technology transfer, explores their impact on common man and the mankind, while at the same time follows their influence on art and examines the question how this new orientation impacts on the coexistence of man with another, between nations and what would be uncovered in the mirror of tolerance.

All these thoughts were interwoven in the introductory remarks of Prof. Marton and Mr. Andrejka, Deputy Mayor of the City. Mr. Ahlers,[734] Vice Rector of the University of Pavol Jozef Šafárik stressed P. J. Šafařík's contributions to the development of science in Slovakia and the Czechlands. Dr. Miloslav Rechcígl, in turn, talked about the aim of the Czechoslovak Society of Arts and Sciences (SVU) and Prof. Alexander Tkáč brought greetings from the Bratislava SVU Chapter. During the ceremonial opening all the universities in the Košice area were duly represented.

The lectures were organized by several major themes, i.e., technology transfer and new sources of energy, population explosion and environment, integrating and disintegrating information science, the art of tolerance, art and tolerance and tolerance in art, and the Prometheus complex in biology and medicine. Detailed program was published in the September 1995 issue of *Zprávy SVU*.[735]

Some thirty lectures were presented along these lines, followed by extensive and highly valuable discussions which created an excellent atmosphere among the participants that intensified from day to day. Here are some of the titles: Problems of technological transfer in the US; Evaluation of scientific work as a presumption for technological transfer; Experience with wind energy in Canada; Using geotechnology to solve some of the environmental problems; Environmental toxic materials and the psychological development of children; Profit and environment; Alternative medicine and environment; Architecture and urbanism and

---

[734] Ivan Ahlers (1938-), professor of general biology, J. P. Šafárik University, Košice.

[735] *Zprávy SVU*, vol. 37, No. 5 (September-November 1995), pp. 12-16.

*The Košice Conference* 243

the environment; Thermodynamic and informatics; Importance of tolerance – gift and responsibility; Importance of tolerance for life; Difficult road for the Slovaks into Europe; Ethnic identity and nationalism; The art of tolerance – Tolerance in art; Teachers and culture; The Slovak greats in America; Effect of psycho-social factors on immunological defense against infectious diseases; Actual ethical-legal problems in medicine; They gave their lives for our health, etc.

As expected, most speakers were Slovaks from Košice or Bratislava, although there was also representation from the Czech Republic (V. Strakoš of Ostrava and P. Pavlovský[736] from Prague), as well as from the US (V. Ličko[737] from San Francisco, M. Rechcígl from Rockville, MD., F. Mucha from New York and Jiří Nehněvajsa from Pittsburgh) and Canada (J. P. Skalný of Toronto, V. Zajíc from Quebec and M. M. Grandtner[738] also from Quebec).

In the evening of August 22, which could be termed as the "Evening of Tolerance," the attendees were treated to a special spiritual lecture by Father Anton Srholec,[739] followed by equally inspiring presentations by Lutheran bishop ThDr. Filo, Dr. Ďurovič and Dr. Gajdoš.

A plenary session, convened in the morning of August 23 in the historical hall of the former "Župný dom,"[740] evoked a lasting impression. This was a historical place, where the first Czechoslovak Government of the National Front met with the Slovak National Council in 1945 and declared its infamous "Košice Program." I had the pleasure of presenting, as a part of the plenary session, a talk on the prominent Americans with Slovak roots.

The socio-cultural program included touring the historical part of the Košice City, a concert at the Budimír's Church, and the excursions to Spiš region and the High Tatras. There was also a gala buffet dinner to

---

[736] Petr Pavlovský (1944-), head, department of theatre and film, FFUK, Prague.
[737] Vojtech Ličko (1932-), professor of biology, University of California, San Francisco.
[738] Miroslav M. Grandtner (1928-), professor of forestry, Laval University, Quebec, Canada.
[739] Anton Srholec (1929-), a noted Catholic priest, writer and the founder of the shelter Rosota for the homeless, who was jailed by communists for many years.
[740] District House.

which the Mayor of Košice, Rudolf Schuster,[741] the Rectors from various Universities, and other dignitaries were invited. The social happening ended with the wine tasting of the enchanted Slovak Tokay wine in a cozy wine cellar and song, with the accompaniment of a guitar, in the charming gardens, amidst a picturesque setting of a renovated historical chapel. The upshot of it all was that everybody dropped their prestigious academic degrees and parted as Karol, Alex, Miriam, Míla or Franta.

The Conference participants also had an opportunity to participate in a special SVU workshop relating to management and financing of research which I had the pleasure of directing with the assistance of Frank Mucha and Jiří Nehněvajsa.[742]

We took advantage of the Košice meeting to also hold our Annual SVU General Assembly Meeting.[743] It was a historical meeting, inasmuch as it was the first meeting of its kind to be held on the territory of the former Czechoslovakia.

Speaking on the whole, the Conference, with its varied programs, was an unqualified success. Prof. Dr. Karol Marton, and his colleagues (Klára Tkáčová, Mariana Martonová,[744] Miriam Gálová, Oliver Racz, Marian Gajdoš, Alexander Tkáč, as well as Dr. J. P Skalný, who represented me on the Organizing Committee, did an excellent job, in terms of logistical arrangements, as well as program preparations.

Cooperation, voluntarism, professionalism, altruism, humility, mutual respect and camaraderie, which I witnessed in every step, was a great inspiration to me. As a consequence, I became afflicted with a serious case of optimism, which, I hoped, would also soon affect the others, with the strong belief that SVU entered a new phase of Renaissance.

Furthermore, I was left with a definite feeling that the ties between the Czechs and the Slovaks are real and unbreakable, and that SVU could strengthen them even more.

---

[741] Ing. Rudolf Schuster, CSc. (1934-) later became President of the Slovak Republic. In the early nineties (1990-92), he served as Czechoslovak Ambassador to Canada.

[742] *Zprávy SVU*, vol. 37, No. 5 (September-October 1995), p. 11.

[743] "The SVU 1995 General Assembly Meeting," *Zprávy SVU*, vol. 37, No. 5 (September-October 1995), 00. 2-4.

[744] Mariana Martonová (1937-), Docent, dept. electrical engineering, Technical University, Košice.

# 41
# *State of the SVU in 1995*

### Report of SVU President Dr. Miloslav Rechcígl, Jr. to the SVU General Assembly Convened in Košice on August 21, 1995[745]

I would like to thank our Košice Chapter for enabling us to hold this year's General Assembly meeting in Košice. This is indeed a historic first as it signifies the first instance of holding such meeting on the soil of Slovakia, and, for that matter, on the soil of former Czechoslovakia.

Considering that we reported on all our past activities in *Zprávy SVU*,[746] I will limit my report to the most important issues. As you will note, the Executive Board was quite busy in the last year. Since the time of our election on October 29, 1994, the Board met on five different occasions. Apart from its regular meetings it had a separate session devoted to the SVU publication program.

1. When we accepted our responsibilities, the Board was keenly aware that the Society was entering its critical period. At the very beginning we had to reexamine the question of the aims and the role of the Society under the circumstances brought about by the far-reaching changes in the old country. When the premature euphoria of the revolutionary days dissipated, it became clear that the future development in the Czechlands, as well as in Slovakia, will require a long-term and sustained patient effort before it would reach the horizons attained during the era of the First Czechoslovak Republic. The Executive Board in its wisdom concluded that the Society, which represents the cream of the Czech and Slovak intelligentsia abroad, has the best potential to offer a helping hand to both nations in the academic arena and through professional contacts worldwide, as well as toward Czech and Slovak immigration, in general.

---

[745] The original Czech version was published in *Zprávy SVU*, vol. 37, No. 5 (September-October 1995), pp. 6-10.

[746] *Zprávy SVU*, vol. 36, No. 6 (November-December 1994), p. 4; *Ibid.*, vol. 37, No. 1 (January-February 1995), pp. 7-11; *Ibid.*, vol. No. 3 vol. 37, No. 3 (May-June 1995), pp. 1-3; *Ibid.*, vol. 37, No. 4 (July-August 1995), pp. 13-16.

To assist in the preservation of their cultural traditions and foster cultural cooperation with the old homeland and propagate Czech and Slovak culture worldwide in academic circles constitute the highest priorities of the Executive Board. Our intention is to devote special attention to young people, be they students from the Czechlands or Slovakia or children of our immigrants abroad. The Executive Board welcomes any new initiatives and suggestions in this connection.

2. From the onset, the Executive Board focused on the evaluation of the current state of the Society and the preparation of a strategic plan and specific agenda for the future. The analysis led to the Executive Board's declaration, titled "SVU Today and Tomorrow," which was subsequently published in *Zprávy SVU*.[747]

3. To enable us to work as a unified team, the Executive Board agreed on its "*modus operandi*" and the division of labor among the officers. The Executive Vice President Jan Skalny[748] was given the responsibility for administrative and management matters. Vice President Věra Bořkovec was to handle local chapters, Katherine David-Fox[749] publications, Eva Maříková Leeds[750] financial matters, Josef Macháč[751] membership, Václav Rajlich[752] computer technology, Dagmar Hasalová-White conferences, and Juraj Slávik,[753] together with Pavel Novák,[754] technical and cultural cooperation between SVU membership abroad and in the old homeland. Blanka Kuděj functioned as Secretary-General and Frank Mucha as Treasurer.

As a newly elected President, I was keenly aware of the fact that my function was not merely a ceremonial one and of routine character, but

---

[747] *Zprávy SVU*, vol. 37, No. 1 (Jan.-Feb, 1995), pp. 1-7.

[748] Jan P. Skalný (1935-), consulting engineer, living in Toronto, Canada.

[749] Katherine O. David-Fox (1964-), assistant professor of history, University of Maryland, College Park.

[750] Eva Maříková Leeds (1953-), assistant professor of finance, Temple University, Philadelphia, PA.

[751] Josef Macháč (1954-), physician, associated with Mt. Sinai Medical Center, New York.

[752] Václav Rajlich (1939-), professor of computer science, Wayne State University, Detroit, MI.

[753] Juraj L. J. Slávik (1929-), program officer, Visiting Program Service, Meridian House International, Washington, DC.

[754] Pavel Novák (1957-), engineer, then associated with the Office of the President, Prague Castle, Prague.

that it would be my responsibility to do everything in my power for SVU to reach its goals and its vision, i.e., a vision based on the thoughts and the initiatives of its members, Society's vision that reflects on the intellectual and professional needs of Czech and Slovaks abroad, as well as in the old country, a vision of the Society that aims to foster and propagate the best fruits of the Czech and Slovak culture, technology and science, as well as humanistic efforts worldwide.[755]

4. Understandably, the Board gave its greatest attention to financial matters. The unsatisfactory state of SVU finances, with which we had taken over the Society's management, required immediate action to stabilize the SVU financial base. The Executive Board was forced to implement a far-reaching financial reform, based on sound accounting and economic principles. A balanced budget was our goal and *sine qua non* for any future SVU undertakings.

With these principles, the Executive Board succeeded drastically to halt the Society's expenses. Through systematic collection of membership dues, the SVU income was significantly increased. The greatest burden on the Society are the members of the European chapters – and here I am not talking about our chapters in Czech and Slovak Republics – who pay late and in grossly inadequate amounts, if at all. The Society founding fathers never contemplated that the Society would financially support or keep alive the activities of local chapters. All the Society documents, from the time of its inception and during its subsequent development, made it clear that all local chapters must be financially self-supporting and finance their own activities. A good example is the Washington DC Chapter which gets its income from the proceeds of their Christmas Bazaar and their annual wine and cheese party. Furthermore, the original chapter guidelines contain a specific language admonishing the chapters to regularly send part of their income to the central Treasury to support the SVU publication program.

The main reason collecting membership dues collectively, with the help of local chapters, came about was nothing else but to lighten the load of SVU Treasurer. Unfortunately, in the last years this practice, instead of assisting his work, it, in fact, made his job more taxing. A collective sending of dues usually came late, without any explanatory notes, making it difficult to ascertain who of the local members actually paid

---

[755] "Rationalizing our Goals and our Mission," *Zprávy SVU*, vol. 37, No. 2 (March-April 1995), pp. 1-5.

and how much, which had its repercussions on the participation of these members in the election process. Initially, the Chapters were allowed to deduct up to 10 % of the money for their assistance but the Chapters later misconstrued this as the support for their local activities and kept most of the monies for themselves which violates previous agreements and is contrary to SVU Bylaws. In conformance with the American laws, none of these members is thus eligible to vote and in fact cannot even be considered a *bona fide* member of SVU. The local chapters thus deprive most of their members of their legitimate right to vote, some of whom may have actually paid their dues locally. This was the reason why the SVU General Assembly recommended to the Executive Board to return to the original collection of dues by the central SVU Treasurer.

To be sure, in all our efforts to balance the SVU budget, the current income from membership dues is barely sufficient for running the Society. It is thus necessary for all members, irrespective where they live, to equally share in the financial support of the Society, as a whole, to correct the present situation in which the financial burden rests almost entirely on the shoulders of American and Canadian members. Even with the resolution of this problem, the Executive Board is concerned that the Society will still need to find additional resources to be able to finance larger projects, particularly publications. It is for these reasons that the Board is attempting to acquire additional resources from external sources.

5. The inadequate financial situation is closely related to the way SVU has administered and managed its affairs. The existing processes and procedures were unnecessarily too complicated, lengthy, expensive and largely ineffective. This is especially apparent in the unnecessary expenses for the two SVU newsletters and the prolonged distribution process. The matters were further complicated by the insufficient system of keeping track of our members. Consequently, the Board considered establishing a new effective database as one of its top priorities. Thanks to the efforts of our Treasurer Frank Mucha we now have a fully functioning database relating to paying members.

6. In order to increase the Society's income, the Executive Board decided to raise the new membership dues to $35 for individuals, $40 for two spouses. The dues in Czech and Slovak Republics remain at $10 for single and $12 for a couple, and the dues for students also remain $5. The Executive Board hopes that the collection of dues centrally,

irrespective of where the members live, will, once and for all, bring order to our bookkeeping and the inventory of SVU members and thus correct the existing problem as to who is entitled to vote and who is not, not to speak about the overall improvement of the SVU financial status.

7. With the aim of revitalizing and rejuvenating the Society, the Board decided on a new membership drive abroad. The drive will concentrate on the younger generation, professionals interested in Czech and Slovak culture, irrespective of their ethnic background, and the descendants of the Czech and Slovak immigrants abroad. We have a new publicity pamphlet and have also revised the application form.[756]

8. Organizationally speaking, apart from bringing order into our haphazard practices, the Executive Board devoted a part of its agenda to the role of various bodies of the Society. The SVU Bylaws give the SVU Council a number of responsibilities and specific rights. The Board respects these stipulations and will support their implementation. The Council is comprised of significant personalities whose talents have not been tapped at all. The Board is thus attempting to revitalize this important body which was neglected in the last few years. Apart from the role they could play in strategic and long-term planning, the Council could also play an important role in the academic area, including their specific function, stipulated by the SVU Bylaws, in the selection process of "SVU Fellows." The Council could also take responsibility for establishing professional sections in the Society and generally devote its attention to strictly academic matters for which the Executive Board lacks time.

9. With respect to local chapters, the Board is well aware of the extensive activities of our chapters in Slovakia and the Czechlands. The Prague SVU Chapter, which showed its effectiveness during the organization of the last two SVU Congresses, initiated a regular lecture series under the chairmanship of Dr. Jaroslava Turková.[757] The Bratislava Chapter, which organized an exceptionally successful conference with central theme " Science and Arts without Borders," continues in its extensive activities under the personal leadership of Prof. Alexander Tkáč. The present conference in Košice, in turn, is primarily the result of the devoted work of the recently established Košice SVU Chapter, headed

---

[756] *Zprávy SVU*, vol. 37, No. 3 (May-June 1995), p. 7.

[757] Jaroslava Turková (1932-2000), biochemist, associated with the Czech Academy of Sciences, Prague; chairperson of the Prague SVU Chapter.

by Prof. Karol Marton. We are also pleased to report on the recently formed SVU chapter in Brno, under the Presidency of Dr. Marie Bobková.[758]

The status of other European chapters is less satisfactory. Their general activities in the last year have considerably slackened and some of them stopped their activities entirely. Considering their continuously reducing number and the increased age of their members, and the lack of younger officers, there is no hope for improvement in the near future. Despite the negative trends, the Board is making an effort to revitalize the inactive chapters and would welcome any initiative from local members in this regard.

In contrast, the number of new members in the US and Canada has risen, especially among the younger generation. Interestingly, a majority of these new "recruits" are not associated with any of the local chapters. One could thus deduce from this that the future of SVU cannot be built primarily on the local chapters. In the US and Canada, the most effective chapters are those that are in the close proximity to Czech and Slovak diplomatic bodies, such as the Czech and Slovak Embassies in Washington, DC, their Missions in New York City, and the Embassies in Ottawa, Canada.

10. In the past, SVU considered publishing as its "Imperative." The Executive Board, which is in full agreement with this emphasis, will pay special attention to this. As the first step in this direction, it renewed the English periodical *Kosmas* which will be publishing English language scholarly articles relating to various aspects of Czech and Slovak culture and occasional scientific and artistic works of our members. There is no intent to duplicate specialized periodicals in any particular discipline of arts or sciences, but rather we have in mind a periodical of high quality that would be written in more readable style to be understood by an intelligent layman, something along the lines of *Scientific American*. As one of a few existing English periodicals devoted exclusively to Czech and Slovak arts, letters and science in the worldwide cultural context. *Kosmas* will serve the SVU business card as well as that of Czech and Slovak culture. Prof. Bruce Garver[759] of the University of Nebraska was named the *Kosmas* new Editor.

---

[758] Marie Bobková (1946-), immunologist, associated with Masaryk University, Brno.
[759] Bruce Garver (1938-), professor of economics, University of Nebraska, Omaha.

Considering the plethora of new magazines and literary revues in the Czechlands and Slovakia in which our members can publish their Czech or Slovak articles, the Executive Board did not consider it cogent, during the period of financial uncertainty, to renew the SVU periodical *Promeny* which played an important role in the past, especially during the time when Czechoslovakia was ruled by the communists.

The Executive Board will again support, however, publications of specific monographs in English and possibly other languages. It would also like to return to the early practice of issuing selected papers from SVU World Congresses. The realization of this is conditioned on the availability of finding additional financial resources.

11. Considerable part of the Executive Board's agenda was devoted to cultural and technical cooperation between Czech and Slovak colleagues and institutions in the home country and those abroad. For this purpose, the Executive Board is attempting to establish a new information network, "SVU Clearinghouse," with gathering and dissemination functions, to be located in Washington, DC.[760]

12. SVU World Congresses from the very beginning belonged to the most important SVU activities. Since the last two Congresses were held in Prague, there was a question whether the subsequent Congress should not be held in the US or Canada. After surveying opinion among SVU members it became clear that the majority of members, with minor exceptions, favored the idea of holding the next Congress again in Europe. Following a lengthy correspondence with the representatives of local chapters regarding the local conditions and the logistics, as well as potential assistance in organizational matters, the Executive Board decided to hold the Congress in Brno in cooperation with Masaryk University.[761]

In conclusion, I would like to thank our members for their understanding and support of our efforts. I would also like to express my sincere appreciation to the Košice organizers for the outstanding Conference and for arranging this year's General Assembly meeting in their lovely city.

..........

---

[760] *Zprávy SVU*, vol. 37, No. 1 (January-February 1995), p. 11; "SVU Information Clearinghouse," *Ibid.*, vol. 37, No. 3 (May-June 1995), p. 6.

[761] As per decision of the SVU Executive Board on June 24, 1995, and reported in *Zprávy SVU*, vol. 37, No. 4 (July-August 1995), p. 16.

I presented the above report in Czech to the SVU General Assembly[762] in Košice, Slovakia on August 21, 1995. The meeting followed the established pattern, starting with the appointment of recording secretary (Milada Tkáčová) and the approval of the minutes from the last General Assembly Meeting. The Assembly then voted the formation of the Resolution committee, consisting of Karol Marton, Alexander Tkáč and Lubomír Ďurovič. After my State of the SVU Report, which came next, followed a report by the SVU Treasurer Frank Mucha, who elaborated on the state of the Society's finances and his efforts to modernize the bookkeeping and to establish a membership database. He also provided the latest guidance on the way the Slovak and Czech chapters could be registered and on the establishment of the SVU accounts in the respective countries. In addition to his report, Mucha also read, for the record, the Secretary-General's report, since Blanka Kuděj could not attend the meeting.

The next order of business was presentations by the chairmen of the SVU Chapters in Košice, Bratislava, Prague and Brno. At the recommendations of the Resolution Committee, the assembly accepted their draft resolution, the text of which was printed in *Zprávy SVU*.[763] The meeting was then adjourned.

---

[762] "The SVU 1995 General Assembly Meeting," *Zprávy SVU*, vol. 37, No. 5 (September-October 1995), pp. 1-4.

[763] *Zprávy SVU*, vol. 37, No. 5 (September-October 1995), pp. 1-2.

# 42
## SVU World Congress in Brno

After two successful congresses in Prague, I felt that we ought to move the next Congress to another location. Brno seemed a logical site. I had the chance to visit Brno in 1995 when we organized a workshop there, following our SVU Conference in Košice. Apart from myself, Prof. Jiří Nehněvajsa of Pittsburgh and Frank Mucha of New York, served as the workshop instructors.[764]

Although my initial preference was to hold the Congress at Palacký University in Olomouc, Prof. Jařáb, then the University Rector, informed me that 1996 was a historical anniversary of the University which meant that they would use all their available facilities for the celebrations and thus they would not have sufficient space for our Congress. We therefore focused on Brno-based Masaryk University, the largest institution of higher learning in Moravia.

Through Jiří Nehněvajsa, who was a graduate of Masaryk University in the late forties, and who knew the city of Brno intimately and had professional contacts there, we met with Prof. Jiří Šrámek, Vice Rector of Masaryk University, and Dr. Jaroslav Bohanes,[765] Director of International Political Institute, associated with the Law Faculty of the University. They both expressed great interest in holding our next SVU World Congress in Brno under Masaryk University's sponsorship. While in Brno, we also met with Dr. Zdeněk Kessler, the Presiding Judge of the Constitutional Court of the Czech Republic, who happened to be Nehněvajsa's classmate during his studies at Masaryk University. Kessler, who spent a number of years in communist jails, was very sympathetic to Czech exiles and promised us the support of the Magistrate of the City of Brno, where he had influence through his daughter, Dagmar Lastovecká, who held the office of Lord Mayor of the City.

---

[764] The workshop was organized by SVU Research Institute. Dr. Zdeněk Slouka, who normally took part in these workshops, was unfortunately too ill to attend.

[765] Jaroslav Bohanes (1922-1998), founder and director of International Political Institute, Law Faculty, Masaryk University, Brno.

Having thus laid the necessary groundwork, it was not difficult to sell the idea to the SVU Executive Board.[766] In the meantime, Rector of Masaryk University, Prof. Eduard Schmidt, informed me in writing that he would gladly accept the honorary chairmanship of the Congress and that Vice Rector Šrámek would assume the responsibility for the logistics of the Congress. The program coordination was assigned to Dr. J. Bohanes, in cooperation with Dr. Marie Bobková, in her capacity as President of the recently established Brno SVU Chapter.

The SVU central organizational committee comprised of myself with the overall responsibility for the Congress, VP Dagmar Hasalová-White who was given responsibility for the coordination of US panels and Secretary General Blanka Kuděj who was appointed the Congress Treasurer.[767]

Early on, Dr. J. Bohanes, unfortunately, fell ill,[768] necessitating organizational changes. Although Vice Rector Šrámek assumed most of the programming responsibilities, an increased burden also fell on our shoulders in the US. I maintained constant contact with Vice Rector Šrámek with whom I had been exchanging messages, at least once a week, usually via FAX. Blanka Kuděj, in turn, maintained a working relationship and contact with Dr. Jana Pilátová of the University International Division, which was under Šrámek's supervision. To my annoyance, Pilátová frequently answered my FAXes that were clearly intended for Vice Rector Šrámek which created some confusion and even misunderstandings. I was particularly annoyed when she began interfering with our scientific program about which she knew little.

---

[766] It should be pointed out that there were a couple of other contenders for the 1996 Congress site, including Washington, DC and the University of South Bohemia. Strong protagonist for the latter was especially Dr. Jaroslava Turková, chairman of the SVU Prague Chapter and the pianist Radoslav Kvapil who had direct ties with the South Bohemia Music Festival. After some debate, the Executive Board came up with a compromise to hold our traditional SVU Congress in Brno for a period of three days, following which the attendees would be transported to southern Bohemia where they would have a choice of participating in one of the topically arranged symposia in Písek, Tábor or České Budějovice, in connection with the Music Festival. The proposed arrangement seemed rather cumbersome so that the South Bohemian component was later dropped.

[767] *Zprávy SVU*, vol. 37, No. 6 (November-December 1995), pp. 1-3.

[768] Dr. Bohanes never completely recovered and did not live to see the Congress as he soon died.

Our correspondence, on the whole, was very professional, and friendly, until we began discussing finances which was aggravated by Pilátová's involvement. Blanka Kuděj was very knowledgeable and did wonders in her correspondence and early negotiations. There seemed to be an agreement on most issues on both sides. So it seemed until we received the so called "tentative budget" which Pilátová prepared.

It was grossly inflated, containing categories and items we never saw before, such as hiring some firm to handle registration (48.000 Kč), production of transparencies (18.000 Kč), leasing City Theatre (69.000 Kč), student help (40.000 Kč), food for Brno organizers (13.500 Kč), retyping of abstracts (15.000 Kč), telephone (30.000 Kč), buffet lunch at the opening (135.000 Kč), printing costs (20.000 Kč), documentary film (40.000 Kč), transportation (5.000 Kč), use of concert hall (8.000 Kč), postage (23.000 Kč), financial reserve (10.000 Kč), and so it went.

It was a shock to all of us on the Executive Board, especially to Blanka Kuděj and me, who had negotiated, in good faith, individual budgetary items before. I was so upset that I could not sleep, as I wrote in my strongly worded FAX to Šrámek at 5 A.M. on July 9, in which I expressed great annoyance of our entire Executive Board over the whole matter, referring to our previous understandings over specific budget items. I stated, in no uncertain terms, that this was not the way business was conducted in America, and for that matter, anywhere in the civilized world. Once an agreement is reached, both sides should stick to it. I reminded him that, based on our previous agreement, we established our registration fee, which cannot be changed at this late hour, having communicated it to all our speakers and participants and in all our public announcements. I admonished him to personally examine every budgetary item, eliminate unnecessary expenditures to bring them down to a reasonable level, along the lines of our earlier agreements. I also asked Blanka Kuděj to scrutinize every item and send Pilátová her recommendations.

Within a week, I had Šrámek's response who apparently took my comments to heart. In his, otherwise conciliatory letter, he stated that "it was time for the two of us to rise above specific details and look at the Congress from the perspective of its totality," indicating his willingness to go the extra mile to resolve the impasse. In my response, I wrote that we need to resolve the matter quickly and proposed, in place of further bickering over individual items, an alternative – a bottom line proposal to offer them $10,000 toward their expenses, irrespective of what they might be. Our offer included the proviso that the amount would include the costs of leasing the theatre for our opening and a festive buffet following the opening for all the participants. We would not otherwise interfere in the way they would spend the monies. I further informed him that we already had a commitment from Dr. Marie Bobková, President of SVU Brno Chapter to provide student volunteers for registration and other needed services, who are willing to do it without any compensation. As I was subsequently informed by Bohanes, my proposal was accepted in its totality.[769]

The official opening of the Congress, which took place in Mahon Theater, one of the most elegant and spacious buildings in Brno, was an impressive sight by any account. The academic procession of the high University brass in historical "talars"[770] and golden chains, led by "pedals" bearing insignia of various universities and faculties, to the tune of trumpets, was an unforgettable sight. The SVU Executive Board members, dressed likewise in academic robes, were part of the procession.

After the national anthems I had the honor of opening the Congress, in my capacity as SVU President. Then came the addresses and greetings of various dignitaries, including the Mayor Lord of the City of Brno. The impressive ceremony was concluded with the performance of the Janacek Quartet and the Children's Choir. The attendees were then treated to a scrumptious buffet where the visitors could rub shoulders with important personalities of the Brno cultural and political scene. A plenary session on the "Cultural Contributions of Moravia from a Worldwide Perspective" followed immediately.

---

[769] After the Congress the University seemed to forget our previous written agreements and submitted us a bill which was completely out of proportion to what we initially agreed to pay, claiming that their expenses exceeded their original estimates. They even had the "chutzpah" to include in their accounting a dinner Vice Rector organized for his coworkers to which Frank Mucha and I were also invited. The notion that they should honor our earlier agreements did not seem to impress them and they were completely oblivious to it. To settle the matter, the SVU Executive Board finally decided to compromise and gave them half of the money they requested toward their expenses. They never acknowledged this gesture on our part, not to speak about expressing any thanks.

[770] University caps and gowns.

The next two and half days were devoted to lectures and discussions, organized in specific sessions by subject, discussion panels, symposia, mini-conferences and the workshops. In social sciences there were panels on such topics as reality in the 20th century literature, confessional tolerance past and present, cultural acculturation, future of written Czech, culture of Great Moravia, problems in Czech transformation from a legal point of view, philosophy, sociology, ethics, pedagogy, etc. The Slovaks, in turn, came with such themes as European enrichment through ethnicity, bio-diplomacy and bio-politics, genetics and ethics, European ethnic identity, limits of tolerance and environment.

Natural sciences were represented by such topics as the role of man in the transformations of nature, environmental changes–hope and threat, Gregor Mendel–the founder of modern genetics. Medical sections included sessions on bio-ethics, contemporary public health, medical education and schooling, growth of cancer cells, modern methods in cardiology, transplantation of cells, tissues and organs, human genetics–a molecular dimension, assisted reproduction, and others.

Of special interest was an international panel, composed of university presidents from abroad and the rectors of several Moravian universities, on current and future problems of university administration and management. Another panel that generated broad interest, particularly among the Congress participants from the Czechlands and Slovakia, dealt with the role and the workings of private foundations. In this connection we had arranged a special workshop, just prior to the Congress, on research "grantsmanship," i.e., the art of the preparation of grant applications and on sources of research funding.

The Brno hosts provided splendid cultural entertainment with several concerts. Thus we heard Dvorak "Biblical Songs" in the beautiful baroque church on Mendel Square, sung by first-rate basso Richard Novak and church concert by JAMU[771] students. In addition, we were treated to a brilliant performance of the pianists, husband and wife team, Vera and Vlastimil Lejka.

There were also special excursions organized into the countryside, including a visit to the word-famous Macocha Abyss, the castle Špilberg, a supper at the rustic Rocky Mill, Znojmo region, the castle

---

[771] Janáčkova akademie múzických umění (Janáček Academy of Music Arts).

Vránovice, a genuine Moravian meal with local specialties and folk music, the palaces of Valice, Mikulov and Lednice, an authentic wine cellar with a scrumptious supper with Moravian music – who could ask for more?

The social events culminated in a magnificent festive party, held in the Špilberg Castle, hosted by Masaryk University, the Magistrate of the City of Brno and several sponsoring Moravian firms. This "mother of parties," as someone referred to it, took place in spacious courts and the mount of the castle, appropriately decorated for the occasion with medieval armor, coat of arms of Moravian nobility and independent trades, flags and other ornaments. After some introductory words by the Mayor of the City and the Rector of Masaryk University, the feast began in earnest. I can hardly find words to describe the scene and the atmosphere of the place. Food and drinks were everywhere, as was music and singing, laughter and noise. One could choose from a variety of meats, from roasting pig to lamb or wild fowl. Moravian prime quality wine of various vintage, beer and liquor were in abundance and late in the evening hours one could find in the deep catacombs of the castle tasty goulash or kielbasa with cabbage. The entertainment was provided by clowns, jugglers, magicians, swordsmen, all dressed in medieval garb, music ensembles, bands, medieval exhibits of crafts and art and magnificent fireworks. To add to the atmosphere, the place was full of young men dressed in medieval costumes, accompanied by elegant hunting dogs.

The last day of the Congress, the Mayor of the City received the SVU leaders in her official seat and awarded us each with commemorative medals of the City and a beautiful book about Brno.

In spite of some of the financial squabbles we had with the University administrators, the SVU Congress was very successful. Dr. Marie Bobková, President of SVU Brno Chapter, was very helpful in smoothing some of the edges and by helping us reduce unnecessary University expenses through common sense and knowing her way around.

# 43
# *State of the SVU in 1996*

## Report of SVU President Dr. Miloslav Rechcígl, Jr. to the SVU General Assembly Convened in Brno, August 14, 1996[772]

Let me first thank the Brno organizers for enabling us to hold our General Assembly meeting in Brno, in conjunction with the 18th SVU Congress. It is a historic event, as it is the first instance of holding our annual meeting on the soil of the Czech Republic.

When the present Executive Board began its term, less than two years ago, the position of the Society was not in an enviable situation. Our finances were in sad shape and there was general apathy among the membership partly due to the unsettling political situation in the old homeland.

The first step the Executive Board took was to determine how bad the situation really was and then prepare a realistic agenda for the future. Our analysis and the proposed course of action were published in *Zprávy SVU*.[773]

First, we had to deal with the notion of some of our members that SVU already fulfilled its mission and that the time has come to cease and desist which brought growing apathy among SVU membership. Through editorials and public discussions we reminded the members of the causes that led to the establishment of the Society in the first place, emphasizing that the defeat of communism does not mean that there is no more need to propagate Czech and Slovak culture abroad. We argued that the situation, when the Czech and Slovak Republics are attempting to establish their legitimate place among the democratic nations, requires external assistance which SVU can provide.

---

[772] The Czech original appeared in *Zprávy SVU*, vol. 38, No. 5 (September-October 1996), p. 4-6.

[773] "Declaration of the Executive Board," *Zprávy SVU*, vol. 37 (Jan-Feb. 1995), No. 1, pp. 1-7.

Administratively, we gave the greatest attention to SVU finances. To correct the deficit it was necessary to stabilize our financial base and institute a far reaching fiscal reform. A balanced budget was our goal and a *sine qua non* for any future fiscal commitment. Through careful planning we succeeded in substantially lowering SVU expenses and through systematic collection of dues we also raised the Society's income. The Executive Board also succeeded in acquiring some donations from external sources, particularly from individual donors.

A still unresolved problem is the relationship with certain West European local chapters, whose members pay their dues late and in insufficient amounts, or not at all. The SVU Bylaws clearly state that every *bona fide* member, irrespective of where she or he lives, must equally share in fiscal responsibilities of the Society so that the major burden does not entirely rest on the shoulders of American and Canadian members. At the recommendation of the General Assembly, the Executive Board decided to return to the original way of collecting the dues, i.e., directly by the central Treasurer. This would automatically correct the problem and negate the question whether or not a given member's dues have been paid and whether he/she is entitled to participate in the elections which was always problematic whenever the dues were collected by local chapters.

Beginning with the year 1996, the Executive Board decided to raise the membership dues to $35 for individuals and $40 for both spouses, while the student rates remained unchanged at $5. The membership dues in the Czech and Slovak Republics were set at $10 for individuals and $12 for both spouses. As for the exemptions from paying dues, these were to be granted only exceptionally for transitory period and only for financial reasons. Retirement alone does not entitle anyone for exemption. Treasurer's establishment of a new membership database has also considerably simplified management of our finances.

The Executive Board has also given great attention to the improvement of our contacts with the membership. As promised, we now regularly inform the members through our newsletter *Zprávy SVU* about our activities and problems that we confront.

In the spirit of rejuvenating the Society, the Executive Board gave impetus to a new membership drive, especially among the younger generation and among the professionals, irrespective of their background, who are interested in Czech and Slovak culture, as well as among the descendants of Czech and Slovak immigrants abroad.

I am pleased to report about the exceptional work of our chapters in the Czech and Slovak Republics. The Prague Chapter, under the chairmanship of Jaroslava Turková, regularly organizes meetings with lectures, as does the Bratislava Chapter under the leadership of Prof. Alexander Tkáč as well as the Košice Chapter under Prof. Karol Marton. The SVU Brno Chapter directed by Dr. Marie Bobková was fully engaged in the preparation of the 18th SVU World Congress in Brno. We are also pleased about the newly established Chapter in Prešov.

Among the most active North American chapters are Washington DC Chapter and the New York Chapter, and to lesser extent Chicago, Cleveland, Pittsburgh and Ottawa Chapters. In Western Europe Munich Chapter appears to be most active.[774]

Publishing has always been considered by the Society as its imperative which the present Executive Board fully endorses. One of the first steps the Board has taken was to reestablish the English periodical *Kosmas – Czechoslovak and Central European Journal* after a three-year lapse.[775] The periodical will be published twice a year in cooperation with the University of Nebraska under the editorship of Prof. Bruce Garver. The price of a single issue was set at $18.

The Executive Board also devoted considerable attention to cultural and scientific cooperation between our colleagues home and abroad. Our plan is to establish an academic network for the purpose of rendering advice and assistance to Czech and Slovak students and researchers studying abroad, especially the USA and Canada, as well as to our members abroad who plan to undertake studies in the Czech or Slovak Republics.

There have been repeated complaints from our members that SVU had focused all its recent activities in Prague. This justified complaint convinced the Executive Board to hold the last year's Annual Meeting in Košice, in conjunction with a conference "Technology-Humanity-Arts-Tolerance,"[776] organized by the Košice SVU Chapter. The conference

---

[774] "SVU Chapters Active in 1996 and their Chairs, " *Zprávy SVU,* vol. 38, No. 3 (May-June 1996), p. 13; "Report on SVU Chapter Activities, *Ibid.*, vol. 38, No. 5 (September-October 1996), pp. 10-11.

[775] "*Kosmas,* notice of resumption of publication," *Zprávy SVU,* vol. 38, No. 2 (March-April 1996), pp. 7-8.

[776] *Zprávy SVU,* vol. 37 (March-Apr. 1995), No. 2, p. 6.

environment, about which we reported in detail in *Zprávy SVU*,[777] was truly outstanding. not only for its high quality program but also for the exceptional hospitality we received there.

The criticism of the so called "Pragocentrism" also led the Executive Board to the decision to convene the present SVU World Congress in Brno with the focus on the cultural contributions of this beautiful and historically important Moravian land. The general success of the Congress, the kind reception of our hosts and the overall mutually agreeable atmosphere confirmed that the decision to hold the Congress in Brno was a wise one.

In conclusion, I would like to thank the members of the Executive Board for their dedicated work and cooperation. Generally speaking, I am very pleased to say that the Society again stands on firm ground.

..........

The above report was presented as part of the proceedings of the General Assembly meeting in Brno on August 14, 1996. The meeting was convened at 5 PM, at which time more than one hundred persons attended, probably making it the largest General Assembly meeting up to that time. Following my report, Secretary-General Blanka Kuděj elaborated on her activities in the past two years and then came the report of VP Dagmar Hasalová White, concerning her function as an overseas program chairperson for the 18th SVU World Congress. Afterwards, the chair persons of the local Chapters in the Czech and Slovak Republics reported on their activities, i.e., Dr. Marie Bobková for the Brno Chapter, Prof. Alexander Tkac for the Bratislava Chapter, Prof. Karol Marton for Košice and Dr. Jaroslava Turková for the Prague Chapter. This portion of the program was concluded by VP Věra Bořkovec who gave a summary report on the activities of other SVU Chapters worldwide. Subsequently the winner of the Hašek Student Award, Jonathan Bolton from the University of Texas, was presented the Award.

Next came the report of the Treasurer Frank Mucha who elaborated on my State of the SVU Report, from the point of view of finances. His report was followed by the auditors' statement which supported his report and recommended its approval so that the outgoing officers could

---

[777] "The Košice Experience," *Zprávy SVU*, vol. 37, No. 5 (Sept.-Oct. 1995), pp. 5-6.

be discharged of their liability. The General Assembly gave their approval by unanimous vote.

The General Assembly also approved a resolution drafted by the SVU Resolution Committee. The text of the Resolution was published in *Zprávy SVU*.[778]

Based on the Report of the Committee of Election Inspectors, the outcome of the elections was announced. All the candidates recommended by the Nominations Committee[779] were elected. The new slate of the elected officers included the following: President – Miloslav Rechcígl, Jr.; Executive VP – Jan Skalný; Vice Presidents – Věra Bořkovec, Milton Černý,[780] Eva Mařiková Leeds, Pavel Novák, Juraj Slávik, Alexander Tkáč, Otto Ulč[781] and Dagmar Hasalová White; Secretary-General – Věra Ulbrecht;[782] Treasurer – Frank L. Mucha.[783]

---

[778] *Zprávy SVU*, vol. 38, No. 4 (July-August 1996), p. 31.

[779] The Nominations Committee comprised Prof. Jiří Nehněvajsa (chairman), Dr. Andrew Eliáš, Dr. Zdenka Fischmann, Dr. Zdeněk Hruban and Prof., Mojmír Povolný, as announced in *Zprávy SVU*, vol. 38, No. 1 (January-February 1996), p. 7.

[780] Milton Cerny (1933-), attorney, with Caplin and Drysdale, Washington, DC.

[781] Otto Ulč (1930-), professor of political science, Binghamton University, Binghamton, New York.

[782] Věra Ulbrecht (1929-2001), librarian, with National Institute of Standards and Technology, Gaithersburg, MD.

[783] For their biographical sketches, see *Zprávy SVU*, vol. 38. No. 3 (May-June 1996), pp. 4-12.

## 44
## *SVU Goes to Texas*

The decision to hold the 1997 SVU Annual Meeting in Texas was my idea and a deliberate one. It stemmed from the unhappiness of some of our members that the previous three congresses were held in Europe and that the time came to hold the next meeting in the US where the majority of SVU members lived. The Executive Board concurred with me that we should accommodate such concerns. I felt that the annual meeting be convened in some geographical area which would be close to a major Czech or Slovak settlement in America, preferably in a rural setting and if we could find a place where they were planning concurrently another Czech or Slovak event so much the better. In this regard Texas came up on the top.

Initially, I discussed the idea of having the meeting in Texas with Clinton Machann[784] whom I knew from earlier days. He was all excited about the possibility and offered his help. He also came with the suggestion of holding our meeting concurrently with the celebrations of the SPJST's 100th anniversary.[785] He approached Howard Leshikar,[786] President of SPJST with the idea who readily agreed to join forces. SVU would offer the academic program while SPJST would provide the social and cultural program. Subsequently I invited the newly named Czech Ambassador, Alexandr Vondra,[787] to the Cosmos Club for lunch where I told him about our impending plans and persuaded him to take part in the event. Leshikar was delighted about it and offered to pay Vondra's expenses.

---

[784] Clinton J. Machann (1947-), professor of English, Texas A&M University, College Station, TX.

[785] Slovanská Podporující Jednota Státu Texas (SPJST) (Slavonic Benevolent Union of State of Texas).

[786] Howard B. Leshikar (1937-), President, SPJST, Temple, TX.

[787] Alexandr Vondra (1961-), Ambassador of the Czech Republic to the US, Washington, DC.

In my discussions with Clint Machann I proposed for the central theme of the Texas Conference: "Czech Americans in Transition: Challenges and Opportunities for the Future." He liked the idea and consented to my request that he take charge of organizing the conference. I offered my assistance in the selection of speakers. We then spent a good four months in putting the program together.[788]

The final program[789] centered on the three key issues of interest to Czech Americans, namely: 1. ethnicity and the preservation of language and culture; 2. Czech American archives and their future; 3. relations between the Czech Americans and the Czech Republic. A detailed write-up about the Conference appeared in September issue of 1997 *Zpravy SVU*.[790]

The conference was convened in Belton, TX, not too far from the SPJST headquarters, located in Temple, TX. It opened on the evening of June 11th, with the SPJST reception in the presence of the new Czech Ambassador, Alexandr Vondra and other dignitaries. The program *per se* started the next day on Saturday at 9 o'clock in the morning at the Bell County Exposition Center. At the completion of the ceremonial opening followed the first section devoted to ethnicity and the preservation of culture. Among the lectures were presentations about Bohemian and Moravian pioneers in the Americas during the colonial times, which I had the pleasure of presenting, cultural legacy of Czech Americans in the early years of the settlement of Texas, the unprecedented Renaissance period of today's Texas, history of SPJST, documentary evidence of the arrival of Czech immigrants in the US, genealogy as a research tool seeking family roots in the Czech Republic, preservation of Czech folklore in America, efforts to preserve cultural traditions in Nebraska and Iowa, social and cultural importance of the first Czech dance halls in Texas, preservation of Czech language in America, Texas Czech, etc.

There was a separate session devoted to Czech American centers, archives and libraries and their future. The first part dealt specifically with the Czech centers in Texas, i.e., Texas Cultural and Heritage Center

---

[788] "SVU Goes to Texas," Preliminary Announcement of the 1997 SVU Annual Meeting," *Zprávy SVU*, vol. 39, No. 1 (January-February 1997), pp. 1-2.

[789] Published in *Zprávy SVU*, vol. 39, No. 4 (July-August 1997), pp. 1-7.

[790] *Zprávy SVU*, vol. 39, No. 5 (September-October 1997), pp. 9-12; "Deep in the Heart of Texas...," *Ibid*, p. 13.

in La Grange, Czech Cultural and Social Center in Houston, Sokol Museum in Ennis and the Chair of the Czech Studies at the University of Texas. The second part comprised a panel discussion about the Czech libraries and archives in the US and Canada. Among them were papers about the Tomas Capek Collection at the Library of Congress, Washington, DC, Masaryk Institute's Library in Toronto, the Archives of Czechs and Slovaks Abroad at the University of Chicago, new Library and Archives at the University of Nebraska, Lincoln, American sources of Czechoslovak history during 1938-1948, readers' clubs in the U.S., Slavonic collections at New York Public Library and the CSA Museum, Library and Archives in Berwyn, IL. A part of the afternoon was reserved for the address by Czech Ambassador Vondra and other personalities of public life.

The Sunday program was just as varied as on the previous day. The main theme was the relations between the U.S. and the Czech Republic. The first part dealt with the historical relations between the two republics in the cultural area, as well as with the diplomacy, particularly during the era of Tomas G. Masaryk's presidency and the exile government of Eduard Benes. Other lectures dealt with the comparison of the minority question in the two countries. There was also a special lecture on the problems of Czech and Czech-American press.

The second part of the Sunday program dealt with the trade relations between the U.S. and the Czech Republic from the fundamental economic issues to personal experiences of the recent economic cooperation between the two countries. The open format of the conference allowed broader discussion, including the Slovak issues.

Apart from the lectures,[791] the participants had the opportunity to attend various cultural and social events that were part of a two day celebration of the SPJST anniversary, all held in the Expo Center. These included: 1. band and orchestra performances each afternoon and evening; 2. folk singing and dance performances; 3. a display of folk costumes; 4. drama presentations depicting events from the history of the

---

[791] Selected papers were later published under the title *Czech-Americans in Transition*. Edited by Clinton Machann. With the preface by Miloslav Rechcígl, Jr. Austin, TX: Eakin Press, 1999. 136 p. My paper was also included (pp. 18-27 and 129-130), as was my bibliography on "Czech-Americans" (pp. 121-128).

SPJST; 5. museum and archival displays; and 6. demonstrations of traditional Czech cooking.

The important outcome of the Conference was a joint SVU-SPJST proclamation[792] regarding the creation of National Heritage Commission with the aim of preserving Czech cultural heritage in America.

---

[792] "The Preservation of Czech-American Cultural Heritage. Proclamation," *Zprávy SVU*, vol. 39, No. 5 (Sept.- Oct. 1997), pp. 1-2.

# 45
# *State of the SVU in 1997*

**Report of SVU President Dr. Miloslav Rechcígl, Jr.
to the SVU General Assembly,
Convened at Belton, TX, July 12, 1997**

In opening this year's Annual Meeting,[793] I wish to first thank our members from distant parts of the country for their participation, and above all to express my sincere appreciation to our Texas colleagues for enabling us to hold our General Assembly, as well as our Conference, in this beautiful part of Texas. Having personally taken part in several of today's activities, I am pleased to say that we have made a good choice in selecting Texas for this year's SVU event.

Inasmuch as this is only an interim report, I plan to be brief. Moreover, the SVU Executive Board has taken pains in informing the membership, in detail, about its various activities through our *Zprávy SVU* (News of SVU)[794] which would make my bit-by-bit reporting here somewhat superfluous. In this connection, we ought to really dispense with these interim Annual Meetings considering that the length of the administrative period for which the officers are elected is actually only for a two-year period.

The decision to hold this year's Annual Meeting in Texas[795] was a deliberate one, stemming, in part, from the unhappiness of some members that the two previous meetings were held in Europe and thus the time has come to hold the meetings in the U.S. where the majority of our SVU members live. We wanted to accommodate such concerns and, furthermore, the Executive Board wanted to convene the meeting in some geographical location which would be close to some major old Czech or

---

[793] Originally published in *Zprávy SVU*, vol. 39, no. 5 (September-October 1997), pp. 2-5.

[794] *Zprávy SVU*, vol. 38, No. 6 (November-December 1996), pp. 5-6; *Ibid.*, vol. 39, No. 1 (January-February), pp. 6-8; Ibid., vol. 39, No. 2 (March-April 1997), pp. 1-2; *Ibid.*, vol. 39, No. 3 (May-June 1997), pp. 1-3.

[795] "Why Have We Chosen Texas for Our 1997 Meeting," *Zprávy SVU*, vol. 39, No. 2 (March-April 1997), p. 3.

Slovak settlement in America, preferably in a rural area and if we could find a place where they were concurrently planning another Czech event, so much the better. This is why Texas came on the top!

Let me say a few words about our aims and priorities. Some of you may recall that soon after the Velvet Revolution in Prague voices were heard that our Society has done its job and that the time has come to cease and desist. The last two SVU Executive Boards did not share that point of view and neither does the present one. The situation in both Czech and Slovak Republics is far from ideal and our Society can still render help with cultural exchanges and with assisting researchers, educators, and students with contacts with American and other universities, as well as other educational and research institutions. Due to the worsened economic situation and other problems, the public image of both Republics in the world arena has also slipped a bit in the last few months and this again is an issue with which our Society can help, as we did during the times when the previous Czechoslovak state suffered under the Communist domination. We have, of course, other reasons for our existence, namely to assist our members abroad, and above all, to do everything we can towards preservation of our cultural heritage abroad.[796] This last goal is the main reason and the basis for organizing the two-day SVU Conference here in Texas.

As far as our long-term plans are concerned, we have begun taking some steps towards rejuvenation of the Society, with emphasis on recruitment of young people, both as members and officers. We would also like to bridge the gap between the exile groups and the descendants of the old immigrants, many of whom are cognizant and proud of their roots. There is a lot we have in common and there is a lot we can offer to each other. This Texas Conference can be the first step towards such cooperation.

As some of you may recall, a few years back, the Society was in financial straits which, thanks to the resolute action of the Executive Board, have been largely remedied. I am pleased to report that the present Executive Board adopted the policy to balance the Society's budget and make it a "sine qua non" for all its activities. One unresolved issue which we would like to correct are the difficulties we are having with certain European chapters, whose members are not forwarding their dues to the Treasurer. Consequently the major financial burden of the Society still

---

[796] "SVU New Initiative," *Zprávy SVU*, vol. 40, No. 1 (January-February 1998), pp. 7-8.

rests on the shoulders of the US and Canadian members which causes obvious resentment among our members in America.

The Executive Board has also made management improvements in the distribution of our newsletter *Zprávy SVU* which until recently was mailed from New York. Since the editorial office is located in Virginia, as is the printer, it made practical sense to move this operation to Virginia, as well. As a result, the delivery of our newsletter should proceed in more timely fashion. The *Zpravy SVU* is the principal means of our communicating with SVU members and through it we systematically keep the members informed of every important event or action the Executive Board takes. We would like to make the newsletter a two-way street, however. To do this, we need more information about individual members and from individual members. There is nothing wrong in sending information about one's successes or one's children's successes. Most members are pleased to read about their countrymen's advances, about the new books they published or awards they won. How else can the Society keep track of what goes on if the members don't let us know. In this connection, the Executive Board has decided to establish and maintain a special registry of prizes and awards won by SVU members, and by Czechs and Slovaks abroad, in general. We appeal to our members to assist us in this endeavor.

We have also made progress with the recently renewed SVU periodical, *Kosmas: Czechoslovak and Central European Journal.*[797] The first issue came out at the end of the last year, the second issue is at the printer's and the third is in preparation. We need to establish a firm subscription base which would permit us to publish the periodical without any additional financial support. The first issue was sent *gratis* to all our paying members with the request, and the hope, that they subscribe to the Journal. We appeal to all our members, who have not done so already, to subscribe to it now. Furthermore, we ask our members that they show the periodical to their colleagues and that they recommend it to their university libraries. This is perhaps the only English periodical devoted to scholarship, humanities, and the arts in the thing Czech or Slovak. We would like to make it a real showcase of Czech and Slovak culture world-wide.

---

[797] "Subscription Form for Kosmas," *Zprávy SVU*, vol. 39, No. 1 (January-February 1997), p. 9.

A decision has also been made to publish a new biographical *SVU Directory* which has been necessitated by numerous changes in members' addresses, as well as the addition of new members since 1992.[798] This recurrent bestseller, in all its editions, is the Society's best business card which can be found in major libraries world-wide and is used as an important reference source in seeking Czech or Slovak expertise anywhere around the world and in any field. I would like to use this occasion to request all those members. who have not done so already, to kindly fill out the biographical questionnaire that was sent to them or that was published in the recent issues of the *Zprávy SVU*. It is not just the updating of addresses but, as you can see for yourselves, by the inspection of the *1992 Directory*, some biographical entries badly need updating. There are cases of individuals, listed as students, who are currently holding position of full professor! This is absurd! I appeal to all of our members to carefully recheck their old entries and send us the appropriate updates. As was announced previously, only those individuals will be included in the *Directory,* who are current with payments of their membership dues.

One of the major decisions taken by the Executive Board has been with reference to the next SVU World Congress. After considering various options, the Board decided to convene the 1998 Congress in Bratislava, Slovakia.[799] There were several compelling reasons for this. Since the last three congresses were held in the Czech Republic, it seemed only right to hold the next Congress in Slovakia. In addition to this argument, the SVU Bratislava Chapter expressed great interest in having the meeting there and submitted a well thought-out proposal, including logistical arrangements, academic program and a variety of social and cultural events.

Being well aware of the fact that some SVU members favor the idea of holding future World Congresses on the North American continent, the Executive Board is recommending that the subsequent 20th SVU World Congress be held in the United States. Because of the numerical significance of that meeting, coupled with the importance of the year 2.000, when it would be held, the Board further recommends that the 20th World Congress be convened in the Nation's Capital, Washington, DC.

---

[798] "Preparation of New SVU Directory," *Zprávy SVU*, vol. 39, No. 2 (March-April 1997), pp. 8-9.

[799] As per the decision of SVU Executive Board on March 29, 1997 and reported in *Zprávy SVU,* vol. 30, No. 3 (May-June 1997), p. 2.

Among other anticipated actions that are on our agenda is the desire to bring SVU into the next century, taking advantage of computer technology. We need to establish our own HomePage. To get us off the ground we need some volunteers among the computer "buffs" who would guide us through the initial steps. Could someone based at an educational institution, include us in their system so that we would not have to pay all those service charges?

An occasional outsider who does not know what we are all about may refer to us as an elitist group. Although we can pride ourselves as having in our midst most of the intellectuals of note, we "ain't no" elitist group. We are a democratic and open society that admits anyone who subscribes to our aims.

Talking about misconceptions in reference to a misrepresentation of our Society, let me relate an incident that happened to me only a few weeks ago. I will paraphrase the narrative to protect the anonymity of the individual in question. I was contacted by a reputable businessman with the preposition that he would join our membership if we would help with his business and purchase his products. His argument was "Something for something. That's the way the world is." I responded as follows: "I beg to differ from your analogy and your conclusions. Our aims are diametrically different from yours. You are a businessman and your goal is to make money. We are a non-profit organization whose principal aim is to foster cultural exchanges with the Czech Republic and Slovakia, help to maintain good Czech/Slovak image in the world, and assist in preserving Czech and Slovak cultural heritage abroad. We do this on a voluntary basis, without any compensation and without any expectations that some day, someone would come to us with profuse thanks for our labors. Everything we do is done in the traditional American spirit of volunteerism, fraternalism, and good will.

On this note I would like to end. Let me thank again the Texas organizers for making it possible to hold our annual Meeting here and our Texas hosts for their hospitality.

·········

I presented the above report to the General Assembly[800] meeting in Belton, TX on July 12, 1997. In addition to my traditional State of the

---

[800] *Zprávy SVU*, vol. 39. No. 5 (September-October 1997), pp. 9-12.

*State of the SVU in 1997* 273

SVU report, there were also reports of the various local chapters. Most interesting report was that of Josef Rostinský from Japan who acquainted the members with the newly established SVU Chapter in Japan. In place of the usually rather general resolution, this time the General Assembly was given a special Proclamation regarding the Preservation of Czech-American Cultural Heritage. This Proclamation, which was later published in *Zprávy SVU*,[801] started SVU on a new path.

---

[801] "Proclamation," *Zprávy SVU,* vol. 39, No. 5 (September-October 1997), pp. 1-2.

## 46
## *Organizing the Bratislava Congress*

As I wrote[802] to Professor Tkáč[803] in December 1996, following our Congress in Brno, there was a prevailing opinion within the ranks of SVU that the next major SVU event be held on the US soil, where the majority of our members lived. Consequently, we decided to hold our 1997 annual meeting with a conference in Texas. As far as the next SVU World Congress was concerned, I felt, however, that I could probably persuade the Executive Board to convene the meeting in Slovakia, provided we could find favorable conditions and the necessary assistance with the logistics and the program there.

By the end of January 1997, Tkáč informed me that he discussed the matter with his Bratislava Chapter, as well as the representatives of the Slovak Technical University, Comenius University, City University Bratislava and the Slovak Academy of Sciences who gave him their spirited approval to the idea of holding the 1998 SVU Congress in Bratislava. They recommended to hold the Congress on 24-30 August. They figured on 300 participants, including 200 from abroad, 50 from Slovakia and 40 from the Czechlands. He indicated that accommodations could be offered in the university dormitories ($8-$10), or hotels ($5-$120) and high quality food in local restaurants ($20-$25).

They could offer a large selection of cultural events of high artistic value (Music Summer, the Philharmonic, Slovak Opera), pointing out that they have excellent contacts with leading opera singers and musicians. He also thought that it may be possible to have the official opening in the Bratislava Castle and a concert in the historic St. Martin House. They would also arrange for a bus excursion to the Slovak Academy of Sciences' Mansion at Smolenice for lunch, followed by a visit to a close-by famous spa of Piešťany. He further mentioned other possible excursions sites, such as Dolná Krupá Mansion, where Ludwig van

---

[802] This narrative is based on authentic correspondence I have kept from that period, in excess of two large ring binders.

[803] Alexander Tkáč was chairman of the Bratislava SVU Chapter.

Beethoven performed or the historic Devin Castle, the one time center of Great Moravian Empire and where Prince Rastislav resided. He indicated that everything could be covered for $ 200-250 per person. With reference to the program he thought that it should be multi disciplinary, covering both arts and sciences, with the participation of personalities from the "spiritual and philosophic sphere."

It sounded so promising, exciting, and fantastic. With such description, I did not have much difficulty in "selling" the idea of having the Congress in Bratislava, even though initially most Executive Board members had an opposing point of view.

About this time, we also learned of the impending celebrations of the 650th anniversary of the ancient Charles University in Prague which was to take place at the end of June and the beginning of July 1998. Some of our members, particularly the former alumni, planned to attend and would not be willing to travel to Europe twice. Consequently, we asked our Bratislava co-organizers to move their proposed Congress dates closer to the Prague celebrations so that interested members could attend both events. Our Slovak colleagues on the Executive Board felt that holding the meeting in Bratislava was desirable, even though it was a bit risky, in view of the sensitive political situation that prevailed in Slovakia under Vladimir Mečiar's rule.[804] During his era, Slovak chauvinistic tendencies were promoted with greater and greater isolationism from the Western World.[805] We were keenly aware of the fact that holding highly visible meetings of the Czechoslovak Society of Arts and Sciences in Slovakia under such conditions might be misconstrued as a provocation. In view of all the sensitivities involved, we made a deliberate decision to send all our official correspondence to Slovakia in

---

[804] Vladimír Mečiar (1942-), who was frequently feared and hated by some, while admired by others, was a populist charismatic Slovak politician who held the post of the first prime minister of Slovakia. It is believed that he had a large role in the split of Czechoslovakia into two separate entities, Slovakia and the Czech Republic, as of January 1993.

[805] A news columnist Tony Barber wrote on November 8, 1997, in his column, "Mečiar Keeps Slovakia out in the Cold" that "just about everything that could go wrong with Slovakia appears to be going wrong. Mečiar's aggressive – some would say authoritarian – style of leadership is the main reason why Slovakia finds itself in trouble. His contempt for civilized political behavior forced NATO and the European Union earlier this year to rebuff Slovakia's application for membership. Slovakia thus earned the dubious distinction of being the only applicant to be turned down on political grounds.

Slovak language and, put our Executive Vice President, Jan P. Skalný, who was a Bratislava native, in charge of our negotiations with Bratislava.

It did not take long and we had Tkáč's concurrence of rescheduling the Congress to 5-10 July 1998, immediately after the conclusion of Charles University's anniversary celebrations. In their letter to Ján P. Skalný,[806] they proposed as the general theme, "Problems of Sciences and Arts on the Eve of the 21st Century." Simultaneously, they recommended that the program be divided into four major schematic blocs, namely natural sciences; new ideas relating to the global political vision; the arts, sciences and inspiration – a dialogue without borders; and philosophy, spirituality and the conscience. One day was to be allotted to each area. Simultaneously, they sent us a rough estimate of the costs involved, i.e., $100 for accommodations, $100 for food, $30 for transportation, $30 for cultural events, and $10 for administrative expenses (invitation letters, program, FAX, telephone).

It all sounded quite logical and I had no problems with their proposal. I responded almost immediately, just before our Executive Board meeting. My only comments were that the accommodations in Prague were a bit less expensive and that their food estimates appeared a little high for Slovakia. I asked them to elaborate on cultural events and recommended that they include an academic procession during the opening ceremony, comparable to that in Prague and Brno. And finally I suggested that the program be expanded, to also include areas of interest to our members abroad, and that they should plan on several parallel sessions simultaneously to accommodate the entire program.

Very little happened for about three months, during the time of Ján Skalný's working assignment in Australia. On his way back, he stopped in Bratislava to meet with the Bratislava Chapter to see how far they progressed. They had apparently a very friendly discussion but he did not bring back any new information.

Inasmuch as our June Executive Board meeting was fast approaching, I wrote an urgent letter to Tkáč, requesting detail budgetary information so that the Board could act on it and to set the amount of the registration fee. In my letter I also restated several principles that should be followed, based on our experiences with the previous congresses, i.e.,

---

[806] Ján P. Skalný (1935-), Executive Vice President of SVU.

there should not be any charge for lecture rooms, most cultural events should be provided gratis, various services, such as assistance with registration, would be performed by unpaid volunteers (graduate students), the cost of accommodations, food, social events. excursions, etc., would be charged separately to individual participants, depending on what they ordered. I also stressed that our members from abroad should not be treated any differently from their own people, keeping in mind that every Slovak or Czech American is not a millionaire, as people in both Republics perceive of us.

A month later, I finally received a response which was rather surprising, both in terms of its contents and its tone. Tkáč wrote, obviously in defensive, but adamant in his demands. He informed us that they encountered all sorts of unexpected difficulties, including financial. Instead of holding the Congress at some university, they now proposed that it be held at SUZA,[807] a special conference center belonging to Slovak Ministry of Foreign Affairs. The Center presumably had all the necessary lecture rooms, equipped with modern audio-visual equipment and could accommodate some 120 guests. There was also a cafeteria there serving 200 visitors. Unfortunately, there would be a charge for individual lecture rooms and all the equipment, and various services, based on hourly basis.

In spite of our previous specific request to the contrary, they would now charge us a composite sum, covering all sorts of costs and expenses, including the usage of the hall for the official opening in the Bratislava Castle, cost of lecture rooms, concert halls, honoraria for performing musicians and other artists, rent of audio-visual equipment, usage of simultaneous translation equipment, transportation, services of students, printing costs, posters, various administrative costs (telephone, FAX, copying, etc.), or, as some of the Executive Board members commented, "everything, including the kitchen sink." They estimated that this would come to about $140 per person. All the individual social and cultural events would be, of course, charged extra. There would be an additional 10% charge for undefined services. Conveniently, the subcontract would be let to a private corporation A. Consults s.r.o., whose director was

---

[807] The acronym stood for Správa účelových zariadení Ministerstva zahraničných vecí.

PhDr. Ondrej Srebala, who happened to also be the general manager of SUZA. A rather convenient arrangement, we thought.

In some ways, I was glad that Tkáč's letter did not reach me before our June Executive Board meeting because otherwise the Board might have decided to cancel the Bratislava Congress altogether. Our Slovak colleagues on the Board, although not happy with the Bratislava response, began to get edgy. On one hand, they were sympathetic to their Bratislava colleagues and became defensive when some Board members started raising criticisms. On the other hand, they realized that we could not charge our members exorbitant overhead without providing anything in return. They also realized that it would be in our interest to keep our registration fee as low as possible to attract overseas members to come to Bratislava.

My immediate concern was to assure the Executive Board at its August meeting not to rescind its earlier tentative approval of holding the Congress in Bratislava. I relied mainly on Skalný and Slávik to help me with this task. At this meeting, as anticipated, there were many questions, but in the end the Executive Board gave its final go ahead to the Bratislava Congress with specific provisos and recommendations that were subsequently communicated to Bratislava Chapter by Skalný. One of the recommendations was to ascertain the possibility whether the location of the Congress could be moved to some university site rather than holding it at SUZA which charged a lot and furthermore was inconveniently located at the outskirts of the city. We wanted to be in the center of the city and be able to be in contact with the local population rather than being isolated in SUZA, as in a prison. We further recommended to get rid of the subcontract and make use of voluntary help. We also did not see any need for the transportation budgetary item since most of our visitors would pay for their own taxis, if needed. With reference to our registration fee, we insisted that it had to include some social and cultural events because no one would be willing to pay just for overhead. Since SUZA was owned by the Slovak Ministry of Foreign affairs, we felt that they should apply pressure on the Slovak Government to exempt us from paying rent for the room usage, etc.

On our end, we had, in the meantime, assigned responsibility for the Congress as follows:

*Organizing the Bratislava Congress*

1. Rechcígl – policy matters, overall planning and organization, "the last resort person," and everything else, as needed.
2. Skalný – remained our main liaison with Bratislava to negotiate the details. In addition, he was given the task of recruiting Slovak professionals abroad to assist with the organization of specific panels.
3. Slávik – A back-up for Skalný. He would also help with finding potential Slovak speakers and other participants among his numerous contacts in Slovakia.
4. Dagmar White – She would assume more active role in the program planning and organizing of panels from overseas, comparable to her role in Brno congress.
5. Věra Ulbrecht – She would assist with mass mailing of invitations to potential overseas speakers and other participants, focusing on the US and Canada.
6. Search for a suitable candidate for Congress Treasurer, the role Blanka Kuděj played at the Brno Congress.[808]

As the first chore, with Skalný's help, I prepared the necessary registration forms, in addition to writing articles about the impending Congress to stimulate interest abroad. Individual Board members were assigned responsibility for organizing specific panels.

With reference to our request to Bratislava for budgetary information, we did not receive a satisfactory response in time for our December Executive board meeting. I was becoming quite frustrated about it so I finally decided to write a personal, rather pointed, letter to Tkáč, in which I went through our earlier discussions and agreements, pointing out how much valuable time was lost and our fear that organizational aspects cannot be possibly completed on time, putting squarely the blame on the Bratislava Chapter. Furthermore, I explained to him that some of our Board members had to come from far distances to attend the scheduled meeting, paying for their own expenses, and thus we should come to a decision regarding the overall Congress budget and finally set the amount for the registration fee, without which we could not start sending out invitations for potential speakers and other participants. Since no information was provided, we had no choice but to postpone

---

[808] The post of the Congress Treasurer was eventually assumed by Secretary-General Věra Ulbrecht.

the matter to another Board meeting, with the obvious loss of precious time.[809]

Later, I realized that my letter was quite strong, so I followed it up with a personal phone call to make sure that Tkáč would not quit on me. Actually, we had quite a friendly and constructive discussion, both trying to explain our positions, without being on the defensive and making an effort to resolve the apparent impasse. Alexander – we were on first basis by then – told me that he understood our situation and that he would make an effort to reduce or eliminate the unnecessary costs. Henceforth, the relationship between us became quite amiable. In due course, the Bratislava organizers sent us a revised budget which, after a few modifications, was accepted by the Executive Board.

The upshot of it was that we agreed to give Bratislava organizers $10,000 from our registration fee, in addition to monies collected from individuals for specific activities and services they ordered, including accommodations, food, bus excursions. In doing so, we had given up on ever receiving a detailed budget. Afterwards, our Secretary-General Věra Ulbrecht, who in the meantime assumed the function of the Congress Treasurer, handled all financial matters, pre-registration of overseas participants and collecting monies for accommodations, etc.

Our subsequent correspondence with Tkáč and Ladislav Macho, who joined the negotiations, focused primarily on the preparation of the program. Keeping in mind our commitment to come up with $10,000 toward the congress expenses, I calculated that we would roughly need between 100-125 participants from abroad to come up with such amount. The simplest way to get people interested to attend our Congress was to offer them the opportunity to present a paper, so we concentrated on that. Although most of our Board members pitched in, it was really left up to me "to deliver." After a number of phone calls and numerous FAXes we finally reached our goal of getting sufficient number of participants from abroad to be able to pay the promised amount, while keeping our Treasury in the black.

Unfortunately, this did not resolve our financial problems altogether, as I found when I arrived in Bratislava. Almost immediately upon my arrival at SUZA, I was confronted by Ondrej Srebala, who

---

[809] Based on our Bylaws, all the decisions by the Executive Board need to be made at the Board meetings, in the presence of the required quorum.

began pointing his finger at me, while shouting that he would put a stop to our Congress unless we pay him what was due to him and to SUZA. He behaved as if he would lose his mind. Frankly, I did not understand what it was all about, until next morning at a special meeting with the leadership of Bratislava Chapter which Srebala hurriedly summoned. This time, I asked Skalný to join me so that I was not alone in the "wolf's den."

As I later found out, Srebala apparently got hold of some of Ulbrecht's records and worksheets, listing our participants from abroad from which he construed that we had actually collected quite a bit more money in excess of $10,000 which, in his opinion, rightly belonged to them, or as Srebala put it, to him. He made another ugly scene at this meeting, insisting again that he be immediately paid or otherwise there won't be any Congress. In my response, I pointed out that his calculations were not correct because they were based on the assumption that all overseas participants paid the same registration fee. This was not true since the spouses were charged considerably less (by $45, in case of members, and $65, in case of nonmembers). Furthermore, a number of participants, listed on the worksheets, cancelled their trip so that we were obligated to return their money. Consequently, the total amount of money was far below Srebala's figures. In addition, I pointed out, that SVU had considerable administrative expenses that had to be deducted from the money collected from registration fee. None of this seemed to make any impression on Srebala who continued with his rage. Finally, I came up with the argument that we had a written agreement with the Bratislava Chapter to pay them $10,000 toward congress expenses, irrespective of the number of our participants. At this point, Dr. Ján Morovič,[810] who had a business and legal background, came to my defense, stating that Bratislava has no legal basis, whatsoever, for any additional demands from us. Agreement is an Agreement which needs to be honored.

This did not sway Srebala, in any way, who continued in his rage, proclaiming that, irrespective of our presumed agreement, to which he was not a party, he had a binding contract with the Bratislava Chapter and that he would take steps to make them pay what they owed him. It was rather an unpleasant scene.

---

[810] Ján Morovič (1945-), Rector of the City University, Bratislava.

We had several additional meetings, which were equally tense, during which I was joined by SVU Treasurer, Frank Mucha. His presence and involvement strengthened my position and generally had a calming effect on the discussions, even though Srebala's position remained unchanged, who now concentrated his anger and demands on the Bratislava Chapter and Professor Tkáč. After our last encounter, Mrs. Tkáč came to me, crying that we need to do something since neither the Chapter, nor Professor Tkáč, have sufficient resources to pay Srebala for the presumed debts. She also mentioned her husband's failing health.

Although Srebala had no legal case against SVU, as a whole, we did not want the Bratislava Local Chapter, nor Professor Tkáč, to unnecessarily suffer any harm, so in the end, Mucha and I proposed a compromise whereby the central SVU would give the Chapter additional $1,500 towards their expenses which was accepted by all parties concerned.

With the exception of the Executive Board, very few other members knew about this dreadful incident and my involvement and what I had to go through in averting a major disaster.

# 47
## *The Unforgettable Memories*

As far as the Congress was concerned, there was a consensus among all of us who took part in the SVU Congress in Bratislava that this was a truly extraordinary event.[811]

Most of the participants arrived in Bratislava on Sunday, 5 July 1998 and were accommodated in modern hotel rooms at SUZA or DRUŽBA. In the afternoon there was an open house at SUZA, i.e., a continuous "Social Get Together" with flowing open face sandwiches and other refreshments, constantly being replenished. This was an opportunity for meeting old friends or making new acquaintances from both sides of the Atlantic. The general mood was festive and very cordial.

Opening ceremony of the 19th SVU World Congress took place at 10 A.M. on Monday, July 6, in the beautiful "Aula" Hall of the Comenius University, Šafárik Square 6. The event started with the academic procession of Rectors, Deans and other university dignitaries, dressed in their colorful academic gowns and golden chains, signifying their university rank, with trumpets playing. It was a marvelous and unforgettable sight.

The large gathering of SVU members and invited guests who filled every available seat of the magnificent hall, was officially welcomed by the Rector of Comenius University Prof. Ing. Ferdinand Devinský, DSc.,[812] who hosted the meeting.[813] He was followed by Dr. Ing. Igor Hudoba,[814] CSc., the Rector of the Slovak Technical University, who greeted the gathering on behalf of the Slovak Conference of University

---

[811] The following narrative is based, in part, on my article, "Unforgettable Moments. Insights and Impressions from the Bratislava SVU Congress, *Zprávy SVU*, vol. 40, No. 4 (July-August 1998), pp. 1-3.

[812] Ferdinand Devinský (1947-), Rector, Comenius University, Bratislava.

[813] *Zprávy SVU*, vol. 40, No. 4 (July-August 1998), pp. 6-8.

[814] Igor Hudoba, Vice Rector, Slovak Technical University, Bratislava.

Rectors, of which he was President.[815] President of the Academy of CR Prof. Dr. Rudolf Zahradník sent a special message of greetings.[816]

The SVU Congress was officially opened by me, in my capacity as President of the Czechoslovak Society of Arts and Sciences.[817] The next speaker was His Excellency Ralph Johnson, the Ambassador of the U.S., who presented his views on the future relations of the US and Slovakia, followed by an enjoyable music interlude by the chorus "TECHNIK." Brief addresses of Dr. Jaroslava Turkova, President of the Prague SVU Chapter and Prof. RNDr. Ing. Alexander Tkáč, President of the SVU Chapter Bratislava and the Chairman of the Bratislava Congress Organizing Committee, followed.[818] The ceremony was closed with "Gaudeamus igitur." In the afternoon there was a plenary session held in the Moyzes Hall at the Music Conservatory, comprised of six major addresses, including those of Juraj Stern,[819] Jozef Tino,[820] Zlatica Plašienková,[821] Ján Morovič, A. Tamir and my own. My talk focused on history and work of SVU, on the occasion of the 40th anniversary of its existence.[822] The festive day was concluded with a reception and a cultural program of folk music and dance at SUZA.

Tuesday morning, Wednesday morning and afternoon and Thursday morning were devoted to academic sessions, many of which reflected the central theme of the 19th SVU World Congress: "Sciences and Arts on the Eve of the 21st Century." In addition, the program included a variety of symposia, and panel discussions on various topics, organized by different disciplines of human endeavor.

Tuesday afternoon was reserved for a guided tour through the historical Old Town, followed by a concert at the St. Martin's Cathedral, with the participation of the opera singer Zuzana Vaseková, Maroš

---

[815] *Zprávy SVU*, vol. 40, No. 4 (July-August 1998), pp. 8-11.
[816] *Zprávy SVU*, vol. 40, No. 4 (July-August 1998), pp. 12-13.
[817] *Zprávy SVU*, vol. 40, No. 4 (July-August 1998), pp. 11-12.
[818] *Zprávy SVU*, vol. 40, No. 5 (September-October 1998), pp. 1-2.
[819] Juraj Stern (1940-), Rector, Economic University of Bratislava, Bratislava.
[820] President, Federation of Slovak Christian Intellectuals, Bratislava.
[821] Zlatica Plašienková (1967-), lecturer in philosophy, Comenius University, Bratislava.
[822] It should be noted that President Václav Havel sent me a special message of congratulation on the occasion, which was published in *Zprávy SVU*, vol. 41, No. 1 (January-February 1999), pp. 1-2.

Kittner, organ, Milan Vonderka, violin, Lucia Majerská, violin, Dimitrij Kopčák, Eva Sochmanová, viola. The music repertoire included music of J. S. Bach, F. Handel, W. A. Mozart, A. Dvořák, F. Schubert and M. Markiezy. The program included words of welcome by Father Anton Srholec and poetry reading by Ladislav Chudik.[823] The Congress participants were then received in the Lord Mayor's Office at the Primacial Palace and treated to the music of W. A. Mozart and Antonín Dvořák by the Bratislava Capella Istropolitana Chamber Orchestra, under the direction of Robert Mareček. The extraordinary evening was concluded by a hospitable reception of scrumptious food and wine.

On Wednesday evening the Congress participants were taken by bus to the Bratislava castle to view the art exhibits and hear music by Mikuláš Schneider, Ludwig van Beethoven, Johannes Brahms, Frederick Chopin and Antonín Dvořák. The performers included two leading opera singers: Zuzana Vaseková, soprano and Peter Mikuláš, baritone and two piano virtuosi: Daniela Varinská and Marian Varinský. A reception with light refreshments to commemorate the 40th anniversary of the Czechoslovak Society of Arts and Sciences followed.

The Thursday afternoon program comprised of two plenary sessions, one of which was devoted to a historical overview of the work of SVU local chapters throughout the world. The academic program was concluded with three keynote addresses, beginning with that of Petr Zuna, Rector of ČVUT in Prague, who talked about the role of the Czech technical universities at the turn of the new millennium. The other two speakers included Father Anton Srholec from Bratislava who talked on the subject "Role of God in the Contemporary World," and Igor Kiss[824] "Is Humanity on the Way Out?" The talks by the representatives of the Catholic and Protestant faiths, respectively, were followed by an extemporaneous presentation of Prof. Pavel Traubner,[825] M.D., Ph.D., Honorary President of the Union of Jews in Slovakia. I formally closed the academic program by expressing thanks to my American collaborators and the Bratislava co-organizers, headed by Prof Tkáč, for the time and effort they put into organizing the 19th SVU World Congress. On

---

[823] Ladislav Chudik (1924-), Slovak actor and pedagogue.
[824] Dean, Evangelical Theological Faculty, Comenius University, Bratislava.
[825] Pavel Traubner (1941-), Dean, Medical Faculty, Comenius University, Bratislava.

Thursday night there was a farewell reception in SUZA with a cultural program, featuring a virtuoso on a cymbal whose mastery cannot be equaled.

Friday was reserved for a bus excursion into the picturesque Slovak countryside, with a guided tour of the Devin Castle and visit of the Smolenice Palace where the participants were served lunch. The group was then taken to Dolná Krupa to view the house of Beethoven and learn about the composer's private life and productive stay in Slovakia. A visit to Modrá and its famous ceramic artistic factory and laboratories "Majolika." followed. The very enjoyable day ended in the small Slovak village of Budmerice where the Congress participants were treated to first rate goulash and other Slovak goodies, accompanied with wholesome Slovak wine and beer. While the eating and drinking was going on, the musicians played the old tunes. Then people began dancing, while others sang.... I almost forgot to mention that we were first welcomed by the honorable Mayor of Budmerice who expressed his joy over our visit in his town and as a token of appreciation presented to me a historical chronicle of Budmerice. As you can imagine, the overall mood was genial, exuberant, enchanted, fantastic, etc. What a way to end the Congress![826]

Mention should also be made of the SVU 1998 General Assembly meeting,[827] convened on Tuesday, July 7 at 12 o'clock noon in the SUZA building, in which it was announced that I was reelected SVU President for the next two years, as was reported in detail in *Zprávy SVU*.[828]

Irrespective of the criteria used, the Bratislava Congress must be judged as a highly successful event, not only in terms of its content and quality but above all, how much it contributed to enhancing understanding between one another, between Czechs and Slovaks, as well as other nationalities, between those in our old country and those abroad, between scientists, artists and humanitarians, as well as across the gender and the age lines. It clearly fulfilled the Society's aim as a cultural,

---

[826] A detailed account of the cultural activities was penned by Alexander Tkáč, as reported in *Zprávy SVU*, vol. 40, No. 5 (September-October 1998), pp. 4-6.

[827] *Zprávy SVU*, vol. 40, No. 5 (September-October 1998), pp. 9-10.

[828] "Rechcígl again at the Helm of SVU," *Zprávy SVU*, vol. 40, No. 6 (November-December 1998), pp. 1-3.

nonpartisan and nonprofit organization, dedicated to principles of free search for truth and knowledge, free contacts among peoples and free dissemination of ideas.

When we got home from Bratislava, someone sent me a copy of the last issue of *Kanadské Listy* which included a curious note[829] that in the halls of the Bratislava SVU Congress echoed a "serious opinion that Dr. Míla Rechcígl would be an excellent candidate for the office of the President of the Czech Republic." Strange, but amusing!

---

[829] *Kanadské Listy*, No. 7-8, July-August 1998, p. 8.

# 48
# *State of the SVU in 1998*

### Report of SVU President Dr. Miloslav Rechcígl
### to the SVU General Assembly
### Convened 7 July 1998 in Bratislava

Allow me to first thank our Bratislava members for enabling us to hold the meeting of SVU General Assembly,[830] thirty-ninth in number, in Bratislava, on the occasion of our SVU World Congress. It is a historic event as we are going to commemorate the 40th anniversary of our Society,[831] which was established in 1958 in the US Capital, Washington, DC. Holding the World Congress in Bratislava is a historical event, in its own right, as it marks the first instance of convening our Congress on the Slovak soil.

As you know from our regular announcements in *Zprávy SVU*, in the first days following the Velvet Revolution, voices began to be heard in the sense that the SVU, which played a significant role during the era of communist oppression, already fulfilled its purpose and the time has come to bring its activities to an end. When the initial euphoria in the Czechlands and Slovakia subsided, the prevailing opinion within SVU substantially changed and the leadership came to the conclusion that the Society has not as yet completed its mission and that it still can accomplish a great deal in the cultural and educational areas, in the homeland, as well as abroad. This belief became even a greater reality following the worsening of the economic situation in both Republics which had an especially negative impact on the situation in education and research area.

The present Executive Board did everything it could to revitalize the Society and to elicit greater interest in the SVU work among SVU membership. The increased number of new members among born Americans,

---

[830] The Czech original appeared in *Zprávy SVU*, vol. 40, No. 5 (September-October 1998), pp. 10-13.

[831] *Zprávy SVU*, vol. 40, No. 5 (September-October 1998), pp. 8-9; "The 40th Anniversary of SVU," *Ibid.*, vol. 40, No. 6 (November-December 1998), pp. 8-9.

which is unquestionably the result of this effort, is a great satisfaction for all of us. This increase took place even though our exile ranks gradually thinned out. Our aim is to especially involve professionally active individuals, regardless of their background, interested in the thing Czech or Slovak. We have had some success in this regard, indicating that the approach has a great potential for our future membership drive. We are also pleased with the rising number of members among professionals in the Czech and Slovak Republics. Our greatest problem is how to inspire our younger generation.

During our two-year administrative period (1996-98), we continued in our efforts to coordinate education, cultural and research activities among Czechs and Slovaks abroad, to propagate Czech and Slovak culture worldwide, and to intensify mutual relations and cooperation between the Czech and Slovak intellectuals in the old countries and those living abroad.

The most important undertaking during our term of office was our Conference in Belton, TX, 12-13 July 1997, in conjunction with SVU annual meeting. The conference was organized on the occasion of the 100th anniversary of the Slavonic Benevolent Union of the State of Texas (SPJST), one of the oldest Czech-American organizations in the US. At this conference, educators, historians, social scientists and librarians together with cultural workers, businessmen and community leaders discussed the key issues of concern of Czech Americans, i.e., the preservation of Czech language, folklore, and folk art, ethnic history, the work of heritage and benevolent organizations, archives, libraries and cultural centers. Holding the Conference, jointly with the historic celebration of the anniversary of SPJST, was an excellent idea because it led to cooperation of two major organizations towards the same goal, i.e., preservation of Czech cultural heritage in North America. In addition, it fostered mutual cooperation between the members of Czech exile with the descendants of the early Czech settlers in America. The conference also resulted in the Executive Board's decision to include the issue of preserving Czech cultural heritage abroad among its top priorities.[832] Because of its general orientation, SVU will not, of course, limit its activities to the Czech cultural heritage but will encompass the Slovak heritage, as well.

---

[832] "SVU New Initiative," *Zprávy SVU*, vol. 40, No. 1 (January-February 1998), pp. 6-7.

Thanks to the thoughtful policy of our Executive Board, the financial situation of the Society has considerably improved, the red ink was replaced with black ink and the balanced budget became the order of the day. The weakest point remain our European local chapters, excluding those in the Czech and Slovak Republics, whose members don't pay their dues to our treasurer in prescribed amounts and are never on time. Consequently, the major financial burden of the Society rests on the shoulders of American and Canadian members.

The Executive Board has also made changes in the way our newsletter *Zprávy SVU* is managed and distributed which led not only to substantial savings but also significantly speeded up the publication schedule and distribution. After a slow start, two issues of the renewed SVU periodical *Kosmas*[833] have been issued and the third one is in press. The preparation of *SVU Biographical Directory*[834] unfortunately was delayed because of the slow response of the members in returning their biographical questionnaires. I again appeal to delinquent members to send in their questionnaires promptly.

With reference to *Kosmas*, until now the Society has had to subsidize it. We would like the periodical to become self-sufficient, relying on its own income. This won't happen without strengthening our subscribers' base. It is for this reason that we distributed the second issue among our American members, in the hope that they would become our regular subscribers. We will gladly send sample issues to our European members who are considering subscribing to the periodical. Library and other institutional subscriptions, are, of course, more important than subscriptions from individuals. We encourage our members to show the periodical to their university libraries and have them order it for their institutions.

Regarding activities of SVU local chapters, I will be brief since VP Věra Bořkovec will report on this separately.[835] I would only like to note that

---

[833] "Kosmas. Czechoslovak and Central European Journal," *Zprávy SVU*, vol. 39, No. 6 (November-December 1997), pp. 20-21; "New Issue of Kosmas," *Ibid.*, vol. 40, No. 6 (November-December 1998), pp. 11-12.

[834] "World Who's Who of Czechs and Slovaks," *Zprávy SVU*, vol. 39, No. 6 (November-December 1997), pp. 4-8.

[835] *Zprávy SVU*, vol. 40, No. 2 (March-April 1998), pp. 9-15; *Ibid*, vol. 40, No. 4 (July August), pp. 13-15.

we have succeeded in establishing a new chapter in Texas[836] and another in Japan, the latter being comprised almost exclusively of Japanese students. The Executive Board has also made a deliberate effort to revitalize several chapters that have been inactive. Among the active chapters, the most effective ones are those that are in close proximity to our Embassies or Missions, as is the case in Washington, DC or New York City. In Europe, most active chapters are those in the Czech and Slovak Republics.

As you have learned from our newsletter, SVU is not far behind technological advances of the day. Largely, through the initiative of SVU President, the Society now has its own Home Page on Internet.[837] Thanks to this page we have gained a number of new members, as well as new *Kosmas* subscribers, and, moreover, several scholars offered to present papers at the Bratislava Congress.

Most effort this year was devoted to the preparation of SVU World Congress in Bratislava. A major part of the year was spent in planning logistical arrangements and organizing the program. Practically, the whole Executive Board took part in this, not to speak about the effort expended to this by our Organizing Committee in Bratislava under the leadership of Alexander Tkáč. Judging from my own observations it is evident that the Bratislava Congress is proceeding extremely well and the local arrangements have far exceeded our expectations. I would like to use this opportunity to thank all persons who have contributed to its success. I will leave it to Prof. Tkáč to name the members of his Organizing Committee.

It should be noted that the Society will hold its next Congress, 20th in number, in the year 2000 in the US Capital, where the Society had its start.

As a parting note, I would like to express my sincere appreciation to the members of the Executive Board for their cooperation. In my judgment, The Board has done an excellent job and all our members can be satisfied with the SVU' current status.

..........

---

[836] "New SVU Chapter in Texas," *Zprávy SVU*, vol. 40, No. 1 (January-February 1998), p. 12.
[837] "SVU HomePage," *Zprávy SVU*, vol. 40, No. 1 (January-February 1998), pp. 6-7.

The above report was presented at the SVU General Assembly[838] in Bratislava on July 7, 1998. It was held in the building SUZA on the Drotárska Street where all the other Congress functions took place. Interestingly, the room was full to the last seat. The usual reports of various local chapters followed, including that of Prof. Alexander Tkáč for Bratislava, Prof. Karol Marton for Košice, Dr. Jaroslava Turková for Prague and Dr. Marie Bobková for Brno. I briefly reported about new chapters in Texas and Japan. SVU Treasurer made his traditional report which was approved after the Assembly heard the Auditors' report.

Subsequently, Dr. Anton Novacký assumed the function of the presiding officer pro tempore, in which capacity he read to the Assembly the outcome of the SVU elections, as prepared by the Election Inspectors, headed by Zdeněk Vich. All candidates, as recommended by the Nominations Committee were elected. The new officers were as follows: Miloslav Rechcígl, President; Jan P. Skalný, Executive Vice President; Eva Vaněk, Secretary-General; Frank Mucha, Treasurer; Věra Bořkovec, Milton Černý, Josef Macháč, Juraj Slávik, Alexander Tkáč, Jaroslav Verner, Dagmar Hasalová White and Petr Zuna, Vice Presidents.

As on other similar occasions, General Assembly approved a special resolution which was published in *Zprávy SVU*.[839]

---

[838] *Zprávy SVU*, vol. 40, No. 5 (September-October 1998), pp. 9-10.
[839] *Zprávy SVU*, vol. 40, No. 5 (September-October 1998), p. 14.

# 49
## *Organizing SVU Minnesota Conference*

Following my election for another two-year term (1998-2000), the first major decision the Executive Board had to make was to select the place for the next SVU Annual Meeting. The prevailing view was that the Meeting be held in the US. Since nobody on the Executive Board came with any concrete suggestions, the selection was essentially up to me.

My preference was to hold the meeting in a new location which would give us the opportunity of establishing a new SVU Chapter in that location. Ideally, it would be in some area where Czech and Slovak immigrants live in large numbers. The obvious location seemed to be somewhere in the Midwest. Having ruled out major cities, like Chicago and Cleveland, it did not take me long to focus on Minnesota. I knew that they had a very active Sokol organization there, as well as a strong genealogy group. Minneapolis was also known for its annual ethnic festivals and the Immigration History Research Center (IHRC) at the University of Minnesota.

As was our custom, I thought of combining our annual meeting with a special conference on some suitable topic which would attract our members, as well as non-members to greater attendance. I would have liked to mimic our experience in Texas where we organized our conference in conjunction with the celebrations of the 100th anniversary of SPJST.

I therefore immediately started inquiring about the possible Czech/Slovak festivals in MN area. My repeated inquiries at MN Sokol and Czechoslovak Genealogical Society were unproductive. They even tried to discourage me from holding our conference in Minneapolis altogether. I had the distinct impression that they worried that we may be encroaching on their territory. I did not get discouraged so easily. I liked the Twin Cities area, Minneapolis and St. Paul, not only because of their active Czech and Slovak community life but also because of the Cities' interest in and linkages with the Czech Republic and Slovakia. Nevertheless, it was clear to me that whatever we would attempt to do in MN, we were essentially on our own.

It must have been sometime in the fall of 1998 when I invited Ambassador Vondra to the Cosmos Club for lunch and gave him a rundown on the SVU Bratislava World Congress and also told him about the possibility of holding our conference in Minnesota. He thought that the place selection was an excellent idea and suggested that we hold it at the time of President Havel's visit to Minneapolis. Our conference would give the President's visit an added dimension and greater visibility among Czech Americans. From our perspective, the SVU Conference would, in turn, gain in importance and would stimulate greater attendance. We tentatively agreed on the joint effort, pending the approval of the idea by Prague Castle. My understanding from my discussion with Ambassador Vondra was that President Havel would personally attend our Conference and also give a talk there.

SVU Executive Board, whom I informed about my discussion with Ambassador Vondra, liked the idea and gave me a green light for further negotiations. I had another meeting with the Ambassador during which I learned that President Havel's trip was planned to coincide with the NATO celebrations in Washington, DC, sometime in April 1999, which he intended to attend. His Minnesota trip was to take place either before or after the Washington event. The main reason for his going to Minneapolis was to give a major address on "Civil Society" at Macalester College with which he would inaugurate a new seminar series. We clearly preferred to have our conference as late as possible to give us more time for the preparation of the program. After considering the available options, we decided on April 24 and 25 which fell on Saturday and Sunday. The dates had to be, of course, approved by Prague.

During my discussions with Ambassador Vondra, the name of Prof. Josef Mestenhauser came up as a possible coordinator of our Conference, who was also being considered for the position of the future Honorary Consul of Czech Republic in Minnesota. Actually I tried to contact Mestenhauser earlier regarding our conference but I was told that he was in a travel status, somewhere in Asia.

After his return, in September 1998, Mestenhauser readily agreed with our plans and accepted our offer to become the Conference coordinator. Apart from logistics, I was hoping that Mestenhauser would also take charge of the preparation of the Conference program. To make his job easier I gave him a draft outline of the proposed eight panels and volunteered to organize two of them myself. But he, in the meantime, landed with the responsibility for the coordination of the entire President Havel's visit, which gave him little time for much else. As time was getting closer to our conference, I became concerned that we would not have the program ready on time. Under the circumstances, I had no choice but to step in and take charge of the program myself.

I put tremendous effort into the preparation of the program and contacted numerous people throughout the US and Canada, using e-mail, whenever possible. Otherwise, I would make the contact by telephone. My best drawing card was, of course, the promised participation of President Havel. I also had a good idea to organize a special presidential symposium to which I invited the respective presidents/chief executive officers of the main Czech organizations in the US. Equally successful were two accompanying panels on the status of Czech/Slovak communities in the US and the preservation of our cultural identity and heritage. It was gratifying that most of the people I invited agreed to participate. With respect to the entire program, after two months of painstaking work, we managed to organize eight separate panels of some ten participants, which was a record by anybody's standards.[840]

In terms of overall logistics, the planning got more and more complicated, as more people got involved. Whereas initially there were to be only two principal players, i.e. SVU and Macalester College, all of a sudden there was a slew of additional organizations which wanted to be involved, particularly the MN genealogists and the local Sokol, which initially were against our holding the Conference in MN. The situation, at times, got so bad, that I had to personally call on Ambassador Vondra to intervene because otherwise SVU would have been pushed further and further away. Nevertheless, at the end, through a series of compromises, most of the differences were resolved, as a result of which we had a very successful Conference indeed. In retrospect, it was a pity that the MN-based Czech/Slovak ethnic organizations did not help us with our Conference and, for that matter, with a few exceptions, did not even take part in it. On the other hand, it was satisfying to see a number of Univer-

---

[840] The final program was published in *Zprávy SVU*. Vol. 41, No. 3 (May-June 1999), pp. 1-7.

sity and other MN-based institutions co-sponsoring our Conference, including Center for Austrian Studies, Department of Educational Policy and Administration, Hubert H. Humphrey Institute of Public Affairs and its Center for Nations in Transition and its International Fellows Program, Immigration History Research Center, Minnesota International Centre, Office of international Programs, MTS Systems corporation, Pharma Nutrients, etc.

# 50
# *In the Limelight of President Havel's Visit*[841]

Those of us, who attended the special SVU Conference in Minnesota,[842] will forever savor the moments of those three memorable days. The SVU Conference was part of a three-day program organized on the occasion of President Václav Havel's visit, culminating with his address on civil society and his meeting with the Czech and Slovak American community. The standing ovation President Havel received from some 3,000 onlookers was electrifying, which gave everybody who could claim origin in the Czechlands a great sense of pride. When the President proudly acknowledged his membership in SVU, while addressing the Czech/Slovak community, it increased the pulse of many a member of our Society and when he subsequently presented SVU President with the Václav Havel Commemorative Medal, in recognition of the Society's work, our members were elated. The program was concluded with songs and dances by performers of the local Sokol, dressed in the authentic national Czech/Slovak costumes, which left the audience in awe and tears in their eyes.

Our two-day Conference started in earnest on Saturday morning, April 24, on the campus of the University of Minnesota and proceeded in two parallel sessions in two large auditoria until late Sunday afternoon. After the words of welcome from Robert Bruininks, Executive Vice President and Provost of the University of Minnesota, the Conference was officially opened by Miloslav Rechcígl, SVU President. The ceremonial opening was concluded with the official greetings from Milan Špaček, Chairman of the Permanent Committee for Relations with Czechs Abroad of the Czech Senate and Jaroslav Karas, representing the similar committee in the Czech House of Representatives. From

---

[841] Based in part on my article in *Zprávy SVU*, vol. 41, No. 4 (July-August 1999), pp. 1–3.
[842] "1999 SVU Minnesota Conference...," *Zprávy SVU*, vol. 41, No. 2 (March-April 1999), pp. 1-5.

Slovakia came official greetings from Rudolf Schuster, Mayor of Košice and Prof. Alexander Tkáč, representing SVU Chapters in Bratislava, Košice and Prešov.

The overall theme of the Conference was "Czech and Slovak America: Quo Vadis?" with the aim of examining major issues that confront us today. This included the questions of historic settlements and present-day communities of immigrants from the territory of former Czechoslovakia and their future, preservation of cultural identity and heritage and mutual relations with the Czech and Slovak Republics. A special panel was devoted to human rights in the Czech and Slovak Republics from the external as well as internal point of view. There was also a Business Forum addressing the questions of trade and business opportunities in both republics. Also held was a journalist panel with the participation of newspapermen from both sides of the Atlantic, and a panel comprised of the younger generation discussing their perspective in viewing the new millennium.[843]

The Conference was attended not only by academics, but also by businessmen, students and community leaders, as well as by official spokesmen of the Czech Republic. Among the guest speakers was Deputy Foreign Minister Martin Palouš, Vice President of the Czech Senate Petr Pithart, Vice Chair of the Senate Permanent Committee for Relations with Czechs Abroad František Mezihorák, and Rector of the Czech Technical University Petr Zuna. The Czechoslovak Foreign Institute in Prague sent its two highest officers, Jaromír Šlápota and Josef Kolinský, President and Director, respectively.

All major Czech ethnic organizations in America were represented. A special Conference Presidential Symposium on the past and future of Czech and Slovak organizations, with participation of their presidents, featured presentations from CSA Fraternal Life, American Sokol Organization, Slavonic Benevolent Order of the State of Texas, Czechoslovak National Council of America, Czechoslovak Society of Arts and Sciences, Council of Free Czechoslovakia, American Fund for Czechoslovak Relief (Refugees), Czech and Slovak Heritage Association of Maryland, National Alliance of Czech Catholics, Czech and Slovak Association of Canada, and American Friends of the Czech Republic.

---

[843] The program of the Conference was published in *Zprávy SVU*, vol. 41, No. 3 (May-June 1999), pp. 1-7.

Never before were so many prominent Czech American ethnic leaders seen together on the same platform. Actually, there were many other ethnic organizations represented at the Conference, including Czech and Slovak Solidarity Council, United Moravian Societies, Moravian Historical Society, Bohemian Benevolent Literary Association of the City of New York, Bohemian Citizen's Benevolent Society of Astoria, Masaryk Club of Boston, Council of Higher Education, Czech Educational Foundation of Texas, American Czechoslovak Club of North Miami, Czech Heritage Foundation, Bohemian National Cemetery Association of Baltimore, Nebraska Czechs of Wilber, Oklahoma Czechs, California Czech and Slovak Club, Friends of Czech Music, Society of Czech Philately, etc. At the state level, there were representations from most areas where Czechs and Slovaks live, i.e., Arizona, Colorado, District of Columbia, Florida, Idaho, Iowa, Kansas, Louisiana, Maine, Maryland, Massachusetts, Michigan, Minnesota, Missouri, Nebraska, New Jersey, New York, North Carolina, North Dakota, Ohio, Oklahoma, Pennsylvania, Texas, Virginia, Washington and Wisconsin, as well as Canada.

The lectures were well prepared and of high quality and many of them generated lively debates. The panel discussions on human rights and the relations between the Czech and Slovak Republics brought out a number of controversial issues which will require specific follow up, both in terms of clarifying different points of view and providing actual data in order to prove or disprove specific points or contentions. The audience was pleased with Deputy Minister Palouš's openness to a dialogue but many a listener felt that time has come for real action, ten years after the Velvet Revolution.

The Conference ended with the crescendo of young voices with their panel discussion on "The Perspectives of the Young in Viewing the New Millennium." It was an enthusiastic group comprised of Czech and Slovak students in the US, as well as former American students in the Czech and Slovak Republics. Everybody who listened to their ideas must have left with the good feeling that the future rests in good hands.

All in all, the Conference and all the related activities in Minneapolis/St. Paul were a great success. It was truly a pivotal event and a historic occasion which will remain in our minds and hearts for many years to come and we are convinced that it may generate increased interest for the preservation of our cultural identity and heritage and, hopefully, lead to the revitalization of our ethnic communities in America.

During the meeting of President Havel with the Czech community representatives, I had the opportunity to greet him on behalf of SVU. My comments are reproduced below:

Mr. President, Ladies and Gentlemen,

It is a distinct honor and great pleasure for me personally to welcome among us, on behalf of the Czechoslovak Society of Arts and Sciences, a distinguished visitor from the Czech Republic, President Václav Havel. I am pleased to say that President Havel has been our member for many years – actually from the time when he was first jailed by the communist regime for his human rights efforts.

Mr. President, we are delighted to welcome you on the Minnesota soil, one of the most important centers of Czech and Slovak life in the Midwest. As you know, our Society has organized, on the occasion of your visit, a special conference, "Czech and Slovak America: Quo Vadis?," to examine some of the timely questions of the day, especially the vitality of our communities in America and the relations with our old homeland.

With respect to the first issue, I can assure you that our America, in spite of the impact of the melting pot, is a vital entity and with our efforts will remain so also tomorrow. Through the SVU initiative, under the newly established National Heritage Commission, composed of our most important organizations in America, we have embarked on a new far-reaching project to survey our monuments and other documented evidence relating to our presence in America in order to preserve for the future the cultural heritage of our fathers which is also an integral part of the Czech and Slovak culture, as a whole.

As to the second question, I can also assure you that we have the heartiest feelings towards our native country or the old homeland of our ancestors. Czech and Slovak America played a key role in the founding of Czechoslovakia over 80 years ago, and provided a helping hand in the liberalization movements during the era of Nazism and communism. Our continued effectiveness is shown by the recent admission of the Czech Republic into NATO.

Mr. President, we have a great interest in maintaining the best relations with our old homeland and feel that your presence here today has contributed greatly toward this end.

Vážený pane prezidente, přejeme Vám mnoho zdaru a hlavně zdraví ve Vaší obětavé práci.

# 51
# State of the SVU in 1999

### Report of SVU President Dr. Miloslav Rechcígl to SVU General Assembly, Convened on April 24, 1999 in Minneapolis, MN[844]

I am delighted to see many of our members at this 40th Annual Meeting of the Czechoslovak Society of Arts and Sciences.[845] It is nice to see so many old-timers who so faithfully attend all our annual meetings, as well as a number of new faces who are in attendance for the first time.

At the outset, I would like to first thank the local organizers, and particularly Jožka Mestenhauser, for making it possible to hold the General Assembly meeting in conjunction with our special conference, "Czech and Slovak America: Quo Vadis?,"[846] on the occasion of President Havel's visit to Minneapolis. Our time is limited to one hour so I will faithfully adhere to the schedule, in order not to jeopardize the activities which follow.

My report will be brief because it will cover only the first eight months of activities of the present Executive Board's two-year administrative period, following our election in 1998.[847]

It will essentially cover the same ground reported in our newsletter *Zprávy SVU*. That the Executive Board has viewed its responsibilities seriously is apparent from the fact that during this short period we held three regular meetings, and the fourth is planned next week.[848]

---

[844] Originally published in *Zprávy SVU*, vol. 41, No. 4 (July-August 1999), pp. 4-6.

[845] "SVU General Assembly," *Zprávy SVU*, vol. 41, No. 4 (July-August 1999), p. 14,

[846] "Special Conference on 'Czech and Slovak America: Quo Vadis," *Zprávy SVU*, vol. 41, No. 3 (May-June 1999} pp. 1-7.

[847] "Rechcígl again at the Helm of SVU," *Zprávy SVU,*vol. 40, N. 6 (November-December 1998), pp. 1-3.

[848] "New SVU Executive Board Meets," *Zprávy SVU*, vol. 40, No. 6 (November-December 1998), pp. 4-6; *Ibid.*, vol. 41, No. 1 (January-February 1999), pp. 3-5; *Ibid.*, vol. 41, No. 2 (March-April), pp. 6-8.

The first action we took was to complete some unfinished business relating to our exceptionally successful SVU World Congress in Bratislava, i.e. reviewing the expenses and paying the bills. It is with great satisfaction that I can report here that our ledger ended in the black, a reflection of the excellent planning of the Congress organizers.

At our election last year, I pledged, on behalf of the newly elected Executive Board, that we shall be fiscally responsible and manage the Society on the basis of a balanced budget. I am pleased to say that we are on target.

As is the custom, at the start of a new administrative period, the Executive Board first reviewed the Society's priorities and set its goals. The results of our deliberations led to a draft of the SVU Mission Statement, which was published in our newsletter,[849] with the request for comments from the membership at large. In brief, the Executive Board agreed to continue emphasis on the previous priorities, i.e., to enhance and promote Czech and Slovak culture abroad, to coordinate and assist the work of SVU members and to promote cooperation between scientists, artists and other professionals, as well as between cultural institutions, in Czech and Slovak Republics and those abroad. In addition to these, two more priorities were added, namely to make a concerted effort toward preservation of Czech and Slovak cultural identity and heritage abroad and assist with development of a civil society.

On October 24, 1998, SVU marked the 40th anniversary of its official founding, which was celebrated a few months earlier, on the occasion of the Bratislava SVU World Congress. President Václav Havel sent us a congratulatory message[850] on the anniversary day, which is reproduced below:

### THE PRESIDENT OF THE REPUBLIC

Dear friends and members of the Czechoslovak Society of Arts and Sciences:

On the occasion of the 40th anniversary of the founding of the Czechoslovak Society of Arts and Sciences let me first of all thank you for the invaluable service that the Society provided during the course of

---

[849] "SVU Mission Statement," *Zprávy SVU,* vol. 41, No. 1 (January-February 1999), pp. 8-9.

[850] *Zprávy SVU,* vol. 41, No. 1 (January-February 1999), pp. 1-2.

its existence to the preservation of the Czech Republic's greatest national treasure, namely to the preservation of those intellectual values which were suppressed and trampled underfoot in our country - along with those who maintained them – and which, thanks to the efforts of your Society were not only able to survive but to further fruitfully develop.

If one only takes into account the number of outstanding personalities who were among the founding members of the Czechoslovak Society of Arts and Sciences in the year 1958 and who continued working for its aims. one has proof enough of the extraordinary character of the Society and I am very proud that in the past I was chosen to be its Honorary Member.

I am deeply convinced that the future activity of the Czechoslovak Society of Arts and Sciences will lead to the enrichment of scholarly understanding and at the same time will contribute to the solution of the most pressing problems the world faces today.

I wish you much success in your praiseworthy endeavors.

**Signed: *Václav Havel***


One of the wisest decisions the new Executive Board made, at the beginning of its administrative period, was to convene the 1999 annual meeting combined with a special conference in Minneapolis/St. Paul area, an area where many a Czech or Slovak immigrant settled at the turn of the 19th and 20th centuries. When we subsequently learned of the possible visit of President Havel to Minnesota, through the cooperation of Ambassador Vondra, we rearranged our schedule so that the conference would coincide with the President's visit and be made part of the overall President Havel's program. In the last two months we worked exceedingly hard to make the program[851] a success and, judging from the comments of the attendees, it is apparent that we have succeeded. It is hard to imagine another comparable event which would have been attended by so many distinguished personalities. While working on the program, Jožka Mestenhauser and I must have exchanged as many as five different e-mail messages a day. I am sure he must be relieved that the ordeal is over.

---

[851] "SVU 1999 Annual Meeting and Special Conference on Czech and Slovak America: Quo Vadis," *Zprávy SVU*, vol. 41, No. 1 (January-February 1999), pp. 9-11; "1999 SVU Minnesota Conference, *Ibid.,* vol. 41, No. 2 (March-April 1999(, pp. 1-4.

Another major effort we have undertaken is the preparation for the 20th SVU World Congress to be held in the Nation's Capital, Washington, D.C. in the year 2000. As the central theme, we have chosen "Civil Society and Democracy into the 21st Century." Apart from the relevant symposia and discussion panels, there will be traditional sessions according to various disciplines. The Washington DC SVU Chapter has assumed responsibility for local arrangements. Věra Bořkovec will coordinate the logistics while Anton Novacky will coordinate the program.

As was recently reported, SVU has just published a new monograph entitled *Czech-Americans in Transition*,[852] based on the SVU Conference in Texas in 1997. It is an excellent publication and we urge you to purchase a copy for yourself and another for a friend. You should also suggest that your librarian order a copy for their public or university library.

The present Executive Board is paying special attention to publications and has undertaken a comprehensive evaluation of the entire SVU publication program with emphasis on periodicals, under the direction of Vice President Josef Macháč. The first task is an in-depth evaluation of the English periodical *Kosmas*, both in terms of management and editorial policies and practices, which is currently in progress.

As a result of our Conference in Texas in 1997, the Society has included among its priorities an effort toward preserving our cultural heritage abroad.[853] SVU has had a long-standing interest in the history of Czech and Slovak Americans and has anxiously followed the disappointing trends in the vitality of our communities, as manifested by the declining interest in Czech and Slovak languages and cultural traditions and the demise of once influential organizations. As the grandparents pass away, the subsequent generations lose interest, not only in the languages of their ancestors, but also in their own family heritage. They have no need for the old Czech or Slovak books, almanacs or calendars and other family treasures which have reminded their parents and grandparents of their old country and which they always held in great reverence. As a result, historic publications and other memorabilia are tossed away and thus permanently lost.

---

[852] "New SVU Book Based on 1997 SVU Conference in Texas," *Zprávy SVU*, vol. 41, No. 1 (January-February 1999) p. 23.

[853] "Preservation of Czech Cultural Heritage in America," *Zprávy SVU*, vol. 40, No. 6 (November-December 1998), pp. 6-8.

It is for this reason that SVU has embarked on the program of making a comprehensive survey of existing memorial sites and documentary material throughout the US which have a bearing on the Czech and Slovak presence in America. To assist in this endeavor, SVU received a grant from the Czech Ministry of Foreign Affairs to survey historic sites and monuments that commemorate important events and personalities of Czech America and to gather information on the existing archives, libraries and other documentary material maintained by various organizations or in private hands. We obviously cannot do this alone and have therefore turned to other major Czech American organizations to assist us in this all-American effort, under a new umbrella organization which we have called National Heritage Commission.

It is also in this spirit that our Society is making a concerted effort to involve young people in our activities. Hopefully, this will lead to revitalizing not only of the SVU ranks but also toward revitalization of all Czech and Slovak America, in general. Towards this end, we have also included in our conference program a special discussion panel, comprised entirely of students and young people, on the topic "The Perspective of the Young in Viewing the Millennium."

In conclusion, let me reiterate, our Society is sound and well. We are always open to new ideas and innovative suggestions. We also welcome volunteers to help us with our large agenda, particularly, but by no means limited to, the younger generation.

..........

I made the above report to the General Assembly meeting on April 24, 1999.[854] I called the meeting to order at 5 PM, one hour later than originally announced, because we did not have the required quorum at that time. Apart from my annual report, there were a few other reports by various SVU officers. The most important item was Ivan Furda's report on the establishment of a new SVU Chapter in Minneapolis which was the direct outcome of our Conference. Furda was elected Chapter chairman. Another item of significance was the approval of SVU resolution, the text of which was later published in *Zprávy SVU*.[855]

---

[854] "SVU 1999 General Assembly," *Zprávy SVU*, vol. 41, No. 4 (July-August 1999), p. 14.

[855] "Resolution approved by SVU General Assembly...," *Zprávy SVU*, vol. 41, No. 4 (July-August 1999), pp. 6-8.

# 52
## *Organizing the Millennium SVU World Congress*

Soon upon assuming the office of SVU President for the 1998-2000 administrative period, it became quite clear to me that our major emphasis should be on the preparation of our anniversary SVU Congress scheduled for the historic year 2000, marking the end of the second Millennium.

Based on my correspondence and contacts with individual SVU members, I was aware of the general feeling, especially among our members in the US and Canada, that the time has come for holding the meeting in America again, considering that four previous Congresses were held in the Czech and Slovak Republics, and that the bulk of our membership resided in America.

Frankly, I had some misgivings about it because I knew quite well that holding the Congress in the US or Canada wouldn't attract as many participants as did Congresses in Prague, Brno and Bratislava. In the first place, many of our members living abroad welcomed the opportunity of visiting their homeland and, secondly, many of our participants, regardless of their background or their ethnic origin, were attracted by numerous cultural sites and events in the beautiful Czech and Slovak cities, not to speak about touring the picturesque countryside. It was obvious to me that we could not possibly mimic the breath-taking academic procession at Karolinum, nor the fabulous fireworks in Brno nor the reception at the Bratislava Castle. My apprehension was magnified by realization that this was our 20th anniversary Congress, a very significant milestone in the SVU history.

The obvious place for holding the Congress was Washington, DC, the place where the first SVU Congress was held in 1962. The idea was readily accepted by the new SVU Executive Board and Vera Bořkovec volunteered to coordinate the Congress' local arrangements. The Washington DC Chapter was also the logical partner and cosponsor in terms of logistics and local arrangements which was made easier by the fact that Vera's husband, Saša Bořkovec, was actually the chairman of the Washington, DC Chapter.

American University, where Věra Bořkovec held a teaching position, appeared as the logical site for holding the Congress. Through Milton Černý's contacts – who held the post of one of SVU Vice Presidents at the time – I had the opportunity to meet with the Dean of the University's Washington Law School who was enthusiastic about holding the Congress on the American University campus and offered the facilities of the Law School for the meetings. We also met with President of the Methodist Theological Seminary, associated with the American University, who also expressed interest in involving the Seminary in our Congress preparation, particularly with reference of co-sponsoring sessions on Bohemian Reformation and historical relations between the Methodists and the Moravian Church.

Soon after, we scheduled a meeting with President of American University, Dr. Benjamin Ladner, who welcomed the idea of hosting our Congress and promised his full support. He immediately appointed his right-hand man, personal assistant Michael Stopford, to be our principal contact. During our meeting with President Ladner, the Czech Ambassador Alexandr Vondra came with us for moral support.

To give the Congress maximum visibility we needed a catchy title for its central theme. We took the advantage of the rapidly approaching new Millennium and picked as our main theme "Civil Society and Democracy into the new Millennium." With the emphasis on civil society we thought we might be able to entice President Havel to attend the Congress. I wrote him a letter inviting him to be a keynote speaker at the official opening. To make the invitation more appealing, American University offered the President an honorary doctorate. Under normal circumstances, he would have probably accepted, but since he had already consented to come to the US a month later during the UN meetings, he declined our offer.

The greatest problem we had was finding a suitable coordinator for planning the program. There was nobody on the Executive Board who was willing to take on such a great responsibility. When Ján Skalný announced his anticipated resignation from our Board, due to family reasons, I suggested Prof. Anton Novacký as his replacement. I knew Anton well from the past, when he served as program chairman during our Congress in Boston in 1986 and later when he accompanied us to Czechoslovakia in 1990 as one of the delegates of the SVU Commission for Cooperation with Czechoslovakia. It was natural to appoint Anton Novacký to the position of Congress program coordinator.

Following the announcement of the Congress in July-August issue of *Zprávy SVU*, I immediately began publicizing the Congress in several Czech newspapers and posting suitable announcements on the Internet. Despite this concerted campaign there was hardly any response from our membership, confirming my initial apprehension about holding the Congress in the US. Nobody came with any suggestions and our call for papers was a dismal failure. Under the circumstances, I realized that a different approach was needed.

Based on my experiences with other congresses, I knew that we'll need to approach all potential speakers individually, inviting them to speak on topics they like. I also realized that Anton Novacký will not be able to handle this without additional help. The best strategy was to find as many knowledgeable individuals as possible in various fields who would be willing to organize their own panels in the areas of their interest. As a starting point, I asked for volunteers from our Executive Board which yielded five possible panels, at best, a long way from what was needed. We spent practically two entire Executive Board meetings discussing possible panel organizers.

The actual work on the program did not start in earnest until after our Executive Board meeting in the fall of 1999. By then, I expected that Anton would have panel organizers in place. But that did not happen. As far as I could ascertain he did not make much progress since our last meeting. It dawned on me that at this late hour it was simply too late to change horses in midstream and furthermore, I realized that, unless I get personally involved, the whole Congress could turn into a disaster.

I spent most of my Christmas holidays at our daughter's in Albuquerque, thinking about various panels we could organize and individuals we could invite. After returning home, I began methodically, day by day, working in front of my computer, composing persuasive invitations and sending e-mails to potential speakers. Knowing only too well that people don't respond to general invitations, I, soon, abandoned the idea of organizing panels by discipline, and focused instead on topical sessions and symposia for which it was easier to find speakers.

Once I secured the person's concurrence, I would immediately inform Anton Novacký about it, and, later on, also send him the speaker's abstract. As per our agreement, he was then supposed to edit individual abstracts and get them ready for publication.

On the whole, I had been pretty successful. By the end of May, I had a number of panels and symposia in place, with some speakers. As part of the program, I also organized a special symposium on "Future of Planet Earth," with participation of three top scientists each from the Czech and Slovak Republics, respectively. To enable them to personally participate I was successful in obtaining for them a special grant support from one of the private foundations which paid for their expenses.

To attract leading scholars and scientists to our Congress I came up with the idea of organizing a two-half day SVU Science Symposium: "Accomplished American Scientists with Czech or Slovak Roots" and a separate plenary session" Czechs and Slovaks Who Made a Difference in the Second Millennium."

Inasmuch as I was planning to leave for the Czech Republic in early June, I made a concerted effort to get everything done before my departure. This related not only to the program per se, but also to the logistics and other SVU-related matters.

While I was methodically working on the panels, I had assumed that Anton would have been diligently working on the abstracts which I had been systematically sending him via e-mail, in addition to those that he may have gathered on his own.

It was therefore to my great dismay when I later found out that he had only some 30 abstracts, a small number indeed, considering that we had over 200 speakers. Frankly, we could not understand what happened to the rest of the abstracts I had sent him earlier.

It was obvious that we could not very well proceed with publishing such a small number of abstracts. In the first place, it would have looked bad and secondly, it would have most certainly infuriated many of our speakers who made a sincere effort to prepare their abstracts and who sent them in on time. Again, I had no choice but to interfere. Without further ado, I sat in front of my computer and began frantically sending out e-mail notices to the respective speakers, asking them for their abstracts and so as not to lose time, I had them sent directly to our VP Dagmar White who was ultimately responsible for getting them published. In this manner, we were able to accumulate quite a large number of missing abstracts.

The last chore which fell on my shoulders was scheduling individual papers, after they were arranged in suitable panels. This turned out to also be an arduous task, more difficult than one would have initially thought. One had to obviously avoid potential conflicts, stemming from the fact that some speakers were presenting more than one paper, while others could be present only at one particular time. Furthermore, we had to also assure that related sessions were not scheduled during the same time period.

As I was heading for Prague, I naively thought that everything humanly possible was done and that the program was completed, except for the printing of the abstracts for which there was sufficient time after my return.

Upon my return from Prague, there were a few surprises awaiting me. Literary, hundreds of e-mail messages awaited me with all sorts of requests, requiring immediate follow-up. Most requests concerned rescheduling papers and even the entire sessions. In addition, some papers were cancelled while new ones were added. I tried to accommodate all the requests and resolve all pending problems, irrespective how difficult, to the satisfaction of the speakers and to make sure that all these changes were reflected in the final program.

# 53
## *Beyond Expectations and Our Dreams:*
### Echoes and Reflections from the SVU Millennium Congress[856]

Upon returning from the last scheduled Congress event – a visit to President Jefferson's home at Monticello – I decided to put down some of my thoughts on the six memorable days at the Congress, while my memory was still fresh.

Speaking as a whole, the Congress was an unqualified success and the organizers' hope that it might be a pivotal event of the historic year 2000 for those interested in the thing Czech or Slovak turned out to be a fulfilled prophecy. There were around 400 registrants, not counting numerous other individuals who sneaked in without paying, making it a record for any SVU Congress held on the American continent.

Only some ten years ago one could hear rumblings among individual SVU members that the Society has done its thing and that the time has come to cease and desist. I doubt there was a single soul at the Congress who would have dared to utter or even contemplate such a thought. What difference ten years make! The vigor and vitality of the Society was self-evident in all of the fifty five scheduled panels. Many a panel was overflowing with listeners so that some of them had to stand or sit on the floor. To be sure, some panels started with only a few individuals but as the time went on they began to fill up, even to capacity. Interestingly enough, even in the less attended panels, as the presentations proceeded, the listeners and the speakers became so engrossed in the proceedings and in intensive discussions that the number of people in the audience did not seem to matter. The people in the audience were not just passive listeners, many of them contributed to discussion, sometimes clarifying points or adding new information. There was something there

---

[856] Originally published in *Zprávy SVU*, vol. 42, No. 5 (September-October 2000), pp. 17-20; *Ibid.*, vol. 42, No. 6 (November-December 2000), pp. 7-11.

for everyone and frequently one had to make hard choices which of the sessions or papers to attend.

The Congress took place in the capital of the US, Washington, DC, where the Czechoslovak Society of Arts and Sciences (SVU) got its start, where the idea of creating the Society was developed, and where the first Society's Congress was held. The present Congress, 20th in number, was organized jointly with the American University where most of the meetings and related activities were held. The Congress was organized under the aegis of both the Czech and Slovak Embassies and Ambassadors Alexandr Vondra, as well as Martin Bútora and his wife personally took part in a number of events. The final program, which appeared as the fourth issue of the 2000 *Zprávy SVU*,[857] covered some 28 pages. Schedule of individual panels with an Addenda to the Program appeared in the subsequent issue.[858]

The Congress started with a bang – a reception at the Slovak Ambassador's residence in McLean Virginia in the late afternoon of August 8. When I first discussed the idea with Hon. Martin Bútora, I had in mind a relatively small group of people attending, 100 at most, considering that it would actually take place the day before the Congress' opening. However, to our amazement, three times as many people actually came, filling every available inch of, otherwise a spacious home. I was told that this was a record attendance for any gathering in the Ambassador's residence. Mrs. Bútorová personally graciously welcomed visitors at the door which gave us a feeling of hospitality and warmth. Because of the distance from the city, the Ambassador arranged for transportation from and to American University by bus. The culinary skills of their new chef were evident in the scrumptious food served.

The official opening of the Congress took place at American University Washington College of Law in the elegant Morella Courtroom, patterned after a classical British courtroom. The program started with a musical piece – *Dance Suite* by Tylman Susato, performed by Annandale Brass, John Wright, conducting – followed with the national anthems. When the Czech "Kde domov můj" was played, followed by "Nad Tatrou sa blýska," a site unseen and the sound unheard since the

---

[857] *Zprávy SVU*, vol. 42, No. 4 (July August 2000), pp. 1-38.
[858] *Zprávy SVU*, vol. 42, No. 5 (September-October 2000), pp. 14-17.

painful separation of the two Republics, there was a visible stir in the audience and one could see an honest tear in the eyes of many. The official welcome was given by President of American University Dr. Benjamin Ladner,[859] who commenced and ended his words with the quotation from Comenius, a real gesture from an American, followed by the greetings of the representatives of Washington College of Law and the Wesley Theological Seminary where some of the meetings were held. I then had the pleasure of officially opening the Congress,[860] which occasion I used to acquaint the audience with the aims of SVU and recapitulate key milestones in its history and activities. Then came the presentations by the Czech and Slovak Ambassadors, Alexandr Vondra and Martin Bútora, respectively, outlining their views on future cooperation of their governments with Czech and Slovaks in the US.

Following a short intermission came the keynote address by Hon. Václav Klaus, Speaker of the House, Czech Parliament, on the perspectives of the Czech Republics in the next continuum, focusing on the economic aspects. His presentation was followed by an address by Hon. Pál Csáky, Vice Premier of the Slovak Republic, who discussed his views on the democratization of Slovakia based on tolerance and the rule of law.

After a buffet lunch, hosted jointly by SVU and the American University, there was a plenary session on the theme "Czech and Slovaks Who Made a Difference in the Second Millennium." Selected speakers gave presentations on the contributions of such outstanding personalities as Jan Hus, Jan Amos Komenský (Comenius), Rabbi Chatam Sofer, Antonín Dvořák, Johann G. Mendel, Sigmund Freud, Thomas G. Masaryk, Milan Rastislav Štefánik, Štefan Osuský and Ján Papánek. All speakers were outstanding personalities in their own right, coming from such institutions as the Academy of Sciences of the Czech Republic, Slovak Academy of Sciences, Charles University, Jewish Museum of Prague, Palacký University, etc.

That evening Congress participants were hosted at a reception at the Czech Embassy which was co-sponsored by the SVU Washington DC Chapter. This reception, which was very successful, was attended by

---

[859] "Welcoming Remarks by President Benjamin Ladner at the Opening of the 20th SVU World Congress," *Zprávy SVU*, vol. 42, No. 5 (September-October 2000), pp. 11-12.

[860] "Remarks by SVU President Miloslav Rechcígl at the Opening of the 20th SVU World Congress," *Zprávy SVU*, vol. 42, No. 5 (September-October 2000), pp. 12-14.

an enormous crowd which made it necessary to open the doors into the garden. There was the customary receiving line and later Ambassador Vondra introduced several distinguished guests from the Czech Republic, i.e., Senator Petr Pithart, Senator Jaroslava Moserová, and the Chief of Staff of the Czech Ministry of Foreign Affairs Martin Vávra.

The next three days were devoted to individual sessions, discussion panels and symposia, organized by subject, discipline, or topic. It is beyond the scope of this article to dwell into detail or even to attempt to summarize proceedings of individual panels. There was such a variety that everybody could find something of interest. A number of people commented that the proceedings of at least some of the panels should be published and disseminated. The SVU Executive Board will definitely make an effort in this direction. Of the various panels I would like to make special reference to the SVU Symposium on the "Future of Planet Earth: Environmental and Sustainable Development in the Czech Republic and Slovakia." This was a carefully planned symposium with the financial assistance of the Trust of Mutual Understanding, and the participation of six leading experts from the Czech and Slovak Republics. The active participants of the Symposium had an opportunity to also meet with the representatives of the National Science Foundation and those of the Environmental Protections Agency and to discuss their program and future cooperation with their American counterparts.

Apart from the strictly academic program, there were a variety of cultural and social events that participants could attend. In connection with the SVU special project on the preservation of the Czech and Slovak heritage in America, the SVU staged a historical photo exhibit of Czech and Slovak communities, arranged by States and cultural institutions. It was beautifully done and Pat DeVoe, who did most of the work, deserves special thanks. Some participants took the advantage of taking part in the arranged and guided tour in the National Gallery of Art. The American University Theater, under the direction of Gail Humphries Mardirosian, staged for the Congress participants an American premiere of Josef Topol's "Hour of Love" (translated by Věra Bořkovec). It was an extraordinary play written by the foremost playwright of the Czech Republic. There was also a showing of a remarkable Mináč's film "All My Loved Ones," depicting the life of the Czech Jewish family at the onset of the World War II. Another film with the Jewish theme from the

World War II was shown in the panel on "The Holocaust." One of SVU members, Suzanne Justman produced this very moving the Emmy-winning film, entitled "Voices of Children." The Congress program also included an annual meeting of the Society which will be addressed elsewhere.

One of the startling phenomena of the Congress was the omnipresence of the young people, or more precisely the young folks in their twenties and the middle-aged folks in their thirties and forties. This was not just a happenstance. The Congress organizers planned for that by selecting several young people who organized panels by themselves. Anybody who attended these panels must agree that they did an outstanding job. Another striking feature of the Congress was the number of visitors from the Czech and Slovak Republics who made the discussions more interesting, more genuine, and more realistic. The fact that the top political leaders from the Czech and Slovak Republics, such as Václav Klaus and Pál Csáky, actively participated at the Congress, is an indication that not only SVU commends greater respect than ever before in the home countries but also that Czech and Slovaks abroad are being viewed more seriously over there.

A number of greetings were received on the occasion of SVU World Congress, including those of President Václav Havel, and Minister of Foreign Affairs Jan Kavan, which are reprinted elsewhere. In addition, the Mayor of Washington, Hon. Anthony A. Williams declared August 9, 2000, as "Czechoslovak Society of Arts and Sciences Day" in Washington, DC. The holding of the Congress was also recognized by the remarks of Hon. James P. Morgan, a Representative of Virginia, published in the *Congressional Record*.

All in all, the Congress more than fulfilled our expectations. Generally, everyone I talked to had a good time. The overall mood was excellent and good humor prevailed most of the time. Occasional problems, such as looking for taxis, were relatively minor, in comparison to everything else which was overwhelmingly positive, exciting, stimulating, encouraging, and enthralling. There was a feeling of warmth, belonging, and camaraderie among all, be they Czechs or Slovaks or anybody else, the young or the old, professionals, political and community leaders alike, irrespective of on what side of the Atlantic one lived Only meetings like this, unassuming, face to face, individuals of good without preconceived notions can overcome the existing and imaginary bee lines or crow lines separating the Czechs and Slovaks abroad from their compatriots in the home countries.

Tolerance, humanity and good will were the underlying tone of the Congress, exquisitely fitting and contemplatively reflecting upon the general theme "Civil Society and Democracy into the New Millennium."

# 54
## State of the SVU in 2000

### Report of SVU President Dr. Miloslav Rechcígl to SVU General Assembly Convened August 10, 2000 in Washington, DC[861]

It is hard to believe that two years have passed. It seems like yesterday when we held our SVU World Congress in Bratislava, soon followed by SVU Conference in Minnesota.

I am delighted to see so many of our members attending this year's annual meeting whose number may very well be a record in SVU history. Because of our extensive agenda, I will keep my report as brief as possible. Our Executive Board has been reporting on its activities on a regular basis in *Zprávy SVU*[862] which makes my task considerably easier.

Two years ago, the Society commemorated the fortieth anniversary of its remarkable history on which occasion we also received a congratulatory message from President Havel.[863]

In his message, President Havel thanked us for the invaluable service that the Society provided during the course of its existence to the preservation of the Czech Republic's greatest national treasure, namely to the preservation of those intellectual values which were suppressed and trampled underfoot in our country – along with those who maintained them – and which, thanks to the efforts of your Society were not only able to survive but to further fruitfully develop. He

---

[861] Originally published in *Zprávy SVU*, vol. 42, No. 5 (September-October 2000), pp. 1-4.

[862] *Zprávy* SVU, vol. 41, No. 4 (July-August 1999), pp. 11-13; *Ibid.*, vol. 41, No. 5 (September-October 1999), pp. 3-4; *Ibid.*, vol. 42. No. 1 (January-February 2000), pp. 5-6; Ibid., vol. 42, no. 2 (March-April 2000), pp. 8-10; *Ibid.*, vol. 42, No. 5 (May-June 2000), pp. 4-5.

[863] *Zprávy SVU*, vol. 41, No. 1 (January-February, 1999), pp. 1-2.

commented on the extraordinary character of the Society and stressed how proud he was of being chosen its Honorary Member. He concluded the statement with his deep conviction that the future activity of the Czechoslovak Society of Arts and Sciences will lead to the enrichment of scholarly understanding and at the same time will contribute to the solution of the most pressing problems the world faces today.

Today, which could be called the eve of the new Millennium, our Society is entering the new era with great expectations, as well as big promise. As you will discern from my account, the SVU activities of the past two years are commendable, giving us a good start for the Third Millennium.

The first thing our Executive Board did, upon assuming its duties, was to reexamine its priorities and to formulate its new Mission statement. The agreed upon priorities are: to enhance and promote Czech and Slovak culture abroad, to assist and coordinate the work of SVU members, to foster cooperation between scientists, artists, and other professionals, as well as between cultural institutions in Czech and Slovak Republics and those abroad, to make a concerted effort toward preservation of Czech and Slovak cultural identity and heritage abroad, and finally to assist with the development of civil society.

Early on, it was decided to hold the Society's annual meeting in Minnesota, which offered a number of advantages – above all its central location in the Midwest – the heart of USA – where a large number of Czech and Slovak immigrants settled. This turned out to be a fortuitous decision as it enabled us to coordinate it with the planned visit of President Havel. This also gave us an opportunity to convene a special SVU Conference on the key issues confronting Czech and Slovak Americans today, under the title "Czech and Slovak America: Quo Vadis?" We set for ourselves three main objectives, i.e., to discuss issues relating to their historical settlements and today's communities, the preservation of their cultural identity and heritage, the future relations between Czechs and Slovaks living in North America, and in the Czechlands and Slovakia.

One of the special features of the conference was a Presidential Symposium entitled "Czech and Slovak Organizations in America, Past and Present," with the participation of the major Czech organizations in America, including CSA Fraternal Life, American Sokol Organization, Slavonic Benevolent Order of the State of Texas (SPJST), Czechoslovak National Council of America, Czechoslovak Society of Arts and Sciences (SVU), Council of Free Czechoslovakia, American Fund for Czechoslovak Relief, Czech and Slovak Heritage Association of Maryland, National Alliance of Czech Catholics, Czech and Slovak Association of Canada, and American Friends of the Czech Republic. Never before in recent history were so many prominent Czech American ethnic leaders assembled on the same platform. In addition to the named organizations, there were some twenty other ethnic organizations represented at the Conference. At the state level, there was representation from most areas in the US where Czechs and Slovaks live, close to 30 states, as well as Canada. Among the prominent guest speakers was Czech Deputy Minister of Foreign Affairs Martin Palouš, Vice President of the Czech Senate Petr Pithart, Senator František Mezihorák and Rector of the Czech Technical University in Prague Petr Zuna.

The SVU MN Conference was part of a three-day program organized on the occasion of President Václav Havel's visit, culminating with his address on civil society and his meeting with the Czech and Slovak American community. When the President proudly acknowledged his membership in SVU during his address, it increased the pulse of many a member of our Society and when he subsequently presented SVU President the Presidential Commemorative Medal, our members were ecstatic.

One of the highest priorities of the current Executive Board was given to SVU publications. A special evaluation committee was established under the chairmanship of Vice President Josef Machac for the purpose of undertaking an in-depth evaluation of SVU periodicals. As a result of their recommendations the *Kosmas*' editorial procedures have been streamlined under the new editor Clinton Machann of the University of Texas A&M and substantially restructured and the publication and the printing operations have been moved to Texas.[864] It is hoped that this will bring about speedier operation in order that the periodical can be published on regular schedule. There have also been considerable improvements in the contents and the quality of *Zprávy*

---

[864] "Kosmas – New Editorial Changes," *Zprávy SVU*, vol. 42, No. 3 (May-June 2000), p. 23.

*SVU* which now regularly bring several new columns, i.e., SVU Calendar, From New SVU Rolls, and Focus on Younger Generation.

The Executive Board also initiated an ambitious monograph publication program. The first monograph, *Czech-Americans in Transition*,[865] based on papers presented in the 1997 SVU conference in Texas, was published under the editorship of Clinton Machann, about half a year ago. Plans are now under way to also publish the Proceeding of the SVU MN Conference, under the editorship of Josef Mestenhauser. Jack and Dagmar White have completed preparation of the third volume of *On All Fronts* which is currently in press. Like the previous two volumes, the current volume is being published with the financial assistance from the SVU, Washington DC Chapter. Furthermore, Vera Bořkovec is readying for publication a special volume of Czech and Slovak Poetry in Exile which will be published in memory of SVU member Frank Marlow.[866] Another commemorative volume will be published in honor of the late Zdenka Fischmann.[867] The latter will be based on Zdenka Fischmann's writings on Czech musicology.

As part of the effort to preserve Czech and Slovak cultural heritage abroad, the SVU has initiated a new project to survey historic sites and monuments, as well as archival material that have some bearing on the Czech presence in America.[868] The project is supported in part by a grant from the Czech Ministry of Foreign Affairs and has been coordinated by Míla Rechcígl. Toward this end, a new National Heritage Commission, comprised of the major Czech-American organizations in the US, has been established, whose role is largely advisory. As a result of this effort, a tentative listing of the major Czech-related sites in the US has been completed under the title "Czech-American Historic Sites, Monuments and Memorials."

---

[865] Clinton Machann, Ed., *Czech-Americans in Transition*. Austin, TX: Eakin Press, 1999. 136 p.

[866] "SVU Publication to Honor Frank Marlow Memory," *Zprávy SVU*, vol. 42, No. 2 (March-April 2000), p. 22.

[867] "Zdenka Fischmann's Bequest to SVU," *Zprávy SVU*, vol. 42, No. 1 (January-February 2000), p. 17.

[868] *Zprávy SVU*, vol. 42, No. 5 (September-October 1999), pp. 7-8; "Survey of Czech and Slovak Historical Monuments in America," *Ibid.*, vol. 41, No. 1 (November-December 1999), pp. 20-21.

As reported in *Zprávy SVU*,[869] our survey received a real boost from the Presidential appointed US Commission for the Preservation of America's Heritage Abroad. In their letter of July 15, Michael Lewan, Chairman of the Commission, wrote to me, in my capacity as SVU President, a letter, which began as follows: "As the Chairman of the US Commission for Preservation of America's Heritage Abroad, it is my pleasure to recognize and endorse the efforts of the Czechoslovak Society of Arts and Sciences (SVU) to preserve Czech cultural heritage in America. I am very impressed with the important work you are doing."

The present Executive Board has also put a deliberate effort in being more responsive and proactive to the needs of students and scholars, and young people,[870] in general. In this connection, new collaborative linkages have been established with several major funding organizations, such as Fulbright Commission and Civil Education Project (CEP). Names of young Fulbright scholars have been published in *Zprávy SVU* and this practice will continue. At the SVU MN Conference one of the distinct features was a panel of young people who discussed issues relating to the new millennium from their perspective.

In terms of new membership, it is noteworthy that practically all new members have come to us via or through Internet. The SVU Home Page,[871] which was recently brought up to date, undoubtedly, has played a major role in this. Equally important have been the frequent announcements on the Internet regarding various specific SVU activities, such as publications and conferences. With suitable outside help, I am hoping that in the foreseeable future we will publish our newsletter on the internet and make our Website more interactive.

---

[869] "Recognition and Endorsement of SVU Project," *Zprávy SVU*, vol. 41, No. 5 (September-October 1999), p. 6.

[870] Regarding young people, as mentioned above, we established a new column in our newsletter *Zprávy SVU*, entitled "Focus on Our Younger Generation." See: *Zprávy SVU*, vol. 41, No. 6 (November-December 1999), pp. 17-19; *Ibid.*, vol. 42, No. 2 (March-April 2000), pp. 1-2.

[871] "SVU Web Sites," *Zprávy SVU*, vol. 42, No. 1 (January-February 2000), pp. 13-14.

*State of the SVU in 2000* 323

With reference to SVU Local chapters, you will recall that we established a new SVU Chapter in Minnesota,[872] which was the direct result of our successful SVU Conference in Minneapolis last year. This reaffirms my own conviction of the importance of convening conferences in new places rather than concentrating on the same locations. I am also pleased to report on the reactivation of the SVU Edmonton Chapter in Canada. Among the US-based Chapters, the Washington DC chapter remains in the forefront. Through its efforts, a new funding drive was commenced that enabled the purchase of a new concert piano donated on its behalf to the Czech Embassy in Washington, DC. This should serve as an example to other SVU Chapters, particularly those in Western Europe, whose members are not even willing to pay their membership dues. Among the European chapters, the activities of the Prague Chapter, under the leadership of Jaroslava Turková[873] and the Brno SVU Chapter, under the chairmanship of Marie Bobková,[874] were particularly noteworthy.

Most of this year's Executive Board's efforts have been devoted to the preparation of the forthcoming SVU World Congress. After preliminary investigations, it was decided to convene the meetings in Washington, DC at American University on August 9-13, 2000. For the central theme we selected, "Civil Society and Democracy into the New Millennium."[875] I shall not dwell into all the work that led to the preparation of the program and the local and logistical arrangements. Suffice to say, it took a tremendous effort and the results speak for themselves. I have only praise for the organizers, particularly Anton Novacký, Věra Bořkovec and Dagmar White. I should also like to acknowledge the tremendous work of our younger generation, Bruce Berglund and Anna Vysoká, in particular, who contributed significantly to our program.

---

[872] "New SVU Chapter in the Midwest of the US," *Zprávy SVU,* vol. 41. No. 4 (July-August 1999), p. 8.

[873] *Zprávy SVU*, vol. 41, No. 4 (July-August 1999), pp. 16-18.

[874] *Zprávy SVU*, vol. 42, No. 3 (May-June 2000), pp. 10-12.

[875] *Zprávy SVU*, vol. 41, No. 4 (July-August 1999), p. 10; *Ibid.*, vol. 41, No. 6 (November-December 1999), pp. 1-2.; *Ibid.*, vol. 42, No. 2 (March-April 2000), pp. 1-4; *Ibid.*, vol. 42, No. 3 (May-June 2000), pp. 1-3.

I am also pleased to report on my visit in the Czech Republic, where I had an opportunity to meet with the members of the Board of the Prague SVU Chapter.[876]

In conclusion, I am happy to say that the Society is sound and well. As always, we are open to new ideas and welcome new initiatives. In parting, let me thank the outgoing Executive Board for their support and their effort on behalf of the Society.

..........

The above report was presented to the SVU General Assembly meeting, convened in the elegant Morrela Courtroom at the American University College of Law in Washington, DC on August 10, 2000. In addition to my State of the SVU Report, brief reports were presented by the representatives of the SVU Local chapters, including that of Dr. Alena Morávková for the Prague Chapter, Dr. Marie Bobková for the Brno Chapter and Dr. Karel Zástěra for the newly established SVU Chapter in Plzeň. Prof. Věra Bořkovec, jointly with Prof. Ivo Feierabend, then introduced to the audience Petra Tichá of Ostrava, a current student at American University, the winner of the Josef Hašek Student Award.

Next was the Treasurer's Report on the state of finances, followed by the Auditors' Report, recommending the approval of the Treasurer's Report. Frank Mucha's statement collaborated SVU President's conclusion that the Society is financially sound and well, thanks to the sound management and fiscal policies of the Executive Board. The Treasurer's Report was then approved unanimously and the retiring officers were discharged of liability.

While this was going on, the Resolution Committee, which worked on the draft resolution, completed its task and presented it to the Assembly. Having been written in superb prose, the resolution was approved without changing a word.[877]

---

[876] "SVU President Visits the Czech Republic," *Zprávy SVU*, vol. 42, No. 5 (September-October 2000), pp. 22-23.

[877] The complete text of the Resolution appeared in *Zprávy SVU*, vol. 42, No. 5 (September-October 2000), pp. 20-21.

As the parting gesture of my Presidency, selected SVU members were awarded SVU Presidential Citations "in recognition for their contributions to SVU, the advancement of the Czechoslovak studies and the furtherance of Czech and Slovak culture worldwide,' The recipients were: Bruce Robert Berglund (from Kansas), Alexej Bořkovec (MD), Věra Bořkovec (MD), Petr and Věra Bísek (NY), Marie Bobková (Brno), Pat Křížek DeVoe (MD), Andrew Eliáš (VA), Jaroslav Folta (Prague), George Glos (VA), Zdeněk Hruban (IL), Blanka Kuděj (NY), Clinton Machann (TX), Karol Marton (Košice), Josef A. Mestenhauser (MN), Josef Macháč (NY), Frank Mucha (NY), Anton J. Novacký (MO), Eva Rechcígl (MD), Jan Skalný (FL), Juraj J. Slávik (DC), Zdeněk Slouka (Prague), Alexander Tkáč (Bratislava), Jan F. Tříska (CA), Jaroslava Turková in memoriam (Prague), Věra Ulbrecht (MD). Eva Vaněk (VA). Zdeněk J. Vich (MD), Zdenka and Marina Vozárik (VA), Anna Vysoká (MN) and Dagmar Hasalová White (VA).

Prof. Jan Tříska, who served in the capacity of Chair of the Nominations Committee,[878] assumed then the role of presiding chair de tempore and reported on the outcome of the elections. The entire slate of nominees, as initially proposed, was elected by an overwhelming margin.[879]

The newly elected officers were Rechcígl as President; Anton Novacký,[880] Executive Vice President; Věra Bořkovec, George Glos,[881] Blanka Kuděj, Josef Macháč, Peter Rafaeli,[882] Alexander Tkáč, Dagmar White, and Petr Zuna, Vice Presidents; Frank Safertal,[883] Secretary-General and Frank Mucha, Treasurer.

---

[878] "SVU Nominations Committee," *Zprávy SVU*, vol. 42, No. 3 (May-June 2000), p. 5.

[879] "Rechcígl Reelected SVU President to Unprecedented 6th Term," *Zprávy SVU*, vol. 42, No. 6 (November-December 2000), pp. 1-.3.

[880] Anton Novacký (1933-), professor of plant pathology, University of Missouri, Columbia.

[881] George Glos (1924-), lawyer, associated with the Library of Congress Law Division, Washington, DC.

[882] Peter A. Rafaeli (1932-), businessman; serves as Honorary Consul of the Czech Republic for the Commonwealth of Pennsylvania.

[883] Frank Safertal (1942-), business consultant, associated with the Bechtel Telecommunications, Frederick, MD.

Following my acceptance speech, the meeting was adjourned.[884]

---

[884] "Rechcígl Reelected SVU President to Unprecedented 6th Term," *Zprávy SVU*, vol. 42, No. 6 (November-December 2000).

# 55
## *The Nebraska Happening*

What happened in Nebraska during the August SVU Conference was unique and truly phenomenal which cannot be expressed by a better term than "Happening" Those of us who came there from other states or foreign countries felt like Alice in Wonderland or, as the Czech say, "u Jiříkova vidění."[885]

The outpouring of kindness, goodwill and friendship was ever present wherever you looked, accompanied by a broad smile and helping hand. You could feel that it was all genuine and not fake.

The preliminary announcements of the Congress appeared regularly in the *Zprávy SVU*[886] in 2001 and the final program was published in its fourth issue.[887] The latter was also printed separately,[888] as did the Abstracts presented at the Conference.[889]

I came there a day earlier "to check on things," arriving in Omaha. I was picked up at the airport and driven to Lincoln, the capitol of Nebraska, where our conference was held. By coincidence, it happened to be my birthday. My Nebraska friends threw me a surprise and joyous birthday party and from that point onward things began rolling.

We were all housed in fabulous, brand-new hotel-like suites in Kaufman Center, on the University of Nebraska campus, comprised of living room, kitchen and two nice rooms, for the price of regular student dormitories. Each room was equipped with all the amenities, including thermostats which allowed one to control temperature in each room.

---

[885] Based, in part, on my editorial article in *Zprávy SVU*, vol. 43, No. 5 (September-October 2001), pp. 1-5.

[886] *Zprávy SVU*, vol. 43, No. 1 (January-February 2001), pp. 1-3; *Ibid.*, vol. 43, No. 2 (March-April 2001), pp. 5-8; *Ibid.*, vol. 43, No. 3 (May-June 2001), pp. 1-3.

[887] *Zprávy SVU*, vol. 43, No. 4 (July-August 2001), pp. 1-18.

[888] *[Program] SVU 2001 North American Conference. Lincoln, Nebraska, August 1-3, 2001*. Lincoln, NE, 2001. 20 p.

[889] *[Program, Abstracts, Biographies of Speakers] SVU 2001 North American Conference*. Lincoln, NE, 2001. 68 p.

Whenever you needed something you simply called the front desk and they would promptly take care of your needs. What a difference from the dormitories we had during our previous conferences and congresses. The prepaid food was served in the Sellick Hall which was situated next to Kaufman Hall where we were staying. The food was excellent and abundant and served in the form of a buffet.

Most of the Conference attendees began arriving on Wednesday afternoon August 1. After registration, which was conveniently placed in Kaufman Center, the participants were treated to a reception in the close-by Wick Alumni Center. Apart from the scrumptious food and good company, we were entertained by music and song. Music performers included Svetlana Yashirin, piano, Budimír Zvolánek, clarinet, and Joel Blahník and Anita Smíšek of Czech Music Alliance. The program included a number of presentations from various Nebraska groups that took part in the Conference organizations, including Ron Stiles, President of the Czech Komenský Club, Helen Pejsar, Nebraska Czechs of Lincoln, Glen Rienche, Czech Language Foundation, Merlin Lawson, Dean of International Affairs UNL, Dean Oliva, College of Fine and Performing Arts, UNL and John Fiala, President Elect, Nebraska Czechs Inc. Carmelee Tuma, Assistant to the Governor of Nebraska brought his personal greetings and presented SVU President with a special proclamation making him "Admiral of Nebraska Navy." It was all in good fun.

The Conference opened the following day in the spacious Nebraska Union Auditorium, with all seats occupied at 8 o'clock sharp. After the four national anthems: (US, Canadian, Czech and Slovak), came the Words of Welcome from the University Dean of Arts and Sciences, Richard J. Hoffmann, on behalf of the Chancellor of the University Harvey Perlman,[890] followed by my official opening, in my capacity as SVU President.

Next on the program came Dr. Mila Šašková-Pierce who was the Chair of the Conference Organizing Committee, and Russell Ganim, Chair of the Department of Modern Languages and Literatures. They were followed by Kate Witek, Auditor of Public Accounts of the State of Nebraska, who brought greetings and a special message from Governor

---

[890] "Words of Welcome by Harvey Perlman, J.D., Chancellor of the University of Nebraska, " *Zprávy SVU*, vol. 43, No. 5 (September-October 2001), pp. 7-8.

Mike Johnson.[891] On the occasion, the Governor proclaimed the days of our Conference, August 1 through the 3rd, 2001, as "Czechoslovak Society of Arts and Sciences Days."[892]

Then came Don Wesley, the newly elected Mayor of Lincoln, who welcomed the participants on behalf of the State Capital Lincoln, mentioning his Czech ancestry who settled in Nebraska in the late 1900s. His name was originally spelled Veselý. This was followed by a message from US Senator Chuck Hagel. The official part of the program was concluded with the greetings of Petr Gandalovič, Consul General of the Czech Republic, who addressed the audience on behalf of the Czech Republic. A message was also received from Pavel Dostál, Minister of Culture of the Czech Republic.[893] The Slovak Ambassador to the US Martin Bútora, who could not attend the Conference sent a special message which was reprinted in *Zprávy SVU*.[894] The program ended with a music performance by Joel Blahník, Anita Smíšek and Maureen Beck, and the Capital City Czech Choraleers.

After a short coffee break and "kolaches," the SVU Conference started in earnest. Three or more sessions usually ran concurrently, following the printed program. All lecture rooms were equipped with the latest equipment. Most sessions were well attended and went smoothly. Each session was usually concluded with a question and answer period and frequently with an animated discussion. Space does not allow description of individual sessions which ran concurrently for two full days, August 2-3. It should be noted that a number of panels were attended by a younger audience, as well as by younger presenters, which was one of the main objectives of the conference.

A special plenary session was devoted to the Presidential Symposium "Role of Ethnic Organizations in Preserving Our Cultural Heritage," which I chaired, with the participation of chief executive officers of ethnic organizations in the US. The session included representatives

---

[891] *Zprávy SVU*, vol. 43, No. 5 (September-October 2001), p. 5.

[892] The text of his proclamation appears in *Zprávy SVU*, vol. 43, No. 5 (September-October 2001), p. 6.

[893] *Zprávy SVU*, vol. 33, No. 5 (September-October 2001), p. 10.

[894] "Message from the Ambassador of the Slovak Republic Martin Bútora to the Participants and Guests of the Nebraska SVU Conference," *Zprávy SVU*, vol. 33, No. 5 (September-October 2001), pp. 8-9.

of the American Sokol Organization, Bohemia Benevolent and Literary Organization of New York, Bohemian Citizen's Benevolent Society of Astoria, Czech and Slovak Heritage Association of Maryland, Czech and Slovak Music Society, Czech and Slovak Society of Oregon, Czech Heritage Society of Texas, Czech Language Foundation of NE, Czechoslovak American National Council of America, Komenský Club, National Czech and Slovak Museum and Library, Nebraska Czechs Inc., Nebraska Czechs of Wilber, Oklahoma Czechs, and Slavonic Benevolent Order of the State of Texas. The Czech Republic was represented by Jaromír Šlápota of the Czechoslovak Foreign Institute and Senator Milan Špaček, Chair of the Permanent Committee of the Senate for Czechs Abroad. Deputy Jiří Karas, Chair of a comparable committee in the Czech House of Representatives was unable to attend.

On Friday afternoon, August 2, the SVU General Assembly meeting was held with the customary State of the SVU Report by SVU President. The latter, as well as the resolution voted by the Assembly are printed separately.

In the evening of the same day the SVU Banquet was held, featuring Mila Rechcígl and Peter Gandalovič as speakers, followed by presentations of SVU Presidential citations to selected organizations that have made contributions to the preservation of Czech and Slovak cultural heritage in the US. These organizations were identical with those which took part in the SVU Presidential Symposium, which is associated with the National Heritage Commission. Additional citations were awarded to Matice Vyššího Vzdělaní (Council of Higher Education), Slovak American International Cultural Foundation, Masaryk Club and individuals: Jiří Eichler, Míla Šašková-Pierce, Tom Zumpfe, John Fiala and Cathleen Oslzly. The latter, who likes to be called "Kačenka," was the chief driving force behind the Conference, received for her extraordinary effort a crystal vase from SVU and an airfare voucher to SVU Congress in Plzeň next year donated to SVU by Tatra Travel.

On Saturday, August 4, many of the Conference participants were bused to Wilber, Nebraska to take part in the famous Wilber Festival. This was a happening in its own right, resembling in many ways a traditional Czech "pout" (fair), except on a much larger scale, accompanied with a traditional American parade and beauty pageant, culminating in the selection of the Czech and Slovak Queen. SVU Secretary General

Frank Safertal, and I, in my capacity as SVU President, had the fun of being driven and waving in the parade with our names and office insignia exhibited on the cars.

Judging as a whole, the SVU conference in Nebraska and everything connected with it was a great success, thanks to local leaders and organizers like Cathleen Oslzly, Míla Šašková-Pierce and her husband Layne, Tom Zumpfe, John Fiala, and Ron and Jitka Stiles, as well as a number of organizations which enthusiastically worked with them as a team. SVU will be forever grateful to them.

Those of you who attended the Nebraska Conference will most assuredly agree that it was a true happening.

# 56
# *State of the SVU in 2001*

## Report of SVU President Dr. Miloslav Rechcígl
## Presented to SVU General Assembly
## Convened 3 August 2001 in Lincoln, NE[895]

Welcome to our 2001 Annual Meeting. Since I don't wish to deprive you of attending any of the exciting events that our Nebraskan friends arranged for us, I will make this year's report brief.

Generally speaking, I am pleased to report that since last year, when the newly elected Executive Board was put in charge of SVU,[896] we have made excellent progress in a number of areas and our finances are sound and well. Thanks to our new Website the SVU visibility and its overall image could not be better.

As customary, the newly elected Executive Board, in its first meeting,[897] reexamined the aims of the Society and decided on its priorities. Considering the aging SVU membership, the Board has selected as its main objective to revitalize the Society with younger people under the new initiative, "Accent on Youth."[898]

Toward this aim, we have established a new Youth Advisory Committee which is busy at work on special projects, including the formation of a separate database and a new page on our Website relating to young people. In addition to Anna Vysoká, who is responsible for this activity, I would like to introduce to you one young man, who is here with us, the

---

[895] Originally published in *Zprávy SVU*, vol. 43, No. 6 (November-December 2001), pp. 9-11.

[896] "Rechcígl Reelected SVU President to Unprecedented 6th Term," *Zprávy SVU*, vol. 42, No, 6 (November-December 2000), pp. 1-3.

[897] "Newly Elected Executive Board Meets," *Zprávy SVU*, vol. 42, No. 6 (November-December 2000), pp. 4-5.

[898] "Memorandum to Young People," *Zprávy SVU*, vol. 42, No. 6 (November-December 2000), pp. 6-7.

*State of the SVU in 2001* 333

SVU Webmaster, Jiří Eichler of Prague. Let the initiative of these young persons serve as an example to others.[899]

The second major priority of the Executive Board has been focus on the computer technology and its application in SVU work. The Executive Board members now communicate among each other entirely via e-mail and, similarly, the Board's contact with SVU Local Chapters, for the most part, is conducted electronically. Those chapters which don't as yet have their e-mail addresses are admonished to add new officers to their boards who have access to a computer.

Technically speaking, our greatest advance has been made in establishing and perfecting a new SVU Website.[900] In close cooperation with the already mentioned SVU Webmaster, Jiří Eichler, we now have a fully functional comprehensive and interactive website which provides information practically on every aspect of SVU work, past and present. In addition, it is becoming an excellent resource on Czech and Slovak matters, in general, including history, literature, culture, conferences, available grants, etc. The thousands of visitors who frequent our Website is indicative of the Website's popularity.

To make the Website as user-friendly as possible, it has been provided with a SEARCH tool which allows the user, by choosing appropriate key words, to readily find names, places and things, in a matter of seconds. Furthermore, we have also established a special SITE MAP which shows a detailed outline of our site, permitting one to access any category or subcategory.[901]

One of the major activities of SVU are regional conferences and world congresses. This year, in its wisdom, the Executive Board chose Nebraska as its site for a conference and traditional annual meeting.[902] It was obviously the best choice, as judged by the program our Nebraskan

---

[899] "SVU Youth Advisory Committee's Recommendations," *Zprávy SVU*, vol. 43, No. 3 (May-June 2001), pp. 10-11.

[900] "A New SVU Web Site Goes Public," *Zprávy SVU*, vol. 43, No. 1 (January-February 2001), pp. 19-20.

[901] "SVU Website – Six Months of Operation," *Zprávy SVU*, vol. 43, No. 3 (May-June 2001,), p. 7.

[902] "SVU announces a Special Conference 'the Czech and Slovak Legacy in the Americas: Preservation of Heritage with the Accent on Youth. Lincoln, NE, August 2-3, 2001," *Zprávy SVU*, vol. 43, No. 1 (January-February 2001), pp. 1-3; *Ibid,* vol. 43, No. 2 (March-/April 2001), pp. 5-8.

friends put together as well as the excellent logistical arrangements. I haven't witnessed such enthusiasm with which they have carried out their tasks for some time. They truly deserve over heartiest thanks.

As far as the next SVU World Congress is concerned, it will be held in Pilsen, Czech Republic in 2002.[903] Our principal contact there is Dr. Ivo Budil, Dean of the Faculty of Humanity Studies.

Let me now turn briefly to other SVU activities. By now, our subscribers have received the second issue of *Kosmas,* under the able editorship and management of Clinton Machann and David Chroust.[904] I am sure you are pleased with its contents. From now on, you should receive future issues on time.

With reference to our newsletter, *Zprávy SVU*, each issue now contains regular features, such as SVU Calendar, From New Membership Rolls, Focus on Younger Generation,[905] etc. The SVU Calendar periodically brings information on the varied SVU activities worldwide. To keep it current it is imperative that local chapters send us their periodic updates in a timely fashion.

As for the other publications, we have two monographs in process: a collection of Zdenka Fischmann's Papers on Musicology and an Anthology of Czech and Slovak Poetry in Exile. Our goal is to have them published within a year.[906]

You will be pleased to know that we are also proceeding with publishing selected papers from the last SVU World Congress under the editorship of Prof. Ján Skalný. Our current plan is to first issue them in the form of a CD and, depending on the interest, we may then also publish the papers in the conventional way.

I also have good news about our *SVU Biographical Directory*. Having solved a number of technical problems relating to the merging of new

---

[903] "Preliminary announcement. 21st SVU World Congress August 2002 in Pilsen, Czech Republic...," *Zprávy SVU*, vol. 43, No. 2 (March-April 2001), pp. 9-11.

[904] "Progress Report on Kosmas by Clinton Machann, Editor," *Zprávy SVU*, vol. 39, No. 4 (July-August 2001), pp. 21-23

[905] *Zprávy SVU*, vol. 42, No. 6 (November-December 2000), pp 15-16; I*bid*, vol. 43, No. 1 (January-February 2001), pp. 11-12; *Ibid.,* vol. 43, No. 2 (March-April 2001), pp. 14-15; *Ibid.*, vol. 43, no. 5 (September-October 2001), pp. 23-24.

[906] "Update on Dr. Fischmann's Papers," *Zprávy SVU*, vol. 43, No. 2 (March-April 2001), p. 11.

biographical data with the old *SVU Directory*, we are now proceeding with the transcription of data as quickly as we can under the capable hands of Jiří Eichler.[907]

I have also made an effort to implement the SVU Fellows category which has been part of the SVU Bylaws but until now nothing has been done about it. Inasmuch as this was the responsibility of the SVU Council, it was necessary to first appoint its Speaker in order to get the process going.[908]

Let me now turn to another of our initiatives, i.e., the SVU efforts toward preserving Czech and Slovak heritage abroad. As part of this undertaking, I had the pleasure of conducting a comprehensive survey relating to Czech historic sites and archival material in the US. This led to two draft reports, "Czech-American Historic Sites. Monuments, and Other Memorabilia" and "Czechoslovak American Archivalia"[909] which were presented to the Czech Ministry of Foreign Affairs, under whose sponsorship and financial assistance they were prepared. The reports generated lots of interest here as well as abroad and suggestions have been made that they be published. It should be noted that the survey was done in cooperation with our National Heritage Commission, comprised of major Czech organizations in America.

A propos, the present Nebraska Conference, with its central theme, "Czech and Slovak Legacy in the Americas," is a part of the SVU continual quest to preserve our national heritage in America. Our aim is to sensitize the Czech and Slovak American community to get them involved in this important effort so that the work of the early immigrants from the Czechlands and Slovakia and their legacy not be forgotten.

Beginning with the year 2001, the first year of the third Millennium, the Society will bestow the annual Andrew Eliáš SVU Human Tolerance Award on an individual whose life and work symbolize the living value

---

[907] "New SVU Biographical Directory," *Zprávy SVU*, vol. 43, No. 4 (July-August 2001), p. 24.

[908] "SVU Fellows, "*Zprávy SVU,* vol. 43, No. 2 (March-April 2001), pp. 18-19.

[909] "Czechoslovak American Archivalia," *Zprávy SVU*, vol. 43, No. 1 (January-February 2001), pp. 17-19.

of human tolerance. The Award shall be accompanied by a prize of $1,000.[910]

With respect to SVU local chapters, I would like to commend our Edmonton Chapter in Canada, particularly its chairman Prof. Pavel Jelen, for their initiative to issue a special CD record with Czech music.[911] The project was brought to fruition, thanks to cooperation with the University of Alberta and the sponsors Dairy Farmers of Canada. The CD features live recording of an Edmonton Symphony Orchestra concert, given on October 29, 1999, conducted by Grzegorz Nowak, Honorary Professor at the department of music.

In conclusion, I wish to express my sincere appreciation to all SVU members who have assisted us with our multi-facet agenda and especially our Nebraskan friends who have made this conference and everything connected with it a big success.

In parting, I wish to reiterate that we always welcome suggestions and volunteers from SVU membership at large, as well as nonmembers, particularly among the younger folks, to help us with our aims. Thanks again and I look forward to seeing you in full force at our SVU World Congress in Plzeň.

..........

The preceding report was presented at the SVU General Assembly meeting[912] in Lincoln. NE, on August 3, 2001, held in conjunction with the SVU's Conference. Apart from the customary reporting of other officials, the statement from the Executive Board was read, concerning the selection of Father Anton Srholec of Bratislava as the first winner of the Eliáš Human Tolerance Award. SVU Student Award to Daniel Neval was also announced.[913] Toward the end of the meeting, the ad hoc

---

[910] "The Czechoslovak Society of Arts and Sciences announces the establishment of annual Andrew Eliáš SVU Human Tolerance Award," *Zprávy SVU*, vol. 43, No. 2 (March-April), pp. 20-21.

[911] "SVU Edmonton Chapter Prepares CD Record with Czech Music, " *Zprávy SVU*, vol. 43, No. 6 (November-December 2001), p. 8.

[912] "42nd Meeting of SVU General Assembly," *Zprávy SVU*, vol. 43, No. 5 (September-October 2001), p. 11.

[913] "SVU Student Award for the Year 2001," *Zprávy SVU*, vol. 43, No. 5 (September-October 2001), p. 9.

Resolution Committee drafted a Resolution which the Assembly approved. The text of the Resolution was published in *Zprávy SVU*.[914]

---

[914] "Resolution of the Czechoslovak Society of Arts and Sciences...," *Zprávy SVU*, vol. 43, No. 5 (September-October 2001), pp. 12-13.

## 57
## *Organizing the Plzeň Congress*

I made the initial contact with Plzeň in the year 2000, during my trip to the Czech Republic, thanks to my acquaintance with Karel Zástěra.[915] He contacted me early in the year with the proposition that the next SVU Congress be held in Plzeň where he then was teaching at the University of West Bohemia. When he heard about my impending visit to the Czech Republic he proposed that I also visit Plzeň and see for myself what the city and the university could offer.

After exchanging a few e-mails with him, I rearranged my schedule and accepted his offer to pick me up upon my arrival in Prague at the Ruzyně airport and drive me to Plzeň. He was accompanied by Ivo Budil, Dean of the Faculty of Humanities at the University of West Bohemia who was his boss.[916]

In Plzeň, I was shown the facilities and was introduced to key people, including Rector Zdeněk Vostracký. I also met with the representative of Mayor of Plzeň. They all expressed great interest in having our Congress held in Plzeň and assured me of their help in the organization aspects, as well as with the preparation of the program. As I understood it, the Faculty of Humanities was to have the major responsibility for the Congress program. This oral agreement between us was later confirmed in writing in a letter Zástěra brought with him to Washington, DC at the time of our Millennium Congress.

---

[915] I first met Zástěra in Washington a couple of years earlier when he was doing some work there. I remember vividly when he came to our house in Rockville for supper on his roller blades, all the way from Georgetown where he was staying. He appeared quite young, in his early thirties, full of energy, ideas and ambitions. He talked a mile a minute, throwing big names into conversation, people whom he knew personally and with whom he associated. Frequently, he made references to Polda Pospíšil. During our first encounter he boasted about his publishing contacts and indicated that he would arrange for my book, on which I had been working (i.e., *Postavy naší Ameriky*), to be published in the Czech Republic. I never heard from him further on his offer.

[916] "SVU President Visits the Czech Republic," *Zprávy SVU*, vol. 42, No. 5 (September-October 2000), pp. 22-23.

My chief contact with Plzeň co-organizers was, at first, exclusively through Zástěra who, in the meantime, also assumed the chairmanship of the newly established SVU Chapter in Plzeň. From our discussions in Washington, I had every indication that the Congress organization in Plzeň is in good hands and assumed that Zástěra would also play a key role. At my request, he sent me a draft statement about the overall plans, including rationalization and the central theme which, after some corrections, was posted on SVU Website. The preliminary announcement of the Congress appeared in the March 2001 issue of *Zprávy SVU*.[917]

With my involvement in the preparation of the 2001 Nebraska Conference, I did not press him more for further details, hoping that their organization committee is in place and running. When I did not hear anything for a while, I sent Zástěra an e-mail requesting an update, to which he responded, with considerable delay, sometime in January 2001, that he had some financial problems which required his immediate attention. Subsequently, he informed me that he was given until the end of May to complete his doctoral dissertation and, as a consequence, he would need to put all his attention to its writing. Frankly, this took me by surprise, since I thought that he already had his doctorate. Be that as it may, I did not bother him for a few months, knowing how busy he must be with his dissertation.

By the end of May, Zástěra sent me a note informing me that he successfully defended his dissertation and that now he would be able to give all his attention to our Congress. Since I did not hear anything from him afterwards, I became quite concerned and decided to contact Dean Ivo Budil directly for explanation. To my dismay, he informed me that Zástěra was no longer an employee of the University and that, from now on, I should be corresponding directly with him.

This was an unexpected turn of events and a great dilemma for me personally, as I considered Zástěra my friend, to whom I was greatly indebted for establishing our contact with the University of West Bohemia. I felt obligated to write to Zástěra to ask him for his side of the story. It took a while before I heard from him and when he finally responded he

---

[917] "21st SVU World Congress August 2002 in Plzeň, Czech Republic with the general theme 'Transformation of the Czech and Slovak Society on the Threshold of New Millennium and its Role in Contemporary World," *Zprávy SVU*, vol. 43, No. 2 (March-April 2001), pp. 9-10.

said that the whole thing must have been a misunderstanding. Somewhat later he wrote again, informing me that he talked to Dean Budil and that everything was straightened out. Simultaneously, he asked me to send him an official letter designating him the chief organizer of the SVU Congress. I found his request somewhat odd, considering that I had just been informed by the University Rectorate that they are assuming the chief organizational responsibility for the Congress.

To make a long story short, after a few additional evasive e-mail messages from Zástěra, which did not throw any new light on the apparent dispute between him and the University, I had no choice but to advise Zástěra that I was unable to send him the requested letter until he first comes to some understanding with the University organizers, since SVU cannot afford to work on two different fronts. Zástěra never responded to this.

With the consent of SVU Executive Board, I subsequently informed Dean Budil that we respect the University decision and from that point onward we corresponded on all Congress matters exclusively with Dean Budil. He became immediately engrossed in the planning and logistical detail. I was hoping that Budil would come to our Nebraska conference and give us an update at our Annual meeting. He could not make it and decided to send Štěpánka Korytová-Magstadt[918] instead. Although she came to the US she did not attend our Conference. This obviously caused some consternation at our meeting and again I became alarmed about the planned SVU Congress.

Later on, I found out in my correspondence with Ivo Budil that some personal reasons prevented Korytová-Magstadt from attending our Conference and assured me that the organization of our Congress is on track. To assure ourselves that the University organizers are taking the matters seriously, we asked our Secretary General Frank Safertal, who was planning a trip to the Czech Republic, to go to Plzeň and find out what was going on. He came back very satisfied, raving about the people he met and what he saw.

First order of business was to prepare a general plan, arrange for logistics and consider various options for cultural and social events.

---

[918] I knew of her, as a young Czech historian who studied in the US and the author of the book, *To Reap a Bountiful Harvest. Czech Immigration beyond the Mississippi, 1850-1900* (Iowa City: Rudi Publishing, 1993).

## Organizing the Plzeň Congress

Most ticklish were the fiscal aspects. Guarded by our unpleasant experiences in Brno and Bratislava, I wanted to avoid anything comparable happening in Plzeň. In time, I had developed a good rapport with Dean Budil and was confident that this time we will be able to agree on these matters.

From the start, I tried to impress on our Plzeň colleagues that it was in our mutual interest to keep the registration fee low in order not to discourage potential attendees. To this end it was necessary to minimize our overhead. As was the case of Brno and Bratislava Congresses, our Plzeň co-organizers wanted to employ a middleman to organize everything. Preliminary estimates showed that such a service would cost between 5 and 10 thousand dollars. It took me a while to convince them that volunteers could do such work better and free of charge. They finally consented to our point of view.

Furthermore, I insisted that lecture halls be provided *gratis* as was the case in most of our previous congresses and conferences. Otherwise, it would have been very costly. After some discussion, usually via e-mail, they obliged and made an effort to obtain sponsors to cover any costs relating to the cost of renting the meeting rooms. Had we held the Congress on the University new campus, a fair distance from the center of town, which had plenty lecture halls, there would not have been any problems at all. Dean Budil and others felt, however, that the Congress should be held in the center of town in the vicinity of hotels where most of our overseas attendees from abroad would be staying.

Our standard practice has been to use the Congress registration fee for paying various expenses, e.g., postage, telephone, copying, printing the programs, etc. For various cultural and social events we normally charged separately which allowed us to keep the registration fee at a modest level. For some unexplained reasons our Plzeň co-organizers did not seem to understand this. We pressed them to itemize individual expenses so that we would know what to charge for various events and activities. Despite our persistent inquiries, they did not seem to understand what we were after and why we needed it, and were giving us only gross estimates.

After some discussion back and forth, and when we came to realization that they won't send us a detailed budget, the Executive Board decided on a different approach. We offered them a package deal whereby we would pay them a total of $10,000, irrespective of their expenses and irrespective of the number of attendees from abroad. They readily accepted.[919]

In order to be able to pay for Congress expenses I knew that we would need about two hundred attendees from the US, Canada and Western Europe. The best way to attract attendees was to give them an opportunity to present a paper at the Congress. So this is what I proceeded to do, i.e., to get as many U.S. speakers as possible.

I had an agreement with Dean Budil that he would assume responsibility for organizing panels with Czech and Slovak participants, while I would coordinate panels from abroad.

In the September 2001 issue of *Zprávy SVU*, I was able to provide more specific information about the upcoming Congress, including the CALL FOR PAPERS.[920]

With the help of individual members of the Executive Board, I compiled a tentative list of possible US panels and then began searching for suitable organizers. Based on previous experience, I knew, only too well, that organizing panels by discipline would not get us too far. So we focused on popular topics instead. We could not find a chemist to talk about chemistry but had no difficulty in assembling a panel of distinguished scientists to talk about their personal lives and experiences. Previously, I also had quite a bit of luck when I approached special interest groups, such as those interested in women's issues, environmentalists, consumer and civil rights advocates or policy makers.

I maintained continuous contact with our panel organizers to check on their progress and regularly sent them suggestions for potential speakers. Surprisingly, a number of panel organizers had difficulties in putting together a panel, comprised of five to six participants. So I had to pitch in and complete the panel for them. I must have received some thirty e-mails a day and sent out an equal number myself. To standardize matters I developed a series of guidelines for the panel organizers.

By the end of March, I finished most of my job. Out of a total of some forty panels, only four or five needed more work. I completed the

---

[919] Only later, it dawned on them that they may have made a mistake after they realized that we would have more than 100 participants from the US. By then, it was, of course, too late to change the rules of the game.

[920] "...Call for Papers," *Zprávy SVU*, vol. 43, No. 5 (September-October 2001), pp. 19-21.

rest in the next few weeks, following which we concentrated on scheduling and then we were "scot-free," as far as the panels were concerned.

There were only a few incidents in the process. One related to the Bohemian Reformation Panel in which several members of the Czech Academy participated. This panel was one of the first to be completed which we advertised in our announcements. Zdeněk David, who organized it, informed me, out of the blue, that all the Academy panelists unexpectedly withdrew in favor of presenting their papers at another conference the Czech Academy organized a week before our Congress. Frankly, this infuriated me and I wrote a protest letter to the President of the Academy. In response, Dr. Illnerová, who was recently elected the new Academy President, informed me that the matter would be corrected, allowing the Academy members to attend our Congress and apologized for the mix-up. Another incident was caused by the organizer of the art panel who got mad for some reason and cancelled the panel after its completion, without even telling us the names and addresses of the participants. Two of the panel members were our own and it took us quite a bit of persuasion to change their mind.

After completion of the panels, I could finally concentrate on the Ceremonial Opening program and the two plenary sessions, and inviting the dignitaries.

Altogether, I must have spent eight months, from September through April, working on the Congress program and related matters, most of the time sitting in front of my computer. I worked very closely with Ivo Budil whose cooperation was exemplary. There was not a day that we would not exchange an e-mail, frequently two, if not more.

# 58
## Plzeň with Flying Colors...
## Commentary on and Echoes from the SVU World Congress in Plzeň

Although there were some initial skeptics who had concerns whether our Plzeň co-organizers, who had no previous experience with such a mammoth undertaking, could swing it, I am delighted to report that our Plzeň Congress was a smashing success, thanks to the persevering efforts and boundless enthusiasm of Dean Ivo Budil and his associates Mgr. Ivona Škanderová and Bc. Marta Varejková. It was the army of his young people – there must have been some fifty of them – all of whom attend the University of West Bohemia, who made the difference. They seemed to be everywhere, handsome with pleasant smiles and helping hand, many of whom spoke flawless English. Most of them sat behind a whole array of computers, both at the registration desk and at the press room. They were not only computer literate; many of them were real pros. Some of these young people were in evidence already upon our arrival at the Prague Airport carrying highly visible signs "SVU World Congress" for easy identification. They were there on Saturday and Sunday, guiding the Congress participants to buses which took them to Plzeň. One of the innovations of this Congress was the daily *Congress Bulletin*, consisting of 6-10 pages, prepared in the SVU Press Room, under the guidance of Mgr. Přemysl Rosůlek and his able student staff. The responsibility for the registration rested on the shoulders of Ing. Jan Černý and his student helpers. The students were also in plain evidence in every academic session tending the audiovisual equipment and making sure that everything moved smoothly. And finally, several young people tended the sale of books, not to speak of the countless invisible mundane activities they were involved with during the organizational phases of the congress. The greatest credit for the organizational aspects goes to Pavel Scholze and Mgr. Sabina Růžičková.

*Plzeň with Flying Colors* 345

The SVU World Congress was held under the auspices of President Václav Havel,[921] in close cooperation with the University of West Bohemia and the City of Plzeň. The official opening was scheduled for Monday, June 24, 2004, however some of the activities already started on Sunday with the opening of the registration desk and the press center on Jungmannova 3. At 10:30 AM, the West Bohemian University Choir, "Nová česká píseň" presented a colorful program of the Renaissance Music, including Monteverdi, Lasso, and Gesualdo, arias from Italian operas (Verdi, Puccini), and illustrations of the 20th century music, i.e., Lukáš, Laburda and Ropek as well as folk songs.

The Congress was ceremoniously opened on Monday, June 24 in the presence of distinguished guests and representatives of the Czech and Slovak political, cultural, and scientific life in the famed Pilsen Theater of Josef Kajetán Tyl. With the sounds of trumpets came the academic procession of the university hierarchy, dressed in academic gowns, followed by dignitaries who were then seated on the platform. The National Anthems of four countries, where the SVU has the largest membership, i.e., Czech Republic, Slovakia, the US and Canada followed. During the playing of the Slovak anthem, many a participant began to sing along, which brought an occasional tear among those present. The official welcome came from Zdeněk Vostracký, Chancellor of the University of West Bohemia, and Mayor Lord of the City of Plzeň, Jiří Šneberger.

SVU President Miloslav Rechcígl then opened the Congress,[922] followed by official greetings and short speeches by Canadian Ambassador Margaret Huber,[923] the Slovak Ambassador to the Czech Republic Ladislav V. Ballek,[924] Ambassador of the US to the Czech Republic Craig R. Stapleton, President of the Senate of the Czech Parliament Petr

---

[921] His message appeared in *Zprávy SVU*, vol. 44, No. 4 (July-August 2002), p. 1.

[922] "Remarks by Dr. Miloslav Rechcígl, Jr., President SVU, at the Opening of SVU World Congress in Plzeň," *Zprávy SVU*, vol. 44, No. 5 (September-October 2002), pp. 10-11.

[923] "Remarks of H. E. Margaret Huber, Ambassador of Canada to the Czech and Slovak Republics at the Opening of the SVU World Congress in Plzeň," *Zprávy SVU*, vol. 44, No. 5 (September-October 2001), pp. 6-7.

[924] *Zprávy SVU*, vol. 44, No. 5 (September-October 2002), p. 5.

Pithart,[925] Ambassador of the Czech Republic to the US Martin Palouš, Ambassador of the Slovak Republic to the US Martin Bútora[926] and President of the Academy of Sciences of the Czech Republic Helena Illnerová. The impressive program was concluded with the key address by Senator Josef Jařáb,[927] the past Chancellor of the Palacký and Central European Universities. All speakers stressed the importance of education and higher learning and the strategic role of Plzeň culturally as well as economically.

After a festive lunch there was a plenary session dedicated to "Tribute to America" with the participation of the Ambassadors from the US[928] and the Czech Republic and the spokesman for Slovakia.[929] The second part of the plenary session was devoted to a special symposium, "Czech and Slovak Americans on Behalf of their Old Homeland" with the participation of the presidents and representatives of the major Czech and Czechoslovak ethnic organizations in the US and Canada that have played a major role in the establishment of Czechoslovakia and in the subsequent liberalization movements. They included Czechoslovak National Council, American Sokol, Alliance of Czech Catholics, Council of Free Czechoslovakia, American Fund for Czechoslovak Refugees, Czechoslovak Society of Arts and Sciences, Czech and Slovak Association of Canada and American Friends of Czech Republic.

---

[925] "Remarks of Hon. Petr Pithart, President of the Senate, Parliament of the Czech Republic at the Opening of the SVU World Congress in Plzeň, " *Zprávy SVU*, vol. 44, No. 5 (September-October 2002), pp. 7-9.

[926] His greetings appeared in *Zprávy SVU*, vol. 44, No. 4 (July-August 2002), p. 2.

[927] The text of his keynote address was published in the Congress Proceedings, *Transformation of Czech and Slovak Societies on the Threshold of the New Millennium and their Role in the Global World*. Selected Papers from the 21st World Congress. Edited by Ján P. Skalný and Miloslav Rechcígl, Jr. Plzeň: Aleš Čeněk, 2004, pp. 23-33.

[928] Address by H. R. Craig Robert Stapleton, Ambassador of the US to the Czech Republic was published in: *Transformation of Czech and Slovak Societies on the Threshold of the New Millennium and their Role in the Global World*. Selected Papers from the 21st World Congress. Edited by Ján P. Skalný and Miloslav Rechcígl, Jr. Plzeň: Aleš Čeněk, 2004, p. 145-50.

[929] Address by Hon. František Růžička, Minister Counselor of the Slovak Republic to the Czech Republic was printed in: *Transformation of Czech and Slovak Societies on the Threshold of the New Millennium and their Role in the Global World*. Selected Papers from the 21st World Congress. Edited by Ján P. Skalný and Miloslav Rechcígl, Jr. Plzeň: Aleš Čeněk, 2004, pp. 51-54.

The first day was concluded with the gala performance by the renown Plzeň Philharmonic Orchestra, in the auditorium of the historic Měšťanská Beseda, Jiří Malát conducting. The program included works of Antonín Dvořák: Violin Concerto in A minor and the New World Symphony in E minor. Featured was a soloist from the US, Janica Martin.

For the following four days, in representative historical halls in the center of Plzeň, numerous lectures, discussion panels and symposia took place in a number of concurrent sessions. On the Czech end, the task of organizing the panels was given to the Faculty of Human Studies of the University of West Bohemia, the Medical Faculty of Charles University in Pilsen, the West Czech Museum, American Center in Plzeň, Beer Brewing Museum, the Museum of Skoda History, and the West Czech Gallery, while the US panels were coordinated by Míla Rechcígl. Altogether there were some eighty panels, half conducted in English and half in Czech or Slovak. It would be virtually impossible to describe the content of each session. Suffice to say, practically every field of human endeavor was covered, from the arts and humanities to social sciences, natural sciences and technology. Most sessions were well attended and all papers I heard were of high quality. The uniformly high quality of papers was noted by everybody I talked to. All the sessions I attended were assisted by young people, usually running the projectors or other audiovisual equipment. They all knew what they were doing and the high tech was visible everywhere, to the envy of many of our colleagues from the US.

Academic panels ended at Friday noon. In the afternoon the concluding plenary session was scheduled. It started with the presentation of the SVU Elias Human Tolerance Awards to Father Anton Srholec,[930] the winner of the 2001 Award, and Prof. Tomáš Halík[931] the winner of the 2002 Award. The presentations were followed by the addresses of each of the laureates.[932] The second part of the plenary

---

[930] "The 2001 Andrew Elias SVU Human Tolerance Award," *Zprávy SVU*, vol. 43, No. 6 (November-December 2001), pp. 1-4.

[931] "The 2002 SVU Andrew Elias Human Tolerance Award Goes to Prof. Tomáš Halík," *Zprávy SVU*, vol. 44, No. 5 (September-October 2002), p. 17.

[932] Prof. Halík's lecture was reprinted in: *Transformation of Czech and Slovak Societies on the Threshold of the New Millennium and their Role in the Global World*. Selected

session was devoted to a panel discussion about the relations between the Czech Republic and the Czechs abroad, with the participation of Senator Jařáb, Senator Jaroslava Moserová, Mojmír Povolný, Radomír Luža, Benjamin Kuras and Petr Bísek. The plenary session was concluded with a brief talk by Dean Budil and with a presentation of an honorary award by Chancellor Vostracký to SVU President in recognition of his efforts toward "the development of academic, cultural and social relations between the Czech Republic and Czech communities abroad." Immediately after the plenary session there was a meeting of the SVU General Assembly.

The culmination of the SVU Congress was the Society's gala banquet on Friday night at the restaurant, "Na špilce," on the premises of the historic Pilsner Urquell brewery, courtesy of the City of Plzeň. Visitors were treated to scrumptious food, and the famous Pilsner Urquell beer, while the band played popular tunes. The occasion was used for presentation of SVU Presidential Citations[933] by SVU President and of SVU Praha Awards[934] by the Chapter President. Regarding the latter, seven SVU members were awarded, i.e., Věra Bořkovec, Jack and Dagmar White, Petr Hrubý, J. Marvan, L. Matějka and myself.

During the duration of the Congress the attendees had an opportunity to choose from a highly interesting and varied cultural program, which, in addition to the Pilsen Philharmonic Orchestra, included a piano recital by virtuoso Professor Radoslav Kvapil, the Jirasky concert, featuring F. Liszt, B. Smetana, F. Chopin, L. Janáček, and C. Debussy, a concert of K. Friesl and D. Tolas, based on the compositions of Antonín Dvořák, Bedřich Smetana, and Zdeněk Fibich, the Stivin's concert, a piano concert by Petr and Martina Karlíček, playing compositions of Franz Schubert, Antonín Dvořak, Bela Bartok, and Franz Liszt, a piano and clarinet concert by Marie Bobková and Budimír Zvolánek, Georges Bizet's opera "Carmen" under the baton of Jiří Štrunc, and the theatrical production of J. Weinberger's play "Kroky po krach čili když se jde, všechno chce," not to speak of a number of classical Czech films. Inter-

---

Papers from the 21st World Congress. Edited by Ján P. Skalný and Miloslav Rechcígl, Jr. Plzeň: Aleš Čeněk, 2004, pp. 34-42.

[933] Presidential Citations were awarded to: Ivo Budil. Ivona Skanderová, Marta Varejková, Ota Safertal, Jiří Eichler. Eva Rechcígl and Nebraska SVU Chapter.

[934] *Zprávy SVU*, vol. 44, No. 6 (November-October 2002), pp. 13-15.

ested people could also sign up for various events in connection with the "Year of Josef Skupa and Jiří Trnka," and view a variety of interesting exhibits in the city galleries. Saturday was reserved for bus excursions through the Plzeň environs with an opportunity to see the historic castles and chateaus, or the renowned spa cities in the western part of the Czech Republic.

Taken as a whole, this was a remarkable event. In addition to the superb academic and cultural program, there were a number of social occasions where the participants could meet their old friends or make new acquaintances that frequently lead to lasting friendships. The hospitality and the friendship of the Plzeň people was clearly visible at every step and one truly felt like being at home and being wanted. As I mentioned in several of my interviews with the reporters, this will be a hard act to follow. The Plzeň organizers, who passed the acid test with flying colors, deserve our sincere thanks and gratitude. They were also successful in attracting a large number of sponsors which made it possible to provide most cultural and social events free of charge. I ascribe their success to the young age and initiative of the organizers, all of whom, starting with Ivo Budil, were below forty years of age.

Proceedings of the Plzeň SVU Congress were later published in several volumes, i.e., *Evoluce člověka a antropologie recentních populací,*[935] *The Transformation of Czech and Slovak Societies on the Threshold of the New Millennium and the Role in the Global World,*[936] and *Transformace české a slovenské společnosti na prahu nového milenia a její úloha v současném globálním světě.*[937]

---

[935] Evoluce cloveka a antropologie recentních populací. Sborník panelu 21. Svetového kongresu Ceskoslovenské společnosti pro vědy a umění. Plzeň, 24.-30. června, 2002. Editori: Vladimír Sládek, Patrik Galeta a Vladimír Blazek. In: Biologická antropologie, Sborník 1 (Plzeň, Aleš Cenek, 2003), 117 pp.

[936] The Transformation of Czech and Slovak Societies on the Threshold of the New Millennium and the Role in the Global World. Selected Papers from the 21st World Congress, University of West Bohemia, Plzeň, Czech Republic, June 23-30, 2002. Edited by Ján P. Skalný and Miloslav Rechcígl, Jr. (Plzeň, Aleš Cenek, 2004), 640 pp.

[937] Transformace ceské a slovenské společnosti na prahu nového milenia a její úloha v soucasném globálním svete. Sborník vybraných príspevku 21. Svetového kongresu Společnosti pro vědy a umění v Plzni 24.-30. Cervna, 2002. Edited by Ivo Budil, Ivona Škanderová and Jana Jantschová (Plzeň, Aleš Cenek, 2004), 400 pp.

# 59
## *State of the SVU in 2002*

**Report of SVU President Dr. Miloslav Rechcígl
Presented to SVU General Assembly
Convened 29 June 2002 in Plzeň, Czech Republic**[938]

I am pleased to present my State of the SVU Report covering the two-year administrative period since the time this Executive Board assumed its office in August 2000. I will be brief because of the time constrain and besides we have regularly been reporting our activities in *Zprávy SVU*.[939]

These were two extraordinary years in terms of SVU growth and development and its accomplishments. This is important symbolically since this period marks SVU entry into the new millennium.

Considering the age structure of the Society the Executive Board selected as its main objective to revitalize the Society with younger people and, with this in mind, it launched a new initiative "Accent on Youth." Success can best be judged by the constantly growing rolls of young people among our membership, as you can verify from our regular reports in our Newsletter. Many of these members are between 20 and 30 years old, all eager to participate in our activities. We have a large group of young people here from Nebraska who, despite high travel and other expenses, managed to come to our Congress. I applaud their effort, enthusiasm and ingenuity.

In this connection, it should be noted that SVU MN Chapter organized a special discussion panel on the issues facing young Czechs and Slovaks living abroad."[940]

---

[938] Based, in part on my original report, published in *Zprávy SVU*, vol. 43, No. 5 (September-October 2002), pp. 22-14.

[939] *Zprávy SVU*, vol. 44, No. 6 (November-December 2001), pp. 11-13; *Ibid.*, vol. 46, No. 1 (January-February 2002), pp. 6-8; *Ibid*, vol. 44, No. 4 (July-August 2002), pp. 19-22.

[940] "MN Chapter Discusses Issues Facing Young Czechs and Slovaks Abroad," *Zprávy SVU*, vol. 44, No. 1 (January-February 2002), pp. 17-18.

Our second priority centered on information technology which is best reflected in the new SVU Website. Thanks to our Webmaster Jiří Eichler we now have a fully functional comprehensive and interactive website providing information about any aspect of SVU work past and present. We have steadily been improving it in an effort to make the site appealing and user friendly. New categories have been added including "SVU Calendar," "Czech and Slovak Issues," News from CR and SR," "Czechoslovak America" and, most recently, an "SVU Forum" has been launched. The popularity of the site is apparent from the counter which records the number of visitors. The SVU Website is not only our best business card but it has become one of the most sought out sources of information about Czech and Slovak matters on the INTERNET.[941]

The most important activity SVU has undertaken was our regional conference in Nebraska. As I pointed out in our Newsletter, "The Nebraska Conference was unique and truly phenomenal which cannot be expressed by a better term than a 'Happening'."[942] The extensive academic program, interwoven with various cultural and social events, large attendance, perfect logistical arrangements, outpouring of friendship and enthusiasm, and ever presence of Kačenka Oslzly, barely express what took place there. A conference like that would be difficult to emulate.

One of the direct outcomes of the conference was the establishment of the new chapter in Lincoln, Nebraska which immediately took off and soon had outdone other chapters with their numerous activities.[943]

After the successful Nebraska Conference we immediately started working on the forthcoming SVU World Congress in Plzeň.[944] It took quite a bit of effort but the fruits of hard work are plainly visible in the fantastic program and all the cultural and social activities arranged by our Plzeň co-organizers. We found an excellent partner in the University of West Bohemia, which, under the leadership of Dean Ivo Budil, has done wonders. I would like to extend my sincere thanks to Dean Budil and his collaborators for their splendid work.

---

[941] "SVU Website," *Zprávy SVU*, vol. 44, No. 2 (March-April 2002), pp. 22-23.

[942] "The Nebraska Happening," *Zprávy SVU*, vol. 43, No. 5 (Sept.-October 2001), p. 1.

[943] "New SVU Chapter," *Zprávy SVU*, vol. 43, No. 6 (November-December 2001), p. 16.

[944] *Zprávy SVU*, vol. 44, No. 1 (January-February 2002), pp. 1-5; *Ibid.*, vol. 44, no. 2 (March-April 2002), pp. 1-8.

The final program of the Congress appeared as the May 2002 issue of *Zprávy SVU*.[945] It also appeared separately, together with the Abstracts of papers and the list of participants.[946]

Let me now turn to our publication program which has always been considered SVU Imperative. I am pleased to see that under the new editorship of Clinton Machann our English periodical *Kosmas* is again published on schedule. Those of you who are subscribers must also be pleased with its content. Our goal is to make the periodical self supporting which can only be accomplished by broadening our subscription base. SVU is currently searching for a suitable candidate for a new Associate Editor for Subscriptions under whose responsibility this will fall.

With reference to our newsletter, *Zprávy SVU* brings regular features such as "From SVU Executive Board," "From New SVU Rolls," "Focus on Younger Generation," "SVU Calendar," etc. In addition to the hard copy, we regularly post an electronic version of the Newsletter on the INTERNET.

Apart from the two periodicals, we are again publishing SVU monographs. *The Taste of a Lost Homeland* is the title of a bilingual anthology of Czech and Slovak exile poetry with translations into English. Twenty one poets are represented. The anthology contains close to a hundred poems, all of which have the theme of nostalgia and love for our homeland which was left behind. The anthology has been published in memory of SVU member Frank Marlow and is edited by Věra Bořkovec.[947]

The second monograph, entitled *Essays on Czech Music,* is based on writings of Czech musicologist Zdenka Fischmann and was prepared for publication by Dagmar White and Judith Fiehler. The SVU published posthumously Dr. Fischmann's work, who was a long-time SVU member, as a tribute to her contributions to Czech music.[948]

Almost completed is the newly revised *SVU Biographical Directory* which brings basic biographic information about SVU members. As was

---

[945] *Zprávy SVU*, vol. 44, No. 3 (May-June 2001), pp. 1-34.

[946] *[Program. Abstracts. Participants] 21st SVU World Congress. 24-29 June 2002. Plzeň*

[947] *Chuť ztraceného domova – The Taste of a Lost Homeland.* A Bilingual Anthology of Czech and Slovak Exile Poetry Written in America. Compiled and edited by Věra Bořkovec. Dedicated to the Memory of Frank Marlow. (Plzeň, TYPOS, 2002), 171 p.

[948] Fischmann, Zdenka E. *Essays on Czech Music.* Edited by Dagmar White and Anne Palmer (Boulder, CO, East European Monographs, 2002), 187 pp.

the case in the past it is anticipated that this publication will again become the top SVU best seller. Some of the initial delays which we experienced were caused by technical difficulties when we attempted to merge the new information with the old data.

And finally, you'll be pleased to know that the Proceedings of the Minnesota and Nebraska SVU Conferences, as well as those of the last SVU Congress in Washington, DC, are readied for publication electronically.

As part of the new SVU initiative aimed at preserving Czech and Slovak heritage abroad, I conducted a comprehensive survey of the Czech and Slovak archival material in the US, after completing a similar survey on "Czech Historic Sites and Monuments in the US,"[949] a year earlier. The results of the second survey were compiled in a draft report, "Czechoslovak-American Archivalia,"[950] and were presented to the Czech Ministry of Affairs under whose sponsorship and financial assistance it was prepared. Both reports generated lots of interest in the US as well as in the Czech Republic and it was recommended that they be published to make the information more widely available. The surveys were carried out in cooperation and under the aegis of the National Heritage Commission comprised of major Czech organizations in the US. In connection with our efforts to preserve Czech and Slovak cultural heritage abroad, thanks to the generosity of John and Lois Fiala, the Society has established, in memory of their son, the new Stephen Fiala Cultural Heritage Award to be awarded annually.

I am pleased to report that our Society also played an active role in the organization of a special conference, "The Czech Republic and Czech Americans: Mutual Ties and Joint Partnership," held at the Czech Embassy in Washington, DC on May 18. The aim of the conference was to strengthen the ties and enhance cooperation between the Czech Republic and Czech Americans.[951]

---

[949] "Czech American Historical Sites, Monuments and Memorials." A Tentative Listing. (Rockville, MD: SVU, 1999. 112 pp. (SVU Information and Reference Series. C. Cultural Heritage Documents No. 1).

[950] "Czechoslovak American Archivalia. US-Based Archival Material Relating to Emigres and Exiles from the Territory of the Former Czechoslovakia and Relevant Holdings Bearing on their Ancestral Land." A Tentative Listing. (Rockville, MD: SVU, 2000). 294 pp. (SVU Information and Reference Series. C. Cultural Heritage Documents No. 2).

[951] "It Takes Two to Tango. Comments on the May Conference at the Czech Embassy," *Zprávy SVU*, vol. 44, No. 4 (September-October 2002), pp. 22-24.

The cultural component, of which I was in charge, enjoyed the most attention and there were many participants who voiced their views. There were three major presentations, i.e., that of Petr Gandalovič, General Consul of New York, Dan Baldwin, Director of the National Czech and Slovak Museum and Library in Cedar Rapids, IA and my own, all dealing with the question of preserving Czech and Slovak cultural heritage in America.

Among other activities, SVU provided a donation towards erecting a new statute honoring President Thomas Garrigue Masaryk in Washington, DC. I had the honor of presenting a check, in the amount of $1,000, to Czech Prime Minister Miloš Zeman on the occasion of his visit to the US Capital.[952] In connection with the Masaryk Memorial which will be unveiled in September of this year, the Society has launched a new drive to raise money for a new Masaryk Youth Incentive Fund.[953] The purpose of this fund is to support short term visits of Czech and Slovak students to America which would lead to collaborative grants with the US or Canadian institutions of higher learning. I should like to stress that all contributions for this cause, as well as other gifts to SVU, are tax deductible.

I would be amiss not to mention another SVU priority aimed at assisting in creating civil society in our old homeland. In the spring of 2001, on the initiative of Dr. Andrew Eliáš as the sponsor, an Annual Andrew Elias SVU Tolerance Award was established. This award includes a prize of $1,000.[954] A while ago you witnessed the presentation of the first two Tolerance awards.

As plainly evident from my report, the last two years were indeed very productive. During this period, SVU's visibility and image has risen to new heights and reached new horizons. Its financial base has been strengthened and a large number of new members, especially young people, were added to its rolls.

I am also pleased to report that SVU local chapters are beginning to catch the prevailing enthusiasm and are making name for themselves. Apart from the already mentioned chapter in Lincoln, NE, special men-

---

[952] "SVU Sponsors President Masaryk Statue in Washington," *Zprávy SVU*, vol. 44, No. 1 (January-February 2002), pp. 13-14.

[953] *Zprávy SVU*, vol. 44, No. 1 (January-February 2002), p. 13.

[954] "Second Year of Andrew Elias Human Tolerance Award," *Zprávy SVU*, vol. 44, No. 1 (January-February 2002), pp. 23-24.

tion needs to be made of the SVU Chapter in Edmonton, Canada which issued a notable CD of Czech music[955] and SVU Chapter in Pittsburgh, PA for its role in unveiling a historic marker commemorating the site of the Pittsburgh Agreement.[956]

In conclusion let me express my sincere appreciation to the outgoing members of our Executive Board for their support and my best wishes to the new officers.

..........

The above report was presented as a part of the SVU General Assembly, convened at the University of West Bohemia in Plzeň, on June 26, 2002. The Assembly was called to order at 4PM by SVU President, who opened the meeting by welcoming the members and thanking the Plzeň co-organizers for their splendid work. The first order of business was the approval of the minutes of the last General Assembly meeting held in Nebraska in 2001 and the naming of the Resolution Committee. Reports by the SVU officers came next, including that of the SVU President.

The fine SVU financial situation, as reported by SVU President, was echoed in the Treasurer's Report, stating that "it is better than last time and better than any other time since 1994, when our current President took charge again of the activities of the Society. The membership, consisting of individual members, spouse membership and student members, is approaching the magic number of 2000. The Society's worldwide membership comprise 49 States of the Union, Canada and 26 individual countries, ranging from Singapore and New Zealand to Bolivia, Brazil, France and there are also local chapters, including three in the Czech Republic and Slovakia each, totaling over 200 members. As has been the tradition of the SVU Congresses, the last SVU Congress did not result in deficit and there is every expectation that the Plzeň Congress was as successful. The stated goals of the Executive Board include fiscal discipline, requiring an annually balanced budget, minimal over-

---

[955] "SVU Edmonton Chapter Prepares CD Record with Czech Music," *Zprávy SVU*, vol. 43, No. 6 (November-December 2001), p. 8.

[956] "Historic Marker Honoring the Pittsburgh Agreement," *Zprávy SVU*, vol. 44, No. 1 (January-February 2002), pp. 15-16.

head and maximal effort to 'live' from current dues, and earned interest, without touching the existing corpus of the Society. This has been made possible by pro-bono service from all the members of the Board and the Council, by scrupulous insisting on external funding of all activities other than publications."

After the approval of the Treasurer's Report and the Assembly absolved the officers of liability, the Resolution Committee presented their drafted Resolution to the Assembly who unanimously voted its approval. The text of the Resolution appeared in the November 2002 issue of *Zprávy SVU*.[957]

Following the Treasurer's Report, Secretary-General Frank Safertal presented the Auditors' Report which recommended that the Treasurer's Report be approved and the retiring officers be absolved of their liability. The approval was granted by unanimous vote of the General Assembly.

As the retiring Executive Board left the podium, Prof. Jan F. Tříska, in his capacity as Chair of the Nominations Committee, assumed the chairmanship of the meeting pro tempore to announce the results of the election of the new officers. The entire slate of officers, as originally proposed by the Nominations Committee, was elected.[958] The newly elected Board comprised the following members: Dr. Miloslav Rechcígl, President; Dr. Ján P, Skalný, Executive Vice President; Prof. Věra Bořkovec, Dean Ivo Budil, John Fiala. Dr. Josef Macháč, Prof. Zlatica Plašienková, Rev. Michael Rokos, Dr. Marc Weiss and Dagmar Hasalová White, Vice Presidents; Frank Mucha, Treasurer; and Frank Safertal, Secretary-General.

---

[957] *Zprávy SVU*, vol. 44, No. 6 (November-December 2002), p. 9.

[958] "SVU Reelects Rechcígl as its President," *Zprávy SVU*, vol. 44, No. 6 (November-December 2002), pp. 1-6.

# 60
## *Reliving the New World Symphony*
*Impressions and Images from the 2003 SVU Conference in Iowa*

When I asked some of the participants of the SVU Conference in Iowa to characterize it in a few words, they usually responded with words like "Grand," "Smashing," "Most interesting and enlightening," "Could not be better," "Uncommonly informative," "Highly enjoyable," "Fun," "First rate," "Extremely well organized," etc. There seemed to be consensus that, until then, it was the most enjoyable conference SVU ever had.[959]

The conference was held on 26-28 June 2003 in Cedar Rapids, Iowa with the general theme "The Czech and Slovak Presence in America: A Retrospective Look and Future Perspectives." It was convened under the patronage of the Presidents of the Czech and Slovak Republics, Václav Klaus and Rudolf Schuster, respectively, with the participation of the representatives of Czech and Slovak Embassies in Washington, DC. Official greetings were also sent by President Václav Havel[960], President Václav Klaus[961] and the Slovak Ambassador to the US, Martin Bútora.[962]

It was organized by the SVU Executive Board with cooperation of the SVU Nebraska Chapter, Coe College, National Czech & Slovak Museum & Library, Cedar Rapids Convention and Visitors Bureau, Department of Languages and Literatures of the University of Nebraska-Lincoln, Federation of Czech Groups of Cedar Rapids, Bíly Clocks Museum, St. Wenceslaus Heritage Society, St. Wenceslaus Parish and the Spillville Historic Action Group. The detailed program was

---

[959] Based, in part, on my report in *Zprávy SVU*, vol., 45, No. 4 (July-August 2003), pp. 1-5.
[960] *Zprávy SVU*, vol. 45, No. 4 (July-August 2003), p. 6.
[961] *Zprávy SVU*, vol. 45, No. 4 (July-August 2003), p. 7.
[962] *Zprávy SVU*, vol. 45, No. 5 (September-October 2003), p. 5.

published in *Zprávy SVU*.[963] The program, with the abstracts and the list of speakers, was also printed as a separate brochure.[964]

Some people began arriving several days before the Conference. The first official event took place on Wednesday night, June 15, with a reception at the National Czech and Slovak Museum and Library, during which Director of the Museum, Gail Naughton, dedicated a new hall bearing the name of Andrew Láska, a long-time SVU member. The reception was concluded with a Czech bagpipe performance by Michael Cwach of the University of South Dakota. Today, in Czech Republic, "České dudy" is primarily preserved by folk music enthusiasts in Southern and Western Bohemia and may be heard in major festivals such as the one in Domažlice and Strakonice.

The ceremonial opening took place on Thursday morning, with the National Anthems, sung by Anita Smíšek. After the words of welcome by the Coe College VP for Student Affairs, Mr. Louis Stark, the Conference was officially opened[965] by Miloslav Rechcígl, SVU President, followed by the greetings of Ambassador of the Czech Republic to the U.S., H.E. Martin Palouš and the Ambassador of the Slovak Republic to the US, H.E. Martin Bútora, the latter being represented by Miroslav Wlachovský, Political Counselor of the Slovak Embassy. Among other dignitaries who greeted the Conference were Senator of the Czech Parliament, the Honorable Jaroslava Moserová and Director of the Cultural Department for the Relations with Czechs Abroad of the Czech Ministry of Foreign Affairs, Dr. Zdeněk Lyčka. The Lord Mayor of Cedar Rapids, the Honorable Paul D. Pate, who was out of town, was represented by Doug Wagner.

The academic program immediately followed, with a break for lunch. Because of the large number of papers given, four to five sessions were running simultaneously in separate lecture halls. Each lecture hall was equipped with the state of the art visual-video equipment, serviced by the Coe College students. Each session had between 3-6 speakers and

---

[963] *Zprávy SVU*, vol. 45, No. 3 (May-June 2003), pp. 1-13.

[964] *2002 SVU North American Conference, "The Czech and Slovak Presence in North America: A Retrospective Look and Future Perspectives." Program and Abstracts. Cedar Rapids, Iowa, 26-28 June 2003.*

[965] "Remarks by SVU President Míla Rechcígl at the Opening of SVU Conference, Cedar Rapids, IA," *Zprávy SVU*, vol. 45, No. 4 (July-August 2003), pp. 9-10.

occasionally also a few discussants. In between the sessions were 15-minute breaks during which "kolaches," coffee and other refreshments were served.

At 4 PM on the first day, sessions were interrupted so that the participants could hear the welcome keynote address by Ambassador Martin Palouš and the words of welcome by the Coe College President James R. Phifer. After a short intermission the SVU General Assembly meeting followed. In the evening, the guests were treated to chuck wagon BBQ and to the tune of an 11-piece popular Czech Plus Band of Cedar Rapids. It did not take long before dancers appeared on the floor, including Ambassador Palouš.

The academic program continued on Friday from 8 AM until 6:15 PM. Friday night was the traditional SVU banquet during which SVU President presented several citations and awards and a number of lucky attendees received a door prize donated by various sponsors. The highly enjoyable evening was concluded with a sing-along, led by Anita Smíšek, as well as tunes of Michael Cwach's bagpipes.

It is beyond the scope of this article to dwell into the subject matter of the various papers presented whose number well exceeded 150. Suffice it to say, that they covered practically every aspect of immigration, settlement, life and contributions of Czech and Slovak Americans. A number of sessions were devoted to their contributions to North America and to the question of how to preserve their cultural heritage. Other sessions dealt with the issues concerning the Czech and Slovak Americans, the echoes of Czech and Slovak history and culture in America and American culture in Czech and Slovak Republics, as well as with the relations with the Czech and Slovak Republics.

On Saturday, those participants who signed up for the tour, had to get up early so that they could get on the excursion bus which took us through the rolling Iowa landscape to Spillville and the environs. Loren Horton, a noted historian of the State Historical Society of Iowa, accompanied the tour, explaining everything about all important sites along the way. It was a memorable day during which we saw the famous Bílý Brothers Clocks and Antonín Dvořák Museums, the St. Wenceslaus Church, the awesome Czech cemetery with the famous Andera crosses, the Dvorak Monument and the schoolhouse purported to be the oldest Czech Catholic parochial school building in the US. This is also the building where Dvorak first performed his Opus 96 and 97. Senator "Jára" Moserová, who came with us on the tour, showed us her music skills on the St. Wenceslaus Church organ on which Dvorak played during his 1893 memorable summer. At noon, lunch was served in the lunchroom of the new school, prepared and served by the members of the St. Wenceslaus Heritage Society. Later the official dedication of a historic Andera Cross on the grounds of the Museum, with active participation of Michael Klimesh, Loren Horton, Mayor of the City, SVU President[966] and Zdeněk Lyčka, was held. Some of the visitors had the opportunity to also see several other Czech settlements, including Ft. Atkinson and Protivin and retraced the historic route of Antonín Dvořák to Spillville.

On our return trip, Loren Horton again accompanied the tour. After a dinner at Coe College, visitors were treated to a special piano and clarinet recital of Vaňhal, Dvořák and Martinů works, performed by Bohumír Zvolánek, clarinet and Erik Entwistle, piano.

Sunday was devoted to sightseeing of Cedar Rapids and the old Bohemian settlements in the vicinity. The bus first took us to the Czech Village for a walking tour of this historic area, following which we stopped for lunch at Zindrick's or Sykora's Café, now operated by SVU member John Rocarek who also donated many of the baked goods at the breaks. Throughout the morning, Jan Stoffer Tursi, Educator and Program Coordinator from the National Czech & Slovak Museum & Library was our able guide.

Mark Hunter, a historian of the Linn County History Center, accompanied us through other areas of Cedar Rapids rich in Czech history and culture. We saw the magnificent St. Wenceslaus Church established in 1873, the Czech National Cemetery and the nearby communities of Ely and Solon. Ely was the home of the first Czech Protestant Church in the US. In Solon, we viewed Sts. Peter and Paul Church and the adjacent Bohemian cemetery, founded by the Czech settlers in the second half of the 19th century. Here we were treated to Czech "koláče" and other goodies prepared for us by the Czech parishioners.

---

[966] "SVU President Míla Rechcígl's Comments at the Andera Crosses Dedication," *Zprávy SVU*, vol. 45, No. 6 (November-December 2003), pp. 12-13.

*Reliving the New World Symphony* 361

The conference, in its totality, was an extraordinary event. In the opinion of many, it was the pivotal event of the year for anyone interested in the thing Czech or Slovak. The organizers prepared a truly outstanding program. Never before has such a comprehensive conference been convened and so many experts on the subject and different community leaders assembled, be it here or abroad. According to my count, just about every state of the Union with significant Czech or Slovak population, was represented, including: California, Colorado, District of Columbia, Florida, Illinois, Indiana, Iowa, Kansas, Maryland, Massachusetts, Michigan, Minnesota, Mississippi, Missouri, Nebraska, New Jersey, New York, North Carolina, Ohio, Oregon, Pennsylvania, South Dakota, Texas, Utah, Virginia, Wisconsin, as well as Canada. There must have been at least 10 participants from the Czech and Slovak Republics. What was remarkable was the presence of many young people. In terms of various organizations represented, I counted at least the following: American Czech & Slovak Club of North Miami, American Friends of Czech Republic, American Sokol, Bohemian Benevolent and Literary Association of New York, Bohemian Citizens' Benevolent Society of Astoria, Czech Slovak Association of Canada, Czech and Slovak Heritage Association of Maryland, Czech and Slovak Music Society, Czech and Slovak Society of Oregon, Czech and Slovak Solidarity Council, Czech Heritage Foundation, Czechoslovak Society of America (CSA), Czechoslovak Society of Arts and Sciences (SVU), Dámská Matice Školská, Federation of Czech Groups of Cedar Rapids, Friends of Slovakia, German Bohemian Heritage Society, Komenský Club, Matice Vyššího Vzdělání, National Czech & Slovak Museum & Library, Nebraska Czechs, Nebraska Czechs of York, Spillville Historic Action Group, Slovak Institute, St. Wenceslaus Heritage Society, Texas Czech Heritage & Cultural Center at La Grange and the Western Fraternal Life Association (WFLA).

All in all, everything was perfect, including the weather. Everything was fantastic, enjoyable, memorable, educational and relaxing. And above all, everyone was so pleasant, friendly and hospitable. No single adjective or noun can express the atmosphere and the prevailing mood. Those SVU members who did not attend cannot imagine what they missed.

Thanks to all the organizers, especially Kačenka Oslzly, for the unforgettable days which will forever stay in our memories.

# 61
# *State of the SVU in 2003*

### Report of SVU President Dr. Miloslav Rechcígl Presented to the SVU General Assembly, Cedar Rapids, IA, 26 June 2003

It is a pleasure to present this year's report on SVU activities.[967] Considering our time pressure, I have planned this report to be brief and to the point.

First, I would like to thank Kačenka Oslzlý and the Nebraska SVU Chapter and our Iowa friends for making the necessary arrangements for the SVU Annual Meeting and the accompanying SVU Conference.

Upon my re-election to the SVU Presidency[968] at the SVU General Assembly Meeting in Plzeň in June 2002, I made several commitments which have become the blueprint for the action plan for the newly elected Executive Board. "Accent on Youth," assisting with the re-establishing civil society in the Czech and Slovak Republics and enhancing cooperation with their institutions, preserving Czech and Slovak heritage abroad and continuing publishing monographs have become our top priorities.[969]

Among specific tasks that I pledged to carry out was the activation of the SVU Fellows program, the reactivation of the SVU Research Institute and finding of a suitable repository for SVU archival material. Faithful to these commitments I am pleased to say that we have made considerable progress in most of these areas. Other than that, we have given great attention to the preparation of our 2003 Conference in Iowa and to improving the management and administrative aspects of SVU periodicals.

---

[967] Based, in part, on my report, published in *Zprávy SVU*, vol. 45, No. 5 (September-October 2003), pp. 2-5.

[968] "SVU Reelects Rechcígl as its President," *Zprávy SVU*, vol. 44, No. 6 (November-December 2002), pp. 1-6.

[969] "From Newly Elected Executive Board," *Zprávy SVU*, vol. 44, No. 6 (November-December 2002), pp. 6-8.

Let me now turn to specifics. As far as our finances are concerned, thanks to the sound fiscal management policies, we are in the black and, as a rule, have drawn primarily on interest rather than on the principal. Being an SVU Treasurer is not an easy task and Frank Mucha deserves our sincere thanks for a job well done.

As for the new initiatives, we have established a new Civil Society Issues Committee which has among its members a number of important personalities, such as Ambassadors Martin Palouš and Martin Bútora and Senator Jaroslava Moserová. Thanks to Lois Herman, we now have a very active Women's Issues Group, comprised of some twenty activists from the US, Czech Republic and Slovakia.[970] You can view their regular postings on the SVU Website, including news releases, statistical and research reports on the women's status in the Czech and Slovak Republics, job openings, conferences, etc. It should be noted that SVU Executive Board, at its meeting on August 10, 2002 approved a special declaration regarding the Women's issues,[971] which, because of historical importance is reprinted below:

## SVU DECLARATION ON WOMEN'S ISSUES

WHEREAS, women constitute half the population of the Czech Republic and Slovakia, and of expatriate Czech and Slovak communities, yet they are underrepresented in government, business, and academia;

WHEREAS, women in the Czech and Slovak republics have witnessed profound changes in the political, economic, social, educational and cultural realms, especially since the collapse of Communism and the latest wave of Accession, under which the Czech Republic and Slovakia will integrate into the European Union;

WHEREAS, the political, socioeconomic, educational and cultural status of Czech and Slovak women and girls is in need of further research, articulation, quantification, funding, public attention, and improvement.

---

[970] "Report to SVU Board from SVU Women's Issues Committee," *Zprávy SVU*, vol. 45, No. 2 (March-April 2003, pp. 17-18).

[971] SVU Declaration of Women's Issues," *Zprávy SVU*, vol. 44, No. 6 (November-December 2002), pp. 14-15.

It has been RESOLVED to establish a Women's Issues Working Group for the purpose of introducing a feminine gender component into the international programs of the SVU World Congress.

It has been further RESOLVED, that the Women's Issues Working Group will strive to ensure that women's issues receive sustained, positive, sensitive, equitable and meaningful consideration in all SVU programs.

It has been further RESOLVED, that in renewed commitment to the SVU mission, the Women's Issues Working Group will reach out to Czech and Slovak women in their homelands and abroad, and work to identify women's issues which unite us, giving primacy to issues that are important in the homelands.

It has been further RESOLVED, that in their capacity as members of the SVU, the Women's Issues Working Group will endeavor to build bridges of understanding between Czech and Slovak women the world over.

Working constructively, through dialogue, with the SVU to incorporate issues pivotal to Czech and Slovak women into SVU programs, the Women's Issues Working Group will provide leadership to, and serve as a forum for, all Czech and Slovak women, helping to empower them and to improve the quality of their lives.

We also have reactivated our Youth Committee which has the responsibility for the SVU initiative "Accent on Youth." Regarding the latter, I also issued a special statement which was published in March 2003 issue of *Zprávy SVU*.[972]

Furthermore, the Executive Board appointed a special SVU Leadership Search Committee with the responsibility to search for new leadership, especially among the younger people.

One of the pressing SVU problems has been the question as to where the Society should deposit its archival material for safe keeping. This was a high priority for us since most of the SVU documents had been kept in cellars, attics and garages of various people for years and there was an imminent danger that they would deteriorate or inadvertently be destroyed. I am delighted to report that, after some negotiations, we

---

[972] "Accent on Youth – No. 1 Priority," *Zprávy SVU*, vol. 45, No. 2 (March-April 2003), pp. 21-23.

successfully deposited most of SVU early documents at the University of Minnesota's Immigration History Research Center (IHRC). I would like to express my appreciation to Daniel Nečas, who is at this meeting, who kindly transported a big load of countless boxes in the University van to Minneapolis.[973]

Another unresolved problem was the SVU Fellows program which, according to our bylaws, falls under the jurisdiction of SVU Council. Although it had been on SVU books for years, the Society was unable to get it off the ground. The main reason for the failure had been a somewhat tedious selection process, based on the nominations of candidates by their peers, requiring laborious documentation. I am pleased to report that we overcame this difficulty by appointing a special Fellows Selection Committee whose function it was to go through the SVU rolls and select suitable candidates for Fellows whose names were then presented to the SVU Council for voting. The outcome of the vote was the election of 41 SVU Fellows.[974]

Emphasis on publications has always been an SVU imperative. The recent two SVU monographs, the *Anthology of Czech and Slovak Exile Poetry*[975] and Zdenka Fischmann's *Essays on Czech Music*,[976] edited by Věra Bořkovec and Dagmar White, respectively, came off the press at the time of our SVU World Congress in Plzeň. Copies of these two important publications can still be purchased and are available at the Registration Desk. We are in the process of preparing two other monographs, one relating to Czech and Slovak Theater Abroad and the other on Czech and Slovak Opera Abroad, under Vera Bořkovec's and Dagmar Hasalová White's editorship, respectively.

You will be also pleased to know about the progress we have made regarding the Plzeň SVU Congress Proceedings. Thanks to the efforts of Dean Ivo Budil, two volumes, containing selected Czech and Slovak papers, have just been published by the University of West Bohemia Press and can be ordered from there. As far as the English papers are

---

[973] "SVU Archives," *Zprávy SVU*, vol. 45, No. 3 (May-June 2003), pp. 23-24.

[974] "SVU Fellows," *Zprávy SVU*, vol. 45, No. 6 (November-December 2003), pp. 4-5.

[975] "An Anthology of Exile Poetry Published by SVU," *Zprávy SVU*, vol. 45, No. 2 (March-April 2003), pp. 15-16; see also: Ibid., vol. 44, No. 6 (November-December 2002), p. 19.

[976] "Essays on Czech Music," *Zprávy SVU*, vol. 44, No. 6 (November-December 2002), p. 18.

concerned, Ján P. Skalný has edited and formatted all papers he has received. Unfortunately, they represent only a fraction of the papers presented. It is imperative that those speakers, who have not yet submitted their papers, do so immediately, otherwise their papers will not be published.[977]

I am sure you had an opportunity to see the new *SVU Directory*[978] which is available for sale at the Registration Desk. This voluminous publication, containing basic information about our Society and biographies of over three thousand members throughout the world, is the result of very hard work and which would not see the light of day without the efforts and technical skills of Jiří Eichler. I would like to thank him publicly for all his assistance and devotion. SVU Directory has always been our top best seller and this edition won't be an exception, I am sure.

Thanks to our editors, Andrew Eliáš and Clinton Machann, respectively, the newsletter *Zprávy SVU* and scholarly periodical *Kosmas* are excellent, both in terms of their content and quality. We have made significant changes on the *Kosmas* Editorial Board, including the appointment of a new Associate Editor, Charles Townsend. In an effort to increase our subscriptions in Europe, with the help of Dean Budil, we are planning to send out sample copies to some five hundred addresses in the Czech and Slovak Republics. I hope this effort will bear some fruit.

The most important public activity the SVU has undertaken in the current administrative period was the organization of the present SVU Conference in Cedar Rapids, Iowa. The site was selected following my wife's and my visit to Nebraska and Iowa last October. Accompanied by Kačenka Oslzlý, who made the necessary arrangements for meeting the key people, we visited all the important places and negotiated the necessary details. As you have been able to see and experience, this is a great event and everything is going smoothly or, as we say in Czech: "jde to jako po másle" (It goes swimmingly). The success is unquestionably due to the one and only person Kačenka. Preliminary announcements of the Conference appeared in *Zprávy SVU*.[979] The final program was

---

[977] "Plzeň SVU World Congress Papers," *Zprávy SVU*, vol. 45, No. 3 (May-June 2003), p. 18.

[978] "New SVU Biographical Directory is Out," *Zprávy SVU*, vol. 45, No. 3 (September-October 2003), p. 11.

[979] *Zprávy SVU*, vol. 45, No. 1 (January-February 2003), pp. 1-3; *Ibid.*, vol. 45, No. 2 (March-April 2003), pp. 1-9.

published in the May and July 2003 issues of *Zprávy SVU*[980] and also separately.

I am also pleased to be able to convey to you the latest news about our 2004 World Congress. Upon exchanging correspondence with the Rector and other responsible officials of Palacký University, I am delighted to report that SVU Executive Board decided to hold the next SVU World Congress in Olomouc, Moravia with the general theme "Moravia from a World Perspective." There are lots of Moravians among our midst so I hope you will be delighted both with the site selection as well as the Congress theme.

I would be amiss if I wouldn't say a few words about our local chapters. You will be pleased to hear that our Cleveland Chapter has reactivated, under the Presidency of Dr. Stanislav Bohonek. Efforts are also afoot to establish a new Chapter in Spillville, Iowa, through the initiative of Michael Klimesh. Among the existing chapters – a big surprise – the Nebraska Chapter, under the leadership of Kačenka Oslzlý, is again Number ONE, in terms of the number of activities and variety of programs.

Mention also needs to be made of the SVU part in the Masaryk dedication ceremony in Washington, DC and in the farewells to Ambassador Martin Bútora, on which occasion SVU presented him a special citation for his accomplishments during his tenure as Ambassador of the Slovak Republic to the US.[981]

Last but not least, I would like to say a few words about the SVU Website. The Website, which is in the third year of operation, flourishes and, in the opinion of many, is the best business card SVU has ever had. It has information on just about everything you need to know about our Society and more. For many, it serves as an encyclopedia and *Vade mecum* on everything relating to Czech and Slovak history and culture, Czechoslovak Americana, Czechoslovak Genealogy on the Net, news releases, grants and aid and much more. Those of you who have not yet seen it please do so. Among the existing media, SVU website is clearly the most effective means of communication with SVU members and the outside world. Thanks to our diligent Webmaster Jiří Eichler, the website

---

[980] *Zprávy SVU*, vol. 45, No. 3 (May-June 2003), pp. 1-13; *Ibid.*, vol. 45, No. 4 (July-August 2003), pp. 10- 13.

[981] "Tribute to Ambassador Bútora and Dr. Zora Bútorová, *Zprávy SVU*, vol. 45, No. 5 (September-October 2003), p. 15 -16.

is systematically updated. He deserves our sincere thanks and appreciation.[982]

In conclusion, let me thank again our Nebraska Chapter and especially their President Kačenka Oslzlý for all they have done to make this meeting a success.

..........

The above report was presented at the General Assembly Meeting[983] in Cedar Rapids. IA on June 25, 2003. The meeting started at 5 PM. When it was announced that the next Congress will be held at Palacký University in Olomouc,[984] considerable debate ensued about the dates for the Congress. the majority expressing preference for holding the meeting in June rather than in September, as was originally proposed by the representatives of Palacký University.

SVU Treasurer Frank Mucha then gave a favorable report on the status of finances, corroborating the SVU President's statement. This was followed by the reports of other officers, including David Chroust's report on *Kosmas,* Kačenka Oslzlý's comments on the organizational aspects of the Iowa Conference, and the reports of the activities of several chapters, i.e., Nebraska, Chicago and Pittsburgh. By this time, the Resolution Committee was ready with their Resolution,[985] which was read and approved by the Assembly. The meeting was then adjourned.

---

[982] "SVU Website in the 3rd Year of Operation," *Zprávy SVU,* vol. 45, No. 3 (May-June 2003), pp. 22-23.
[983] "General Assembly Meeting," *Zprávy SVU,* vol. 45, No. 5 (September-October 2003), pp. 6-7.
[984] "2004 SVU World Congress," *Zprávy SVU,* vol. 45, No. 5 (September-October 2003), p. 12.
[985] *Zprávy SVU,* vol. 45, No. 5 (September-October 2003), pp. 7-8.

# 62
## *Organizing the Congress in Olomouc*

First steps toward organizing the Olomouc Congress took place at SVU Conference in Cedar Rapids, Iowa which was attended by Dean Ivo Bartecek and Karel Konečný of Palacký University. They brought with them a proposal to hold the Congress in September-October 2004. For a variety of reasons most of my colleagues did not like the dates, being concerned that we would get a very low attendance from the US. This issue was discussed at our General Assembly Meeting in Cedar Rapids. The consensus of the participants was to hold the meeting earlier.

Another matter of contention was the central theme of the Congress. Dean Bartecek proposed that it be "Czech Science in Exile." We did not like the topic because it seemed too narrow and we feared that we would not get enough people from US and Canada to participate in the Congress. Instead we proposed "Moravia in the World's Context" as the central theme. Dean Bartecek was initially not too thrilled about it, arguing that he received a special grant for the topic he proposed, and that it could not be used toward paying the Congress expenses if our topic was chosen. Later, when we met with him, he changed his mind and accepted our proposal.

Jointly with our Treasurer, Frank Mucha, I met with Ivo Bartecek and Karel Konečný to discuss the matter further and the upshot of the meeting was that they agreed to change the date provided they would get concurrence from their University Rector.

Rector of Palacký University, Jana Mačáková, later agreed with the change, and the new dates of the Congress were set for June 28–July 3, 2004.[986] Subsequently I spent quite a bit of time, corresponding with my Olomouc colleagues about the logistics and the fiscal matters. The latter point, just as in previous Congresses in CR and SR, again became a major stumbling block.

---

[986] "From Executive Board Meeting," *Zprávy SVU*, vol. 45, No. 5 (September-October 2003), pp. 8-10.

It was fortuitous that unexpectedly I received an invitation from the Czech Academy of Sciences in Prague to attend their conference in November 2003[987] which enabled me to visit Olomouc and discuss the Congress on a personal basis. Karel Konečný took me "under his wing" and showed me the University and other important sites in the historic part of Olomouc and the environs. I was impressed with what I saw. He also introduced me to key people at the University and in the city. I was treated as a VIP.

Ivo Barteček impressed me as a capable organizer and manager who was a real doer who had important contacts and exerted influence. They arranged a special meeting for me with the University chief fiscal person Ing. Pauer, to talk about financial matters, relating to our Congress, including the budget which he drafted. It was a strange meeting. Although he appeared very cordial, he was obviously a very shrewd businessman. He tried to impress me with his knowledge and experience with administering international conferences at the University, such as American medical conventions. He pictured fabulous meetings for me which he helped to organize which would have rivaled the most expensive conferences in the US. I tried to bring him down to earth, explaining that we are a non-profit organization and that our sole income comes from the dues of our members who are not millionaires, by any means. We obviously talked on different levels and no real discussion really took place between us and I was becoming restless. Ing. Pauer then produced his so called budget which shocked me. It was not really a complete budget but rather a list of budgetary items, most of which seemed to be irrelevant and if you would add them up it reached tens of thousands of dollars.

To make a long story short, after an hour of useless talk, I hurriedly ended the meeting, thanked him for his effort and left with the thought that we'll need to think about the matter some more and that we will need to involve other university administrators.

I was quite upset about my encounter and could not sleep that night. I got up in the middle of night, sat behind the desk and began listing acceptable expense items and prepared a reasonable draft budget that would be acceptable to SVU.

---

[987] *Zprávy SVU*, vol. 45, No. 5 (September-October 2003), pp. 18-19.

The next morning, just before my planned trip to Suchdol, Moravia, I spent about an hour with Karel Konečný, who was to accompany me on my trip, telling him about my unsatisfactory meeting with Ing. Pauer, including his unrealistic and, for us, unacceptable assumptions. I knew Karel Konečný from before and by then we were good friends so that I could talk to him quite openly. I explained our fiscal situation and gave him a draft budget which I put together the previous night which I thought would be acceptable for us. I also indicated that further discussions with Ing. Pauer would be quite pointless and that I would prefer to discuss these matters strictly with Dean Bartečkem and him. Karel seemed to understand my rationale and my arguments and promised to come to me later after he had a chance to talk to Ivo Bartečkem.

Soon after my return to the US, we scheduled our SVU Executive Board meeting for the early part of December 2003.[988] I was pleased that just before the meeting I received a general concurrence from Ivo Barteček with my fiscal assumptions but he did not send the detailed budget I had requested. Subsequently we exchanged correspondence back and forth via e-mail and when his detailed budget did not arrive, I made a proposition to him to the effect that SVU would make available to him $10,000 towards the Congress expenses, irrespective of the costs and the number of participants from abroad with no questions asked. We had similar arrangements with other universities in ČR and SR when we organized our congresses there. Dean Barteček accepted our offer. It also took a while before we received any details regarding the logistics, including accommodations, and any concrete suggestions for possible cultural and social events. Eventually, the information came and our Board was quite pleased with their proposal.

In the meantime, Otakara Safertal from Bethesda agreed to serve as our Congress Treasurer which took some arm twisting. Finally we were in the position to get our registration forms ready and advertise our Congress in earnest on SVU Website, our newsletter *Zprávy SVU* and external press, and start the arduous task of searching for potential speakers and other participants.

---

[988] "From Executive Board Meeting," *Zprávy SVU*, vol. 46, No. 2 (March-April 2004), pp. 16-18.

*Organizing the Congress in Olomouc* 373

The first preliminary announcement of the Congress with the "Call for Papers" appeared in November 2003 issue of *Zprávy SVU*,[989] followed by two additional announcements.[990] The March 2004 issue also carried a special invitation from Dean Ivo Barteček.[991]

During our Christmas vacation in New Mexico I had some time to think about possible panels which I presented to our Executive Board meeting in January 2004. The Board generally agreed with my ideas and several Board members volunteered to organize a panel or two. The major task of organizing the panels was, however, on my shoulders.

Since that point on I worked really hard spending some ten hours daily in front of my computer. To be sure, it was not just the concern for having a rich and excellent program which made me work so hard, but it was also the need of getting sufficient number of participants from abroad to be able to meet our commitment to Olomouc to give them $10,000 which I hoped would come from the registration fees. The most effective way of getting people to attend the Congress was to offer them the possibility of being put on the program. This was the second reason why I tried so hard to work on the program.

To my surprise, which really should not have been any surprise at all, hardly anybody responded to my general announcements and call for papers on our website and in our newsletter. I had similar experiences before.

Thus I had no choice but to start sending out individual e-mails, addressing them by individuals' names, preferably by their first names, and fitting the invitations to their particular backgrounds and interests. Initially I tried to recruit additional panel organizers because I could not very well handle the preparation of the program by myself. This met with mixed results. Most of the recruited panel organizers had little experience and got discouraged early on when people did not respond to their e-mails. The problem was accentuated by the fact that they did not

---

[989] "2004 SVU World Congress, Palacký University, Olomouc, Czech Republic, 25 June – 2 July 2–4. Call for Papers," *Zprávy SVU*, vol. 45. No. 6 (November-December 2003), pp. 1-4.

[990] "All Roads Lead to Olomouc...," *Zprávy SVU*, vol. 46, No. 1 (January-February 2004), [pp. 1-2; "22nd SVU World Congress...," *Zprávy SVU*, vol. 46, No. 2 (March-April 2004), pp. 1-15.

[991] "Invitation to Olomouc. By Ivo Barteček, Dean, Philosophical Faculty UP," *Zprávy SVU*, vol. 46. No. 2 (March-April 2004), pp. 2-5.

keep me informed of what they were doing and only after repeated e-mails did they inform me that they did not make any progress and consequently had given up on the idea of organizing panels of their own. In the end, the task fell again on my shoulders. I should also add that some of our panel organizers, almost exclusively, found their speakers in the Czech and Slovak Republics which did not help us financially since they were paying considerably lower registration fee than the overseas participants. We had an added problem with the Czech and Slovak participants because some of them were not willing to pay registration fee at all. Nevertheless, some panel organizers came through splendidly, while others managed, with my help, to complete their panels.

The difficulty in finding willing speakers was, in part, due to the fact that we started too late, less than six months before the meetings. Frankly, it was the shortest time we ever had for the preparation of the Congress program. Many of the invitees had other plans and some of them who intended to come to the Czech Republic, could not very well afford to come twice. Another reason for turning us down was the cost of travel, since our Congress was scheduled in the midst of the tourist season when everything is expensive, especially the airline tickets. Thus cost of travel from New York City to Prague was around $1,000 a person.

I had to use my utmost imagination and my psychological skills to persuade people to come to Olomouc. I knew quite well from my previous experience that to invite some scientist or artist to talk about some aspect of their work or research would not work. What seemed to work best was to select some interesting topic which would attract potential speakers because they worked in the area and were anxious to show their knowledge and their prominence in the field.

Some of the topics, which I thought might be appealing to the speakers, were:

Czech and Slovak Scientists Abroad: Their Life Stories and Experiences
The American Presence in the Czech Republic and Slovakia
The Bat'a Symposium
Comenius Symposium

In addition to our Academic Program, I had to devote attention to the Opening Ceremony, two Plenary sessions and SVU General Assembly meeting. For the Opening Ceremony, apart from the participation of the Rector of Palacký University and Lord Mayor of Olomouc, my plan was to invite several ambassadors and other dignitaries. In my private meetings with Ambassador Martin Palouš and Ambassador Rastislav Káčer, I received assurances of their participation.

For the Monday Plenary session, initially, I thought of devoting it to: "Notable Moravians Who Changed the World," having in mind such personalities as Comenius, Husserl, Freud, Masaryk, Janáček and Gődel. Unfortunately, I had to give up, on an otherwise good idea, because I did not have sufficient time to find suitable speakers of sufficient caliber from abroad who would be willing to come to Olomouc on such short notice. Consequently I decided to replace it with a symposium on "Czech and Slovak Scientists Abroad: Their Life Stories and Personal Experiences." As for our final plenary session I planned it on the basis of SVU Award ceremony, followed by the official conclusion of the Congress, with the participation of the key SVU and University representatives.

The final program of the Olomouc Congress was published in the May 2004 issue of *Zprávy SVU*,[992] with an addendum, detailing the program of the Opening Ceremony, in the subsequent issue.[993]

---

[992] "SVU World Congress, Palacký University, June 27-July 4, 2004," *Zprávy SVU*, vol. 46, No. 3 (May-June 2004), pp. 1-18.

[993] *Zprávy SVU*, vol. 46, No. 4 (July-August 2004), pp. 14-15.

# 63
## *The Olomouc Happening*

There is no better way to describe it. Those who were there will most certainly concur with this characterization of the SVU World Congress held at the Palacký University on June 27–July 4, 2004, while those who were not there cannot imagine what a great event they missed. Had we taken a poll there is no question that the consensus would be that this was the best Congress SVU ever had. After every event there are always some people who complain about something. This time, I have not heard any complaints whatsoever, which is truly remarkable, and is the best indicator of how the Congress participants felt.[994]

Preliminary Announcements of the Congress program appeared in *Zprávy SVU*.[995] The final program was published in *Zprávy SVU*[996] and also a separate brochure, together with the Abstracts and the list of speakers.[997]

Some people began arriving on Saturday, June 26, including our family, but the majority came the next day. Although it was a bit cloudy at first, on our arrival in Olomouc we were welcomed by sunshine. After checking in the hotel Arigone, which was conveniently located across from the recently renovated old university (Konvikt), where most of the Congress meetings were held, we went to the University Arts Center where the registration desk was located. It was a busy place getting ready for the reception the following day.

On Sunday, as the guests were arriving for the social get-together, they were greeted with champagne and excellent Moravian wine. At five o'clock sharp, Rector of Palacký University Prof. Jana Mačáková came,

---

[994] Based, in part, on articles in *Zprávy SVU*, vol. 46, No. 4 (July-August 2004), pp. 1-4.

[995] *Zprávy SVU*, vol. 45, No. 6 (November-December 2003), pp. 1-4; *Ibid.*, vol. 46, No. 1 (January-February 2004), pp. 1-3; *Ibid.*, vol. 46, No. 2 (March-April 2004), pp. 1-15.

[996] *Zprávy SVU*, vol. 46, No. 3 (May-June 2004), pp. 1-18.

[997] *[Program and Abstracts of the] 22nd World Congress of Czechoslovak Society of Arts and Sciences*, Palacký University, Olomouc, June 26- July 4, 2004. Central Theme: Moravia from World Perspective (Olomouc, Centrum pro ceskoslovenská studia pri Katedre historie Filozofické fakulty Univerzity Palackého, 2004), 166 pp.

# The Olomouc Happening 377

elegantly dressed, wearing a golden chain signifying her university rank. Upon Dean Barteček's introduction, who also wore a ceremonial chain, in his capacity as Dean of the Philosophical Faculty, the Rector welcomed the participants, and then it was my turn to say a few words on behalf of SVU. At this point a mother with her young son and daughter stepped forward, all dressed in beautiful native Moravian costumes from Haná Region who symbolically offered me bread and salt, which represents the traditional Moravian welcome. After accepting this gesture, the guests were then invited to help themselves from a festive table overflowing with delicious refreshments. Afterwards, the visitors had the opportunity to view an exhibit on "Czechs in America" organized by Ivan Dubovický and David Kraft.

The next day started early with a press conference at the government Regional Center where the ceremonial opening of the Congress was held. It was a beautiful, newly constructed modern building equipped with all the amenities, fitting the occasion. After the national anthems, Ivo Barteček,[998] who was the master of ceremonies, read the personal message from President Václav Klaus[999] expressing thanks to SVU for its meritorious work toward preserving democratic values. The University Rector Jana Mačáková[1000] then heartily welcomed the Congress participants, followed by brief addresses of the former Rector Josef Jařáb,[1001] Lord Mayor of the City Ing. Martin Tesařík and Governor of the Olomouc Region Ing. Jan Březina. I then had the pleasure to offi-

---

[998] "Speech by Ivo Barteček, Dean of the Philosophical Faculty, Palacký University Olomouc," in: *Moravia from World Perspective. Selected Papers from the 22nd World Congress of the Czechoslovak Society of Arts and Sciences.* Palacký University, June 26 to July 4, 2004. Vol. 1. Opening, English Panels Culture and Education, The Arts, The Humanities). Edited by Tomáš Motlíček and Miloslav Rechcígl, Jr. (Ostrava, Repronis, 2006), p. 12.

[999] "Message from Mr. Václav Klaus, President of the Czech Republic," in: *Moravia from World Perspective. Selected Papers from the 22nd World Congress of the Czechoslovak Society of Arts and Sciences, op. cit.,* p. 8.

[1000] "Words of Welcome by the University Rector Prof. Jana Mačáková," *Zprávy SVU,* vol. 46, No. 4 (July-August 2004), pp. 8-9.

[1001] "Remarks by Josef Jařáb, Rector Emeritus, Palacký University Olomouc & Central European University in Budapest and Warsaw," in: *Moravia from World Perspective. Selected Papers from the 22nd World Congress of the Czechoslovak Society of Arts and Sciences, op. cit.,* pp. 13-15.

cially open the Congress as SVU President,[1002] followed by additional greetings by Senator Hon. Jaroslava Moserová, Dr. Evelyn Early, representing US Ambassador William J. Cabaniss, the Czech Ambassador to the US Martin Palouš,[1003] the Slovak Ambassador to the US Rastislav Káčer,[1004] and Dr. Ivan Dubovický, representing the Ministry of Foreign Affairs. Greetings were also received from Helena Illnerová, President of the Academy of Sciences of the Czech Republic.[1005] This part of the program was concluded by the performance of the children's choir 'Campanella.' After an intermission the participants witnessed the awarding of the University honorary doctorate to Jiří Louda which included an impressive academic procession with colorful caps and gowns and university insignia, ending with everybody singing "Gaudeamus igitur."

The ceremony was followed by a gourmet buffet lunch, hosted by the Governor of the Olomouc Region. In the afternoon there was a plenary session with the theme "Czech and Slovak Scientists Abroad: Their Life Stories and Personal Experiences" in which selected scientists from the US gave testimony of their lives, professional career and achievements. The evening was devoted to a piano recital by Jaroslava Pecháčová.

The following three and half days were devoted to the academic program comprised of various topical or disciplinary sessions, symposia and discussion panels, about two thirds in English and one third in Czech or Slovak. There was something for everybody among the plethora of themes that included such topics as How to Run a University American Style, Symposium on John Amos Comenius, Bohemian Reformation, The Czechoslovak Jewish Community – Its Spiritual, Cultural, Political an Economic History, The Holocaust, Eduard Beneš Symposium, Baťa

---

[1002] "Remarks by SVU President Miloslav Rechcígl at the Opening of SVU World Congress," *Zprávy SVU*, vol. 46, No. 4 (July-August 2004), pp. 10-11.

[1003] "Greetings by H. E. Martin Palouš, Ambassador of Czech Republic to the USA," in: *Moravia from World Perspective. Selected Papers from the 22nd World Congress of the Czechoslovak Society of Arts and Sciences, op. cit.*, p. 16.

[1004] "Greetings by Slovak Ambassador to the USA H.E. Rastislav Káčer...," *Zprávy SVU*, vol. 46, No. 6 (November-December 2004), pp. 8-9.

[1005] "Greetings by Helena Illnerová, President of the Academy of Sciences of the Czech Republic," in: *Moravia from World Perspective. Selected Papers from the 22nd World Congress of the Czechoslovak Society of Arts and Sciences, op. cit.*, pp. 21-22.

and Batism, Women's Issues, The American Presence in the Czech Republic, Emigration and Czechs Abroad, The Moravian Texas, etc. Among various disciplines, all areas were covered, from the arts, humanities, social sciences to science. medicine and technology. The Czech panels were organized under the common theme "Mors Moravicus."[1006] Because of space limitation it is impossible to discuss what transpired in each session. Suffice it to say that the talks which I heard or which were reported to me were extremely interesting and invariably of high quality.

Apart from the academic sessions, the visitors had the opportunity to take part in one of the guided tours through the historic part of the city, usually scheduled in the morning. Practically every afternoon was planned for book presentations which were published on the occasion of the Congress.

The evenings were reserved for some cultural or social event. On Tuesday at five o'clock there was a piano recital by Marek Keprt, followed by a ballet performance honoring Antonín Dvořák at the Moravian Theatre. On Wednesday at five o 'clock a chamber concert by Budimír Zvolánek, Mathew Krejčí and Marie Bobková, took place. At night of the same day we had the Society's banquet, followed by an evening performance of a delightful baroque opera (Tomáš Hanzlík's Endymio). On Thursday night there was a cymbal recital by Edita Keglerová, followed by an organ concert by Petr Planý.[1007]

On Friday afternoon we had the final plenary session which consisted of the SVU Award ceremony, concluding speeches and General Assembly meeting. The Congress was concluded by a social get-together and festive buffet hosted by the Lord Mayor of the City.

On Saturday the participants could participate in one of the two planned bus excursions, one to view the Holštýn Castle, Rožnov pod Radhoštěm and Kopřivnice and the other Bouzov medieval castle, Loštice and Velké Losiny. Those who partook in one of these could testify how much they enjoyed it.

---

[1006] "Program konference Mars Moravicus. Neklidná léta Moravy," *Zprávy SVU*, vol. 46, No. 4 (July-August 2004), pp. 11-14.

[1007] Music program at the Congress was described in *Zprávy SVU*, vol. 46, No. 6 (November-December 2004), pp. 12-14.

I should also mention that there was a special meeting during the Congress between the SVU leadership and the representatives of the Senate Permanent Committee on the Relations with Czechs Abroad.

Everybody commented on the convenience of having all the meetings in one building equipped with elevators, allowing easy access for the participants. Just as was the case during the Plzeň SVU Congress, it was a pleasure to see young people attending panels, as well as performing various Congress chores. Mrs. Ludmila Vašková and her daughter, who were responsible for registration, stayed at the registration desk for the duration of the Congress and with great efficiency and pleasant smiles handled the requests of the participants.

The invisible hand of Ivo Barteček, who had the ultimate responsibility for the Congress, was clearly in evidence and whenever need arose he appeared on the scene and like a music conductor directed all the events smoothly and at strategic points brought them to a crescendo with efficiency, zest and poise. The logistical arrangements were the domain of Dr. Karel Konečný who handled everything superbly with flexibility, calm and ease.

Everybody was charmed by the beauty of the historical part of Olomouc which has been largely refurbished and "renovated" to give it its original picturesque medieval look. In this respect it resembles Prague on a smaller scale but without the tourists and without commercialization. It is amazing that the city has not, as yet, been discovered by tourists and foreigners. The food in the city restaurants was excellent and considerably cheaper than in Prague.

Wherever we went we were met with cordiality, kindness and hospitality common to Olomouc inhabitants. In many ways, the people, here, resemble the mid- and south-westerners in America and, considering that lots of folks actually immigrated to these parts from Moravia, supports this supposition.

All in all, it was a great event. As I mentioned to Olomouc reporters, the Congress not only fulfilled our expectations, it greatly exceeded them. I can talk about it only in superlatives and would give it an A+.

The Congress proceedings were published in an impressive two-volume set entitled *Moravia from World Perspective*.[1008]

---

[1008] *Moravia from World Perspective. Selected Papers from the 22nd World Congress of the Czechoslovak Society of Arts and Sciences.* Palacký University, June 26 to July 4, 2004. Vol. 1. Opening, English Panels Culture and Education, The Arts, The Humanities). Edited by Tomáš Motlíček and Miloslav Rechcígl, Jr. (Ostrava, Repronis, 2006), 434 p.; Vol. 2. English Panels. Czech Panels (Social Sciences, Science, Medicine and Technology, Czechs and Slovaks Abroad. Edited by Tomáš Motlíček and Miloslav Rechcígl, Jr. (Ostrava, Repronis, 2006), 432 p.

# 64
## *State of the SVU in 2004*

I am pleased to present to you our traditional State of the SVU Report,[1009] covering our two-year administrative period. I shall be brief and to the point as everybody is anxious to get ready for the evening feast, hosted by the Lord Mayor of the City of Olomouc.

It will be a very positive and the most optimistic report I have ever presented at any of our General Assembly meetings. Our Executive Board worked hard and the results show it.

At the outset of our two-year term, we decided on our priorities and set the course following our action plan which became the blue print of all our actions.[1010]

Accent on Youth[1011] became our number one priority and I am pleased to say that we have succeeded in recruiting a large number of young people, mostly students, both here and abroad. Some of our young people have become an integral part of the SVU apparatus of which our diligent SVU Webmaster Jiří Eichler is a prime example.

Assisting with the reestablishment of civil society in the Czech Republic and Slovakia has been another high priority for us. Here too, we have made head-ways, thanks to our agile leader Lois Herman who set in motion the SVU Women's Issues Group.[1012] For those of you who are not familiar with this SVU effort I invite you to view the frequent announcements of this Group on our SVU Website. You will be amazed what this group has been doing and what they have accomplished to date. In respect to the reestablishment of the civil society on the territory of former Czechoslovakia, SVU has also continued to award its

---

[1009] Based, in part on my report to the General Assembly meeting in Olomouc on July 2, 2004, published in *Zprávy SVU*, vol. 46, No. 5 (September-October 2004), pp. 5-7.

[1010] *Zprávy SVU*, vol. 44, No. 6 (November-December 2002), p. 6-8.

[1011] "Accent on Youth – No. 1 Priority," *Zprávy SVU*, vol. 45, No. 2 (March-April 2003), pp. 21-24.

[1012] *Zprávy SVU*, vol. 45, No. 2 (March-April 2003), pp 17-18.

symbolic annual Andrew Eliáš Humanitarian Award [1013] and this year is no exception.

Another SVU priority has been our continuing efforts to preserve the Czech and Slovak heritage abroad. Toward this end we held an impressive SVU Conference in Cedar Rapids, Iowa last year with the general theme "The Czech and Slovak Presence in North America: A Retrospective Look and Future Perspectives."[1014] It was an unqualified success, thanks to the superb cooperation of SVU Nebraska Chapter and its dynamic President Kačenka Oslzlý. Some of you may still recall my glowing report in the SVU newsletter which I appropriately entitled "Reliving the New World Symphony."[1015]

In the fall of last year we had another important event bearing on our priority to preserve the Czech and Slovak Heritage Abroad. In cooperation both with the Czech and Slovak Embassies in Washington, DC, we convened a special Working Conference on Czech and Slovak American Archival Materials and their Preservation,[1016] held on the premises of the two Embassies. It was an extraordinary event, attended by archivists from the major archival institutions in America and the Czech and Slovak Republics that had collections of such materials. as well as the representatives of the three respective governments.[1017] Proceedings of this remarkable Conference were published [1018] in record time, thanks to Pražská edice and its director David Kraft. One of the outcomes of the Conference was the establishment of the Czech & Slovak American

---

[1013] "Third Elias SVU Human Tolerance Award," *Zprávy SVU*, vol. 45, No. 1 (January-February 2003), pp. 20-21.

[1014] "2003 SVU Conference. 'The Czech and Slovak Presence in North America: A Retrospective Look and Future Perspectives." Cedar Rapids, IA, 26-28 June 2003," *Zprávy SVU*, vol. 45, No. 1 (May-June 2003), pp. 1-10.

[1015] *Zprávy SVU*, vol. 45, No. 4 (July-August 2003), pp. 1-5.

[1016] "Working Conference on Czech and Slovak American Archival Materials, Washington, DC, 22-23 November 2003," *Zprávy SVU*, vol. 45, No. 5 (September-October 2003), p. 18; *Ibid.*, vol. 45, No. 6 (November-December 2003), pp. 20-22.

[1017] "A Successful Archival Conference, " *Zprávy SVU*, vol. 46, No. 1 (January-February 2004), pp. 20-22.

[1018] *Czech and Slovak American Archival Materials and their Preservation.* Proceedings of the Working Conference held at the Czech and Slovak Embassies in Washington, DC on November 22-23, 2003. Edited by Miloslav Rechcígl, Jr., President, SVU (Prague, Prague Editions, 2004), 168 pp.

Archival Consortium (CSAAC). The SVU agreed to host the Consortium's WebPage on its WebSite.[1019]

In this connection I would also like to mention two other important publications which I compiled and edited, namely that of the *Czech-American Historic Sites, Monuments, and Memorials*,[1020] and the *Czechoslovak American Archivalia*.[1021] The results of these comprehensive surveys the SVU undertook, in cooperation with the National Heritage Commission, comprised the major Czech ethnic organizations in the US. These important documents have been published by the courtesy of Palacký University, thanks to the efforts of Docent Ivo Barteček, Dean of the Philosophical Faculty.

You may recall that in my acceptance speech at the General Assembly in Plzeň I pledged to carry out two specific tasks. One dealt with the activation of the SVU Fellows program[1022] and the other related to finding a suitable repository for SVU archives.[1023] Faithful to these commitments I am pleased to report that we have accomplished both. After overcoming the initial impasse, as you know, the SVU Council approved the first group of SVU Fellows some of whom are here today and I would like them to stand up. To be selected a SVU Fellow is a distinct honor and we congratulate them on their professional achievements which is the basis for their selection.

One of the unresolved SVU problems for years was the question what to do with the Society's archival materials which in years have grown into geometric proportions. Some of the documents were kept in people's cellars or attics where they collected dust and invited pests, with the imminent danger of being destroyed and forever lost. As you will remember from my last year's report, after some looking around and negotiations, we successfully deposited most of SVU early records at the

---

[1019] "SVU Hosts Archival Consortium Webpage," *Zprávy SVU*, vol. 46, No. 4 (July-August 2004), p. 24.

[1020] Miloslav Rechcígl, Jr., ed., *Czech-American Historic Sites, Monuments, and Memorabilia,* Olomouc-Ostrava: Centrum pro československá studia při Katedře Filozofické fakulty University Palackého v Olomouci, 2004. 142 p.

[1021] Miloslav Rechcígl, Jr., ed., *Czechoslovak Archivalia*. Olomouc- Ostrava: Centrum pro československá studia při Katedře Filozofické fakulty University Palackého v Olomouci, 2004. 2 vols. (206 p. & 368 p.)

[1022] *Zprávy SVU*, 45, No. 6 (November -December 2003), pp. 4-6.

[1023] *Zprávy SVU*, vol. 45, No. 3 (May-June 2003), pp. 23-24; Ibid., vol. 45, No. 6 (November-December 2003), p. 16.

University of Minnesota's Immigration History Research Center (IHRC) where they are well taken care of and preserved for the future and will be available to scholars for research.[1024] In this connection, I would like to express my appreciation to another young member of SVU, Daniel Nečas, assistant curator of the Center for making this possible.

Publication program has always been the Society's imperative. Here too, we have achieved success. After overcoming a series of technical difficulties, we succeeded in publishing our popular *SVU Biographical Directory*[1025] last year. This is a vade-mecum of information about our members, as well as our Society. You have an opportunity to see it here at the meetings and purchase it for yourself. This indispensable source of information should not be missing in your libraries.

You also have the opportunity at these meetings to see and purchase selected papers from our last SVU World Congress,[1026] published by the University of West Bohemia Press, thanks to the efforts of Docent Ivo Budil, Dean of the Faculty of Humanities. In addition to the English volume, there also were issued two other volumes from the Congress in Czech.[1027] [1028]

Under the rubric of publications also the three other publications belong which I discussed earlier, in connection with SVU activities relating to the preservation of our cultural heritage abroad.

---

[1024] SVU Archives," *Zprávy SVU,* vol. 45, No. 3 (May-June 2003), pp. 23-24.

[1025] *Czechoslovak Society of Arts and Sciences, Inc.* 8th ed. Compiled and edited by Miloslav Rechcígl, Jr., Eva Rechcígl and Jiří Eichler (Washington, DC, 2003), 368 p.

[1026] *The Transformation of Czech and Slovak Societies on the Threshold of the New Millennium and the Role in the Global World.* Selected Papers from the 21st World Congress, University of West Bohemia, Plzeň, Czech Republic, June 23-30, 2002. Edited by Jan P. Skalný and Miloslav Rechcígl, Jr. (Plzeň, Aleš Čeněk, 2004), 640 p.

[1027] Evoluce člověka a antropologie recentních populací. Sborník panelů 21. Světového kongresu Československé společnosti pro vědy a umění. Plzeň, 24.-30. června, 2002. Editoři: Vladimír Sládek, Patrik Galeta a Vladimír Blazek. In: Biologická antropologie, Sborník 1 (Plzeň, Aleš Čeněk, 2003), 117 p.

[1028] Transformace ceské a slovenské spolecnosti na prahu noveho milenia a její úloha v soucasném globálním svete. Sborník vybraných príspevku 21. Světového kongresu Spolecnosti pro vedy a umeení v Plzni 24.-30. cervna 2002. Edited by Ivo Budil, Ivona Škanderová and Jana Jantschová (Plzeň, Aleš Cenek, 2004), 400 p.

Among the planned publications, Věra Bořkovec is working hard on a monograph relating to Czech and Slovak Theatre Abroad and Dagmar White on another monograph on Czech Opera Abroad.[1029]

With reference to our periodicals, both *Kosmas*[1030] and *Zprávy SVU* newsletter have continued their excellent coverage, under the editorship of Clinton Machann and Andrew Eliáš, respectively. As for the visibility and external contact, the SVU Website,[1031] thanks to the diligence of our Webmaster, Jiří Eichler, is the most effective means of communication we have, at least with those who have access to computers.

I would be amiss not to say a few words about our Local Chapters. Generally speaking, we have witnessed considerable increase and improvement in activities. You will be pleased to hear that we have established a new chapter in Spillville, IA,[1032] under the leadership of Michael Klimesh, who is here today, and that the Cleveland Chapter in Ohio has been reactivated.

Last but not least, I am pleased to report that our finances are in the black and that we have been operating with a balanced budget. To be a Treasurer is a difficult and thankless job, and I would like to express my sincere appreciation to Frank Mucha for doing the impossible.

..........

The above report was given as a part of the proceedings of the forty-sixth General Assembly meeting in Olomouc on July 2. There were also individual reports of various SVU Chapters, including Bratislava, Brno, Prague, Plzeň, New York, Washington, DC, Texas, Nebraska, Spillville, IA and Cleveland, OH. There was also the traditional Treasurer's Report and the Report of the Auditors of the Accounts. They were approved by the General Assembly as was the Resolution drafted by the

---

[1029] "Planned Monograph on Czech Opera in America," *Zprávy SVU*, vol. 46, No. 1 (January-February 2004), 19-20.

[1030] *Zprávy SVU*, vol. 45, No. 1 (January-February 2003), pp. 21-22; *Ibid.*, vol. 46, No. 2 (January-February 2004), pp. 17-18; "Kosmas – Spring 2004," *Ibid.*, No. 4 (July-August 2004), 20-21.

[1031] "SVU Website in the 3rd Year of Operation," *Zprávy SVU*, vol. 45, No. 3 (May-June 2003), pp 22-23.

[1032] "New SVU Chapter," *Zprávy SVU*, vol. 45, No. 6 (November-December 2003), p. 17.

Resolution Committee. The text of the Resolution was reprinted in *Zprávy SVU*.[1033]

Afterwards the outcome of the elections of officers for the 2004-06) administrative period was announced. The entire slate of candidates, as originally proposed by the Nominations Committee,[1034] was elected.

---

[1033] "Resolution of the Czechoslovak Society of Arts and Sciences (SVU) on the Occasion of the Forty-sixth Annual Meeting, Olomouc, July 2, 204," *Zprávy SVU*, vol. 46, No. 5 (September-October 2004), pp. 8-9.

[1034] "SVU Nominations Committee," *Zprávy SVU*, vol. 46, No. 2 (March-April 2004), p. 5.

# 65
## Organizing the 2005 SVU Conference

My first thought following the announcement of my reelection[1035] to SVU Presidency for the 2004-2006 period was the question of where to hold the next year's Conference. This was a matter of high priority, considering that we had only a few months for making the necessary arrangements. This was also the main item on the agenda of the first meeting of our newly elected SVU Executive Board.

Although in the past I usually had some idea of possible sites for the SVU Conferences, this time I had nothing specific in mind. We tossed around a number of possibilities during the Board meeting but these were all wild guesses and no one came up with any concrete suggestions. Several Board members thought that the Conference should be held in Canada since we did not have any SVU event there for over a decade. This was, however, a long shot, considering that most Canadian SVU Local Chapters have not been too active lately. Other Board members favored the idea of having the Conference in Houston, TX where they have just opened a new Czech Cultural Center.[1036]

Frankly, the only thing which came out of our meeting was an agreement on the criteria that should govern the selection of the Conference site. Above all, the Board felt it was important to find a place where we had some members who would assist with the local arrangements. In the past, when Local Chapters were involved, they would usually assume responsibility for arranging the conference program. We also preferred a place where they would not charge us for lecture rooms. There was obviously an advantage in convening the conference at some university because the participants could stay in student dorms which were relatively inexpensive.

The most ideal site was a small college setting such as was Coe College, where the SVU held its 2003 Conference. I would have also

---

[1035] *Zprávy SVU*, vol. 46, No. 5 (September-October 2004), pp 1-4.

[1036] "From the First Executive Board Meeting," *Zprávy SVU*, vol. 46, No. 5 (November-December 2004), pp. 15-17.

liked to have the conference in an area close to some Czech/Slovak community, especially during the time of their festival or other community event.

Since none of the Board members volunteered to find a suitable conference site, it was essentially up to me to do the searching. I first approached various SVU Local Chapters but without much luck. The Edmonton Chapter initially expressed some interest but was unwilling to help with the preparation of the program. Furthermore, they suggested that the conference be held in Banff, a popular ski resort in Alberta, which would have been quite expensive. The Pittsburgh Chapter indicated that they may be interested in the future but not now.

I then followed up on the Houston idea but did not get anywhere because of the lack of interest from the Texas side. The best they could do would be to rent us their facilities, which would not be cheap, and without any assistance with the local arrangements or the program. I thought that I could always depend on my friend Clinton Machann of Texas A&M University but he turned me down also, because he was unusually busy the coming year.

Inasmuch as one of our Board members, Joe Kohn, held a professorial appointment at Princeton University, I asked him to look into the possibility of having our Conference at his university. At first, it looked quite promising but later the University insisted that we would have to have a million dollar insurance which was quite expensive. Another possibility was the neighboring Rider College which, however, could only offer rather outdated dorms which were not air-conditioned. This would have been a problem if our conference were held in summer time, as we planned. David Chroust from Texas A&M University suggested that we could possibly hold the conference in one of smaller colleges in Texas where he had some acquaintances. The problem with this idea was that this would be "in the middle of nowhere" and with little logistical help.

Frankly, by then, I was getting a bit desperate. Sometime in October 2004, I happened to attend one cultural event at the Slovak Embassy in Washington where I met an old acquaintance of mine, Robert Petrik, Honorary Consul of Slovakia for Florida. I knew that he was also an active officer of the American Czech-Slovak Cultural Club (ACSCC) in North Miami which organized various cultural events throughout the year. It occurred to me that we could possibly join forces and hold our conference together with their Club. When I approached Bob with the idea, he was quite receptive and thought that he could get support from his Board. By happenstance, a week later, we were visited by Cecilia Rokusek, professor at Gulf Coast University at Fort Myers, Florida, whom we knew well from the time of our Iowa Conference in 2003. As it turned out, she was also an officer of the Florida-based ACSCC Club and a good friend of Bob Petrik. She liked the idea of combining our Conference with some of the Club's cultural event and thought that both organizations would benefit from it.

The Club Board members had a meeting soon after during which they overwhelmingly approved our joint endeavor. The only problem was that their planned Festival was scheduled for 19 March 2005 which would not give us much time for the preparation of the conference program. Nevertheless, I thought that we would make it if we would put great effort into it, especially if we would restrict the Conference program to one day with the invited speakers. The SVU Executive Board approved the idea in their October meeting.[1037]

Interestingly, there was a possibility that the Czech Minister of Defense Karel Kűhnl might attend our conference and I was asked to send him an official letter of invitation. Unfortunately, he could not make it. With the help of Jiří Stanislav, whom I knew when he still lived in Canada, an arrangement was made with the Czechoslovak Association of Legionnaires to send their three representatives to the Conference.

In November, I interrupted my busy schedule for about a week, to drive with Eva to Florida, to spend Thanksgiving with our son's family and again in the mid December, to fly to New Mexico, to celebrate Christmas holidays at our daughter's family. By that time, I already had enough speakers for a one day program. Inasmuch as new e-mails continued coming in with suggestions for additional papers, it was obvious to me that we will need to modify our Conference program to accommodate all the new speakers.

The first general announcement of the Florida Conference, together with preliminary registration forms, appeared in the November 2004 issue of *Zprávy SVU*.[1038]

---

[1037] "From Executive Board," *Zprávy SVU*, vol. 46, No. 6 (November-December 2004), pp. 5-8.

[1038] *Zprávy SVU*, vol. 46, No. 6 (November-December 2004) pp. 1-5.

After Christmas I worked really hard to get the program finished as soon as possible. The number of speakers was increasing daily, and so was the number of panels which I had to continuously modify to fit in various topics, some of which were outside the general theme of the Conference. Since we had a number of speakers from the Czech and Slovak Republics, who preferred to talk on some subject relating to their home country, I had to add several new panels with such titles as "Echoes from the Old Country" and Czech and Slovak Issues."

I put together all panels except one which was originally proposed by Peter Filip of the University of Southern Illinois. He came to me with the idea of organizing a special symposium on university collaboration between the Czech Republic and the US. This sounded promising, particularly when he indicated that he already had commitment from several University Rectors to participate. The idea indeed came to fruition. In addition to the Technical University of Ostrava, the University of West Bohemia in Plzeň and the University of Southern Illinois at Carbondale, which he proposed, I was able to get participation from the University of South Bohemia in České Budějovice, the Catholic University of Ružomberok and the University of Florida. I was hoping that we would also have a sizeable representation from Palacký University in Olomouc, including Dean Ivo Barteček, Prof. Miloš Trapl and Dr. Karel Konečný but, at the end, only Karel Konečný attended.

In the January 2005 issue of *Zprávy SVU*, I published the "2005 Conference Update," in which I could be more specific and talk about the speakers we were getting and what sessions were planned.[1039] The write-up which was written in a popular journalistic style, must have had some impact, because we were, all of a sudden, swamped with requests from additional potential speakers, as well as from other people who were interested in coming.

In the meantime, Bob Petrik left for a 3-4 week trip to Africa, and as a consequence Cecilia Rokusek became my chief contact with the Florida organizers. Upon consultation with her, we decided to extend our Conference program to Saturday afternoon and also include Sunday morning, with two sessions running concurrently, to be able to fit in so

---

[1039] "2005 SVU Conference Update: 'Czech and Slovak Heritage on Both Sides of the Atlantic,' North Miami, FL, 17-20 March 2005," *Zprávy SVU*, vol. 47, No. 1 (January-February 2005), pp. 1-6.

many speakers, whose number, by then, exceeded sixty. By early February, I had the program more or less finished.

I also had the responsibility for collecting and editing the speakers' abstracts which was quite a chore, on which I must have spent a good three weeks. What remained were the last minute changes and the final scheduling of the papers to avoid conflicts. Once that was done I was able to complete the program brochure.

At the end, we had altogether ten panels. The most important session, titled Presidential Plenary Session, was devoted to the subject of "Preserving Czech and Slovak Heritage Abroad." It was scheduled for Saturday afternoon and featured addresses by the two Ambassadors, H.E. Martin Palouš and H.E. Rastislav Káčer, representing the Czech and the Slovak Republics, respectively. They were followed by a major address by Prof. Rudolph Vecoli, Director of the University of Minnesota's Immigration History Research Center (IHRC), where the SVU deposited its archival material. I was the next speaker and used this occasion to announce the establishment of the new Czech and Slovak Studies Fund at the IHRC to assist the Czech and Slovak scholars and students to work at the Center.

It must have been in the latter part of January 2005, when I was approached by David Kraft of Prague, the publisher of my book *Postavy naší Ameriky*, but whose main interest was in organizing exhibits, with the idea that he would be willing to organize, on the occasion of our Florida Conference, a special exhibit on "Czechs in America." I thought it was a great idea and encouraged him to do it. With the financial help of the Czech Foreign Ministry, the exhibit material arrived safely in Florida in sufficient time to get the exhibit readied for our Conference. Another last minute arrangement was an art exhibit of George Hořák's paintings which were hung in the main Club room for everybody to see.

Through my contacts in Prague Castle, I was able to arrange President Václav Klaus' sponsorship of our Conference and later I also succeeded in getting sponsorship from the Slovak President Ivan Gasparovič. In the case of the Slovak President it took a little longer because the arrangements had to be made through the Slovak Ambassador Rastislav Káčer in Washington. I would have liked for them to also attend the meetings but they already had other plans. In addition I also succeeded in having our Conference sponsored by the US Commission

*Organizing the 2005 SVU Conference* 393

for the Preservation of America's Heritage Abroad, a Presidentially-appointed Commission, which had collaborative links with both the Czech and the Slovak Republics. I actually met with the Chairman of the commission, H.E. Warren Miller, in the hope that I could persuade him to personally participate in our Conference.

By early March, I had everything done, at least as far as the lecture program was concerned. As for the cultural events, that was entirely in the hands of Cecilia Rokusek and Bob Petrik. They also were responsible for all the local arrangements and the logistics.

The final program was printed in the March 2005 issue of *Zprávy SVU*.[1040] It was also published, together with the Abstracts, as a separate brochure.[1041] Frankly, it was a record, if not a miracle, what we were able to accomplish in a matter of a few months.

---

[1040] *Zprávy SVU*, vol. 47, No. 2 (March-April 2005), pp. 1-17.

[1041] [Program and Abstracts]. Special Conference and Festival, North Miami, Florida, 17-20 March 2005. Central Theme: "Czech and Slovak Cultural Heritage on Both Sides of the Atlantic" (North Miami, FL, SVU, 2005), 50 p.

# 66
## *SVU Extravaganza in Florida*[1042]

*"Here comes the sun... always behind rain*
*Rain brings tears, the sun warms away pain*
*Gone now the doubts that seemed to loom ahead*
*Now bright sunshine to fill my life instead!"*

The Czechs, as well as the Slovaks, have the saying :"Po dešti vždy slunce svítí," which is comparable to American gardeners' popular quote "The sun always shines after the rain." The Floridians have, of course, modified it to their own favorite sayings, such as "Sun shines on Florida, as the rain pours on the rest" or "Sun shines and the fun never sets in Florida beaches," etc. All these sayings are quite appropriate in characterizing our joint SVU Conference and the ASCC Festival held in North Miami on 17-20 March, 2005.

Just as a number of my friends did, such as the Czech Ambassador Martin Palouš or Slovak Ambassador Rastislav Káčer, my wife and I decided to combine our trip to the Conference with a brief vacation on Florida beaches. Miami is about 1100 miles from Washington, DC which, we figured, would take us ca. 18 hours by car, i.e., roughly two days, with one night stop-over in some motel on the way, if we had an early start. We left on Tuesday morning. To avoid traffic around Richmond, we left a few hours after midnight so that by the midst afternoon we made it to Brunswick, Georgia where we stayed over night. When we left Washington, the temperature was 32 degrees F., while in Georgia, it rose above 40, which was still pretty cold. After a few hours of sleep we decided to move on. The temperature, in the meantime, dropped down again and it began raining. It looked miserable and the drive was difficult, as the rain changed into a downpour. Nevertheless, we drove on and when we reached Jacksonville, Florida, the temperature began rising rapidly. Upon coming to our destination in North Miami at noon on

---

[1042] Originally published in *Zprávy SVU*, vol. 47, No. 3 (May-June 2005), pp. 1-5.

Wednesday, it climbed to 85 degrees. The overflowing sunshine with the blue sky above was a marvelous sight and wonderful welcome.

After checking in the Windsor Inn, we drove immediately to the American Czech-Slovak Cultural Club which was only a few blocks away, to see what the place looked like and also to ascertain how the Conference preparations were proceeding. The Club was located on a four-acre lot, on a grassy meadow, adjacent to a spacious yard for outdoor activities and a large picnic area covered by ancient banyan trees. These are East-Indian fig trees of the mulberry family with branches that send out shoots which grow down to the soil and root to form secondary tree trunks. With Spanish moss hanging over the branches, the trees give a majestic and somewhat mystery, if not spooky, appearance.

The extensive property was bordered by a small brook which apparently was used in the old days by the legendary Al Capone, the original owner of the place, for shipping whisky to other locations during the prohibition era. The Club building was apparently purchased by the Czechs, sometime after the war, and was refurbished into a meeting place for their American Czechoslovak Social Club, with a restaurant, bar, library and sport and picnic facilities. They had dances there, with Czech music bands, serving Czech cuisine with Czech beer. As I was informed, Alice Masaryková, the daughter of President Tomáš Garrigue Masaryk, used to come to the Club occasionally, when she lived in the area in her retirement, as did such personalities as Minister Jan Masaryk and the Czechoslovak Ambassador to the UN Ján Papánek.

The main Club room reminded one of a typical Czech American Sokol Hall with pictures and paintings of prominent Czechoslovak figures, such as Tomáš G. Masaryk, Edvard Beneš and Rastislav Štefánik, intermingled with the paintings of typical Bohemian landscapes, picturesque panoramas of Prague and castles, the Tatra mountains, the Czech and Slovak State insignia, flags and much more. You really had a warm and melancholic feeling that you were at home, even though a few decades ago.

When we arrived, our Florida co-organizers had obviously still plenty to do, considering that they were in the midst of paving the yard and the Club road with a fresh layer of asphalt. Only late that afternoon, they started erecting a huge tent and setting up a generator for the electricity in preparation for the Waldemar Matuška concert, scheduled for Friday night. I was a bit concerned about the timing because one of our sessions was scheduled to take place in the tent on Thursday afternoon. Robert Petrik, President of the Club was running around, instructing the Club employees to get the Club ready for the avalanche of people expected the next day. He did not shy away from doing much of the physical work himself. I also had a chance to pitch in by moving and arranging tables and chairs in the Club. The Czech chef, with several helpers, were engaged in preparing all sorts of typical Czech dishes, such as duck with sauerkraut and dumplings, sirloin tip with dill sauce, paprika chicken, goulash soup, "kolatches," etc., everything in huge quantities, expecting some 200 people. Honestly, I don't know how they managed to cook all these dishes in their relatively small kitchen. As I understand it, more people came than were expected, but everybody got served, nevertheless.

Cecilia Rokusek, professor at the Gulf Coast University at Ft. Myers, was responsible mainly for the logistics of the Conference, including the registration. She must have taken off a week from her University responsibilities to be able to handle all the chores. I am sure that she welcomed my wife's help in preparing the registration material. Mrs. Callahan from Nebraska, who later sat at the Registration desk for the duration of the Conference, without taking a break; was a marvelous help throughout the Conference.

Despite all the work that had to be done, the Floridian organizers did not seem to get excited and somehow finished everything on time so that our Conference could get started on Friday morning, as scheduled. Frankly, I was amazed by both their somewhat easy-going attitude, calmness, poise and humor – characteristics, which are quite different from us who live in the eastern part of the US where everything is urgent and has to be organized to the last detail beforehand. I suppose, if we lived in the Florida environment, we could get acclimatized to the Southern way of doing things with ease.

From the point of view of the American Czech-Slovak Cultural Club, the SVU Conference brought them a new dimension, by acquainting their members, many of whom having descended from early settlers from the territory of former Czechoslovakia, with the outstanding contributions of Czechs and Slovaks worldwide, as well as bringing them new information in the area of history, literature and the arts, sciences, technology, business and medicine. The SVU members, on the other hand, benefited by being exposed to the ways Czech and Slovak Americans maintain the Czech and Slovak historic and family traditions, from one generation to the next, especially the folklore, music, and the cuisine. It was a happy marriage with genuine cordiality and good spirit.

By combining the SVU efforts with those of the Florida-based American Czech-Slovak Cultural Club, we were able to put together an outstanding academic program, combined with highly enjoyable and entertaining cultural events. The general theme of our joint program was "Czech and Slovak Heritage on Both Sides of the Atlantic." This was our fifth SVU conference devoted to the subject of Czech and Slovak Americans – a subject, obviously, close to our heart, and one of SVU priorities. The conference was co-sponsored by the US Commission for the Preservation of America's Heritage Abroad and was held under the aegis of President of the Czech Republic Václav Klaus[1043] and President of the Slovak Republic Ivan Gasparovič. The academic program was organized into several major topics, including Czech and Slovak Historic Tradition, Czech and Slovak Contemporary Issues, Echoes from the Old Country, Czechs and Slovaks in the New World, and Presidential Symposium on Preserving Czech and Slovak Heritage. The latter session featured the Ambassador of the Slovak Republic to the U.S., H.E. Rastislav Káčer, the Czech Ambassador to the U.S., H.E. Martin Palouš, and the Director of the Immigration History Research Center (IHRC) at the University of Minnesota, Prof. Rudolf Vecoli. I used the occasion, in my capacity as SVU President, to announce the establishment of the new Czech and Slovak Archival Fund which is reported in more detail elsewhere.

Apart from the various sessions bearing on the general theme of the Conference, there was a special symposium and a discussion panel relating to Czech and Slovak Universities and their Cooperation with the Institutions of Higher Learning, with the participation of University Rectors and other high-level university officials from the University of West Bohemia in Plzeň, University of South Bohemia in České Budějovice, Technical University in Ostrava and the Catholic University

---

[1043] President Klaus' message was reprinted in *Zprávy SVU*, vol. 47, May-June 2005), p. 7.

in Ružomberok. The US institutions were represented by the University of Florida and the University of Southern Illinois in Carbondale, both of which have active cooperative agreements with Czech and Slovak Universities.

The attendees had an opportunity to view two special exhibits, one on "Czechs in America," organized by curator David Kraft and the second showing the paintings of Miami-based George Hořák. The new SVU publications, which were exhibited in the Club's library, included Jan Vičar's Imprints: Musical Studies and Lectures from the 1990s, Rechcígl's *Czech American Historic Sites, Monuments and Memorabilia* and a two-volume set *Czechoslovak American Archivalia,* all published through the courtesy of Palacký University in Olomouc. Also shown was a newly issued video cassette and DVD, featuring the highlights of the 22nd SVU World Congress in Olomouc in June 2004. Other exhibited works included SVU Biographical Directory, a collection of Selected English Papers from the SVU World Congress in Plzeň and the Proceedings of the Working Conference on Czech and Slovak American Archival Materials and their Preservation, held in Washington DC in November 2003.

The cultural program featured Czech country and western singers, Slovak folk dancers from Masaryktown, FL, the Europa Band from Orlando, Czech folk singers from Key West, etc. Other heritage events included ethnic food and craft demonstrations, folk art booths, ethnic food tasting, an accordion jamboree, and last but not least, the Miss Czech and Slovak Florida Pageant.

The latter was a highly enjoyable and charming event, involving young ladies, mostly college students, dressed in Czech and Slovak picturesque folk costumes ("kroje") from different parts of Bohemia, Moravia and Slovakia who had to demonstrate their poise and particular skills and respond to questions before a group of judges. These young ladies, each of them accompanied by a court of young charming princesses, also attired in beautiful Czech/Slovak costumes, had to demonstrate their knowledge of and love for the heritage of their ancestors. In their presentations, they were all sincere and very natural. They obviously believed in what they were saying to the point that some of the older folks had a tear in their eyes. This is certainly one of the best unassuming ways to assure that the children will acquire the love for the roots of their ancestors.

The Matuška Concert on Friday night was a real hit. The tunes he and his wife Olga sang were familiar to most of the audience who frequently joined them in singing. Music seemed to be ever present during the duration of the Conference and the Festival. During dinners and lunches, two noted Slovak singers Jozef and Dodo Ivaška sang a medley of traditional Bohemian, Moravian and Slovak folk songs.

There were some 150 pre-registrants for the Conference but a number of additional attendees registered later at the registration desk. Some of the cultural events drew as many as 300-400 visitors. Even though the nearby beaches attracted a large number of our members, there was always a sizeable audience in most sessions.

We were glad to see so many people from the Czech Republic and Slovakia. Apart from the two Ambassadors, the roster of attendees included DCM from the Slovak Embassy Miroslav Wlachovský, Senator Jaroslava Moserová from Prague, Senator and the former Rector of the Technical University in Ostrava Václav Roubíček, Rector Josef Průša and Past Rector Zdeněk Vostracký of the University of West Bohemia, Vice Rector Vladimír Papoušek and Docent Michael Bauer of the University of South Bohemia, Vice Rector Dalibor Mikuláš of the Catholic University of Ružomberok, Mayor of Ružomberok Hon. Juraj Čech and his Deputy Pavlík. Palacký University in Olomouc was represented by historian Dr. Karel Konečný and the head of the musicology department Dr. Jan Vicar. The Conference was also attended by the Director of the Czech Academy's Institute for Contemporary History Oldřich Tůma and the historian of the Slovak Academy of Sciences Slavomír Michálek. There was also an official representation from the Cs. obec legionářská (Czechoslovak Association of Legionnaires) at the Conference, led by Col. Ing. Jan Horal, who used the occasion to award medals to selected individuals. Also in attendance was Eva Střížovská, Editor-in-Chief of *Český Dialog*, and her assistant. Czech media were also there, including ČTK, the Radio Prague and the Czech TV, who were very busy, recording the proceedings and interviewing the participants.

For the Conference participants relatively inexpensive accommodations were reserved in close-by motels and for those who wanted to extend their stay on the beach, rooms were reserved at an ocean resort.

Overall speaking, it was a grand event. I did not find a single person who did not enjoy it. Above all, everybody had a good time and there was plenty of opportunity to rub shoulders with pretty important people from the Czech and Slovak Republics, as well as from the US. The joint SVU Conference and the ACSCC Festival clearly demonstrated that it is possible to arrange concurrently a high level academic event with cultural and social community activities, to the benefit of both. Those of you who missed this great event will regret that you were not there!

In conclusion, I would like to again express my sincere appreciation to Bob Petrik and Cecilia Rokusek who have really outdone themselves to make the event such a memorable happening. They were also very helpful to me in the preparation of the Conference program.

# 67
# *State of the SVU in 2005*

## Report of SVU President Dr. Miloslav Rechcígl
## Presented to SVU General Assembly Meeting,
## North Miami, Florida, March 18, 2005

Our Bylaws require that the SVU President annually presents a report on the status of the Society to the membership, usually at the General Assembly meeting held in conjunction with our traditional Conferences or World Congresses. This year's report[1044] will necessarily be shorter than others because we have hardly completed the third quarter of our two-year administrative period. I am sure this will be welcome news to most of you who are eager to get ready for our special social occasion this evening.

I would like to start by giving thanks to Robert Petrik and Cecilia Rokusek and the American Czech-Slovak Cultural Club for hosting this Conference. They have worked very hard and you can see the fruits of their labor all around you.

As has been our practice, the first thing the newly elected Executive Board did, was to acquaint the new Board members with our *modus operandi* and collectively decided about the division of labor of individual Board members. We went over the Society's Mission Statement, reexamined the SVU priorities, worked out strategy and outlined individual tasks. Most of our priority areas remain the same as before, including the Accent on Youth, fostering cooperation with cultural institutions in the Czech and Slovak Republics, helping to rebuild the civil society in the Czech and Slovak Republics and making concerted efforts toward the preservation of our heritage abroad. In addition, we are in the process of developing our program with the goal of publishing more English titles in Czech and Slovak history, literature, the arts and culture. Obviously most of these projects are still in *statu nascendi*.

---

[1044] *Zprávy SVU*, vol. 47, No. 4 (July-August 2005), pp. 10-12.

The two most important immediate tasks were to find a suitable location for our 2005 Conference and 2006 World Congress. The first task was actually much more difficult than the second one because no one had any ideas where to start and none of our Local Chapters volunteered to host the Conference. It was by happenstance and through my acquaintance and friendship with Robert Petrik, whom I frequently saw at various functions at the Czech or Slovak Embassies, that we struck on the idea of combining forces and holding our Conference jointly with the American Czech-Slovak Cultural Club, of which he was an officer. This was a brilliant idea as the present versatile and stimulating academic program and highly enjoyable socio-cultural events clearly demonstrate. Frankly, we were amazed at the interest the Conference generated, here as well as abroad, and are thrilled by the caliber of people attending.

As for the location for the SVU 2006 World Congress we had an excellent candidate from the start. The University of South Bohemia, which is represented here by their Vice Rector Prof. Vladimír Papoušek and Dr. Michael Bauer, actually came to us with the proposition of holding the Congress on their campus. Based on their plan, the SVU Executive Board accepted their proposal to hold the next SVU World Congress in České Budějovice 25 June – 1 July 2006.[1045]

SVU has always considered publishing as its highest imperative, which is reflected in its very active publication program. In 2004 alone, the Society published, through the courtesy of the University of West Bohemia in Plzeň, the Palacký University in Olomouc and the Prague Editions Ltd., six new monographs, i.e., two collections of Czech papers and one collection of English papers from the SVU World Congress in Plzeň,[1046] a monograph on *Czech-American Historic Sites, Monuments, and Memorials*[1047] and a two-volume set on *Czechoslovak American*

---

[1045] "2006 SVU World Congress Featuring "Czech and Slovak Culture in International Context," *Zprávy SVU*, vol. 46, No. 6 (November-December 2004), p. 19; "2006 SVU World Congress. University of South Bohemia, České Budějovice, Czech Republic, 25 June – 2 July 2006...," *Ibid.*, vol. 47, No. 4 (July-August 2005), pp. 13-17.

[1046] "English Papers from the Plzeň SVU Congress Are Now Available for Sale," *Zprávy SVU*, vol. 47, No. 2 (March-April 2005), p. 24.

[1047] Miloslav Rechcígl, Jr. *Czech-American Historic Sites, Monuments, and Memorabilia* Olomouc-Ostrava: Centrum pro československá studia při Katedře historie Filozofické fakulty Univerzity Palackého v Olomouci, 2004. 142 p.

*Archivalia*[1048]; and the *Proceedings of the Working Conference on Czech and Slovak American Archival Materials and their Preservation*,[1049] respectively. The long awaited *SVU Biographical Directory,* comprised of some 3,000 biographical entries of members, listing addresses, telephone numbers and e-mails is now available in the US for purchase.

As was announced in our newsletter, Selected Papers from the 2003 SVU Iowa Conference have been posted on our SVU Website.[1050] This is our first attempt at electronic publishing, which saves the Society high publication costs and the inherent problems with distribution and storage.

I am pleased to report, that we have also recently completed editing the Proceedings of the SVU 2004 World Congress, in Olomouc, which will soon be published, through the courtesy of the Philosophical Faculty of the Palacký University.[1051] Two additional monographs, one on *Czech and Slovak Theatre Abroad* and the second on *Czech Opera Abroad*, edited by Věra Bořkovec and Dagmar White, respectively, are in preparation. SVU also cosponsored Jan Vičar's monograph *Imprints: Essays on Czech Music and Aesthetics*[1052] and co-produced Video Cassette and DVD, highlighting proceedings and depicting memorable events of the 22nd SVU World Congress. which are available at this Conference.[1053]

---

[1048] Miloslav Rechcígl, Jr. *Czechoslovak American Archivalia.* Vol. 1. Government Repositories, University-based Collections, Collections Maintained by Public Museums and Libraries, Collections of Ethnic and Other Related Organizations; Vol. 2. Personal Papers and Collections, Repositories Abroad Bearing on the Subject, Virtual Archives on the Internet. Appendixes (Olomouc-Ostrava: Centrum pro československá studia při Katedře historie Filozofické fakulty Univerzity Palackého v Olomouci, 2004. 206 p. & 368 p.

[1049] Czech and Slovak American Archival Materials and their Preservation. Proceedings of the Working Conference held at the Czech and Slovak Embassies in Washington, DC on November 22-23, 2003. Edited by Miloslav Rechcígl, Jr., President, SVU. Prague, Prague Editions, 2004. 168 p.

[1050] "SVU Enters the Electronic Publishing Age," *Zprávy SVU, vol.* 47, No. 1 (January-February 2005), pp. 20-24.

[1051] "Publishing Papers from the Olomouc SVU Congress," *Zprávy SVU*, vol. 46, No. 5 (November-December 2004), p. 10.

[1052] Jan Vičar, *Imprints: Essays on Czech Music and Aesthetics.* Prague: Togga and Olomouc: Palacký University, 2005. 270 p.

[1053] *22nd SVU World Congress, Palacký University, Olomouc, June 26-July 4, 2004. Video Cassette and DVD.* A 40-minute documentary vividly highlighting proceedings and depicting memorable events of the Congress.

The Society has also systematically pursued its efforts toward the preservation of Czech and Slovak Heritage abroad, of which the present Florida Conference is a formidable example. Prior to this Conference, we convened, jointly with the Czech and Slovak Embassies in Washington, a special Working Archival Conference,[1054] which was prompted by our genuine concern for the deplorable state and the uncertain fate of Czech and Slovak archival materials in America, many of which are in danger of being destroyed or lost.[1055] As a result of that Conference, the SVU, jointly with other organizations, launched a concerted effort aiming at the preservation of the Czech and Slovak documentary and other archival materials in America for the future. Toward this end, we have established a Consortium, comprised of the major archival institutions and other interested organizations, to provide a platform and forum for communication and discussion of issues among the Consortium members and to establish working linkages and encourage cooperation among the archival institutions, To keep the public informed and to provide an effective means for contact and communication, the SVU created a special Web page for the use by the Consortium members, as part of the SVU Website.[1056]

Among specific recommendations, the referenced Archival Conference stressed was the dire need to financially assist archival institutions with cataloguing and other functions to make the archives accessible for use by scholars. Inasmuch as our Society deposited its archival materials at the renown Immigration History Research Center (IHRC) at the University of Minnesota, the SVU Executive Board decided to establish at that Center a special Czech and Slovak Archival Study Fund to assist scholars and students to come to the Center and study the materials. The Fund[1057] will officially be established at the special Presidential Plenary Session at this Conference, with the participation of the Czech and Slovak Ambassadors, the Director of the IHRC Center and the SVU

---

[1054] "Working Conference on Czech and Slovak American Archival Materials, Washington, DC, 22-23 November 2003...," *Zprávy SVU*, vol. 45, No. 5 (September-October 2003), pp. 17-18; *Ibid.*, vol. 45, No. 6 (November-December 2003), pp. 20-21.

[1055] Miloslav Rechcígl, "Preserving Czech and Slovak American Archival Material," *Kosmas* 17, No. 2 (Spring 2004), pp. 95-96.

[1056] "SVU Hosts Archival Consortium Webpage," *Zprávy SVU,* vol. 46, No. 4 (July-August 2004), p. 24.

[1057] "SVU Establishes a Special Studies Fund," *Zprávy* SVU, vol. 47, No. 3 (May-June 2005), pp. 21-22.

President. We are hoping that the SVU donation will attract other Czech and Slovak organizations to contribute to this important endeavor.

Among other ongoing efforts, I would like to compliment our agile Lois Herman for keeping us current on various activities striving to improve the status of women worldwide.[1058] Please have a look at her postings on the SVU Website.

Organizationally speaking, SVU is in the process of revitalizing some of its dormant Local Chapters and in creating new ones. Among other, it is hoped that the highly successful present Conference here in North Miami will give the impetus for establishing a new SVU Chapter in Florida.

In conclusion, I am pleased to state that SVU finances are in the black and that we have been operating with a balanced budget. We are indebted to our Treasurer Frank Mucha for doing an excellent job. Overall speaking, the prestige of our Society could not be better and the same is true about its visibility, the latter being due, in part, to our highly effective SVU Website, diligently maintained by SVU Webmaster Jiří Eichler.[1059]

.........

The above report was presented to the SVU General Assembly meeting in North Miami on March 18, 2005. There were also individual reports of SVU Local chapters, including Washington DC, Pittsburgh, New York, Nebraska, Chicago, Texas and Iowa. Karel Konečný of Palacký University reported that they were in process of establishing a new Chapter in Olomouc. The Treasurer's Report came next, which showed that the Society managed its fiscal affairs on a balanced budget and its finances were in the black. Vladimír Papoušek, Vice Rector of the University of South Bohemia in České Budějovice, followed with a brief report on the preparation of the next SVU World Congress to be held on their University campus in June 2006. The Resolution Committee, which was busy, in the meantime, drafting the Resolution,

---

[1058] "SVU Women's Issues Program Celebrates Second Anniversary," *Zprávy SVU*, vol. 47, No. 2 (March-April 2005), pp. 22-23.

[1059] "Four Years of the SVU Website," *Zprávy SVU*, vol. 48, No. 4 (July-August 2006), pp. 26-27.

completed its task. The Resolution was unanimously approved and its text can be found in January 2006 *Zprávy SVU*.[1060]

---

[1060] "Czech and Slovak Heritage on Both Sides of the Atlantic. Resolution...," *Zprávy SVU*, vol. 48, No. 1 (January-February 2006), p. 11.

# 68
## *Organizing the 2006 SVU World Congress*

It was as early as the 2003 SVU Conference in Cedar Rapids when I was first approached about the idea of holding a future SVU World Congress in České Budějovice in South Bohemia. Vladimír Papoušek[1061] and Michal Bauer,[1062] who were attending the Conference, proposed that we consider holding the 2004 SVU World Congress at the University of South Bohemia at České Budějovice, with which they were associated. Inasmuch as we had already picked Palacký University at Olomouc for the site of the next Congress in 2004, they asked me to consider their University for the subsequent Congress, to be held in 2006. I told them that we would certainly consider the idea and asked them to make sure to attend the next year's Congress in Olomouc, to see what is involved and how such Congress is organized.

They came indeed and during the meetings they assured me that they would not have any difficulties in organizing a comparable Congress in České Budějovice. Their Rector, who was originally supposed to attend the 2004 Congress, could not come. I asked them to send us an official letter of invitation, signed by the Rector, stating their University's willingness to host the Congress so that I could present it to our newly elected SVU Executive Board for action. Simultaneously, I requested a similar letter from the Mayor of the City of České Budějovice.

Upon my return from Olomouc to the US, I reminded Papoušek of the urgency of sending me the invitation letter since our Board was to meet on August 14. Furthermore, I reminded them of our discussion concerning the conditions under which we would consider having the next congress at their University. The conditions, which were patterned on our previous agreements with the officials of Palacký University in Olomouc, included the following points:

---

[1061] Professor of Bohemistics and Vice Rector for International Relations at the University of South Bohemia in České Budějovice.

[1062] Docent Michal Bauer taught Bohemistics at the University of South Bohemia.

1. University would furnish lecture rooms free of charge;
2. University would provide the audio-visual and other technical equipment gratis, including the servicing of the equipment;
3. University would provide students' assistance free of charge;
4. University would arrange for publishing special daily newsletter during the duration of the Congress;
5. University would arrange for printing of the Congress Program and the Abstracts;
6. University would take responsibility for preparing the cultural program, as well as for the social events. Half of the costs for these activities will be covered by the University and the other half by the Congress participants;
7. University accepts the SVU President's offer of one-shot financial contribution by SVU towards the Congress expenses – in the amount of $10,000. The University (together with its sponsors) will cover the rest of the expenses;
8. University will provide a concrete offer on the availability of accommodations at the University dorms and local hotels at lower rates for the Congress participants;
9. University will provide transportation from and to Prague-Ruzyne airport, to be paid by the Congress participants;
10. University will organize one or two bus excursions through the countryside on the second Saturday and Sunday, following the conclusion of academic program.

A few days before the Board meeting came the following letter, written in a typical non-idiomatic "Czenglish,"[1063] from Prof. Václav Bůžek, Rector of the University of South Bohemia.

*University of South Bohemia České Budějovice Rectorate*
Branišovská 31, 370 05 České Budějovice
Phone: +420 387 772 030, Fax: +420 385 3 10 373

---

[1063] Czenglish, a portmanteau of the words Czech and English, is any poor or 'broken' English spoken by native Czech speakers.

Miloslav Rechcígl
SVU President
Czechoslovak Society of Arts and Sciences
1703 Mark Lane
Rockville
MD 20852-4106
USA

České Budějovice, July 12, 2004

Dear Mr. Rechcígl,

I would like to take this opportunity to present you, the main authority of the Czechoslovak Society of Arts and Sciences, our suggestion. We would be very pleased and it would be a great honour to us to host the World Congress of SVU at our University.

The University of South Bohemia České Budějovice was established in 1991, when two previously unrelated institutions, College of Education, and the Faculty of Agronomy. Agricultural University. Prague combined to form its backbone and three other faculties were created to join them.

Although we do not have a long time tradition of the university education. the history of the present Pedagogical Faculty thus dates back to 1948, and that of the Faculty of Agriculture to 1960. We have a lot of successful departments, well respected in the Czech Republic as well as in the world. The University has about 7,500 students.

We would like to assure you the University has both technical facilities and personnel to organize the event of such importance. The University campus is near the historical center. The town of České Budějovice is originated in 1265. The visitors have a possibility to visit the town of Česky Krumlov, protected by the UNESCO, to see the Hluboka Chateau or visit the beautiful nature of Sumava Mountains. We believe the congress participants would find here a friendly and inspiring environment.

You are sincerely welcome to visit the University of South Bohemia. We are ready to present our facilities and background to you before you make the final decision. We would like to assure you we would endeavour to fulfill your expectations.

Looking forward to receiving your reply.

Yours sincerely,

*Prof. PhDr. Václav Bužek, CSc., Rector*

I responded affirmatively, stating that we are indeed very much interested in having our Congress at their University, pending the receipt of more detailed information concerning the logistics and local arrangements.[1064] Simultaneously, I wrote to Doc. Michal Bauer requesting additional information in order that the Executive Board could make a decision regarding their proposal. Specifically, I asked him to provide information on these points:

1. Submit the name of the University's coordinator to be responsible for logistics, local arrangements and for the organization of social and cultural events;
2. Submit the name of the University coordinator to be responsible for academic program;
3. Suggested dates for the Congress and the overall schedule of major events;
4. Availability of lecture rooms and a large hall for the opening of the Congress;
5. Availability of accommodations in the University dorms and local hotels;
6. Suggested general theme for the Congress;
7. Proposed social and cultural program;
8. Proposed excursion bus tours through the South Bohemian landscape.

---

[1064] "From the First Executive Board Meeting," *Zprávy SVU*. Vol. 46, No. 5 (September-October 2004), pp. 15-17.

After several urgent reminders, I finally received a substantial response from Vice Rector Papoušek, containing the following information:

1. Jana Zbíralová, who works in the Rectorate for me, will be responsible for logistics;
2. I will assume responsibility for the coordination of the academic program. We expect about 20-30 sections;
3. I recommend the last week of June 2006 as the dates for the Congress;
4. Less expensive accommodations will be provided for the Czech participants and for interested people from abroad in University dorms. Hotel accommodations will be provided in city hotels;
5. Lecture rooms will be provided on the University campus. The University shares buildings and space with the Czech Academy of Sciences which will participate with us in the congress preparation;
6. General theme of the Congress is "Czech Culture and Science in International Context;"
7. For cultural program, we are preparing a theatrical production and concert in the South Bohemian Theatre;
8. For bus excursion we are preparing trips to Hluboká and Český Krumlov and a guided tour of the Budvar brewery;
9. We will organize the main banquet on Friday. Besides that the City and other sponsors will finance social-get together on the first Saturday and a festive buffet on Monday.

The Executive Board[1065] was generally pleased with the overall plans but would have liked to have more details. I sent several e-mails about this to Docent Michal Bauer, as well as to Vice Rector Papoušek, but did not get response. I also wrote to them with the request for more general information about the Congress, and about the University, which I needed for my lead article in the next issue of the SVU newsletter.

---

[1065] "From Executive Board," *Zprávy SVU*, vol. 46, No. 6 (November-December 2004), pp. 5-8.

Since the information did not arrive by our deadline, I had to improvise and write an article of my own.

As the year 2004 was coming to an end and the new year 2005 was approaching, I had to refocus my energies and start working on he program for the upcoming SVU Conference, scheduled for May 2005 in Florida. For practical purposes, I had to postpone any further work on the Congress preparations, until after the Conference. Both Papoušek and Bauer attended the Florida Conference but I was too busy to be able to discuss with them, in detail, what progress they had made so far. Nevertheless, during our brief conversation, they assured me that everything was under control and not to worry. They sounded very optimistic, if not out right enthusiastic.

As it turned out, I did not hear from the University of South Bohemia until mid summer 2005, when, on August 18, I received an e-mail message from Jana Zbíralová, apologizing for not responding to my e-mails and giving as an explanation the fact that the University was closed for summer and that she herself had no access to Vice Rector's e-mail box. I re-sent her my previous e-mail messages which she promptly answered and in considerable detail. Since then I exclusively corresponded with her regarding various issues relating to our Congress. We exchanged quite a few e-mails regarding accommodations, both in the University dorms and the local hotels. One thing that confused the picture was the fact that the largest hotel in the city, Hotel Gomel, was booked by the New York-based Tatra Travel, in the hope that our Congress participants would opt to stay there. Consequently, the hotel representatives refused to negotiate special rates for us. As I mentioned to Mrs. Zbíralová, we found the Tatra Travel hotel offer too high and gave preference for the University dorms and smaller hotels with which the University had arrangements.

By this time, we were finally able to publish a joint announcement with Prof. Papoušek in our newsletter *Zprávy SVU*.[1066]

Although we were initially under the assumption that the Congress would take place on the University campus, Zbíralová, all of a sudden, wrote to us that the University, which is not centrally located, is considering holding the Congress in the center of the City, in a newly built cultural conference center "Bazilika," which would presumably allow

---

[1066] *Zprávy SVU*, vol. 47, No. 5 (September-October 2005), pp. 1-5.

having all Congress lectures under one roof. Since it was more than 20 minutes by trolley from the University campus, it would have been impractical for the Congress participants to eat at the University cafeteria. We thus had a choice of either having our meals individually in one of the smaller restaurants in the City or in the Hotel Gomel, as a group, which could seat as many as 200 visitors in one sitting. Frankly, I did not like this arrangement because it would probably be quite costly and impractical. If we had taken our meals individually, it would have also cost us precious time and we would lose the needed audience in the Congress lecture room. Regarding accommodations, since the Hotel Gomel was not a consideration, Zbíralová came with the suggestion of having our people stay in the newly constructed Hotel Uran, which was apparently willing to give us special rates.

It was early in September when I received notifications from both the Office of the Czech President, and that of the Slovak President, informing us that President Klaus and President Gasparovič, respectively, agreed to sponsor our Congress. This was great news as it would enhance the visibility of the Congress.

By this time, Blanka Kuděj, who has served as SVU Secretary-General, and who also held the position of Congress Treasurer, complied with my request to serve as treasurer of the forthcoming Congress and take on the responsibility for the registration process. I therefore requested Zbíralová to send any future correspondence to her as well. As per Executive Board decision, "all participants from America and the Western countries, including the foreigners and the Czech and Slovak ex-patriots from abroad, irrespective of where they lived, would be required to register with Blanka Kuděj and pay the designated registration fee." I also told her that we anticipated difficulties from the participants from Western Europe, especially from Switzerland, Germany, Austria and England, who, in the past, did not want to pay our registration fee which was higher than what the participants from the Czech Republic were charged.[1067] They preferred to register with the University directly because under those conditions they would pay less. This was against

---

[1067] My anticipations, unfortunately, turned out to be correct in case of the present Congress and we actually lost several panels on account of this when the Austrians and Germans refused to pay our registration fee.

our policy. We wanted the Western European participants to pay the same registration fee as we charged the US and Canadian participants.

It took me a while to convince Mrs. Zbíralová to accept our policy to register our members from the US and from abroad by ourselves, and also collect monies from them beforehand. With reference to our registration fee for the overseas participants, since the University previously agreed to accept our offer to receive from SVU a one-shot contribution of $10,000 toward Congress expenses, the question of what we would charge our overseas members was strictly our own affair. They initially planned to post their Czech-written registration form on their website and let our people fill it out and have them send their money directly to České Budějovice. Based on our experience, we knew that hardly any of the potential Congress participants would bother searching for their website and those who did, would, as a rule, have all sorts of questions which had to be answered. I finally convinced them that this would not work, not to speak of the language problem. I must have exchanged tens of e-mail messages back and forth, to get this point settled.

Since there were still a number of issues unresolved and since I also felt I should have a look by myself at the physical layout of the University and the City of České Budějovice, and check on the available accommodations, the food places, lecture halls, and logistics, I began thinking about visiting České Budějovice as soon as it was practicable. To be sure, I had a standing invitation from Vice Rector Papoušek to visit them. After exchanging a few e-mails, we decided to set my visit for the latter part of October 2005. My plan was to leave Washington on Wednesday, October 23, arrive in Prague early on Thursday and then travel to České Budějovice, stay over night there and go back on Friday night.[1068]

As per my arrangement with Jana Zbíralová, I was picked up by the University car at the Prague Ruzyně airport in the early hours on Thursday and then immediately taken to České Budějovice. Vice Rector Papoušek came along with the University driver which gave me the opportunity to discuss with him the details of my visit and to learn the latest news about their plans. We drove fast so that by 10 o'clock we were already on the University campus. I quickly put my things in my

---

[1068] "SVU President's Sojourn in Czech Republic and Slovakia," *Zprávy SVU,* vol. 48, No. 1 (January-February 2006), pp. 8-10.

reserved room at the University hostel "Bobik" and hurried back to meet with Vice Rector Papoušek who then took me to see the University Rector Prof. PhDr. Václav Bužek. I acquainted him with the aims and history of SVU and our plans for the World Congress next year. He was supportive of the effort and promised to make the University resources available to us.

Subsequently, we met with Jana Zbíralová who worked in the Rector's office and was apparently Papoušek's "Girl Friday," a very capable young woman, who seemed to handle all the logistical problems with ease. We were joined by Ing. František Vrtiška, director of the University dorms and cafeterias who outlined various options regarding the available accommodations and the food services at the time of our Congress. He then took us around to show us various dorms (K1, K2, K3 and K4) on the campus, including the Hostel "Bobík," as well as their new "hotel" facility "Uran" located in the center of the City.

After lunch I had a scheduled meeting with Mgr. Juraj Thoma, deputy mayor of the Statutory City České Budějovice, whom I informed about the upcoming Congress of our Society and also briefed him about SVU. He seemed quite impressed and looked, with great interest, through our *Biographical SVU Directory* which I gave him. The upshot of our discussion was his promise to provide the City's support to our Congress to make it a truly memorable event in České Budějovice and indicated that he would talk to the Mayor about it.

Later that afternoon, I met with Michal Bauer who was charged with the responsibility to organize the Czech panels for the academic program. To my surprise, he had actually done quite a bit in terms of number of panels planned. However, I did not actually see the make up of individual panels. I gave him several suggestions for additional panels in areas that were missing from the program, such as music, arts, etc. Afterwards, Bauer took me around and showed me the memorable sites of the City. Before going to bed that night, I stayed up for several hours to go over the material we discussed during the day, particularly with reference to accommodations and the food services available to the Congress participants and drafted a number of questions to be clarified the following day.

On Friday, the University chauffeur drove Papoušek and me to see the hotel "U tří lvů" which offered SVU a special deal, and then we proceeded toward the newly constructed City Cultural Center, named "Bazilika," located on the first floor of the modern IGY Centre complex. The organizers planned to use the Bazilika for the opening of the SVU Congress and perhaps for other meetings, if suitable sponsors could be found to cover the costs which were quite high. We met with the Bazilika manager Eva Čepičková who took us around and showed us the beautiful auditorium and the adjacent rooms where the "rout" could be held, as well as the meeting and exhibit rooms. It all looked very modern and quite luxurious and they were obviously anxious to have us as the "first tenants." Afterwards, I sat down with Papoušek and Zbíralová to discuss various options available to us and then proceeded to have a look at one more hotel, "Atlas."

The last item on our busy schedule was a meeting in Papoušek's office with the representatives of the Biological Centre of the Academy of Sciences of the Czech Republic, located next to the University "campus." Besides us two, the meeting was attended by Prof. RNDr. Zdeněk Brandl, CSc, Vice Rector for Academic Affairs, Prof. RNDr. Libor Grubhoffer, CSc., Dean of the Biological Faculty and Doc. RNDr. Jan Šula, CSc., Director of Entomology Institute of the Academy. It was a very productive meeting, the result of which was their commitment to actively participate in our Congress and to organize a number of scientific panels. They recommended that all the panels be in English with which I had no qualms whatsoever.

The two days I spent in České Budějovice were quite hectic. I found the visit extremely useful since it clarified a number of points for me and corrected some wrong assumptions I had. Having seen the available facilities and the physical layout of various sites and having learned about the costs involved, I came to several conclusions that differed considerably from my previous ideas:

1. The Congress should take place on the University campus which had all the needed resources.
2. The Congress participants should stay, as much as possible, in the University dorms which were quite nice, relatively inexpensive and located directly on the campus. Those members who would prefer to stay in a hotel, should use one of the three hotels with which the University negotiated special rates.

3. The participants should have their meals at the University cafeteria which was in the vicinity of the dorms. Apart from the convenience, the cafeteria prices of the meals were reasonable.
4. The Congress opening could be held in the "Bazilika," if the University would find a suitable sponsor, otherwise it should be held at the University auditorium on the campus. Should the Bazilika be chosen, the University would have to arrange for transportation.

After my return to the US, Mrs. Zbíralová informed me via e-mail that Vice Rector Papoušek, based on our discussions, essentially accepted all my recommendations. They would use the Conference center Bazilika just on Monday. June 26, for the opening of the Congress and Friday afternoon, June 30, for the concluding plenary session and the concluding banquet. This would provide a beautiful setting for the opening and large capacity to host all Congress participants and invited guests. The regular academic program, consisting of various panels, symposia and workshops, would be held on the University premises and space shared with the Czech Academy of Sciences. The main Academy hall, which would accommodate as many as 200 people, would be used for larger sessions.

There were still some remaining issues concerning the scheduling of the major events of the Congress which prevented us from posting this information on SVU Website. The major point of contention was the scheduling of the Monday gala lunch ("rout"), which they planned for the midst of the afternoon, some two hours after the conclusion of the official opening of the Congress. This was not acceptable to us since we feared that we would lose many of our visitors, particularly VIPs. Furthermore, they had reserved only two hours for our plenary session that afternoon which was insufficient for the program we planned. It took me several e-mails back and forth to clear this up, including a letter to Vice Rector Papoušek who was my last resort.

I was finally able to complete our registration form, which was posted on SVU Website, together with an update of the Congress preparation. Frankly, only then, could we start the registration in earnest. I was glad when in January we received a letter from the Slovak Academy of Sciences, informing us of their decision to co-organize the Congress with us, along the lines of the Academy of Sciences of the Czech Republic, as per my earlier agreement with the Czech Academy President Václav Pačes.

As this was going on, we simultaneously began working on our academic program. Although our entire Executive Board initially comprised our American program committee, I found it impractical and unwieldy. Consequently I established instead a four-member group, consisting of Zdeněk David, Karel Raška, Dagmar White and myself, to which I later added Cecilia Rokusek. The group was quite useful in terms of bouncing various ideas around, but in terms of performance, only a few concrete suggestions led to the establishment of the actual panels. As for myself, starting sometimes in December, I spent most of my time in front of my computer, sending out invitation letters and answering e-mails to persuade individuals to participate. I'd say that I must have sent out, on average, at least 10-20 invitation letters daily. To get the potential speakers interested I had to constantly think of some new attractive panels and symposia in which they could participate and be the center of attention. Obviously, I tried to find additional panel organizers but, for the most part, I was on my own.

Everything seemed to move smoothly from that point on until the receipt of an alarming letter from Jana Zbíralová, dated February 2, 2007, in which she informed us, as per their Questor's[1069] decision, that the University will levy on all our events a special tax at the level of 19%. This created quite an uproar in our Executive Board, because this was not in our earlier agreement and, furthermore, it was too late, since the prices of individual activities had been publicized both in our newsletter and on the SVU Website and a number of our members had already registered. To now go back to the members, demanding more money from them would be unthinkable. I protested immediately but since no answer came back, I decided to send Papoušek, in the name of SVU Executive Board, a strongly phrased letter, which is reproduced below:

Dear Vladimír:

On the instructions of the SVU Executive Board, I wish to inform you that the Society has put all the organizational work relating to

---

[1069] University Treasurer.

the planned 2006 SVU World Congress, including the publicity, preparation of the English panel program and invitation of potential participants, on hold, pending the satisfactory resolution of the apparent crisis which has been precipitated by today's official communication from your University. The Board finds the notion of taxing our non-profit organization, which makes a concerted effort to enhance the image of the Czech Republic abroad, particularly in the cultural area, outrageous and the additional University demands, which go beyond our original agreement, unacceptable.

The University should bear in mind that this matter may negatively impact not only on the reputation of SVU but also on the image of the University of South Bohemia worldwide. Furthermore, the ill-advised University action may also seriously affect the relations between the United States and the Czech Republic.

It would therefore be in the best interest of the University to get this matter satisfactorily resolved as soon as possible.

Sincerely yours,

*Míla Rechcígl*
SVU President

cc. H.E. Ambassador of the Czech Republic to the United States.

The letter was quite effective because in a matter of hours I had a response from Papoušek informing me that, in his capacity as Vice Rector, he overruled the University Questor and that no additional tax would be charged. Furthermore, he assured me that from now on the University will honor all our previous agreements.

I should mention that I had sent, some time ago, a special letter of invitation to President Klaus, as I did to President Gasparovič, to attend our Congress and take part in the official opening. After several reminder notices, I received a notification from the Prague Castle that President Klaus agreed to come to our Congress and give a talk at the official opening. This was, of course, great news, which I immediately transmitted to České Budějovice. Papoušek and his colleagues were thrilled with the news, since President Klaus had not as yet visited their campus, not to speak of the City of České Budějovice.

My work on organizing the panels was progressing very well so that, by April 11, I was able to send a draft listing of the English papers, arranged by panels, to Vice Rector Papoušek who was quite impressed by the variety of papers distributed in some 40 panels. Apart from specific panels, organized by discipline or subject, I organized a Plenary Session on "Diplomatic Relations between the North America and Czech & Slovak Republics," with the participation of at least five Ambassadors. There was also a special Presidential Symposium on "University Leadership on Both Sides of the Atlantic," with the participation of university Presidents, Rectors, Provosts, and other high-level university representatives from the US and the Czech and Slovak Republics, and a discussion panel on the "University Partnerships and Cooperation between the US and the Czech and Slovak Republics" and much more.

In addition to organizing the panels, I also assumed the responsibility for collecting the abstracts from individual authors and for editing them and, in some cases, for translating them into English. This task was completed by May 2, when I also sent the corrected Abstracts, together with the final program, to České Budějovice for printing.

In connection with my work on the panels, one curious incident is worth mentioning. It was early in March when I received an urgent e-mail letter from Prof. Awah Njume William of the Cameroon Universities Arts and Cultural Union with an abstract from the delegates of this Union. It appeared that the eight students, listed on the abstract, planned to personally participate in the Congress. It looked odd but, after consulting with my colleagues, I took it seriously. They subsequently submitted their registration form but without money. When I pressed them on the point, they assured me that they would deposit the money in our bank account if we would give them the SVU account number. Our Treasurer got suspicious at that point and decided to set up a separate account for them. Soon after, I received a request from Prof. Njume to provide an affidavit for their participants, signed by me, certifying that they have no criminal record so that they could apply for the Czech visa. Obviously, I was not willing to do that because I did not know any of them personally. It seems that these Cameroonians wanted to get to the Czech Republic and stay there and used our Congress as a pretense to enter the country.

*Organizing the 2006 SVU World Congress* 421

With the completion of the academic program, you would think that my responsibilities were over. Well think again and have a look at the reminder list of various chores that I still had to do. The list bears the date of April 23, 2006.

1. Prepare 3rd issue of *Zprávy SVU* devoted to SVU Congress
2. Write Preface for Congress Program
3. Assure that Election Ballots are sent to SVU membership by Secretary-General
4. Write "State of SVU in the Year 2006 Report."
5. Prepare agenda for the Ceremonial Opening of the Congress.
6. Prepare my Opening Remarks at the Official Opening of the Congress
7. Prepare agenda for SVU General Assembly meeting
8. Assure that SVU congress Resolution is drafted
9. Prepare agenda for the Concluding Plenary session and for the Award Ceremony.
10. Make changes in the June 25 Sunday program, taking into account that most people won't be arriving before 1 PM.
11. Check with J. Eichler whether the CD containing our revised SVU Directory will be ready for the Congress.
12. Arrange for meeting between Raška, Mucha and myself in lieu of Executive board meeting that had to be cancelled because of the lack of quorum.
13. Make arrangements for Book Presentation at the Congress.
14. Contact Z. Vich regarding counting of the election ballots
15. Make last changes in the Congress program
16. Finalize Panel on the Experiences and the Role of CZ and SL diplomats abroad
17. Check on missing abstracts and contact the speakers who have not submitted them
18. Edit and correct abstracts and get them ready for the printer

19. Finalize the Major Events during Congress and contact V. Papoušek
20. Appoint Chairs of panels, as needed
21. Get the Minutes of the last General Assembly meeting
22. Schedule panels to assure there are no conflicts
23. Send final program to Papoušek for printing
24. Get Presidential Citations ready
25. Contact Local chapters regarding submission of their Annual Reports
26. Resolve the question of the participation of Cameroon students
27. Check with Mucha on Auditor's Report
28. Send reminder notices to speakers who have not yet pre-registered with Blanka Kuděj
29. Prepare instructions for Panel Chairs
30. Check with Matajs on audiovisual equipment at the University lecture rooms.
31. Contact Procházková regarding her award and ascertain her presence

As I was working on the agenda for the program for the Official Opening of the Congress, based on our previous experience, I planned to start the Congress with the welcome by the University Rector, followed by the greetings of the Lord Mayor of the City and the Governor of the Region. Afterwards I planned to officially open the Congress, followed by greetings of selected VIPs. The last item was to be the keynote address by President Václav Klaus. When I sent the draft program of the Official Opening to Vice Rector Papoušek, I received an unexpected response. He informed me that President Klaus was planning to stay only an hour during the Official Opening of the Congress, since he had other activities planned for him by the Regional Governor, and consequently that he would have to be put on the program as the first speaker, following the welcoming talk by the University Rector and the Governor of the Region. At the conclusion of the President's speech, there would be a break, during which the President and his entourage would leave. I was to open the Congress in the second part of the program.

Frankly, this made us all, not only frustrated, but outright mad, because with such an arrangement, the President would not take part in our Congress at all, considering that the latter would officially start only after his departure. This was unacceptable to us and I made it known, in no uncertain terms, to the University and the Governor's Office, as well as to the Office of the President. What made us also furious was the fact that it was actually SVU which arranged for President Klaus to come to České Budějovice to attend the Congress, which was conveniently forgotten, and now the Regional Governor et al. wanted to take over. They apparently, presumably with the University knowledge, had everything planned beforehand in minute detail, behind our backs. A "one-upmanship" of the worst kind! I told them that we would not stand for this and insisted, as a compromise, to have me open the Congress first, followed by Rector's and Governor's welcome and then have the President talk. Not to belabor the point, after several fiery phone calls, they finally accepted my proposition. The rest is history.

# 69
## SVU Scores a "Home Run" in České Budějovice[1070]

SVU Congresses and Conferences of late have been remarkably successful. The just completed 23rd SVU World Congress, held in the South Bohemian Metropolis České Budějovice, has not been an exception. While the Czech soccer team did not perform as well this year in the World Cup as expected, one can say, without any reservation, that the SVU Congress was a real hit, and, in fact, "scoring a home run."

The University of South Bohemia, which hosted the Congress, provided visitors from all over the world a truly warm welcome. The warmth of the welcome was also reflected in the temperature which exceeded 33 degrees Celsius, making it one of the hottest seasons in the city's and region's history. Fortunately, there was a gentle breeze which made it agreeable in the shade to some, or even pleasant to others. In the evening, and in the subsequent days, the temperature dropped down significantly, partly due to minor and intermittent showers, so that the lack of air conditioning in the city was not a problem.

The Congress, as a whole, was a remarkable event, both in terms of its contents, a plethora and variety of topics and high quality of individual papers. There was a general consensus that this was the best Congress SVU ever staged.

Although a few of us already arrived on Saturday, June 24, the majority of overseas attendees began arriving on Sunday in the early afternoon. Most of them came directly from the Prague-Ruzyně airport in one of the buses provided by the University. The buses brought them to the University campus, in the vicinity of the University Hostel "Bobík," where the registration desk was located, which enabled participants to register immediately upon their arrival. The registration went smoothly because most of the oversees participants were already pre-

---

[1070] Originally published in *Zprávy SVU*, vol. 48, No. 4 (July-August 2006), pp. 1-7.

## SVU Scores a "Home Run" in České Budějovice

registered in the US, thanks to the efficient work of Blanka Kuděj and her husband Svaťa.

After registration, the Congress participants moved their bags to their rooms in one of the University dorms which were conveniently located next to the Hostel "Bobík." Having done so, most of them then hurried to the close-by city bus stop to take part in the guided tour through the historic part of the city. Immediately after the tour, which lasted about three hours, there was a Social-Get-Together which was attended by a large crowd of overseas, as well as local Congress participants. The food was plentiful and the famous local beer "Budvar" enhanced the prevailing joyous atmosphere and exuberant mood.

The long day was crowned with the final event on the famous České Budějovice square, bearing the name of its founder the Bohemian King Přemysl Otakar II. Here our Congress participants were treated to a concert performed by a noted South Bohemian Chamber Philharmonic which performed Carl Orff's "Carmina Burana." It was a fabulous performance by one of the leading orchestras in the Czech Republic. Afterwards, most of us went to bed, but, as I later learned, a sizeable group ended up in one of the local pubs to get more taste of famous Czech brew.

The SVU Congress officially opened on Monday, June 26, with a ceremony held in the recently completed cultural center "Bazilika" in the midst of the City to which the Congress participants were transported by the University buses. The kickoff time was at 10 AM but several of us, who were responsible for the organization and preparation of the Congress, were there earlier so that we could take part in the scheduled press conference. Subsequently, together with Rector Václav Bůžek, I had the pleasure of welcoming President and Mrs. Klaus upon their arrival in front of the building and escorting them to one of the Bazilika's elegant receiving rooms. Here already were assembled a group of Ambassadors from both sides of the Atlantic, together with other VIPs. After a few formalities of small talk, I raised a glass of champagne and toasted the President, and others joined me. He reciprocated, commenting on the importance of the SVU Congress and the role SVU has played on behalf of the Czech Republic.

We were then taken to the head table in the large Bazilika Hall which was already full to the last seat by the Congress participants. The academic procession followed, consisting of University Presidents, Rectors, Provosts and Deans from overseas, as well as from the Czech Republic and Slovakia, dressed in their traditional academic attire, to the tune of Janacek's music. It was a wonderful sight.

In my capacity as SVU President, I then officially opened the Congress,[1071] followed by the welcoming speeches of the University Rector Václav Bůžek[1072] and the Governor of the České Budějovice Region Jan Zahradník.[1073] Afterwards, President Klaus presented a brief address in English.

After a short recess, the ceremony continued with the greetings and short messages from a number of Ambassadors from the US,[1074] Canada and the Czech[1075] and Slovak Republics and other dignitaries, including President of the Czech Learned Society,[1076] Scientific Secretary of the Slovak Academy of Sciences,[1077] Vice President of the Academy of Sciences of the Czech Republic[1078] and the Rector of Charles University.[1079] The whole proceedings were very impressive and, as some people who saw it on TV, commented, "it had majestic look."

As the academic procession left the hall, followed by the audience, the Congress attendees were treated to an enormous "rout," the Czech

---

[1071] "Remarks by SVU President Miloslav Rechcígl at the Opening of SVU World Congress," *Zprávy SVU*, vol. 48, No. 4 (July-August 2006), pp. 9-10.

[1072] "Welcoming speech by Rector of the University of South Bohemia Prof. Václav Bůžek," *Zprávy SVU,* vol. 48, No. 4 (July-August 2006), pp. 11-12.

[1073] "Welcoming Address by Governor of České Budějovice Region RNDr. Jan Zahradník, to be published in the Congress Proceedings.

[1074] "Ambassador Cabannis' Introductory Remarks for the 23rd World Congress of Czechoslovak Society of Arts and Sciences 2006," *Zprávy SVU*, vol. 48, No. 4 (July-August 2006), p. 13.

[1075] "Greetings of Ambassador of the Czech Republic to the United States H. E. Petr Kolář," *Zprávy SVU*, vol. 48, No. 5 (September-October 2006), p. 13.

[1076] "Greetings from President of the Learned Society of the Czech Republic RNDr. Jiří Grygar," *Zprávy SVU*, vol. 48, No. 4 (July-August 2006), pp. 13-14.

[1077] "Greetings by President of the Slovak Learned Society SAV Prof. MUDr. Fedor Ciampor, DrSc.," *Zprávy SVU*, vol. 48, No. 4 (July-August 2006), p. 14.

[1078] "Greetings by Vice President of the Academy of Sciences of CR Prof. PhDr. Jaroslav Pánek, DrSc.," *Zprávy SVU*, vol. 48, No. 5 (September-October 2006), pp. 14-15.

[1079] "Greetings by Rector of Charles University Prof. RNDr. Václáv Hampl, DrSc.," to be published in the Congress Proceedings.

word for a festive buffet. The tables were overflowing with a large variety of warm and cold dishes, meats, salads, assorted cheeses, sweets, hors d'oeuvres, vegetable trays with tangy dips, stuffed mushroom caps, marinated foods, mini quiches, meatballs, wines, soft drinks and ever present "Budvar" beer. In spite of large crowds, I am sure, nobody went hungry. Here you had the chance of meeting many interesting people from the Czech Republic and Slovakia, as well as from overseas.

At about 2:30 PM the attendees reassembled in the main hall where the Plenary Session, which I chaired, was about to start. The theme of the session was "Diplomatic Relations between North America and the Czech and Slovak Republics." The panelists comprised the respective Ambassadors from the Czech and Slovak Republics, the United States and Canada. It was a highly informative and amiable session in which the Ambassadors, not only charted the official course of their Governments' positions and actions but also a meeting in which they showed their human side and talked about their experiences in their assigned country posts to which they showed an obvious attachment, admiration and love.

When it ended, most attendees were taken back by the University buses to the University grounds. A sizeable group, however, went with me to the Theology Faculty building where an exhibit of the "Czech Bible through the Course of Centuries" was housed. Together with the Faculty Dean, the City Bishop and the director of the exhibit we opened the exhibit. It was a beautiful display of rare texts from the time of the Sts. Cyril and Methodius to date. The exhibit was open during the duration of our Congress so that other Congress participants could view it at their convenience.

Those who previously purchased tickets had supper at the University "menza" (cafeteria) but, as I suspect, most of the attendees skipped it because they were still full from the scrumptious "rout." The busy day ended "with a crescendo" at the University Congressional Hall in "Bobik" where the piano virtuoso Radoslav Kvapil gave a memorable performance of Mozart, Smetana. Suk and Martinů's works. It should be noted that Radoslav Kvapil, who is our SVU member, performed this gratis.

The days that followed were just as exciting as the first two. The attendees could select from as many as twelve concurrently run academic sessions from Tuesday morning till Friday noon, held on the premises shared by the University of South Bohemia and the Czech Academy of Sciences. Lack of space does not allow me to give a description of individual panels. Suffice it to say that practically every area of human endeavor was covered, ranging from history, literature, philosophy, the arts, education, politics, law, business, economics, trade, and the media to natural sciences and engineering, medicine, agriculture, and environment.

This time, there was a strong representation of medicine and natural sciences, including three medical panels, one on mental health, two on public health, another on neurosciences, five in biological sciences and another in physical sciences and engineering. Most of the panelists were scientists of international standing.

Apart from specific disciplines, the program featured a number of highly stimulating symposia. One dealt with the "University Leadership on Both Sides of the Atlantic," in which high-level university officials participated, including presidents, chancellors, vice presidents, rectors, provosts and deans.

Equally enticing was a panel on "University Partnerships and Cooperation between the US and ČR and SR," in which the university representatives with active programs in the referenced countries recounted their experiences with collaborative arrangements and projects. In another symposium, members of the Czech and Slovak diplomatic core discussed their experiences and the role in representing the Czech and Slovak Republics abroad. Among the Czech symposia, one of the most interesting ones was a two-day seminar on the Czech archives and resources relating to history of Czechs abroad. A number of leading archivists took part in the seminar, including Jiří Křesťan of the Czech National Archives and Milena Secká from the Náprstek Museum.

An entire section of the Congress was devoted to Czechs and Slovaks abroad in which such topics as emigrations and re-emigration, US settlements and communities, Czechs and Moravians in Texas, cultural contributions of Czechs and Slovak emigrants, and preservation of national heritage abroad were discussed.

What was unique among the English panels this time was the fact that a considerable proportion of the panelists were individuals with interest in some aspect of Czech and Slovak culture or affairs without having roots or any Czechoslovak background.

Two other events need to be mentioned. In the early afternoon on Tuesday, there was a book showing ("knižní prezentace") during which recently published SVU publications were shown and discussed by Dean Ivo Barteček and myself. They included the Proceedings of the last SVU Congress in Olomouc, bearing the title *Moravia from World Perspectives. Selected Papers from the 22nd SVU World Congress,* published in two volumes by Repronis in Ostrava in 2006. Also shown were recently issued two CDs – one containing *Selected Papers from the 2003 SVU North American Conference, Cedar Rapids, Iowa*, and another containing a revised *SVU Directory.*

At about the same time on Wednesday, Prof. Joseph Kohn and his colleagues made a presentation of the planned Václav Havel Library. Inspired, in part, by the American model of Presidential Libraries, the Václav Havel Library will house Havel's works and papers, document the complex battle for democracy and freedom in the second half of the 20th century, and stimulate discussion, research, and publications on the ongoing struggle for human rights and the challenges of post-communist political and civic engagement.

Practically every evening a concert or other cultural attraction was featured. Thus on Tuesday night there was a performance of South Bohemian Philharmonic with the repertoire of music works by Mozart, Dvořák, Pablo Sarasate and Beethoven. The added attraction was the noted Czech violin virtuoso Pavel Šporcl. After this concert, the Congress attendees could go to the Přemysl Otakar II Square where a special program, entitled "Co Čech, to muzikant" (Every Czech a Musician) was given. On Wednesday night, there was a special performance in the Bobik's Congressional Hall by two SVU members, Budimír Zvolánek – clarinet and Marie Bobkova – piano. Later that evening one could view on the city courtyard Theatre J. K. Tyl performing the play "Světáci." On Thursday evening, one could attend the Theatre Street Festival "Kvelb," a popular puppet theatre. If you preferred, you could have instead attended a flute recital, featuring Hana B. Colombo – flute, and Fabrizio Vanoncini – organ. Their program consisted of music by Vivaldi, three music pieces by Bach, and one piece by Handel. On Friday night, the Congress attendees could again hear the music performance by

South Bohemian Philharmonic which played Edvard Hagerup Grieg, Josef Mysliveček, Antonín Dvořák and Bedřich Smetana. And finally, on Sunday night, there was a swing concert "Muses on the River," featuring Zatrestband from Třešť which presented popular music and songs from Jerry Herman, Jaroslav Ježek and Frank Sinatra.

At the conclusion of the academic program on Friday noon, the Congress attendees moved to the cultural center "Bazilika," where the remainder of the Congress program was held and where it was concluded. It started at 2 PM with a Plenary Session over which I had the pleasure to preside. The first item on the agenda was a keynote address by the President of the Czech Academy of Sciences Václav Pačes who talked on "Czech Science in the Globalized World: Challenges and Pitfalls." After his thoughtful and brilliant presentation came a discussion panel "What Have We Learned and Where We Are Going" in which Zdeněk Brandl, Vladimír Papoušek, Libor Grubhoffer. Michael Bauer, Václav Pačes, Karel Raška and I took part.

During the SVU Award Ceremony, which followed, I had the pleasure of acknowledging several individuals for their assistance in organizing the present Congress by awarding them SVU Presidential Citations, i.e., Prof. Vladimír Papoušek, Prof. Libor Grubhoffer, Docent Michal Bauer, Vladimir Matajs, Zuzana Galatíková, Gabriela Dudová, Blanka and Svaťa Kuděj, Cecilia Rokusek, Karel Raška and George Tesař. Presidential Citations were also presented to Clinton Machann, Andrej Eliáš (absent) and Jiří Eichler for their continuous and sustained contributions to the Society. Last but not least, two other individuals were singled out for a special recognition by awarding them "Beyond the Call of Duty Award" for "they have always been there, whenever needed, always loyal and always dependable: Frank Mucha, SVU Treasurer and Eva Rechcígl, my wife."

The occasion was also used to present SVU Fellow certificates to several Fellows who have been honored with such distinction and who were present at the meeting. They were: Prof. Václav Pačes – for his achievements in the area of biological sciences, Prof. Leopold Pospíšil – for his achievements in social sciences, Prof. František Sehnal – for his contributions to biological sciences, Prof. Václav Vítek – for his contribution in engineering and Prof. Josef Jařáb – for his contributions to humanities.

The Award Ceremony was concluded with the presentation of Andrew Elias Humanitarian and Tolerance Award to the noted Czech journalist Petra Procházková for her humanitarian work and for calling to public attention violations of human rights.[1080] After acceptance of the award, together with an honorarium of $ 1000, she gave a talk in Czech on "Iluze západu o dopadu humanitární pomoci" (Illusion in the West about the impact of humanitarian aid), based on her personal experiences.

The very busy afternoon ended with the SVU General Assembly meeting, followed by a press conference. Then came a beautiful music performance by the South Bohemian Chamber Philharmonic, mentioned earlier and a "rout," hosted by SVU member Jan Seyfried,[1081] for which we are very grateful to him.

Some of us also took the advantage of the two scheduled excursions on Saturday and Sunday, to Český Krumlov and Hluboká, respectively, which was a pleasant way of finishing our sojourn in South Bohemia.

All in all, the Congress and everything else connected with it was great. The memories of the beautiful South Bohemian region and its friendly and hospitable people will stay with us forever. Thanks again to everyone for making it such a memorable and unforgettable event.

---

[1080] "2006 SVU Elias Humanitarian and Tolerance Award," *Zprávy SVU*, vol. 48, No. 5 (September-October 2006), pp. 18-19.

[1081] Jan Seyfried (1926-), vice president and director, Dominio Securities Ames, Ltd., Toronto, Canada.

# 70
## State of the SVU in 2006

It is a pleasure to present our traditional State of SVU Report[1082] to our distinguished General Assembly, meeting here, in the historic city of České Budějovice. First, I would like, however, to express our sincere appreciation to Lord Mayor of the City and the Governor of the Budějovice Region for letting us use this fantastic facility, the elegant cultural center's "Bazilika" for our meeting.

This report covers the usual two-year administrative period, since the time the present Executive Board was elected at the SVU World Congress in Olomouc in June 2004.

I am pleased to report we had two very successful years. As has been our practice, we started our term with the review of SVU Mission Statement and developing an action plan and dividing responsibilities among the individual Board members. The Executive Board essentially has continued with the priorities that were developed earlier, i.e., an Accent on Youth initiative, institutionalizing cultural cooperation with ČR and SR, fostering preservation of Czech and Slovak heritage abroad, sponsoring publication projects, and assisting with the development of civil society in ČR and SR. To this we added another priority, namely to search for new SVU leadership to assure the Society's continuity in the future.

These priorities were, of course, superimposed over the usual processes relating to the running of the Society, such as holding regular Board meetings, organizing our annual Conference and SVU World Congress, maintenance of SVU membership rolls and finances, coordinating local chapter activities, issuance of SVU periodicals and keeping our SVU Website up to date.

The most immediate task of the newly elected Executive Board was selecting a suitable site for the 2005 SVU Conference, as well as that for the next SVU World Congress in 2006. Interestingly, we had decided on the latter before picking the site for the 2005 Conference which was only a few months away.

---

[1082] Originally published in *Zprávy SVU*, vol. 48, No. 5 (September-October 2006), pp. 6-10.

There was really only one site that met the specific criteria and conditions set by the Executive Board, namely North Miami, Florida. It was decided to join forces with the local American Czech and Slovak Cultural Club and to hold a joint Conference & Festival on the premises of their Club in North Miami on the weekend of 17-20 March 2005. The Conference, with its general theme "Czechs and Slovaks in America: Challenges and Opportunities,"[1083] and sponsored by Presidents Václav Klaus and Ivan Gasparovič, of Czech and Slovak Republic, respectively, generated lots of excitement and publicity. It attracted a half dozen University Rectors from the Czech and Slovak Republics and other dignitaries, including the Czech and Slovak Ambassadors in the US. I had the pleasure of organizing the academic program, while Cecilia Rokusek and Bob Petrik handled the logistics and cultural and social events. The combination of a beautiful setting in the vicinity of sunny beaches of Florida, the involvement of the local Czech and Slovak community, the interesting academic program and enjoyable cultural activities led to a very successful event which was characterized as "SVU Extravaganza in Florida."[1084]

Although we began forming plans already in 2004 for the SVU World Congress, to be held at the University of South Bohemia on 25-June- 2 July 2006,[1085] we did not start the organizational work and programming until fall 2005, until a number of administrative aspects were resolved. After some back and forth correspondence with our co-organizers in České Budějovice regarding financial arrangements and logistics, only then did the preparation and organizational work begin in earnest. In October 2005 I went to České Budějovice to iron out the remaining bottlenecks and negotiate the details.[1086]

Afterwards I devoted some time to correspondence with the Prague Castle and the Bratislava Castle to get sponsorship of the Congress by both the Czech and Slovak Presidents and also to assure President Klaus' personal participation in the Congress. While this was going on, we

---

[1083] [Program and Abstracts]. Special Conference and Festival, North Miami, Florida, 17-20 March 2005. Central Theme: "Czech and Slovak Cultural Heritage on Both Sides of the Atlantic" (North Miami, FL, SVU, 2005), 50 p.

[1084] *Zprávy SVU*, vol. 47, No. 3 (May-June 2005), pp. 1-7.

[1085] "2006 SVU World Congress featuring Czech and Slovak Culture in International Context," *Zprávy SVU*, vol. 46, No. 6 (November-December 2004), p. 19.

[1086] "SVU President's Sojourn in Czech Republic and Slovakia, "*Zprávy SVU,* vol. 48, No. 1 (January-February 2006), pp. 8-10.

began, together with our colleagues in České Budějovice, developing plans for local arrangements. After completion of the logistical details, we could finally focus on the preparation of the program. Docent Michal Bauer was given responsibility for the coordination of the Czech and Slovak panels, while I took charge of organizing the English-language panels. It was an arduous task which in my case took more than four months of steady work in front of the computer, sending out hundreds of personal invitation letters and responding to a plethora of e-mails. I presume Docent Bauer and his colleagues must have spent quite a bit of time on their panels as well. That the hard work paid off is plainly evident from the versatile program and the high quality of individuals papers.

As has been stressed on a number of occasions, publishing monographs and periodicals is the SVU's imperative. In the last two years we have certainly gone a long way to meet this objective. The first task in this area was to get selected papers from the Olomouc SVU World Congress ready for publication.[1087] I had the pleasure of editing the English papers, while Docent Ivo Barteček edited the Czech papers. Most of you must have seen the results of this work in viewing the impressive Congress collections, published by Palacký University, under Docent Barteček's leadership.[1088]

With our Webmaster Jiří Eichler's help, SVU produced a CD containing *Selected Papers from the 2003 SVU North American Conference, Cedar Rapids, Iowa,*[1089] this being our first electronic attempt in publishing. In the same vein, we proceeded with the electronic production of the revised *SVU Biographical Directory.*[1090] I presume some of you purchased these two CDs which were available for sale here. While doing this, we have simultaneously begun working, with our Webmaster, on a

---

[1087] "Publishing Papers from the Olomouc SVU Congress," *Zprávy SVU*, vol. 46, No. 5 (September-October 2004), p. 10.

[1088] *Moravia from World Perspective. Selected Papers from the 22nd World Congress of the Czechoslovak Society of Arts and Sciences.* Palacký University, June 26 to July 4, 2004. Edited by Tomáš Motlíček and Miloslav Rechcígl, Jr. (Ostrava, Repronis, 2006). 2 vols.

[1089] SVU Enters the Electronic Publishing Age," *Zprávy SVU* vol. 47, No. 1 (January-February 2005), pp. 20-24.

[1090] "New SVU Biographical Directory on CD, *Zprávy SVU*, vol. 48, No. 2 (March-April 2006), p. 8.

Biographical Data Base[1091] comprised of biographical sketches of selected SVU members, which has been posted on SVU Website.

Among new SVU monographs, Vice President Vera Bořkovec was given the responsibility for putting together and editing a book on "Czech and Slovak Theatre Abroad,"[1092] while Vice President Dagmar Hasalová White assumed responsibility for preparing a comparable volume on "Czech Opera Abroad." I should also mention that, on the occasion of my 75th birthday, SVU honored me by publishing a selection of my writings, under the title *Czechs and Slovaks in America*,[1093] as a part of the East European Monographs series. Description of the book appeared in November 2005 issue of *Zprávy SVU*.[1094] SVU also sponsored musicologist Jan Vičar's monograph on *Czech Music and Aesthetics*,[1095] which was available at the SVU Conference in Florida. With reference to the present Congress, plans are in motion to also publish selected papers.

Mention should also be made of two significant monographs, published by the Prague SVU Chapter and by the British Chapter. The former published a small anthology of the Czech exile prose from the fifties,[1096] while the latter published a series of biographical sketches of selected personalities in the Czech Britain.[1097]

As far as SVU periodicals are concerned, Andrew Eliáš and Clinton Machann deserve our thanks for publishing our newsletter *Zprávy SVU* and the English periodical *Kosmas*. Both periodicals have been issued in

---

[1091] "SVU Biographical Data Base, "*Zprávy SVU*, vol. 47. No. 5 (September-October 2005), pp. 19-20.

[1092] Věra Bořkovec, ed., *Czech and Slovak Theatre Abroad: In the USA, Canada, Australia and England.* Boulder, CO: East European Monographs, 2006. 128 p.

[1093] Miloslav Rechcígl, Jr., *Czechs and Slovaks in America. Surveys, Reflections and Personal Insights Relating to the History and the Contributions of Czech and Slovak Immigrants in America and their Descendants.* Published on the occasion of Dr. Rechcígl's 75th birthday. Boulder, CO: East European Monographs, 2005. 317 p.

[1094] "New Book about Czechs and Slovaks in America," *Zprávy SVU*, vol. 47, No. 6 (November-December 2005), pp. 20-21.

[1095] Jan Vičar, Imprints: *Essays on Czech Music and Aesthetics.* Prague: Togga and Olomouc: Palacký University, 2005. 270 p.

[1096] *Poštovní schránka domov. Malá antologie exilové povídky padesátých let.* Vybral a uspořádal Michal Přibáň. K vydání připravila Alena Morávková. Praha: SVU, 2005. 85 p.

[1097] Milan Kocourek and Zuzana Slobodová. *Česko-slovenská Britanie.* Pro SVU Londýn vydalo nakladatelství Carpio v Třeboni r. 2006. 356 p.

a timely fashion and have been praised by the readers for their interesting content and high quality.

As pointed out earlier, the preservation of Czech and Slovak cultural heritage belongs among SVU top priorities. In this regard, our Florida Conference dealt exclusively with this subject, as did one entire section of this Congress' program. Some of you, who attended the SVU Florida Conference, will recall that at that meeting I announced the establishment of a special SVU Czech and Slovak Studies Fund at the University of Minnesota's Immigration History Research Center (IHRC).[1098] The purpose of the Fund is to prepare an inventory of SVU Archives which were deposited there and to provide financial assistance to students and scholars conducting research in the Archives. To be sure, it was meant as seed money to attract other Czech and Slovak organizations to assist with the maintenance and development of IHRC's Czech and Slovak collection. I had the pleasure of presenting our $10,000 check to Rudolph Vecoli, the Director of IHRC at a special ceremony, attended by both the Czech Ambassador Martin Palouš and the Slovak Ambassador Rastislav Káčer. I should also like to mention that in July 2005 the University of Minnesota sent their truck to pick up the remaining archival materials maintained in our house.[1099]

Organizationally speaking, you will be pleased that we have established two new SVU Chapters: one in Olomouc, under the leadership of Evžen Weigl, and another in North Miami, Florida,[1100] with Blanka Kuděj, serving as its President. The former was the direct result of our SVU World Congress held at Palacký University in 2004, while the latter was, similarly, an outcome of the Florida Conference. In this connection, I am happy to also report that our colleagues at the University of South Bohemia are planning to establish a new chapter there, under the leadership of Prof. Vladimír Papoušek. With all this good news, I am a bit concerned about the future of some of our older chapters which are rapidly aging with their officers, some of whom held the office for several decades without any intention of stepping down. Unless the younger generation will soon take over they may phase out into oblivion as some other chapters have done. Consequently, I urge all the officers

---

[1098] "SVU Establishes a Special Studies Fund," *Zprávy* SVU 47, No. 3 (May-June 2005), pp. 21-22; *Czech the News*, Spring 2005, pp. 6-7.

[1099] "Additional SVU Archival Material Moved to IHRC," *Zprávy* SVU 48, No. 1 (January-February 2006), pp. 10-11.

[1100] "Florida SVU Chapter," *Zprávy SVU*, vol. 48, No. 2 (March April 2007), p. 20.

of the respective chapters who have reached the venerable age of seventy or over, to voluntarily step down and let the younger generation take over before it is too late.

With respect to SVU membership, a number our members passed away, while others are aging, I am pleased to report, however, that we have recruited a significant number of new members, a preponderance of whom came from the younger generation, particularly students.[1101] I am gratified that our Blue Ribbon SVU Leadership Search Committee has also made a real effort to rejuvenate the future SVU Executive Board which is reflected in the voting ballots.

It should be noted that most of the new SVU members are young Americans, usually associated with universities, with interest in Czech or Slovak culture or affairs. Inasmuch as we cannot in the future count on new immigration waves from the old countries, it is clear that the future of our Society will depend on these types of people, i.e. university-based professors and students pursuing studies on Czech or Slovak matters and other professionals in the US and Canada involved in some work or business with the Czech and Slovak Republics, who may not even have any Czech or Slovak roots. Although some of these professionals may have some working knowledge of Czech or Slovak, for the most part, they are primarily English-speaking people. For this reason, and considering that younger people in the Czech and Slovak Republics are being trained in English, the English language needs to remain the SVU's "lingua franca" in the future. It should also be noted that the main source of revenue of the Society comes from the US and Canada, in comparison with the small contributions coming from Europe. With the exception of a few newly established chapters in the Midwest and the South of the US, hardly any established local chapters have been recruiting new members. Practically all new members have been recruited individually and have no association with any SVU chapters.

As part of our Civil Society emphasis, SVU established a special SVU Tolerance and Humanitarian Award, thanks to the generous donation of Andrew Eliáš. This award is given annually to an individual whose life and work symbolizes the values of human tolerance and humanitarianism. It was a pleasure to present last year's award to Jan Figel, Slovak

---

[1101] "New SVU Biographical Drive," *Zprávy SVU*, vol. 47, No. 5 (September-October), pp. 18-19.

Commissioner at EU for Education.[1102] This year's award was given to Petra Procházková, a prominent Czech journalist who concentrated her efforts on bringing the worst violations of human rights to public attention.[1103]

In the area of civil rights, I would also like to commend Lois Herman for her leadership role in promoting the women's issues idea, not only in terms of organizing an effective force within SVU but also for systematically contributing to our Women's Issue Sub-Website.

From the time I was given the chief responsibility of heading and managing the Society, I made a deliberate effort to assure that we have a solid financial base and that we manage our precious financial resources wisely. In this regard, I would like to commend our Treasurer Frank Mucha who was my principal ally in this effort, who made sure that our books are carefully maintained and that we operate with a balanced budget. As a result of this policy, I am pleased to say that our finances are sound. We do not depend on anyone, we don't owe anything to anyone and we stand on our own two feet. The Society's image could not be better and its visibility is high, thanks, in part, to our splendid SVU Website,[1104] managed by our always dependable Webmaster Jiří Eichler.

---

[1102] "Andrew Eliáš SVU Human Tolerance Award. Presentation to Jan Figel," *Zprávy SVU*, vol. 48, No. 4 (July-August 2006), pp. 24-26.

[1103] "2006 SVU Eliáš Humanitarian and Tolerance Award," *Zprávy SVU* 48, No. 5 (September-October 2006), pp. 18-19.

[1104] "Four Years of the SVU Website," *Zprávy SVU*, vol. 48, No. 4 (July-August 2006), pp. 26-27.

# 71
# *The End of an Era: Míla Rechcígl Bids Farewell*[1105]

The improbable and unexpected really happened. Long-term SVU President Míla Rechcígl, who served continuously as SVU President from 1994 to 2006, after his initial sojourn in 1974-1978, decided to relinquish his post after completion of his current term.

In his parting words at the General Assembly meeting, convened on the occasion of the 23rd SVU World Congress at the University of South Bohemia in České Budějovice, on June 30, 2006, he said the following:

> Before I leave, I would like to again express my sincere appreciation to the members of the outgoing Executive Board who worked diligently with me in the last two years on the SVU agenda. As most of you know, I have served in the office of SVU President continuously since 1994, i.e., twelve years altogether. If you add to this four more years when I served as SVU President during the 1974-1978 period, that makes it sixteen years which is an incredibly long period by any standard. It's time for change and have a younger person take over, and this is the reason why I decided not to be a candidate in the next term.
>
> The older members among you will remember that when I first became President in 1974, the Society was at a brink of financial crisis, which threatened the Society's very existence. With hard work and perseverance we managed to overcome the impending disaster to the point that within a year the SVU finances were in the black. I was brought back sixteen years later – in 2004 – when the Society was again at a very critical point. There was general apathy among the membership, partly due to the unsettling political situation in the old homeland. There was even talk about abolishing the Society, based on the belief that SVU already fulfilled its mission and that the time had come to cease and desist. With coming years we were successful in overcoming these trends. The Society has

---

[1105] Reprinted from *Zprávy SVU* 48, No. 5 (September-October 2006), pp. 1- 3.

been revitalized and brought to higher and more glowing horizons than ever before – to the point that, presently, SVU is considered the most influential organization of its kind which promotes Czech and Slovak culture globally and that fosters cooperation between the old homeland and the Western World. As I mentioned in my 2006 State of the SVU Report, the Society's image could not be better.

I am pleased that we can pass on the reign to our successors with the Society being in excellent shape, in terms of its reputation, as well as organizationally and financially.

I wish my successors all the best, with the hope that they take good care of our Society and continue its mission, as originally foreseen by its founders.

Most of the members who attended the General Assembly were unaware that such an event would take place and were stunned by the announcement, believing that Rechcígl would want to keep the function as long as he could. Although Rechcígl has made occasional hints that he would hand over the reign of the Society as soon as a suitable successor could be found, none of the members took him seriously.

The General Assembly meeting started at 4:15 P.M. As customary, it met one hour after the scheduled time, in order to meet requirements of quorum. Actually, the "Bazilika" main hall, where the meeting was held, was so crowded with people that it is quite possible that enough people would have already been present at 3 o'clock so that the meeting could have started at the scheduled time.

After opening the meeting and welcoming the members and guests, SVU President Rechcígl, who presided over the meeting, appointed Cathleen Oslzlý as Recording Secretary and then named the SVU Resolution Committee, consisting of Zdeněk David, David Chroust and Vladimír Papoušek to draft a resolution to be voted on by the Assembly. At the request of attending scientists, he also named a second resolution committee, consisting of Prof. Thomas A. Miller, Prof. František Sehnal and Prof. Jaroslav Drobník to prepare an additional resolution dealing specifically with the environmental and ecological issues.

Next on the agenda was the approval of the Minutes of the previous Annual meeting, held in North Miami, FL in March 2005, which was presented to the Assembly by Dr. Blanka Kuděj who authored the document. Rechcígl then called on the Assembly to honor the memory of the deceased members in the last two years by standing.

Then followed the reports of the individual SVU Chapters, including Prague, Brno, London, Munich, New York, Texas, Nebraska, New York, Chicago, Pittsburgh, Cleveland and Florida and the report of the Student Award Committee, given by Vice President Vera Bořkovec. Afterwards, SVU President presented his traditional State of SVU Report for the last 2-year administrative period. His report, which is published separately, was received with applause and approval by the Assembly.

SVU Treasurer Frank Mucha was then asked to give his report on the status of SVU finances, followed by the report of the Auditors of Accounts. At the recommendation of the SVU auditors, the Treasurer's Report was approved by the Assembly and the outgoing Executive Board was granted "Absolutorium."

By this time, both Resolution Committees completed drafting their resolutions which were presented to the General Assembly for vote. Both Resolutions were approved as drafted.[1106][1107]

Following the established procedures, the outgoing President Rechcígl, after his concluding remarks, appointed a new presiding officer pro tempore. He selected for this purpose Prof. Zdeněk Slouka, a former SVU President (1992-1994) and a member of the Nominations Committee. His function was to inform the Assembly of the outcome of the recent SVU elections, based on the Report of the Inspectors of Elections, chaired by Zdeněk Vich. All candidates, as originally proposed by the Nominations Committee, chaired by Prof. Petr Zuman, were elected.

After announcing the outcome of the elections, Prof. Slouka asked the newly elected SVU President Karel Raška to assume his new function, while the outgoing President Míla Rechcígl symbolically handed him the gavel.

..........

---

[1106] "Czech and Slovak Heritage on both Sides of the Atlantic. Resolution of the Czechoslovak Society of Arts and Sciences (SVU), on the Occasion of its Twenty-third World Congress...,"*Zprávy SVU*, vol. 48, No. 5 (September-October 2006), pp. 10-11.

[1107] "Resolution of the Czechoslovak Society of Arts and Sciences (SVU)," *Zprávy SVU*, vol. 48, No. 5 (September-October 2006), pp. 11-12.

After returning to the US, a great burden fell from my shoulders, since I no longer was SVU President. Besides removing a great stress and pressure of deadlines, under which I was continuously since 1994, I also gained precious time. I imagined I should be able now to do things which I could not do before or, at least, with a higher degree of concentration.

Nevertheless, I had committed, to my successor Karel Raška, to prepare the next two issues of the SVU newsletter, for which I still had some material and which deserved to be published. I completed these tasks in record time. The July-August issue was finished by July 19 and the September-October issue was done by August 3. There were, of course, several other chores relating to SVU, I had to take care of, including signing a certificate for the student award winner, etc., not counting frequent inquires from the new SVU President, which I answered promptly.

Frankly, I did not expect any particular accolades from the SVU upon my retirement. I was therefore pleasantly surprised when the editor of SVU periodical *Kosmas*, Prof. Clinton Machann, wrote the following editorial in the upcoming Fall 2006 issue of *Kosmas*[1108]:

> This issue of *Kosmas* contains items that we believe will be of special interest to members of our sponsoring organization, SVU, who have been around since the early days. In our lead article, Francis D. Raška reviews the complex history of the Council of Free Czechoslovakia, which was established in early 1949, one year after the Communist takeover. The story of this first political organization of its type to be formed by political exiles from a Soviet-dominated European country certainly deserves to be told, and one of the individuals involved in this story is the father of a man who deserves recognition from us at this current historical moment. Míla Rechcígl served as President of SVU during the years 1974-78 and then again 1994-2006. The extent of his service to our organization is so great that it cannot be easily summarized, but as editor of *Kosmas* I want to add my own thanks to the expressions of appreciation being offered to him by the SVU officers and council members who have worked with him for many years.

---

[1108] "Editor's Notes," *Kosmas. Czechoslovak and Central European Journal,* 20, No. 1 (Fall 2006), p. iii.

Regarding *Kosmas*, President Rechcígl not only offered consistent support during difficult times, but over the years he has made his own scholarly contributions as well. Appropriately enough, his contribution to this Fall 2006 issue is a bibliography of SVU publications, many of which he himself had a hand in writing or editing and compiling–often with the help of his wife Eva. I am sure that many join me in hoping that Mila and Eva Rechcígl will continue to offer their valuable help and advice to those of us who continue with SVU projects in the future. As most readers know, a farewell message from our former president can be found in the September-October 2006 issue of the SVU newsletter *Zprávy*.

I received several other personal messages and e-mails of thanks and appreciation from my friends. Among them was also a letter from Director of Political Affairs in the Office of the Czech President Václav Klaus that read as follows:

### *Office of the President of the Czech Republic*
In Prague, August 11, 2006

Dear Mr. Rechcígl:

Please accept our greetings on the occasion of the completion of the concluding term of office as President of the Czechoslovak Society of Arts and Sciences.

As the founding member and many-years-President of the Society, you have done a lot in leading the Czech and Slovak scientists and artists here at home, as well as abroad, in successfully fostering our joint spiritual wealth and strengthening the moral and historical awareness about culture of our nations in the world.

Dear Mr. Rechcígl, it was a great pleasure to work with you during the duration of your Presidency and I look forward to continue in our collaboration also in the future.

Please accept our wishes for continued good health and lots of success in the work on your future projects.

Ladislav Mravec
Director of the International Relations Sector
Office of the President

A very kind and thoughtful personal letter came from the Ambassador of the Czech Republic to the US, Petr Kolář:

**Petr Kolář**
***Ambassador of the Czech Republic***
*3900 Spring of Freedom Street, Washington, DC 20008*
October 19, 2006

Dear Dr. Rechcigl, *Milý Milo,*

Allow me to congratulate you on your long-time service to the Czechoslovak Society of Arts and Sciences as you pass the SVU presidency on to your successor. Your meritorious work with SVU has helped make it the dynamic and active organization that it is today.

Under your guidance and with your indefatigable enthusiasm, SVU has attained a tradition of excellence in promoting the Czech and Slovak Republics, while fostering the cross-cultural sharing of information, ideas, and artistic and scientific property. During your tenure as President, SVU conducted first-rate activities, including the highly successful SVU World Congress in České Budějovice in summer 2006.

I know that you will remain extremely active in SVU, but I thank your for your accomplishments connecting not only Czechs, Slovaks, and Americans, but in promoting SVU worldwide. I wish you great success in your ongoing SVU participation and in your new pursuits.

Warm regards,

Petr Kolář, Ambassador

In the same spirit was a letter from Effie Rosene, Executive Director of the Czech Cultural Center in Houston, informing me that the Center planned to present me Comenius Award. Unfortunately they picked September 16 for the presentation which conflicted with the first meeting of the newly elected SVU Executive Board which I offered to hold in our house in Rockville. Since I could not be there in person, Mrs. Rosene kindly sent me the citation by mail. See below:

### *The Czech Cultural Center Houston*

is proud to present the
## COMENIUS AWARD
to
### Miloslav Rechcígl, Ph.D.

In recognition of his achievements in fostering the principle which Jan Amos Komenský espoused especially "Teaching thoroughly all things to all men," we honor Miloslav Rechcígl, Ph.D. for his dedication to a successful professional career as a biochemist and his dedication to his avocation of teaching, researching and promulgating his Czech culture by informing the public and the Czech-American community by means of his dedication and long association with the Czechoslovak Society of Arts and Sciences of the history, language and culture of their heritage in order to preserve in their minds the meaning and impact of their heritage on their lives. We salute him and are proud to claim him as one of our own.

In witness thereof, I have set my hand
Effie M. Rosene
Chairman of the Board
Czech Cultural Center Houston, Texas

# Part V
# Special Topics

# 72
# *SVU Aims and its Mission*

The rationale for founding the SVU can be found in its proclamation by the SVU Preparatory Council:[1108]

### *Struggle for the Soul of Man*

The Czechoslovak Society of Arts and Sciences has its beginnings in the tenth year of our exile, resulting from the concern about the dismal events the Czech and the Slovak culture had suffered in the home country. The Communist regime of Czechoslovakia obstructs the scientific and artistic development and, in many areas of cultural life, it actually destroys the wealth of our thousand-years-long tradition. The cultural efforts of the Czechs and Slovaks in America and elsewhere in the free world have been slowed down by foreign environment, denationalization processes and the lack of new immigrants. Above all, it has been slowed down by the sad state of the national culture in the home country, which is the natural center of its cultural life.

The world political events, defined by the geopolitical location of Czechoslovakia behind the Iron Country, and the fear, provoked by the threat of extinction of the world civilization by atomic war, don't give us much hope for liberation by political or military means. Therefore the dynamic ideological struggle in the cultural sphere, the struggle for the soul of man is of much greater importance than ever before. If such struggle is a novelty for large and powerful nations, it is certainly nothing new for us, the Czechs and the Slovaks. It is the traditional way of our struggle, which we had used for centuries for our own survival. It was actually František Palacký who expressed this principle elegantly in the following words: 'Whenever we were winning, it was always through the superiority of our spirit, rather than through physical power and whenever we succumbed, it was because of the lack of spiritual effort, moral courage and boldness.'

---

1108 "Struggle for the Soul of Man," *Co jest SVU, Zprávy SVU – Special issue* (1958), 5.

> SVU does not seek the noise of publicity, neither does it follow political gains. The main interest the Society is in supporting and coordinating the work of individual scientists and artists and in the preparation of suitable ground for the fruits of their labor. To be effective, SVU will need advice, help and collaboration of all, who are convinced that the nations live and die with their culture and therefore it is the shared responsibility of all friends of Czechoslovakia to strive so that the riches of the Christian and our national tradition will not remain buried within us. We consider it for certain that moral and cultural advance must precede our political liberation.

Václav Hlavatý elaborated on the scheme further by stating the following:

> After ten years of exile it is finally clear what should have been our guide from the beginning. The best policy for a small nation is in the area of nonpolitical orientation, i.e., in the cultural sphere. This recognition led to the establishment of the Czechoslovak Society of Arts and Sciences. If it is not possible for a small nation to assert itself politically, it is necessary to assert itself in an area where quality matters rather than quantity.
>
> Everybody among us, who is concerned about his nation, from which he came, has two obligations toward that nation: the moral obligation and cultural obligation. These two obligations are the only possible weapons one has in the ideological struggle between dictatorship and democracy. Both of these competing ideologies suffer certain stagnation. On the Communist side, one can discern that the ideological makeup of the dictatorship stops being the main guiding force and that practical considerations take over. In case of democracy, it is clear that its basis is morality in the relations between men and the respect for the human free thought. This broad framework must be, however, filled with the appropriate economic and political measures, if it should not end as a cliché. It is our moral responsibility to aid the former, either through the fulfillment of one's life or through creative work. How we shall fulfill this obligation, will decide on the future character of our nation. Our moral mission will influence the future free generations in our homeland.

In the preamble of the Proclamation were these words:

*SVU Aims and its Mission*

Czechs and Slovaks settled, for time immemorial, on the important site of the Central Europe, created distinct and irreplaceable cultural environment. In it, great ideas originated and, through its lands, European cultural streams penetrated and joined.

Twenty years of calm and peace during the era of the Masaryk Republic, when the Czechoslovak peoples again associated themselves, based on their old tradition, with the number of free and the progress-loving nations, was interrupted by another war and renewed violence, to which there is no end. Already more than ten years, the creative energy of the Czech and Slovak nation has been constricted by international Communism, which disables our home country from contributing towards the development of the free mankind, at the moment when searching for new ways of doing things makes every contribution so much more important.

Under these conditions we, in the free world, must maintain viable continuity with the treasures of our Christian and European civilization, which took centuries to build. It is our solemn obligation to keep creating moral values, scientific and artistic, so that, one day, they could resuscitate the free culture, when Czechoslovakia again is politically free. It is our obligation to erect one of the bridges which will outlast even the life of its builder, which will link the free generations of the past, the present and the future, across the abyss that opened up among them by today's lack of freedom.

So much for the rationale. In terms of its purpose, the following statement was put in the SVU Bylaws: "The Society is a cultural, educational, literary and artistic, non-political and non-profit organization for public benefit. Its purpose shall be the effort to maintain and develop a free Czechoslovak culture."

In term of its activities, the SVU Bylaws elaborate it as follows:

1. Support and cooperation of scholarly, educational, literary and artistic activity and cooperation with institutions having similar aims;
2. Publication of scholarly, educational and literary works and works of art and the eventual issuance of periodicals or other publications;
3. Organizational of general membership meetings and of conferences for special purposes;
4. Lecture and information activities;

5. Establishment of a document center (Library and Archives of the Society). These activities shall be carried on by the Society with particular regard to the Czechoslovak ethnic groups throughout the free World.

The activities of the Society shall be directed toward benefiting, enlightening and educating the public and shall, therefore, be open to the public, except as to item 3 above.

With coming years, the Society became involved in just about all of the activities listed above. It conducted meetings of its various organs, including Executive Board, the SVU Council and the General Assembly. It sponsored regional conferences and SVU World Congresses and each of its local; chapters organized lecture programs and other activities. The Society also published periodicals and the newsletter, as well as monographic publications, Congress proceedings, etc. At one time, it also had its own library. Its enormous archival holdings have been deposited for safe keeping in the University of Minnesota IHRC. The Society also collaborated with other organizations in joint projects and after the Iron Curtain was torn down, the Society established collaborative links with the Czech and Slovak most important cultural institutions, as well as with individuals in various universities.

When it became fashionable in the US government agencies, as well as in the public sector, to prepare detailed Mission Statements,[1109] which happened during my presidency, we also prepared such statement which elaborated SVU priorities and its strategies. See below.

---

[1109] Mission statement is a brief description of a company's fundamental purpose. A Mission statement answers the question, "Why do we exist?" The mission statement articulates the company's purpose both for those in the organization and for the public. However, all mission statements will "broadly describe an organization's present capabilities, customer focus, activities, and business makeup." The difference between a mission statement and a vision statement is that a mission statement focuses on a company's present state while a vision statement focuses on a company's future. Every business should have a mission statement, both as a way of ensuring that everyone in the organization is "on the same page" and to serve as a baseline for effective business planning

## SVU Mission Statement

### WHO WE ARE

SVU is an independent nonprofit international and cultural organization dedicated to the pursuit of knowledge, free dissemination of ideas, and to fostering of contact among people. The Society brings together scholars, scientists, artists, writers, students, lawyers, businessmen and others, throughout the world, who are interested in the Czech Republic and/or Slovakia, their histories, peoples or their cultural and intellectual achievements.

### WHAT ARE OUR AIMS AND GOALS

1. **To enhance and promote Czech and Slovak culture:**
   a) by organizing meetings, public lectures, conferences, seminars, workshops, etc.;
   b) by sponsoring and/or publicizing concerts, exhibits, and other cultural events;
   c) by publishing scholarly, educational and literary works, as well as periodicals and newsletters;
   d) by compiling selected bibliographies and other information briefs;
   e) by establishing a documentary center;
   f) by maintaining liaison between cultural institutions in the Czech and Slovak Republics and their counterparts abroad, and
   g) by cooperating with similar organizations on joint activities.

2. **To coordinate and assist with the work of SVU members:**
   a) by periodically reporting on their activities in its newsletter;
   b) by enabling members to present results of their work and research at its world congresses, annual conferences, etc.;
   c) by preparing biographical directories of members with the listing of their accomplishments;
   d) by establishing a clearinghouse regarding members' interests and making effective use of their expertise;
   e) by using its extensive worldwide network to provide members with advice and contacts.

3. **To promote cooperation between scientists, artists, and other professionals, as well as between cultural institutions in the Czech and Slovak Republics and those abroad:**

a) by maintaining contact with major cultural institutions in the Czech and Slovak Republics and their counterparts abroad;
b) by keeping track of study and research opportunities worldwide;
c) by providing advice on the art of "grantsmanship";
d) by preparing specific study and research guide;
e) by assisting with joint projects.

**4. To assist with the preservation of Czech and Slovak cultural heritage abroad:**

a) by mapping historical sites relating to Czechs and Slovaks abroad;
b) by surveying and collecting archival material relating to Czechs and Slovaks abroad;
c) by fostering studies and research on Czechs arid Slovaks abroad;
d) by organizing conferences, seminars and workshops with the focus on Czechs and Slovaks abroad;
e) by sponsoring relevant publications;
f) by working with other organizations with similar aims.

**5. To assist with development of a Civil Society:**

a) by using new forms of communications media to provide the transfer of knowledge about the current development of Czech and Slovak society as they exist in their homeland and throughout the world;
b) by serving as a facilitator in the creation of such civil society.

**6. To revitalize the SVU ranks with young people and to assist young people generally.**

It should be noted that we added several new priorities, which were the result of the changes in Czechoslovakia and its Successor States since 1989, such as collaboration with the Czech and Slovak Republics and the assistance with development of a Civil Society in those countries. With reference to Czechs and Slovaks abroad, the Society established a new priority to launch an effort to preserve their cultural heritage.[1110] And finally, a great emphasis was placed on the young people, this initiative being called "The Accent on Youth."[1111]

---

[1110] "Preserving Czech Cultural Heritage in America," *Zprávy SVU*, vol. 41, No. 6 (November–December 1999), pp. 6-8.

[1111] "Accent on Youth – No. 1 Priority," *Zprávy SVU*, vol. 45, No. 2 (March-April 2003), pp. 21-23.

# 73
# *Organizational Aspects of the Society*

At the time of the SVU's founding, when Dr. Jaroslav Němec held the function of the Secretary-General, he went to great detail in describing just about every important organizational aspect of the Society. Inasmuch as most of his ideas were adopted and subsequently maintained, it is of interest to go through some of them.

One of the first documents he prepared dealt with the principles that should be embodied in the new SVU Bylaws. The document is quite interesting because it also shows what the organizers had originally in mind:

### Principles Guiding the New SVU Bylaws

| | |
|---|---|
| The Name: | Academy of Sciences and Arts – associated with CNCA[1113] (AVU) [Society of Arts and Sciences) (SVU)] |
| Relation to CNCA: | AVU is autonomous in professional and financial aspects |
| Seat | Undefined |
| Language: | Czech, Slovak, English |
| Purpose: | Support expansion of arts and sciences, publish results of scientific research, inform the world public about the Czechoslovak artistic and scientific issues and problems, establish contacts with other scientific and artistic organizations, carry out research relating to immigrant history, propagate arts and sciences among the immigrant communities, etc. |
| Members: | Individual members Institutional members |
| Kind of membership: | Founding members |

---

[1113] The acronym for Czechoslovak National Council of America

|  |  |
|---|---|
|  | Honorary members |
|  | Regular members |
|  | Corresponding members |
|  | Associate members |
| Rights of Members: | Only regular members have the active and the passive election right. The other members don't have this right but, otherwise, they have similar rights as regular members. |
| SVU organs: | General Assembly; Executive Council; Membership Committee; Conciliation and Arbitration Committee; Auditors of Accounts; Committees established by General Assembly, as needed. |
| Internal Division: | Branches, Classes, Sections |

Another of Němec's documents are the Guidelines regarding the activities, authority and duties of the Regional Secretaries of SVU. The document is dated September 2, 1960 and is co-signed by Prof. Václav Hlavatý, in his capacity as the SVU President. Here are some excerpts:[1114]

### Activities, Rights and Duties of the SVU Regional Secretaries

The function of the Regional Secretary was established by the SVU Preparatory Council at their Charter meeting on October 24, 1958. The definite sanction did not occur until April 16, 1960, when it was included in the SVU Bylaws, originally as the Article 22, which states that 'The duty of the Regional Secretaries is the recruitment of new members, responsibility for the SVU interests in their regions, and continued working contact with the SVU General-Secretary and the SVU Press Secretary.' According to the original Article 14 of the Bylaws, the Regional Secretaries were simultaneously members of the SVU Council and, as such, they had also comparable rights and responsibilities as the other members of the Council.

The Bylaws don't spell out specific functions and responsibilities of the Regional Secretaries. They become clear, however, when one considers the reasons for the establishment of these positions. The Society wanted

---

[1114] Pokyny předsedy SVU, vztahující se k činnosti, právům a povinnostem oblastních jednatelů SVU, Bloomington, Ind., September 2. 1960.

to decentralize the SVU work with regard to geographical spread of its members and have its representatives in places where there was the largest concentration of SVU intellectuals. One can accomplish much more through personal contact than through correspondence. Besides that, a single person who is thoroughly familiar with the local conditions, can provide meaningful suggestions for the expansion of SVU activities of the region, for establishing local chapters and can effectively coordinate and control the work of the region.

Specifically, the responsibilities of a Regional Secretary include:

1. *Represent SVU in one's region* – This means participation as SVU representative in the Society's meetings, make contact with the leading scientists and artists, be in touch with universities and colleges, have contact with the local press, accept invitations by scientific, artistic and cultural organizations to their activities, and represent SVU in all important events organized by democratic organizations of Czechs and Slovaks abroad, etc.

2. *Promote SVU in one's region* – Use one's knowledge and one's contacts for the promotion of SVU in press and on radio, accept invitation to give lectures about the Society, or find other speakers from among the SVU members, offer local institutions lectures about Czechoslovak sciences and arts, and in case that there is no suitable speaker in the area, find one in other regions, with the help of the Secretary-General, etc.

3. *Conduct a membership drive* – Under no circumstances, should we invite to membership persons who are known for their anti-democratic thinking, not even then if it concerns recognized experts in science or arts. We are a democratic organization. Similarly, we ought to avoid inviting people who are generally considered controversial because of serious defect in character, or persons who are prosecuted for some criminal act, irrespective of their, otherwise, professional standing.

4. *Interest other organizations in membership in SVU* – To be sure, these organizations must be democratic. Their importance lies not only in obtaining their membership fee, which is actually the same as that for individual members, but in the fact that they recognize the professional authority of SVU. Such a membership is also the best prerequisite for possible collaboration.

5. *Establish local chapters, and give assistance with and control their activities* – The right to form local chapters is given by the Bylaws. The details are spelled out in the Rules of Procedures. The chapter can be

formed by at least 5 members who live in the same area so that they can regularly meet. To form a chapter, one needs the consent of the Regional Secretary. In an area where there is no Regional Secretary, the Secretary-General must give his concurrence. If they disapprove of the idea, the local members can still appeal to the SVU Executive Board. If at all possible, the Regional Secretary should take part in the Chapter's meetings to provide advice and through his initiative get them started on various activities, removes obstacles and disputes and has the authority, with his veto power, to stop any decision by the chapter which could bring harm to the Society. The Regional Secretary should not, however, accept any function locally.

6. *Inspire scientific and artistic work of members in his region.*

7. *Organize services for members in his region* – This could be social service, such as finding employment or fiscal assistance, legal help, help with research, etc. For the purpose of evaluation of one's studies in Czechoslovakia, SVU established a special Evaluation Committee, under the chairmanship of Dr. Rudolf Šturm. The Evaluation Committee always welcomes the input from a Regional Secretary on applications from his region.

8. *Work with Secretary-General* – Every third month, Regional Secretary is required to provide report to Secretary-General about the situation in his region. He has to inform him immediately upon founding a local chapter and keep him abreast on all important events and gained experiences in his region. He should consult him on all basic questions and send him suggestions and incentives on possible SVU activities.

9. *Be in contact with Press Secretary* – He should inform the Press Secretary of all events in his region that ought to be publicized, especially with reference to the activities of the local chapter and individual SVU members.

10. *Request (through Secretary-General) reimbursement from SVU Treasurer for his administrative expenses.* The expenses above $25 have to be approved by Secretary-General. It is recommended that the regions make an effort to be self-sufficient, for example from the income of the activities of local chapters.

On another occasion, Němec prepared a set of guidelines concerning the conduct of lectures by local chapters. The document is undated but it probably comes from the same time period as the above, i.e., 1960:[1115]

### Suggestions Concerning the Conduct of Lectures by Local Chapters

An important part of the activities of local chapters is the organization of lectures. The themes can vary but they ought to be in conformance with the program and the mission of SVU.

For successful lecture activities a realistic evaluation of local situation and possibilities should be done first. The situation in an immigrant and exile community, as a rule, is considerably different from the pre-war situation in Czechoslovakia and consequently one should carefully think through the whole idea. The Washington DC Chapter learned their lesson when they started their lecture series last year, about whose successful outcome you must have heard. Inasmuch as I assume that every local chapter will, sooner or later, initiate their own lecture program, I thought it appropriate to acquaint you with our experiences learned.

1. Watching the organizational life in Washington, DC since 1948 showed that public lectures, especially those that were not accompanied with film or slide showing, as a rule, were poorly visited, unless the speaker was unusually liked or the topic was exceptionally attractive. The attendance was usually a reflection of a good will and friendship, or friendly relations with the organizers or to the speaker, rather than an expression of interest in the subject matter of the talk. As a result, almost all our Washington-based organizations stopped sponsoring lectures altogether, except, of course, for commemoration of our national holidays, i.e., March 7 and October 28.

2. The Washington DC Chapter faced the problem of how to attract the interest of the public. After thinking it through, the organizers came with the following prerequisites for running a successful lecture program:[1116]

a) interesting topic

b) high-caliber speaker

---

[1115] Poznámky a podněty k přednáškám v pracovních skupinách SVU.

[1116] When I became Secretary of the Washington DC Chapter, we added another innovation, i.e., after each lecture, we served coffee and pastries, baked by our ladies. This made the meeting more cordial and more enjoyable because the people stayed around and talked to each other and thus became better acquainted with each other.

c) location, equipment and the overall appearance of the lecture room/hall

d) lectures would always be a part of the official meetings of the chapter and, as such, they would be open only to SVU members, to the members of their family and to specially invited guests.

Having this in mind, the Chapter initiated an interesting series of lectures, entitled "Contributions to the Development of the Idea of the Czechoslovak state in the years 1938-1948." The speakers who appeared on the program included such personalities as Minister Dr. Ladislav Feierabend, Ambassador Dr. Juraj Slávik, Ambassador Dr. Štefan Osuský, Dr. Jozef Lettrich, Dr. Arnost Heidrich, Prof. Vratislav Bušek, Minister Václav Majer, the names everybody in the Czechoslovak community readily recognized. The program continues and the plan is to have these lectures published.

The talks were held in the elegant Alliance Room, All Souls Church and the last lecture (Prof. Bušek) was combined with a joint dinner in the Army-Navy Club, one of the choice Clubs in the Washington area. This way, the lectures also became a social event.

Not making the lectures public proved to be a good idea. It made them so much more attractive. It is a fact that people give preference to meetings which have some sort of "numerus clausus" rather than meetings that are accessible to everyone. The exclusion of the public had another advantage: Since the talks were open to SVU members only, and to the members of their families and specially invited guests, there was a control over the audience which assured that the chairperson could manage the debate, which was always lively, without unnecessary confrontation with individuals who might have a personal grudge against the speaker. Since the lecture was a part of a regular Chapter meeting, the speaker's talk became an internal part of the proceedings, and consequently could not be released without the consent of the Chapter and the speaker had thus an assured "copyright."

3. The actual organization of the lectures was also worked out into great detail which became important in practice later. The process was as follows:

a) As already mentioned, invited were only SVU members, members of their family in the region where the chapter functioned. In addition, the speaker could designate additional people who could be invited plus individuals whom the leadership of the chapter recommended.

*Organizational Aspects of the Society* 461

Uninvited people could request admittance from a person who was specifically designated for this purpose. The invited guest was informed that he would not be permitted to attend future meetings, if he missed two lectures without a valid excuse.

b) At the entrance to the lecture hall there was a list of regulars and the invited guests and every visitor had to sign his name upon entry. Next to the sign-up list was a kitty for voluntary contributions to cover the administrative costs. Experience showed that whoever signed the roster also put some money in the kitty. Who was not on the list was not allowed to enter. The sign-up lists allowed a control over those present but it also gave a way of keeping track of the interest among the members.

c) As already mentioned, the lectures were a part of the official meetings, As a rule, each meeting was started by the Chapter chairman who then went through a regular agenda, permitting vote on issues at hand, after which he introduced the chairman pro tempore who took over the lecture part of the meeting, including the discussion. This is the way it was done in Washington.[1117] Each lecture was chaired by someone else, which had a purpose. The chairman pro tempore, who presided over the lecture, was responsible for every detail of the lecture component and his chairing the session was, in a way, a reward for his labors. The audience seemed to like this arrangement, while the chairperson benefited by recapitulating some part of history and also becoming familiar with the organizational rules and routine and, within the Chapter itself, we gained a degree of decentralization.

d) Before starting the lecture, the chair person gave a brief biography of the speaker. The information usually came from the speaker himself. It was not recommended to extol the speaker too much, as it was considered wrong to bring in adverse comments. Three minutes were usually provided for the speaker's introduction.

e) Before beginning his talk, the speaker was required to give the original copy of his speech to the presiding officer. This was a condition *sine qua non*. The reasons for this rigor were:

   i) The preparation of a written manuscript gave guarantee that the speaker will come prepared and that he won't improvise;

---

[1117] Actually, I served as Secretary of the Chapter at that time.

ii) The lecture was a part of an official meeting and. as such, it belongs to the SVU, as a part of the proceedings;

iii) In the case of Washington Chapter, the manuscript was also required because there was intention to publish it.

The manuscript was not requested until the time the speaker began his talk, because the Society did not want to be responsible for the contents of the lecture, and consequently no SVU officer read it, nor approved it.

f) The lecture itself was planned exactly for one hour, because experience showed that this was the maximum time listeners were willing to listen.

All the Washington lectures were recorded on a tape. This way the lecture was recorded even in points that differed from the written text but, even more importantly, the debate was recorded. Besides that, since the speakers were individuals who played important roles in the Czechoslovak political life, or in some area of Czechoslovak sciences or arts, the recorded tape itself had historical value.

g) It is the responsibility of the presiding officer to assure that the speaker is nor interrupted, so that he has the entire hour for his presentation and can finish it without embarrassment.

h) After the completion of the lecture, the presiding officer allows the debate to proceed and also directs it. The debate must be matter-of-fact and comments that have nothing to do with the topic are not tolerated. If more than one person wishes to talk, it is up to the presiding officer to decide on the order and the allotted time limit. If the presiding officer anticipates that the debate may swerve outside the academic limits, he can request that all questions and comments be first given to him, after which he will decide about their acceptance.

Those who would deviate from the orderly and proper discussion are rebuked or divested from further debate and, in serious situations, can be asked to leave the room or the meeting may be adjourned.

i) The conduct of the entire meeting, including the lecture component, must be dignified. For psychological reasons it is necessary to avoid unsuitable jokes, unseemly fraternizing, etc. The members and guests must realize that they are attending a serious working session of an organization whose mission is important and serious.

The Washington meetings and lectures were conducted quite formally. The approach had a good psychological effect on the audience and there was general feeling that this is the only way to assure freedom of speech for the speaker and the listener, how to assure matter-of-factness and the decent conduct of the proceedings.

j) At the conclusion of the debate, the presiding officer thanks the speaker and the attendees and hands over the meeting to the chairman of the chapter, or with his concurrence, he adjourns the meeting.

The experience gained in Washington may be applicable in many other places but it is understandable that some changes may be needed.

# 74
## *SVU Membership*

The Table below shows the number of SVU members at different time periods. Since the Society did not keep running tallies on its membership, it took some doing to resurrect these numbers. Until 1971, the figures are essentially based on the various reports of the SVU Secretary-Generals in a given time period. The later figures are based on the SVU Directories. To be sure, these two sets of sources may not be always comparable but, nevertheless, the combined figures show similar trends. Since it usually took several years to prepare a given SVU Directory, when it finally came out, it couldn't obviously be up to date. It should also be noted that, at any one time, the reported numbers may not include all members because their application forms might have been in the hands of the membership committee. On the other hand, the numbers may include names of individuals who had recently deceased. I would also like to point out that it is difficult, if not practically impossible, to reconcile these numbers with the Treasurer's reports because many of the members paid their dues irregularly and some actually paid in lump sum for several years of membership. The European chapters muddle the water even more, because their members usually paid their dues locally, of which the central treasury saw very little. Nevertheless, for symbolic and psychological reasons, the SVU Executive Board agreed to have them be included in the *SVU Directory*, although legally they cannot be considered *bona fide* rightful members of the Society.

Be that as it may, as the Table shows quite clearly, an upward movement in the SVU membership, with coming years, is plainly discernible, indicating the vitality and the growth of the Society. It is also of interest that the Society had a sizeable membership, even before it was actually officially established in October 1958, at which time the total membership already exceeded 300.

## Table 1
## Number of SVU Members in Retrospect

| Date | No. of Members | Source |
| --- | --- | --- |
| 1957 | 57 | Secretary-General (SG) |
| June 16, 1958 | almost 200 | SG |
| October 24, 1958 | over 300 | SG |
| December 31, 1959 | 325 | SG |
| April 15, 1960 | 370 | SG |
| June 15, 1960 | 386 | SG |
| October 1, 1960 | 403 | SG |
| April 19, 1962 1st Congress) | 521 | SG |
| September 1963 | 615 | SG |
| September 1964 | 726 | SG |
| March 1965 | 800 | SG |
| September 1965 | 855 | SG |
| June 1966 | 970 | SG |
| September 1966 | 1,000 | SG |
| November 1968 | 1,200 | SG |
| November 6, 1970 | 1,365 | SG |
| November 3, 1971 | 1,482 | SG |
| 1983 | 1,559 | SVU Directory 1983 |
| 1988 | 1,933 | SVU Directory 1988 |
| 1992 | 2,167 | SVU Directory 1992 |
| 2003 | 3,014 | SVU Directory 2003 |
| 2006 | 3.087 | SVU Directory 2006 |

When transposed into a graph form, one gets a better visual of the rising trend line, indicating the moving average.

**SVU Membership**

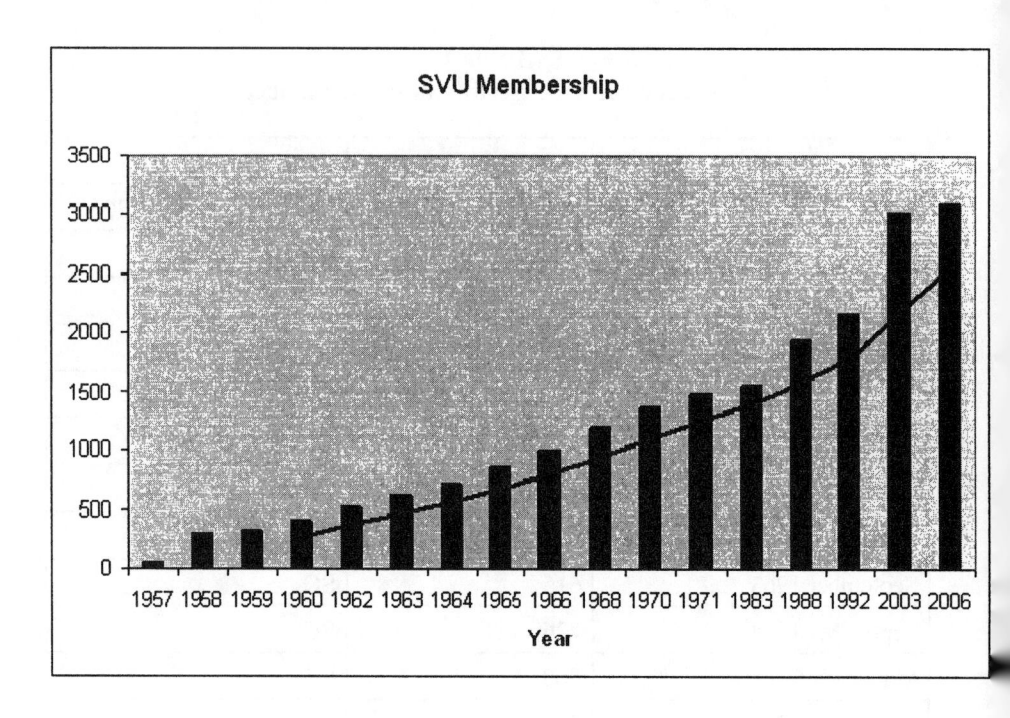

[Bar chart showing SVU membership from 1957 to 2006, rising from near 0 in 1957 to over 3000 in 2006. Years shown: 1957, 1958, 1959, 1960, 1962, 1963, 1964, 1965, 1966, 1968, 1970, 1971, 1983, 1988, 1992, 2003, 2006.]

From the very beginning, SVU could not decide whether the new organization should be limited only to the outstanding experts in a given field, or whether the membership should be broader and also include "friends of sciences and arts." The 1960 Bylaws distinguished two membership categories: the regular members and the associate members. A regular member would be a person who attained some academic degree. There were only a few exception to this principle, i.e., the journalists, artists or noted cultural workers. Individuals who did not meet these criteria were included in the category of associate members. In practice, such distinction meant that only regular members had the voting rights. The associate members were, however, permitted to participate in the elections of the local chapters.

As Jaroslav Němec pointed out in one of his situation reports, the two distinctly different types of membership were important in the formative years of the Society since it prevented individuals lacking education to make judgments on technical matters. With coming years, it was learned that this concern was not as great as the drafters of the Bylaws originally thought, while, on the other hand, two different categories of membership caused some apprehension among the members because some of the associate members felt the stigma of being inferior to their colleagues who were in the other category.

Although the Society claimed to have members as early as 1957, they were not really officially members yet because at the recommendation of the SVU Preparatory Council it was decided to have a newly appointed Membership Committee to go though all the applications and make the determination to which of the two categories an individual belongs. This process began in June 1961 and was completed by the end of October of that year. Once the Committee finished their task, it was up to the SVU Council to make the final determination. As stated in the report of the Secretary-General,[1118] by the end of 1961, every member would know where he/she belongs and would also be recipient of the SVU membership card.

There were several attempts to analyze the composition of the SVU membership. In one of these analyses,[1119] Secretary-General John G. Lexa made a comparison between August 1965 and January 1970, at which times the Society had 855 and 1293 members, respectively. The age group containing the largest number of members was between 30 to 50 years in both cases, with a 1.2% increase in the latter. The age group between 60 and 70 years remained more or less the same for both situations (20.6% in 1970 and 20.2% in 1965. The number of members in the ages from 70 to 80 marked an increase of 4.3% in 1970, amounting to 20.2% of the total membership. In contrast, in the age group between 50 and 60 years, there was a slight decline in the number of members in 1970, in comparison with 1965 (23.4 % vs. 25.6%), and this was also true about the age group between 40 and 45 years, where the difference was even greater, amounting to 5% (10.7% vs. 15.8%). The percentage of the youngest group (between 20 and 30 years) remained again very low (1.9% in 1965 vs. 2.7% for 1970).

In the follow-up analysis[1120] of November 11, 1970, it was concluded that, although the number of the youngest members (20-30 years)

---

[1118] "SVU in the Fall 1971 – Report of Secretary-General," *Zprávy SVU*, vol. 3, No. 8 (October 1961), pp. 73-74.

[1119] "Statistics," *Zprávy SVU*, vol. 12, No. 1 (January 1970), pp. 6-7.

[1120] "Statistical Report about the Number of SVU Members, *Zprávy SVU*, vol. 12, No. 10 (December 1970), pp. 81- 83.

doubled, when compared with the previous year, it amounted to only 6% of the total membership. The largest number of members remained in the group between 40 to 60 years, i.e., around 54%.

With reference to the small percentage of young people in the formative years, the Society made a serious effort to remedy the situation, particularly in the years 2002-2006, when we made the "Accent on Youth" the SVU Number One Priority. As a result of that effort, a number of new young people were recruited, some of whom assumed significant responsibilities in the Society. The increase in the membership among young is clearly noticeable in my last 2006 report on the new members, which, by some fluke, did not appear in print until the March 2007 issue of *Zprávy SVU*.[1121]

Of interest is also the statistical breakdown of SVU membership by countries. Thus in December 1970, the statistics showed 73% of members living in the US, as compared to 10.3% in Canada, 2.5% in Switzerland, 2.8% in Germany, 2.4% in England, 1.2% in France, 0.8% in Austria, 0.6% in Italy, and lesser numbers in other countries.

If we look at actual numbers of members living in various countries, on the basis of SVU Directory from 2003, we get the following picture:

North America
- U.S.A.     ca 1842
- Canada     ca 307
- Mexico     1

Central America     5
South America     8
Europe
- Czech Republic     310
- Switzerland     112
- Slovak Republic     102
- Germany     79
- Austria     46
- United Kingdom     30
- Sweden     21

---

[1121] "New SVU Members," *Zprávy SVU*, vol. 49, No. 2 (March-April 2007), pp. 7-12.

## SVU Membership

|  |  |  |
|---|---|---|
|  | Netherlands | 15 |
|  | France | 14 |
|  | Italy | 12 |
| Oceania |  |  |
|  | Australia | 42 |
|  | New Zealand | 6 |
| Asia |  | 14 |
| Africa |  | 7 |

So in comparison with 1970, some 33 years later, the majority of SVU members still lives in the US, although their percentage is lower by 12 percentage point, which is largely due to the new members in the Czech Republic and Slovakia.

From the very beginning, the Society was considered a joint endeavor of Czechs and Slovaks. It was for this reason that during the original discussions in 1954, Dr. Branislav Štefánek[1122] was included. Subsequently, other known Slovaks joined, such as Dr. Mikula,[1123] Dr. Mamatey[1124] and Dr. Andic.[1125] Nevertheless, it is the fact that the percentage of Slovaks, because of their then complicated internal situation, had a lower number than one would expect from the ratio of Slovaks vs. Czechs in Czechoslovakia. The Society tried to remedy the situation by seeking addresses of professional Slovaks in the US, especially in university settings, and inviting them to membership.

Within the Society, the relationship between the Czechs and Slovaks always was and has been more than brotherly. In fact, nobody ever paid any attention to the differences in ethnic background. Slovaks occupied high positions in the SVU hierarchy on most Executive Boards, whose membership was not based on any political motivation nor on

---

[1122] Branislav Anton Štefánek (1923-1983), journalist, editor, Radio Free Europe, Munich, Germany; son of noted Slovak sociologist Anton Štefánek.

[1123] Felix Mikula (1907-1979), former professor of dogmatic theology at Charles University; former aide to the Archbishop Josef Beran.

[1124] Victor S. Mamatey (1917-2007), professor of history at Florida State University in Tallahassee.

[1125] Vojtech E. Andic (1910-1976), professor of economics at Union University, Albany, NY.

maintaining some arbitrary ratio, but rather on the assessment of the individual's performance. Take for example, Vojtech E. Andic, who worked for the Society from the very beginning, who in the period 1966-68 held the difficult post of Secretary-General and later became SVU Vice President. Architect Emil Royco, in turn, who was SVU Treasurer for six years (1966-1972), was originally Treasurer of the Washington DC Chapter. Actually, I had the pleasure of recruiting him into the Society, when I first met him during the First SVU Congress in Washington in 1962. The third example is Andrew Eliáš, who succeeded me as chairman of the publication committee, who qualified for that position by his previous engagement as a program organizer of the 4th SVU Congress in 1968. Later, he became Editor of *Zprávy SVU*. The Slovaks, of course, held other important functions within the Society. For example Rev. Felix Mikula organized SVU Munich Chapter and for a number of years held the post of Vice President in the Society, just as did Prof. Jaroslav Pelikán,[1126] Prof. Victor S. Mamatey, Dr. Michael Šumichrast,[1127] a former SVU Treasurer and Chairman of the Washington DC Chapter.

In later years, the number of Slovaks began increasing in more rapid pace, under the influence of changed conditions in Czechoslovakia, and due to the influx of new refugees.

To complete the picture of the SVU membership, it would be in order to mention the names of at least some better known members, such as: Madeleine Korbel Albright, Vratislav Bušek, Peter Demetz, Karl W. Deutsch, Francis Dvorník, Václav Hlavatý, Roman Jakobson, Zdeněk Kopal, Josef Korbel, Vladimír Krajina, Frank Král, Henry Kučera, Nicholas Lobkowicz, Jan Milič Lochman, Otakar Machotka, Jiří Nehněvajsa, Otakar Odložilík, Jaroslav Pelikán, Leopold Pospíšil, Jan F. Tříska and René Wellek among the university professors; Rudolf Firkušný, Karel Husa, Karel B. Jirák, Rafael Kubelík, Eva Líková, Oskar Morawetz, Jarmila Novotná, among musicians, composers and singers; F. V. Foit, A. Kohout-Lecoque, Oskar Kokoschka, Albin Polášek, Antonín Raymond, Koloman Sokol, Ladislav Sutnar, Jan Zach, among the visual artists and architects; Jarka Burian, Hugo Haas, Jára Kohout,

---

[1126] Jaroslav Pelikán (1923-2006), professor of ecclesiastical history at Yale University.

[1127] Michael Šumichrast (1921-2007), director of economics of the National Association of Home Builders, Washington, DC.

*SVU Membership* 471

Jan Rubeš, Jiří Voskovec, among the dramatic artists; Cardinal Josef Beran, Přemysl Pitter, Bishop Jaroslav Škarvada, Matthew Spinka, Karel Vrána, Jarold K. Zeman, among theologians; Jan Čep, Egon Hostovský, Pavel Javor, Petr Den, Zdeněk Němeček, among the writers; Ivan Herben, Josef Josten, Ferdinand Peroutka, Pavel Tigrid, among journalists, etc.

The list of "prominents" greatly expanded by the influx of the post-sixty-eighters, a la Karel Ančerl, Jan Beneš, Miloš Forman, Vojtěch Jasný, Jiří Kolář, Milan Kundera, Arnošt Lustig, Mirek J. Plavec, Jan Roček, Emil Skamene, Petr Skalník, Vladimír Škutina, Josef Škvorecký, Jan Švejnar, Otto Ulč, etc. And when the Iron Curtain fell down and the democracy returned to Czechoslovakia and its Successor States, the membership rolls where enriched by such personalities, as Ferdinand Devinský, Libor Ebringer, Miroslav Ferenčík, Norbert Frištacký, Stanislav Hanzl, Josef Jařáb, Radoslav Kvapil, Zdeněk Lojda, Ladislav Macho, Václav Pačes, Radim Palouš, Jiří Petr, František Sehnal, František Šmahel, Juraj Švec, Alexander Tkáč, Jaroslav Valenta, Otto Wichterle, Rudolf Zahradník, Petr Zuna and others. I would be amiss not to also include a number of our honorary members from Czechoslovakia, including Václav Černý, Václav Havel, Bohumil Hrabal, Zdeněk Rotrekl, Jaroslav Seifert, Eugen Suchoň and Dominik Tatarka.

The membership was not limited to the Czech or Slovak natives, by any means, but also included a number of noted personalities of other nationalities, such as Peter Brock, R. V. Burks, Louis E. Faucher, Feliks Gross, Alfred French, D. Carleton Gajdusek, Tadeusz Z. Gasinski, Thomas T. Hammond, Frederick G. Heymann, Miroslav Hryhorijiv-Gregory, Owen V. Johnson, Andrzej Korbonski, Heinrich Kuhn, Heinrich H. Kunstmann, Rado L. Lencek, Paul R. Magocsi, Roman Olynyk, Lawrence D. Orton, Marija Petrovska, Rostislav Pletnev, Ivan L. Rudnytsky, Howard A. Rusk, Emil Schieche, H. Gordon Skilling, Ronald G. Slaby, Roman S. Smal-Stocki, S. Harrison Thompson, Charles Townsend, Elizabeth W. Trahan, Betty M. Unterberger, Rudolf Urban, Piotr S. Wandycz, Robert S. Wechsler, Stanley B. Winters and William E. Wright.

# 75
## SVU Finances

As pointed out in Němec's reminiscences, the planning of SVU started without any money. In 1957, the organizers received a small loan of $35 from the Washington Chapter of the Czechoslovak National Council of America, which was not too difficult, considering that Jaroslav Němec headed the latter, frankly, it might even have been his own money. The organizers were not deterred by the paucity of fiscal resources, even when they received a letter from one of our own well known economists, stating "I like your idea very much but I won't become your member because it is useless. You have no financial means and consequently you cannot accomplish anything!"

Němec and his colleagues did not give up so easily. They persevered and used their own money for postage and other administrative expenses. In terms of publication projects, which they considered as number one priority, they knew that it could get expensive but they hoped that they would be able to persuade some of our millionaires and other wealthy countrymen to finance it. So they went, with the hat in their hands, literally begging for assistance. In spite of their eloquence and their persuasive case, the result was deplorable. One benefactor gave them $300 once and for all, another said that he will contribute once he sees what they can do and whether they are worth it, the third one wanted to think it over and after several years of thinking, he passed away, leaving all his property to the State and that's the way it went. In the end, it was clear that the SVU was on its own.

The organizers realized that to accomplish their goals will be a slow process because they could only count on the membership dues of the members and a few occasional gifts. As a result, all the work for SVU, from the very beginning, had to be done gratis.

The growing membership, nevertheless, expected from its leadership some sort of activities and the realization of the goals. To be sure, initially there was not only lack of finances but there was also a paucity of volunteers to do the work. When the SVU began publishing *Zprávy SVU* in 1959, this was a step forward, as it brought in more members and with them also more money from their membership dues, even though the cost of publishing the newsletter was quite high.

A basic turn in the SVU situation came with the organization of the First SVU Congress in Washington, DC in 1962, initially opposed by some of the Board members, as well as those of SVU Council. They talked about the almost certain fiscal debacle, as well as scientific debacle and the megalomaniac plans of the Washingtonians, by which they meant Němec and me. Nevertheless, with the aid of Professor Hlavatý, the idea was finally approved and to the surprise of many, the Congress was a great success.

The Congress clearly demonstrated that the SVU is a viable institution. It brought in many new members, as well as more gifts and higher donations. It led to the establishment of the SVU Office in New York and a part-time secretary and thus relieving the Secretary-General and other officers of some administrative chores. The membership fees and smaller donations covered most SVU administrative expenses. Other income came from selling publications and then from larger gifts from private individuals and institutions. Another important milestone in the SVU history was publishing papers from the first and second Congresses which further enhanced the SVU image and reputation worldwide, particularly when the first book reviews extolled the importance and the quality of these volumes.

Of course, as time went on, with exceptionally good planning, the Society was beginning to make profit on its Congresses, as well as Conferences. In fact, the SVU World Congresses were planned in such a way so that they were self-sufficient. In other words, they had to pay for themselves and bring in a revenue, as well. With reference to publications, the Society made a determined effort to find private publishers who would publish the Society monographs at their own expense, which was achieved by choice topics and having outstanding authors. The Society also solicited assistance from external sources, government institutions and private foundations.

In the last decade or so, the Society always operated on the balanced budget and, as a rule, each year ended up with a surplus. One could thus say that the Society stands entirely on its own feet, it has no debts, and is not subservient to anyone. Frankly, during my presidency, I never felt that money was an obstacle to almost anything we wanted to do. If one had a good product and was able to sell it, you did not need any extra money. That was my philosophy. Consequently, we put the emphasis on quality and on highly interesting and attractive topics.

That is the SVU financial success story in brief. Having said that, it is of interest to look at some figures from the time of the formative years of the Society, which clearly show that the Society, in the early days, operated on "a shoestring budget."

Thus, in January 1960, Secretary-General Šturm[1128] reported that the SVU had a total of $700 in its account and no debts. The amount should have been probably higher, since some of the Regional Secretaries had not, as yet, mailed the Secretary General their membership applications and checks of recent members.

As per the Situation Report of Secretary-General Němec,[1129] dated June 15, 1960, SVU had approximately $800 in its bank account. It was anticipated that approximately $1,400 would be collected from the membership fees and, based on previous experience, additional $500 was expected from donations. In term of expenses, printing costs of *Zprávy SVU* were estimated at $600 and administrative expenses $500. Consequently $1,600 was available for various SVU activities. The amount would increase with the admittance of new SVU members.

As shown in the subsequent report,[1130] dated October 1, 1960, the estimate for publishing *Zprávy SVU* was underestimated. According to November Report the figure was changed to $1,000. This meant that half of a member's dues, i.e., $2.50, was spent on *Zprávy SVU*. The administrative expenses (office supplies, postage) did not exceed $500 and SVU, of course, did not reimburse anyone for their work. In terms of income, most of it came from membership dues, or better said, from the dues of US and Canadian members. The SVU initially did not ask people living outside the American continent to pay dues, because for some people $5 membership fee seemed a bit high. To be sure, the Society hoped that this situation would soon change because it did not seem fair to have the entire financial burden on the shoulders of its US and Canadian members.

---

[1128] Rudolf Šturm, Situation Report for the members of the Preparatory Council, January 12, 1960.

[1129] Jaroslav Němec, Situation Report of SVU Secretary-General, June 15, 1960.

[1130] Jaroslav Němec, Situation Report of SVU Secretary-General, October 1, 1960.

*SVU Finances*

Of some interest is the Treasurer's Report[1131] of the same period (April 1960). In it, he writes that "The SVU income in the first months in 1959 was meager. The Society had no solid financial foundation and it began its work without any subvention. The Society was still *in statu nascendi*, the state of formation, it only now carried out its membership drive and the new members began sending in their dues and gifts. Fortunately, the expenses in this period were not high. Practically, the only expenses we had, were for postage, buying paper, mimeographing material, etc. On May 31, 1959 we recorded our lowest balance in our banking account, amounting to $34.52. With a few larger gifts in June 1959, SVU achieved somewhat firmer ground. Credit for it goes to Mr. Kubát who gave SVU a donation of $300, Mr. Thomas Baťa, who donated $100 and Mr. Bedřich Čecha,[1132] who also gave us $100.

In the fall of 1959, all members received a statement of the status of their membership dues. It had a positive outcome, especially during September and October, when a large majority of delinquent members paid their dues. With additional personal reminders, the number of delinquents decreased to 38. Later another reminder was sent in March 1960, to which most addressees responded positively. As of today, we have only 14 delinquents who have not paid their 1959 dues.

During the current and the past year, to the SVU administrative expenses were added expenses in connection with our *Zprávy SVU*. The printing of one issue cost us initially $82.50. Ivan Herben succeeded to negotiate the price downward to $70. For distribution we are being charged $15. The income from advertisements and gifts relating to *Zprávy* lowers the costs approximately to $65 per issue.

In summary, here is a brief overview of our finances:

**The Year 1959**

| | | |
|---|---|---|
| Membership dues paid by 273 members | Total | $546.00 |
| Gifts from 103 members | Total | $1224.65 |
| 15 members owe dues for 1959 | | |

---

[1131] Oldřich Černý, Financial Report, Washington, DC, April 1, 1960.

[1132] Bedřich Čecha (1906-), long-time president of the Hamilton branch of the Czechoslovak Association of Canada (CSAC).

**The Year 1960**

| | | |
|---|---|---|
| Membership dues paid by 72 members | Total | $218.00 |
| Gifts from 18 members | Total | $113.00 |
| Advertisements | | $20.00 |
| | Overall Total | $2,021.65 |

**Expenses**

| | | |
|---|---|---|
| Administrative (December 1958-1/4/1960) | Total | $405.29 |
| Zprávy SVU[1133] | | $513.25 |
| Distribution of Zprávy SVU | | $98.41 |
| Special issue of Zprávy SVU | | $100.00 |
| | Overall Expenses | $1,116.95 |
| Cash as of April 1, 1960 | | $904.70 |

I don't want to leave the impression that everything was always rosy with the SVU finances. Actually, when I assumed the presidency of the Society in 1974, the Society was at the brink of bankruptcy, brought about by poor management. Frankly, it is now difficult to comprehend how that could happen, considering that, in 1969, the Society had reserved $12,000 for publications, which was 75% of its assets. Be that as it may, it took me and our Executive Board tremendous effort to turn things around and put the Society on firm ground again. For details see the chapter dealing with my presidency.

Something, almost comparable, occurred when I was brought back to the SVU leadership in 1994, when the Society was again at a very critical point. There was general apathy among the membership, partly due to the unsettling political situation in the old homeland and there was even talk about abolishing it. All this had detrimental effects on the Society's finances. We succeeded in turning the situation around and actually bring the Society to even higher horizons than ever before. When I retired form the post of SVU President for the second time, after continuous twelve years of service, I was pleased that I could pass on the reign to my successors, with the Society being in excellent shape, in terms of its reputation, as well as organizationally and financially. In fact, financially the Society was in the best shape ever.

---

[1133] SVU Treasurer's figures for printing Zprávy SVU seem considerably lower than those reported by the Secretary-General. Perhaps they did not cover the whole year.

# 76
## The Non-political Character of the SVU

One characteristic that differentiates SVU from other Czechoslovak organizations abroad was its non-political character. The founders of the Society felt so strongly about this that the matter was put into the SVU Bylaws.

The issue came up so frequently in discussions that the responsible SVU officers had time and time again to publicly address it and defend the Society's stand. One can find references to it in practically every speech of most SVU Presidents. Some even wrote editorials in *Zprávy SVU* and in public media. The most adamant people in SVU about this issue were Jaroš Němec, René Wellek and myself.

It was the political climate prevalent in the Czechoslovak exile that actually led to the establishment of the SVU. In the mid fifties the Czechoslovak exile was divided into different political groups and subgroups, based on the original political parties that existed during the era of the Czechoslovak Republic and a number of other newly formed associations and private clubs. The situation got so bad that the adherents of one camp would not talk to people in other camps and publicly attacked each other, blaming others for the misfortunes that brought Czechoslovakia under the Communist rule. It was this poisonous atmosphere that led Czechoslovak intellectuals abroad to the realization that enough is enough and that time has come to change the negativism into a positive mode, the result of which was the establishment of an independent non-political organization under the name of the Czechoslovak Society of Arts and Sciences in America, as SVU was originally called.

The politicians viewed the establishment of the new organization with great suspicion, considering it a threat to their own political activities. They accused SVU leaders, especially its first President Prof. Václav Hlavatý, of building for themselves a new platform for their ambitions to take over the exile and make them principal players in Czechoslovakia after the fall of Communism. This was obviously nonsense and the Society had no choice but to fight against such accusations, not so much by rhetoric, but by its own deeds and actions.

Despite the fact that the accusations against SVU persisted for a number of years, one politician after another, sooner or later, joined the SVU ranks, following the old saying: "If you cannot beat them, join them." Politicians, who joined SVU, included such personalities as Petr Zenkl, Jaroslav Stránský, Václav Majer, Adolf Procházka, Josef Černý, Jozef Lettrich, Juraj Slávik and Ján Papánek. Among politicians the first person to break their ranks was Ladislav Feierabend who joined SVU at the very beginning and who held the function of the first President of the SVU Washington DC Chapter in 1958. To be sure, he did not belong to those politicians who tried to besmirch the SVU name.

It is of note that it was actually SVU that offered politicians of different camps the first official platform where they could meet and openly discuss political issues in a civilized manner in an academic atmosphere. The first such opportunity was provided to them in the series of lectures and debates, organized by the SVU Washington DC Chapter, relating to political events, covering years 1938 to 1948. Later, when the Society began organizing its bi-annual Congresses, the programs regularly included lectures, symposia and discussion panels on politics and political affairs, in which a number of political personalities took part.

In the sixties, some "do-gooders" in Canada started spreading stories that SVU was run by Social Nationalists, because people like Ivan Herben, Vratislav Bušek, Vladimír Krajina, who belonged to that party in Czechoslovakia, were in leadership role of the Society. Němec retaliated to that by saying that one could make a similar case for the People's Party, basing it on the role of its former members in the SVU affairs, like Adolf Procházka, Felix Mikula or Rudolf Šturm. And one could make similar claims for other political parties. When I began playing an important role in SVU, I certainly could not have been accused of being a National Socialist or an adherent of the People's Party, considering that my farther belonged to the Agrarian Party which he represented in the pre-war Czechoslovak Parliament as the youngest member of that body, not to speak of the fact that I always considered myself an independent in my political thinking.

The nonpolitical character of SVU had a different connotation for different people. Some thought it referred to avoidance of politicking while others, who were in majority, had complete abstinence from political activities in mind.

On and off, the Society was criticized for not taking part in public demonstrations and political rallies, organized, for example, by the Czechoslovak National Council of America and/or the Council of Free Czechoslovakia. Some of the ardent politicians went as far as accusing the Society of lack of patriotism, if not worse. It is a paradox that the same people, who initially accused SVU of politicking, now made a concerted effort to pull the Society with them to the political arena.

The accusations that SVU lacked patriotism was utter nonsense, of course, since the Society regularly participated, together with other ethnic organizations, in the traditional memorials, such as the anniversaries of Masaryk's birth, the founding of Czechoslovakia, etc. Moreover, numerous lectures and discussions at the SVU Congresses and Conferences, as well as its publications, have done more for making the American public aware of the situation in the communist Czechoslovakia than empty speeches of politicians. Proceedings in an academic setting and atmosphere were judged far more objective and far more credible than some public demonstration which was generally viewed with suspicion. For this reason, the SVU activities were taken seriously by the Communist regime in Czechoslovakia, which considered the Society as its arch enemy.

An example of how the Communist regime felt about the SVU was the Prague Radio broadcast of March 18 1960, in which they savagely attacked SVU, using as a pretense the SVU program lecture series, initiated by the Washington DC Chapter, on "the Idea of the Czechoslovak State in the "period of 1938-1945,"[1134] in which they grouped the SVU members with the Neo-Nazi Revanchists.

During the Fourth SVU World Congress in Washington, DC in 1968, which took place soon after the infamous Soviet invasion of Czechoslovakia, there was a Press Conference with Prof. Ivan Sviták who just arrived from Austria, bringing with him the proclamation of Czech intellectuals, who just escaped from their invaded homeland. His testimony and the wording of the proclamation, entitled "Manifest against Aggression," brought excitement among the newsmen in America, as well as overseas, as was evident from the published

---

[1134] "Invisible Work," *Zprávy SVU,* vol. 2, No. 4 (April 1960), pp. 1-2.

commentaries.[1135] Even the Soviet Press TASS carried a statement about our Congress, referring to the participants "who escaped from Czechoslovakia, with the retreating Hitler Army and who now form a reactionary part of the Czechoslovak emigration."

It is of interest that our Society was the only Czechoslovak organization abroad which was so brutally attacked. The explanation is easy: They were afraid of our influence in the academic circles. They knew well that our university professors could and would speak freely and open the students' eyes with truth about the Soviet imperialism. A free word for Moscow was more dangerous than some weapon. A free word – the truth – penetrates the strongest armor. The largest army won't stop it and neither can police arrest it.

Upon my election to SVU presidency, the Communist regime in Prague reported that "some kind of a Society of Arts and Sciences at its Congress in Washington, DC elected for its new President some Zionist by name of Reczkziegel." To be sure, the term "Zionist" in the Communist vocabulary was the worst swearword which was used for their worst enemies only, which had nothing to do with the individual's religious background or his stand. To make it more persuasive, they messed up the spelling of my name so that it would more resemble a name of German Jewish origin.[1136]

In terms of specific disputes over the non-political nature of SVU, one incident comes to mind more than anything else. It actually occurred during the first term of my presidency in 1976, when we were organizing our Bicentennial Congress. Sáša Bořkovec, who served as one of the Vice Presidents on our Executive Board, had the responsibility for coordinating the Congress program. One of his panel organizers, Prof. Joseph Zacek of the State University of New York in Albany, presumably on his own volition and without Bořkovec's knowledge,[1137] invited several speakers from Czechoslovakia which caused an outcry among

---

[1135] "Echo of Invasion of Czechoslovakia at the Congress," *Zprávy SVU*, vol. 10, No. 7-8 (September-October 1968), pp. 45-46.

[1136] It was published in the periodical *Život strany*, which was a political organ of the Czechoslovak Communist Party.

[1137] Actually when later asked about this, Prof. Zacek vehemently denied this, claiming that he informed Bořkovec, at the very beginning, of his plan to invite speakers from Czechoslovakia (Record of Secretary-General John G. Lexa's telephone conversation with Prof. J. F. Zacek about Palacký Symposium, dated November 26, 1976).

the Czechoslovak exile politicians, when it became known. As a result, SVU was practically accused of collaboration with the communists. I still vividly recall receiving letters from several politically oriented Czechoslovak organizations abroad, as well as from individuals. These letters caused quite a furor among the members of our Executive Board, who felt that these organizations had no business interfering in the affairs of our Society.

Jaroš Němec, who regularly attended our Board meetings, guided us to restrain and subsequently drafted a public statement [1138] in an effort to pacify the leaders of the Czechoslovak political exile. As it turned out, at the end, none of the intended speakers from Czechoslovakia showed up at the Congress and the few papers from that country that were read, had nothing to do with politics. They dealt entirely with the historian František Palacký (1798-1876), which was the theme of the symposium. Nevertheless, the harm was done. Although the SVU public statement, referenced above, seemingly appeased the SVU critics, the Symposium chairman, upset by the attacks from the politicians, severed his ties with our Society, as did several other historians, complaining of the censorship and unjustly blaming SVU for the entire incident. You never win in situations like this. This was also the last time we let the politicians or outsiders interfere with the Society's affairs.

In spite of its nonpolitical nature, SVU has always been in the forefront whenever there was a question of violations of human rights or personal freedom. During the occupation of Czechoslovakia in 1968, SVU sent out a Memorandum[1139] to 1000 universities in the free world protesting against the occupation and against the decline of public morality in the world, and pleaded for help for the increasing numbers of refugees escaping from Czechoslovakia.[1140]

In 1977, SVU protested against persecution of Czech and Slovak intellectuals and the Chartists,[1141] at which time, it also issued a special

---

[1138] "Declaration of SVU Executive Board," *Hlas Národa*, Saturday, May 21, 1977, p. 11.

[1139] "SVU Memorandum to Universities of the World," *Zprávy SVU*, vol. 10, No. 9 (November 1968), pp. 57-58.

[1140] The entire text of the Memorandum has been reprinted in the Chapter "Jaroslav Němec's Presidency."

[1141] "Prohlášení SVU k Chartě 77" (SVU Proclamation regarding the Charter 77), *Zprávy SVU*, vol. 19, No. 2 (March-April 1977), pp. 1-2.

proclamation on the need to pursue free inquiry and exchange of ideas.[1142] The text of the proclamations follows.

## AN ASSERTION OF THE NEED TO INTENSIFY THE PURSUIT OF FREE INQUIRY AND EXCHANGE OF IDEAS

PREAMBLE

The Czechoslovak Society of Arts and Sciences in America, Inc. (the Society), a nonpartisan, nonprofit, cultural organization, is dedicated to the principles of free search for truth and knowledge, free contacts among peoples and free dissemination of ideas. The Society associates scientists, scholars, artists, and writers throughout the world who, either because of their national origin or because of their particular interests and calling, pursue activities related to Czechoslovakia, her peoples and their contribution to the world culture.

RESOLUTION

Assembled in Washington, D.C. in commemoration of the Bicentennial Anniversary of the American Revolution, the members of the Society greatly cherishing their status as free men;
Proudly affirming their allegiance to the fundamental rights invested in the Declaration of Independence and the United States Constitution;
Sincerely joining in the celebration of the American Revolution;
Gratefully remembering the role of the American people in establishing a free and democratic Czechoslovakia;
Deservingly pointing out the contribution of Czechs and Slovaks to American and world culture;
Unwaveringly pledging their travail and endeavors to the cause of freedom and human dignity.

HAVE RESOLVED

TO REAFFIRM their faith in the free search for truth and individual happiness as the fundamental basis of any political system preserving the dignity of man;

---

[1142] "SVU Proclamation on the Need to Intensify the Pursuit of Free Inquiry and Exchange of Ideas," *Zprávy SVU*, vol. 19, No. 2 (March-April 1977), pp. 2-3.

TO EXPRESS their deep concern over the loss of freedom of assembly, inquiry and expression in Czechoslovakia and other countries of the world;

TO WELCOME the efforts of Czech and Slovak artists and scientists, dedicated to the principles of intellectual and creative freedom, who in the present difficult conditions in Czechoslovakia strive to fulfill their mission so important for all nations;

TO URGE all scientists, scholars, artists and writers throughout the world to ask and work for reestablishing of these fundamental rights in Czechoslovakia as well as elsewhere in the world;

TO CALL on all men of good will to join them and work together for application of the principles enunciated in the United Nations Universal Declaration of Human Rights and upholding universal belief in the worth and dignity of each human being.

Approved by General Assembly of the Czechoslovak Society of Arts and Sciences in America, Washington, D.C., August 12, 1976

Miloslav Rechcígl, Jr., Ph.D.  John G. Lexa, J.D.

President  Secretary-General

In 1985, the SVU Executive Board approved a special statement for presentation to the US delegation, attending the Cultural Forum in Budapest on 15-October-15 November,[1143] in which the Society appealed to the governments, signatories of the Final Act of Helsinki, to adopt the following recommendations:

– to develop and implement policies and programs protecting those whose views may not agree with official cultural policies of their governments;

– to strive toward the removal of all barriers to the pursuit of artistic creativity and of scientific research, including those limiting public display or publication of resulting works;

– to insist that persecution and discrimination against artists and

---

[1143] *Zprávy SVU*, vol. 27, No. 6 (November-December 1985), pp. 3-4.

scientists on the basis of their non-conformity to existing ideological tenets be stopped;

– to allow the broadest development of the limitless possibilities and talents of all people so that each human being can find opportunity for self-fulfillment and satisfy his yearning for respect and human dignity. In 1992, on the occasion of the XVI SVU World Congress in Prague, when Czechoslovakia considered to breakup into two separate entities, SVU strongly urged the Nation against such action.[1144] And when the country broke up on the last day of December 2002, SVU issued a special statement, in which it stressed that it will continue supporting federation of spiritual values and enhance the unity of democratically thinking people without regard to their geopolitical location.[1145] Subsequently, SVU launched an effort toward reestablishing civil society in the old homeland, which was also the theme of the SVU Millennium Congress in Washington, DC in 2000.

At that Congress, the issue of the non-political natures of SVU was revisited, resulting in the issuance of the following statement[1146] by the SVU General Assembly:

Since its inception, the Society has been true to its nonpolitical character and intends to do so in the future. This, in no way, mitigates the Society's firm adherence to fundamental values and principles of a democratic political culture.

Projecting its past record into the future, the Society shall protect its nonpolitical stance by

a) not subscribing to any political ideology nor affiliating with any political party, movement, group, or their functions, while cooperating with all who share and promote the values held by the Society, and

b) not allowing itself to be guided by or to become the instrument of any government of other power based organizations, while

---

[1144] "*Zprávy SVU*, vol. 44, No. 5 (September-October 1992), p. 1

[1145] "SVU Executive Board's Position towards the Czechoslovak Question," *Zprávy SVU*, vol. 45, No. 1 (January-February 1993, p. 5.

[1146] "SVU Resolution on the Occasion of its Anniversary World Congress in Washington, DC, August 8-13, 2000," *Zprávy SVU*, vol. 47, No. 5 (September-October 2000), pp, 20-22,

maintaining friendly and productive relations with those of democratic persuasion and record. In all of its undertakings, the Society shall continue its efforts toward enhancing the values of human tolerance and of freedom of spirit and thought. Without them, cultural growth falters and enlightened democracy decays.

# 77
## SVU Goes International

When the SVU was first conceived, it was supposed to be essentially an organization consisting of Czechoslovak exile intellectuals who left their native land after the communist takeover. In the formative years of the Society one could surmise that the entire membership was constituted only by Czech and Slovak-speaking members. Consequently all the proceedings in those days were naturally conducted in the members' native tongue. Furthermore, the initial membership of the Society was primarily based on the membership in the US and Canada, which explains why the Society's original name was "Czechoslovak Society of Arts and Sciences in America."

The situation began changing at the time we began organizing the first SVU Congress in 1962. As the program coordinator, I invited not only native Czechs and Slovaks, but also individuals of other nationalities, specializing in the thing Czechoslovak. This was quite logical since there were a number of professionals in America, especially in the US, who were knowledgeable about Czechoslovakia, some of whom holding distinguished positions in various universities throughout the country. I was also keenly aware of the fact that by involving such people we would enhance the prestige of our Society on the academic forum.

This notion received general acceptance in the Society and the SVU Bylaws were soon changed to read that "SVU member can become anyone interested in Czechoslovak culture." From that point on, the Society stopped being just another ethnic organization and assumed a professional status. At the insistence of our members in Europe, in due course, the Society also dropped the suffix "in America" in its official name.

When I organized the first two SVU Congresses in 1962 and 1964, I insisted that all papers be presented in English, pointing out that our aim should not be to merely talk among ourselves but to speak to the world, if we want to make any impact in the academic world and enhance the image of Czechoslovakia, which was one of the SVU goals. My arguments were strengthened when I succeeded in identifying a number of prominent Americans who took an active part in our Congresses, who had to make their presentations in English. There was some opposition, of course, but with Jaroš Němec's help, who agreed with my position, and with the voice of Prof. Václav Hlavatý and Prof. René Wellek, it did not take much effort to get agreement from the Society's Executive Board.

I felt the same way about the SVU publications and when I became Chairman of SVU Publication Committee, and, de facto, the SVU publication director, I stressed the importance of publishing English titles. The idea was not always easy to sell, because some members accused us of betrayal and lack of patriotism, feeling that it is SVU's responsibility to publish mainly in Czech or Slovak. People like Ladislav Radimský,[1147] who, in the early days of the Society, was responsible for its long-term plans, felt very strongly about this and he frequently got into a verbal dispute with me regarding this issue.

I have preserved one of my early memoranda from 1962,[1148] in which I made a valiant effort to explain to the SVU leadership why we need to pursue the international course:

### MEMORANDUM TO SVU LEADERSHIP

One of the most important and unresolved issues of our Society is its Mission. According to the Article 2 of our Bylaws, "SVU is a cultural, nonpolitical and nonprofit organization whose purpose is to maintain and develop free Czechoslovak culture." Different members interpret this statement differently. There are usually two seemingly opposing viewpoints. Some members are of the opinion that the main purpose of the Society is, above all, to maintain the Czech and Slovak language and foster publications in these languages. The adherents of the second viewpoint maintain that the purpose of the Society is to promote Czechoslovak culture on the international forum.

The first group is limited to Czechoslovaks or, exceptionally, also to individuals of other ethnic groups provided they have mustered Czech or Slovak languages. The second group tends to be international, favoring publishing in world languages, especially English. In this connection, it should be noted that during the First SVU

---

[1147] Czech exile writer and poet, writing under pseudonym Peter Den.
[1148] "Naše úkoly" (Our Aims), February 1962.

Congress in Washington in 1962, all lectures were presented in English, as will also be the case of the Second Congress planned for 1964.

These two opposing viewpoints, most certainly, each has enough followers. In my judgment, limiting ourselves to one or the other viewpoint would be wrong because it would unnecessarily lead to a dispute among the Society members. Although I myself prefer the emphasis on the international orientation of SVU rather than on a narrow, "chauvinistic "and bit parochial approach, I believe that a compromise is possible and desirable among the two positions.

Should our Society survive beyond our generation, we need to maintain international orientation. It is a fact that the children and grandchildren of most of our members don't speak Czech or Slovak. Limiting ourselves to our native languages would necessarily lead to the demise of our Society with the departure of our current generation. Apart from saving SVU from its eventual demise, there are other reasons why we should maintain the international orientation. The Czechoslovak culture has not been given sufficient international recognition it deserves, primarily because little is known about it. This is the most important mission of SVU – to propagate Czechoslovak culture in world languages, especially in English so that the world learns about us. In doing so, we need to be objective and critical and avoid any undue chauvinistic exaggeration. Toward this goal, SVU publication activities are of paramount importance. I recommend establishing a publication committee to guide the future SVU publication program and also launching an English periodical....

Having said that, I am also keenly aware of a large number of our writers and poets abroad who continue writing in their native tongue. They also deserve our support and the Society should provide it. As for myself, I would favor establishing within SVU an association of Czechoslovak writers abroad. They could have their own meetings and organize working conferences, etc. There are lots of literary magazines abroad, one of which could be used as their forum, rather than creating a new one.

I am pleased to say, that I prevailed in my arguments to follow the international course. The academic program of all subsequent SVU Congresses was based, as a rule, on English presentations and most of the monographs that were published under SVU auspices were also written in the English language. Beginning with the 9th SVU Congress, we began calling them the SVU World Congresses to emphasize their international orientation and scope.

# 78
## *Directing the SVU Publication Program*

During the 1962 SVU election of the new officers, which took place at the General Assembly meeting in Washington, DC on April 20, 1962, on the first day of the SVU Congress, I was elected "publikační referent"[1149] It was undoubtedly the successful outcome of the Congress program which I organized and the way I negotiated publishing the Congress Proceedings which led to my selection for this responsible position. I knew about it beforehand since Jaroš Němec discussed it with me and he was also the driving force for my election behind the scenes. I was naturally pleased by my election which was quite an honor, considering my relatively young age, in comparison with the rest of SVU leadership.[1150]

As the first step I established a publication committee, composed of Prof. Peter Demetz,[1151] Dr. Jaroslav Němec and myself who served as the Committee's Chairman. It did not take long before we had a concrete plan ready, which was favorably commented on the first page of the December 1962 issue of the SVU Newsletter.[1152]

Our plan started with the Proceedings of the First SVU Congress to be published by the publishing house Mouton and Co. in the Hague, Netherlands. By that time I already negotiated all the details with the publisher with the understanding that the book would be printed entirely at the publisher's expense. With the tentative title *The Czechoslovak*

---

[1149] Publication Secretary. I should point out that in those days all General Assembly meetings were conducted in Czech.

[1150] The newly elected Executive Board included such distinguished members as Prof. René Wellek, President, Prof. Vratislav Bušek, Rafael Kubelík and Dr. Felix Mikula, Vice Presidents and Prof. Rudolf Šturm, Secretary-General, Oldřich Černý, Treasurer and Ivan Herben, Press Secretary.

[1151] Professor and Chairman, Dept. of Germanic Languages, Yale University, New Haven, CT.

[1152] *Zprávy SVU*, vol. 4, No. 10 (December 1962), pp. 87-88.

*Contribution to World Culture,* the book was to be based on selected papers presented at the Congress that were thematically related to the title.

The second publication on our list was a collection of Prof. René Wellek's essays on the occasion of his sixtieth birthday. I again negotiated its publication with the Dutch publisher at their expense. I suggested the tentative title *Essays on Czech Literature* which was accepted. Prof. Demetz assumed the responsibility for preparing the book for print and for writing the introduction.

The third proposed publication was to be a collection of lectures presented in the program of the Washington DC Chapter relating to the Idea of Developing the Czechoslovak State 1938-1948. Our tentative title for this publication was: *Czechoslovakia 1938-1948. Sources and Documents.* Václav Hlavatý was to find out whether Indiana University, where he was a professor, would be interested in publishing it.

The fourth publication on our agenda was a collection of papers on the occasion of Václav Hlavatý's seventieth birthday. I took it upon myself to find a publisher and began searching for a suitable editor among Hlavatý's pupils.

In our report we also mentioned that we were contemplating the issuance of a scholarly periodical in English, stating that the Czechs and Slovaks abroad were the only ethnic group lacking such periodical. In comparison, several good revues existed in the Czech and Slovak languages, such as *Perspektivy, Nový život, Sklizeň* and *Svědectví*. We had in mind a scholarly journal on Czechoslovak topics with the aim of increasing interest in and promoting development of the Czechoslovak studies, primarily in the area of history, economics, literature and the arts. We thought that one of the American universities with interest in Slavic Studies would be an ideal publisher, while SVU would serve as an editorial board.

The report ended with the good news regarding the improved health of Jaroslav Němec to the degree that he commenced working on another demanding project Who is Who in Czechoslovak Sciences and Arts in the Free World. We concluded with a plea to our membership to fully cooperate by sending him their biographies and reprints of their works.

On the occasion of the Second SVU Congress I presented to the General Assembly Meeting,[1153] on September 30, 1964 a comprehensive report of our efforts in the publication area[1154]. First, I reported on the successful publishing of René Wellek's *Essays on Czech Literature*, published in The Hague, with Prof. Demetz's introductory essay.[1155] The selling price for SVU members was $3.50 compared to the regular price $6.45.

Secondly, I mentioned that our collection of selected lectures from the First Congress would be published in a matter of days under the title *The Czechoslovak Contribution to World Culture*.[1156] Apart from the originally presented papers, seventeen additional papers were included to make the book more comprehensive in terms of coverage, including an extensive bibliography relating to Czechoslovak culture.

About the same time, SVU was to issue Egon Hostovsky's novel *Tři noci* (Three Nights) in the Czech language.[1157] Its English translation was simultaneously published by Cassel & Co. in London. SVU also sponsored a collection of Slovak and Czech poems of Miloslav Zlámal,[1158] published in Toronto under the title *Zpěvy z modrých hor* (Songs from the Blue Mountains).

I was also pleased to report on my successful negotiations with Indiana University Press regarding Václav Hlavatý's Festschrift. The book bearing the title *Perspectives in Relativity and Geometry* was put together with the assistance of university professors–mathematicians, under the editorship of Prof. Banesh Hoffmann of Queens College, New York. The book was scheduled for publication in early 1965 with projected 400-500 pages. It was expected that some forty scientists would contribute papers to Hlavatý's Festschrift.

---

[1153] Held at Columbia University, New York.

[1154] *Zprávy SVU*, vol. 6, No. 4 (April 1964), pp. 25-26; *Ibid.*, No. 8. (Oct. 1964), p. 64.

[1155] René Wellek, *Essays on Czech Literature*. Introduced by Peter Demetz. The Hague: Mouton & Co., 1963. 214 p.

[1156] *The Czechoslovak Contribution to World Culture*. Edited by Miloslav Rechcígl, Jr. The Hague/London/Paris: Mouton & Co., 1964. 682 p.

[1157] Published by SVU in 1964. Egon Hostovský (1908-1973) was the foremost Czech writer living in exile at that time.

[1158] Slovak poet living in Toronto, Canada.

Our report also made reference to Dr. Němec's progress towards the preparation of the planned *Who is Who among the Czechs and Slovaks Abroad*. With reference to planned publication *Czechoslovakia 1938-1948. Sources and Documents*, based on the Washington lectures, little progress was made.

Among the planned projects I informed the Assembly that we were contemplating issuing another Festschrift on the occasion of the seventy fifth birthday of Prof. Francis Dvorník.[1159] We had in mind an international collection of papers in Byzantine and Slavic studies. An editorial board composed of Otakar Odložilík,[1160] Prof. Roman Jacobson,[1161] Dmitrij Obolensky[1162] and Prof. George Soulis[1163] was already in place[1164].

In my concluding remarks I recommended establishing a committee of university professors – historians for the purpose of preparing a detailed Czechoslovak history in English. We wanted to emulate the prestigious *Cambridge History of Poland*. In the same light we wanted to encourage writing a history of Czechs and Slovaks abroad, a compilation of doctoral dissertations relating to Czechoslovakia, periodical issuance of bibliographies of works of Czechoslovak scholars and scientists, as well as bibliography of works relating to Czechoslovakia, and prepare a list of Czech and Slovak manuscripts in English and other foreign languages suitable for publication. I also admonished the SVU members to establish a financial reserve so that the Society could publish books on its own and serve as a publishing house.

I remained in charge of the publications through 1968. I still have in my possession my report as chairman of the publication committee to

---

[1159] Rev. Francis Dvorník (1893-1976) belongs among the most renown scholars in the area of Byzantine Studies.

[1160] Professor of History, University of Pennsylvania, Philadelphia, PA.

[1161] Professor of Linguistics, Harvard University, Cambridge, MA.

[1162] Professor, Oxford University.

[1163] Professor, Indiana University.

[1164] To my great regret this Festschrift never materialized. We depended too much on Prof. Odložilík who unfortunately could not get the project off the ground. I am sure I could have done it myself but was reluctant to venture into the field of Byzantine Studies and Slavistics of which I was a novice. My regret was so much greater since I already had a commitment from our Dutch publisher to publish the Festschrift, at their expense.

the General Assembly at the Fourth SVU Congress on Sept. 30, 1968.[1165] By then the Publication Committee was quite large, comprising of Dr. Paul L. Horecký,[1166] Prof. Henry Kučera,[1167] Dr. Jaroslav Němec, Dr. Jaroslav G. Polach, Prof. Peter A. Toma,[1168] and Dr. Miloslav Rechcígl, Chairman.

In it I reported that by the end of 1966 Indiana University published a collection of essays honoring Prof. Václav Hlavatý on his seventieth birthday. As was reported earlier, it was edited by Prof. Banesh Hoffmann and his editorial board. It was available to SVU members from Indiana University at the reduced price of $9.00. The book otherwise sold for $15.00.[1169]

At the time of my report, Mouton and Co. published lectures from the Second World Congress which I also edited. The two volume set, with the title *Czechoslovakia Past and Present*,[1170] contained some two thousand pages. It was available to SVU members from the publisher with 40% savings.

With the consent of the Executive Board, my wife prepared the second edition of *SVU Directory*.[1171] Just as was the case with the first edition, it contained the basic data of SVU members (place and date of birth, position and affiliation, private address, education, specialization and interests). The *Directory* was appended with a geographic index, as well as the grouping of the members on the basis of their specialization or interests. In addition, it contained all important data about the Society, its aims, early history, current organization, activities and list of SVU publications. It was available to SVU membership for $3.00 and there

---

[1165] Convened in Washington, DC at Georgetown University.

[1166] Chief of Slavic and East European Division at the Library of Congress, Washington, DC.

[1167] Professor of Slavic Linguistics, Brown University, Providence, RI.

[1168] Professor of Government, University of Arizona, Tucson, Arizona.

[1169] *Perspectives in Geometry and Relativity*. Essays in Honor of Václav Hlavatý. Bloomington, IN: Indiana University Press, 1966. 491 p.

[1170] *Czechoslovak Past and Present*. Edited by Miloslav Rechcígl, Jr. *Vol. I. Political, International, Social and Economic Aspects. Vol. II. Essays on the Arts and Sciences.* The Hague/Paris: Mouton & Co., 1968. 1-880 pp., 881-1889 pp.

[1171] Czechoslovak Society of Arts and Sciences in America, Inc. *Directory*. 2nd ed. Compiled and edited by Eva Rechcígl. New York: SVU, 1968. 100 p.

was every expectation that it will become SVU bestseller as was the first edition.

In addition to the above, SVU sponsored several other publications, including Prof. Otakar Machotka's short stories *Povídky exulantovy*[1172] and German written monograph by Dr. Antonín Kratochvíl,[1173] *Die komunistische Hochschulpolitik in der Tschechoslowakei.* It further sponsored a book of essays relating to the Masaryk Republic, entitled *Padesát let* (Fifty Years), under the editorship of Ivan Herben and František Třešňák.[1174]

Prof. Jiří Nehněvajsa, who assumed editorship of the *Who is Who among Czechs and Slovaks Abroad,* sent out a questionnaire with the request for updates. It was hoped that it would be ready for the fiftieth anniversary of the Czechoslovak Republic.

I also reported on the progress Prof. Henry Kučera made with respect to the collection he was preparing on the occasion of the fiftieth anniversary of the Czechoslovak Republic[1175] and informed the Assembly of Mr. Josef Žanda's progress on the compilation of *Rejstřík Zpráv SVU 1956-1966*[1176] and on my editorial work relating to the papers presented at the Third World Congress.

During the time I was in charge of SVU publications, several other monographs were published by SVU, including V. N. Duben's 1964 bibliography of Czech and Slovak periodicals abroad,[1177] Vladimír

---

[1172] Published by "Naše Hlasy" in Toronto, Ont., Canada in 1968. Otakar Machotka (1899-1970) held the position of Professor of Sociology at the State University of New York at Binghamton, NY.

[1173] *Die kommunistische Hochschulpolitik in der Tschechoslowakei.* München: Fides-Verlagsgesellschaft, 1968. 271 p. Antonín Kratochvíl was a specialist on Czech literature with Radio Free Europe, Munich Germany

[1174] *Padesát let: Soubor vzpomínek a úvah na Masarkovu republiku.* Toronto, Ont., Canada: "Naše Hlasy," 1968. 206 p.

[1175] This information was apparently not based on facts. As it turned out, very little progress was made on the project which, in fact, never materialized. I very much regretted this because I had already negotiated with our publisher in the Netherlands that he would publish the volume at their expense.

[1176] Index to SVU newsletter, *Zprávy SVU 1956-1966.*

[1177] V. N. Duben, *Czech and Slovak Periodicals outside Czechoslovakia as of September 1964.* New York: SVU, 1964. 208 p.

Vaněk's short stories,[1178] V. N. Duben's 1968 bibliography of Czech and Slovak periodicals abroad [1179] and a pamphlet on Cardinal Josef Beran.[1180] In addition, SVU also sponsored Pavel Javor's collection of poetry[1181] and Josef Martínek's poems.[1182]

I would be remiss not to also mention our effort to sponsor a special SVU Literary Competition which I proposed in 1965. Although a lot of thinking and preparation[1183] went into this project, I am sorry to say that it never materialized because of differences in opinion among the Executive Board members. I made another effort to resurrect the competition in 1968, on the occasion of the 50th anniversary of the Czechoslovak Republic. The idea was to recognize the best scholarly manuscript on the Czechoslovak theme. My proposal was accepted and the competition was publicly announced[1184] but it produced no results because of the apparent lack of interest among the SVU members.

---

[1178] Vladimir Vaněk, *Kniha povídek*. New York: SVU, 1965. 118 p.

[1179] V. N. Duben, *Czech and Slovak Periodicals outside Czechoslovakia, as of September 1968*. New York: SVU, 1968. 28 p.

[1180] *Se souhlasem milionů: Kardinál Josef Beran čestným členem SVU*. New York, 1966.

[1181] Pavel Javor, *Nedosněno, nedomilováno*. New York: Universum Press Co., 1965. 104 p.

[1182] Josef Martínek, *Verše ze zásuvky a verše zapomění*. New Jersey: Universum Press, 1968. 80 p.

[1183] My letter to the members of the Publication Committee of April 8, 1965; "Návrh Publikační komise SVU na organizování soutěže SVU v oborech vědy a umění."

[1184] *Zprávy SVU*, vol. 9, No. 7-8 (September–October 1967), pp. 53-55; *Americké Listy*, September 22, 1967.

# 79
## *Zprávy SVU*

The first order of business of the newly formed Czechoslovak Society of Arts and Sciences in America in 1958 was to establish a newsletter in order that the leadership could communicate with its members. This led to *Zprávy SVU* (News of SVU) which commenced publishing in September 1959.

Interestingly, as Jaroš Němec told me and also wrote in his reminiscences,[1185] he and the small group of his friends who gave the impetus for establishing SVU, initially, wanted to publish a literary-cultural periodical in the Czech and Slovak languages, or an English technical journal that would cover most of the scientific disciplines. Because of the lack of financial resources, neither of these ideas materialized. Under these circumstances, they therefore welcomed when the editor Ivan Herben came up with his initiative to publish a newsletter, on a monthly basis, which would become the main connecting link among and with the SVU members and that he indicated his willingness to assume responsibility for such newsletter.

He presumably promised that he would get sufficient material for each issue, that he would arrange for its printing, that he would take care of the proofs and, with the aid of his wife, Milena Herben, he would also assume responsibility for sending it out, as well as taking care of all the administrative work. SVU would have to pay only for the printing costs. That was the deal! No wonder that the SVU leadership accepted his offer.

The above narrative is based on J. Němec's reminiscences. In his report of the working session of the Organization Council in New York in February 1959, he, however, presents a slightly different scenario.[1186] In the section entitled "SVU Magazine," he writes:

---

[1185] *Zprávy SVU*, vol. 25, No. 7 (January-February 1983), pp. 1-3.
[1186] Record of the meeting of the members of the SVU Preparatory Council, held on February 15 in New York in Dr. Bušek's residence.

Secretary-General recommended publishing SVU magazine for which he provided the following rationale – Secretary-General and Treasurer and other officers must contact the SVU membership at least ten times a year about various SVU matters. If we would count only on 300 members, it would mean that we would spend $150 on postage, $50 on paper and another $50 for mimeographing material, altogether $250. Such an expense would enable us to issue a mimeographed magazine of 32 pages four times a year. If we would wish a better quality product, we would still be able to have a magazine of 24 pages for that price. Secretary-General and possibly other SVU officers would provide the organizational news material but the additional material for the magazine, i.e., about 20 pages, would have to be provided by the magazine's editorial board. This board would also be responsible for the arrangement of the entire issue. Secretary-General was willing to type the material himself on the mimeographing sheets, running the mimeographing machine, as well as for the distribution of the magazine. Dr. Radimský or Ivan Herben would be most competent to take on the editorial responsibility, perhaps with the help of some friends. One of the members of the editorial board would need to be from the Washington area to help with the process. Dr. Němec's idea was readily accepted, with the recommendation that Ivan Herben be appointed the editor.

Be that as it may, the fact is that Ivan Herben was appointed the editor of the new SVU newsletter and by September 1959, the first issue could be ready. To make it official, Herben was subsequently also elected the Society's Press Secretary. He was, obviously, no novice in this business by any means, having come from a prominent journalist family, and who himself previously served as editor of *Svobodné slovo* in Czechoslovakia after the World War II.

In his introductory essay "Pouze Zpravodaj" (Only a Newsletter),[1187] he made it clear that this would be just a cultural newsletter rather than a magazine. He wanted to be sure that this periodical would not be viewed as competition with a number of existing Czech and Slovak magazines abroad.

---

[1187] "Only a Newsletter," *Zprávy SVU,* vol. 1, No. 1 (September 1959), pp. 1-2.

*Zprávy SVU*

He rationalized the establishment of the SVU newsletter in these words:[1188]

> The SVU does not want to publish another magazine. It only wants to serve its members and make contact with them. We are aware of the fact that SVU, and this is true about other organizations as well, cannot create anything on its own. It is not even capable to fulfill the mission of carrying the torch of free Czechoslovak culture and its traditions. The Society comprises, however, creative members in the vineyards of arts, letters and science, the bearers of this torch. The SVU, as a whole, can only bring their works to the attention of the world, with some lesser newborn pains and utilize their creative capabilities for the good name of free Czechoslovakia. Science and arts were meant to be created, not at the gatherings of crowds but within four walls of the work room of the makers. SVU can only open the door of these work rooms into the free world. SVU can only help with providing information, gathering documentary material, coordination and last, but not least, by promoting competition.
>
> The *Zprávy SVU* does not wish to be anything else. Above all, it wants to be a living link among the members, as well as a bond, which will connect the readers with the Home Nation and its spiritual traditions. This is one of the ways how to remind our young scientists and artists, who may be drowning in the sea of the foreign, albeit kind, environment, of their appurtenance with Czechoslovakia and their responsibilities to their Nation, from whose spiritual traditions they are drawing genius and inspiration for their scientific or artistic work in the Western World.

He also stated that he had assumed the difficult task of keeping track of the "creative work of exile," by keeping the SVU members informed of what had been written and what is in progress and made an appeal to the membership to regularly keep sending him news items of their publication activities, as well as lectures, artistic work, etc. He customarily sent out postcards to individual members to remind them of this.

---

[1188] "Service to Members," What is SVU, *Zprávy SVU – Special issue*, 1959, p. 4.

As promised, Herben served not only as an editor-in-chief, but also as a language editor and proofreader, as well as the administrator of *Zprávy SVU*. He was capable of finding benefactors for the Zprávy expansion and for paying for the supplement "Četba." Reading). He remained in that function until June 1963, when he retired on account of bad health and moved to California. Under his stewardship the *Zprávy SVU* was truly a professional periodical.

How the members felt about *Zprávy SVU* is evident from Rudolf Šturm's Situation Report[1189] of January 12, 1960, when he served as the Society's Secretary-General:

> *Zprávy SVU* has been published since September 1959 and, just these days, Ivan Herben took his fifth issue to the printer. Besides five numbers, a separate unnumbered issue was published for the purposes of a membership drive The response of the membership to the newsletter was overwhelmingly positive – they like the newsletter, which is becoming an indispensable bond of the intellectual component of the Czechoslovak community in the free world. The Press Secretary is doing an outstanding job.

When Herben contemplated retiring, he wrote in his parting words,[1190] that in exile he learned what the "trifle: or "piddling" work is, which was so often stressed by T. G. Masaryk, adding:

> I wish to assure my successor that it is a mere drudgery to rewrite and transcribe news items, sent by individual members; that it is toilsome to hunt for information in American and compatriot newspapers; to search continuously in dictionaries and encyclopedias for the correct translations of technical English terms; that there is endless correspondence with delinquent members – that it takes all one's free time, often at the expense of one's personal comfort – nevertheless, on the other hand, one, for ever, gains the feeling of the job well done and personal satisfaction of fulfilled responsibility. And what more can one ask for in exile? Unless he, of course, went abroad just to have a good life...

---

[1189] Situation Report for the members of the SVU Preparatory Council, January 12, 1960.
[1190] "In Saying Goodbye," *Zprávy SVU*, vol. 5, No. 6 (June 1963), pp. 51-52.

In saying good bye to his friends and collaborators, Herben thanked Jaroš Němec, the first Secretary-General and co-founder of SVU and Rudolf Šturm, the 2nd Secretary-General, for their assistance. I was gratified that he also mentioned my name for my continuous help, characterizing me as "The SVU Hope."

After he resigned from his function, on June 23, 1963, he wrote: "You must understand that I am concerned about the fate of *Zprávy SVU*. After all, it is "my baby," having spent almost five years working on it with genuine love, while being exposed to all sorts of criticisms and swear-words." Frankly, I believe it. His immediate successor was Vojtěch Nevlud, journalist with the Voice of America in Washington, DC who, in bidding Herben farewell and thanking him for his work, stated that "without Ivan Herben there would not be any *Zprávy SVU* and the SVU itself would not be such a successful organization."[1191]

Just as Herben, his successors had to struggle with the same problems, such as printing costs, printer's delays, postal strikes, lack of information, distribution problems, lack of cooperation from the members, while, at the same time, they were confronted with criticism. Editing of the *Zprávy SVU* did not bring any profit nor glory, and only rarely did the editor receive a word of thanks.

His successors, obviously, were not on the par with Herben, but, nevertheless, on the whole, they did a credible job. The editors of *Zprávy SVU*, in chronological order, were as follows:

September 1959 – June 1963: Ivan Herben

September 1963 – November 1963: Vojtěch Nevlud

May 1964 – September 1966: Vladimír S. Walzel

October 1966 – June 1968: Josef Čermák

September 1968 – December 1969: Jan Lorenc

January 1970 – December 1974: Editorial Board (Vratislav Bušek, Rudolf Šturm, Vojtech E. Andic, Jiří Škvor, John G. Lexa)

February 1975 – May 1975: Andrew Eliáš and others

June 1975 – April 1977: Editorial Board (Jaroslav Němec, Jaromír Zástěra, Zdenka Vozáriková, M. Oravec)

---

[1191] *Zprávy SVU*, vol. 5, No. 7-8 (September-October 1963), p. 58.

May 1977 – December 1978: Editorial board (M. Oravec, Zdenka Vozáriková, Jaromír Zástěra)
January 1979 – October 1980: Jaroslav Pecháček
November 1980 – December 1982: Hana Demetz
January 1983 – June 1985: Jaroslav Němec, with the assistance of Irena Lettrich
July 1985 – October 1988: Libuše Zorin
November 1988 – June 2007: Andrew Eliáš

Although the specifics have not been spelled out, it was understood, from the very beginning, that the chief goal of the newsletter was to facilitate contacts among the SVU members, and write information about them. When Herben was in charge, he tried to expand it to include information about books and their authors, for which he created a Supplement called "Četba." It should be noted that for this purpose he never used the SVU funds, his support coming from some of the benefactors he himself found. When the SVU began publishing a separate literary periodical *Proměny*, the above Supplement stopped being issued.

With time, the *Zprávy SVU* changed into a more structured newsletter, by bringing information about the work of SVU leadership, outcome of the General Assembly meetings, activities of the Executive Board, as well as those of the SVU Council, activities of various Committees and specialized subject sections, publications program of the Society, the finances. In addition, the newsletter brought information about the activities of various local chapters from around the world, and above all, about the activities of individual SVU members and their accomplishments.

Because of the lack of space, we had a policy not to print book reviews, because the right place for the former were the other SVU periodicals (*Proměny* or *Kosmas*). For the same reason, the editors avoided publishing any material relating to nonmembers or for that matter to various cultural events that had no bearing on our Society.

In terms of number of pages, the original newsletter consisted of 8 pages per issue. When. in September 1976, it became a bimonthly, each issue carried 16 pages, at least until the end of my presidency 1978. Afterwards, however, the number of pages differed from issue to issue, ranging from 16 to 56 pages, not counting the Congress issues, which were naturally longer. Inasmuch as the printer normally charged for the cost of paper on the basis of the number of large sheets used, it was apparent that the Society was really wasting quite a bit of money, because in some cases it was below and other times, over the limit.

In terms of the contents, during the period from 1979 till 2004, the editors seemed to ignore the original guidelines and began including all sorts of extraneous material which frequently had nothing to do with the Society matters, which explains why some of the issues were so humongous. The upshot of it was that the cost of publishing *Zprávy* became excessively high which seriously affected the Society's budget. Consequently, upon my return to SVU presidency in 1994, the first thing I did was to limit the number of pages in the newsletter to 24 which was "religiously" adhered to until my retirement in 2006.

Actually, during the time of editorship under Ivan Herben, he was constantly concerned about the costs of the newsletter and, whenever needed, he was usually able to get the additional money from his friends' donations. In 1960, the annual cost of publishing 10 issues of *Zprávy SVU* was in the neighborhood of $900. With the $2 SVU membership dues, at that time, the Society would not have made it. Consequently, the membership dues, starting with January 1960, were increased to $5 annually. It is hard to understand why Herben's successors did not pay any attention to finances.

. . . . . . . . .

As for myself, I have been involved with the *Zprávy SVU* from the very beginning, first as a contributor of brief notes relating to my own research activities at NIH, which Ivan Herben periodically requested and then, as the program chairman of the first two SVU Congresses and subsequently also publication chair, I was regularly providing him, and his successors, with reports of our activities. I also provided the Editor of *Zprávy SVU* information about various other projects, in which I became involved, such as *SVU Directory*, inventory of Czech and Slovak intellectuals abroad, etc. Later on, I also began writing obituaries of important SVU members. When I became SVU President, in 1974, I started the practice of publishing in the newsletter my annual reports to the General Assembly, as well as regular reports from our Executive Board meetings, the practice, which my successors, more or less, then followed.

When I returned to presidency in 1994, my involvement in the *Zprávy SVU* began to gradually increase. All the announcements and write-ups about SVU Congresses and Conferences were the products of my pen, which, since 1996, I wrote in English. Reports of the SVU Executive Board, which I also wrote, were also since then penned in English. This was inevitable, considering that our English *SVU Bulletin* ceased its publication in 1994.

On entering the new Millennium in January 2000, most of the text in *Zprávy SVU* appeared in English. Inasmuch as I was the main source of information about the SVU-related matters, much of the material appearing in *Zprávy SVU* came from me. Frankly, I not only wrote every article which had something to do with SVU, but I also contributed information about the new members, about the activities of selected members and their honors and accomplishments, and wrote most of the obituaries.

In the past there did not seem to be much order or system in the material that was published in the *Zprávy*. What was eventually published depended primarily on the material the editor received from some SVU officer or a member. Since in the last number of years I generated quite a bit of material myself, I began grouping it into regular columns. The first page of the newsletter was reserved for some editorial or an important announcement, such as SVU World Congress, Call for Papers, etc. This was usually followed by such columns as the News from Executive Board, New Faces on Executive Board, News of SVU Members, Honors to SVU Members, Accent on Youth, From New SVU Rolls, In Memoriam, New SVU Publications, Publications of SVU Members, SVU Calendar, Activities of Local Chapters, depending, of course, on the availability of the news material. Nevertheless, there was an order to it and, in fact, each issue was carefully planned to assure that we had something to say in most of the above listed columns.

In terms of information, there is no question that in the last two administrative periods (2002-06), the *SVU Zprávy* was the best. The only criticism I would find was the column on "Activities of SVU Members," which was rather skimpy for lack of information. This was, of course, generally, ever since the times of Herben's retirement, because none of his successors went to the length Herben did. in trying to get personal information from individual SVU members.

In terms of readability, the *Zprávy SVU* was clearly the best during Herben's era. As a professional journalist and writer, he had the knack for writing and he knew what would appeal to our readers and knew how to put it in prose. He was also less wordy and thus more effective, which none of his successors were able to emulate. Being employed by the Radio Free Europe, he also had access to the latest information about Czechoslovakia and what was happening on the cultural scene, so that his articles were always timely and to the point. Among his successors, only Jan Lorenc came close, who also was a professional journalist, associated with Radio Free Europe. He also was innovative, as one can see from the overall appearance of his individual issues, in which he experimented with various graphics and design. At the time of his retirement, he advocated that the future SVU newspaper be published in English rather than in Czech and Slovak, to make it more effective in the English-speaking world. This actually happened but it took thirty years!

As an afterthought, I have decided to dedicate this chapter to Ivan Herben, as a tribute for all he has done on behalf of the SVU. Although the *Zprávy SVU* carried his obituary,[1192] when he died on October 25, 1968, the SVU did not really acknowledge his many accomplishments.

---

[1192] "Ivan Herben," *Zprávy SVU*, vol. 10, No. 9 (November 1968), p. 63.

# 80
# *SVU Directory*

From its inception, SVU had in its plans to publish a biographical directory of Czechs and Slovaks abroad. It was supposed to be in the form of Who's Who, patterned after a typical Who's Who publication in the US. Among various titles proposed were titles like "Who's Who among Czechs and Slovaks Abroad" or "Who's Who among the Czech and Slovak Intellectuals Abroad."

The project was sequentially assigned to a number of individuals, none of whom was able to get it off the ground, including Jaroslav Němec, Jiří Nehněvajsa and others.

Because of the inherent difficulties in compiling a comprehensive biographical directory that would include Czech and Slovak intellectuals worldwide, I realized that it would take years for such a project to be completed. Consequently I proposed to the SVU leadership, in my capacity as the chairman of Publication Committee, to prepare, in the interim period, a directory of SVU members which, I thought, could be done with relative ease, since we had access to names and addresses of SVU members.[1193]

The idea was accepted without opposition, particularly when I volunteered Eva and myself to undertake the job. The first task was to prepare a questionnaire which was mailed to all SVU members. The questionnaire was based, in part, on AAASS[1194] questionnaire and directory of their members. As I recall, most SVU members returned the questionnaire more or less on time, following which Eva and I prepared

---

[1193] The Society was actually contemplating issuing some kind of an information brochure with addresses of SVU members, on the occasion of the Second World Congress in 1964. The letters were actually sent out to membership, under the signature of Treasurer Oldřich Černý, who was put in charge of the project, with the request for information. Apparently nothing came out of it, since there is no mention of it in *Zprávy SVU*, except for the initial announcement - *Zprávy SVU*, vol. 6, No. 6 (June 1964), p. 48.

[1194] American Association for the Advancement of Slavic Studies.

individual entries on 3x5 cards and Eva then typed them in a manuscript form.

Individual entries included the member's name, position, affiliation and place of employment, business phone, private address with a telephone, place and date of birth, academic degrees with the name of institution and year when they were awarded, specialization and interests and major publications. When this was completed, we prepared a geographical index, based on places where the members lived and a subject index, based on their specialization and expertise. For printing we used a Baltimore firm, owned by Mr. Hlubucek, which had a good reputation and frequently printed announcements for Czech ethnic organizations in the area.

The Directory[1195] was completed on schedule, in time for the Third SVU Congress in 1966. It had 80 pages and looked very professional. It was well received and most copies were sold out among the members. Because it provided such valuable information it became an SVU bestseller.

Because of the constant turnover among the members, we soon decided to work on the revised edition which came out in 1968.[1196] Several other editions were published subsequently, in longer intervals, i.e., in 1972,[1197] 1978,[1198] 1983,[1199] 1988,[1200] and 1992.[1201] The later editions

---

[1195] *Czechoslovak Society of Arts and Sciences in America, Inc. Directory*. Compiled and edited by Eva Rechcígl. New York, 1966. 80 p.

[1196] *Czechoslovak Society of Arts and Sciences in America, Inc. Directory*. 2nd ed. Compiled and edited by Eva Rechcígl. New York, 1968. 100 p.

[1197] *Biographical Directory of the Members of the Czechoslovak Society of Arts and Sciences in America, Inc.* 3rd ed. Compiled and edited by Eva Rechcígl and Miloslav Rechcígl, Jr. New York. 1972. 134 p.

[1198] *Biographical Directory of the Members of the Czechoslovak Society of Arts and Sciences.* 4th ed. Compiled and edited by Eva Rechcígl and Miloslav Rechcígl, Jr. Washington, DC, 1978. 137 p.

[1199] *Biographical Directory of the Members of the Czechoslovak Society of Arts and Sciences.* 5th ed. Compiled by Eva Rechcígl and Miloslav Rechcígl, Jr. Washington, DC, 1983. 193 p.

[1200] *Biographical Directory of the Members of the Czechoslovak Society of Arts and Sciences.* 6th ed. Compiled by Eva Rechcígl and Miloslav Rechcígl, Jr. Washington, DC, 1988. 285 p.

were more extensive and also provided basic information about the Society and its activities. I included a section on SVU history and milestones in its development, list of its officers, a bibliography of its publications and the SVU Bylaws.

The most extensive and most impressive version of these was the seventh edition, published in 1992, under the title *SVU Biographical Directory, Organization and the Biographies of Members*, comprised of almost 400 pages. The first part, of some 80 pages long, featured a historical overview of the Society from its inception till 1992. It included sections on the purpose and scope of the Society, milestones in the history of the Society, chief executive officers of the Society, local chapters, interests groups, SVU Research Institute, Society activities, SVU workshops, special projects, SVU publications and awards.

The biographical section, which comprised the second part, was followed by subject classification of members based on their expertise, a geographical index and a list of deceased members. The appendix, which constituted the third part, included the SVU Bylaws and selected SVU Resolutions.

The seventh edition came out in the most opportune time, i.e., soon after the Velvet Revolution. It became the most sought out publication, as it listed the leading Czech and Slovak intellectuals throughout the world which came in very handy to Czech and Slovak scholars and scientists in the old country who were eager to establish professional contacts with the outside world.

The seventh edition was also unique in another respect. It was computerized which would facilitate future revisions, so we hoped.

Unfortunately, when in the late nineties we began contemplating issuing another revision, things did not turn out as we had hoped. Even though we had the *Directory* data on a diskette, we encountered all sorts of problems when we tried to merge old data with the new. We even selected a computer expert as one of SVU Vice Presidents to help us with this but to no avail. He was too theoretical and even experienced difficulties in accessing the data from the old diskette.

---

[1201] *SVU Directory. History, Organization and Biographies of Members*. 7th ed. Compiled by Eva Rechcígl and Miloslav Rechcígl, Jr. with technical assistance of Michaela Harnick. Washington, DC, 1992. 390 p.

*SVU Directory*

Most people we consulted were of the opinion that the old data on the diskette cannot be transcribed and merged with new data because the old data were not in the form of a database and recommended that we start from scratch. This would have meant retyping the entire old *Directory* onto a new data base which would have been an enormous task, not to speak of the errors that would have been introduced in the process.

Although I was not much of an expert in these matters, I did not feel that this approach made much sense. We had several knowledgeable persons on our Executive Board, none of them, however, had a sensible solution. As a consequence, work on the revised edition was temporarily suspended.

It was not until I became acquainted with Jiří Eichler, a young student in Prague, that the project began moving again. Jiří began experimenting with the merging of the old data with the new addresses of members, which worked. Subsequently he transcribed some of the new entries from the new 3x5 cards that Eva and I supplied and then tried to merge them with the data on the old diskette. Lo and behold it worked. As I understand it, he was able to do it because the individual pieces of information were separated by semicolons.

Once he mastered the technique, the rest seemed relatively easy, even though a bit tedious, as he had to first transcribe the new entries from our cards. His goal was to complete the task by the end of the calendar year 2001. This would give us sufficient time to publish the Directory by June 2002, in time for our Congress.

Because of the recurrent delays in getting updated biographical data from individual members, we missed the deadline by a whole year. Through Jiří Eichler's contacts, we had the *Directory* finally printed in Prague,[1202] so that it became available for sale on the occasion of SVU Conference in Nebraska in June 2003.

---

[1202] *SVU Directory 2003*. Organization, Activities, and Biographies of Members. Compiled and edited by Miloslav Rechcígl, Jr., Eva Rechcígl, and Jiří Eichler. Washington, DC: SVU Press, 2003.368 p.

# 81
## *Proměny*

Initially, the SVU did not plan to publish its own literary magazine. In fact, at the General Assembly meeting[1203] in Toronto, Canada on September 7, 1963, there was a serious discussion about the need to combine Czechoslovak cultural magazines abroad. The recommendation was made that SVU attempt to discuss and negotiate with some publishers regarding combining their magazines into one representative magazine, with the financial support from SVU. The Executive Board was specifically assigned responsibility for this task. It was only after this effort failed that the Society decided to do it alone with the idea of publishing a representative Czechoslovak literary and cultural magazine abroad.

In announcing[1204] the new magazine, the SVU, in an unsigned article, put it in these words:

> SVU decided to publish a quarterly, devoted to issues of maintaining and fostering free Czechoslovak culture. The magazine will bear the title '*Proměny*,' and it will make an effort to keep track and interpret metamorphoses of modern times in the light of everlasting values of our national tradition. '*Proměny*' will print samples of the original and the translated prose, short belles lettres, essays, studies, articles, relating to arts and sciences, and critically follow the cultural production which would be of interest to Czechs and Slovaks. Besides that, we will, of course, continue publishing our *Zprávy SVU*, which will be devoted exclusively to news items about the activity of the Society and its members.

The editing responsibility was entrusted to Dr. Ladislav Radimský who can be reached at this address: 205 East 82nd Street, New York 28, NY, where you should also send your manuscripts and other editorial

---

[1203] "SVU General Assembly," *Zprávy SVU*, vol. 5, No. 7-8 (September-October 1963), pp. 59-60.

[1204] "*New SVU Periodical*," *Zprávy SVU*, vol. 5, No. 9 (November 1963), p. 76.

mail. The first issue is scheduled to come out after the New Year 1964. The annual subscription is $4 for members and $5 for nonmembers. Subscription, gifts for the Proměny publishing fund and administrative costs is $5 for members. Lexa, 47-16 Austel Place, Long Island City, New York 11101.

In the follow up announcement,[1205] Ladislav Radimský informs the reader that the first issue of the quarterly *Proměny* will come out in January 1964 and then proceeds to explain the basis for choosing the name "Proměny" – it is, as he says, "the only Czech word – just as the Slovak word "Premeny" – which comes close in meaning to the foreign words, such as 'transfiguration,' 'transubstantiation' and 'metamorphosis' and thus describe the mission of the magazine which attempts to spiritualize the man, standing against the changing world, in the context of everlasting values of our national tradition."

Ladislav Radimský was no novice in this area. Although he was trained as a lawyer and although he spent most of his life in diplomatic service of the Czechoslovak Government, his real love was literature and writing. He was literary active since the thirties and his literary critical studies regularly appeared in *Lidové noviny, Kritický měsíčník, Naše doba, Listy pro umění a kritiku*, magazine *Kvarta* and *Zahraniční politika*. In 1932, he received the first Melantrich Prize for his monograph *Tvůrcem snadno a rychle* in an anonymous competition, judged by F. X. Šalda and Otakar Fischer. He continued writing, usually under his pseudonym Petr Den. In exile, he regularly contributed his essays to various periodicals, such as *České Slovo, Nový Život, Studie. Sklizeň, Archy, Perspektivy, Books Abroad, Rencontres,* etc. Voice of America and Radio Free Europe frequently broadcasted his reflections and essays.

In 1961, he became editor of the new periodical *Perspektivy*, published in New York by Frantisek Švehla.[1206] He published altogether six issues, containing studies, reflections, and commentaries regarding the political and social situation in exile, situation in Czechoslovakia, and various issues in philosophy, psychology and history of science and art. Book reviews were also included as was a separate section, bringing new poetry and prose and news about recent publications.

---

[1205] *Zprávy SVU*, vol. 5, No. 10 (December 1963), p. 87.

[1206] František Švehla (1912-1991), printer and owner of the Universum Press and publisher of *Americké Listy* and *Perspektivy*, Long Island, NY.

Radimský[1207] was obviously an experienced editor and, in the opinion of many, the best qualified person for the editorship of the new SVU periodical. As it turned out, the new periodical *Proměny* proved they were right. Interestingly, there was some overlap between the *Perspektivy* and *Proměny*, so that at one time Radimský actually edited both periodicals at the same time.

The first issue of *Proměny* brought samples of incredible poetic output (Radimský's words) of Gertruda Goepfertová-Gruberová,[1208] Pavel Javor,[1209] and the poet Ferdinand Pessoy, whose verses probably appeared in Czech for the first time. René Wellek was represented with his essay about two traditions of Czech literature, Věra Stárková[1210] with her philosophical analysis of the French existentialism in literature and Dr. Ernest Šturc[1211] with his study on economic expansion of Free Europe. The issue ends with critical notes about publications, and presentations that were of interest.

True to his word, as he announced in March 1964 in *Zprávy SVU*,[1212] the second issue of *Proměny* was already at the printer for distribution in April, as originally scheduled. With the variety of topics, it topped the previous issue. It began with a poem by the noted Prague writer who celebrates the City; Jan Čep's essay ponders the truthfulness of poetic expression; Rafael Kubelík discusses his new requiem "Libera nos," Klement Šimončič publishes his translation of lyric composition from a computer; Václav Hlavatý gives his interpretation of the theory of relativity and talks about his own relations with Albert Einstein; and professor V. E. Andic writes about immigration. In the belles lettres part, Egon Hostovský presents his completed chapter from his still unpublished literary biography. In addition, the reader could also find a study about the role of nationality in culture, a beginning discourse about our exile culture and its goals, as well as a number of critical notes.

---

[1207] Above all, Radimský was also an ardent advocate of the usage of the Czech and Slovak languages and did not favor the international and English orientation of SVU.

[1208] Gertruda Goepfertová-Gruberová (1924-), poet and artist living in Munich, Germany.

[1209] The pseudonym of Dr. Jiří Škvor.

[1210] Věra Stárková (1914-1979), philosopher, writer and poet residing in England.

[1211] Ernest Šturc (1914-1980), economist with the International Monetary Fund, Washington, DC.

[1212] *Zprávy SVU*, vol. 6, No. 3 (March 1964), p. 22.

The third issue of *Proměny* was also on time and, in fact, it was very timely, as well, as it greeted the visitors of the Second SVU Congress. The issue brought unpublished poetry of E. J. Popera, Gertruda Goepfertová-Gruberová, František Listopad[1213] and Milada Součková. Robert Vlach commemorated here the 75th birthday of the Russian poet Anna Achmatová and translated some of her poems. Pavel Želivan[1214] used the occasion of Galileo Galilei's anniversary to analyze the changes the Renaissance scientist brought about in science and in the minds of modern man. Jaroslav Jíra[1215] contributed an article about two Czech artists in Paris. Vratislav Bušek wrote an analysis of population statistics relating to Czechoslovakia. Juraj Slávik wrote about American army in Czechoslovakia in 1945 on the basis of unpublished memoirs of American Ambassador in Prague Steinhardt, while Josef Anderle examined the question what led to the Slovak independence twenty-five years ago. In the section entitled "Discourse and polemics," one could find Sláma's epigrams and the first contributions about the exile culture. As usual, the issue was concluded with book reviews of relevant publications in Czechoslovakia, as well as those abroad.

I went through some detail in describing the contents of the first three issues of *Proměny* to give the reader the feel of the new periodical. The subsequent issues were, more or less, done in similar style.

Some people thought that *Proměny*, in its conception under Radimský resembled the periodical *Sklizeň*, published in the mid-sixties by Antonín Vlach in Norman, Oklahoma. I see very little analogy, except perhaps for the literary and history of art component. I would say, that *Proměny* resembled most the periodical *Perspektivy*, which Radimský also edited.

If one goes through individual issues of *Proměny*, one can readily see, besides new poetry and prose and literary criticisms, essays on art, articles and studies related to other fields, including philosophy, religion, psychology, philology, translations, sociology, politics, geopolitics, international relations, liberalization efforts on behalf of the homeland,

---

[1213] František Listopad (1922-), poet, prosaic and journalist living in Portugal.

[1214] Pavel Želivan (1925-), pseudonym of Karel Vrána, Catholic priest and theologian, residing in Rome, Italy.

[1215] Jaroslav Jíra (1896-1968), art historian and journalist.

economics, industrial development, law, problems of immigration, architecture, music, natural sciences, technology, etc.

At the time when *Proměny* entered its sixth volume in 1969, Radimský wrote[1216] that in the periodical of the twenty issues that were published up to that point, some 140 different authors participated, which he considered a record among the Czech and Slovak periodicals abroad. According to Radimský, practically all known writers who lived outside Czechoslovakia participated, as did many new authors, previously not known. Furthermore, the periodical *Proměny* is almost the only periodical abroad which follows the book production in the old Homeland. All twenty issues of *Proměny* contained book reviews, whose total exceeded 140.

Ladislav Radimský edited *Proměny* for 7 years (1964-1970). He would have, no doubt, continued editing beyond that year, had he not died prematurely on September 9, 1970.[1217]

His successor was Dr. Jiří Škvor from Canada, who had a doctorate in Slavic literature and who was also a noted poet, writing under the pseudonym Pavel Javor. He was editor for 8 years (1971-78).

Then came Dr. Ladislav Matějka, Professor of Slavic Languages and Literatures at University of Michigan at Ann Arbor, who edited the periodical, with the assistance of Josef Staša, for 4 years.

The last editor was Dr. Karel Hrubý of Switzerland, a sociologist by training, who edited the periodical for 10 years (1983-92), being assisted by Zdenka Brodská, after which the journal stopped being issued.

It is beyond the scope of this chapter to go into the description of the contents and the merits of the periodical during the time of Radimský's successors, or, for that matter even during the times when Radimský was the editor. This will have to await until some graduate student will choose this subject as the topic of his dissertation. Suffice it to say, that Radimský's successors made a valiant effort to maintain the philosophy of the magazine along Radimský's lines. They, obviously, lacked Radimský's flare and enormous breadth of knowledge of the Czechoslovak literature and cultural history, as well as his grasp for the contemporary literary scene, both in the free world and in the home

---

[1216] "140 Authors in Proměny," *Zprávy SVU*, vol. 10, No. 10 (December 1968), p. 67.

[1217] "Dr. Ladislav Radimský 3.4.1898 in Kolín - 9.9.1970 in New York," *Zprávy SVU*, vol. 12, No. 7 (September 1970), p. 1.

country, not to speak about his extensive network of collaborators and contacts. Beyond that, as a former diplomat, he had the gentle touch and knew how to deal with the contributors.

Regarding the latter, I recall several occasions when his successors got into a hassle with potential contributors when they refused to publish their polemical manuscripts, which went so far that the matter had to be elevated to the level of the Executive Board. Having looked at the manuscript, the Board agreed with the Editor's decision to refuse publishing the paper.

During my second term SVU presidency[1218] in the seventies, our Executive Board introduced a number of changes in the way the periodical was managed. To make the periodical pay for itself we felt it necessary to increase its subscription base. In our opinion, this could be best achieved by publicizing it and making its content more interesting. With this in mind, the Board decided to augment the editorial office by appointing three assistant editors and 7-member editorial board. The stylistic editing was entrusted to a language editor and the design to a graphic artist. In retrospect, *Proměny* was an outstanding journal and, in a way, it was SVU's institution, which attracted, not only the known Czech and Slovak literary figures, but also the new aspiring authors from all over the world and also, frequently, brought in forbidden Samozdat manuscripts from the Communist Czechoslovakia. It clearly played an important role during the times when Czechoslovakia was under the Communist control. It ceased publication after the Velvet Revolution in 1994 because the SVU leadership felt that it was not needed anymore.

---

[1218] "Reorganization of Proměny," *Zprávy SVU*, vol. 19, No. 3 (May-June 1977), pp. 4-5.

# 82
## SVU English Periodical

The idea of publishing a periodical in the English language under SVU sponsorship must have occurred to a number of SVU members but nobody came forth with a concrete plan to implement it. To my knowledge, I must have been one of the first SVU officers who brought it to the attention of SVU leadership. In fact, I still have my report regarding this matter, dated Spring 1962.[1219] As Chairman of SVU Publication Committee I brought it to the attention of SVU Council in 1962, as reported in *Zprávy SVU* [1220] as well as by the ethnic press.[1221]

In my report I stated that our Publication Committee is seriously considering the idea of publishing an English scholarly periodical on Czechoslovak subjects, pointing out that Czechs and Slovaks are the only ethnic group in the US and Canada who do not have such a journal. In comparison, there are plenty revue magazines in Czech and Slovak languages, such as *Perspektivy, Nový život, Sklizeň* and *Svědectví*. With its focus on Czechoslovak topics it would enhance the image of Czechoslovakia which has been greatly tarnished by the communist regime. The periodical would have an added benefit by fostering greater interest in the Czechoslovak area studies and enhancing scholarship relating to the country's history, literature, economics, etc. I further noted that our Publication Committee was of the opinion that the easiest and the ideal way to realize this idea would be if some American university would be willing to sponsor such a periodical, while SVU would provide the editorial board function. The report ends with my appeal to SVU members to come up with a concrete suggestion which university could assume such a role.

As I recall, no concrete suggestion was proposed, as far as SVU was concerned, so the Executive Board was reluctant to take on such

---

[1219] Miloslav Rechcígl, "Naše úkoly" (Our Mission), Spring 1962.
[1220] *Zprávy SVU*, vol. 4, No. 10 (December 1962), pp. 87-88.
[1221] *Naše Hlasy*, January 12, 1963.

burden on its own. Thus the idea was tabled until the time I became SVU President (1974-78).

On August 29, 1977 I sent a letter[1222] to selected SVU members, as well as nonmembers, soliciting their views on publishing an English periodical under SVU auspices. The text of the letter follows:

> I hope that you will excuse the informality with which I am writing to you. In order to save time and effort I had the letter duplicated and am sending it to several key people in the area of Czechoslovak studies.
>
> A number of our members suggested that the Society consider the possibility of publishing a scholarly periodical in English (and perhaps in other international languages) which would be devoted solely to Czechoslovak studies. The purpose of this communication is to solicit your views on the feasibility and the wisdom of such an idea. After you have had a chance to think about it a bit, which I would very much appreciate, if you would send me your comments regarding this matter.
>
> Specifically, would you please comment on the following points:
>
> 1. Is there a need for such a periodical? Is there enough scholarly material which would assure publishing this periodical on a regular basis? How often should it be published? How many pages should be devoted to one issue?
>
> 2. Would there be a market for such a periodical? How many institutions would subscribe to it (In US, elsewhere in the world) ? How many individuals would subscribe to it? What should be the price of an individual issue?
>
> 3. Assuming that the Society would be willing to sponsor such a periodical, should it do it on its own, or jointly with some University Press or Area Studies Department? In the latter case, could you suggest a suitable institution which might be interested in such a venture?
>
> 4. What should be the nature of the proposed periodical? Should it cover all major disciplines or be limited to history, philosophy, literature, linguistics, economics, and social sciences? Should it have special features, such as "Current Events (with emphasis on Czechoslova-

---

[1222] SVU President Miloslav Rechcígl's letter of August 29, 1977 addressed to selected addressees.

kia)," "Book Review section," "Bibliography section," Letter to the Editor," "Czechoslovak studies (in progress) in brief," etc. Should it be published exclusively in English?

5. How large should the editorial board be? Should it be organized by disciplines or by sections? What type of individuals should serve on the Board? Should the Board he international in scope? Any thought you might have on possible members on the board, including the editor-in-chief would be greatly appreciated.

6. Would you be willing to assist us in getting the periodical off the ground? What specifically would you be interested in doing?

7. Any other comments you might wish to make regarding this matter would be most welcome.

The list of addressees who were sent the above letter read like Who's Who. It included such people as Alfred French of University of Adelaide, George Gibian of Cornell, William E. Harkins of Columbia, Frederick G. Heymann of Calgary, Roman Jakobson of Harvard, Heinrich Kunstmann of University of Munich, Vladimir Kusín of University of Scotland, Radomír Luža of Tulane, Paul R. Magocsi from Toronto, Ivo Moravčík of University of Alberta, Frank Munk from Portland State, G. H. Seton-Watson of University of London, H. Gordon Skilling of University of Toronto, Josef Škvorecký of Toronto, Ivan Sviták of California State University, Otto Ulč of State University of New York, René Wellek of Yale, Thomas G. Winner of Brown University and Stanley B. Winters of New Jersey Institute of Technology.

Interestingly, most individuals I contacted responded and some of them in lengthy letters. Generally speaking, a large number of them were a bit skeptical, particularly with reference to finances and also whether there would be enough material for publishing and whether there would be enough subscribers.

For example, René Wellek, in his letter of September 8, 1977, wrote:

To tell you truth, I am a skeptic. I doubt that such periodical of good quality would last more than a year. I doubt one would find sufficient number subscriptions, except for the largest libraries (there are only some 70 of them in the US) and individuals don't subscribe, if the periodical was too expensive (which it would have to be to look nice, with diacritical marks, etc.) It could be done, if we would find financial support from some university foundation. I am retired now and have no influence. I don't think there is a Center for Czechoslovak Studies. There are several scholars scattered in the US, England, Germany and elsewhere but to launch a new periodical would be difficult.

I recommend that we don't get involved in this until we would have a financial guarantee for at least five years and the editors would have on hand manuscripts for at least 4-5 issues.

I would like to offer my help, as a member of editorial board to evaluate contributions in the area of literature, criticism, etc. The experience with *Proměny* does not give me much encouragement.

Similarly Roman Jakobson, who listed all his official positions after his name, i.e., S. H. Cross Prof. of Slav. Langs. & Lits. & of Gen. Ling, Emeritus, Harvard Univ., Institute Prof., Emeritus, MIT, in his letter of October 13, 1977, wrote as follows:

A scholarly periodical envisioned is a nice thing, but I must confess that I am afraid as to the practical, especially financial, possibilities. I know that Professor Thomas Winner of Brown University has been preparing a similar journal of Czech literary studies. If you contact him, you will probably hear what the outlooks and difficulties are. I am ready to help you as much as I can, but I am concerned about the number of various Slavistic periodicals and about the difficulties all these are experiencing at present."

G. H. N. Seton-Watson, Professor, SSEES at the University of London, in his letter of September 14, stated:

I have every sympathy for your projected enterprise, but I fear that I am not able to give you any useful advice. I am afraid that in this country the market would be exceedingly small, as libraries are being forced to cut down even on existing periodical subscriptions. I would guess that the wider the range of intellectual disciplines the better would be the chances of the review.

My feeling is that the decisive factor would be the number of Czechoslovak exiles of intellectual and literary ability who are available, and the amount of work that they would all be willing to put in. With a hard core of people, something might be achieved; but if you rely too much on academic well-wishers who are not themselves one hundred per cent committed, you would find the result disappointing.

For my own part, I regret that I cannot undertake any regular commitments as I am already overstretched.

Nevertheless, several letters were quite positive, if not enthusiastic, including letters from Vladimír Kusín, Ivo Moravčík and John Bradley. So eventually I succeeded in persuading the Executive Board of the need to publish an English scholarly periodical which would publish studies and essays relating to Czechoslovakia and its culture.

Before proceeding with the endeavor, the SVU Executive Board felt that "we need to articulate carefully the purpose of the proposed periodical with the clear notion of the audience to which it will address itself. We should have concrete plans regarding the organization and the substantive content of the periodical and to select an appropriate title for it. We should also have a rough estimate of the number of potential subscribers and the costs involved, in order to have an idea of the overall financial requirements."[1223]

Toward this end, our Board established an Organizing Czechoslovak Scholarly Periodical Committee, comprised of Ivo Moravčík, Vladimír V. Kusín and William E. Harkins. Our guideline to the Committee was: "It should be a first-rate journal with outstanding contributors and international audience. A reputable advisory board (e.g., Drs. Jakobson, Wellek, Seton-Watson, Skilling, Jaroslav Pelikán, Robert Auty, etc.) and equally reputable working editorial board were considered *sine qua non*."

As my term, as SVU President, was nearing to an end, there was not enough time to get the periodical off the ground. By the time Jan Tříska assumed the SVU Presidency (1978-1980), our membership had more English-speaking people than ever before which also created a more favorable climate for an English-language journal but, yet, there were doubts. At my suggestion, Tříska's Executive Board approved the

---

[1223] SVU President Miloslav Rechcígl's letter of February 20, 1978 to Dr. Ivo Moravčík, Dr. Vladimír V. Kusín and William E. Harkins.

idea of first publishing an English newsletter with the title *Bulletin*, under the editorship of Dr. Zdenka Fischmann of California.

With this success, I approached Tříska's Executive Board with the proposal to also go ahead with launching a scholarly English periodical. The Board approved the idea, in principle, but no money was allocated for the new effort. It was not until Leopold Pospíšil's Presidency (1980-82) that the idea materialized. In the fall of 1981 the SVU Council voted the necessary funds and in 1982 the first issue came out.

The new periodical bore the name *Kosmas* with the subtitle *The Journal of Czechoslovak and Central European Studies*. As for the title, as was explained in the preface, "although the periodical's broad coverage might warrant calling it "Cosmos," the title of *Kosmas* was chosen to honor the scholar and monk of that name who practiced many arts and sciences and wrote the memorable *Chronica Bohemorum* which has survived nearly one millennium as an eloquent treatise on early medieval Bohemia. No lesser authority than Frantisek Palacký, the "Father of the Nation" and eminent leader of the Czech national revival, bestowed on Kosmas the epithet: 'The Virtual Herodotus of this Country'."

At my recommendation, John F. N. Bradley of the University of Manchester was appointed the first editor. He was assisted with a prestigious advisory board which included names like Prof. Jean-Baptiste of the University of Paris, Prof. D. J. Footman of the University of Oxford, Prof. S. Koerner of the University of Bristol, Prof. Z. Kopal of the University of Manchester, Sir Cecil Parrott of the University of Lancaster, Prof. O. Šik of the University of St. Gallen, Prof. Seton-Watson of the University of London, etc. There were also Executive Members, who included Prof. F. M. Barnard, Prof. V. M. Fic, Prof. S. Fischer-Galati, Prof. W. E. Harkins, Prof. G. Liška, Prof. V. S. Mamatey, Prof. V. Mastný, Prof. M. Novak, Prof. F. E. Prinz, Prof. P. S. Wandycz, who functioned as the Editorial Board.

In announcing the new periodical, SVU used the following announcement:

### KOSMAS – JOURNAL OF CZECHOSLOVAK AND CENTRAL EUROPEAN STUDIES

Published at the University of Manchester for the Czechoslovak Society of Arts and Sciences Inc. in Washington, DC, USA

Editor: John F. N. Bradley, Department of Government, University of Manchester, Manchester, M13 9PL, Great Britain

The journal is an interdisciplinary cultural forum for scholars and scientists of Czech and Slovak descent and for others interested in the studies of Czechoslovakia in particular, and Central Europe in general. It is sponsored by the University of Manchester and financially supported by the Endowment 1981 set up by the Czechoslovak Society of Arts and Sciences. It is managed by an editorial council consisting of the Editor; Professor L. Pospíšil; Professor J. Nehněvajsa; Dr. K. Absolon; and Dr. M. Rechcígl, Jr. Issues appear twice a year, in the spring and autumn of every year.

Publication is in English and manuscripts for consideration should be sent to the Editor, K.JCCES, Department of Government, University of Manchester, Manchester M13 9PL, Great Britain. They should not exceed twenty pages, should be typed double-spaced and submitted in duplicate. To insure uniformity of style it is suggested that reference to books should be as follows: Jan Milič Lochman, *Duchovní odkaz obrození*. Prague: Kalich, 1964. References to publications in periodicals, e.g.: A. Tallentire, "Radiation resistance of bacterial spores." J. Appl. Bact., 33, 1970, pp. 141-147. Footnotes should be at the back of the text.

Subscriptions $ 20.00 for one year (two issues): members and students $ 10,00. Cheques should be made payable to K.JCCES and sent to Frank. J. Marlow, Esq., 4217 Noble Avenue, Sherman Oaks, California 91403, U.S.A.

After two volumes, for reasons unknown to me, the new Executive Board replaced Bradley with Zdeněk Suda of the University of Pittsburgh as the periodical editor. He remained editor until the end of 1988.[1224]

---

[1224] He was followed by Paul I. Trenský (1989-1992) who dropped the name *Kosmas* and published the journal under the periodical's subtitle. After the lapse of four years, during my return to SVU Presidency, the periodical resumed publication under the editorship of Prof. Bruce Garver (1996-1998) of the University of Nebraska in Omaha. He was subsequently replaced by Professor Clinton Machann of the University of Texas A&M (2000-), under whose editorship the periodical was published again under its original title *Kosmas*.

# 83
## *The SVU Local Chapters*

Soon after SVU was established, the SVU founders saw it fit to start organizing local SVU Chapters, first in the US and Canada. They were usually organized in places where the Society had the largest concentration of members in a given area. The purpose of these chapters was to provide a vehicle for the local members to meet and hold their activities, as appropriate, and in doing so help to publicize SVU locally and contribute to the Society's aims. In this sense, a new paragraph was added to SVU Bylaws, stating that "Local Chapters shall be associations of not less than five members of the Society living in the same area, who associate themselves (as a chapter) with the concurrence of the Executive Board in order to enhance the purpose of the Society by mutual cooperation and in accordance with local possibilities." In time, governing guidelines were written up to provide directions and rules on how the local chapters were to be organized and run.

From the very beginning, two principal rules guided the chapters. First, to be eligible for membership locally, one had to be a full-pledged SVU member, i.e., a member who pays regularly his/her membership dues to SVU Treasurer. And second, that the chapter would finance its own activities from its own resources, without burdening the central Treasury of the Society. With reference to the second point, the local chapter guidelines included a statement that local chapters should, furthermore, assist the Society, as a whole, with financing its publication program, for which the Society does not have sufficient resources.

The first SVU local chapter was organized in 1959 in the Metropolitan Washington area, comprising Washington, DC and the adjacent counties of Maryland and Virginia, namely Montgomery and Frederick Counties, in case of the former and Arlington and Fairfax Counties, in the latter. I have already described the founding of the Washington DC Chapter elsewhere.[1225]

---

[1225] See my chapter "Recruited to SVU."

The second SVU chapter was established in Chicago, IL also in 1959. From the very beginning the Chapter planned to publish a collection of papers relating to the development of Czechoslovak sciences and arts and the cultural contribution of Czechoslovakia to the free world. The idea came from Dr. Jaroslav Tuzar.[1226] On the occasion of the Czechoslovak Day in Chicago, traditionally organized by the Czechoslovak National Council of America, the SVU Chapter had a very successful exposition, arranged by architect Vladimír Richter and Mrs. Heinz.

About the same time, the regional secretary for New York readied a meeting for SVU members living in New York City and the environs for the purpose of establishing a New York Chapter. The Chapter was officially established on March 26, 1960.[1227] At the time of its founding, there were already some 80 SVU members living in the New York Metropolitan area, some of whom were more than an hour from the City, which made it difficult to attend the meetings. To attract them to the first meeting, they invited two outstanding speakers, Dr. Mojmír Drvota, an expert on film and theatre, and Dr. Miroslav Poseděl, a psychiatrist of note. The second meeting, held on November 20, was devoted to a discussion with the theme "World without God," with the participation of Petr Den and Dr. Jaroslav Stránský of London.[1228] During that meeting, Dr. John G. Lexa was elected chairman of the New York Chapter. As part of the celebrations of the 28th of October, the New York Chapter organized a lecture by Prof. Vratislav Bušek on "Three Czechoslovak Constitutions" from the year 1920, 1948 and 1960. They concluded their program for the year on December 8, with a lecture by Ing. Pavel Blaho on "Slovakia in Czechoslovak Republic."

For April 1961, the New York Chapter planned an afternoon concert of the chamber music of Antonín Dvořák, as a part of the "Dvořák Year." On October 20, the Chapter sponsored a discussion evening about the recently published monograph, *In the Governments of the Second Republic*, written by Dr. Ladislav Feierabend, with the participation of the author. And on November 26, they organized a lecture by Josef

---

[1226] Jaroslav Tuzar (1915-2003, professor of mathematics at Northeastern Illinois University who studied under Prof. Hlavatý in Prague.

[1227] "New York SVU Chapter," *Zprávy SVU*, vol. 2, No. 5 (May 1960), p. 40.

[1228] "World without God," *Zprávy SVU*, vol. 2, No. 6 (June 1960), pp. 45.

Zelenda, accompanied with two original films from Abyssinia. In January, 1962, the essayist Petr Den (Dr. Ladislav Radimský) talked about "Essay as a Literary Form" and he accompanied his exposition with examples from his book "Počítadlo" (Abacus). In May, the Chapter organized a narrative about Czech and English poetry of the nestor of Czech-American journalists Josef Martínek.[1229] They concluded their summer season with a concert in the Husův Dum (The Hus House) in Manhattan, playing compositions of Vaňhal, Dušek, Smetana and Dvořák. In the fall, they organized a music evening entitled "Czech Musicians in Exile or Music that You Cannot Hear anywhere." After the introduction by Ivan Herben, the attendees listened to taped music compositions of Karel Husa. Karel B. Jirák, Jaroslav Ježek and Bohuslav Martinů, the compositions that had not yet been publicly released.

The year 1959 marked also the planning activities of establishing the first SVU chapter in Europe, namely that in Munich, Germany. The preparations were made, in collaboration with the Association of Czechoslovak Political Refugees and with the group associated with the periodical *Archa*. The chapter was not established until 1961, however. Their first activity reported in *Zprávy SVU* (May 1961 issue) was the lecture by Prof. Edward Fischer[1230] of Free University in Ludwigsburg, on "Secrets of Atom." Two additional lectures soon followed by Director of American Fund for Czechoslovak Refugees, Dr. Jaroslav J. Brázda[1231] who spent the previous year in India. The lectures, bearing the title "India and the Far East," were accompanied by colorful slides. The final lecture of the year was that of Prof. Edward Fischer, who talked this time on the subject of "Effects of uncontrolled chain reaction and possible protection against radioactive contamination of atmosphere and the land surface."

As early as 1959, there were efforts to also establish a new chapter in Pittsburgh, PA,[1232] when three SVU representatives visited the city, i.e., Prof. Vratislav Bušek, Dr. Jaroslav Němec and Dr. Jaroslav Polach. At the meeting, held at the University of Pittsburgh's Czechoslovak

---

[1229] Joseph Martínek (1889-1980), journalist and poet.
[1230] Edward Fischer (1888-1967), engineer in Munich, Germany.
[1231] Jaroslav J Brázda (1924-1982), European Director, American Fund for Czechoslovak Refugees, Munich, Germany.
[1232] "SVU in Pittsburgh," *Zprávy SVU*, vol. 1, No. 4 (December 1959), p. 27.

Hall, they made presentations about the aims of the Society and its activities, following which there was a lively discussion, in which Prof. Josef Macek,[1233] Milan Getting and Prof. Václav Mareš[1234] of the State Pennsylvania University took part. In spite of the successful outcome of the meeting, the Pittsburgh Chapter was not established until 1961. It was finally established, thanks to the efforts of the regional secretary Prof. Vojtech Andic, at the meeting with the local SVU members, at the beginning of the year, where also Marie Provazníková,[1235] chair of the SVU Education Committee, participated.[1236]

In June 1960, Ivan Herben visited Cleveland and Toronto to lay the groundwork for establishing SVU chapter there. In Cleveland he met with some twenty existing or potential members, with the help of editor V. Hyvnar[1237] and Antonín Šuster,[1238] who lived in that City. The meeting went very well and the attendees were already talking about possible program. In Toronto, the local organizers arranged a special "Acquaintance evening and discussion," chaired by poet Pavel Javor from Montreal. A number of people participated in the discussion, including Mrs. Valerie Bílá-Beck, Dr. Josef Čermák,[1239] Jaromír Petříček,[1240] poet Miloslav Zlámal, and the regional secretary Dr. Mario Hikl.[1241] After the discussion, they established an organizing committee to plan the charter meeting of the future Toronto Chapter.

Soon after, the Chapter organized a discussion evening about theatre, under their newly elected chairman Miloslav Zlámal.[1242] Two

---

[1233] Josef Macek (1887-1972), professor of economics at Pittsburgh University, formerly from Prague College of Business.

[1234] Václav E. Mareš (1902-1998), professor of economics at Pennsylvania State University.

[1235] Marie Provazníká (1890-1991), chairwomen of Sokol.

[1236] *Zprávy* SVU, vol. 3, No. 3 (March 1961), p. 22.

[1237] Václav Hyvnar (1922-2001), editor of *Novy Svět* and future President of the National Alliance of Czech Catholics in Cleveland.

[1238] Anthony J. Šuster (1924-1970), business executive.

[1239] Josef Čermák (1924-), lawyer, barrister and solicitor, Toronto, Canada.

[1240] Jaromír Petříček (1920-), high school teacher in Toronto, Canada.

[1241] Mario J. Hikl (1923-1992), Canadian attorney and publicist, Ottawa.

[1242] Miloslav Zlámal (1922-1997), Slovak-born businessman, journalist and poet who wrote equally well in Slovak and in Czech.

Czech actresses participated in the program, namely Mrs. Susan Douglas Rubes (the wife of Jan Rubeš) and the young Markéta Mareš who had just had her debut in Toronto. For their second discussion evening, they invited the editor Josef Pejskar[1243] from the Munich Editorial Offices of Radio Free Europe to speak about the work and the aims of Radio Free Europe. At the next discussion evening on March 4, 1961, Ambassador Dr. Jan Papánek talked about the mission of the United Nations. On April 20, the chapter met at the International Institute to hear reports on the artistic, literary and scientific works of their members. Soon after, SVU Secretary-General Jaroslav Němec[1244] was invited to Toronto by the agile Chapter, not only to present a talk and participate in the discussion, but also to open the first art exhibit the Chapter organized in the International Institute of Toronto. Three exile artists participated, namely Jaroslav Šejnoha, Anna Škvorová-Vaništová and Antonín Lněnička.[1245] The entire program was a big hit and the lecture room was so full that no seats were left unoccupied. The exhibit was opened in the presence of the official representatives of the City of Toronto, as well as Canadian Press.

On October 1, 1961, the SVU Chapter in Chicago[1246] organized, jointly with the Czechoslovak National Council of America, a concert of Antonín Dvořák's chamber music, on the occasion of Dvořák's 120th birthday. As part of the program, Prof. Karel B. Jirák gave a talk about Dvořák's work, while Mrs. Prokop-Fried[1247] and Mrs. Jiřina Tuzar[1248] sang his Moravian Songs. Also on the program was Dvořák's "American Quartet," which he composed during his stay in Spillville, IA, performed by the Otakar Šroubek's Quartet. In February 1962, the Chapter organized a lecture by Professor Václav Hlavatý, entitled "With Abacus around the World," accompanied with a film about his global trip. On another occasion, the Chapter hosted Professor Roman Jakobson,[1249] the

---

[1243] Josef Pejskar (1912-1999), journalist, editor, Radio Free Europe, Munich, Germany.
[1244] "SVU Secretary-General in Toronto," *Zprávy SVU*, vol. 3, No. 6 (June 1961), pp. 53-54.
[1245] Antonín Lněnička (1921-), artist and painter living in Ontario, Canada.
[1246] *Zprávy SVU*, vol. 3, No. 9 (November 1961), p. 94.
[1247] Marie Prokop-Fried (1906-), opera singer and painter.
[1248] Georgia Tuzar (1915-), a concert singer.
[1249] Roman Jakobson (1896-1982), professor of linguistics at Harvard University.

founder of the famed Prague Linguistic Circle, who gave a talk about the subject. In the early fall, the Chapter organized another exhibit during the Czechoslovak Day, in which were exhibited also the paintings by the artist Gen. Oskar Pejša.[1250] In October, the Chapter arranged a special evening with Dr. Milada Součková,[1251] who then taught Czech language and literature at the University of Chicago. Present was also the University Dean Prof. Robert Streets and Prof. Joseph Malik,[1252] a native of Texas, chairman of Russian Department at the University of Arizona in Tucson. The evening was also dedicated to the memory of the Czechoslovak students, killed or persecuted following their peaceful demonstration by Nazis on the 17th of November 1939. The 17th of November tradition was remembered by Jaromír Zástěra,[1253] the recently released Communist prisoner.[1254]

Due to the visit of Professor Hlavatý in Montreal, Canada a new chapter was established in that city in 1961. Jiří Škvor was elected its first chairman, while Dr. Oskar Sýkora[1255] became the secretary.[1256] Ivan Herben visited Montreal in January 1962 where he met with the new regional secretary Dr. Ivan Bujna for the purpose of giving them advice on the new membership drive they planned for the Montreal area. Toward the end of May 1963, the Montreal members met again to elect new officers. Dr. Jaroslav Frei[1257] was elected chairman, Dr. Josef Kalenda[1258] vice chairman, Ing. Vladimír Brož[1259] secretary and Dr.

---

[1250] Oskar Pejša (1896-1979), Gen., former Czechoslovak military officer and artist.
[1251] Milada Součková (1899-1983), writer.
[1252] Joseph Malik (1920-1998), head of the Russian Department at the University of Arizona in Tucson.
[1253] Jaromír Zástěra (1930-1984), student at Loyola University.
[1254] *Zprávy SVU*, vol. 4, No. 9 (November 1962), p. 83.
[1255] Oskar P. Sýkora (1929-), professor of prosthetics at McGill University in Montreal, later held similar position at Dalhousie University, Halifax, N.S.
[1256] *Zprávy SVU*, vol. 4, No. 4 & 5 (April-May 1962), p. 44.
[1257] Jaroslav V. Frei (1929-), professor of pathology at the University of Western Ontario, London, Canada.
[1258] Josef Kalenda (1905-), architect and chief designer with the Canadian National Railways in Montreal.
[1259] Vladimír J. Brož (1927-), industrial engineer with the Canadian National Railways in Montreal.

Ivan Trebichavský[1260] treasurer. A day before the meeting, Radio Canada broadcasted an interview with Dr. Jiří Škvor about the SVU activities in Canada and in the US.[1261]

The above gives the reader a composite picture of how the first local chapters were organized during the formative years of the Society. Gradually, additional chapters were established in other locations in the US, Canada and elsewhere in the world. These include, in chronological order, chapters in: Boston, MA (1965), Los Angeles, CA (1966), London, England (1967), Albany, NY (1969), Cleveland, OH (1969), Ottawa, Ont., Canada (1970), Battawa, Ont., Canada (1971), Edmonton, Alta., Canada (1971), Stuttgart, Germany (1972), etc.

The founding of the Swiss Chapter (1972) and those in Australia, i.e., Melbourne (1972) and Sydney (1972) had something to do with the personal visits by Dr. Jan Mládek, whose job in the International Monetary Fund enabled him to travel around the globe. When I became SVU President, we also created a chapter in Wellington, NZ (1976) and another in Vancouver, B.C., Canada (1977). In subsequent years, additional chapters were founded in Pretoria, South Africa (1979), San Francisco, CA (1979), Vienna, Austria (1980), Hartford, CT (1983), and Perth, Australia (1983).

After the Velvet Revolution, SVU began establishing new chapters in the former Czechoslovakia and then in the Successor States, the Czech Republic and Slovakia. The first chapter was established in Prague (1992). Originally it was a chapter for the entire Czechoslovakia but when the country split, it became the Prague Chapter, while the Slovaks created their separate chapter in Bratislava (1993). When I returned to SVU Presidency in 1994, I gave the impetus to establishing a new chapter in Košice (1994), Brno (1995), Plzeň (2002), Olomouc (2004) and České Budějovice (2006).

I was also instrumental in establishing a number of new chapters in the Southwest and the Midwest of the US, namely Central Texas (1997), Minneapolis (1999), Lincoln, NE (2001), Spillville, IA (2003) and North Miami, FL (2005).

---

[1260] Ivan Trebichavský (1910-1973), journalist living in Montreal, Canada.
[1261] *Zprávy SVU*, vol. 5, No. 5 (May 1963), pp. 45-46.

# 84
# *In the Background But Not in the Shadows*

After four years of intensive work as SVU President (1974-78), I was really exhausted and felt strongly that I should step down and let somebody else run the Society's affairs. I also felt very strongly about the need of continuous turnover among the SVU officers.

By getting out of the limelight, I had obviously no intentions of disappearing into oblivion. I clearly wanted to continue my work but on my own terms and without pressure. In addition, there were several new activities to which I wanted to devote my energies without interruption.

As a past SVU President, I was invited to all meetings of the SVU Executive Board which I faithfully attended and had my voice heard, when appropriate. I regularly provided advice to my successors and was always available to them upon request. Most presidents who succeeded me in the office of SVU President availed themselves of my offer and availability and were in constant contact with me during their term, except perhaps Igor Nábělek.

One activity to which my wife and I devoted continuous attention was the systematic updating of *SVU Directory*. After publishing the 4th edition in 1978, we prepared three subsequent editions, one in 1983, another in 1988, still another in 1992 and finally, the eighth edition in 2003.

In the early eighties I launched a new effort under the SVU sponsorship, i.e., to collect historical and biographical information on Czech and Slovak personalities abroad, with particular emphasis on America. I have viewed this as a long-term endeavor which is still ongoing, as of this writing. Related to this undertaking were two of my publications, *Educators with Czechoslovak Roots* and *US Legislators with Czechoslovak Roots from Colonial Times to Present with Genealogical Lineages*, published by SVU in 1980 and 1987, respectively.

In terms of new initiatives, during Tříska's presidency, I suggested that SVU start publishing *The SVU Bulletin*, a new newsletter for the increasing number of English speaking members. The newsletter was launched in 1980, three times a year, under the editorship of Zdenka Fischmann of Los Angeles.

About the same time, I proposed to Tříska's Executive Board the idea of publishing a new SVU periodical in English which would publish scholarly articles relating to Czechoslovakia and Czechoslovak culture. By then, I had already corresponded with a number of SVU members as well as nonmembers, soliciting their view on the idea and also for suggestions for a possible editor. Although the Executive Board approved the concept, the idea did not materialize until the time of Pospíšil's presidency. It was formalized in the fall of 1981 when the SVU Council voted the necessary funds for the new endeavor. The new periodical was to bear the name *Kosmas* with a subtitle *The Journal of Czechoslovak and Central European Studies*. The name Kosmas was patterned after the first Bohemian chronicler who lived in the Czechlands in the years 1045-1125. Prof. John F. N. Bradley of the University of Manchester was appointed the editor with the assistance of prestigious international advisory and editorial boards.

The third major initiative that I had something to do with, was the idea of establishing the SVU Research Institute. My idea was that the Institute would be a research arm of the Society and the chief instrument to attract grant funds and to provide mechanism for the review, conduct, evaluation, and coordination of research projects in the arts and sciences relating to Czechoslovak culture. I felt strongly that it should be an integral part of the Society, while being financially independent. We spent endless debates on this proposal in the meetings of the Executive Board during Nehněvajsa's presidency until it was approved in 1988. The Institute was formally incorporated in 1989, at which time the Institute's Board of Trustees was also appointed. The realization of the idea remained dormant until the time of the new Tříska's presidency when Prof. Zdeněk Slouka was appointed the first director of the Institute. As narrated elsewhere, the SVU Research Institute subsequently played an important role in the SVU program to assist Czechoslovakia.

After I retired for the second time from SVU presidency, which lasted twelve years (1994-2006), I returned to my old love of gathering information about prominent Czech Americans, which I had to interrupt in 1994 because of my Society's management responsibilities. This time

I planned to be more systematic and work toward a specific goal of actually preparing a publishable manuscript. I started with the title "Notable Americans with Czech Roots," but later changed it to "Czech American Biography."

The idea was to compile an authoritative dictionary of notable personalities of Czech origin who have influenced and shaped American history and culture. This was a monumental undertaking, which would encompass biographies of significant men and women from the Colonial times to the present. The undertaking was not to be viewed as a traditional "Who's Who," consisting of chance listings of individuals, based on their current popularity or whether they financially contributed toward its publication. Instead it was planned as an objective, systematic and comprehensive effort to include all important persons in specific fields of human endeavor. Accordingly, the resulting *Vade mecum* would be organized into specific sections by profession or area of expertise. Apart from the deserving individuals who were born on the territory of the historic Czech Lands, the plan was to include distinguished personages of Czech ancestry, irrespective of when or where they were born.

Besides that, I intended to complete the history of SVU, on which I began working, in connection with my Memoirs, soon after I retired from the Government Service. After rethinking the matter, I decided to publish the SVU history separately. Although I had written a large number of chapters before, there were still a significant number to be written. Beyond that, I had to also reread each chapter from the point of view of documentation to assure that each event, activity or personality is footnoted with appropriate reference.

# 85
## *From an Understudy to a King-Maker*

From the earliest days of SVU and ever since I first met Dr. Jaroslav Němec, I worked with him very closely. He was my true mentor and under his tutelage I became familiar with every facet of the Society's business and acquainted myself with all major SVU figures. Jaroš involved me in just about everything and frequently consulted with me on various problems the Society faced. It was he who ingrained in me the concept of keeping the Society apolitical. I, in turn, convinced him of the need of emphasizing the English language in our congresses and conferences, as well as publications, and opening the Society to scholars and scientists of other nationalities; thus making SVU a truly international organization.

We obviously talked often and openly about individual personalities in SVU and their suitability for various offices. Although a mere "rookie," Jaroš took my suggestions seriously and, more frequently than not, followed my advice.

One of my earliest suggestions that had a great impact on the future of SVU was the selection of Prof. René Wellek for SVU President in 1962. I still remember quite vividly the evening when Jaroš and I took Prof. Wellek to a local pub in Georgetown[1262] to "feel him out" and eventually persuade him to accept the nomination. Initially, he had some apprehensions because he felt he was not close enough to the Czechoslovak American community but after a few hours of intensive discussion we persuaded him to accept. One of the arguments I used was our desire and determination to make the Society a genuinely scholarly institution which would enjoy world reputation and my conviction that he was the best candidate for it because of the respect he held in scholarly circles. His lack of contact with the Czech community abroad was, in our judgment, an asset rather than a detriment. As it turned out, Prof. Wellek's selection was the best selection we could have made. Under his Presidency, the visibility and prestige of SVU rose substantially. From a

---

[1262] An elegant section of Washington, DC.

relatively obscure ethnic organization, we suddenly gained the status of a respected academic institution with international reputation.

The second time I influenced the selection of a SVU President was in 1978, the last year of the second two-year term of my Presidency. When the Nominations Committee, headed by Dr. Jan Mládek, began searching for my successor, there was no suitable candidate among the active members of SVU. They were looking for new blood, i.e., an established professional, reputable in his field, known for his initiative, capable of continuing the work that I had started. I suggested, as a possible candidate, Jan F. Tříska. Of the various people whom I knew by their reputation, I thought that Tříska, a professor of political science at Stanford University, would be an excellent choice. This led to his invitation to Washington to discuss the matter and to acquaint him with the SVU agenda. Although he expressed great interest when I first spoke to him by telephone, upon arrival in Washington, Jan had an apparent change of heart and we almost lost him. It took an enormous effort to change his mind until he finally consented to accept the nomination. He frequently reminded me of the "pressure cooker" approach which the Nominations committee used in order to change his mind.

Two years later, the Society faced a similar problem when we sought a suitable successor to replace Tříska. As the Chairman of the Nominations Committee, I recalled seeing an old letter in my files from Leopold Pospíšil. In spite of its arrogant tone, I was impressed by the sender's ideas and vitality. Nobody from my circle of friends knew him personally but I had a feeling that this fellow has what it takes to make a good President. We thus took a chance by inviting him to Washington for a chat. We met in the prestigious Cosmos Club, of which I was a member. Almost instantaneously we became friends. He was sure of himself, ambitious, with plenty of ideas. He was very successful in his field of anthropology and held full professorship at Yale, one of the Ivy League schools. As we talked, it became clear to me that he was the person we were seeking. Polda, as he liked to be called, was elected and served two very successful terms as SVU President.

He was followed in Presidency by Jiří Nehněvajsa of Pittsburgh University, whom I knew personally from the previous SVU Congresses. He achieved success at a relatively young age and soon became known as one of the largest recipients of grant money in social sciences. His character and temperament was very much like that of Pospíšil's, with whom he also shared the Moravian ancestry. Following my recommendation, he was nominated for the next SVU President and then served successfully for 2 two-year terms.

As he was nearing the completion of his second term, there was a general feeling among the SVU leadership that the time had come for nominating a Slovak to the SVU Presidency. Actually the idea was not entirely new, as we made an effort earlier in that direction but could not find a suitable candidate. I recall in the late sixties when Jaroš and I tried to talk Victor S. Mamatey[1263] in becoming a candidate but he refused because he felt that he "did not have what it takes" to be an effective president, on par with Prof. Wellek and Prof. Hlavatý. We also considered offering the presidency to Jaroslav Pelikán, an eminent church historian and theologian at Yale University, who enjoyed almost the same reputation as did René Wellek. Although he served as SVU Vice President before, Prof. Pelikán, who was of Slovak ancestry, turned down our offer, because of his preoccupation with writing scholarly books and new administrative duties, having just bean elected Dean of the Yale Graduate School.

During the second term of Nehněvajsa's administrative period, the most visible Slovak in SVU circles was Igor Nábělek, professor of audiology at the University of Tennessee, who served as Vice President on Nehněvajsa's Executive Board. He was thus a logical choice to succeed Jiří who favored his candidacy. As was customary, Jaroš Němec, Jan Mládek and I, as members of the Nominations Committee, invited Igor to Washington to discuss his candidacy. Unfortunately, Nábělek, for some unknown reason, did not heed to our wishes, which, in retrospect, was a bad mistake. From our perspective, we did not have the opportunity to learn what kind of person he was and "what made him tick," while he, in turn, missed the chance of learning the intricacies and responsibilities of the SVU Presidency from the most knowledgeable individuals in SVU. I am convinced that some of the later misunderstandings between him and the SVU Presidential Collegium were caused by the insufficient background and lack of experience on his part.

The indecisiveness of the Board during the critical days, following the Velvet Revolution in Prague, and the rapidly changing political scene

---

[1263] Professor of History, University of Georgia, Athens, GA.

in the Home country convinced the Society "Elders" that a new more experienced SVU leadership is needed to cope with the fluid situation in Czechoslovakia. Consequently, we recommended to the Nominations Committee to nominate the experienced Jan F. Tříska for the next SVU President. As discussed elsewhere, after some difficulties, he got eventually elected to that post.

The most active and effective SVU member during Tříska's Presidency was Zdenek J. Slouka, professor of international law and relations at Lehigh University. It was therefore only natural to nominate him as Tříska's successor upon conclusion of his term of office. As chairman of the Nominations Committee, I did exactly that.

After my return to SVU Presidency in 1994, it was not my intention to stay in that position as long as I actually did. I wanted to hand over the "reigns" of the Society as soon as it was practicable, i.e., once we found a suitable candidate who could follow in my footsteps. Frankly, I was ready to do so after the first two terms but no suitable candidate was in sight. It was not until 2006, when I became sure that we have a candidate with the desired Presidential characteristics and about whom I was convinced he could carry the Society to further horizons.

Apart from influencing the choice of SVU President, I also affected the choice of many other SVU officers, including the selection of program coordinators and logistical chairpersons of various Congresses and Conferences. The reason for it was obvious since I knew practically everybody in SVU from my work on the *Biographical Directory of SVU Members*. I also had a significant influence on the selection of honorary and founding members, the highest recognition the Society could render. I have always pushed for the selection of individuals who were universally recognized by their peers as leading scholars or scientists in their area of expertise. As I look over the rostrum of the honorary members, it is apparent that I had some say about the selection of most of them, including Prof. Francis Dvornik (1963), Max Brod (1964), Prof. Otakar Odložilík (1966), Prof. Roman Jakobson (1966), Oskar Kokoschka (1968), Prof. Matthew Spinka (1970), Prof. René Wellek (1977), Dr. D. Carleton Gajdusek (1980), Prof. Karl W. Deutsch (1980), Prof. Gordon Skilling (1980), Prof. Wesley W. Posvar (1980), Prof. Ivan A. Getting (1980), Tom Stoppard (1980), Prof. Victor S. Mamatey (1982), Prof. Karel Husa (1982), Jaroslav Seifert (1984), Václav Havel (1984), Milan

Kundera (1984), Prof. Jan Milič Lochman (1985), Prof. Mikuláš Lobkowicz (1986) and Prof. Leopold Pospíšil (1988). The reason for my effectiveness in the selection process was my familiarity with who was who among our people worldwide and the fact that I always did my homework well beforehand.

# 86
# *The Rebellious Local Chapters*

It was in the early seventies that someone proposed the local chapters could be of assistance with the collection of dues locally and thus lighten the burden of SVU Treasurer. To make the idea more enticing, those chapters that agreed to do this, were to be rewarded for their help with a nominal portion of the money collected, 5 to 10 percent, as I recall. Most European chapters opted for this mode of paying SVU dues, while in the US only a couple of chapters participated.

Initially, the arrangement seemed to work but not for long. As time progressed, some of the chapters, instead of helping, they made the job progressively more difficult for the Treasurer. At first, they began squabbling about the small "reward" for their "hard work" and began demanding a bigger cut from the proceeds. Their demands were becoming more and more vocal, as time went on, to the point that the Swiss Chapter refused to turn in the membership dues altogether.

Leopold Pospíšil, who was SVU President at that time, refused to yield to their demands, pointing out the unconstitutionality of the matter. There was even talk about dissolving the Swiss Chapter,[1264] if the Swiss Chapter would not conform. Secretary General Blanka Glos was instructed by the Executive Board to send them a strongly-worded letter to make the situation right. President Pospíšil, Dr. Jaroslav Němec and SVU Treasurer Frank Marlow subsequently met in Vienna with the leadership of the Swiss Chapters during which the Chapter agreed to repay the money they owed to the SVU Treasury.[1265]

Subsequently the situation more or less quieted down, until it surfaced again into open, during the last months of Jan F Třiska's Presidency. The subject was unexpectedly brought up at a hurriedly convened meeting of SVU Council in Prague, at the conclusion of the SVU World

---

[1264] Record of the meeting of SVU Executive Board, held on April 16 and 17, 1982, Washington, DC in Blanka Glos' residence, Falls Church, VA.

[1265] Record of the Meeting of SVU Executive Board, held on September 10 and 11, 1982 in Barton House, Arlington, VA.

*The Rebellious Local Chapters* 539

Congress in June 1992. I do recall some of the unpleasant exchanges that took place between Tříska and Hrubý.[1266] As far as I know, no written records were kept of the meeting. Subsequently, Hrubý came with the claim that he and Tříska reached an agreement, according to which Tříska was supposed to essentially accept the Swiss position and their demands to keep a sizeable portion of the membership dues for themselves. Tříska always vehemently denied this assertion[1267]. The subject was certainly not brought up at the SVU General Assembly meeting in Los Angeles on October 22, 1992, which I attended, as verified by the report of the meeting.[1268] Hrubý, nevertheless, kept bringing up his unsubstantiated assertion even during the ensuing Zdeněk Slouka's Presidency (1992-1994).

Since it was generally known that I would become the next SVU President, Hrubý and Krejčí[1269] tried to get me on their side during our SVU World Congress in 1994 in Prague. Frankly, they ruined the entire social gathering in the Valdstein Garden (Valdštejnská zahrada) for me, arguing over the same issues, over and over again, including the presumed agreements with Tříska, pressuring me to the point that it made me pretty mad. I tried to keep my cool, and when we finally parted I told them that, as far as I was concerned, I found their position unacceptable and harmful to the entire SVU.

The matter received special attention during the 1994 General Assembly meeting, held a few months later in New York City, where I assumed the SVU Presidency. At the recommendation of the outgoing Secretary-General Marlow, the Assembly ruled that the practice of collecting dues locally was not beneficial to the Society and that it should be stopped and that the dues henceforth should be again exclusively collected centrally by SVU Treasurer, the way the founding fathers

---

[1266] Karel Hrubý (1923-), was the chairman of the Swiss Chapter.

[1267] Later, I came across Hrubý's letter to Tříska, dated July 23, 1992, in which he makes specific reference to his discussion with Tříska in Prague, during which, as he wrote, they did not come to any agreement, and consequently requested that the matter and Hrubý's proposal be brought to the attention to the Executive Board for resolution and approval. From this letter it is quite clear that Hrubý's assertions of some kind of an agreement between Tříska and himself were all products of his imagination.

[1268] "SVU General Assembly in Los Angeles," *SVU Bulletin*, vol. 14, No. 4 (October 1992), pp. 4-5.

[1269] Jaroslav Krejčí (1916-) was chairman of the British Chapter.

originally meant it.[1270] The newly elected SVU Executive Board accepted the Assembly's recommendation as its new policy.

---

[1270] *Zprávy SVU*, vol. 36, No. 6 (November-December 1994), pp. 2-3.

# 87
## *SVU Research Institute Activated*

The creation of a semi-autonomous research institute within SVU was originally my idea, with which I had toyed for a number of years. It was finally approved in 1988 but did not get implemented, however, until 1991, after we found a suitable individual to direct it.

I envisioned it as a research, training and education arm of the Society, comparable to the function the National Research Council performs in relation to its parent National Academy of Sciences. It was to be financially independent and raise its own funds for various training and research projects.

The Institute was duly incorporated in Washington, DC in 1989 and simultaneously a new Board of Trustees was established to set its policy. In Referendum of Members which decided on its approval, the following justification was provided:

> Through the dedicated efforts of its members, the Czechoslovak Society of Arts and Sciences has matured into a respectable forum for the promotion of intellectual activity in the arts and sciences.
>
> By means of the World Congresses, work of the local chapters, and publication activities, the Society has encouraged intellectual pursuits and facilitated the exchange of ideas especially among its members. However, in order for the Society to expand its research activities and carry them out more effectively, it is necessary to take the next step to provide a more permanent research environment and to enable the Society to attract external grant funding for projects.
>
> The creation of a research institute can provide the catalyst necessary to improve the intellectual achievement environment and the mechanism through which additional resources could be effectively developed and channeled. A research institute would also be a symbolic statement to the larger Intellectual world – and to ourselves – that, as a Society of arts and sciences, we are becoming more effective in fostering our aims.

Of course, symbolism alone does not justify creating a research institute. There are also concrete, practical reasons to do so at this time. The Society does not have the appropriate structures to be able to raise significant funds for research and to professionally administer projects. The present relationship between our Society and the National Endowment for Democracy has provided the first opportunity for the Society to become involved in externally funded projects. At the same time, however, that relationship has also served to emphasize that the present limitations of the Society structure make the necessary project administration and oversight functions somewhat awkward and unprofessional. For most long term projects, a desirable feature of the institute would be a board of directors and officers with longer terms to provide stability and continuity. A research institute, established as an integral part of the Society, would enable the Society to raise funds, conduct systematic research, and take advantage of the expertise of the members of the Society.

In order to continue to grow and prosper, the Society needs to attract new members from a wider community, particularly persons not of Czechoslovak origin. A research institute would be a catalyst for attracting new members by opening up the intellectual endeavors of the Society to a wider segment of the intellectual world, beyond the present membership.

The stature and reputation of the Society demand an appropriate structure to accommodate these needs. A research institute, properly administered, would create the environment necessary to reach these goals and could make the Society a nationally, or even internationally, recognized point of intellectual convergence for research in arts and sciences related to Czechoslovak culture. The time to act is now.

Therefore, the Executive Board, proposes that the Society establish the Research Institute of the Czechoslovak Society of Arts and Sciences, Inc.

The specific language in the Bylaws regarding the establishment and the functions of the new SVU Research Institute read as follows:

It shall be the function of the SVU Research Institute to be the research arm of the Society and the chief instrument to attract grant

## SVU Research Institute Activated

funds and to provide the mechanism for the review, conduct, evaluation and coordination of research projects in the arts and sciences relating to Czechoslovak culture. The Institute shall be an integral part of the Society, but it shall be financially independent of the Society. The Institute shall be managed by a Director under the guidance of the Institute Governing Board according to policies to be established by the Society.

The Institute Governing Board will be comprised of the past presidents of the Society who declare their willingness to serve in that capacity. Additional members may be co-opted by the Institute Governing Board with the approval of the Executive Board of the Society. The Director shall be nominated by the Institute Governing Board and appointed by the Executive Board of the Society for the duration of four years. He may be revoked by the Executive Board of the Society upon the recommendation of the Institute Governing Board.

Members of the Institute Governing Board and the Director may be reappointed at the end of their terms. The Institute Governing Board may appoint, on the recommendation of the Director, other officers of the Institute.

To get it off the ground, the original Board comprised exclusively of the Past SVU Presidents, i.e., Prof. René Wellek, Dr. Jaroslav Němec, Prof. Francis Schwarzenberg, Dr. Miloslav Rechcígl, Prof. Leopold Pospíšil and Prof. Jiří Nehněvajsa. In March 1990, at the recommendation of the Collegium of Presidents, the Executive Board expanded its membership[1271] to also include Dr. Madeleine Korbel Albright,[1272] Dr. Alexej Bořkovec, Dr. Thomas G. Gibian Dr. Ladislav Matějka, Dr. Anton J. Novacký,[1273] Dr. Michael Novak,[1274] Dr. Jaroslav J. Pelikán[1275]

---

[1271] *Zprávy SVU*, vol. 32, No. 2 (March-April 1990), pp. 15-16.

[1272] Professor of International Affairs, School of Foreign Service, Georgetown University, Washington, DC; later US Secretary of State.

[1273] Professor of Plant Pathology, University of Missouri, Columbia, MO.

[1274] Prominent theologian, writer and publicist of Slovak ancestry, Washington, DC.

[1275] Sterling Professor of History, Yale University, New Haven, CT.

and Dr. Zdeněk J. Slouka,[1276] with the understanding that the original Past Presidents could stay on if they wished.[1277]

In January, 1991, upon the recommendation of the Institute's Board of Trustees, the SVU Executive Board appointed Prof. Zdeněk Slouka as the first Executive Director of the Institute, to serve for a four-year term.

In the first year of its operation,[1278] the Institute concentrated on: (a) strengthening its cooperative links with other institutions in the West, a process already begun by the SVU Commission for Cooperation with Czechoslovakia, now superseded by the Institute; (b) expanding its cooperation with Czech and Slovak academic and research institutions and related governmental agencies; (c) launching its first externally funded training projects. The Institute became directly and actively involved in a number of cooperative programs and initiatives. The Institute's Director was a member of the Board of Directors of the Charter 77 Foundation and of the American Czech-and-Slovak Education Fund, and serves as a Trustee of the Independent Journalists' Center sponsored by The New York Times Foundation and operating a training program in Prague. Close working contacts were simultaneously developed between the Institute and various Czech and Slovak academic and research institutions. The Institute's Director served as the foreign consultant to the Working Group for the Formulation and Design of National Science Policy, a group responsible for developing the strategy and the structure of the national science, technology and education establishment.

Slouka also made an effort to establish, within the Institute, an SVU Information Service in Prague for the purpose of expanding and deepening links between the US and the Czechs and Slovaks in professions, where it counts most, with the hope that it would trigger more permanent bi-national relationships. The core of our plan was simple. Using our extensive network of SVU members in the US and the institutional and professional setting in which they operate, we would collect in one

---

[1276] J. B. Cohen Professor of International Relations, Lehigh University, Lehigh, Bethlehem, PA.

[1277] No new Past Presidents were to be added in the future to the Institute's Board of Trustees unless specifically appointed by the SVU Executive Board.

[1278] Based on the Memo, dated 11 April 1992, addressed to the Board of Trustees, SVU Research Institute, from Zdeněk J. Slouka, Director, SVU Research Institute. Subject: Director's First Year's Report.

terminal on the US side information of the following type: on specific study and research opportunities in the US, on major areas of ongoing research in a variety of disciplines, on training opportunities in various professions, and on individual researchers and scholars in the US interested in joint research/study projects with their Czech and Slovak professional counterparts. At the US terminal, this information would be programmed for computer use and transmitted to the second terminal in Prague. At the Prague end, an interested local client would be able to find out, for instance, what is going on in the US in his/her specialized field, what is the cutting edge of a given discipline, what are the most recent publications in a given field, etc. And moreover: who is doing what, and where in the US may be interested in a professional partnership with Czech and Slovak researchers.

To this end, Slouka applied for a special grant from the USIA but, to my knowledge, nothing came of it, which was a great pity because SVU was uniquely suited for its programmatic function, i.e., to be a bridge between Czechoslovak professionals and those in the US. The Society itself was a pool of bilingual, and often bi-cultural, professional talent. Our members had a well-trained habit of volunteering their services and then performing them professionally and throughout 1990, many SVU members and all officers visited Czechoslovakia for extended periods, renewed lost contacts and established new ones, and accumulated considerable understanding and knowledge about the contemporary conditions in Czechoslovakia.

# 88
# The SVU Research Institute's First Workshop

In 1990, SVU conducted several highly successful seminars in the Czech Republic under the aegis of the SVU Commission for Cooperation with Czechoslovakia. After the activation of the SVU Research Institute, this function was taken over by the Institute.

This is the report of the first two workshops held in Prague in 1991, which really set the stage for the whole series of workshops that followed.[1279]

Descriptive Summary

*Preparatory work*: In the US, 1-17 July 1991; in Prague, 18 July – 23 August 1991.

*Workshop dates*: Workshop I – 16-21 September 1991, Workshop II – 23-28 September 1991.

*Location*: Charles University, Karolinum, Celetna Street, Prague, Czech Republic

*Workshop schedule*: Monday-Friday 9-12, 13-15. All sessions conducted jointly by both workshop instructors. Individual consultations: 15:00 – on and on Saturdays.

*Participants*: workshop I – 34. Workshop II – 35. Of the total of 69, 54 were faculty members of Charles University, 13 from the Technical University and 2 from the University of Agriculture (all in Prague). Breakdown by disciplinary categories: social sciences and humanities – 21; natural and physical sciences – 31; health fields, engineering, law – 17.

---

[1279] Based on the Interim Report. Workshops on US Practice in Research Management. Prague: SVU Research Institute, December 1991; see also my notice, "From the SVU Research Institute," *SVU Bulletin*, vol. 13, No. 3 (August 1992), p. 5.

*Instructors*:

(1) Miloslav Rechcígl, Jr. (Ph.D., Cornell University, 1958), Research Review Director, Office of the Science Advisor, U.S. Agency for International Development, Washington, DC.

Fields of expertise pertinent to project: biomedical sciences, biochemistry, biotechnology, nutrition, agriculture, research management, international development

(2) Zdenek J. Slouka (Ph.D., Columbia, 1965), Cohen Professor of International Relations, Lehigh University, Bethlehem, PA; First Director of Lehigh Center for International Studies

Fields of expertise pertinent to project: political science, international relations, international political economy; science policy, comparative research/ education systems.

Workshop Outlined

The workshop design and the eventual outcome of the workshop process, need to be measured against the objective of the project, namely, to familiarize Czech and Slovak scientists with modern methods of scientific research and research management. This is, in fact, a two-pronged objective. First, there is an intrinsic value in sharing US research experiences with talented Czech and Slovak scientists isolated for so long – in fact, throughout their professional lives – from their western colleagues. Whether or not the workshop experience would eventually translate into more effective research performance in the participants' laboratories and study rooms is, of course, beyond our present ability to evaluate.

The second prong is sharper. A good understanding of American methods of research management is a prerequisite for the Czech and Slovak scientists seeking to re-enter, via US, their international scientific communities as partners in joint research ventures or as participants in institutional research program in the West in general and the US in particular. So far, many of those who attempted that re-entry failed in the very first stage. Their research proposals clearly revealed, both in the concepts employed and in the overall design, the Czech and Slovak scientists' unfamiliarity with modern research methods and their imperatives. In this respect, the workshops' outcome would eventfully be measurable by the participants' successful entry into international scientific enterprises.

Concentrating on the US research scene and emphasizing what is termed above "the second prong," the workshop instructors covered the following topics:

> US research information sources (types and access to research related literature, library information centers, information on research priorities, magnitude and directions of research in specific fields, leading researchers and research institutions, etc.)

> Organization of US research (universities, research universities, private research institutes and organizations, governmental research establishments, industry; co-operative links among them, etc.)

> Research design (placing a research project within its field and relating it to other concurrent or recent research efforts; project timetable; quality control; etc.)

> Research proposal as a mirror of a sound research design (methods of preparing a proposal; role of research offices in US universities; compliance with guidelines and regulations of sponsoring agencies and of host institutions; etc.).

> The use and function of the peer review system; different modes of employing peer review by governmental agencies and other institutions supportive of research projects.

> Special topics: research priorities as a function of science policy; scientific collaboration; research ethics; environmental concerns; intellectual property rights; fiscal; management; administration of grants and contracts.

The workshop presentations and ensuing discussions were supplemented by a collection of US research directories, guidelines and descriptions of various research programs and projects, as well as by samples of actual research proposals that have been funded and entered the public domain.

Workshop Participants

As will become clear further below, the selection of workshop participants drawn, in the first two workshops, from Czech and largely only Prague institutions, was a critical element affecting the process and the outcome of the workshops. In this respect some background comments are necessary.

Following what amounts to half a century (1939-1989) of gross political interference with Czech and Slovak science and education, the entire system of scientific research is now seriously out of balance. Most of the relatively good research is done in some of the disciplinary research institutes of the sprawling Czechoslovak Academy of Sciences (ČSAV) while the universities, ultimately responsible for the training of new generations of scientists and scholars, are singularly weak in the research domain.

During our preparatory work for the workshops in the summer of 1991, we had an opportunity to discuss the academy/university schism with the leadership of the academy, including its president, with several university rectors, pro-rectors, deans, department heads, as well as with individual scientists and faculty members at both the ČSAV. and the universities. Responding to their general suggestions and to the recommendations of the leadership of Charles University, we decided to aim the workshops primarily at the university faculties where the need to strengthen the research dimension is greatest.

We have also agreed with the responsible administrators of Charles University that while they would make the final selection of the participants, the selection itself would be guided by several criteria. Among them were at least a good passive knowledge of English, previous documented experience in research, and evidence (by way of an abstract) of preparation for a future viable research project. Unfortunately, and most likely due to the inexperience of some of our Prague colleagues in organizing similar projects, many participants did not meet these criteria.

Workshop Schedule

Monday A.M.
I. General Introduction – Z. Slouka (ZS)
    B. SVU – M. Rechcígl (MR)
    C. Purpose of Workshop – ZS & MR

II. U.S. Information Sources
    A. Information Sources – MR
    B. Information Services – ZS

Monday P.M.

III. Organization of Research in U.S.
- A. Generalities – MR
- B. University-Based Research – ZS
- C. Federal Research Labs – MR
- D. Industrial Research – ZS & MR

IV. Research Support
- A. Sources of Support
    1. Government Agencies – MR
    2. Private Foundations – ZS
    3. Corporate Funding – ZS
- B. Instruments of Support – MR

Tuesday A.M.

V. Public Policy – Research Priorities
- A. Introductory Comments and Structural Aspects – ZS & MR
- B. Setting up Research Priorities by the Government – MR
- C. Private Sector Considerations – ZS
- D. Research Priorities in Czechoslovakia – Workshop Participants – MR & ZS

Tuesday P.M.

VI. Review of Research Proposals
- A. Government Sponsored Programs – MR
- B. Programs Sponsored by Private Foundations and Corporations – ZS

VII. Preparation of Research Proposals. Part 1.
- A. Fundamentals – MR & ZS
- B. Preparation of Curriculum Vitae – Workshop participants – MR

Wednesday A.M.

VIII. Regulatory Aspects and Special Concerns
- A. Governmental Requirements and Regulations – MR
- B. Grantee's and Contractor's Compliance – ZS

IX. Administration of Grants and Contracts
    A. At Government Level – MR
    B. At Researcher's Institutional Level – ZS

Wednesday P.M.
X. Preparation of Research Proposals. Part 2.
    A. Natural, Technical and Applied Sciences – MR
    B. Social Sciences and Humanities – ZS

Thursday A.M.
XI. Why Are Research Proposals Rejected
    A. Government-Sponsored Programs – MR
    B. Programs Sponsored by Foundations and Corporations – ZS

Thursday P.M.
XII. Preparation of Research Proposals. Part 3.
    A. Natural, Technical, and Applied Sciences – MR
    B. Social Sciences and Humanities – ZS

Friday A. M.
XIII. Summation and General Discussion

Workshop Evaluation

    Judging from their reactions during the workshop sessions, their almost perfect attendance, their comments during the individual consultations, as well as from the follow-up correspondence and requests for various research guidelines and other materials, the Czech participants considered the workshops a valuable experience. It is indeed very likely that the Prague workshops have contributed quite significantly to the quality of their future research work.

    From the instructors' perspective, the outcome of the first two workshops has been less satisfactory as measured against our own expectations. This refers primarily to our primary objective, that is, to help active university researchers in honing their research designs so as to make them meet US standards in form and method, thus enabling the scientists to enter into various cooperative ventures within their US and other Western colleagues and institutions. From all the participants, only two and possibly three may, as a result of the workshops, achieve that end.

Perhaps, it is not inappropriate to stress the very novelty of the entire workshop project and, indeed, its path-breaking character. In the US, people learn about research management and about research support system within their scientific and scholarly experience; there certainly are no textbooks and no formalized classroom inscription in this area. Just as obviously, nothing even remotely resembling the Prague workshops has ever been offered in Czechoslovakia. In the absence of applicable models and tested tools, the workshop instructors had to develop their own approaches and materials and learn from their own experience.

# 89
## *The Second Series of Workshops*

Following the successful conclusion of our workshops in 1991, we decided to start a second phase, for which Zdeněk Slouka secured an external grant support from the Mellon Foundation. The workshops were again sponsored by the SVU Research Institute in close collaboration with the respective institutions in the Czech and Slovak Republics. As previously, the theme of the workshops dealt with the US methods of research management. The narrative is based on the Final Report submitted to Mellon Foundation.[1280]

Organizational Background

The 1992 Mellon grant project was intended to utilize the funds on the approved activities in the following one or two years. We started a fairly intensive preparation, in both the US and in the Czech and Slovak lands, in early 1993. Unfortunately, the effort was largely wasted due to radical changes in the whole Czech and Slovak academia, particularly due to severe budget cuts in the academic and research establishments of both regions.

During the year of 1993, the Czech Academy of Sciences announced the closing of 21 of its 86 research institutes. At least 2,000 of the Academy's 8,800 scientists and associated professional employees were dismissed and these cuts came on the top of an earlier 36 percent reduction in the Academy's workforce. The cuts followed a government decision to reduce the Academy's budget by about one quarter of its previous year's level.

In the universities the situation was fairly similar and the cuts perhaps even more dramatic. The budgets for most major universities in both regions of former Czechoslovakia were reduced to about 70 percent of the level of the previous year, which actually, in view of the increas

---

[1280] The 1992-1996 Report. Workshops on US Practice in Research Management and Grantsmanship. Prague: SVU Research Institute, September 1996.

ing costs, represented a 50 percent reduction, necessarily resulting in wide-spread shifts and dismissals of professional staff members.

After numerous consultations with the representatives of Czech and Slovak academies and universities, we found that probably as many as 50 percent of those applying for admission to the workshops were on their way out of the academia and mostly heading for various emoluments with private and chiefly foreign firms. That, of course, would significantly undermine the potential effectiveness of the workshop program which was intended to raise the capability of scientific researchers and university professors to link with, learn from, and contribute to the work of their American colleagues.

Consequently, we have decided to delay the opening of the workshop series until the situation in the Czech and Slovak academic establishment may have stabilized.

The subsequent intervals between the several workshops were still due to some continuity flux in the local academic environment as well as to some difficulties in matching the calendars of Czech and Slovak scientists and scholars with the availability of the team of American instructors.

Workshop Calendar and Attendance

*One-week workshop: June 1992*, at Charles University, Prague

*Instructors*: Drs. Rechcígl and Slouka

*Attendance*: 82 professors and research scientists from Charles U. and its divisions in Hradec Králové and Plzeň, and from Palacký U. (Olomouc), Masaryk U. (Brno), and Komenský U. (Bratislava)

*One-week workshop: June 1994*, at the Czech Academy of Sciences, Prague

*Instructors*: Drs. Rechcígl and Slouka, and Mr. Frank L. Mucha, Mgr. Columbia University, NY)

*Attendance*: 33 professors and scientists from a wide range of Czech and Slovak universities and research institutes

*Three workshops of varying durations* (4–7 days) conducted in August 1995 at the Technical U. (Košice, Slovakia) and at Masaryk U. (Brno)

*Instructors*: Dr. Rechcígl, Mr. Mucha, Prof. Jiří Nehněvajsa (University of Pittsburgh)

*Attendance*: 77 professors and scientists from a wide range of institutions of the workshop

*Two one-week workshops, August 1996*, at Masaryk University, Brno
*Instructors*: Dr. Rechcígl and Mr. Mucha
*Attendance*: 70 participants. Apart from professors and scientists, these workshops were also open to postgraduate students

*Twelve consulting sessions held during July and August 1996* at the Czech Academy of Sciences, Prague
*Instructor*: Prof. Slouka
*Attendance*: 62 participants from a variety of academic institutions
*Note*: These were one-day and two-day working sessions organized for interested workshop participants developing their own research projects.

## Location of Workshops

As the above paragraphs already indicate, we have considerably expanded the geographical reach of the workshops to Slovakia and Moravia. Although this extension of the workshops outside Prague added to the organizational tasks and to some costs, it was necessary due to two closely related factors. First, researchers and scholars from Prague have greater access to information about American methods of research management and better opportunities to individually contact their American professional counterparts. (Even in Prague this process of interlinked cooperative research ventures is by no means ideal but it is still way ahead of other Czech and Slovak academic communities. Second, and as a direct reflection of the first point, there is a very strong interest in the workshops in academic communities such as Bratislava and Košice in Slovakia, in Brno and Olomouc in Moravia, and in the "outlaying" regions of Bohemia such as České Budějovice, Plzeň, Hradec Králové, Liberec and others.

Obviously, we could not cover them all, but we did cover Košice (with participants from other Slovak academic communities) and Brno (again with participants from other Moravian academic communities).

## Participants – Structure Economists

Originally, as per the basic 1992 proposal, we intended to conduct workshops organized according to the professional disciplines of the participants, i.e., separately for economists, social scientists, physical scientists, etc. This proved largely impossible primarily due to timing and to the fact that in other various disciplines the needs for the kind of information we offer through the workshops widely differ. First, since the calendars of the various research institutes and university divisions are not aligned, the scheduling of the disciplinary oriented workshops proved unworkable. Second, we realized after several discussions with our institutional and university colleagues, that such disciplinary differentiation is not really absolutely necessary because the basic principles of well-managed academic research and grantsmanship do apply to all fields, and moreover, as we discovered during the discussions, people from various disciplines significantly contributed to the discussions and better understanding of the overall process. Thus we have reverted to our previous pattern of a disciplinary mix.

In Slovakia (the workshop based in Košice) the participants were somewhat unevenly divided, as followed: medical and related fields 11, informatics and electrotechnics 10, chemistry 5 and then, briefly, pedagogy 2, ecology 2, natural sciences 1, social sciences and philosophy 2, mathematics and air engineering 3, music compositions 1, and production management 1.

In Moravia (the workshop based in Brno at Masaryk University) the participation pattern differed in only some categories: medical and related fields 14, natural sciences 7, informatics and cybernetics 4, pedagogy 6, weapon technology 3, agronomy 2, and then each discipline represented by one representative: economics, philosophy, geodesy, engineering, and music. The second Brno workshop, as well as the first Prague workshop, and the individual consultations had similar disciplinary patterns.

This disciplinary breakdown does, at least partly, reflect some realities: that, in fact, professionals in some disciplines, e.g. economics, agronomy, etc., lately have found their professional contacts abroad and thus have a lesser need for institutional interlinks through the workshops, while others, as in medical research, in natural sciences, and in several other fields do need and want to expand their professional horizons.

Participants – Structure II

In the previous workshops conducted under the Mellon sponsorship, our efforts were largely, if not exclusively, directed toward researchers and scholars already well-established in their fields but, because of their professional high standing, they also have already established reasonably good contacts and direct individual communication with their professional colleagues in America and elsewhere in the West. For that reason, we have included among the participants in the latter part of the workshop series a significant number of postgraduate students heading for academic careers. At the concluding workshop in Brno, some 50 percent participants fell into this category. Of course, not all of the postgraduates will necessarily end up in the academia. But those who will, probably a majority of them, may be better armed for their future academic tasks.

Those postgraduates who opted for preparing their own research proposals were given an opportunity of having their proposals reviewed by an external panel of American scientists, arranged by Drs. Rechcígl and Mucha.

The high value given the workshops by the participating Czech and Slovak academic institutions is best evidenced by the fact that some of these institutions, Masaryk University in Brno in particular, gave regular academic credits to participating postgraduates – 2 credits for workshop attendance, 2 additional credits for tasking and successfully completing a final examination, and still 2 more credits for preparing a professional research proposal.

The Instructors

The second phase of the Mellon-supported workshops was arranged and organized by the Research Institute of the Czechoslovak Society of Arts and Sciences (SVU) (founded and incorporated in Washington, D.C., in the 1950s), in cooperation with the International Institute of Political Sciences of the Masaryk University in Brno, with SVU Chapter in Brno and with Slovak universities and SVU Chapters. For the second phase of workshops we have expanded and reorganized the team of instructors (individually identified further below), all of them with extensive experience in research management and grantsmanship, all of them fully bi-lingual in English and Czech/Slovak, and all of them leading members of SVU:

DR. MILOSLAV RECHCÍGL, JR., Ph.D. (Cornell) in natural sciences. As the
    Director of Research Review, Dr. Rechcígl for many years managed

innovative research programs at the US Agency for International Development (AID) and directed an external peer review of AID research proposals. Dr. Rechcígl led the entire workshop series as its key participant. He currently serves as the President of SVU in his second two-year term. He also served in the same function for four years in 1974-78.

DR. JIŘÍ NEHNĚVAJSA, Professor of Sociology, University of Pittsburgh. Dr. Nehněvajsa was in his field as a teacher and researcher for well over thirty years. He also served for four years (1984-88) as President of SVU. Dr. Nehněvajsa covered three of the workshops (in Košice and Brno) and performed this function exceedingly well. Although unknown to us, at the time, he had already been diagnosed as suffering from terminal cancer. He was still determined to cover the last workshop in Brno, as well and was scheduled as one on the instructors' team – "the doctors are giving me up to six months, so it should work," he told us shortly before the last August 1996 team's departure for Brno. It did not work. Dr. Nehněvajsa died within the next few days.

MR. FRANK L. MUCHA, Columbia University, NY. For many years, Mr. Mucha has been responsible, as the deputy director of the Research Foundation for Mental Hygiene at Columbia, for administering grants and for directing the privately endowed health foundation. Mr. Mucha very actively carried out his load as one of the workshop instructors throughout the presently reported second phase (Prague, Košice, Brno) and was praised for his performance by his colleagues as well as by the workshop participants. Mr. Mucha currently serves, in his third year, as the Treasurer of SVU.

DR. ZDENĚK J. SLOUKA, Cohen Processor emeritus, Lehigh University in Bethlehem, PA. After thirty years of teaching and research at Columbia University, Wellesley College and Lehigh University, Dr. Slouka was the instructor of the workshop program. During the second phase, Dr. Slouka served as the Prague organizer of the workshop series and as a research consultant for over 60 Czech and Slovak academics. He could do so because he now spends most of his time in Prague and serves as an international advisor to the President of the Academy of Sciences. He also served for two years (1992-94) as President of SVU. In 1990 Dr. Slouka chaired the SVU Commission for Cooperation with Czechoslovakia and, since 1991, he has been the director of SVU Research Institute, the primary mechanism for arranging the workshop program.

## General Observations and Comments

Most of the following paragraphs are based on written reports by the workshop instructors on the workshop process itself and on their individual experiences, and also summarizes the situation in research academics in the Czech Republic and Slovakia.

## Workshop Content

The workshops covered the following areas:

1. US information sources – both published sources and information services
2. Organization of research in the US – university-based research, Federal research laboratories, and industrial research
3. Research support – sources and instruments
4. Public policy and research priorities – structural aspects, setting research priorities by the US Government, private sector considerations, and comparison of US research priorities with those in the Czech Republic and Slovakia
5. Preparation of proposals – I. Fundamentals
6. Review of research proposals – government sponsored vs. programs of private foundations and corporations
7. Regulatory aspects and special concerns – governmental requirements and regulations, compliance by grantees and contractors
8. Administration of grants and contracts at all levels
9. Preparation of proposals – II. Comparisons between natural sciences, social sciences and humanities
10. Why are research proposals rejected

In addition to a number of reference volumes provided for the needs of participants, documents prepared specifically for the workshops included the following: list of US information sources relating to research management and grantsmanship – list of commonly used US acronyms in the field – glossary of terms used in the US – instructions for the preparation of resumes.

## Workshop Process

Dr. Rechcígl provided key leadership on each workshop session while Dr. Nehněvajsa and Mr. Mucha further expanded on each point raised by Dr. Rechcígl.

Questions and comments by the participants were encouraged at any time during the presentations and the participants, indeed, availed themselves of this opportunity quite amply. As one of the instructors reported, "the discussions were lively and relevant and served as another indicator of the strong interest of the participants. All three of us noted that the kind of information we were able to share with our colleagues was quite new to them so that the workshops appear to have served a significant function."

Another member of the instructors team commented that, "in addition to formal meetings, there were on subsequent days informal meetings with individual participants or small groups to discuss their specific research interests. Some participants brought along drafts of their research proposals which will, however, require a follow-up by the instructors. (Dr. Rechcígl prepared a list of twelve items representing steps and conditions for a serious follow-up. These, of course, would come after the conclusion of the second workshop phase and consequently do not constitute a part of this report.

## Instructors' Comments on Needs and Capabilities

In Košice, representatives from the Medical School and the Technical University requested a special afternoon workshop focused on the understanding and usage of Internet for the purposes of locating sources of information and funds for their research and educational needs. The special session was conducted in the Computing Center of the Technical University. During three-and-a-half hours we were able to review the technical capabilities of the Center, discuss possible remedies to their difficulties, and bring to their attention various soft-ware programs and Service Centers in the US.

In all workshop locations, Prague, Brno and Košice, there was a pronounced hunger for information – the Czech and Slovak institutions have no, or only meager, publications on US research system, on US science policy, and on US research institutes and universities. Nor do they have information about grant opportunities, grant agencies, and foundations. The publications that have been used in this and the previous workshop series, already somewhat out of date but still informative, we have left at Masaryk University for teaching and other uses.

Problem of Assessment

We do know from our experience and from the continuing and, in fact, rising interest in the subject matter of the workshops on the part of Czech and Slovak academic institutions and research centers that the workshops were indeed on target. However, we have not yet found a method of a more precise assessment of the specific results of our work – namely, how many and who of the participants would be able to convert into actual projects the information and the contacts with their professional colleagues in the US., gained through the workshops. The preparation and execution of such projects is, of course, a long-time affair, whether they are cooperative projects or individual undertakings, and we have no mechanism to monitor such subsequent workshop spin-offs. We do know, mostly from personal contacts and occasional correspondence, of some specific cases in which the workshops led directly to transnational undertakings. These, however, are rather sporadic and probably not representative.

# 90
## *SVU Workshop for the Administrators*

This workshop was conducted in Prague on February 3-7, 1997. It was in response to the participants of earlier workshops that we offer a special workshop for university administrators responsible for stimulating, supporting and administering academic research – the "training for trainers" idea. This fully coincided with our own understanding of the academic scene. The description of the workshop is based on our Closing Report to the Mellon Foundation.[1281]

The Aim of Workshop

The primary aim of the workshop was to acquaint high-level personnel of Czech and Slovak universities with the multiple functions of "Research and Grants Offices" at US academic institutions. Universities in the Slovak and Czech Republics do have officers and offices responsible for "science and research" but their functions are chiefly in record-keeping – who is doing what, where, etc. As we learned through earlier workshops, many faculty members did not even know about the existence of such office at their institutions. As one of them remarked, using the old saying – "a mystery wrapped in an enigma."

When describing the American model of a "Research and Grants Office" and its functions, we were not suggesting that Czech and Slovak universities adopt it. We were very much aware that models such as this cannot be transplanted across economic, social, political, and generally cultural boundaries. In the workshop sessions, we stressed this point clearly and repeatedly. But we also suggested that the American model may contain elements which, creatively adapted, may indeed fit into the Czech and Slovak institutional context.

The secondary but not negligible aim of the workshop, not particularly emphasized but visible, was somewhat different. In increasing numbers, Czech and Slovak scientists seek opportunities for longer-term

---

[1281] SVU Research Institute. Closing Report. Prague, February 11, 1997. Submitted to Andrew W. Mellon Foundation.

research projects in the US, either on individual grants from American sources, or as cooperative projects with their professional American colleagues. In either case, they need to know how the American "research and grants" system operates, and their own institutional "science and research office" should be adequately armed to guide them. Some of the working scientists are outstanding in their fields. Their failure to effectively interlink their research efforts with their American colleagues and institutions is often due to their inadequate understanding of the American system.

The Organization of Workshop

As briefly mentioned above, the local preparation and overall organization of the special workshop required more time and effort than in the previous cases.

On November 4, 1996, an announcement of the workshop was sent to twenty-nine university presidents (rectors) in the Czech and Slovak Republics, inviting them to designate the "science and research" people within their administrative staff for workshop attendance.

On November 15, another memorandum went out to all addresses, specifying the time and place of the workshop. They were selected on the basis of previous inquiries regarding various academia calendars and selecting the most suitable time.

All prospective participants were clearly informed of conditions: while workshop attendance is free, travel, meals and housing are the responsibility of the participants or their institutions.

To ease the participants' financial burden, we have arranged housing for twenty-two out of town participants in Prague university facilities in locations close to the site of the workshop – the Czech Academy of Sciences.

Also in November, registration and housing forms went to all prospective participants.

During the three-month organization time, the details of the workshop agenda were worked out (by mail, fax and e-mail) between the workshop organizer (Slouka, Prague) and the instructors (Rechcígl, Washington, DC) and Mucha (New York). Also during this period, the instructors prepared materials to be distributed to workshop participants.

A fully equipped conference hall was reserved at the Academy of Sciences and also secured were the usual paraphernalia, i.e., an overhead projector, an electronic projector connected to our P.C., etc.

The only problems plaguing the workshop organization were periodic changes in the list of registered participants.

## The Participants

From the twenty-nine academic institutions invited to designate their "science and research" people, twenty-four responded positively. In the end, however, only nineteen were represented due to various causes beyond our control, as explained further below. The following list of institutions is arranged neither alphabetically nor geographically, largely due to the translation into English of the names of universities and their locations. Slovak universities are marked with an (S).

Masaryk University – Brno
Technical University – Ostrava
Technical University – Brno
Mendel University of Agriculture and Forestry – Brno
Czech Technical University – Prague
Matej Bel University – Banská Bystrica (S)
University of West Bohemia – Pilsen
University of Pardubice – Pardubice
Technical University – Liberec
University of South Bohemia – České Budějovice
University of Economics – Prague
University of Economics – Bratislava (S)
Silesian University – Opava
Technical University – Zvolen (S)
University of Ostrava – Ostrava
Technical University -Košice (S)
University of Chemical Technology – Prague
Charles University – Prague
National Center of Higher Education Studies, Ministry of Education – Prague

Our list of duly registered individual participants shows forty names but only thirty-three actually attended. The absentees were held back either by illness or by travel difficulties from distant regions – a nationwide railroad strike started just before the opening of the workshop.

In summary, among the registered participants were:
1) Seven university vice-presidents (pro-rectors) responsible for the science and research area;
2) Twenty-five deans, associate deans, and others in comparable positions;
3) Eight academics active in the research and grants field but without formal responsibilities.

The number of participants is higher than the number of institutions represented because some universities sent two or more people.

## The Auspices

The workshop was conducted under the formal auspices of the Czech Technical University (ČVUT), one of the largest and most prestigious universities of its kind in central Europe. The newly installed Rector of ČVUT, Prof. Petr Zuna (a worthy successor to the recently deceased ČVUT President Stanislav Hanzl), fully participated in the opening of the workshop, as did Prof. Václav Pačes,[1282] Vice President of the Czech Academy of Sciences, on behalf of the Academy behalf.

## Workshop Schedule and Process

During the five-day workshop week, general sessions were conducted daily for 3-4 hours, while the afternoons and the last day were reserved for individual and small-group consultations. All sessions were held at the Academy of Sciences.

The workshop followed a fairly tight agenda, planned by the instructors in the preceding three months.

---

[1282] Václav Pačes (1942-), biochemist, director of the Institute of Molecular Genetics of the Academy, Prague. He and I were in correspondence for a number of years and I first met him at a private breakfast at Villa Lana, attended by him, Professor Otto Wichterle and myself. In 2005, Professor Pačes was elected President of the Academy.

All three instructors fully participated in all workshop sessions and were available for subsequent consultations as needed. The workshop, while sticking to its agenda, was run in an informal manner to generate discussion, questions, and comments – and the participants used this amply. We abandoned the idea of having the workshop video-taped and, after editing, having the copies of the video-tape distributed to universities. There were two reasons for this decision. The-video-taping would disrupt the proceedings and would inhibit free discussion. Further, its cost would go well beyond our available budget.

DAY 1
(A) The first day – Monday, February 3, following a 25 min. formal opening (Zuna, Pačes, Rechcígl, Slouka), was fully devoted to a description of a generalized American model of a university "research and grants office" – with the necessary caveats: not for adoption, but for possible adaptation of some of its elements. The model was presented with the aid of previously prepared transparencies on an overhead projector.

The material presented was based on the instructor's experience at Columbia University, Wellesley and Lehigh Universities/ and further on recent information we obtained for this purpose from Dr. Peter Likins, President of Lehigh University and formerly a member of the Science Advisor Board to President Bush.

Also, during the first day, we were able to show and explain one of the models of the symbiotic, highly productive relationship between academic research and corporate needs, drawing on the example of the Benjamin Franklin Partnership functioning throughout Pennsylvania for well over a decade.

The first day workshop proceedings were led primarily by Slouka and were richly supplemented by comments by the other two instructors, Rechcígl and Mucha.

(B) The second through the fourth day the workshop program was in the hands of Dr. Rechcígl, who had agreed to assume the responsibility for running the agenda, with the other two instructors joining in the presentation, commenting, supplementing.

In general, the agenda was designed to cover all the functions which the American "research and grant office" needs to encompass.

## DAY 2

Information sources, publications, information via INTERNET, information services.

U.S. organization of research: university research, research in federal laboratories, individual research.

Sources of financial support: federal agencies, private foundations, corporate sources.

## DAY 3

Science policy: infrastructure, setting the priorities, the role of public opinion and the voices of the scientific community. (Supplemented by materials chiefly derived from Bruce L. R. Smith, *American Science Policy since World War* II,[1283] with stress on the role of universities and individual scientists in the formation of science policy).

Preparation of research grant proposals.

Evaluation of proposals – criteria: Federal agencies, private and corporate foundations.

## DAY 4

Guidelines and regulations: governmental requirements, foundation policies and guidelines, university control over compliance, research ethics.

Administration of research grants and contracts.

Why are research proposals turned down?

## DAY 5

Individual consultations.

While throughout the workshop proceedings we abstained from presenting the generalized American model research management as something that should and could be grafted onto the Czech and Slovak academic institutions, this dimension did come out rather vividly – as we had hoped – through the numerous comments by the participants.

---

[1283] Washington, DC: The Brookings Institution, 1990.

The Instructors
Frank L. Mucha, M.B.A., Columbia University, New York
Miloslav Rechcígl, Jr., Ph.D., A.I.D, Washington, D.C.
Zdeněk J. Slouka, Ph.D., Professor Emeritus, Lehigh University, PA

Materials and Facilities

Almost 3,000 pages of texts and various data pertaining to specific agenda items were distributed (free) to workshop participants.

Some two dozen pertinent U.S. reference volumes (from the Foundation Center, NY, Dryx, other US publishers) were laid out during the workshop for participants' inspection. (Most were graciously loaned to the workshop from the remaining collection of the Prague office of IREX and from the Foundation Information Center also in Prague).

The Czech Academy of Sciences provided – at minimal cost – an overhead projector and electronic components allowing projection of materials from our own computer programs.

# 91
## *Demands for Autonomy of European Chapters*

Had we thought that the newly established SVU policy of restoring the exclusive right for collecting membership dues by SVU Treasurer would once and for all settle the question of separatism of European Chapters, we were grossly mistaken.

Out of the blue, after returning to the US from our successful SVU World Congress in Bratislava in July 1998, we received a letter from Dr. Karel Hrubý[1284] of Switzerland, co-signed by Dr. Jaroslava Turková[1285] of Czech Republic. In this letter, we were informed of the meeting of European Chapters, i.e., Brno, Germany, Prague, Switzerland and Great Britain and their joint "agreement." The meeting presumably took place on June 28, 1998 in Prague, at the time when I was actually visiting the city.[1286]

To the letter was attached a joint proposal for establishing a "special status for European Chapters in the world Czechoslovak Society of Arts and Sciences." Hrubý's letter created quite a stir, if not an uproar among the Executive Board members. The thought that the Executive Board would accept it was preposterous. To give an autonomy to one region was unacceptable, as it might have precipitated similar demands from other regions, resulting in eventual breakup of SVU. In the minds of some, it immediately brought the analogy to Henlein's demands for the autonomy of the Sudetenland.

This whole thing was apparently orchestrated by Karel Hrubý, taking the other individuals for a ride. The former still held a grudge against Tříska and SVU leadership, which was accentuated by the Executive

---

[1284] Chairman of SVU Swiss Chapter.

[1285] She was Chairman of the Prague SVU Chapter at the time.

[1286] This was obviously a secretive meeting to which neither I nor any other high-ranking SVU officer was invited. This also explains why Jaroslava Turková refused to arrange a meeting between me and the Prague SVU Chapter arguing that nobody from the Chapter leadership was in Prague at that time which clearly was not true.

Board's decision to terminate publishing the periodical *Proměny* which Hrubý edited.

Several individuals who attended the infamous clandestine meeting in Prague were clearly misinformed what it was about and what they were getting into, as they later confided to me. Both Jarka Turková and Marie Bobková were clearly quite embarrassed by the whole thing, indicating that they were told that the main purpose of the agreement was a closer cooperation between individual European chapters rather than a call for an autonomy. Marie Bobková subsequently sent Hrubý a retraction in which she completely distanced herself and the Brno Chapter from Hrubý's proposal. As I subsequently learned from my Slovak friends, the Slovak Chapters were also initially invited to the Prague meeting but they declined to attend. It was also transparent that the Prague meeting was a solo action of a few individuals, without the knowledge of, or approval by, the respective chapters. With reference to the Prague Chapter, as far as I have been able to discern, none of its members I talked to knew anything about it, not to speak of any approval of the so called European joint proposal. The matter was obviously not discussed nor voted on in any of their meetings. Prof. Petr Zuna, Rector of the Czech Technical University in Prague, who, at the time, served as SVU Vice President on our Executive Board, representing the Czech Republic, sent us a letter in which he strongly voiced his disagreement with any proposal for autonomy for European Chapters.

It was at this juncture that I wrote a special Memorandum to the SVU Executive Board in which I restated the whole case (see below).

## MEMORANDUM

To: SVU Executive Board

From: SVU President

Subject: Hrubý's Proposal to Give Autonomy to European Chapters

**Merits of the Idea**
The proposal calls for a drastic overhaul of the Society which would seriously disrupt its integrity. No rationale or explanatory justification was put forward. The accompanying letter makes only a general reference to "closer cooperation and coordination of European chapters."

The proposal comes at a time when the Society is rapidly losing its members because of their old age or death. The situation was further aggravated by the fact that a number of SVU Chapters have become inactive and several of them actually ceased to exist altogether, e.g. Vienna Chapter. Giving autonomy to some chapters under these circumstances would further weaken the Society and most likely lead to its eventual breakup. Some members see an analogy in the Munich Agreement which forced Czechoslovakia to give up its border regions to Nazi Germany, resulting in the rapid dissolution of the Czechoslovak State.

Historically, the Society was established on the basis of individual memberships and, as the SVU Bylaws stipulate, admittance to membership is only conducted centrally. According to the Bylaws, dues were to be collected centrally, as was reaffirmed by the recommendation of the SVU General Assembly in 1994 and by the action of several Executive Boards. The recurrent disputes with some of the European chapters have been over the lack of the conformance of some of the European members with the Bylaws, and the rulings by the Executive Board regarding this matter. Because of this, and on the advice of SVU legal counsel, European members who have not paid their dues to the Treasurer have lost their membership rights, including the right to participate in SVU elections.

Local chapters, as envisioned by the SVU founding fathers, were never intended to be separate or, for that matter, distinct legal entities. According to SVU Bylaws, they are organized only with the concurrence of the Executive Board for the sole purpose "to enhance the purposes of the Society." The local chapters' guidelines specifically state that the local chapters must find their own resources for financing their local activities. The original guidelines, as prepared *by* the Society's founder, Dr. Jaroslav Němec, also made a strong recommendation that local chapters make a deliberate effort to periodically contribute money to the SVU Treasury to help the Society with its publication program.

For its various activities, the Society depends primarily on its membership dues. Prior to 1994, the Society finances were in the red. It took almost four years of hard work to balance the SVU budget which allows us to carry out basic activities but not much more. For example, if the *Kosmas* were to be published twice a year, as was originally planned, our budget would most likely be in red again, not to speak about the greatly increased expenses if we were to launch a regular publication program of monographs, etc.

As the situation now stands, most of the financial burden of the Society lies almost entirely or the shoulders of American and Canadian members. Very little revenue comes from Europe and if Hrubý's proposal were to be implemented, the disproportion between the American and European members would get even worse. The SVU Bylaws do not give regional privileges to any one group over others and it would be certainly incorrect and unethical to tax some individuals more than others. It would also make little sense to give special privileges to European members, who *are* in minority over American members, who are clearly in majority. An analogy to the Munich Agreement and its consequences is really not so farfetched.

The arguments that SVU members in Switzerland and Germany don't make as much money as our American members, which was used as the basis for not forwarding their membership dues to the central Treasury, are also fallacious. Their standard of living is just as high there, if not higher, than it is here in the US. Similarly, the European chapters can just as easily collect money locally for their activities, as it is done by the American chapters. In this connection, we need to be also reminded of our legal counsel's admonishment that "It is unlawful under the US law, or Swiss law, for any individual to refuse funds that were designated to SVU."

All SVU members, irrespective where they live, should have equal rights and privileges. To give special privileges to Europeans would be unacceptable to most of our members. There is already an increased resentment among the American members that they have to foot most of the Society expenses, while the European chapters pay hardly anything, while retaining all the privileges.

In other words, it is not possible to give special privileges to one group over another and it would certainly be unwise to grant privileges to a minority at the expense of a majority. If we were to consider giving privileges to one group, we would have to provide same privileges to other groups as well, The idea of regionalism or "regionalization" of the entire Society would be, however, most unwise because it would add another administrative layer which would create a nightmare for the SVU leadership, not to speak about the irrationality of the idea in view of the diminishing membership worldwide and inactivity of a large number of our local chapters.

## Legal Aspects

The proposal is clearly contrary to SVU Bylaws and, if implemented, would be in clear violation of the Articles of Incorporation, and the Laws of the District of Columbia. Furthermore, this matter is beyond the jurisdiction of the Executive Board. The only way to effect any changes would require a special Referendum of Members, conducted along the existing Laws of the District of Columbia.

## Responsibilities of the Executive Board

It is obvious that the Executive Board will need to take some action regarding this matter. It is in the interest of the Society to reach some understanding with European Chapters, however, this cannot be done at the expense of destroying SVU's integrity and its effectiveness. The response of the Executive Board cannot therefore be done hastily. The matter will require a very careful analysis and study, as well as innovative thinking.

In any case, as the SVU Bylaws stipulate, the Executive Board can carry out its responsibilities only in conformance with the SVU Bylaws. Furthermore, it must act in accordance with the Laws of the District of Columbia because otherwise the Society may not only lose its tax-deductible status but be open to legal proceedings, as would be the individual Executive Board members themselves.

The Executive Board members need to be mindful of the fact that it would not take much effort to dismantle the Society just as it was not difficult to dissolve the Czechoslovak State.

I personally promised Dr. Němec, a few days before he died, that I will do my utmost to preserve the Society's integrity, as a whole, and foster its further development along the ideas of the founding fathers. In my capacity as the SVU President, it is my responsibility to do no less.

*Miloslav Rechcígl*
SVU President

Before taking any official action on Hrubý's proposal, the Executive Board felt it prudent to send the matter to SVU Collegium of Presidents for their counsel. In addition, we constituted a special committee of lawyers to look into the matter.

The response from the Collegium of Presidents[1287] came in January 1999 in a letter signed by Leopold Pospíšil who served as their spokesman. The letter is reproduced below.

### Recommendation of the Collegium of Presidents Concerning the Request by Dr. Hrubý and Associates

Dr. Miloslav Rechcígl, the President of the Czechoslovak Society of Arts and Sciences invited the counsel of the former Presidents of the Society (as is his right according to Article 20 of the SVU bylaws) regarding the answer to the request of Dr. Hrubý and four co-signatories, all chairmen of European local chapters of the Society (Brno, Germany, Great Britain, Prague and Switzerland). He asked Prof. Leopold Pospíšil to chair the Collegium of President's deliberations. The following is the response of the Collegium's majority, after its serious and thoughtful review of the request, its legality and possible consequences.

The Society has been founded and incorporated in Washington, D.C. USA with the purpose of furthering educational, literary, scientific, and artistic activities of its individual members in order to maintain and develop a free Czechoslovak culture. It is strictly a non-profit and non-political organization for public benefit (Art. 2). Thus it is an association subject to the laws of the District of Columbia and the USA, and therefore its Executive Board and individual members have to abide by their laws and are responsible for their actions to these laws and regulations, no matter where they may be. It is therefore impossible that its members could disregard these laws and statutes if living abroad. Foreign laws and regulations certainly cannot bind the members of the Society. In other words the legal responsibility of all the members of the Society rests totally with the Society's center in Washington D.C. Consequently a local chapter may not initiate activities which represent novelty to the current practice, and only subsequently inform the Executive Board about it.

Members of the Society, as individuals, are being admitted to the membership centrally, that means by the Membership Committee, appointed by the Executive Board (Art. 7). They cannot be admitted by local and

---

[1287] As stated in Article 20 of SVU Bylaws, the President of the Society shall have the right to invite the counsel of the former presidents of the society - who shall form the Collegium of Presidents - in matters of basic importance to the Society.

foreign chapters, registered there and abide by the laws of the foreign countries, as Dr. Hrubý and associates' request demands (2b, c, d). This would not only be contradictory to the Society's by-laws, but also to the terms of its American incorporation.

From the above it is obvious that local chapters are not legal entities, they are not members of the Society; only individuals are. They cannot be fiscally independent, administering their income and expenditures as they please, and collecting dues (as Dr. Hrubý's request demands; e., f.), because the Society is a registered non-profit organization subject to the regulations of the District of Columbia of the USA. Thus for all the monetary transactions its leadership is responsible to the U.S. requirements for non-profit corporations. Certainly the local chapters may not retain arbitrary portions of the Society's members' dues according to their wishes (request 3), and send collectively the rest to the Society's treasurer. Indeed, any Society's member is free to decide whether he or she will participate in the activities of the local chapter or not. Certainly he or she is not subject to the powers of the local chapter's chairman. These requirements provide for the equality of all of the Society's membership, no matter in what part of the world they may reside. As a consequence the activities of the various chapters have to be financed by the contributions of their members, in other words they have to originate from the chapters' own resources. This has been a long practice of the American chapters, which from their income even supported the central Society's administration in its publication and meeting programs. If any additional funds for legitimate activities of the chapters are needed, the chapters can always petition the Executive Board for financial support. There simply cannot be a discrepancy between the European and American chapters. No one can reasonably argue that local chapters in Germany, Switzerland, and Great Britain are economically severely disadvantaged vis-à-vis those in the United States. Have they attempted a fund raising activity to finance their local projects? The situation in the Czech and Slovak Republics has been solved by having adequately lowered their membership dues.

The request of Dr. Hrubý and associates goes even beyond the autonomy of local chapters, by demanding a unification of the European chapters into a "coordination board" (request 4. and 5.), headed by a special European vice-president, seated on the Executive Board of the Society and, unlike the rest of the Board members, elected exclusively. by the "European Election Committee." This sort of resulting dualism reminds one of the Austro-Hungarian Empire. Furthermore the request changes the nature of the Society's Council by demanding that each local chapter appoint a representative, usually its chairman, to the Council's membership (request 4). This demand cannot be justified by regional or political differences between Europe and the USA, neither by the fact that the locus of the Czechoslovakian culture is in Europe. The Society deals with maintenance and development of the Czechoslovak culture (Art. 2) and not with political entities. It is non-political, and scientific, and scholarly endeavors of its members can be pursued anywhere and by anybody, irrespective of political or regional boundaries. The requested political segmentation of the Society is contradicting its scientific and scholarly goals.

Most of the changes suggested by Dr. Hrubý and associates would require a radical change in the constitution and by-laws of the Society. Some of them would even preclude the Society's incorporation in Washington D.C. Such changes would require a referendum of all the Society's members, and therefore the demand upon the Executive Board (request 6.) to institute these changes is irrelevant and has to be rejected a priori. Furthermore, the request seems to be a concept of Dr. Hrubý, subsequently signed by the four other representatives of Brno, Germany, Great Britain and Prague. Indeed, one of the signatories (the representative the Moravian Chapter of Brno) has subsequently withdrawn her support for Hrubý's request. So the latter does not even represent wishes of members of the five chapters. It is a request composed by Dr. Hrubý and possibly supported by only a few individuals at best.

And finally, the most surprising legal point. The Society's bylaws stipulate (Art. 6) that: "A member who has not paid the membership dues for the current year may not assert or exercise his rights." Furthermore Article 8 states that "the membership of member of the Society shall terminate:... 4. If the member has failed to pay his/her membership dues for two years despite the demands of payment" According to the information supplied to the Chair of the Collegium by Frank L. Mucha, the treasurer of the Society, Dr. Hrubý has not paid his dues since 1996. Even then the Swiss chapter sent only a lump sum to the treasurer, not specifying the names of the paying members. Therefore Dr. Hrubý is not only incompetent to "exercise his rights" of membership according to the Article 6, but, indeed, according to Article 8, he ceased to be a member of the Society. Therefore any dealings with him (legally a non-member), and other non-paying individuals (e.g. J. Krejčí's last payment was in 1994!) should be regarded as inconsequential and in violation of the above stated explicit stipulation of the Society's bylaws.

Signed in January 1999

*Leopold Pospíšil*

To make a long story short, the upshot of this was that the Executive Board rejected Hrubý's proposal on the basis that "it would require changes in SVU Bylaws that would not be popular among SVU membership." As a conciliatory gesture, it offered to European Chapters the possibility of requesting financial aid for specific projects for which they don't have sufficient resources.

# 92
## *Preserving Our Cultural Heritage*

On July 12 and 13, 1997, I had the pleasure of organizing, jointly with Clinton Machann, a SVU Conference, entitled "Czech-Americans in Transition: Challenges and Opportunities for the Future." The conference was held in conjunction with the historic celebration of the 100th anniversary of the Slavonic Benevolent Order of the State of Texas (SPJST) in Belton, Texas.[1288]

At this conference, educators, historians. social scientists, librarians, and other scholars joined with business people and community leaders to discuss key issues facing Czech-Americans and Slovak-Americans today: the preservation of language, folklore and folk art; ethnic history and genealogy; fraternal and cultural activities; the establishment and maintenance of archives, libraries, and cultural centers.

As a result of the deliberations, the Conferees came up with the Proclamation,[1289] co-signed by Presidents of SVU and SPJST, which had the following language:

### *The Preservation of Czech-American Cultural Heritage*

United in a commonality of purpose, the undersigned believe that this historic event will mark the beginning of a warm friendship and mutually beneficial cooperation between the SPJST and SVU. Like other citizens of the United States and Canada, nations which thrive on cultural and racial diversity, the members of our organizations realize that there is no conflict between our loyalty to and love for the country where we live and our desire to preserve the rich and distinctive cultural heritage of our ethnic origins. We are also hopeful that activities such as the conference in Belton will enhance the social, cultural, political, and commercial relations between North America and Central Europe.

---

[1288] *Zprávy SVU,* vol. 39, No. 4 (July-August 1997), pp. 1-15.

[1289] "The Preservation of Czech American Cultural Heritage - Proclamation," *Zprávy SVU,* vol. 39, No. 5 (September-October 1997), pp. 1-2.

In this spirit, we will do our best to preserve the Czech, as well as the Slovak, cultural heritage in North America, and we call on all interested men and women to help us in this endeavor – particularly in efforts to encourage our children to learn about their heritage and to establish and promote cultural and language programs at universities throughout the United States and Canada, as well as educational exchanges with the Czech Republic and Slovakia.

Following the Velvet Revolution of November 1989, the members of many Czech and Slovak organizations in the United States and other Western countries felt that their work was done, but this feeling was premature. Our work has only begun, and cooperation among our various organizations is essential. We propose to establish a Cultural Heritage Commission, which would initially consist of representatives from the SVU and SPJST and later incorporate representatives of other major Czech and Slovak organizations in North America.

Signed by

*Miloslav Rechcígl, Jr.*　　　　　*Howard Leshikar*
SVU President　　　　　　　　　SPJST President

Two months after this conference I suggested to the Czech Ambassador Alexandr Vondra, who participated at the Texas Conference, to have a follow-up Conference which we entitled "The Czech Republic and Czech Americans on their Way to a Common Future," to which he readily agreed. The Conference was held at the Czech Embassy in Washington on 18-19 October 1997.[1290] At the official invitation of Ambassador Vondra, officers and representatives of Czech American organizations throughout the US met with the embassy officials and government representatives from the Czech Republic, including Senator Michal Žantovský, to discuss strategies for broader cooperation. Close to 100 participants gathered for two days to discuss the ways of preserving the rich heritage of the past generations of Czech-Americans. Promoting strong relations between the Czech Republic and the United States also

---

[1290] "Czech Embassy Conference – Czech Republic and Czech Americans on their Way to a Common Future (1997), SVU Website, http://www.svu2000.org/issues/97-conference.htm

ranked high on the agenda of the conference reflecting the historic moment for the ČR: an invitation to become a member of the NATO marks the return of the Czech Republic to the family of Western nations. The participants showed strong support for this cause.

The Conference approved two resolutions, one calling for the US Senate to give its full and unequivocal support to the candidacy of the Czech Republic, Hungary, and Poland for admission to the North Atlantic Alliance. The resolution on the preservation of Czech-American cultural heritage emphasized support for the establishment of the cultural Commission.[1291] A partial text of the latter Resolution is reproduced below:

> ...We who have participated in the Washington conference resolve to support the Czechoslovak Society of Arts and Sciences and the Slavonic Benevolent Order of the State of Texas in establishing the Cultural Heritage Commission. The Commission will aid already existing organizations in gathering and disseminating information, coordinating and publicizing their efforts to preserve Czech heritage, and suggesting new strategies for joint action (e.g., surveying historic sites of particular significance to Czech-Americans). The continuing neglect and destruction of archival records, gradual decline of the Czech language in America, and disappearance of some of the traditional Czech-American organizations make this an urgent mission.
>
> The Washington Conference reflected Ambassador Vondra's commitment to meet and confer with the guardians of Czech heritage, pride, and culture in the United States with the goal of strengthening cultural, economic, and political ties between Czechs and Americans. Topics of discussion included issues related to the preservation and development of the Czech heritage in the United States, including historical sites and monuments; the political influence of the Czech-American community; and the possibility of future economic and political cooperation between Americans and Czech business and political leaders.
>
> United in a commonality of purpose, we believe that this historic event will strengthen ties between the United States and the Czech

---

[1291] The complete text of the resolution was published in *Zprávy SVU*, vol. 40, No. 1 (January-February 1998), pp. 8-9.

Republic. Like other citizens of the United States, a nation which thrives on cultural and racial diversity, the members of our organizations realize that there is no conflict between our loyalty to and love for the country where we live and our desire to preserve the rich and distinctive cultural heritage of our ethnic origins. We are also hopeful that activities such as this conference will enhance the social, cultural, political, and commercial relations between the two countries.

In this spirit, we will do our best to preserve the Czech cultural heritage in North America, and we call on all interested men and women to help us in this endeavor – particularly in efforts to encourage our children to learn about their heritage – and to establish and promote cultural and language programs throughout the United States, as well as educational exchanges with the Czech Republic.

Armed with a strongly worked resolution from the 1997 Embassy's Conference, I then went ahead with approaching the major Czech-American organizations with the request that they join the newly established Commission.

Knowing how sensitive various organizations and their officers are, I was very careful in my correspondence not to give an impression that we want to somehow rule their organization but rather stressing that the proposed Heritage Commission is just an umbrella organization whose main task was to assure that something is being done towards preserving our common cultural heritage. We had no interest in interfering with any of their ongoing activities. The Commission was to aid already existing organizations in gathering and disseminating information, coordinating and publicizing their efforts to preserve Czech heritage, and suggesting new strategies for joint action (e.g., surveying historic sites of particular significance to Czech-Americans). I pointed out that the continuing neglect and destruction of archival records, gradual decline of the Czech language in America, and disappearance of some of the traditional Czech-American organizations make this an urgent mission.

On the advice of our legal counsel, we planned the Commission as an informal and voluntary entity, without any bylaws or incorporation. Otherwise, because of various legalities we would not have been able to come to a quick agreement.

Just about all major societies, I contacted, enthusiastically accepted our invitation and promised their support. The list of the organizations that joined is given below:

>Czechoslovak Society of Arts and Sciences (SVU)
>Slavonic Benevolent Order of the State of Texas (SPJST)
>Czechoslovak National Council of America (CNCA)
>American Sokol Organization (ASO)
>CSA Fraternal Life (CSA)
>Western Fraternal Life Association (WFLA)
>Czech Catholic Union (CCU)
>Farmers Mutual Protective Association of Texas (RVOS)
>Czech Heritage Society of Texas (CHST)
>Czech Educational Foundation of Texas (CEFT)
>Texans of Czech Ancestry (TOCA)
>Czech and Slovak Heritage Association of Maryland (CSHA)
>Bohemian Benevolent Literary Association of the City of New York (BBLA)
>Moravian Heritage Society (MHS)
>Nebraska Czechs, Inc.
>Nebraska Czechs of Wilbur (NCW)
>Oklahoma Czechs
>American Czech-Slovak Cultural Club of North Miami (ACSCC)
>American Friends of Czech Republic (AFoCR)
>Czechoslovak Foreign Institute, Prague (CSUZ)
>Náprstek Museum, Prague

Of all the organizations I contacted, only genealogists dragged their feet, particularly the Czechoslovak Genealogical Society International. We had an endless back and forth correspondence with them, during which they demanded all sorts of information on legal aspects, size of our paying membership and even inquiring about our finances. They finally gave us a negative response, claiming that they have their own work to do, and their own priorities to follow, of which the preservation of Czech/Slovak cultural heritage in America is not one. Not even the intervention of the Czech Ambassador affected their position. Considering their unexplainable attitude, I subsequently severed my association with them, although I used to be their member from the very beginning and was a frequent contributor to their periodical.

·········

There was still another Conference in the Czech Embassy in Washington, DC, bearing on the subject of the preservation of our cultural heritage, i.e., held on 17-18 May 2002, with the theme "The Czech Republic and Czech Americans Mutual Ties and Joint Partnership, with the aim of strengthening ties and cooperation between the Czech Republic and Czech Americans. Unfortunately, it was run, more or less, like a show-and-tell sort of a meeting, without any substantive conclusion or recommendations.[1292]

---

[1292] For the description and the critique of the Conference see my article, "It Takes Two To Tango. Comments on the May Conference at the Czech Embassy," *Zprávy SVU*, vol. 44, No. 4 (September-October 2002), pp. 22-24.

# 93
# *The MZV Grant*

At the same time I was inviting Czech American organizations to join our Heritage Commission, I began toying with the idea of assembling the relevant information on the existing historic sites and other memorabilia that had some bearing on the Czech presence in America. Since no such listing existed, it was obvious to me that we'll need to conduct a survey around the country to gather such information and to also ascertain what is actually known and what descriptive materials are available, if any.

I was aware that such an undertaking would not be easy and furthermore that I could not do it on my own. That's when I thought of the idea of getting external support to be able to pay for various trips to visit specific sites, the number of which could be considerable. I realized that corresponding alone would take forever and, moreover, it would not, necessarily, bring the desired information. With external support, enlisting other organizations in the endeavor would also be easier.

At the suggestion of Ivan Dubovický, who was then at the Czech Embassy in Washington, I applied, in the name of SVU, for a grant from the Czech Ministry of Foreign Affairs (Ministerstvo zahraničních věcí České republiky – MZV). The substantive parts of the grant proposal are reproduced below.

### Proposed Project Proposal

Project Title: Preservation of Czech Cultural Heritage and Propagation of the Czech Republic in America

Submitting Institution: Czechoslovak Society of Arts and Sciences (SVU)

Principal Investigator: Miloslav Rechcígl, Jr., Ph.D.

1. Aim and Objectives

The overall aim of this project is to preserve Czech cultural heritage in America and by doing so to enhance the social, cultural, political, and commercial relations between the US and the Czech Republic, and to propagate the good name of the Czech Republic in North America and worldwide.

Specific objectives are: (a) to carry out a comprehensive survey of all Czech-related organizations in the US and their activities; (b) to make a comprehensive survey of historic sites commemorating important events in the Czech-American history; (c) to note various festivals and other events bearing on the folk life and cultural activities of Czech Americans; (d) to conduct a comprehensive survey of all Czech related archives and libraries in the US and to search for any additional archival and other documentary material relating to American Czechs maintained by various organizations and in private homes; (e) to conduct a survey of all current newspapers, newsletters, periodicals, and other publications relating to Czech Americans; (f) to organize a suitable conference with an exhibit on "Czech Cultural Heritage in America"; (g) to prepare a selective bibliography on Czech Americans and a comprehensive Czech-American Guide describing the Czech presence in America; (h) to publish a newsletter, tentatively called "Czech American Cultural Heritage."

2. Background

It has been estimated that there are some 1.5 million Czechs in the US. By other estimates, the figure would exceed the two million mark. This is the largest Czech community abroad and its size far exceeds all the other Czech communities abroad if combined. A community of this size can be potentially a strong force that could facilitate better understanding of Americans of the Czech Republic and thus enhance cultural, business and political relations and cooperation between the two countries.

Cities like Chicago, Cleveland and New York could at one time boast of flourishing Czech life. However, due to the inevitable effects of the "melting pot," this distinct life is steadily fading away. As the old great grandparents die, the subsequent generations lose interest not only in the Czech language but also in their own family heritage. From generation to generation, many of these families have kept old Czech books, almanacs, anniversary publications, calendars, posters and other family treasures which have reminded them of their old country and which they have held in great reverence. Some of these publications are long out of print and cannot be located even in the Náprstek Museum in Prague. This type of material, often containing important historical information which is irreplaceable, obviously has very little value for the descendants, particularly if they do not know the Czech language.

If we look at the Czech American community, as a whole, the situation is equally alarming. As the community leaders get older, it is difficult to replace them with young blood. In case of various societies, a given society may cease and desist with death of its chief executive officer. Furthermore, to make matters worse, a number of Czech American societies have lost the PURPOSE for meaningful existence, other than mere socializing. Oddly enough, this trend has been accentuated following the Velvet Revolution, when a number of organizations reached the conclusion that their work is no longer needed.

The Czechoslovak Society of Arts and Sciences, which has had a long interest in the history of Czech and Slovak Americans, has anxiously followed these trends in the Czech American community. In doing so, it began to see some signs of hope, coming from the rural areas of the US where many early immigrants settled, such as Texas and Nebraska. In fact, the developments in Texas impressed the writer (MR) so much that he referred to it as "The American Czech Renaissance."

This realization led to the decision by the SVU to convene a special Conference in Belton, TX on 12-13 July 1997, entitled "Czech-Americans in Transition: Challenges and Opportunities for the Future," in conjunction with the historic celebration of the 100th anniversary of the Slovanská podporující Jednota Státu Texas (SPJST). A direct product of the conference was a joint proclamation by the two societies to establish a Cultural Heritage Commission for the purpose of coordinating a joint effort towards preserving Czech cultural heritage in America. The idea soon caught on and the topic became one of the principal issues discussed in the October 1997 Conference convened by the Ambassador in Washington, D.C. At the end of the Conference the delegates resolved to support the SVU and the SPJST in an effort to launch such an effort with the participation of the major Czech organizations in the U.S. There was a consensus that such an endeavor would not only help to preserve Czech cultural heritage in America but also revitalize the Czech-American community as a whole, and enhance the relations and cooperation between the US and the Czech Republic.

3. Scope and the Work Plan of the Project

The planned project is envisioned as a long-term and broadly based effort, involving close cooperation with the members of the Cultural Heritage Commission and the representatives of the individual Czech-American organizations, as well as with the Czech Embassy in Washington, DC and the Department of Cultural Relations and Czechs Living Abroad of the Czech Ministry of Foreign Affairs in Prague. The later phases would entail the actual transfer of Czech-related archival material to selected places for safekeeping, preservation of specific historical sites and monuments, educational efforts to keep the Czech language alive and introduction of specific courses in various US institutions of higher learning focusing on Czech Republic and Czech culture.

The immediate task at hand is to constitute the planned Commission which we have tentatively named in Czech as "Výbor pro záchranu českého kulturního dědictví v Americe" and to formulate an agenda. This will be handled mostly through correspondence, by telephone, and personal contact. At the same time a broad campaign will be launched through the Czech newspapers abroad to familiarize the Czech-American community with the planned endeavor.

Once the initial steps have been completed, we shall concentrate on identifying all existing Czech-related organizations in the US, establishing contact with them and then gathering basic information about each. This is a prerequisite for the successful carrying out of the project. Apart from correspondence and telephone contact, this phase will require some library research.

Subsequent specific tasks will necessarily involve personal visitation and travel. They include:

Survey of Existing Czech-Related Archives and Libraries in the US, such as those in Washington, DC (Library of Congress), Chicago, IL (University of Chicago Library – Archives of Czechs and Slovaks Abroad; CSA Museum & Library), Cedar Rapids, IA (National Czech and Slovak Museum and Library), Temple, TX (SPJST Museum and Library), Austin, TX (University of Texas – Institute of Texan Cultures), Minneapolis, MN (CGSI Library), Lincoln, NE (University of Nebraska – Czech Heritage Collection), Nazareth, PA (Moravian Historical Society Museum), Bethlehem, PA (Moravian Museum and Archives), etc.

Survey of Other Archival and Documentary Materials maintained by various organizations in private collections, e.g., holding of the Sokol, CNCA, SVU, WFLA, NACC, RVOS, CESAT, KJT, KJZT, AFCR, CW, CCU, Matice vyššího vzdělani, etc.

Survey of Newpapers, Newsletter, Periodicals, and Other Publications

Survey of Historic Sites and Monuments Bearing on Czech Americans, e.g., American entry of the first colonist from Bohemia (North Carolina), Augustine Herman's Bohemia Manor (Maryland), statue of J. A.

Comenius (Moravian College, Bethlehem, PA), the oldest Czech Catholic Church in the US (St. Louis, MO), location of Czechoslovak Declaration of Independence (Philadelphia, PA), etc.

Organize a Special Czech Cultural Heritage Conference with Exhibit
During the course of conducting archival surveys, simultaneous efforts will be made to examine various alternatives for the storage and safekeeping of the documents for the future, including locations both in the US and the Czech Republic. Some of the documents might also be shipped at this time to specific sites for safekeeping.

4. Staff and Resources
The project will be coordinated by Miloslav Rechcígl Jr., the current President of the Czechoslovak Society of Arts and Sciences (SVU) and Coordinator of the Cultural Heritage Commission. He is recognized as an expert in the field of Czech American history and has conducted extensive research in this area. In his capacity as the SVU President he has also developed extensive collaborative networks and linkages with numerous professionals and representatives of the entire Czech American community.

In the course of this project he will be assisted by the members of the Cultural Heritage Commission, as well as by the selected members of various Czech American organizations.

# 94
## *Survey of Czech-American Historic Sites*

This survey was the first part of our large effort to preserve Czech and Slovak cultural heritage abroad, undertaken by SVU, in cooperation with the National Heritage Commission. I had the pleasure of directing it, and, in fact, also carrying it out. The effort was endorsed by the US Commission for the Preservation of America's Heritage Abroad and the Czech Ministry of Foreign Affairs provided partial funding.

The effort was prompted by the concern for the sad state of Czech historical monuments and memorabilia, as well as for the continuous loss of historically important archival materials regarding the life and work of the Czech immigrants and their descendants. Although the focus is on Czech memorabilia, considering the frequent difficulties in separating Czech from Slovak materials, the relevant Slovak and Czechoslovak materials were also to be included. We eventually hoped to enlarge the project to cover all Slovak materials with cooperation from the Slovak-American organizations.

Although some of the Czech ethnic organizations provided us with some useful information, for the most part, I was left with the responsibility of finding the required information. Some is based on the personal visitation of the relevant sites, while other comes from a variety of secondary sources, published or unpublished. The task was completed by the end of 1999.

The results of the survey were included in a special report, entitled "Czech-American Historic Sites, Monuments, and Memorabilia. A Tentative Listing."[1293] The report, which contained some 112 pages, was

---

[1293] "Czech-American Historic Sites, Monuments, and Memorials. A Tentative Listing. Compiled and edited by Miloslav Rechcígl, Jr., Ph.D., President, Czechoslovak Society of Arts and Sciences (SVU) with the assistance of the major Czech-American organizations associated in the National Heritage Commission. Rockville, MD: SVU, 1999. (*SVU Information and Reference Series: Cultural Heritage Doc. 1*).

printed only in a few copies and was made available only to the Czech Ministry of Foreign Affairs.

It is a tentative listing of historic sites and monuments that have some bearing on Czech immigrants in America, their lives and activities in their new homeland. The sites include historical buildings, schools, museums, churches, cabins, synagogues, cemeteries, libraries, community halls, parks, gardens, statues, historic markers, commemorative plagues, etc. The listing was arranged by individual states and cities. Whenever possible, each entry included location of the site with a descriptive material and an historical account.

This was the first attempt ever to compile such listing, and, as such, it is obviously not complete. In some instances, because of the pressure of time, I could not do more than simply identify the site, while in other cases, the exact address may be missing. Moreover, it is more than certain that a number of other Czech-related sites may exist which I have not been able to identify. Information which came from secondary sources will need to be verified and the current status of such sites will need to be ascertained.

The revised and considerably enlarged report was later published as a monograph, under the title *Czech-American Historic Sites, Monuments, and Memorials*,[1294] by the Palacký University in Olomouc in 2004, on the occasion of SVU World Congress.

The compendium was organized alphabetically by the individual States of the Union and within each State by the cities or villages in which some historic sites could be found. Whenever possible or available, entries included information on the following: location, description, historical significance, and Registry (if relevant).

As is clearly evident from the listing, the Czechs have been in the US from the very beginning. In fact, evidence indicates that the first colonist from Bohemia, named Joachim Ganz, put foot on American soil – the Roanoke Island, NC – as early as 1585, some 35 years before the arrival of the Pilgrims on the Mayflower. Although this first settlement on the US territory on the Outer Banks features a Festival Park with Adventure Museum, Settlement Site and History Garden, there also

---

[1294] Miloslav Rechcígl, Jr., *Czech-American Historic Sites, Monuments, and Memorials*. Olomouc-Ostrava: Centrum pro československá exilová studia při Katedře historie Filozofické fakulty Univerzity Palackého v Olomouci, 2004. 142 p.

should be a historic marker here dedicated to the Bohemian adventurer and scientist Joachim Gans. In contrast, there are a number of places in New York and in Maryland which remind one of the work of the first permanent settler in America, Augustine Herman from Prague, who became famous for executing the first accurate map of Maryland and Virginia. Moravian Brethren, too, left visible footprints in Pennsylvania, Ohio, North Carolina and many other locations, some of which unmistakably bear Czech or Bohemian names, which are included in the present compendium.

Although many of the early settlements disappeared or were incorporated into larger towns, a number of them still exist today. With the increased interest in preserving America's ethnic heritage, there is an effort on the way to save as many historical buildings and other monuments and sites of historical value as possible, as well as to mark the lost sites with historic markers.

# 95
# Survey of Czechoslovak-American Archivalia

The survey of the existing archival materials bearing on the Czech and Slovak presence in America was sponsored by SVU, in cooperation with the major Czech-American organizations, associated with the National Heritage Commission. The undertaking was part of the overall SVU effort toward the preservation of the Czech and Slovak cultural heritage abroad. The survey, which had full endorsement by the US Commission for the Preservation of the America's Heritage Abroad, received partial financial support from the Ministry of Foreign Affairs of the Czech Republic.

The focus of the survey was on the US-based archival materials and library holdings relating to émigrés and exiles from the territory of former Czechoslovakia and the relevant holdings bearing on their ancestral land. Although the initial focus was exclusively on the Czech element, I soon discovered the difficulty of differentiating archival material into Czech or Slovak, considering that many an individual played a role in Czechoslovakia, as a whole, irrespective of his or her ethnic background. Consequently, I decided to cover, in our survey, all emigrant and exile groups from the territory of former Czechoslovakia, irrespective of their ethnicity.

My initial approach was to prepare detailed survey forms and then send them to all Czech-related organizations and institutions which were thought of having archival material or publications bearing on the Czech presence in America. Despite the considerable effort put into this, including extensive follow-up via letters, telephone and electronic contact, the result was "zilch." The probable explanation for this is the fact that practically all ethnic organizations are run by volunteers and amateurs without much professional training. Furthermore, most of their holdings are relatively small and no inventories exist. Interestingly enough, even such major Czech repository as the National Czech & Slovak Museum and Library in Cedar Rapids does not, as yet have inventory. In case of the Archives of Czechs and Slovaks in Exile, as maintained by the University of Chicago, for which no inventory exists, I was told that it would take at least $100,000 to prepare one. The situation with the holdings maintained by the ethnic organizations is even worse. For example, I have been trying for several years to have the chief executive officer of one major Czech organization tell me what kind of material they keep in their archive but without success.

Be that as it may, I soon discovered that a majority of Czech, and for that matter, Slovak, repository collections are, for the most part, university or government-based. It is therefore logical to search for and through various Slavic and East European collections maintained at selected American universities and other institutions. Some of these collections have been inventoried in detail, which is reflected in our listing. In addition, we also found several public libraries and other institutions possessing Czech-related material. Thus, the various Moravian archives, which have an obvious connection with the Bohemian Brethren, Unitas fratrum, and Moravia, have not been systematically inventoried or studied by Czech scholars. To be sure, they would have to be fluent in German. The same thing can be said about various archives relating to German-speaking people, such as Leo Baeck Institute or other American Jewish archives. Czech scholars, who are knowledgeable of German language and Hebrew, would find it worthwhile to explore these rich albeit unknown information resources.

I completed the task in the early part of the year 2000 with the preparation of the Report, "Czechoslovak American Archivalia. US-Based Archival Material Relating to Émigrés and Exiles from the Territory of the former Czechoslovakia and Relevant Holdings Bearing on the Ancestral Land. A Tentative Listing."[1295] Four years later, a revised and an enlarged edition was published by Palacký University in Olomouc.[1296]

---

[1295] Miloslav Rechcígl, Jr., *Czechoslovak American Archivalia. US-Based Archival Material Relating to Émigrés and Exiles from the Territory of the Former Czechoslovakia and Relevant Holdings Bearing on their Ancestral Land.* A Tentative Listing. Rockville, MD: SVU, 2000). 294 p. (SVU Information and Reference Series. C. Cultural Heritage Documents No. 2).

[1296] Miloslav Rechcígl, Jr., *Czechoslovak American Archivalia.* Olomouc-Ostrava: Centrum pro československá exilová studia při Katedře historie Filozofické fakulty Univerzity Palackého v Olomouci 2004. 2 vols. (206 p. & 368 p.).

The listing was divided into seven major categories, i.e., government repositories, university-based collections, collections maintained by public museums and libraries, collections of ethnic organizations, personal papers and collections, repositories abroad bearing on the subject, and finally the virtual archives on the Internet. Rules governing each of these categories are quite different; some allowing an easy access, while other require specific permission. Holdings at government institutions are usually maintained exceptionally well and this is also true about most of the university-based collections.

The largest category in our listing is entitled "Personal Papers and Collections" These are personal papers and other documents of prominent personalities maintained in various repositories, usually under an individual's name. The compilation is based strictly on the compiler's familiarity with the individuals' names and their accomplishments. As a rule, these are distinct collections and you wouldn't find them under Czech or Slovak collections. For a researcher these collections may be of greater value than general Czech and Slovak collections.

Since a number of archivalia and library holdings bearing on the subject are also kept in selected institutions in the Czech and Slovak Republics, as well as in other European countries, we thought it appropriate to include such major repositories in our listing. Some of these repositories have already inventoried their stock and actually published catalogs of their holdings.

Now that computers are gaining momentum in practically every walk of life, we deemed it necessary to also include in our listing the virtual archives on the Internet. So far, only one reputable archive exists bearing on thing Czech or Slovak. With time, more such archives will be in evidence.

Just as in the case of Czech-American historic sites, one should consider the present listing as tentative. The user should realize that this is the first effort of its kind and that no compilations of Czech or Slovak materials heretofore existed. It has taken the compiler an enormous effort, including correspondence, personal or telephone contact, and above all, a systematic and painstaking research to find relevant collections, based on the compiler's intimate knowledge of Czech and Slovak ethnic immigration history. The compiler is well aware that this is only a beginning and that the work will have to continue.

Nevertheless, the listing represents an important step forward. It is a firm foundation to which more information can be added. Frankly, one cannot but be impressed with the information that has already been gathered. There is plenty of information on hand for many years of scholars' intensive work.

With the increased interest in preserving America's ethnic heritage, there is an effort a foot to save as many historical buildings and other monuments as possible. We should be equally, if not more so, concerned with preserving our spiritual legacy, i.e., archival material and other precious documents bearing on the life and contributions of our ancestors. It is not so much the material that is already being maintained in some government or university archives, but it is the material about which we don't know which is hidden in some box or stashed away in an old file in the basement or cellar of a former officer of some ethnic organization. It is a challenge for anyone to find these lost treasures!

# 96
## SVU Archives Repository

Ever since its founding in 1958, our Society has been concerned with what to do with its archival material, the volume of which has steadily been increasing. The situation came to focus after the Society abolished its office in New York and the materials, including books, were brought to Washington where they were stored in individual members' houses – basements, attics and garages. This was only a temporary measure until the Society would find a permanent place for their storage.

After the end of my two-term Presidency in 1978, I myself accumulated a large amount of SVU documents which I kept, to my wife's dismay, in my study. In as much as I have continued working for the Society in various capacities, I kept accumulating more and more material so that, after several years, there were so many boxes in my room that we had difficulty walking around, not to speak about the possibility of cleaning the room.

In spite of the seriousness of the situation, none of the SVU Presidents, nor any other officer, came forth with an idea for the solution. It was not until my return to SVU Presidency in the mid nineties, when I made the preservation of our Czech and Slovak heritage abroad one of our priorities, that I became very involved in the matter.

After conducting a comprehensive survey of Czechoslovak-related archival materials in the US, I came to the realization that many of the materials in the US are in great danger of being destroyed or lost, unless they are deposited in some permanent repository for safekeeping. SVU would be one of the victims.

From that point on, I began searching for a suitable place where the SVU archives could be deposited so that the materials could be preserved for the future. I talked to a number of my friends and acquaintances at various universities and other institutions and, in addition, browsed on INTERNET for pertinent information. I did not confine my search to the US alone but also considered the possibility of moving the materials to the Czech or Slovak Republics.

Among the various possible sites that came to mind were institutions like Hoover Institution in California, Balch Institute for Ethnic Studies in Philadelphia, Immigration and History Research Center (IHRC) in Minnesota. National Czech & Slovak Museum and Library in Cedar Rapids, Czech and Slovak Archives in Exile at the University of Chicago, Library of Congress and several university libraries that maintained Czech and/or Slovak collections.

In the Czech Republic, I broached the subject with archivists at the Academy of Sciences of CR, the Czech National Archives, the Náprstek Museum, The Institute of Contemporary History, all located in Prague, and at the Czechoslovak Exile Studies Archives at Palacký University in Olomouc. Of these institutions, the Czech Academy, the State Central Archives and the Palacký University were eager to get our materials. Under normal circumstances, I am sure, we would have considered their offers quite seriously. However, after what I heard from my colleagues of their experiences with the Czech and Slovak repositories, I was reluctant to move our material there, partly because their repositories were not up to par with the modern American facilities and partly because of their overwhelming and hopeless bureaucracy. There was also the question of transportation and its costs which would be considerable.

Of the American repositories, from the very beginning I favored the Immigration History Research Center (IHRC) at the University of Minnesota,[1297] which I had the chance to see in 1999, on the occasion of SVU Conference, in which President Havel participated.

For over 35 years, the Center has worked hard to collect, preserve and make available to researchers, from all over the United States and the world, archival materials documenting the experience of various immigrant communities, including the Czechs and Slovaks – and their descendants in America. The IHRC recently moved to the Elmer L. Andersen Library on the Minneapolis West Bank Campus of the University of Minnesota. The building is a new, state-of-the-art archival facility where the documents find a safe home, designed to provide an ideal environment for their preservation (constant air temperature and humidity, minimal exposure to light and dust, security features, etc).

---

[1297] Now located at the following address: Immigration History Research Center, University of Minnesota, 311 Elmer L. Andersen Library, 222-21st Avenue South, Minneapolis, MN 55455.

The collections receive professional care by the IHRC staff, which includes a Czech-born archivist. Once the materials are sorted, organized, placed in non-acidic file folders and containers, and catalogued, their location at a major research university provides opportunities for academic researchers to generate scholarly articles and books contributing to the better knowledge of the history of the ethnic Americans.

In the meantime, I also became acquainted with the Czech IHRC archivist Daniel Nečas who introduced me to his superiors. They were very much interested in SVU-related materials, as well as in my father's correspondence, which I kept in our basement since his death in 1973. We then engaged in correspondence, discussing the conditions, which led to their firm offer to accept our material, as well as that of my father, for their archives. They did not ask for any money for the maintenance, although they hinted that other organizations had given the IHRC financial support and even created special study funds to enable the students and scholars to do research in their archives. Our Executive Board subsequently gave its approval for the SVU materials to be transferred and deposited in the IHRC archives.

The IHRC arranged for the transport of our material to Minnesota. Actually they sent their Czech archivist Daniel Nečas, accompanied by his father-in-law, with a moving van to pick up the material. The transfer took place around November 2, 2002, just before the start of severe winter for which the state of Minnesota is famous.

They filled the van completely, up to the rim, with some 100 packing boxes and several filing cabinets, a sizeable volume of which came from our house. The other boxes came from Thomas Gibian's attic, and George Glos' and Andrew Eliáš' basements. Additional material was brought to our house by Věra Bořkovec and Dagmar White.

In announcing this to our membership,[1298] we pointed out that the material that we had deposited in IHRC repository related primarily to SVU central archives, with realization that lots of additional SVU materials was still kept by individual SVU Local Chapters, as well as by former SVU officers. It would be an obvious advantage if all SVU material would be kept together in one place. Consequently, I called on all SVU officers to kindly assemble all of their historical material and send it to University of Minnesota to be included in SVU Archives.

---

[1298] "SVU Archives," *Zprávy SVU*, vol. 45, No. 3 (May-June 2003), pp. 23-24.

It did not take long and the IHRC Website announced the acquisition of our archival material on their Website,[1299] which read as follows:

### IHRC Acquires Archive of the Czechoslovak Society of Arts and Sciences (SVU)

Three major archival collections have arrived at the IHRC. Dr. Miloslav Rechcígl, Jr., of Rockville, MD, currently serving as president of the Czechoslovak Society of Arts and Sciences (SVU: *Společnost pro vědy a umění* donated his own papers, the papers of his father, Miloslav Rechcígl, Sr., and the archival records of the SVU.

### SVU Archive, ca. 1958 – present. Ca. 75 linear ft, manuscript and print materials

This acquisition makes the IHRC the repository of the records of one of the most significant Czechoslovak organizations founded by the post-World War II exiles from the former Czechoslovakia. The SVU, headquartered in Washington, DC, was formed in 1958 after a period of preparatory negotiations by Dr. Jaroslav Němec and others in the Czech and Slovak American communities. Originally, it was viewed as an initiative within the well-established Czechoslovak National Council in America, focusing on constructing a platform for the newly arrived intellectuals from Czechoslovakia, among them well-known literary scientists René Wellek, professor of linguistics at Yale; Roman Jakobson, professor of linguistics and Slavic studies at Harvard and MIT; music conductor Rafael Kubelík; physicist Václav Hlavatý (collaborator with Albert Einstein); Max Brod, interpreter, editor and one of the closest people to Franz Kafka; pianist Rudolf Firkušný; writer Egon Hostovský; Alice Masaryk, daughter of the first Czechoslovak president; diplomat Ján Papánek; and many others. The organization still exists today with membership of several thousand in dozens of countries.

The collection contains the archive of the early SVU records (maintained by long-time SVU Secretaries General Jaroslav Němec and John Lexa), meeting agendas and minutes, executive committee elections records, personal files of SVU members,

---

[1299] IHRC Website

correspondence pertaining to organizing the SVU World Congresses (beginning with the Washington, DC, Congress of 1962), membership applications, event announcements and programs, detailed information about the SVU publication program, which was under the direction of Miloslav Rechcígl, Jr., etc. Also well covered are the presidency terms Dr. Rechcígl, Jr., has served as the SVU president (1974-1978, 1994-present). The print section of the collection encompasses the published production of the organization, including complete or near complete sets of the SVU newsletter, *Zprávy SVU*, the *SVU Bulletin*, the *Proměny* (Metamorphosis) journal, the *Kosmas* journal, and various monographs, almanacs and commemorative publications. Audio-visual material includes photographs, tapes of Voice of America radio programs, recordings of lectures, interviews, etc.

The SVU archive, presently comprising ca. 75 linear feet of archival and published material, is a major addition to the IHRC Czech and Slovak American collections, an excellent resource for the study of the Czech and Slovak exile communities in the United States and Canada as well as in other countries of the world where emigrants from the former Czechoslovakia found their new homes after World War II. President Rechcígl plans to arrange for more archival material – pertaining to both national (and international) SVU headquarters as well as his presidency and the organization's local chapters – to be deposited at the IHRC in the future.

Most of the documents that had been deposited in SVU Archives came primarily from the collections maintained by Dr. Jaroslav Němec, Dr. John G. Lexa, Prof. René Wellek, Prof. Leopold Pospíšil and Miloslav Rechcígl, Jr. I made therefore another urgent appeal to SVU Local Chapters and past SVU officers to send to IHRC any material relating to SVU activities, reminding them that such material has historic value and that SVU cannot afford to have it lost.[1300]

In the middle of July 2005, Daniel Nečas, Assistant Archivist of the University of Minnesota's Immigration History Research Center (IHRC), came to Rockville, MD to pick up the remaining documents, publications and other SVU archival materials and my own correspon-

---

[1300] "SVU Archival Material - Urgent Message for SVU Local Chapters and Past SVU Officers," *Zprávy SVU*, vol. 45, No. 6 (November-December 2003), pp. 16.

dence that had been kept in our house. The load comprised some 100 packed boxes, weighing over a ton.[1301] With the addition of this material to our archives in IHRC, most of the centrally maintained SVU material has thus been preserved for the future. Since the local chapters have also accumulated significant material, I made again an appeal to them to send it to Minnesota so that all the material can be kept together.

One of the major unresolved issues that was brought up by our Working Archival Conference in Washington in 2003 was the paucity of funds to prepare inventories of the existing archival collections and to enable scholars and students to conduct research in the archives. Having this in mind, SVU, which has recently deposited its archives at the University of Minnesota's Immigration History Research Center (IHRC), has used the occasion of the SVU Florida Conference in 2005, to announce the establishment of a special Czech and Slovak Archival Study Fund at IHRC. In my capacity as SVU President, I had the pleasure of presenting a check, in the amount of $10,000, to Director of the Center, Prof. Rudolph Vecoli, at the banquet, attended by some 300 persons, including the representatives from the Czech and Slovak Embassies and other dignitaries, from the Czech and Slovak Republics, as well as a number of the Czech/Slovak American community leaders.[1302]

It was hoped that the SVU's example would be infectious to inspire other Czech and Slovak ethnic organizations to join in this important and noble endeavor. When the Fund will reach the level of $25,000, the University of Minnesota will start matching these donations with their own money. Just before I stepped on the platform to announce the SVU donation, I was gratified to get a commitment from Prof. Jan Hird Pokorný, on behalf of the American Fund for Czechoslovak Relief (AFCSR), to give a comparable amount to IHRC next year.

---

[1301] "Additional SVU Archival Material Moved to IHRC," *Zprávy SVU*, vol. 48, No. 1 (January-February 2006), pp. 10-11.

[1302] "SVU Establishes a Special Studies Fund," *Zprávy SVU*, vol. 47, No. 3 (May-June 2005), pp. 21-22.

# 97
# Working Archival Conference

In the days 22-23 November 2003, SVU together with the Embassies of the Czech and Slovak Republics in Washington, DC, organized a special working conference related to the preservation of Czech and Slovak archives in America. This was practically my own undertaking from thinking up the idea, developing the program, finding the speakers, and arranging with the two Embassies to help with the logistics and the local arrangements.

This was indeed a Czech-Slovak endeavor because the first day the Conference took place on the grounds of the Czech Embassy and on the second day at the Slovak Embassy with the Czech Ambassador Martin Palouš and Slovak Ambassador Rastislav Káčer participating.

This was truly a working conference, as clearly expressed by the Czech Senator Moserová, who said that this was the first useful conference of this year, one which made sense and had a definite purpose. The Conference was attended by specialists and representatives of the most important archival institutions both in America and in the Czech and Slovak Republics which deal with the documentation of Czech and Slovak America or with the relationships between Czechoslovakia and its successor states and America. The importance of the Conference was evident in that Czech and Slovak media reported the proceedings each day and even carried an interview with me, in my capacity as the coordinator of the Conference.

"There are many archival materials throughout America and we are afraid that they might be destroyed...ninety percent of the material can be found in the basements and attics of individuals and society officers, which gave impetus for the Conference," as I informed the CTK (Czech Press). I went on to say that often these individuals and society presidents are not aware of the importance of historical documents and their progeny will simply discard them.

One of the purposes of the Conference was to bring this impending danger to the attention of Czech and Slovak ethnic organizations in America (numbering several hundred) and to inspire them to a cooperative effort to preserve these valuable documents for the future. After all, we are dealing with some basic information about the life, suffering and work of the Czechs and Slovaks in America, about the work of Czechoslovak exiles in America, and about the relations between the US and our homeland, which must be preserved because they are an indispensable part of Czech, Slovak and American culture. These documents are irreplaceable and many exist only in the original.

The United States has truly a great interest in preserving these documents which was proven by the presence of so many representatives of important American institutions and the fact that the Conference was organized under the auspices of the U.S. Commission for the Preservation of America's Heritage Abroad, with its Chairman Warren L. Miller in attendance. It should be noted that Mr. Miller had been appointed to this function by the President of the US.

The representatives of the Czech Republic, as well as the representatives of the Slovak Republic, have the same interest and many of their archival institutions would welcome receiving these materials. As I pointed out, there is so much material that it cannot be deposited in a single archive. What matters is that the material be deposited in a secure place that is well taken care of and available to the public, regardless of where it is deposited.

This unique Conference, doubtlessly, served its purpose and surpassed even the expectations of the organizers.[1303] It was the first time that the most important "players" on both sides of the Atlantic were able to meet. These were not only archivists and scholars, but also government representatives, community leaders and members of various Czech and Slovak ethnic organizations in America. This was the first important step taken for forming a working base for cooperative work toward the single goal of preserving these valuable documents for the future.

Most of us, who attended the conference met for the first time and left as good friends. Most of us acquired a lot of new information and have established working linkages with our counterparts in Europe and in America. This was not just a "show-and- tell" type of meeting, as many conferences are, but a working conference in which issues were presented, discussed and solutions sought. To assure follow-up, the

---

[1303] "A Successful Archival Conference," *Zprávy SVU*, vol. 46, No. 1 (January-February 2004), pp. 20-22.

conference attendees agreed upon a future agenda and concrete steps, as was spelled out in the joint Resolution,[1304] and appointed a follow-up committee so that the conference recommendations are carried out. The text of the Resolution follows:

## RESOLUTION

Recommendations by the Attendees of the
Working Conference on CZ & SL American Archival Materials
and their Preservation Washington, DC, November 22-23, 2003

1. We assert the importance of archival materials relating to Czechs and Slovaks in America and to relations between the US and the historical Czech and Slovak homelands, including the states of Czechoslovakia, the Czech Republic and the Slovak Republic;

2. We should launch a concerted effort to preserve these materials for future generations;

3. We recommend the establishment of working linkages and encourage cooperation and collaboration among the many archives related to Czechs and Slovaks supported by universities, public libraries, and various other private and governmental institutions on both sides of the Atlantic;

4. We advocate the establishment of an information system designated to help interested people, including potential researchers as well as potential donors, inform each other about the availability of archival materials and the status and policies of archival institutions;

5. We recommend the publication of Miloslav Rechcígl's comprehensive report entitled "Czechoslovak American Archivalia. US-Based Archival Material Relating to Émigrés and Exiles from the Territory of Former Czechoslovakia and Relevant Holdings Bearing on their Ancestral Land," which outlines the basis of Czech and Slovak American archival materials in the US and the Czech and Slovak Republics;

---

[1304] "Recommendations by the Attendees of the Working Conference on Czech and Slovak American Archival Materials and their Preservation. Washington, DC, November 22-23, 2003, *Zprávy SVU*, vol. 46, No. 1 (January-February 2004), pp. 22-23.

6. We recommend the publication of the proceedings of the Working Conference on Czech and Slovak American archival materials and their Preservation;

7. We recommend the establishment of a coordinating committee to follow up on the recommendations of the working Conference and prepare guidelines for future activities related to the archives.

8. Finally, We thank SVU and the Czech and Slovak Embassies for organizing the conference and for the Embassies' hospitality, in the hope and confidence that these institutions will assist us in carrying out the important tasks outlined above.

As a result of the conference, the participants unanimously agreed to launch a concerted effort leading to the preservation of the Czech and Slovak documents and other memorabilia for the future, irrespective of where they may be. This goal, of course, was feasible and attainable only with the participation and cooperation of the entire Czech and Slovak community in the US and Canada. We therefore made an appeal to Czech and Slovak ethnic societies to lend their hand to this important endeavor.[1305] The mechanism for such cooperation we already had in place in the recently created National Heritage Commission. The Czech and Slovak ethnic societies that were not members as yet were encouraged to join our ranks so that we can indeed launch a united national effort to save our precious cultural heritage.

We also appealed to individuals who had possessions of any documentary material or other memorabilia bearing on the Czech and Slovak presence in North America or on the relationship between America and Czechoslovakia and its successor states, to please let us know. The type of material, for which we are looking, included correspondence, oral histories, diaries, memoirs, speeches, photographs, reprints, notebooks, newspaper clippings, obituaries and other announcements, certificates and various family documents, posters, records of meetings, club financial records, various types of publications, almanacs, calendars, annuals, old newspapers and periodicals, etc.

---

[1305] "Preserving Czech and Slovak American Archival Material," *Kosmas*, vol. 17, No. 2 (Spring 2004), pp. pp. 95-96.

I was gratified that in a matter of a few months my publisher in Prague, David Kraft, had the Proceedings of the Conference published.[1306]

.........

Several specific recommendations of the Conference have already been implemented, including the establishment of a new umbrella organization, "Czech & Slovak American Archival Consortium" (CSAAC), encompassing the major institutions that maintain such archival materials. The Consortium's official website "Czech & Slovak American Archivalia," hosted by SVU, can be accessed on the following address: http://www.svu2000.org/archivalia/index.htm

Another recommendation of the Conference was to prepare a tentative Directory of Czech and Slovak related archival materials in America. Thanks to the efforts of SVU, which conducted a comprehensive survey in this regard, and which I had the pleasure to direct, and in fact, to carry out, such a Directory now exists. It was published a few months ago, under the title Czechoslovak American Archivalia,[1307] through the courtesy of the Center for Czechoslovak Exile Studies of the Philosophical Faculty at Palacký University in Olomouc, as a two-volume set, which was available for everyone to see at the new book exhibit at the recent SVU Conference in Florida. It is a listing of US-based archival materials and library holdings relating to émigrés and exiles from the territory of former Czechoslovakia and relevant holdings bearing on their ancestral land. The first volume encompasses US government repositories, university-based collections, collections maintained by public museums and libraries, collections of ethnic and other cultural organizations. The second volume covers personal papers and collections, including notable personalities, as well as lesser known individuals, emigrants and exiles, who have distinguished themselves in

---

[1306] *Czech and Slovak American Archival Materials and their Preservation.* Proceedings of the Working Conference on Czech and Slovak American Archival Materials, held at the Czech and Slovak Embassies. Washington, DC, 2003. Prague: Prague Editions Ltd., 2004. 168 p.

[1307] Miloslav Rechcígl, Jr., *Czechoslovak American Archivalia.* Olomouc-Ostrava: Centrum pro československá exilová studia při Katedře historie Filozofické fakulty Univerzity Palackého v Olomouci 2004. 2 vols. (206 p. & 368 p.).

public life, and professions. It is an indispensable resource for scholars and students.

To keep the public informed about the activities of the Consortium and to provide an effective means for contact and communication among the Consortium members, the SVU offered to create a special webpage for the use of the Consortium, as a part of the SVU Website.[1308] The archival WebPage is up and running and can be accessed on the following address: http://svu2000.org/archivalia/

Apart from the basic information about the Consortium, its membership and its aims, the webpage provides separate categories on the Consortium activities, meetings, publications, and other news. Special category is devoted to Headline News. There are also links to major archival institutions in North America, Czech and Slovak Republics and other parts of the world. The Webpage also features Queries which enables anybody interested in the subject to ask questions or to respond to inquiries from others.

---

[1308] "SVU Hosts Archival Consortium Webpage," *Zprávy SVU*, vol. 46, No. 4 (July-August 2004), pp. 24.

# 98
# SVU Fellows

To my knowledge, the idea of recognizing SVU members' achievements by electing them SVU Fellows was originally my idea which can be traced to the time of my second-term SVU Presidency (1977-1978).

In the original SVU Bylaws, the Society had two types of memberships: 1) a regular membership intended for scientists, artists, persons with academic education, as well as persons preparing themselves for scientific or artistic careers, and other cultural workers; and 2) supporting membership for those members who did not meet criteria for regular membership.[1309]

With time, this conception was found unsatisfactory because it led to bitterness which was frequently justified, and raised questions regarding the criteria used for making the differentiation. Some people were offended because the supporting membership gave them the stigma of inferiority. Yet, many of these individuals have made significant contributions to the SVU development. As expected, this differentiation also brought about some animosity between the members in the two categories.

I saw a simple solution to this dilemma: by recognizing selected members' achievements in their particular scientific, scholarly or artistic field by electing them to the status of SVU Fellow, there would not be any need for having a dual SVU membership.

In due course, the SVU Bylaws were modified, first by abolishing the differentiation between regular and supporting memberships and substituting them with a single membership, and later,[1310] by establishing SVU Fellows category to recognize scientific or other achievements of selected SVU members.

---

[1309] "Bylaws of the Czechoslovak Society of Arts and Sciences, Inc.," in: *SVU Biographical Directory*. 4th edition. Compiled and edited by Eva Rechcígl and Miloslav Rechcígl, Jr. Washington, DC: SVU, 1978, pp. 126-136.

[1310] Approved by Referendum of Members of February 1991.

Although the SVU Fellows category has been on the SVU books as Article 26 of the new Bylaws[1311] for a number of years, none of the SVU Presidents made any effort to activate the provision.

When I returned to SVU Presidency in the mid-1990s, the activation of the SVU Fellowship was a part of my agenda but because of other priorities I kept postponing it, partly because I had to first reactivate the SVU Council. This was of paramount importance because, based on our Bylaws, it was the Council which actually had the jurisdiction over the selection process of SVU Fellows.

I first approached Leopold Pospíšil, former SVU President, with the request to draft criteria for the selection of the Fellows. Since he was a member of the prestigious National Academy of Sciences, I felt he would have the best qualifications to do this. Unfortunately, what he came up with was rather restrictive, making it almost impossible to elect a significant number of SVU Fellows, unless they already were members of renown academies of humanities and sciences, such as the National Academy of Sciences, National Academy of Engineering or the Institute of Medicine. So I put the matter on the back burner again.

After Zdeněk Slouka's election to the post of the speaker of the SVU Council, I decided to enlist his assistance, I asked him to draft the new selection criteria, as well as to prepare a simple election process. He accomplished the task to my satisfaction. The Executive Board accepted his proposal which was officially announced in our newsletter[1312] and was also posted on SVU Website. The process was described as follows:

### NOMINATION AND ELECTION OF SVU FELLOWS

Members of the Society may be elected Fellows of the Society in recognition of their outstanding record as scholars, scientists, educators, technologists, writers or artists, or in other appropriate creative fields. Any one or more SVU members acting as Sponsor(s) may propose a candidate for SVU Fellowship to the Fellows

---

[1311] "Bylaws of the Czechoslovak Society of Arts and Sciences," in *SVU Directory. History, Organization and Biographies of Members.* Compiled by Eva Rechcígl and Miloslav Rechcígl, Jr. Washington, DC: SVU Press, 1992, pp. 372-385.

[1312] Miloslav Rechcígl, "SVU Fellows," *Zprávy SVU*, vol. 43, No. 2 (March-April 2001), pp. 18-19.

Nominations Committee of the SVU Council (further "the Committee") for election by the Council.

A. INITIAL PROPOSAL OF CANDIDACY. The initial proposal should contain the name, the address, the professional field and the current position of the candidate. Upon the receipt of the proposal, the Committee shall provide the Sponsor(s) with guidelines for establishing the candidate's dossier. The initial proposal, in the form of a letter addressed to the Committee should be submitted by mail, fax, or e-mail to the Speaker of the Council: Zdeněk J. Slouka, Lucemburská 43, 130 00 Prague 3, Czech Republic, tel./fax 0 11-420-2-6272070.

B. REVIEW AND NOMINATION. The completed candidate's dossier shall be evaluated by at least two experts in the candidate's field, chosen ad hoc by the Committee. Where the expert evaluations and other data so warrant, the Committee shall nominate the candidate to the SVU Council for election.

C. ELECTION OF FELLOWS. The nomination of a Fellow to the Council shall be accompanied by a synopsis of the candidate's dossier and of its evaluation. The votes of the members of the Council shall be in writing, their anonymity ensured by the standard double-envelope method. The ballots shall be mailed to the Speaker of the Council for transmission to the Committee. Only votes received within thirty days from the date of the Committee's submission of the nomination to the Council shall be counted as valid. The Fellow shall be elected by a simple majority of valid votes.

Even though we repeatedly carried out announcements of the establishment of the SVU Fellows category, surprisingly, there was hardly any response. As much as I could figure out, the reason for it was the rather cumbersome process, with the burden being entirely put on the shoulders of a nominating person. Perhaps, the outcome would have been different if we had let individual candidates apply for the Fellowship themselves.

After a few additional years of impasse, I took a different approach. I approached the SVU Council with the idea that we establish a high-level Fellows Nomination Committee, which would be responsible to the Council, with the purpose of selecting eligible candidates for SVU Fellow. Their list would then be submitted to the SVU Council for vote.

The Council readily accepted the idea and we then proceeded to form Fellows' Committee, comprised of reputable scholars and scientists. The Committee comprised of the following individuals: George Bekey (Engineering), Petr Zuman (Natural Sciences), Vlado Šimko (Medicine), Jan Uhde (The Arts), Zdeněk David (Humanities) and Josef A. Mestenhauser (Social Sciences).

After some prodding, the Committee came up with some fifty candidates whose names were then sent to the Council for vote. Zdeněk Slouka, in his capacity as the Speaker of the SVU Council, had been entrusted with conducting the elections.

We had to go through several rounds of voting, in order to satisfy the Bylaws' requirement that the Fellows be elected by the majority of votes cast, with the participation of the majority of the Council members.

At the end, the following forty-two Fellows were elected:

BAŽANT, Zdeněk Pavel – Engineering
BEKEY, George – Engineering
BUDIL, Ivo – Social Sciences
BÚTOROVÁ, Zora – Social Sciences
ČERNÝ, Petr – Natural Sciences
ČERYCH, Ladislav – Social Sciences
DEMETZ, Peter – The Humanities
EBRINGER, Libor – Natural Sciences
FORMAN, Miloš – The Arts
HAVEL, Ivan – Natural Sciences
HRUBAN, Zdeněk – Medicine
HUDLICKY, Tomas – Natural Sciences
HUSA, Karel – The Arts
JAŘÁB, Josef – The Humanities
KOHN, Joseph J. – Natural Sciences
KOMENDA, Stanislav – Natural Sciences
KVAPIL, Radoslav – The Arts
LOCHMAN, Jan Milič – The Humanities
LOJDA, Zdeněk – Medicine
LUSTIG, Arnošt – The Arts
MACHÁČ, Josef – Medicine

MACHO, Ladislav – Medicine
NOVOTNÝ, Vladimír – Engineering
PAČES, Václav – Natural Sciences
PALOUŠ, Radim – The Humanities
PELIKÁN, Jaroslav Jan – The Humanities
POVOLNÝ, Mojmír – Social Sciences
POSPÍŠIL, Leopold Jaroslav – Social Sciences
RECHCÍCL, Jack – Natural Sciences
SEGERT, Stanislav – The Humanities
SEHNAL, František – Natural Sciences
SIS, Peter Alexander – The Arts
SKAMENE, Emil – Medicine
ŠKVORECKY, Josef Václav – The Arts
SOKOL, Koloman – The Arts
ŠVEJNAR, Jan – Social Sciences
TŘÍSKA, Jan F. – Social Sciences
VALENTA, Jaroslav – Engineering
VANÍČEK, Petr – Engineering
VIEST, Ivan M. – Engineering
VÍTEK, Václav – Engineering
WANDYCZ, Piotr S. – The Humanities

# 99
# *SVU Website*

When I consider the amount of effort that went into its development and the impact it made on SVU, as well as on the public, I frequently thought that the SVU Website would be "my greatest legacy."

Actually the idea of SVU having its own HomePage had been under discussion. for some time, especially during my Presidency in the nineties, because I wanted the SVU to enter the new technological age as soon as possible. When no volunteer on our Executive Board stepped forward, I decided to go ahead on my own and soon was able to set up a HomePage,[1313] through my association with the Federation of East European Family History Societies (FEEFHS). The SVU interest in ethnic history, combined with my long-term involvement in genealogical research, enabled the Society to qualify for membership in FEEFHS and through them establish our HomePage on the web – without the necessity of paying expensive service fees. The SVU HomePage was then accessed on the following URL address: http://feefhs.orglczs/svu/frg-svu.html.

Our first HomePage included information on the aims and objectives of the SVU, its history, and various activities, including the forthcoming SVU World Congress in Bratislava. It also provided information on how to become a member and where to subscribe to our periodical *Kosmas*. Further, it listed the names, addresses and telephone/fax numbers, as well as e-mail addresses of the individual members of the SVU Executive Board. Detailed information was also provided on all SVU Local Chapters throughout the world.

Having one's own HomePage does not necessarily assure that everybody will be able to access it unless the interested individual knows the SVU web address. Consequently, it was necessary to contact the major "search engines" on the Internet with the request that the SVU HomePage be included in their system and give them the necessary data for indexing. Beyond that I also contacted the relevant webmasters

---

[1313] "SVU HomePage," *Zprávy SVU*, vol. 40, No. 1 (January-February 1998), pp. 6-7.

managing specialized HomePages that focus on Central and East Europe, with the request to link with the SVU HomePage. Several of them have already done so, including electronic "Newyorské Listy," electronic "Britské Listy," electronic Prague-based "Neviditelný pes," and the Czech Heritage Society of Texas.

As per our announcement in the January 2000 issue of *Zprávy SVU*[1314] I made a major revision of our HomePage so that it would be up-to-date and also make it more informative. Frankly, I would have done it earlier but had to wait for the outcome of elections of our local chapters, so that the information would be up-to-date, not to speak of the fact that it took some time for our intermediary to make the technical changes. The newly revised HomePage provided basic information about SVU, including its history and the milestones in its development, its aims and objectives, its varied activities and accomplishments, current priorities, the makeup of the Executive Board, and a list of local chapters and their officers. It also brought information on the latest publications and the current projects, as well as an update on the preparations for the SVU World Congress in the year 2000.

Since I had to go through an intermediary, it was always a rather cumbersome process to make any changes in or add new information to our HomePage. I therefore appealed to our members for technical advice of how to streamline the process. I would have also welcomed any advice and assistance from our computer experts as to how to make the page interactive, how to make modifications at will and how to link it with other sites.

In addition to the above SVU HomePage, using relatively simple software on Internet "hometown.aol.com," I was able to establish another Web Page, entitled "Czech-American Cultural Heritage," in which one could find information on the SVU efforts towards preserving our cultural heritage abroad. I was also pleased to report to the membership that our two Chapters in the Czech Republic have been working on developing their own customized HomePages.

As we were entering into the new century, I encouraged every SVU Chapter to adopt new technologies and have ready access to e-mail and Internet in order to speed up communication with the SVU headquarters

---

[1314] "SVU Web Sites," *Zprávy SVU*, vol. 42, No. 1 (January-February 2000), p. 14.

and the rest of the world. Accordingly, some of their officers should at least have basic computer skills.

..........

Our new SVU Website saga began on 19th August 2000, right after the SVU World Congress in Washington, DC, when I mentioned our current difficulties to Jiří Eichler of Prague, who was attending the Congress. Jiří, who understood computers, expressed great interest in helping us out with a new website, even though he had never prepared one before.

In the first phase of our collaboration, we must have exchanged hundreds of e-mails, of which some 700 came from me regarding web postings, suggestions, corrections, and updates. By the end of the first week Jiri placed an experimental HomePage on "mujweb.cz" server which did not charge.

I constantly was sending him new material which Jiří diligently kept posting, while making improvements on Website's appearance and its structure. Because of some technical difficulties we began testing a new version on a larger server at "geocities.com." In the beginning of October 2000, the SVU HomePage already consisted of 71 pages in 5 categories: Headline News, SVU Organization and its Work (with already 13 subcategories and 16 active sections), SVU Calendar, and How to Become SVU Member. The site was technically fine, however, when the server wanted us to start putting advertisements on our pages we decided to rent a space which would be entirely under our control, free of any advertisements, and which would be maintained by a professional server around the clock.

On Wednesday 25th October 2000, at 10:50 AM Prague time, the new SVU Website showed up at its registered address www.svu2000.org. After necessary tests, it was publicly announced with its official birth date on 28th October 2000.[1315] It featured the Lincoln Memorial on the main page, Czech and Slovak national flags, SVU original logo, and a moving belt with SVU Chapter locations across the

---

[1315] "A New SVU Web Site Goes Public," *Zprávy SVU,* vol. 43, No. 1 (January-February 2001), pp. 19-20.

screen The website consisted of 10 main categories with numerous subcategories and approximately 260 pages.

During the first year of operation, SVU Website had been visited by more then seven thousand visitors, and the traffic was increasing continually. It provided not only a comprehensive and systematic library of SVU-related information, but the SVU2000.org domain had also become an attractive source of information for the general public interested in Czech and Slovak matters, such as Czech and Slovak Issues, Genealogy, Czechoslovak America, Czechophilia, or Grants and Aid. It was registered in all major search engines, bringing more visitors who searched for Czech and Slovak related sources. As of October 2001, the SVU Website had over 400 pages in 148 active subcategories and sections under 19 main categories. Since January 2001, SVU Publications category had contained electronic version of SVU News (*Zprávy SVU*) in PDF format, with an interactive table of contents in each issue.

Thanks to the feedback from SVU members and friends, we were successful in improving the website's user-friendliness. In the spring of 2001, the website was rebuilt in order to give every category and page their own address. At the end of May 2001, an internal search option was first tested, and soon, an effective Google search module was installed on SVU Website's main page. It provided a full-text search to visitors, looking for a particular keyword through all pages of the SVU Website, including all issues of the electronic version of SVU Newsletter. This tool was followed by a standard drop-down menu providing fast direct links also to website's subcategories, and also a website map giving an outline of the content. To commemorate the first anniversary, SVU Website was newly redesigned.

What does the traffic statistics say? The 2001 summer's winner was definitely the SVU Conference in Nebraska. All pages related to this happening were on the top positions in traffic for three months. However, most visitors again soon began requesting their No. 1 choice – Czechoslovak Genealogy Sites on the Internet. Also three of my documents from the SVU Information and Reference Series section came to the top: Czech and Slovak Genealogy, Czech Societies in the US, and Czech Americans. Later in the year the popularity of the SVU Calendar increased and reached top position. Among categories, the top five were: SVU Calendar, Who Are We & What We Do, Czechoslovak America, Czech and Slovak Issues, and Other Links.

The peak time for visits was between 7 PM and 11 PM Prague time, which is 1 PM to 5 PM Eastern Time, and throughout the year, the traffic on weekends is lower than during weekdays. More than 40% of visitors come from the United States, and almost 20% from the Czech Republic. Frequent visitors come from Slovakia, Canada, Germany, Switzerland, Austria, UK, Australia, and recently also from Japan, Taiwan, and Saudi Arabia. The SVU Website has also been repeatedly visited by people connected to the Internet from the following countries (order by number of visits): Hungary, Poland, Spain, Cyprus, Mexico, Belgium, Germany, Croatia, Estonia, Ireland, Italy, Netherlands, Finland, Luxembourg, Argentina, Sweden, France, Uruguay, Denmark, South Africa, Israel, New Zealand, Russia, Brazil, Yugoslavia, Bosnia and Herzegovina, Romania, Philippines, Morocco, Norway, Portugal, Greece, Venezuela, Macedonia, United Arab Emirates, and Chile.

Generally speaking, I put an inordinate effort into the website in the 2001 calendar year. There was not a day that I would not send an e-mail to Jiří Eichler with some new idea or suggestion how the Website could be improved – with the aim of making it more user-friendly and as informative as possible. We made a very good team. I supplied text and he did the posting and took care of all technical aspects. After I exhausted various SVU topics, I began working on other Czech/Slovak related topics which would attract the attention to and the utility of our Website, including such items as "Czech & Slovak Issues," "Conferences," "Grants and Aid," "Czechoslovak America" and "Genealogy." Many, if not most, of the narratives were written by me.

Some older materials had to be scanned and then carefully proofread before they could be posted, which took a considerable amount of time. Some of the postings were projects by themselves, such as "Czechoslovak Americana on the Net," which was one of the subcategories under "Czechoslovak America, was a Mega listing of various Internet sites relating to Czechs, Slovaks, Ruthenians and other nationalities in America that had their roots on the territory of the former Czechoslovakia.

On the day of its first anniversary, the SVU Website was quite an impressive site, both in terms of its contents and its looks. It had 20 main categories, each of which was further subdivided into subcategories and possibly sub-subcategories. The main categories, listed in the left column, were: "Who Are We And What We Do," "How to Join SVU," "SVU Milestones," "SVU Calendar," "Local Chapters," "Focus on Youth," "Executive Board," "President's Corner," "SVU Awards," "Picture Gallery," "SVU Forum," "Czech & Slovak Issues," "Czechoslovak America," "Conferences," "Grants & Aid," "Genealogy," "Other Links," "SVU Contacts. The heading of the 20th category, "Headline News," appeared in the right hand column, listing individual press items below.

Our website has proved to be extremely useful to us for many reasons. It has made SVU much more visible worldwide and brought us quite a large number of potential members. It also brought SVU prestige by offering useful information that could not be found elsewhere to numerous visitors.

Since its first posting, the SVU Website underwent a series of improvements and a number of new useful categories and subcategories[1316] were added. Since 2004, it also began hosting the Archival Consortium WebPage.[1317]

In 2005, we posted on SVU Website Selected Papers from the 2003 SVU Iowa Conference. This was the first SVU attempt at electronic publishing. It saved the Society high publication costs and inherent problems with distribution and storage.[1318] In order to speed up the process, the newly revised 2006 *SVU Biographical Directory* was also published electronically and was available on CD.[1319]

---

[1316] SVU Website - First Anniversary," *Zprávy SVU*, vol. 44, No. 2 (March-April 2002), pp. 22-23; "SVU Website in the 3rd Year of Operation," *Ibid.*, vol. 45, No. 3 (May-June 2003), pp. 22-23; "Four Years of the SVU Website," *Ibid.*, vol. 48, No. 4 (July-August 2006), pp. 26-27.

[1317] SVU Hosts Archival Consortium Webpage," *Zprávy SVU*, vol. 46, No. 4 (July-August 2004), p. 24.

[1318] "SVU Enters the Electronic Publishing Age," *Zprávy SVU*, vol. 47, No. 1 (January-February 2005), pp. 20-24.

[1319] "New SVU Biographical Directory on CD," *Zprávy SVU*, vol. 48, No. 2 (March-April 2006), p. 8.

# 100
## *Bibliography of SVU Publications*

This bibliography, which I had written, and which covers the SVU publications since the Society's very beginnings to date (2006), is based in part on my article, "Publications of the Czechoslovak Society of Arts and Sciences (SVU): Formative Years and Bibliography."[1320]

### CONTENTS
1. Periodicals
2. SVU Directories
3. Congress and Conference Publications
4. Monographs
5. Occasional Papers
6. Publications Sponsored by SVU
7. Audiovisual Materials

### BIBLIOGRAPHY

**1. Periodicals**

*Zprávy SVU,* Vol. 1-48 and ff., 1959-2006 and *ff.* Bimonthly (free to members).

*SVU Bulletin* (Los Angeles Chapter*),* Vol. 1 -23, 1969- 1991. Quarterly.

*SVU Bulletin,* Vol. 1-15, 1980-1994. Quarterly.

*Promeny-Premeny (Metamorphoses).* Vol. 1-29, 1964-1992. Quarterly.

*Kosmas – Czechoslovak and Central European Journal.* Vol. 1-19 and ff., 1982-2006-and ff. Semiannually.

**2. SVU Membership Directories**

*Czechoslovak Society of Arts and Sciences* in *America, Inc., Directory.* Compiled and edited by Eva Rechcígl (New York, 1966), 80 p.

*Czechoslovak Society of Arts and Sciences* in *America, Inc., Directory.* 2nd ed. Compiled and edited by Eva Rechcígl (New York, 1968), 100 p.)

---

[1320] Miloslav Rechcígl, Jr., "Publications of the Czechoslovak Society of Arts and Sciences (SVU): Formative Years and Bibliography," *Kosmas*, vol. 20, No. 1 (Fall 2006), pp. 83-102.

Czechoslovak Society of Arts and Sciences in America, Inc. *Biographical Directory of the Members of the Czechoslovak Society of Arts and Sciences in America, Inc.* 3rd ed. Compiled and edited by Eva Rechcígl and Miloslav Rechcígl, Jr. (New York, *1972),* 134 p.

Czechoslovak Society of Arts and Sciences. *Biographical Directory of the Members of the Czechoslovak Society of Arts and Sciences.* 4th ed. Compiled and edited by Eva Rechcígl and Miloslav Rechcígl, Jr. (Washington, DC, 1978), 137 p.

Czechoslovak Society of Arts and Sciences. *Biographical Directory of the Members of the Czechoslovak Society of Arts and Sciences.* 5th ed. Compiled and edited by Eva Rechcígl and Miloslav Rechcígl, Jr. (Washington, DC, 1983), 193 p.

Czechoslovak Society of Arts and Sciences. *Biographical Directory of the Members of the Czechoslovak Society of Arts and Sciences, Inc.* 6th ed. Compiled and edited by Eva Rechcígl and Miloslav Rechcígl, Jr. (Washington, DC, 1988), 285 p.

Czechoslovak Society of Arts and Sciences. *Biographical Directory of Members of the Czechoslovak Society of Arts and Sciences, Inc.* 7th ed. Compiled and edited by Eva Rechcígl and Miloslav Rechcígl, Jr. (Washington, DC, 1992), 390 p.

*Czechoslovak Society of Arts and Sciences, Inc.* 8th ed. Compiled and edited by Miloslav Rechcígl, Jr., Eva Rechcígl and Jiří Eichler (Washington, DC, 2003), 368 p.

### 3. Congress and Conference Publications

*Abstracts of The First Congress of the Czechoslovak Society of Arts and Sciences in America Inc., Washington, D.C., April 20-22, 1962* (Washington-New York, 1962), 40 p.

*Catalogue of Books of the CSASA Exhibition. The First Congress of the Czechoslovak Society of Arts and Sciences in America. Inc., April 20-22, 1962, Washington, DC* (Washington, DC. 1962), 12 pp.

Czechoslovak Society of Arts and Sciences in America. *Program [of the] Second Congress Columbia University, September 11-13, 1964* (New York, 1964), 28 p.

*Abstracts of Papers of the Second Congress of Czechoslovak Society of Arts and Sciences in America, Inc., Columbia University, New York, September 11-13, 1964* (Washington, DC, 1964), 66 p.

*Catalogue of Books* on *Display. Exhibit of Books and Periodicals. The Second Congress, Columbia University, New York City, September 11-13, 1964,* (New York, 1964), 29 p.

Czechoslovak Society of Arts and Sciences in America. *Program [of] The Third Congress, Columbia University, September 2-4, 1966* (New York, 1966), 32 p.

*Bibliography of SVU Publications* 621

*Abstracts of Papers [of the] Third Congress of the Czechoslovak Society of Arts and Sciences* in *America, Inc., Columbia University, New York, September 2-4, 1966* (New York, 1966), 72 p.

Czechoslovak Society of Arts and Sciences in America. *Program of The Fourth Congress, Georgetown University, Washington, DC, August 30–September 1, 1968* (New York, 1968), 30 p.

*Abstracts of Papers of The Fourth Congress of the Czechoslovak Society of Arts and Sciences* in *America, Inc., Georgetown University, Washington, DC, August 30–September 1, 1961* (New York, 1968), 69 p.

*Art Exhibition: Koloman Sokol – Oskar Kokoschka.* Smithsonian Institution, Arts and Industrial Bldg., Washington, DC, Aug. 26-Sept. 16, 1968, 12 p.

*Abstracts of Papers of The Fifth Congress of the Czechoslovak Society of Arts and Sciences* in *America, Inc., New York University, New York, NY, November 10-12, 1970* (New York 1970), 98 p.

Czechoslovak Society of Arts and Sciences in America. *Transkript I. Evropské konference, Horgenu.* Transcribed by Libuše Králová. (New York, 1971), 185 p.

Czechoslovak Society of Arts and Sciences in America. *Program of the Sixth Congress, George Washington University, Washington, DC. November 10-12, 1972* (Washington, DC, 1972), 38 p.

Czechoslovak Society of Arts and Sciences in America. *Program of the Seventh Congress, New York University, New York, NY, November 15-17, 1974* (New York, 1974), 15 p.

Czechoslovak Society of Arts and Sciences in America. *Program of the Eighth Congress, George Washington University, Washington, DC, August 12- 15, 1976* (Washington, DC, 1976), 26 p.

Czechoslovak Society of Arts and Sciences in America. *"Contributions of Czechs and Slovaks in North America,"* The Central Theme of the Eighth Congress of the Czechoslovak Society of Arts and Sciences in *America: Abstracts of Papers* (Washington, DC, 1976), 70 p.

Czechoslovak Society of Arts and Sciences. *Abstracts of Papers [of] The Ninth World Congress, Cleveland State University, Cleveland, Ohio, October 26-29, 1978* (Cleveland, Cleveland State University Press, 1978), 80 p.

Czechoslovak Society of Arts and Sciences. *Abstracts of Papers [of] The Tenth World Congress, Georgetown University, Washington, DC, October 17-19, 1980* (Washington, DC, 1980), 71 p.

*Arts and Crafts of Czechoslovakian Artists Abroad.* Exhibition of Paintings, Drawings and Craft: by Czech and Slovak Artists Abroad Organized by Czechoslovak Society of Arts and Science: in America on the Occasion of its 10th Congress, Washington, DC, October 16-20, 1980. 13 leaves.

Czechoslovak Society of Arts and Sciences. *Program [of] The Eleventh World Art Congress, University of Pittsburgh, PA, October 28-31, 1982* (Pittsburgh, PA, 1982), 26 p.

*Art SVU.* Czechoslovakian Artists Working Abroad. An exhibition of Fine Arts by Czechs and Slovaks Living Outside Czechoslovakia, organized by the Czechoslovak Society of Arts and Sciences on the occasion of its 11th Congress at the University of Pittsburgh, Pittsburgh PA, October 1982. 6 p.

Czechoslovak Society of Arts and Sciences. *Program of the Twelfth World Congress, The Royal York Hotel, Toronto, Ont., October 25-28, 1984.* 38 p.

Czechoslovak Society of Arts and Sciences. *Abstracts of the 12th World Congress, The Royal York Hotel, Toronto, Ont., October 25-28, 1984.* 90 p.

Thirteenth World Congress of the Czechoslovak Society of Arts and Sciences. *Art Exhibition,* September 18-21, 1986, Art Gallery, Dodge Library, Northeastern University, Boston, MA. 6 leaves.

Thirteenth World Congress of the Czechoslovak Society of Arts and Sciences. *Program of the Thirteenth World Congress, Northeastern University, Boston, MA, Sept. 18-21, 1986.* 32 p.

Czechoslovak Society of Arts and Sciences. *Abstracts of the Papers Presented at the Thirteenth World Congress, Northeastern University, Boston, MA, September 18-21, 1986.* 111 p.

Czechoslovak Society of Arts and Sciences. *Program of the Fourteenth World Congress, National 4-H Center, Chevy Chase, MD, September 15-18, 1988.* 26 p.

Czechoslovak Society of Arts and Sciences. *Program and Abstracts of Papers of the 14th World Congress. National 4-H Center, Chevy Chase, MD, September 15-18, 1988.* 101 p.

The Fourteenth World Congress of the Czechoslovak Society of Arts and Sciences. Art Exhibition. September 15-18,1988, National 4-H Center, Chevy Chase, MD. 4 p.

Czechoslovak Society of Arts and Sciences. *Program of the Fifteenth World Congress, Royal York Hotel, Toronto, Ont., Canada, October 11-14, 1990.* 30 p.

Czechoslovak Society of Arts and Sciences. *Abstracts of Papers [of the] 15th World Congress, Toronto, Ont., Canada, October 11-13, 1990.* 76 p.

The Fifteenth World Congress of the Czechoslovak Society of Arts and Sciences. *Art Exhibition: Canadian Artists of Czech and Slovak Origin.* Royal York Hotel, Toronto, Ont., Canada. Opening Oct. 12th and 13th, 1990. 20 p.

Program. SVU World Congress, Prague – Bratislava, Czechoslovakia, June 26- July 2, 1992. 20 p.

*Czechoslovakia, Europe and the World: Arts and Sciences in the International Context – Československo, Evropa a svět: Věda a umění v mezinárodních souvislostech.* Program of the 16th SVU World Congress, Prague – Bratislava, June 26 – July 2, 1992. Organized in cooperation with the Council of Learned Societies of ČSFR (Prague, 1992), 110, 22 p.

*Czech and Slovak Contribution to the World Culture. Abstracts of Papers Presented at the 17th SVU World Congress, Prague, Czech Republic, June 26-29, 1994.* Organized in cooperation with the Council of Learned Societies of CR (Prague, 1994), 137, 64 p.

*Abstracts of Papers Presented at the 18th SVU World Congress, Brno, Czech Republic, August 26-29, 1996* (Brno, 1996), 181 p.

[Program and Conference Participants]. Czech-Americans in Transition: Challenges and Opportunities for the Future. Annual Meeting and Conference of the Czechoslovak Society of Arts and Sciences (SVU). The Bell Co. Exposition Center, Belton, TX, July 12-13, 1997. 12 p.

*Problems of Sciences and Arts on the Eve of the 21st Century. Abstracts of Papers Presented at 19th SVU World Congress of the Czechoslovak Society of Arts and Sciences. Bratislava, July 5-10, 1998* (Bratislava, 1998), 94 p.

[Program and Speakers]. Special SVU Conference: Twin Cities of Minneapolis and St. Paul, MN, April 24-26, 1999. Central Theme: "Czech and Slovak America: Quo Vadis?" 20 p.

Program of the 20th Anniversary SVU World Congress. Central Theme: "Civil Society and Democracy into the New Millennium." American University, Washington, DC, August 9-13, 2000. Special offprint of *Zprávy SVU.* 40 p.

*Abstracts of the 20th World Congress of the Czechoslovak Society of Arts and Sciences (SVU). Central Theme: Civil Society and Democracy into the New Millennium. August 8-13, 2000, American University, Washington, D.C.* 232 p.

[Program, Abstracts, Biographies of Speakers]. SVU 2002 North American Conference, Lincoln, Nebraska, August 1-3, 2001. "The Czech and Slovak Legacy in the Americas: Preservation of Heritage with the Accent on Youth." Lincoln, NE, SVU, 2001.

Program kongresu SVU 24.-28 června 2002 v Plzni. 10 p.

[Program, Abstracts, List of Participants and Lecturers] Československá společnost pro vědy a umění, 21. Výroční světový kongres pod záštitou prezidenta České republiky Václava Havla na téma Transformace České a slovenské společnosti na prahu nového milenia a její úloha v současném globálním sv.t.. 24.-30. 6. 2002, Plzeň. 160 p.

[Program, Abstracts and Biographies of Speakers]. 2003 SVU North American Conference, Cedar Rapids, Iowa, 26-28, June 2003. Central Theme: "The

Czech and Slovak Presence in North America: A Retrospective Look and Future Perspectives." 76 p.

[Program and Abstracts]. 22nd World Congress of Czechoslovak Society of Arts and Sciences, Palacky University, Olomouc, June 26- July 4, 2004. Central Theme: Moravia from World Perspective (Olomouc, Centrum pro Československá studia při Kated ř e historie Filozofické fakulty Univerzity Palackého, 2004), 166 p.

[Program and Abstracts]. Special Conference and Festival, North Miami, Florida, 17-20 March 2005. Central Theme: "Czech and Slovak Cultural Heritage on Both Sides of the Atlantic" (North Miami, FL, SVU, 2005), 50 pp.

Czech and Slovak Culture and Science in International Context. (Academic Sessions and Abstracts of) 23rd World Congress of Czechoslovak Society of Arts and Sciences, University of South Bohemia, Ceske Budejovice, Czech Republic, June 25- July 2, 2006 (České Budějovice, Tiskárna Johanus 2006), 151 p.

Schedule of the 23rd World Congress of Czechoslovak Society of Arts and Sciences, University of South Bohemia, Ceske Budejovice, Czech Republic, June 25- July 2, 2006 (České Budějovice, Tiskárna Johanus, 2006), 8 p.

## 4. Monographs

Jirák, Karel B. *Antonín Dvořák,* 1841-1961 (New York, NY, 1961), 31 p.

Duben, V. N. *Czech and Slovak Periodical Press Outside Czechoslovakia: Its History and Status as of January* 1962 (Washington, DC, 1962), 99 p.

Heidrich, A. *International Political Causes of the Czechoslovak Tragedies of 1938 and 1948. Part I* (Washington, DC, 1962), 27 p.

Štěrba, F. C. *Česi a Slováci v Latinské Americe* (Washington, DC, 1962), 61 p.

Masaryková, Alice G. *Hudba v Spillville* (New York, 1963), 19 p.

Šejnoha, Jaroslav. *Svědectví a skazky z umění výtvarného* (Toronto, Ont., 1963), 13 p.

Wellek, René. *Czech Literature at the Crossroads of Europe* (Toronto, Ont., 1963), 15 p.

Wellek, René. *Essays on Czech Literature* (The Hague, Mouton & Co., 1963), 214 p.

Rechcígl, Miloslav, Jr., ed. *The Czechoslovak Contribution to World Culture* (The Hague-Paris-London, Mouton & Co., 1964), 862 p.

Duben, V. N. *Czech and Slovak Periodicals Outside Czechoslovakia as of September* 1964 (New York, NY, 1964), 208 p.

Zlámal, Miloslav. *Zpěvy z modrých hor* (Toronto, Ont., 1964), 66 p.

Vaněk, Vladimír. *Kniha povídek* (New York, NY, 1965), 118 pp.

Rechcígl, Miloslav, Jr., ed. *Ten Years of the Czechoslovak Society of Arts and Sciences* in *America, Inc.,* 1956-1966 (Toronto, Ont., "Nase Hlasy," 1966), 20 pp.

*Se souhlasem milionů: Kardinal Josef Beran čestným čenem SVU.* Trans. A. Rozehnal and V. E. Andic (New York, NY, 1966), 16 p.

Duben, V. N. *Czech and Slovak Periodicals Outside Czechoslovakia, as of Sept.* 1968 (New York, NY, 1968), 28 p.

*Rejtsřík Zpráv SVU* 1959-1966: *A Comprehensive Index to the First* 8 *Volumes of the Society's Newsletter.* Compiled by Josef Žanda (Washington, DC, 1968), 45 p.

Rechcígl, Miloslav, Jr., ed. *Czechoslovakia: Past and Present. Vol. I: Political, International, Social, and Economic Aspects* (Hague-Paris, Mouton, 1968), 880 p.

Rechcígl, Miloslav, Jr., ed. *Czechoslovakia: Past and Present. Vol. II: Essays on the Arts and Sciences* (Hague-Paris, Mouton, 1968), pp. 882-1889.

Machotka, Otakar. *Povídky exulantovy* (Toronto, Ont., "Naše Hlasy"), 81 p.

Comenius, J. A. *Diogenes the Cynic.* Trans. M. C. Mittelstadt (New York, NY, 1970), 73 p.

Duben, V. N. *České a slovenské noviny a časopisy* (New York, NY, 1970), 28 p.

Jelínek, Ivan. *Sochy* (New York, NY, 1970), 114 p.

Lokay, Miroslav. *Československé legie v Itálii* (New York, NY, 1970), 31 p.

Jakobson, Roman. *Studies in Verbal Art: Texts in Czech and Slovak* (Ann Arbor, MI, University of Michigan, 1971), 412 p.

Bušek, Vratislav, ed. *Comenius: A Symposium Commemorating the 300th Anniversary of the Death of Jan Amos Comenius (Komenský)* (New York, NY, 1972), 184 p.

Comenius, J. A. *The Labyrinth of the World and the Paradise of the Heart: With a Facsimile of the 1663 Czech Original.* Trans. Matthew Spinka (Ann Arbor, MI, University of Michigan, 1972), 203 p.

French, Alfred, comp. *Anthology of Czech Poetry. Intr.* by René Wellek (New York, NY, SVU and Ann Arbor, MI, Dept. of Slavic Languages and Literatures, University of Michigan, 1973), 372 pp.

Fisher, John H., et al. *Czechoslovak Military Justice Abroad during the Second World War* (New York, NY, 1975), 47 p.

Jeřábek, Esther. *Czechs and Slovaks in America: A Bibliography* (New York, SVU and Chicago, IL, CNCA, 1976), 448 p.

Rechcígl, Miloslav, Jr., ed. *Studies in Czechoslovak Culture and Society* (Meerut-2, India, Sadhna Prakashan, 1976), 460 p.

Rechcígl, Miloslav, Jr., ed. *Studies in Czechoslovak History* (Meerut-2, India, Sadhna Prakashan., 1976), 458 p.

*O Janáčkovi*. R. Firkušný – R. Kubelík – F. Smetana – K. B. Jirák. Vydala místní skupina SVU v Chicagu. Chicago, IL, Velehrad, 1978. 24 p.

Orten, Jiří. *Elegie – Elegies*. Trans. Lyn Coffin (New York, NY, 1980), 111 p.

Rechcígl, Miloslav, Jr. *Educators with Czechoslovak Roots: A U.S. and Canadian Faculty Roster* (Washington, DC, 1980), 122 p.

Seifert, Jaroslav. *Morový sloup – The Plague Monument*. Trans. Lyn Coffin (New York, NY, 1980), 57 p.

Čapek, Milič and Karel Hrubý, eds. *T. G. Masaryk: Perspective: Comments and Criticism* (New York, NY, 1981), 282 pp.

Chada, Joseph. *The Czechs in the United States* (New York, NY, 1981), 292 pp.

Harkins, William, ed. *Czech Prose: An Anthology* (Ann Arbor, MI, University of Michigan, 1983), 321 pp.

Czechoslovak Society of Arts and Sciences. *Index k Zprávám SVU: Ročníky I-X (1959-1968)*. Compiled by Josef Žanda (Washington, DC, 1985), 68 pp

Engliš, Karel. *An Essay on Economic Systems: A Teleological Approach*. Trans. Ivo Moravčík (Boulder, CO, East European Monographs, 1986), 159 pp.

Novák, Arne. *Czech Literature*. Rev. ed. Edited with Supplement by William E. Harkins (Ann Arbor, MI, University of Michigan, 1986), 382 p.

Rechcígl, Miloslav, Jr. *U.S. Legislators with Czechoslovak Roots from Colonial Times to Present: With Genealogical Lineages* (Washington, DC, 1987),65 p.

*Kultur und Gewalt: Erfahrungen einer Region* (Kendat, Cambria, 1988), 72 pp.

*Společnost a kultura* (Lancaster, Lancaster U. Press, 1990), 198 p.

Hrubý, Petr. *Daydreams and Nightmares: Czech Communist and Ex-Communist Literature,* 1917-1987 (Boulder, CO, East European Monographs, 1990), 362 p.

*On All Fronts: Czechs and Slovaks in World War II*. Edited by Lewis M. White (Boulder, CO, East European Monographs, 1991), 296 p.

*SVU Sydney 1972-1992*. Záznamy z dvacetileté činnosti Místní skupiny Společnosti pro vědy a umění v Sydney. Sestavili Oliver Fiala a Jan Jirásek za ediční spolupráce členů výboru SVU, Sydney 1990-1992 (Sydney, 1992), 142 p.

*Na všech frontách*. Upravili V. N. Duben a Lewis M. White. Pod záštitou SVU. S fiananční podporou washingtonské skupiny SVU (Praha, Melantrich, 1992), 331 p.

Sommer, Karel. *UNRRA a Československo*. S finanční podporou Washingtonské skupiny SVU (Opava, Slezský ústav AV ČR, 1993), 112 p.

*Sborník Československé společnosti pro vědy zemědelské, lesnické, veterinární a potravinářské*. Sborník příspevků ze 17. světového kongresu SVU, konaného v Praze 26.6 až 29.6. 1994. Uspořádal Rudolf Jánal. (Praha, 1994), 238 p.

*Czech and Slovak Contributions to Perinatal Medicine.* Summary of Reports Presented at a Symposium During the 17th Congress of Czechoslovak Society of Arts and Sciences, May 26-29, 1994, Prague. Czech Republic. In: *Physiological Research*, vol. 44, Issue 6, 1995, pp. 339-360.

*On All Fronts. Czechoslovaks in World War II.* Part 2. Edited by Lewis M. White With the financial support of the SVU Washington, DC Chapter (Boulder, CO, East European Monographs, 1995), 303 p.

*The Bohemian Reformation and Religious Practice.* Vol. 1. Papers from the XVIIth World Congress of the Czechoslovak Society of Arts and Sciences, Prague 1994. Edited by David R. Holeton (Prague: Academy of Sciences of the Czech Republic, 1996), 95 p.

*Trvalé udržitelné lesnictví v České republice, na Slovensku a ve svetě – Sustainable Forestry in the Czech Republic, Slovakia and the World.* Sborník referátu z konference lesnické sekce konané v Praze dne 26. června 1994 v rámci 17. Světového kongresu Společnosti pro vědy a umění – Proceedings of the Conference of the Forestry Section, held in Prague, June 26, 1994 in association with the 17th World Congress of the Czechoslovak Society of Arts and Sciences. Redigovali Miroslav M. Grandtner a Bohuslav Vinš. (Praha – Zbraslav: Národní lesnický komitet, 1996), 78 p.

*Technologia – Humanita – Umenie – Tolerancia.* Konferencia SVU Košice – Vysoké Tatry, August 1996. Redigovali Klára Tkáčová a Karol Marton (Košice, Miestna skupina SVU Košice, 1996), 83 p.

*Setkáni a Hovory.* Almanach Společnosti pro vědy a umění v Mnichově. Z příspěvků členů a přátel SVU sestavul Štěpán F. Kadlec (Praha: Tiskárna České akademie věd v Praze, 1997), 267 p.

*Symbioza v poznáni pro trvalé udržitelné lesnictví.* Sborník referátů z 2. konference lesnické sekce konané v Brně dne 27. srpna 1996 v rámci 18. Světového kongresu Společnosti pro vědy a umění. Redigovali Bohuslav Vinš a Miroslav M. Grandtner (Praha – Zbraslav: Národní lesnický komitét, 1998), 44 p.

*The Bohemian Reformation and Religious Practice.* Vol. 2. Papers from the XVIIIth World Congress of the Czechoslovak Society of Arts and Sciences, Brno 1998. Edited by Zdenek V. David and David R. Holeton (Prague: Academy of Sciences of the Czech Republic, 1998), 165 p.

*The Bohemian Reformation and Religious Practice.* Vol. 3. Papers from the XIXth World Congress of the Czechoslovak Society of Arts and Sciences, Bratislava 1998. Edited by Zdenek V. David and David R. Holeton. Prague: Academy of Sciences of the Czech Republic, 2000. 238 p.

Machann, Clinton, ed. *Czech-Americans in Transition.* Austin, TX: Eakin Press, 2000. 136 p.

*On All Fronts. Czechoslovaks in World War II.* Part 3. With the financial support of the SVU Washington, DC Chapter. Edited by Lewis M. White (Boulder, CO, East European Monographs, 2000), 333 p.

Fischmann, Zdenka E. *Essays on Czech Music.* Edited by Dagmar White and Anne Palmer (Boulder, CO, East European Monographs, 2002), 187 p.

*Chuť ztraceného domova – The Taste of a Lost Homeland.* A Bilingual Anthology of Czech and Slovak Exile Poetry Written in America. Compiled and edited by Věra Bořkovec. Dedicated to the Memory of Frank Marlow. (Plzen, TYPOS, 2002), 171 p.

Evoluce člověka a antropologie recentních populací. Sborník panelů 21. Světového kongresu Československé společnosti pro vědy a umění. Plzeň, 24.-30. června, 2002. Editoři: Vladimír Sládek, Patrik Galeta a Vladimír Blažek. In: Biologická antropologie, Sborník 1 (Plzeň, Aleš Čeněk, 2003), 117 p.

The Transformation of Czech and Slovak Societies on the Threshold of the New Millennium and the Role in the Global World. Selected Papers from the 21st World Congress, University of West Bohemia, Plzeň, Czech Republic, June 23-30, 2002. Edited by Ján P. Skalný and Miloslav Rechcígl, Jr. (Plzeň, Aleš Čeněk, 2004), 640 p.

Transformace české a slovenské společnosti na prahu nového milenia a její úloha v současném globálním světě. Sborník vybraných příspěvků 21. Světového kongresu Společnosti pro vědy a umění v Plzni 24.-30. června, 2002. Edited by Ivo Budil, Ivona Škanderová and Jana Jantschová (Plzeň, Aleš Čeněk, 2004), 400 p.

Czech and Slovak American Archival Materials and their Preservation. Proceedings of the Working Conference held at the Czech and Slovak Embassies in Washington, DC on November 22-23, 2003. Edited by Miloslav Rechcígl, Jr., President, SVU. (Prague, Prague Editions, 2004), 168 p.

Setkání a hovory 1997-2004. Z příspěvků členů a přátel SVU z let 1997-2004. K 20ti letému výročí založení. Sestavili Ivan Cikl a Ladislav Pavlík (Mnichov, SVU Německo, 2004). 326 p.

*Poštovní schránka domov.* Malá antologie exilové povídky padesátých let. Vybral a uspořádal Michal Přibáň. K vydání připravila Alena Morávková. Praha: SVU, 2005. 85 p.

Rechcígl, Miloslav, Jr. *Czechs and Slovaks in America. Surveys, Essays, Reflections and Personal Insights Relating to the History and Contributions of Czech and Slovak Immigrants in America and their Descendants.* Arranged by Karen Rechcígl and Jack E. Rechcígl. Published on the occasion of Dr. Rechcígl's 75th birthday. Boulder, CO: East European Monographs, 2005. 317 p.

Czechoslovak Society of Arts and Sciences. Palacky University, June 26 to July 4, 2004. Vol. 1. Opening, English Panels Culture and Education, The Arts, The

Humanities). Edited by Tomáš Motlíček and Miloslav Rechcígl, Jr. (Ostrava, Repronis, 2006). 434 p.

Moravia from World Perspective. Selected Papers from the 22nd World Congress of the Czechoslovak Society of Arts and Sciences. Palacký University, June 26 to July 4, 2004. Vol. 2. English Panels. Czech Panels (Social Sciences, Science, Medicine and Technology, Czechs and Slovaks Abroad. Edited by Tomáš Motlíček and Miloslav Rechcígl, Jr. (Ostrava, Repronis, 2006), 432 p.

Kocourek, Milan and Zuzana Slobodová. Česko-slovenská Britanie. Pro SVU Londyn vydalo nakladatelství Carpio v Třeboni r. 2006. 356 p.

Bořkovec, Věra, ed. *Czech and Slovak Theatre Abroad: In the USA, Canada, Australia and England.* Boulder, CO: East European Monographs, 2006. 128 p.

## 5. Occasional Papers

1. Mamatey, Victor S. *Building Czechoslovakia in America:* 1914-1918 (Washington, DC, 1976), 17 p.
2. Polach, Eva B. *The SVU List* of *Lectures, Studies and Other Materials* (Washington, DC, 1976), 34 p.
3. Lewis, Brackett. *Eyewitness Story* of *the Occupation of Samara, Russia, by the Czechoslovak Legion in June* 1918 (Washington, DC, 1977), 20 pp.
4. Duben, Vojtěch N. *Czech and Slovak Press: Its Status in* 1978 (Washington, DC, 1978), 62 p.
5. Schwarzenberg, František. *František Palacký* (Washington, DC, 1978), 26 p.

## 6. Publications Sponsored by SVU

Javor, Pavel. *Nedosněno, nedomilováno* (New York, NY, Universum Press Co., 1965), 104 p.

Hoffmann, Banesh, ed. *Perspectives in Geometry and Relativity: Essays in Honor of Václav Hlavatý* (Bloomington-London, Indiana University Press, 1966), 491 p.

Herben, Ivan and František Třešňák, eds. *Padesát let: Soubor vzpomínek a úvah na Masarykovu republiku* (Toronto, Ont., "Naše Hlasy," 1968), 206 p.

Kratochvíl, Antonín. *Die kommunistische Hochschulpolitik in der Tschechoslowakei* (München, Fides-Verlagsgesellschaft München, 1968), 271 p.

Martínek, Josef. *Verše ze zásuvky a verše zapomenuté* (New Jersey, Universum Press Co., 1968), 80 p.

Brabec, Jiří, ed. *Slovník českých spisovatelů* (Toronto, Ont., 68 Publishers, 1982), 537 p.

Drtina, Prokop. *Československo můj osud* (Toronto, Ont., 68 Publishers, 1982), 2 vols.

Absolon, Karel B. (After Karla Bufková-Wankelová), *Series* 1. *Moravian Tales, Legends, Myths: The Tale* of *the Bad Macocha and The Fable* of *the Underground Punkva River* (Rockville, MD, KABEL Publishers, 1984), 60 p.

Absolon, Karel B. *Developmental Technology* of *Gastric Surgery* 1521 *to Present* (Rockville, MD, KABEL Publishers, 1985), 170 p.

Kovtun, Jiří. *Slovo má poslanec Masaryk* (München, Edice Arkýř), 211 p.

Kosková, Helena. *Hledání ztracené generace* (Toronto, Ont., 68 Publishers, 1986), 368 p.

Prečan, Vilém, ed. *T. G. Masaryk and Our Times* (Hannover, CSDS, 1986), 112 p.

Prečan, Vilém, ed. *Ten Years* of *Charter 77* (Hannover, CSDS, 1986), 111 pp.

Richterová, Sylvie. *Slovo a ticho* (München, Edice Arkýř, 1986), 155 p.

Kovtun, Jiří. *Masarykův triumf: Příběh konce velké války* (Toronto, Ont., 68 Publishers, 1987), 714 p.

Mešťan, Antonín. *Česká literatura,* 1785- 1985 (Toronto, Ont., 68 Publishers, 1987), 456 p.

Rotrekl, Zdeněk. *Skrytá tvář české literatury* (Toronto, Ont., 68 Publishers, 1987), 250 p.

Křesadlo, Jan. *Fuga Trium* (Toronto, Ont., 68 Publishers, 1987), 371 p.

*ACTA.* Čvrtletnik Čs. dokumentačního střediska nezavislé literatury. Vol. 1 (1987), Nos. 1-4; Vol. 2 (1988), Nos. 5-8; Vol. 3 (1989), Nos. 9-12.

*Demokracie pro všechny: Dokumenty Hnutí za občanskou svobodu* (Scheinfeld, CSDS), 19 p.

*Democracy for All: Documents* of *the Movement for Civil Liberties* (Scheinfeld, CSDS), 20 p.

Fuchs, Jiřina. *Jiří Karger: A Retrospective* (Los Angeles, CA, Framar Publishers, 1988), 104 p.

Prečan, Vilém, ed. *Acta creationis: Unabhangige Geschichtsschreibung in der Tschechoslowakei 1969-1980* (Scheinfeld, CSDS, 1988), 252 p.

Provazníková, Marie. *To byl Sokol.* Za redakční spolupráce Otilie Kabešové (München, České slovo, 1988), 252 p.

Synek, Miroslav. *Naděje* a *zklamání: Pražské jaro* 1968 (Scheinfeld, CSDS, 1988), 157 p.

*About Theatre* (Stockholm, CSDS & Charter 77 Foundation, 1989) 96 p. *(Voices from Czechoslovakia, 3-4)*

Havel, Václav. *Do různých stran: Eseje* a *články z let* 1983-1989. Ed. by Vilém Prečan (Scheinfeld, CSDS & Charter 77 Foundation, 1989), 526 p.

*Charta 77, 1977 – 1989: Od morální k demokratické revoluci: Dokumentace.* Ed. by Vilém Prečan (Bratislava, CSDS & Archa Publishers, 1990), 525 p.

*Demokratická revoluce: Stav a výhledy světa – jaro* 1989 (Prague, Institute for Contemporary History & Scheinfeld. CSDS. 1990), 123 p.

Čulík, Jan. *Seznam publikací vydaných v hlavních exilových nakladatelstvích 1971-1990* (Prague, Institute for Contemporary History & CSDS, 1992), 53 p.

Gruša, Jiří. *Cenzura* a *literární život mimo masmedia* (Prague, Institute for Contemporary History & CSDS, 1992), 26 p.

*Milan Šimečka – Bibliografie díla za léta 1975-1990.* Compiled by Milan Drápala (Prague, Institute for Contemporary History & CSDS, 1992), 48 p.

Prečan, Vilém. *Independent Literature and Samizdat* in *Czechoslovakia* in *the 1970s and the 1980s* (Prague, Institute for Contemporary History & CSDS, 1992), 20 p.

Vladislav, Jan. *O edici Kvart po letech* (Prague, Institute for Contemporary History & CSDS, 1992), 12 p.

A series of brochures published to mark the opening of an exhibition of independent literature published in samizdat and in exile, 1948-1989 (Prague, Památník národního písemnictvi, January-June 1992).

Rechcígl, Miloslav, Jr. *Postavy naší Ameriky.* Z iniciativy senátní Stálé komise pro krajany žijící v zahraničí a za finanční podpory Senátu Parlamentu České republiky (Praha, Pražská edice, 2000), 356 p.

Rechcígl, Miloslav, Jr. Czech-American Historic Sites, Monuments, and Memorabilia (Olomouc-Ostrava: Centrum pro československá studia při Katedře historie Filozofické fakulty Univerzity Palackého v Olomouci, 2004), 142 p.

Rechcígl, Miloslav, Jr. Czechoslovak American Archivalia. Vol. 1. Government Repositories, University-based Collections, Collections Maintained by Public Museums and Libraries, Collections of Ethnic and Other Related Organizations (Olomouc-Ostrava: Centrum pro československá studia při Katedře historie Filozofické fakulty Univerzity Palackého v Olomouci, 2004), 206 p.

Rechcígl, Miloslav, Jr. Czechoslovak American Archivalia. Vol. 2. Personal Papers and Collections, Repositories Abroad Bearing on the Subject, Virtual Archives on the Internet. Appendixes (Olomouc-Ostrava: Centrum pro československá studia při Katedře historie Filozofické fakulty Univerzity Palackého v Olomouci, 2004), 368 p.

Vičar, Jan. Imprints: Essays on Czech Music and Aesthetics. (Prague: Togga and Olomouc: Palacký University, 2005), 270 p.

## 7. Audiovisual Materials
### a. Records and Tapes
Veit, Vladimir. Ve lví stopě. Recorded in Vienna, Austria, April 1985.

## b. Video Cassettes

*SVU a čs. výtvarníci v exilu.* Prepared by Jindřich Bernard, Emil Purgina and Vladimír Škutina; videotaped at the SVU World Congress' Art Exhibit, Boston, MA, Sept. 18-21, 1986. (Provides material about selected painters and a few sculptors of Czechoslovak descent living in the West.)

*Jihoafrické rozhovory.* Vladimír Škutina (Commentary), Jindřich Bernard (Camera).

*Rudolf Firkušný.* Interviewed by Vladimír Škutina; videotaped by Jindřich Bernard.

*Jaroslav Seifert na Západě.* Videotaped by Jindřich Bernard (1987). (Includes excellent readings of some of Seifert's poems; scenes from the Nobel Prize Award presentation in Stockholm, 1984; Seifert himself, sharing his thoughts about art and life).

*Rozhovor s Janem Papánkem.* Interviewed by Pavel Pecháček; videotaped by Michael Baumbruck. (Recollections about his life and Czechoslovakia).

*Rozhovor s Karlem Steinbachem.* Interviewed by Pavel Pecháček; videotaped by Michael Baumbruck. (Reflections about cultural and political life in post World War I Czechoslovakia).

*Koncert Karla Kryla.* Produced by Milan Leimberger (Los Angeles); videotaped in Chicago, 1988, during his tour in the U.S.

*22nd SVU World Congress, Palacký University, Olomouc, June 26-July 4, 2004.* Video Cassette and DVD. A 40-minute documentary vividly highlighting proceedings and depicting memorable events of the Congress.

## c. CDs and DVDs

CD recording of Edmonton Symphony Orchestra concert, featuring Czech music, given on October 28, 1989, conducted by Grzegorz Nowak. Includes Smetana's "Má Vlast" and Janacek's "Moravian Dances."

SVU World Congress, Olomouc, Czech Republic, 2004. Opening Ceremony. Prepared by Philosophical Faculty of the Palacký University in Olomouc.

Selected Papers from the 2003 SVU North American Conference, Cedar Rapids, Iowa, 26-28 June 2003. Prepared by Charles Townsend, Kačenka Oslzlý, Míla Rechcígl and Jiří Eichler (Washington, DC, SVU Press, 2006).

SVU Directory. Compiled by Miloslav Rechcígl, Jr., Eva Rechcígl and Jiří Eichler. Revised 8th ed. (Washington, DC, SVU Press, 2006).

## d. INTERNET

SVU Website: Czechs and Slovaks Worldwide and their Culture. Text: Mila Rechcígl; Webmaster: Jiří Eichler. URL: http://www.svu2000.org/

Brno Local Chapter. URL: http://www.svu.vutbr.cz/

České Budějovice. URL: http://www.svu.vutbr.cz/

Cleveland Local Chapter. URL: http://www.geocities.com/clevelandsvu2004/

*Bibliography of SVU Publications* 633

Lincoln, NE Local Chapter. URL: http://www.unl.edu/SVUNebraska/
Olomouc Local Chapter. URL: http://www.svukongres2004.upol.cz/
Plzeň Local Chapter. URL: http://www.svu.zcu.cz/:
Prague Local Chapter. URL: http://www.kav.cas.cz/SVU/
Spillvile Local Chapter. URL: http://www.czechoslovaksmidwest.org/

# Appendices

# *Appendices*

## Table 1
### Chief Executive Officers of the Society

| Period | President | Secretary General |
|---|---|---|
| 1958-1959 | Prof. Václav Hlavatý | Dr. Jaroslav Němec |
| 1959-1960 | Prof. Václav Hlavatý | Prof. Rudolf Šturm |
| 1960-1962 | Prof. Václav Hlavatý | Dr. Jaroslav Němec |
| 1962-1964 | Prof. René Wellek | Prof. Rudolf Šturm |
| 1964-1966 | Prof. René Wellek | Prof. Rudolf Šturm |
| 1966-1968 | Prof. Václav Hlavatý | Prof. Vojtech E. Andic |
| 1968-1970 | Dr. Jaroslav Němec | Dr. John G. Lexa |
| 1970-1972 | Dr. Jan V. Mládek | Dr. John G. Lexa |
| 1972-1974 | Prof. František Schwarzenberg | Dr. John G. Lexa |
| 1974-1976 | Dr. Miloslav Rechcígl | Dr. John G. Lexa |
| 1976-1978 | Dr. Miloslav Rechcígl | Dr. John G. Lexa |
| 1978-1980 | Prof. Jan F. Tříska | Dr. Vera Z. Bořkovec |
| 1980-1982 | Prof. Leopold J. Pospíšil | Blanka S. Glos |
| 1982-1984 | Prof. Leopold J. Pospíšil | Ing. Miloš K. Kučera |
| 1984-1986 | Prof. Jiří Nehněvajsa | Ing. Miloš K. Kučera |
| 1986-1988 | Prof. Jiří Nehněvajsa | Ing. Miloš K. Kučera |
| 1988-1990 | Prof. Igor V. Nábělek | Ing. Miloš K. Kučera |
| 1990-1992 | Prof. Jan F. Tříska | Frank Marlow |
| 1992-1994 | Prof. Zdeněk J. Slouka | P. Machotka/V. Bořkovec |
| 1994-1996 | Dr. Miloslav Rechcígl | Dr. Blanka Kuděj |
| 1996-1998 | Dr. Miloslav Rechcígl | Věra Ulbrecht |
| 1998-2000 | Dr. Miloslav Rechcígl | Eva Vaněk |
| 2000-2002 | Dr. Miloslav Rechcígl | Frank Safertal |
| 2002-2004 | Dr. Miloslav Rechcígl | Frank Safertal |
| 2004-2006 | Dr. Miloslav Rechcígl | Frank Safertal |

## Table 2
### SVU General Assembly Meetings

| Meeting | Location | Date |
|---|---|---|
| 1st | New York, NY | 16 April 1960 |
| 2nd | New York, NY | 16 December 1961 |
| 3rd | Washington, DC | 20 April 1962 |
| 4th | Toronto, Ont. | 7 September 1963 |
| 5th | New York, NY | 11 September 1964 |
| 6th | Chicago, IL | 18 September 1965 |
| 7th | New York, NY | 2 September 1966 |
| 8th | Montreal, P.Q. | 1 July 1967 |
| 9th | Washington, DC | 30 August 1968 |
| 10th | New York, NY | 4 October 1969 |
| 11th | New York, NY | 13 November 1970 |
| 12th | New York, NY | 6 November 1971 |
| 13th | Washington, DC | 10 November 1972 |
| 14th | Toronto, Ont. | 17 November 1973 |
| 15th | New York, NY | 15 November 1974 |
| 16th | Los Angeles, CA | 24 October 1975 |
| 17th | Washington, DC | 12 August 1976 |
| 18th | Ottawa, Ont. | 7 October 1977 |
| 19th | Cleveland, OH | 26 October 1978 |
| 20th | Los Angeles, CA | 26 October 1979 |
| 21st | Washington, DC | 17 October 1980 |
| 22nd | Montreal, P.Q. | 23 October 1981 |
| 23rd | Pittsburgh, PA | 29 October 1982 |
| 24th | Cambridge, MA | 4 November 1983 |
| 25th | Toronto, Ont. | 25 October 1984 |
| 26th | Thun, Switzerland | 11 August 1985 |
| 27th | Boston, MA | 18 September 1986 |

| Meeting | Location | Date |
|---|---|---|
| 28th | Los Angles, CA | 18 September 1987 |
| 29th | Washington, DC | 15 September 1988 |
| 30th | Bethlehem, PA | 13 October 1989 |
| 31st | Toronto, Ont. | 11 October 1990 |
| 32nd | Chicago, IL | 21 September 1991 |
| 33rd | Los Angeles, CA | 24 October 1992 |
| 34th | Washington, DC | 11 December 1993 |
| 35th | New York, NY | 29 October 1994 |
| 36th | Košice, SR | 21 August, 1995 |
| 37th | Brno, ČR | 28 August 1996 |
| 38th | Belton, TX | 12 July 1997 |
| 39th | Bratislava, SR | 7 July 1998 |
| 40th | Minneapolis, MN | 24 April 1999 |
| 41st | Washington, DC | 10 August 2000 |
| 42nd | Lincoln, NE | 3 August 2001 |
| 43rd | Plzeň, ČR | 28 June, 2002 |
| 44th | Cedar Rapids, IA | June 26, 2003 |
| 45th | Olomouc, ČR | July 2, 2004 |
| 46th | Miami, FL | March 18, 2005 |
| 47th | České Budějovice, ČR | June 30, 2006 |

## Table 3
## SVU World Congresses

| No. | Location | Date | Program Coordinator |
|---|---|---|---|
| I | Washington, DC | April 20-22, 1962 | Miloslav Rechcígl |
| II | New York, NY | Sept. 1-3, 1964 | Miloslav Rechcígl |
| III | New York, NY | Sept. 2-4, 1966 | Antonín L. Vaněk |
| IV | Washington, DC | Aug. 30-Sept. 1, 1968 | Andrej Eliáš |
| V | New York, NY | Jan. 13-15, 1970 | John G. Lexa |
| VI | Washington, DC | Nov. 10-12, 1972 | Otakar A. Horna |
| VII | New York, NY | Nov. 15-17, 1974 | M. Fryščák/J. G. Lexa |
| VIII | Washington, DC | Aug. 12-15, 1976 | Alexej B. Bořkovec |
| IX | Cleveland, OH | Oct. 26-29, 1978 | Stanislav Maršík |
| X | Washington, DC | Jan. 17-19, 1980 | W. E. Harkins |
| XI | Pittsburgh, PA | Oct. 28-31, 1982 | Zdenka Pospíšil |
| XII | Toronto, Ont. | Oct. 25-28, 1984 | Thomas G. Winner |
| XIII | Boston, MA | Sept. 18-21, 1986 | Anton J. Novacký |
| XIV | Washington, DC | Sept. 15-18, 1988 | Frank Meissner |
| XV | Toronto, Ont. | Oct. 11-14, 1990 | Stanislav Maršík |
| XVI | Prague, ČSFR | June 26-July 1, 1992 | A. Eliáš/J. F. Tříska |
| XVII | Prague, ČR | June 26-29, 1994 | Miloslav Rechcígl |
| XVIII | Brno, ČR | Aug. 25-29, 1996 | D. H. White/Rechcígl |
| XIX | Bratislava, SR | July 5-10, 1998 | Miloslav Rechcígl |
| XX | Washington, DC | Aug. 9-13, 2000 | Miloslav Rechcígl |
| XXI | Plzeň, ČR | June 23-30, 2002 | Rechcígl/Budil |
| XXII | Olomouc, ČR | June 27-July 3, 2004 | Rechcígl/Barteček |
| XXIII | České Budějovice, ČR | June 26-July 2, 2006 | Rechcígl/Papoušek |

## Table 4
## SVU Local Chapters in Retrospect

| Location | Founded | Chair | Secretary |
|---|---|---|---|
| Washington, DC | 1959 | Dr. Ladislav K. Feierabend | Dr. Miloslav Rechcígl |
| Chicago, IL | 1959 | Prof. Joseph Čada | Marie Heinz |
| New York, NY | 1960 | Dr. John G. Lexa | Milan Vojtek |
| Toronto, Ont. | 1961 | Miloslav Zlámal | Mirko Janeček |
| Munich, Germany | 1961 | Dr. Antonín Kratochvíl | Olga Kopecká |
| Montreal, P.Q. | 1961 | Prof. Jiří Škvor | Dr. Oskar Sýkora |
| Boston, MA | 1965 | Prof. Svatava P. Jakobson | Dr. Václav Mostecký |
| Los Angeles, CA | 1966 | Dr. Joseph Zahradka | Ing. Ladislav A. Krátký |
| London, England | 1967 | Dr. Jaroslav Stránský | Dr. B. R. Bradbrook |
| Albany, NY | 1969 | Prof. Vojtech E. Andic | Prof. Mojmír Frinta |
| Cleveland, OH | 1970 | Ing. Ferdinand J. Bastl | Dagmar V. Poseděl |
| Ottawa, Ont. | 1970 | Dr. Jaroslav A. Bouček | Ing. Jaromír A. Kouba |
| Battawa, Ont. | 1971 | Antonín Cekota | Antonín Šuler |
| Edmonton, Alta. | 1971 | Prof. Ivo Moravčík | Vladimír Valenta |
| Stuttgart, Germany | 1972 | Prof. Josef Kratochvíl | Ludvík Císař |
| Switzerland | 1972 | Dr. Přemysl Pitter | Dr. Zorka M. Černá |
| Melbourne, Australia | 1972 | Oto Sitnai | |
| Sydney, Australia | 1972 | Dr. Oliver Fiala | Dr. Jan H. Jirásek |
| Wellington, N.Z. | 1976 | Dr. Ivan Cikl | Jar. Zahrádka |
| Vancouver, BC | 1977 | Otto J. Juren | Jan Drábek |
| Pretoria, So. Africa | 1979 | Karel Smrčka | Jaroslava R. Smrčka |
| San Francisco, CA | 1979 | Pavel Kryška | Ing. Jaromír Malý |
| Vienna, Austria | 1980 | Dr. Věra A. Běhalová | Ivan Medek |
| Pittsburgh, PA | 1983 | Dr. Hana F. Romováček | Alena Něničková |
| Hartford, CT | 1983 | Prof. Josef Kalvoda | Martha M. Krahula |
| Perth, Australia | 1983 | Dr. Peter A. Hrubý | Stanislav Menšík |
| Praha, ČR | 1992 | Dr. Rudolf Zahradník | Prof. Rudolf Janál |
| Bratislava, Slovakia | 1993 | Prof. Alexander Tkáč | Ing. Ján Morovič |
| Košice, Slovakia | 1994 | Prof. Karol Marton | Doc. Miriam Gálová |
| Brno, ČR | 1995 | Dr. Marie Bobková | Dr. Jaroslav Bohanes |
| Central Texas, TX | 1997 | Prof. Clinton Machann | James W. Mendl |
| Tokyo, Japan | 1998 | Prof. Joseph N. Rostinský | |
| Minneapolis, MN | 1999 | Dr. Ivan Furda | Anna Vysoka |
| Plzeň, ČR | 2000 | Dr. Ivo Budil | Ivona Škanderova |
| Lincoln, NE | 2001 | Dr. Jitka Stiles | Dr. Míla Šašková-Pierce |
| Spillville, IA | 2003 | Michael Klimesh | JoAnn Dostal |
| Olomouc, ČR | 2004 | Dr. Evžen Weigl | Karel Konečný |
| Miami, FL | 2005 | Dr. Blanka Kuděj | Thomas Gral |
| České Budějovice, ČR | 2006 | Dr. František Sehnal | Zuzana Galatíková |

## Table 5
## *Major SVU Awards*
### Recipients of the SVU Honorary Membership

| Awardee | Area of Distinction | Gen. Assembly | Election |
|---|---|---|---|
| Zdeněk Němeček (in mem.) | Literature | New York, NY | 1960 |
| Jan Lowenbach | Music | New York, NY | 1960 |
| Josef Martínek | Journalism | New York, NY | 1960 |
| Albin Polášek | Fine Arts | New York, NY | 1960 |
| Alice Masaryková | Social Work | Washington, DC | 1962 |
| Prof. Vladislav Brdlík | Agr. Economics | Washington, DC | 1962 |
| Marie Heritesová | Music | Washington, DC | 1962 |
| Prof. Francis Dvorník | History | Toronto, Ont. | 1963 |
| Max Brod | Literature | New York, NY | 1964 |
| John Slezák | Public Service | New York, NY | 1964 |
| Prof. Howard A. Rusk | Medicine | New York, NY | 1964 |
| Prof. Karel B. Jirák | Music | Chicago, IL | 1965 |
| Josef Cardinal Beran | Theology | New York, NY | 1966 |
| Rafael Kubelík | Music | New York, NY | 1966 |
| Prof. Otakar Odložilík | History | New York, NY | 1966 |
| Prof. Roman Jakobson | Linguistics | New York, NY | 1966 |
| Oskar Kokoschka | Fine Arts | Montreal, P.Q. | 1967 |
| Prof. Johannes Urzidil | Literature | Montreal, P.Q. | 1967 |
| Koloman Sokol | Fine Arts | Montreal, P.Q. | 1967 |
| Prof. Václav Hlavatý | Mathematics | Washington, DC | 1968 |
| Prof. Vratislav Bušek | Law | Washington, DC | 1968 |
| Prof. S. Harrison Thompson | History | Washington, DC | 1968 |
| Dr. L. Radimský (in mem.) | Literature | New York, NY | 1970 |
| Prof. Matthew Spinka | History | New York, NY | 1970 |
| Ladislav Sutnar | Fine Arts | New York, NY | 1970 |
| Prof. René Wellek | Literary Criticism | Washington, DC | 1972 |
| Dr. Jaroslav Němec | Medical Jurisprudence | Washington, DC | 1972 |
| Rudolf Firkušný | Music | New York, NY | 1974 |
| Dr. Carleton Gajdusek | Medicine | Ottawa, Ont. | 1977 |

# Appendices

| Awardee | Area of Distinction | Gen. Assembly | Election |
|---|---|---|---|
| Prof. František Král | Veterinary Medicine | Ottawa, Ont. | 1977 |
| Ferdinand Peroutka | Journalism | Ottawa, Ont. | 1977 |
| Dr. Miroslav Rechcígl, Jr. | Biological Sciences | Cleveland, OH | 1978 |
| Prof. Karl W. Deutsch | Political Science | Washington, DC | 1980 |
| Prof. H. Gordon Skilling | Political Science | Washington, DC | 1980 |
| Prof. Wesley W. Posvar | Political Science | Washington, DC | 1980 |
| Dr. Ivan A. Getting | Engineering | Washington, DC | 1980 |
| Michael Butor | Literature | Washington, DC | 1980 |
| Tom Stoppard | Literature | Washington, DC | 1980 |
| Prof. Karel Husa | Music | Pittsburgh, PA | 1982 |
| Prof. Victor S. Mamatey | History | Pittsburgh, PA | 1982 |
| Jaroslav Seifert | Poetry | Toronto, Ont. | 1984 |
| Václav Havel | Literature | Toronto, Ont. | 1984 |
| Milan Kundera | Literature | Toronto, Ont. | 1984 |
| Prof. Jan Milič Lochman | Theology | Thun, Switz. | 1985 |
| Prof. Mikuláš Lobkowicz | Philosophy | Thun, Switz. | 1985 |
| Cardinal J. Tomko | Theology | Thun, Switz. | 1985 |
| Miloš Forman | Film | Thun, Switz. | 1985 |
| Prof. Václav Černý | Philosophy | Boston, MA | 1986 |
| Sir Cecil Parrott (in mem.) | Literature | Boston, MA | 1986 |
| Avigdor Dagan | Literature | Boston, MA | 1986 |
| Dr. Ján Papánek | International Relations | Boston, MA | 1986 |
| Dr. Jan Mládek | Economics | Los Angeles, CA | 1987 |
| Prof. Josef V. Škvorecký | Literature | Washington, DC | 1988 |
| Prof. Leopold J. Pospíšil | Anthropology | Washington, DC | 1988 |
| Eugen Suchoň | Music | Washington, DC | 1988 |
| Dominik Tatarka | Literature | Washington, DC | 1988 |
| Bohumil Hrabal | Literature | Bethlehem, PA | 1989 |
| Jiří Kolář | Fine Arts | Toronto, Ont. | 1990 |
| Prof. Zdeněk Kopal | Astronomy | Toronto, Ont. | 1990 |
| Oskar Morawetz | Music | Toronto, Ont. | 1990 |
| Prof. Jaroslav Pelikán | Theology | Toronto, Ont. | 1990 |
| Thomas Cech | Biochemistry | Los Angeles, CA | 1992 |
| Michael Novak | Theology | Los Angeles, CA | 1992 |
| Zdeněk Rotrekl | Literature | Los Angeles, CA | 1992 |

## Recipients of the SVU Founding Membership

| Awardee | Recognition for Service | Gen. Assembly | Election |
|---|---|---|---|
| Ivan Herben | Editor, *Zprávy SVU* | Toronto, Ont. | 1963 |
| Prof. Rudolf Šturm | Secretary General SVU | New York, NY | 1974 |
| Přemysl Pitter (in mem.) | President, Swiss Chapter | Ottawa, Ont. | 1977 |
| Dr. John G. Lexa (in mem.) | Secretary General SVU | Ottawa, Ont. | 1977 |
| Dr. Jiří Škvor | Editor, *Proměny* | Cleveland, OH | 1978 |
| Joseph A. Zahradka (in mem.) | President, Los Angeles Chapter | Cleveland, OH | 1978 |
| Mme. Lida Brodenová | Promotion of Czech Music | Washington, DC | 1980 |
| Arch. Emil Royco | Treasurer, SVU | Washington, DC | 1980 |
| Emilia Royco | Community and Cultural Work | Washington, DC | 1980 |
| Alexander Heidler (in mem.) | Pastoral Work | Washington, DC | 1980 |
| Vlasta Vráz | Community and Cultural Work | Pittsburgh, PA | 1982 |
| Prof. Vojtech E. Andic | Secretary General SVU | Pittsburgh, PA | 1982 |
| Josef Zanda (in mem.) | Archivist SVU | Pittsburgh, PA | 1982 |
| Dr. Mojmír Vaněk | President, Swiss Chapter | Pittsburgh, PA | 1982 |
| Dr. Karel Steinbach | Cultural Work | Cambridge, MA | 1983 |
| Olga D. Komers | Secretary, Swiss Chapter | Thun, Switz. | 1985 |
| Ing. Ladislav Krátký | Secretary, Los Angeles Chapter | Boston, MA | 1986 |
| Marie Provazníková | Cultural Work | Boston, MA | 1986 |
| Prof. Edith Vogel Garrett | Promotion of Cz. Music | Boston, MA | 1986 |
| Vlasta Vlažná | Cultural Work | Boston, MA | 1986 |
| Dr. Jaroslav G. Polach | President Washington, DC Chapter | Washington, DC | 1988 |
| Frank Marlow | Treasurer, SVU | Washington, DC | 1988 |
| Prof. Joseph Čada | Cultural Work | Bethlehem, PA | 1989 |
| Dr. Zorka Černá (in mem.) | Cultural Work | Bethlehem, PA | 1989 |
| Zdena Salivarová | Cultural Work | Toronto, Ont. | 1990 |
| Zdenek Hruban | Cultural Work | Los Angeles, CA | 1992 |

## 1976 Bicentennial SVU Awards

Thomas John Baťa, President and Chief Executive Officer, Bata Shoe Organization

Eugene A. Cernan, U.S. Astronaut, NASA.

Carl Ferdinand Cori, M.D., Professor Emeritus of Pharmacology, St. Louis University; Nobel Laureate in medicine and physiology.

Rev. Msgr. Francis Dvorník (In memoriam) D.D., D. Litt., former Professor of Byzantine History, Harvard University, Dumbarton Oaks.

Rudolf Firkušný, pianist and music composer.

Miloš Forman, filmmaker.

John Havlicek, basketball star with Boston Celtics.

Hon. Roman Hruska, U.S. Senator from Nebraska.

Francis Gladys Knight, Director, U.S. Passport Office, Department of State.

Rafael Kubelík, music conductor and composer.

Jarmila Novotná, opera singer, formerly with Metropolitan Opera.

Rev. Jaroslav Jan Pelikan, D.D., Ph.D., Sterling Professor of History and Religious Studies and Dean, Graduate School, Yale University.

Rudolf Serkin, pianist, former Director, Curtis Institute of Music.

Hon. John Slezak, former Undersecretary, U.S. Army.

Hon. John K. Tabor, former Undersecretary, U.S. Department of Commerce.

Hon. Charles A. Vanik, U.S. Congressman from Ohio.

Andy Warhol, artist and filmmaker.

René Wellek, Ph.D., Sterling Professor Emeritus of Comparative Literature, Yale University.

# List of Illustrations

Figure 1. Dr. Jaroslav Němec in 1956, at the time he began organizing SVU.

Figure 2. Prof. Václav Hlavatý. The First SVU President (1958-59, 1959-60, 1960-62).

Figure 3. Prof. Václav Hlavatý and Dr. Jaroslav Němec

Figure 4. Banquet, 1st SVU Congress, Washington, DC, 1962 – Prof. René Wellek, Mrs. Wellek, Prof. V. Hlavatý, Mrs. Hlavatý, Dr. J. Němec, Editor Ivan Herben.

Figure 5. Banquet (photomontage), SVU Annual Meeting, Toronto, Canada, 1963.

Figure 6. Prof. René Wellek. The Second SVU President (1962-64, 1964-66).

Figure 7. Prof. V. E. Andic, Prof. V. Hlavatý and Prof. R. Šturm at the 3rd SVU Congress, New York, NY, 1966.

Figure 8. Dr. Míla Rechcígl as SVU Vice President in 1969.

Figure 9. Dr. Rechcígl on the occasion of his Election as SVU President in 1974.

Figure 10. SVU Secretary-General Dr. John G. Lexa and SVU President Dr. Míla Rechcígl, at the 8th SVU World Congress, Washington, DC, 1976.

Figure 11. Six SVU Presidents at the 9th SVU World Congress, Cleveland, OH, 1978 – From the left: Dr. Jan Mládek, Prof. Jan F. Tříska, Prof. René Wellek, Dr. Rechcígl, Prof. Schwarzenberg, Dr. J. Němec

Figure 12. Prof. Jan F. Tříska, SVU President (1978-80, 1990-92).

Figure 13. Prof. Leopold J. Pospíšil, SVU President (1980-82, 1982-84).

Figure 14. Three SVU Presidents: Prof. F. Schwarzenberg, Dr. J. Němec and Prof. L. Pospíšil

Figure 15. Prof. Jiří Nehněvajsa, SVU President (1984-86, 1986-88).

*List of Illustrations* 647

Figure 16. SVU Executive Board Meeting, 1986. From left: Josef Staša, Dr. J. Němec, Dr. Jan V. Mládek and Prof. Zdeněk Suda.

Figure 17. Prof. Igor Nábělek, SVU President (1988-90).

Figure 18. SVU Fact Finding Mission in Czechoslovakia in 1990. From left: Prof. Anton Novacky, Mrs. Eva Rechcígl. Dr. Míla Rechcígl and Prof. Jan F. Tříska.

Figure 19. Dr. Rechcígl speaking at the Czechoslovak Academy of Sciences in Prague in 1991, on the occasion of the 100th anniversary of the Czech Academy.

Figure 20. After Rechcígl's receipt of the Academy's Josef Hlávka Medal in Prague in 1991. From left: Dr. Jiří Ullschmied, Dr. Jaroslav Folta, Mrs. MarieVodičková, Mrs. Eva Rechcígl and Dr. Míla Rechcígl.

Figure 21. At President Havel's Reception, Czechoslovak Embassy, Washington, DC, 1992. From left: Dr. Míla Rechcígl, President Václav Havel and Czech Ambassador Rita Klímová.

Figure 22. Opening of the 16th SVU World Congress in Prague, 1992. President Václav Havel is on extreme left. Dr. Rechcígl sits on the right side from him.

Figure 23. SVU World Congress, Prague, 1992 – US Ambassador Shirley Temple Black Bids Farewell to Czechoslovakia.

Figure 24. Two SVU Presidents at the SVU World Congress in Prague in 1992: Prof. Jan F. Tříska and Dr. M. Rechcígl.

Figure 25. Zdeněk J. Slouka, SVU President (1992-94).

Figure 26. SVU World Congress in Brno in 1996.

Figure 27. SVU President Dr. Rechcígl at the SVU World Congress in Brno in 1996.

Figure 28. SVU President Dr. Rechcígl Speaks at the SVU Conference in Texas, 1997.

Figure 29. Conference at the Czech Embassy, Washington DC, 1997. From left: former Amb. Michael Žantovský, Dr. Míla Rechcígl and Amb. Sáša Vondra.

Figure 30. SVU President Dr. Rechcígl Addresses SVU World Congress in Bratislava, 1998.

Figure 31. SVU World Congress in Bratislava, 1998. The last three persons on the right: Vice Rector Prof. Alexander Tkáč, Rector Petr Zuna and SVU President Dr. Mila Rechcígl.

Figure 32. Dr. Rechcígl receiving Medal on behalf of SVU from President Havel at the SVU Conference in Minnesota, 1999.

Figure 33. SVU World Congress, in Washington, DC in 2000. From left: Dr. Mila Rechcígl, Václav Klaus and Amb. Martin Palouš.

Figure 34. At SVU World Congress in Washington, DC, 2000: SVU President Dr. Rechcígl and Senator Petr Pithart.

Figure 35. Amb. Sáša Vondra at Mila Rechcígl's 70th Birthday Party in Rockville, MD, July 30, 2000.

Figure 36. SVU World Congress in Plzeň, 2002. From left: Dean Ivo Budil and Mrs. Eva Rechcígl.

Figure 37. SVU World Congress in Olomouc, 2004. SVU President Dr. Míla Rechcígl is welcomed with the traditional bread and salt.

Figure 38. SVU World Congress in Olomouc, 2004. From left: Rector Jana Mačáková, Dean Prof. Ivo Barteček and SVU President Míla Rechcígl.

Figure 39. SVU President Rechcígl receiving Jan Masaryk Medal from the Czech Ministry of Foreign Affairs at the Czech Embassy, Washington, DC, 2005. From left: Dr. Míla Rechcígl, Mrs. Eva Rechcígl and Amb. Martin Palouš.

Figure 40. Organizers of SVU World Congress in České Budějovice, 2006: Vice Rector Vladimír Papoušek and SVU President Míla Rechcígl.

Figure 41. SVU World Congress in České Budějovice, 2006: Mrs. Klaus, Rector Václav Bužek and President Václav Klaus.

Figure 42. SVU World Congress in České Budějovice, 2006: Banquet.

Figure 43. Dr. Rechcígl on his retirement from SVU Presidency, 2006.

Figure 44. Dr. Míla Rechcígl's Family.

# *Bibliographic Note*

### Primary Source

Apart from my own memory and personal interviews, I relied primarily on the correspondence and other archival material – "SVU Archives" and the "Miloslav Rechcígl, Jr. Papers" – maintained at the University of Minnesota's Immigration History Research Center (IHRC), as well as my own personal documents which I keep.

### Secondary Sources

Various SVU serial publications were used, including SVU newsletters: *Zprávy SVU*, vol. 1-49 (1958-2007), and *SVU Bulletin*, vol. 1-15 (1980-94); SVU periodicals: *Proměny*, vol. 1-29 (1964-92), and *Kosmas*, 1 -20 (1982-2007).

SVU Biographical Directories, vol. 1 - 8 (1966-2003).

Published proceedings of various SVU World Congresses, since 1962 to 2006, including Programs, Abstracts, and Selected Papers.

Various monographic publications published by the Society – their listing appears elsewhere, under the title "Bibliography of SVU Publications."

### Specific References

Specific books, pamphlets, speeches, letters, and unpublished papers cited in the text are indicated in the relevant Footnotes on particular pages.

# *Author's Biography*

Miloslav Rechcígl, Jr. is one of the founders and past Presidents of many years of the Czechoslovak Society of Arts and Sciences (SVU), an international professional organization based in Washington, DC. He is a native of Mladá Boleslav, Czechoslovakia, who has lived in the US since 1950. After receiving a scholarship, he went to Cornell University where he studied from 1951-58, receiving his B.S., M.N.S., and Ph.D. degrees there, specializing in biochemistry, nutrition, physiology, and food science.

He then spent two years conducting research at the National Institutes of Health as a postdoctoral research fellow. Subsequently he was appointed to the staff of the Laboratory of Biochemistry at the National Cancer Institute.

During 1968-69 he was selected for one year of training in a special USPHS executive program in research management, grants administration, and science policy. This led to his appointment as Special Assistant for Nutrition and Health in the Health Services and Mental Health Administration. In 1970 he joined the Agency for International Development as Nutrition Advisor and soon after was promoted to the position of Chief of Research and Institutional Grants Division. Later he became a Director with the responsibility for reviewing, administering and managing AID research.

He is the author or editor of over 30 books and handbooks in the field of biochemistry, physiology, nutrition, food science and technology, agriculture, and international development, in addition to a large number of peer-reviewed original scientific articles and book chapters.

Apart from his purely scientific endeavors as a researcher and science administrator, Dr. Rechcígl devoted almost 50 years of his life to the Czechoslovak Society of Arts and Sciences (SVU). In 1960-62 he served as secretary of the SVU Washington D.C. Chapter. He was responsible for the first two Society's World Congresses, both of which were a great success and which put the Society on the world map.

He also edited the Congress lectures and arranged for their publication, under the title *The Czechoslovak Contribution to World Culture* (1964, 682 p.) and *Czechoslovakia Past and Present* (1968, 2 volumes,

1900 p.). The publications received acclaim in the American academic circles and greatly contributed to the growing prestige of the Society worldwide.

Dr. Rechcígl was also involved, one way or another, with most of the subsequent SVU World Congresses, including the recent SVU Congresses in Prague, Brno, Bratislava, Washington, Plzeň, Olomouc and České Budějovice. Prior to his last term as the SVU President (2004-06), he held similar posts during 1974-76, 1976-78, and again in 1994-96, 1996-98, 1998-2000, 2000-02, 2002-04. In 1999, in conjunction with President Havel's visit to Minnesota, he organized a memorable conference at the University of Minnesota on "Czech and Slovak America: Quo Vadis?"

Together with his wife Eva, he published eight editions of the *SVU Biographical Directory*, the last of which was printed in Prague in 2003. He was instrumental in launching a new English periodical *Kosmas – Czechoslovak and Central European Journal*. It was his idea to establish the SVU Research Institute and to create the SVU Commission for Cooperation with Czechoslovakia, and its Successor States, which played an important role in the first years after the Velvet Revolution of 1989. Under the sponsorship of the Research Institute he and his colleagues conducted a series of seminars about research management and the art of "grantsmanship" for scientists and scholars, as well as for the administrators, and science policy makers, at Czech and Slovak universities, the Academies of Sciences.

He was also instrumental in establishing the National Heritage Commission with the aim of preserving Czech and Slovak cultural heritage in America. Under its aegis, he has undertaken a comprehensive survey of Czech-related historic sites and archival materials in the US. Based on this survey, he has prepared a detailed listing, "Czech-American Historic Sites, Monuments, and Memorials" which was published through the courtesy of Palacký University in Olomouc (2004). The second part of the survey, bearing the title "Czechoslovak American Archivalia," was also published by Palacký University (2004).

In this connection, he also organized several important conferences, one in Texas in 1997, the second in Minnesota (1999), the third in Nebraska (2001) and another in Iowa (2003). Through his initiative, a special Working Conference on Czech & Slovak American Materials and their Preservation was also held at the Czech and Slovak Embassies in Washington, DC in November 2003. It was an exceptionally successful conference which led to the establishment of the new Czech & Slovak American Archival Consortium (CSAAC). Most recently, he also organized, jointly with the ACSCC of North Miami, a conference on "Czech and Slovak Heritage on Both Sides of the Atlantic," 17-20 March 2005. The conference was co-sponsored by the US Commission for the Preservation of America's Heritage Abroad, under the aegis of both Presidents of the Czech and Slovak Republics.

Among historians, Dr. Rechcígl is well known for his studies on history, genealogy, and bibliography of American Czechs and Slovaks. A number of his publications deal with the early immigrants from the Czechlands and Slovakia, including the migration of Moravian Brethren to America. In the last few years he has been working on the cultural contributions of American Czechs and Slovaks. A selection of his biographical portraits of prominent Czech-Americans from the 17th century to date has been published in Prague, under the title *Postavy naší Ameriky* (Personalities of our America) (2000; 350 p.)On the occasion of his 75th birthday, SVU published a collection of his essays, *Czechs and Slovaks in America*.

In 1991, on the occasion of its 100th anniversary, the Czechoslovak Academy of Sciences awarded him the Hlavka Memorial Medal. In 1997 he received a newly established prize "Gratias agit" from the Czech Minister of Foreign Affairs. In 1999, on the occasion of President Václav Havel's visit to the US, President Havel presented him, on behalf of SVU, the Presidential Memorial Medal. More recently, he was given an honorary title "Admiral of the Nebraska Navy" by the Governor of Nebraska and the key to the Capital of Nebraska by the Mayor of Lincoln and the SVU Prague Chapter awarded him 2002 Praha SVU Award. In 2005 Minister of Foreign Affairs of the Czech Republic honored him by awarding him Jan Masaryk Medal for his contributions in preserving and fostering relations between the Czech Republic and the United States.

# *Index*

## – A –

Absolon, Karel B., 51, 84, 85, 126, 131, 522, 630
Achmatová, Anna, 513
Aggleton, Art, 150
Ahlers, Ivan, 242
Albert, Carl, 41
Albrecht, Catherine, 196, 216
Albright, Madeleine Korbel, 154, 470, 543
Ančerl, Karel, 471
Anderle, Josef, 31, 37, 51, 147, 196, 211, 214, 513
Andic, Vojtech E., xi, 15, 19, 22, 31, 33, 34, 52, 55, 63, 71, 77, 88, 469, 470, 501, 512, 625, 637, 641, 644, 646
Auty, Robert, 520

## – B –

Babický, Vaclav, 203
Baker, Russell 167
Baldwin, Dan, 354
Ballek, Ladislav V., 345
Barber, Tony, 275
Barnard, F. M., 521
Barry, Robert R., 41
Barteček, Ivo, xii, 370, 371, 372, 373, 377, 380, 384, 391, 429, 434, 640, 648
Basch, Antonín, 13, 31, 52
Basora, Adrian, 229
Bastl, Ferdinand J., 641
Baťa, Thomas John, 39, 105, 475, 645
Batt, Judy, 195
Bauer, Michael (Michal), 399, 402, 407, 410, 412, 415, 430, 434
Baumbruck,Michael, 632
Bažant, Zdeněk Pavel, 611
Beadle, George, W., 47

Beck, Curt F., 52
Beck, Maureen, 329
Bednar, Charles S., 14, 131
Bednář, Vratislav, 173
Běhalová Věra A., 641
Bekey, George, 611
Beleš, J., 55
Bělohlávek, Jiří, 207
Bělohradský, V., 133
Benda, Antonín, 75
Benedík, Jaroslav, 173
Beneš, Edvard (Eduard Benes), 266, 378, 395
Beneš, J., 171
Beneš, Jan, 471
Beneš, Václav 7, 15, 33
Beran, Josef Cardinal, Archbishop of Prague, 21, 48, 469, 471, 496, 625, 642
Berglund, Bruce Robert, 323, 325
Bernard, Jindřich, 138, 632
Bílá-Beck, Valerie, 526
Bílek, Petr, 223
Bílek, V., 223
Bínová, Veronika, 203
Bísek, Petr, 227, 325, 348
Bísek, Věra, 325
Black, Shirley Temple, 205, 206, 647
Blahník, Joel, 328, 329
Blaho, Pavel (Paul), 52, 524
Blažek, Vladimír, 628
Bobková, Marie, 250, 254, 256, 258, 261, 262, 292, 323, 324, 325, 348, 379, 429, 570, 641
Boehmer, Alois, 13
Bohanes, Jaroslav, 253, 254, 256, 641
Bohonek, Stanislav, 368
Bondy, Francois, 109
Borecký, Ladislav, 222
Bořkovec, Alexej B. (Sáša), 86, 87, 105, 106, 107, 114, 153, 154, 157,

158, 237, 308, 325, 308, 480, 543, 640
Bořkovec, Věra Žandová, 108, 113, 121, 136, 146, 221, 246, 262, 263, 290, 292, 305, 307, 308, 315, 321, 323, 324, 325, 348, 352, 356, 366, 386, 403, 435, 441, 598, 628, 629, 637
Borsody, Stephen, 44, 52
Borovský, K. H., 91
Bouček, Jaroslav A., 116, 641
Brabec, Jiří, 629
Bradbrook, Bohuslava R., 106, 148, 641
Bradley, John F. N., 52, 127, 520, 521, 522, 531
Brandl, Zdeněk, 416, 430
Brázda, Jaroslav J., 525
Brdlík, Vladislav, 5, 6, 7, 15, 16, 642
Brechler, Josef, 172
Břeň, Halina, 217
Březina, Jan, 377
Březina, Jiří, 174
Brilla, Jozef, 203, 204, 208
Brock, Peter, 471
Brod, Max, 536, 599, 642
Brodenová, Lída, 13, 105, 125, 644
Brodská, Zdenka, 514
Brodská, Zora, 203
Brouček, Stanislav, 170, 201
Browes, Pauline, 150
Brož, Vladimír J., 528
Brožek, Josef, 33, 53
Bruegel, John Wolfgang, 52
Bruininks, Robert, 297
Bruna, J., 55
Brychta, Ivan, 14
Budil, Ivo, xii, 202, 334, 338, 339, 340, 341, 342, 343, 344, 348, 349, 351, 356, 366, 367, 385, 611, 628, 640, 641, 648
Bufková-Wankelová, Karla, 630
Bujna, Ivan, 528
Burian, Jarka, 470

Burks, R. V., 471
Bušek, Vratislav, xi, 5, 7, 15, 16, 19, 20, 21, 24, 26, 31, 33, 36, 38, 46, 52, 64, 71, 74, 76, 77, 79, 460, 470, 478, 490, 501, 513, 524, 525, 625, 642
Bútora, Martin, xii, 313, 314, 329, 346, 357, 358, 364, 368
Bútorová, Zora, 313, 611
Bůžek, Václav, 408, 410, 415, 425, 426, 648

– C –
Caliguiri, Richard S., 129
Cardew (nee Kruliš-Randa), Angelika K., 33
Carter, President Jimmy, 117, 118, 124
Case, Clifford P., 41
Cech, Thomas, 643
Celler, Emanuel, 41
Cerman, J., 172
Cernan, Eugene A., 645
Cholrad, Vladimír, 169
Chroust, David, 334, 369, 389, 440
Chudik, Ladislav, 285
Chvatík, Květoslav, 142
Cibulka, J., 173
Ceithaml, Joseph, 95
Cekota, Antonín (Anthony), 33, 36, 38, 641
Chada, Joseph (Josef Čada), 16, 22, 122, 626, 641, 644
Chytil, F., 48
Ciampor, Fedor, 426
Cihlář, Antonín, 14
Cikl, Ivan, 628, 641
Cilka, Ingrová, 14
Coffin, Lyn, 122
Colombo, Hana B., 429
Comenius, John Amos (See also: Jan Amos Komenský), 5, 15, 32, 49, 52, 66, 67, 68, 74, 75, 76, 79, 147,

148, 150, 196, 200, 203, 205, 222, 314, 315, 375, 378, 445, 625
Conant, James B., 42
Cori, Carl Ferdinand, 645
Cotier, Georges, 109
Cotti, F., 143
Csáky, Pál, 314, 316
Cwach, Michael, 358, 359
Cywinski, B., 138

– Č –

Čada, Josef (Joseph Chada), 16, 22, 122, 626, 641, 644
Čambalík, Jozef, 12
Čapek, Josef, 12
Čapek, Karel, 11, 84, 133, 145, 150
Čapek, Milič, 5, 31, 33, 52, 122, 626
Čech, Juraj, 399
Čecha, Bedřich, 475
Čep, Jan, 471, 512
Čepičková, Eva, 416
Čermák, Josef, 39, 501, 526
Černá, Zorka M., 12, 13, 641, 644
Černohorský, Bohuslav Matěj, 130
Černý, George, 13
Černý, Jan, 344
Černý, Josef, 478
Černý, Milton, 263, 292, 308
Černý, Oldřich, 8, 13, 15, 16, 21, 475, 490, 506
Černý, Petr, 611
Černý, Václav, 471, 643
Čerych, Ladislav, 611
Čipera, John D., 114
Císař, Ludvík, 641
Čulík, Jan, 631

– D –

David, Zdeněk V., 343, 418, 440, 611, 627
David-Fox, Katherine O., 246
Dagan, Avigdor, 643
Dahrendorf, Sir Ralf, 195
Dalecká, Zdenka, 13

Davenport, Marcia, 60
De Ridder, Peter, 30
Delors, J. J., 168
Demetz, Hana, 502
Demetz, Peter, 33, 37, 470, 490, 491, 492, 611
Den, Petr (Peter), 43, 52, 471, 487, 511, 524, 525
Deutsch, Karl W., 470, 536, 643
Devinský, Ferdinand, 283, 471
DeVoe, Pat Křížek, 315, 325
Diensbier, Jiří, 167
Dirkson, Everett McKinley, 41
Dittrich, Zdeněk R., 52, 142, 146
Dodd, Thomas J., 41
Dolanská, Marie, 36
Dolanský, Ladislav, 139, 141, 146
Dorival, Bernard, 109
Dostal, JoAnn, 641
Dostál, Pavel, 329
Douglas Paul. H., 41
Drábek, Jan, 10, 641
Drábek, Jaroslav (Jáša), 10, 11, 12, 13, 52
Drábek, Jaroslav A., Jr., 13
Drápala, Milan, 631
Dresler, Jaroslav, 33
Dressler, Milan, 173
Drobník, Jaroslav, 440
Drtina, Prokop, 629
Drtina, Richard, 127
Drvota, Mojmír, 524
Dubček, Alexander, 58, 59
Duben, Vojtěch N. (see also: Nevlud, Vojtěch),
Dubovický, Ivan, 377, 378, 584
Ducháček, Ivo, 31
Dudová, Gabriela, 430
Dunn, Leslie C., 52
Dušek, Jan Ladislav, 525
Dvořák, Antonín, 25, 28, 34, 39, 130, 143, 145, 205, 257, 285, 314, 347, 348, 359, 360, 379, 429, 430, 524, 525, 527, 624

Dvořák, Eduard, 139
Dvořáková, Jarmila, 42
Dvorník, Rev. Msgr. Francis, xi, 31, 38, 52, 53, 56, 105,470, 493, 536, 642,645

– Ď –
Ďurica, Milan S., 108
Ďurovič, Lubomír, 133, 146, 193, 222, 243, 252

– E –
Early, Evelyn, 378
Eben, Petr (Peter), 130, 206
Ebringer, Libor, 222, 471, 611
Eichler, Jiří, xiii, 330, 333, 335, 348, 351, 367, 368, 382, 385, 386, 405, 421, 430, 434, 438, 509, 615, 617, 620, 632
Einstein, Albert, 512, 599
Eliáš, Andrew (Andrej), 52, 63, 153, 154, 157, 166, 174, 192, 198, 199, 237, 263, 325, 335, 336, 347, 354, 367, 383, 386, 430, 431, 435, 437, 438, 470, 501, 502, 598, 640
Engliš, Karel, 71, 93, 137, 626
Entwistle, Erik, 360
Eret, Gen. Josef P., 13, 36
Eubank, Keith, 52

– F –
Fabšic, Jiří J., 116
Falk, Čestmír, 200
Faltus, Anna, 104
Fanderlík, Velen, 22
Farrand, Robert W., 145
Faucher, Louis E., 471
Fehl, Philipp, 52
Feierabend, Ladislav K., 10, 11, 12, 13, 14, 19, 52, 460, 478, 524, 641
Feierabendová, Jana, 13
Felsenfeld, Oscar, 52
Ferenčík, Miroslav, 471
Ferjenčik, Mikuláš, 12

Fiala, Jiří, 13
Fiala, John, 328, 330, 331, 353, 356
Fiala, Lois, 353
Fiala, Oliver, 626, 641
Fiala, R., 222
Fiala, Silvio E., 115
Fiala, Stephen, 353
Fibich, Zdeněk, 348
Fic, Victor Miroslav, 52, 116, 521
Fiehler, Judith, 352
Figel, Jan, 437, 438
Figulus-Kallik, Gerta, 67
Filípek, Jan, 99
Firkušný, Rudolf, xi, 5, 6, 29, 42, 470, 599, 626, 632, 642, 645
Fischer, Edward, 525
Fischer, Otakar, 511
Fischer-Galati, Stephen A., xiii, 53, 127, 521
Fischerová, Eva M., 223
Fischerová, Daniela, 206
Fischmann, Zdenka E., 78, 87, 99, 123, 131, 210, 263, 321, 334, 352, 366, 521, 531, 628
Fischmeister, Ladislav, 13
Fisher, John H., 625
Flier, Michael S., 123
Florescu, Radu K., 52
Foel, Earl W., 140
Foit, F. V., 470
Folta, Jaroslav, 200, 201, 202, 212, 225, 227, 325, 647
Footman, D. J., 521
Ford, Gerald R., 100
Forman, Miloš, 471, 611, 643, 645
Fousek, Marianka S., 52
Francis, Cyril Lloyd, 115
Frank, Philipp, 31
Frei, Jaroslav V., 528
French, Alfred, 52, 74, 76, 121, 471, 518, 625
Freud, Sigmund, 314, 375
Freudenberger, Herman, 53
Fried, V. 48

Friedrich, Rudolf, 143
Frinta, Mojmír S., 31, 33, 52, 641
Frištacký, Norbert, 471
Fryščák, Milan, 80, 131, 220, 640
Fuchs, Jiřina, 630
Fuchs, V., 128
Fugii, Noriko, 130
Furda, Ivan, 306, 641

– G –
Gajdoš, Marian, 243, 244
Gajdusek, D. Carleton, 113, 471, 536, 642
Galatíková, Zuzana, 430, 641
Galeta, Patrik, 628
Gálová, Miriam, 222, 244, 641
Gandalovič, Petr, 329, 330, 354
Ganim, Russell, 328
Garrett, Edith Vogl, 33, 644
Garver, Bruce, 250, 522, 261
Gasinski, Tadeusz Z., 471
Gasparovič, Ivan, 392, 397, 413, 419, 433
Gavora, Ján, 86, 106, 108, 114, 118
Gaydos, Joseph M., 129
Getting, Ivan A., 130, 536, 643
Getting, Milan, Jr., 126
Gibian, George, 52, 53, 518
Gibian, Thomas G., 146, 153, 154, 157, 158, 193, 210, 221, 237, 238, 543, 598
Glos, Blanka S., 126, 538, 637
Glos, George, 132, 325, 598
Gődel, Kurt, 375
Goepfertová-Gruberová, Gertruda, 43, 512, 513
Goetz, Petr, 172
Gosztony, P., 138
Gral, Thomas, 641
Grandtner, Miroslav M., 243, 627
Greksák, Misoslav, 222
Gross, Feliks, 52, 471
Grubhoffer, Libor, 416, 430
Gruša, Jiří, 141, 631

Grygar, Jiří, 232, 426
Grygar, Mojmír, 218

– H –
Haas, Hugo, 470
Hajda, Jan, 11, 14, 31, 33
Hajda, Joseph, 52
Halaga, O. R., 223
Hagel, Chuck, 329
Hahn, Henry, 140
Hájek, Igor, 148
Hájek, Jiří, 107
Halford, Ralph S., 42
Halík, Tomáš, 347
Halleck, Charles A., 41
Hammond, Thomas T., 471
Hanák, Harry, 52, 149
Hančil, Vladislav, 168, 201
Hanic, František, 169, 223
Haňka, Ladislav R., 130
Hanzl, Stanislav, xii, 168, 230, 471, 565
Hanzlík, Tomáš, 379
Hapala, Milan E., 14, 52
Harkins, William E., 33, 52, 53, 121, 124, 127, 136, 518, 520, 521, 626, 640
Harnick, Michaela, 202, 508
Harwit, Martin, 145
Hasal, Milan J., 13
Hašek, Josef, 12, 13, 324
Hasil, Jiří, 223
Hauner, Milan L., 108, 196
Hauzenblas, J. W., 14
Havel, Dáša, 158
Havel, Ivan, 158, 611
Havel, Václav, xii, 57, 107, 143, 147, 148, 149, 158, 160, 161, 163, 165, 180, 195, 197, 201, 203, 205, 206, 218, 229, 231, 284, 294, 295, 297, 300, 302, 303, 304, 308, 316, 318, 320, 345, 357, 429, 471, 536, 630, 643, 647
Havlicek, John, 645

Heidler, Alexander, 125, 644
Heidrich, Arnošt, 11, 13, 460, 624
Heim, Michael L. 91, 123, 211
Heinz, John, 129
Heinz, Marie, 524, 641
Hejný, Frank, 14
Heller, Jan, 173
Herben, Ivan, xi, 5, 6, 7, 11, 12, 15, 17, 18, 19, 21, 23, 29, 36, 37, 38, 45, 82, 471, 475, 478, 490, 495, 497, 498, 500, 501, 502, 503, 504, 505, 525, 526, 528, 629, 644, 646
Herben, Milena, 497
Heritesová, Marie, 642
Herman, Augustine, 101, 231
Herman, Jerry, 430
Herman, Lois, 364, 382, 405, 438
Hersch, Jeanne, 109
Hexner, Ervin, 13, 31
Heymann, Frederick G., 31, 33, 53, 471, 518
Hlaváčková, Libuše, 203
Hlavatý, Václav, xi, 3, 5, 6, 7, 8, 15, 18, 19, 21, 22, 23, 24, 25, 26, 28, 29, 31, 38, 47, 48, 49, 53, 55, 56, 64, 450, 456, 470, 473, 477, 487, 491, 492, 494, 512, 524, 527, 528, 535, 599, 629, 637, 642, 646
Hlávka, Josef, 199
Hikl, Mario J., 22, 526
Hnilička, Milo P., 31
Hnízdo, Borek, 146, 149
Hodin, Josef Paul, 52
Hodža, Milan, 195
Hoffmann, Banesh, 492, 494, 629
Hoffmann, Richard J., 328
Hoffmeister, Ferdinand S., 55, 71
Holanová, Miroslava, 203
Holbík, Karel, 52
Holeton, David R., 147, 627
Hollar, Wenceslav, 49
Holoubek, Ivan, 173
Horák, Bohuslav, 22
Hořák, George, 392, 398

Horáková, Milada, 22
Horal, Jan, 399
Horecký, Paul L., 494
Horna, Otakar A., 73, 640
Horský, Igor, 43
Horton, Loren, 359, 360
Hošek, Erik, 52
Hostovský, Egon, 42, 45, 471, 492, 512, 599
Howell, Roger, 52
Hrabal, Bohumil, 471, 643
Hrabík, Helena, 47
Hradílek, Antonín, 55
Hrdlička, Aleš, 102
Hrdý, I., 199
Hron, Frantisek, 230
Hruban, Zdeněk, 47, 139, 195, 214, 263, 325, 611, 644
Hrubý, Karel, 40, 108, 122, 124, 131, 133, 141, 193, 514, 539, 569, 570, 572, 573, 574, 575, 576, 577, 626
Hrubý, Petr (Peter A.), 348, 626, 641
Hruska, Roman L., 41, 102, 645
Hryhorijiv-Gregory, Miroslav, 471
Hujer, Karel, 33
Huber, Margaret, 345
Hudlický, Tomáš, 611
Hudoba, Igor, 222, 283
Hunter, Mark, 360
Hus, Jan, 32, 139, 314
Husa, Karel, 81, 145, 470, 525, 536, 611, 643
Husák, Marie, 99
Husserl, Edmund, 375
Hyvnar, Václav, 526

– I –

Iggers, Wilma A., 52
Illnerová, Helena, 343, 346, 378
Ingrová, Cilka, 13
Ivaška, Dodo, 399
Ivaška, Jozef, 399

# Index

**– J –**

Jakobson, Roman, 74, 75, 76, 470, 493, 518, 519, 520, 527, 536, 599, 625, 641, 642
Jakobson, Svatava P., 641
Janáček, Leoš, 29, 81, 119, 120, 130, 375, 426, 632
Jánal, Rudolf, 232, 641
Janeček, Mirko, 641
Janisch, R., 200
Jansa, Miloš A., 10, 13
Jánský, Ladislav, 172
Jantschová, Jana, 628
Jařáb, Josef, xii, 150, 195, 253, 346, 348, 377, 430, 471, 611
Jarolím, John S., 14
Jaroš, Bohumil, 93
Jasný, Vojtěch, 471
Javits, Jacob J., 41
Javor, Pavel (see also: Škvor, Jiří) 38, 43, 46, 128, 471, 496, 512, 514, 526, 629
Jedličková, Bohuslava, 203
Jelen, Pavel, 336
Jelínek, Ivan, 625
Jeřábek, Esther, 93, 110, 114, 625
Ješina, Čestmír, 11, 14, 93, 136
Ježek, Jaroslav, 430, 525
Jíra, Jaroslav, 8, 14, 15, 16, 20, 33, 52, 513
Jirák, Karel Boleslav, 5, 25, 26, 29, 31, 33, 47, 52, 81, 130, 195, 470, 525, 527, 624, 626, 642
Jirásek, Jan H., 626, 641
Johnson, Ralph, 284
Johnson, Owen V., 471
Johnson, Mike, 329
Josten, Josef, 42, 471
Juren, Otto J., 641

**– K –**

Kabeš, Vladimír M., 135, 136, 158
Kabešové, Otilie, 630
Káčer, Rastislav, xii, 375, 378, 392, 394, 397, 436, 602
Kadlec, Štěpán F., 627
Kadrik, Mary, 105
Kafka, Franz, 124, 599
Kalb, Marvin, 59
Kalenda, Josef, 528
Kalvoda, Jan, 230
Kalvoda, Josef, 641
Kameníčková, Věra, 195
Kaminsky, Howard, 33, 52, 53
Kann, Robert A., 52
Karas, Jiří, 330
Karas, Joža, 46
Karfík, L. 203
Karger, Jiří (George), 55, 193, 210, 211, 630
Karlíček, Martina, 348
Karlíček, Petr, 348
Kaše, František, 14
Kaše, Karel, 14
Kašpar-Pátý, Jaroslav, Col., 14
Kavan, Jan, 316
Kavka, Jiří, 43
Keating, Kenneth B., 41
Keeler, Virginia, 105
Keglerová, Edita, 379
Keleti, George, 146
Keprt, Marek, 379
Kertesz, Stephen Dent, 53
Kessler, Zdeněk, 229, 253
Kirk, Grayson, 42
Kisch, Bruno Z., 31, 53
Kisch, Guido, 52
Kiss, Igor, 285
Kittner, Maroš, 285
Klaus, Václav, xii, 314, 316, 357, 377, 392, 397, 413, 419, 422, 423, 425, 426, 433, 443, 648
Klaus, Livia, 425, 648
Klener, Pavel, 230
Klíma, Ivan, 57
Klíma, Michal, 167
Klímek, Adolf, 14

Klimeš, Jan, 14, 28
Klimesh, Michael, 360, 368, 386, 641
Klimešová, Naďa, 14
Klímová, Rita, 158, 647
Klír, George, 166
Knight, Francis Gladys, 105, 645
Kočan, Anton, 174
Kocourek, Milan, 435, 629
Kočvara, Štefan, 14, 52
Koeppl, Evžen C., 14
Koerner, S. 521
Kolafa, Josef, 14
Kofroň, J. 171, 172
Kohák, Erazim V., 33, 52, 123, 124, 133
Kohn, Hans, 53
Kohn, Joseph J., 216, 219, 389, 429, 611
Kohout, Jára, 470
Kohout, Pavel, 57, 107
Kohout-Lecoque, A., 470
Kokoschka, Oskar, 60, 470, 536, 621, 642
Kolaja, Jiří, 31, 52, 71
Kolář, Jiří, 122, 471, 643
Kolář, Petr, xii, 426, 444
Kolegar, Ferdinand, 31, 52
Kolinský, Josef, 298
Kollecas, Karen Rechcígl, iii, 28, 628
Kollecas, Kristin, iii
Kollecas, Paul, iii
Komenda, Stanislav, 611
Komenský, Jan Amos (see also: Comenius), 5, 15, 32, 49, 66, 67, 68, 74, 75, 76, 147, 148, 150, 196, 200, 203, 205, 222, 314, 315, 375, 378, 445, 625
Komers, Olga D., 644
Konečný, Karel, 370, 371, 372, 380, 391, 399, 405, 641
Koníček, Zdeněk, 108, 115
Kopal, Zdeněk, 470, 521, 643
Kopčák, Dimitrij, 285
Kopecká, Olga, 641

Korbel, Josef, 45, 52, 55, 171, 470
Korbonski, Andrzej, 123, 211, 471
Korecký, Bořivoj, 115
Korytová-Magstadt, Štěpánka, 340
Kosek, Helena, 137
Kosková, Helena, 137, 630
Košler, Miroslav, 230
Kouba, Jaromír A., 641
Kouba, Martina, 108, 115
Kováč, D., 223
Kovanda, Karel, 223
Kovařík, Jiří 173
Kovaříková, Alena, 203
Kovtun, Jiří (George), 130, 132, 630
Kracíkova, Jarmila, 99
Kraft, David, 377, 383, 392, 398, 606
Krahula, Martha M., 641
Krajina, Vladimír, 114, 470, 478
Král, František (Frank), 5, 6, 113, 470, 643
Králová, Libuše, 621
Králové, Dvůr, 80
Kraml, Jiří, 200
Krátký, Ladislav A., 99, 641, 644
Kratochvíl, Antonín, 88, 495, 629, 641
Kratochvíl, Josef, 641
Krč, Jan, 216
Krejčí, Jaroslav, 109, 124, 133, 142, 146, 149, 195, 539, 576
Krejčí, Mathew, 379
Krekic, Boris, 123
Kremenliev, Boris, 52
Křesadlo, Jan, 630
Kresanek, Jozef, 75
Křesťan, Jiří, 428
Kreysa, Frank J., 14
Křikavová, Dagmar, 203
Křivánek, Ladislav, 128
Krondl, Anthony, 134
Krupka, Jan, 128
Kryla, Karla, 632
Kryška, Pavel, 641
Kubálek, Antonín, 120

Kubelík, Rafael, xi, 6, 7, 15, 16, 21, 36, 470, 490, 512, 599, 626, 642, 645
Kubín, George, 55
Kučera, Henry, 31, 33, 52, 126, 470, 494, 495
Kučera, Josef, 10, 14
Kučera, Miloš K., 131, 136, 138, 146, 165, 637
Kuchař, Jan Křtitel, 130
Kuchel, Thomas H., 41
Kuděj, Blanka, 226, 227, 246, 252, 254, 255, 262, 279, 325, 413, 422, 425, 430, 436, 440, 637, 641
Kuděj, Svaťa, 425, 430
Kuhn, Heinrich, 471
Kuklík, Jan, 223
Kundera, Milan, 57, 471, 537, 643
Kunstmann, Heinrich H., 471, 518
Kupová, Václava, 203
Kuras, Benjamin, 348
Kusín, Vladimír V., 518, 520
Kvapil, Radoslav, xii, 254, 348, 427, 471, 611
Kvetko, Marvin, 85
Kvídera, George J., 166, 193
Kybal, Milič, 13, 34
Kyncl, K., 146

– L –

Ladner, Benjamin, 308, 314
Lajda, Brano M., 14, 77, 78, 93, 106
Landa, Vladimír, 168, 170
Lapka, Miloslav, 173
Lasch, Jindra H., 99
Laška, Václav, 47
Lastovecká, Dagmar, 253
Lausche, Frank J., 41
Lawson, Merlin, 328
Leeds, Eva Maříková, 246, 263
Lederer, Ivo John, 53
Leimberger, Milan, 632
Lejka, Vera, 257
Lejka, Vlastimil, 257

Lejková, Milada, 14
Lemberg, Hans, 142
Lencek, Rado L., 52, 471
Leshikar, Howard B., 264, 579
Lettrich, Irena, 502
Lettrich, Jozef, 6, 11, 12, 14, 85, 460, 478
Lewan, Michael, 322
Lewis, Brackett, 111, 629
Lexa, John G. (Hanuš), xi, 24, 31, 33, 40, 41, 63, 66, 67, 68, 70, 71, 77, 78, 79, 80, 82, 86, 89, 105, 106, 108, 113, 114, 167, 467, 480, 483, 501, 511, 524, 599, 600, 637, 640, 641, 644, 646
Liberský, Frank, 14
Lichardus, Branislav, 206
Ličko, Vojtech, 243
Likins, Peter, 566
Líková, Eva, 470
Liška, G., 521
Liška, Jiří, 91
Lišková, Marta, 14
Listopad, František, 43, 513
Lněnička, Antonín, 527
Lobkowicz, Nicholas, 52, 470, 537, 643
Lochman, Jan Milič, 109, 123, 133, 147, 148, 229, 470, 522, 537, 611, 643
Lojda, Zdeněk, 164, 167, 171, 172, 201, 203, 471, 611
Lokay, Miroslav, 68, 625
Lomský, Igor, 14
Lorenc, Jan, 501, 505
Louda, Jiří, 378
Lovecky, Georgine B., 154
Lowenbach, Jan, 21, 642
Lukáš, Zdeněk, 230
Lustig, Arnošt, 130, 471, 611
Luža, Radomír, 196, 348, 518
Lyčka, Zdeněk, 358, 360

– M –
Jana Mačáková, 370, 376, 377, 648
Macek, Josef, 54, 526
Macek, Milan, 172
Macháč, Josef, 246, 292, 305, 320, 325, 356, 611
Machann, Clinton J., 264, 265, 266, 320, 321, 325, 334, 352, 367, 386, 389, 430, 435, 442, 522, 578, 627, 641
Macho, Ladislav (Laco), 169, 222, 280, 471, 612
Machotka, Otakar, 6, 7, 15, 16, 31, 33, 470, 495, 625
Machotka, Pavel, 91, 210, 211, 217, 219, 221, 637
Macků, Zdeněk A., 223
Mader, Pavel, 173, 222
Magocsi, Paul R., 471, 518
Majer, Jiří, 201
Majer, Václav, 11, 14, 460, 478
Majerská, Lucia, 285
Malát, Jiří, 347
Malik, Joseph, 528
Malý, Jaromír, 641
Mamatey, Victor S., 6, 15, 45, 52, 55, 92, 111, 196, 469, 470, 521, 535, 536, 629, 643
Maňhal, Gertruda, 14
Mardirosian, Gail Humphries, 315
Mareček, Robert, 285
Mareš, Markéta, 527
Mareš, Václav E., 53, 526
Markiezy, M., 285
Markuš, Jozef, 169
Marlow, Frank J., xi, 91, 99, 123, 126, 133, 193, 211, 212, 214, 321, 352, 522, 538, 539, 628, 637, 644
Maršík, Stanislav (Stanley) J., 118, 121, 122, 141, 146, 193,640
Martin, Janica, 347
Martínek, Josef (Joseph), 16, 21, 43, 496, 525, 629, 642

Martinů, Bohuslav, 29, 101, 150, 359, 360, 427, 525
Marton, Karol, 241, 242, 244, 250, 252, 261, 262, 325, 627, 641
Martonová, Mariana, 244
Marvan, J., 348
Marynchak, Arnošt, 14
Masaryková, Alice, 37, 395, 624, 599, 642
Masaryk, Jan, 8, 60, 84, 395
Masaryk, Thomas (Tomáš) Garrigue, 7, 32, 37, 43, 60, 91, 92, 93, 98, 122, 123, 129, 145, 266, 314, 354, 375, 395, 451, 479, 495, 500, 626, 630
Mastný, V. 521
Matajs, Vladimír, 422, 430
Matějka, Ladislav, xi, 31, 33, 40, 53, 74, 121, 348, 514, 543
Materna, Anthony, 55
Matoušek, Karel, 14
Matuška, Waldemar, 396, 399
Matuška, Olga, 399
McCormack, John W., 41
Měchurová, Lenka, 200, 201, 203, 212, 222, 225
Mečiar, Vladimír, 275
Medek, Ivan, 641
Meissner, Frank, 11, 31, 86, 106, 143, 640
Meissner, M. 105
Mendel, Johann Gregor, 135, 257, 314
Mendl, James W., 641
Menšík, Stanislav, 641
Messer, Thomas, 71
Měšťan, Antonín, 133, 137, 630
Měšťan, Jaromír, 43
Mestenhauser, Josef A., 211, 217, 218, 219, 220, 294, 302, 304, 321, 325, 611
Mezihorák, František, 298, 320
Mičátek, Mikuláš, 109
Michal, Jan M., 33, 53
Michal, Jaromír J., 14

*Index* 663

Michálek, Slavomír, 399
Michalička, Jan, 130
Mikloško, Josef, 207
Mikula, Felix, 21, 36, 469, 470, 478, 490
Mikuláš, Dalibor, 399
Mikuláš, Peter, 285
Miller, Thomas A., 440
Miller, Warren L., 393, 603
Mináč, Matej, 315
Minden, George, 56
Mittelstadt, Michael C., 68, 625
Mládek, Jan V., xi, 14, 31, 71, 72, 73, 75, 76, 78, 82, 83, 84, 88, 105, 118, 119, 147, 529, 534, 535, 637, 643, 646, 647
Mlynárik, Ján, 141
Mlynář, Zdeněk, 107
Moravčík, Ivo, 137, 518, 520, 626, 641
Morávková, Alena, 628
Morawetz, Oskar, 39, 470, 643
Morgan, James P., 316
Morovič, Ján, 222, 281, 284, 641
Morse, Wayne, 41
Morton, George, 54
Moseley, Edwin M., 53
Mosely, Philip E., 54
Moserová, Jaroslava (Jára), 315, 348, 358, 360, 364, 378, 399, 602
Mostecký, Václav, 3, 4, 5, 7, 15, 641
Motlíček, Tomáš, 377, 381, 434, 629
Motyca-Dawson, Francis, 145
Moulisová, Yveta, 203
Moyzes, Mikuláš, 130
Mráček, Jaroslav J., 55, 123
Mravec, Ladislav, 443
Mucha, Frank Ladislav, 210, 211, 217, 243, 244, 246, 248, 252, 262, 263, 282, 292, 324, 325, 356, 364, 369, 370, 386, 405, 421, 422, 430, 438, 441, 554, 555, 557, 558, 560, 563, 566, 576
Muenzerová, Zdenka, 43, 87

Munk, František, 6, 54, 133, 518
Munz, Otto John, 14
Mysliveček, Josef, 430

– N –

Nábělek, Igor V., 131, 136, 138, 146, 149, 165, 192, 193, 530, 535, 637, 647
Nábělek, Vojtech, 131
Naughton, Gail, 358
Naughton, James, 148
Naus, Jan, 173
Naylor, Herbert, Maj., 14, 121
Nečas, Daniel, 366, 385, 598, 600
Nečas, Oldřich, 200
Nehněvajsa, Jiří, xi, 6, 31, 33, 54, 126, 131, 136, 138, 141, 142, 146, 153, 154, 157, 243, 244, 253, 263, 470, 495, 506, 522, 534, 543, 554, 558, 560, 637, 646
Němcová, Jarmila, 14, 22
Němec, Igor, 229
Němec, Jaroslav (Jaroš), xi, 3, 4, 5, 6, 7, 8, 9, 10, 11, 14, 15, 19, 20, 21, 22, 26, 28, 29, 31, 33, 40, 53, 63, 67, 70, 74, 76, 77, 82, 83, 88, 106, 118, 119, 131, 132, 146, 149, 153, 154, 157, 166, 210, 455, 456, 458, 466, 472, 473, 474, 477, 478, 481, 487, 490, 491, 493, 494, 497, 498, 501, 502, 506, 525, 527, 533, 535, 538, 543, 571, 573, 599, 600, 637, 642, 646, 647
Němec, Jiří, 141
Němeček, Zdeněk, 21, 642
Něničková, Alena, 641
Neresnický, J. (see also: Slávik, Juraj), 43
Nettl, Paul, 54
Neumann, Bishop St. John Nepomucene, 119, 120
Neumann, Matěj, 14
Neval, Daniel, 336

Nevlud, Vojtěch (see also: Duben, Vojtěch N.), 10, 12, 13, 14, 31, 34, 52, 111, 495, 496, 501, 624, 625, 626, 629
Niederle, Jiří, 168
Nosek, Jindřich, 14
Novacký, Anton J., 136, 139, 166, 169, 193,292, 305, 308, 309, 310, 323, 325, 543, 640, 647
Novák, Arne, 136, 626
Novak, Jan, 143, 195
Novak, Michael, 102, 105, 521, 543, 643
Novák, Miroslav, 124, 141
Novák, Pavel, 246, 263
Novak, Richard, 257
Novák, Vítězslav, 67
Novotná, Jarmila, xi, 6, 7, 15, 42, 470, 645
Novotney, J., 93, 105
Novotný, Antonín, 57, 58
Novotný, Jan Maria, 6
Novotný, Vladimir, 166, 612
Nowak, Grzegorz, 336, 632

– O –

Obolensky, Dmitrij, 493
Odložilík, Otakar, 31, 42, 67, 470, 493, 536, 642
Olejníček, Jiří, 173
Olynyk, Roman, 53, 471
Oravec, M., 501, 502
Orten, Jiří, 122, 626
Orton, Lawrence D., 471
Oslzlý, Kačenka (Cathleen), 330, 331, 351, 362, 363, 367, 368, 369, 383, 440, 632
Osuský, Štefan, 314, 460

– P –

Pačes, Václav, xii, xvii, 418, 430, 471, 565, 566, 612
Pacner, Karel, 202
Palach, Jan, 139

Palacký, František, 101, 111, 449, 481, 521, 629
Palic, Vladimír, 14
Palouš, Martin, xii, 158, 298, 299, 320, 346, 358, 359, 364, 375, 378, 392, 394, 397, 436, 602, 648
Palouš, Radim, xii, 164, 168, 171, 172, 196, 201, 471, 612
Pánek, Jaroslav, 426
Pánková, Dana, 203
Pantůčková, Jitka, 200
Papánek, Ján, 53, 75, 233, 314, 395, 478, 527, 599, 643
Papánek, Štefan, 105
Papoušek, xii, Vladimír, 223, 399, 402, 405, 407, 411, 412, 414, 415, 416, 417, 418, 419, 420, 422, 430, 436, 440, 640, 648
Pařízková, J., 173
Parrott, Sir Cecil, 521, 643
Pasák, Tomáš, 203
Pate, Paul D., 358
Patočka, Jan, 107
Páty, Libor, 170
Paukert, Karel, 60, 120, 130
Pavlásek, Tomáš J. F., 128
Pavlík, Ladislav, 628
Pavlovský, Petr, 243
Pech, Stanley J., 53
Pecháček, Jarsolav, (?? Should be Jaros?) 121, 502
Pecháček, Pavel, 121, 149, 632
Pejša, Oskar, 528
Pejsar, Helen, 328
Pejskar, Josef, 527
Pelikán, Jaroslav Jan, 31, 105, 470, 520, 535, 543, 612, 643, 645
Perlman, Harvey, 328
Peroutka, Ferdinand, 84, 113, 471, 643
Pessoy, Ferdinand, 512
Petr, Jiří, 471
Petříček, Jaromír, 526

# Index

Petrik, Robert, 389, 390, 391, 393, 396, 400, 401, 402, 433
Petrla, Zdeněk, 22
Petrovska, Marija, 471
Phifer, James R., 359
Pierce, Layne, 331
Pilátová, Jana, 254, 255
Pilip, Ivan, 229, 230
Pírek, Zdeněk, 167
Pistorius, George, 33
Pithart, Petr, 298, 315, 320, 346, 648
Pitter, Přemysl, 114, 471, 641, 644
Planý, Petr, 379
Plašienková, Zlatica, 284, 356
Plavec, Mirek J., 232, 471
Pletnev, Rostislav, 471
Polach, Eva B., 93, 111, 629
Polach, Jaroslav G., 3, 4, 9, 10, 11, 14, 18, 19, 20, 33, 71, 91, 92, 494, 525, 644
Polášek, Albin, 21, 195, 470, 642
Popera, E. J., 513
Porter, Robert, 148
Poseděl, Dagmar V., 118, 641
Poseděl, Miroslav, 524
Pospíšil, Leopold Jaroslav, xi, 31, 54, 125, 126-135, 136, 153, 154, 157, 237, 338, 430, 470, 521, 522, 531, 534, 535, 537, 538, 543, 574, 577, 600, 609, 612, 637, 643, 646
Pospíšil, Zdenka, 129, 146, 147, 193, 237, 640
Posvar, Wesley W., 130, 536, 643
Povolný, Dalibor, 174
Povolný, Mojmír, 16, 53, 263, 348, 612
Powell, Adam C., 41
Pravda, Alex, 149, 195
Pražák, Čeněk, 133
Prečan, Vilém, 138, 141, 170, 630, 631
Prinz, F. E., 521
Přibáň, Michal, 628
Procházka, Adolf, 33, 53, 478

Procházková, Petra, 422, 431, 438
Procházka, Theodore, 11, 14, 31, 33
Procházková, Zora, 12
Procházka, Zorka, 14
Prokop-Fried, Marie, 527
Provazník, K., 172
Provazníková, Marie, 12, 15, 526, 630, 644
Proxmire, William, 41
Průša, Josef, 399
Ptáček, Zdeněk, 14
Puchmajer, Líba, 120
Purgina, Emil S., 136, 140, 632

– R –

Racz, Oliver, 244
Radimský, Ladislav, xi, 7, 8, 11, 15, 37, 40, 52, 63, 67, 487, 498, 510, 511, 512, 513, 514, 525, 642
Raditsa, Bogdan, 53
Rafaeli, Peter A., 325
Rajlich, Václav, 246
Rakušan, Karel, 115
Raška, Francis D., 421, 442
Raška, Karel, 418, 430, 441, 442
Raymond, Antonín, 470
Reagan, Ronald, 124, 129, 143, 144
Rechcígl, Eva, iii, xiv, 9, 11, 18, 27, 49, 73, 76, 111, 120, 126, 132, 137, 164, 166, 167, 169, 193, 202, 212-213, 325, 348, 430, 443, 494, 506-509, 608, 609, 619-620, 632, 647, 648
Rechcígl, Gregory, iii
Rechcígl, Jack E., iii, 612, 628
Rechcígl, Kevin, iii
Rechcígl, Lindsey, iii
Rechcígl, Miloslav, Jr., xii, xiii, xvi, 14, 45, 46, 48, 49, 56, 57, 63, 64, 65, 67, 71, 73, 76, 77, 78, 115, 116, 118, 119, 120, 121, 122, 125, 126, 127, 132, 133, 137, 142, 147, 148, 149, 153, 154, 157, 158, 162, 163, 166, 167, 169, 170, 174, 175,

176, 193, 194, 197, 205, 206, 212-
213, 214, 215, 217, 218, 219, 220,
224, 230, 241, 242, 243, 244, 257,
266, 285, 287, 299, 300-301, 312,
313, 314, 316, 327, 328, 329, 330,
345, 347, 358, 360,452, 459, 461,
470, 473, 476, 478, 479, 480, 481,
483, 486, 487, 488, 502, 503-504,
505, 515, 529, 530-532, 533-537,
539, 541, 542, 543, 570, 573, 574,
608, 609, 610, 637, 640, 641, 643,
646, 647, 648
Rechcígl, Miloslav, Jr., directing SVU
    publication program, 30-35, 50-54,
    490-496, 506-509, 516-522, 613-
    618, 619-633
Rechcígl, Miloslav, Jr., organizing
    SVU Congresses and Conferences,
    26-29, 41-44, 198, 199, 200, 201,
    202, 203, 225-228, 253-256, 264-
    265, 274-282, 293-296, 302-306,
    307-311, 338-343, 370-375, 388-
    393, 407-423
Rechcígl, Miloslav, Jr., elected to
    SVU Presidency, 82-86, 237-240
Rechcígl, Miloslav, Jr., as SVU
    President, 87-95, 106-112, 245-
    252, 259-263, 268-273, 288-292,
    318-324, 332-337, 350-356, 363-
    369, 382-387, 401-406, 432-438
Rechcígl, Miloslav, Jr., conducting
    workshops, 546-552, 553-561,
    562-568
Rechcígl, Miloslav, Jr., preserving
    cultural heritage, 329, 335, 578-
    583, 584-588, 589-591, 592-595,
    596-601, 602-607
Rechcígl, Miloslav, Jr., leaving SVU
    Presidency, 439-445
Rechcígl, Miloslav, Sr., xiii, 598, 599
Redisch, Walter, 33
Relochová, Jiřina, 173
Reszler, Andre, 109, 138
Řezníček, H. K. S., 54

Ribicoff, Abraham, 41
Richter, Vladimír, 524
Richterová, Sylvie, 132, 630
Rienche, Glen, 328
Rocarek, John, 360
Roček, Jan, 53, 471
Rokos, Rev. Michael, 356
Rokusek, Cecilia, 390, 391, 393, 396,
    400, 401, 418, 430, 433
Romováček, Hana F., 216, 641
Rosene, Effie M., 445
Rostinský, Joseph N., 273, 641
Rosůlek, Přemysl, 344
Rotrekl, Zdeněk, 471, 630, 643
Rouček, Joseph S., 6, 7, 33
Roubíček, Václav, xii, 399
Rowen, Carl T., 42
Royco, Emil, 12, 14, 55, 63, 71, 77,
    124, 125, 470, 644
Royco, Emilia, 104, 124, 125, 644
Rozehnal, Alois, 53, 625
Rubeš, Jan, 7, 39, 471, 527
Rubes, Susan Douglas, 527
Rudnytsky, Ivan L., 471
Ruffieux, Roland, 109
Ruml, J., 167
Rupník, Jaques, 143
Rusk, Howard A., 471, 642
Růžena, Bohuslava, 52
Růžička, František, 346
Růžičková, Sabina, 344

– S –

Sádlík, Josef, 14
Safertal, Frank, 325, 331, 340, 356,
    637
Safertal, Otakara, 348, 372
Salivarová, Zdena,644
Savage, Timothy, 167
Schattschneider, David A., 147
Schejbal, Gen. Josef, 11
Schieche, Emil, 471
Schlosberg, Květa G., 14
Schmidt, Eduard, 254

*Index* 667

Schneider, Joseph Z., 33
Schneider, Mikuláš, 285
Scholze, Pavel, 344
Schuster, Rudolf, 150, 244, 298, 357
Schwarzenberg, František, 7, 15, 16, 29, 55, 77, 82, 84, 85, 86, 88, 105, 106, 111, 119, 124, 141, 153, 154, 170, 543, 629, 637, 646
Scott, Louise, 147
Screvane, Paul R., 42
Scruton, Roger, 146
Shillinglaw, Draga, 91
Secká, Milena, 428
Seemanová, Eva, 172
Segert, Stanislav, 91, 99, 123, 147, 211, 612
Sehnal, František, 430, 440, 471, 612, 641
Seifert, Jaroslav, 121, 122, 134, 139, 207, 471, 536, 626, 632, 643
Serkin, Rudolf, 645
Seton-Watson, G. H., 518, 519, 520, 521
Seyfried, Jan, 431
Sirek, Anna, 115
Sirek, Otakar V., 115
Sis, Peter Alexander, xiii, 612
Sitnai, Oto, 641
Skalická, Marie, 203
Skalický, Karel, 109, 133
Skalník, Petr, 471
Skalný, Jan P., 243, 244, 246, 263, 276, 278, 279, 281, 292, 308, 325, 334, 346, 348, 349, 354, 367, 385, 628
Skamene, Emil, 471, 612
Skilling, H. Gordon, 128, 471, 518, 520, 536, 643
Skolek, Jaroslav, 201, 203
Skřivánek, John M., 33
Skupa, Josef, 349
Slabý, A., 173
Slaby, Ronald G., 471
Sládek, Jaromil, 14

Sládek, Vladimír, 628
Sládková, Gertrude, 14
Slámečka, Vladimír, 48, 53, 166
Slávik, Juraj, 14, 37, 460, 478, 513
Slávik, Juraj L. J., Jr., 14, 278, 279, 325, 246, 263, 292, 325,
Slezák, John, 105, 125, 642, 645
Slobodnik, Dušan, 208
Slobodová, Zuzana, 435, 629
Slouka, Zdeněk J., xi, xii, xvi, 149, 154, 157, 161, 162, 163, 165, 166, 193, 196, 198, 202, 211, 214, 216, 217, 219, 220, 222, 223, 224, 225, 229, 237, 253, 325, 441, 531, 536, 539, 544, 545, 547, 549, 553, 554, 555, 558, 563, 566, 568, 609, 610, 611, 637, 647
Smal-Stocki, Roman S., 54, 471
Smetana, Bedřich, 29, 75, 145, 207, 348, 427, 430, 525, 632
Smetana, František, 81, 626
Smíšek, Anita, 328, 329, 358, 359
Smith, Bruce L. R., 567
Smith, Margaret Chase, 41
Smith, W. Stanford, 105
Smrčka, Jaroslava R., 641
Smrčka, Karel, 641
Smutná, Inka (see also: Steinský-Sehnoutka, Georgina), 38, 43
Sochmanová, Eva, 285
Sofer, Chatam, 314
Sokol, Koloman, 60, 470, 612, 621, 642
Sommer, Karel, 626
Součková, Milada, 513, 528
Soukup, J., 171
Soulis, George, 493
Sovík, Thomas P., 148
Spáčil, Dušan, 84
Spačková, Jana, 75
Spinka, Matthew, 33, 54, 74, 75, 76, 471, 536, 625, 642
Srba, Antonín, 78
Srebala, Ondrej, 278, 280, 281, 282

Srholec, Anton, 223, 243, 285, 336, 347
Staller, George J., 31
Staněk, J., 171
Stanislav, Jiří, 390
Stankiewicz, Edward, 47
Stapleton, Craig R., 345
Stark, Louis, 358
Stárková, Věra, 43, 512
Staša, Josef, 131, 136, 514, 647
Steigl, Jan, 173
Stein, František, 108, 115
Steinbach, Karel, 11, 60, 73, 77, 84, 632, 644
Steinský-Sehnoutka, Georgina (see also: Smutná, Inka), 39
Stejskalová, Zora, 173
Stern, Josef Peter, 53
Stern, Juraj, 284
Stevenson, Adlai E., 41
Stewart, T. D., 33
Stloukal, Milan, 203
Stiles, Jitka, 331, 641
Stiles, Ron, 328, 331
Stoppard, Tom, 536, 643
Stránský, Jan, 85
Stránský, Jiří, 230
Stránský, Jaroslav, 85, 478, 524, 641
Stránský, Zdenek, 173
Strakoš, V., 243
Straškraba, Milan, 173
Streets, Robert, 528
Střížovská, Eva, 399
Suchoň, Evžen (Eugen), 81, 471, 643
Suda, Zdeněk, 86, 87, 129, 131, 133, 157, 166, 237, 522, 647
Suk, Josef, 427
Susato, Tylman, 313
Sutnar, Ladislav, 42, 470, 642
Sviták, Ivan, 59, 479, 518
Svoboda, Frank J., 42
Svobodová, Ivana, 203
Svoboda, Ludvík, 58, 59
Sýkora, Oskar P., 528, 641

Synek, Miroslav, 47, 630
Szalatnay, Louisa, 14

– Š –

Šabat, Jaroslav, 66, 77, 81
Šafařík, Pavel Josef, 241, 242
Šalda, F. X., 511
Šašková-Pierce, Míla, 328, 330, 331, 641
Šebor, Miloš M., 33, 46, 77, 106, 107, 116
Šejnoha, Jaroslav, 33, 38, 46,527, 624
Šetlík, Jiří, 150
Ševela, Ladislav, 163, 164, 167, 171, 172
Šik, O., 521
Šimečka, Milan, 631
Šimek, Pavel, 195
Šimko, Vlado, 193, 217, 218, 611
Šimončič, Klement, 512
Šimunková, Hermenegilda, 173
Šipoš, E., 48
Šístek, Anna, 115
Šístek, Otakar, 115
Šístek, Vladimír, 114
Škanderová, Ivona, 344, 348, 349, 385, 628, 641
Škarvada, Bishop Jaroslav, 471
Škodáček, J., 223
Škrábánek, Robert L., 54
Škutina, Vladimír, 133, 138, 471, 632
Škvor, Mrs. A. 128
Škvor, Jiří (see also: Javor, Pavel), xi, 7, 15, 21, 32, 37, 38, 39, 40, 43, 46, 63, 65, 71, 77, 86, 106, 121, 125, 501, 512, 514, 528, 529, 641, 644
Škvorecký, Josef Václav, xi, 86, 87, 93, 106, 107, 126, 130, 136, 471, 518, 612, 643
Škvorová-Vaništová, Anna, 527
Šlápota, Jaromír, 298, 330
Šlechtová, Jana, 203
Šmahel, František, 200, 201, 471
Šneberger, Jiří, 345

# Index

Špaček, Milan, 297, 330
Šporcl, Pavel, 429
Šrámek, Jiří, 253, 254, 255
Šroubek, Otakar, 527
Štefánek, Branislav Anton, 3, 124, 133, 469
Štefánik, Milan Rastislav, 314, 395
Štefanovič, Milan, 150
Štěpánková, Hana, 203
Štěrba, F. C., 624
Šturc, Ernest, 14, 31, 74, 86, 87, 105, 106, 107, 126, 512
Šturm, Rudolf, xi, 19, 20, 22, 31, 33, 36, 37, 38, 42, 45, 46, 63, 71, 77, 78, 79, 87, 88, 125, 458, 474, 478, 490, 500, 501, 637, 644, 646
Šturman, Pavel, 14
Štrunc, Jiří, 348
Šula, Jan, 416
Šuler, Antonín, 641
Šumichrast, Michael (Miša), 45, 85, 121, 131, 146, 157, 470
Šuster, Antonín (Anthony) J., 526
Šustrová, Milena, 43
Švachula, V., 173
Švec, Juraj, 471
Švehla, Antonín, 120
Švehla, František, 511
Švejda, Agnes F., 14
Švejda, M. Norma, 33
Švejnar, Jan, 471, 612
Švestka, Miroslav J., 14

– T –

Tabor, John K., 645
Táborský, Edward (Eduard), 7, 15, 31, 33, 54
Táborský, V., 173
Talacko, Joseph V., 53
Tamir, A., 284
Tatarka, Dominik, 471, 643
Tesař, George, 430
Tesařík, Martin, 377
Thoma, Juraj, 415

Thompson, S. Harrison, 54, 471, 642
Thornburgh, Richard L., 129
Tichá, Petra, 324
Tigrid, Pavel, 53, 109, 133, 201, 206, 229, 230, 471
Tino, Jozef, 284
Tkáč, Alexander, xii, 208, 222, 230, 242, 244, 249, 252, 261, 263, 274, 276, 277, 278, 279, 280, 282, 284, 285, 286, 291, 292, 298, 325, 471, 641, 648
Tkáčová, Klára, 244, 627
Tkáčová, Milada, 252
Toma, Peter A., 53, 87, 126, 494
Tománek, Godfrey, 134, 148
Tomko, Cardinal J., 643
Topol, Josef, 315
Townsend, Charles, 471, 632
Trahan, Elizabeth W., 471
Traubner, Pavel, 285
Trebichavský, Ivan, 529
Trenský, Pavel (Paul) I., 166, 174, 198, 199, 202, 218, 522
Třešňák, František, 495, 629
Tříska, Jan F., xi, 53, 121, 123, 124, 125, 131, 153, 154, 157, 166, 169, 170, 174, 176, 192, 193, 195, 197, 198, 199, 210, 212, 213, 214, 215, 216, 237, 238, 325, 356, 470, 520, 521, 530, 531, 534, 536, 538, 539, 569, 612, 637, 640, 646, 647
Trnka, Jiří, 349
Trpiš, Milan, 121, 166
Tuma, Carmelee, 328
Tůma, Oldřich, 399
Tumlíř, Jan, 33
Turchan, Otto Charles, 88, 99
Turková, Jaroslava, 249, 254, 261, 262, 284, 292, 323, 325, 569, 570
Tursi, Jan Stoffer, 360
Tuzar, Jaroslav, 524
Tuzar, Jiřina (Georgia), 527

– U –
Uhde, Jan, 611
Uhlířová, Jarmila, 71
Ulbrecht, Věra, 263, 279, 280, 325, 637
Ulbrichová, Marie, 171, 173
Ulč, Otto, 53, 263, 471, 518
Uličný, Oldřich, 223
Ullschmied, Jiří, 197, 201, 203, 225, 647
Unterberger, Betty M., 471
Urban, Louis, 105
Urban, Rudolf, 48, 471
Urbánek, Zdeněk, 158
Urzidil, Johannes, 642

– V –
Vaculík, L., 57
Valenta, Jaroslav, 201, 202, 229, 471, 612
Valenta, Jiří, 123
Valenta, Vladimír, 641
Valert, Mia, 196
Valocký, Dušan Q., 223
Van den Beld, Ant., 124
Vaněk, Antonín L., 66, 640
Vaněk, Eva, 292, 325, 637
Vaněk, Mojmír, 109, 123, 644
Vaněk, Vladimír, 53, 496, 624
Vaňhal, Johann Baptist 360, 525
Vaníček, Petr, 612
Vanik, Charles A., 119, 645
Vanoncini, Fabrizio, 429
Varejková, Marta, 344, 348
Varinská, Daniela, 285
Varinský, Marian, 285
Vaseková, Zuzana, 284, 285
Vašková, Ludmila, 380
Vávra, Martin, 315,
Veit, Vladimir, 137, 631
Vecoli, Rudolph, 392, 397, 436
Vejvoda, Jaroslav, 140
Velinský, Stanislav J., 53
Verner, Jaroslav, 292

Vernerová, Andrea, 176
Veverka, Anna M., 105
Vičar, Jan, 398, 399, 403, 435, 631
Vich, Zdeněk J., 292, 325, 421, 441
Viest, Ivan M., 211, 216, 221,612
Vinš, Bohuslav, 627
Vítek, Václav, 430, 612
Vlach, Antonín, 513
Vlach, Robert, 43, 513
Vladislav, Jan, 631
Vlasák, Pavel, 168
Vlažná, Vlasta, 644
Vodičková, Marie, 647
Vodrážka, Frank J., 105
Vojtek, Milan, 22, 641
Volková, Bronislava, 196
Vonderka, Milan, 285
Vondra, Alexandr (Sáša), xii, 264, 265, 266, 294, 295, 304, 308, 313, 314, 315, 579, 580, 647, 648
Voskovec, Jiří, 471
Vostracký, Zdeněk, 338, 345, 348, 399
Vozárik, Marina, 325
Vozárik, Zdenka, 325, 501, 502
Vrána, Karel, 471, 513
Vráz, Vlasta, 34, 644
Vrbová, Miroslava, 173
Vysoká, Anna, 323, 325, 332, 641

– W –
Wagner, Doug, 358
Wagner, Murray L., 147
Walter, Emil, 53
Walzel, Vladimir S., 45, 501
Wandycz, Piotr S., 44, 53, 54, 471, 521, 612
Warhol, Andy, 645
Wechsler, Robert S., 471
Wehle, Kurt, 31
Weigl, Evžen, 173, 641
Weinberg, Gerhard L., 53
Weiss, Marc, 356
Welclová, Emilie, 21

*Index* 671

Wellek, René, xi, 6, 26, 31, 32, 36, 37, 38, 39, 40, 42, 43, 45, 47, 48, 54, 55, 74, 76, 83, 88, 106, 119, 126, 131, 134, 153, 470, 477, 487, 490, 491, 492, 512, 518, 520, 533, 535, 536, 543, 599, 600, 624, 625, 637, 642, 645, 646
Wesley, Don, 329
White, Dagmar Hasalová, 13, 105, 143, 193, 246, 254, 262, 263, 279, 292, 310, 321, 323, 325, 348, 352, 356, 366, 386, 403, 418, 435, 598, 628, 640
White, Jack, 321, 348
White, Lewis M., 626, 627, 628
Wichterle, Otto, xii, xvi, 199, 206, 471, 565
Wiedermann, Bedřich Antonín, 130
Wilder, Thornton, 135
Williams, Anthony A., 316
Wilson, Woodrow, 60
Winner, Thomas G., 131, 134, 518, 640
Winters, Stanley B., 471, 518
Witek, Kate, 328
Wlachovský, Miroslav, 358, 399
Wright, John, 313
Wright, William E., 471

– Y –
Yashirin, Svetlana, 328
Young, Stephen M., 41

– Z –
Zaborski, Jerzy, 33
Zach, Jan, 16, 22, 33, 470
Zahrádka, Jar., 641
Zahradka, Joseph A., 91, 99, 641, 644
Zahradník, Jan, 426
Zahradník, Rudolf, xii, 229, 284, 471, 641
Zajíc, Vladimír D., 128, 243
Zástěra, Karel, 324, 338, 339, 340

Zástěra, Jaromír, 119, 501, 502, 528
Zbíralová, Jana, 411, 412, 413, 414, 415, 416, 417, 418
Zelenda, Josef, 525
Zeman, Jarold K., 471
Zeman, Miloš, 354
Zeman, V., 128
Zeman, Z. A. B., 54
Zenkl, Petr, 14, 478
Zielenec, Josef, 230
Zinner, Paul H., 54
Zlámal, Miloslav, 38, 39, 492, 526, 624, 641
Zorin, Libuše, 502
Zuman, Petr, 441, 611
Zumpfe, Tom, 330, 331
Zuna, Petr, xii, 225, 229, 230, 285, 292, 298, 320, 325, 471, 565, 566, 570, 648
Zvolánek, Budimír, 328, 348, 379, 429
Zvolánek, Bohumír, 360

– Ž –
Žáčková, Jaromíra, 42
Žáček, Joseph Frederick, 53, 480
Žanda, Josef, 77, 495, 625, 626, 644
Žantovský, Michael, xii, 579, 647
Želivan, Pavel, 22, 513
Žiar, Mariam, 43
Žižka, Rev. Arnošt, 42

# *Illustrations*

**Figure 1. Dr. Jaroslav Němec in 1956, at the time he began organizing SVU.**

**Figure 2. Prof. Václav Hlavatý. The First SVU President (1958-59, 1959-60, 1960-62).**

Figure 3. Prof. Václav Hlavatý and Dr. Jaroslav Němec

Figure 4. Banquet, 1st SVU Congress, Washington, DC, 1962 - Prof. René Wellek, Mrs. Wellek, Prof. V. Hlavatý, Mrs. Hlavatý, Dr. J. Němec, Editor Ivan Herben

Figure 5. Banquet (photomontage), SVU Annual Meeting, Toronto, Canada, 1963.

Figure 6. Prof. René Wellek. The 2nd SVU President (1962-64, 1964-66).

Figure 7. Prof. V. E. Andic, Prof. V. Hlavatý and Prof. R. Šturm at the 3rd SVU Congress, New York, NY, 1966.

**Figure 8. Dr. Míla Rechcígl as SVU Vice President in 1969.**

Figure 9. Dr. Míla Rechcígl on the occasion
of his Election as SVU President in 1974.

Figure 10. SVU Secretary-General Dr. John G. Lexa, and SVU President
Dr. Míla Rechcígl at the 8th SVU World Congress, Washington, DC, 1976.

Figure 11. Six SVU Presidents at the 9th SVU World Congress, Cleveland, OH, 1978 - From left: Dr. Jan Mládek, Prof. Jan F. Tříska, Prof. René Wellek, Dr. Rechcígl, Prof. Schwarzenberg, Dr. Němec.

Figure 12. Prof. Jan F. Tříska, SVU President (1978-80, 1990-92).

Figure 13. Prof. Leopold J. Pospíšil, SVU President (1980-82, 1982-84).

**Figure 14. Three SVU Presidents: Prof. F. Schwarzenberg, Dr. J. Němec, and Prof. L. Pospíšil**

Figure 15. Prof. Jiří Nehněvajsa, SVU President (1984-86, 1986-88).

Figure 16. SVU Executive Board Meeting, 1986.
From left: Josef Staša, Dr. J. Němec, Dr. Jan F. Mládek and Prof. Zdeněk Suda.

Figure 17. Prof. Igor Nábělek, SVU President (1988-90).

Figure 18. SVU Fact Finding Mission in Czechoslovakia, 1990. From left: Prof. Anton Novacky, Mrs. Eva Rechcígl. Dr. Míla Rechcígl and Prof. Jan F. Tříska.

Figure 19. Dr. Rechcígl speaking at the Czechoslovak Academy of Sciences in Prague in 1991, on the occasion of the 100th anniversary of the Czech Academy.

Figure 20. After Rechcígl's receipt of the Academy's Josef Hlávka Medal, Prague, 1991. From left: Dr. Jiří Ullschmied, Dr. Jaroslav Folta, Mrs. Marie Vodičková, Mrs. Eva Rechcígl and Dr. Míla Rechcígl.

Figure 21. At President Havel's Reception, Czechoslovak Embassy, Washington, DC, 1992. From left: Dr. Míla Rechcígl, President Václav Havel, and Czech Ambassador Rita Klímová.

**Figure 22. Opening of the 16th SVU World Congress in Prague, 1992. President Václav Havel is on extreme left. Dr. Rechcígl sits on the right side from him.**

**Figure 23. SVU World Congress, Prague, 1992 - US Ambassador Shirley Temple Black Bids Farewell to Czechoslovakia.**

Figure 24. Two SVU Presidents at the SVU World Congress in Prague, 1992.
- Prof. Jan F. Tříska and Dr. M. Rechcígl.

Figure 25. Zdeněk J. Slouka, SVU President (1992-94).

Figure 26. SVU World Congress in Brno, 1996.

Figure 27. Dr. Rechcígl at the SVU World Congress in Brno, 1996.

Figure 28. Dr. Rechcígl Speaks at the SVU Conference in Texas, 1997.

Figure 29. Conference at the Czech Embassy, Washington, DC, 1997.
From left: former Amb. Michael Žantovský, Dr. Míla Rechcígl and Amb. Sáša Vondra.

Figure 30. Dr. Rechcígl addresses SVU World Congress in Bratislava, 1998.

Figure 31. SVU World Congress in Bratislava, 1998.
The last three persons on the right: Vice Rector Prof. Alexander Tkáč,
Rector Petr Zuna and SVU President Dr. Rechcígl.

Figure 32. Rechcígl Receiving Medal on Behalf of SVU from President Havel at the SVU Conference in Minnesota, 1999.

Figure 33. SVU World Congress, in Washington, DC, 1992.
From left: Dr. Rechcígl, Václav Klaus and Amb. Martin Palouš (1992).

Figure 34. SVU World Congress in Washington, DC, 2000:
SVU President Dr. Rechcígl and Senator Petr Pithart.

Figure 35. Amb. Sáša Vondra at Míla Rechcígl's 70th Birthday Party
in Rockville, MD, July 30, 2000.

Figure 36. SVU World Congress in Plzeň, 2002.
From left: Dean Ivo Budil and Mrs. Eva Rechcígl.

Figure 37. SVU World Congress in Olomouc, 2004.
SVU President Rechcígl is welcomed with the traditional bread and salt.

Figure 38. SVU World Congress in Olomouc, 2004. From the left:
Rector Jana Mačáková, Dean Prof. Ivo Barteček and SVU President Míla Rechcígl.

Figure 39. Rechcígl Receiving Jan Masaryk Medal from the Czech Ministry of Foreign Affairs at the Czech Embassy, Washington, DC, 2005.
From left: Dr. Míla Rechcígl. Mrs. Eva Rechcígl and Amb. Martin Palouš.

Figure 40. Organizers of SVU World Congress in České Budějovice, 2006: Vice Rector Vladimír Papoušek and SVU President Míla Rechcígl.

**Figure 41. SVU World Congress in České Budějovice, 2006:
Mrs. Klaus, Rector Václav Bužek and President Václav Klaus.**

Figure 42. SVU World Congress in České Budějovice, 2006: Banquet.

Figure 43. Dr. Rechcígl on his retirement from SVU Presidency, 2006.

**Figure 44. Dr. Rechcígl's Family.**
1st Row: Kevin Rechcígl, Lindsey Rechcígl, Kristin Kollecas and Paul Kollecas.
2nd Row: Nancy Palko Rechcígl, Eva Rechcígl and Karen Rechcígl Kollecas.
3rd Row: Prof. Jack Rechcígl, Gregory Rechcígl, Dr. Míla Rechcígl and Ullyses Kollecas.